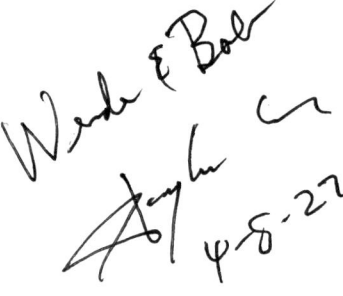

# Seeking Tong-Shaan, Encountering Gum-Shaan:

## What it Meant to Be Cantonese in China and America, 1850–1900

### Volume 1
### The Gum-Shaan Chronicles,
### The Early History of Cantonese-Chinese America, 1850-1900

by

Douglas W. Lee, PhD

The contents of this work, including, but not limited to, the accuracy of events, people, and places depicted; opinions expressed; permission to use previously published materials included; and any advice given or actions advocated are solely the responsibility of the author, who assumes all liability for said work and indemnifies the publisher against any claims stemming from publication of the work.

All Rights Reserved
Copyright © 2023 by Douglas W. Lee, PhD

No part of this book may be reproduced or transmitted, downloaded, distributed, reverse engineered, or stored in or introduced into any information storage and retrieval system, in any form or by any means, including photocopying and recording, whether electronic or mechanical, now known or hereinafter invented without permission in writing from the publisher.

Dorrance Publishing Co
585 Alpha Drive
Pittsburgh, PA 15238
Visit our website at www.dorrancebookstore.com

ISBN: 978-1-6393-7094-8
eISBN: 978-1-6393-7905-7

## DEDICATION

Honoring the past, with respect and appreciation
My Father:            My Mother:
Lee Jung Won          Lee Ching Lai-Jun
(1894–1967)           (1904–1972)

Nurturing the future, with love and trust
My two sons
Douglas Warren "Parky" Lee Jr.
George Paul Lee

# TABLE OF CONTENTS

Foreword
pp. vii-ix

Preface
pp. xi-xxviii

Acknowledgments
pp. xxix-xxx

Introduction
pp. 1-43

Chapter 1:
Central Gwongdung: The Cantonese Homeland and Fountainhead
pp. 45-118

Chapter 2:
The Cornerstone of Cantonese Identity:
*Yuet* Language and Cantonese Speech
pp. 119-166

Chapter 3:
Cantonese Ethnicity: A Series of Ethnic group
and Speech Community Identity Labels
pp. 167-240

Chapter 4:
Cantonese Culture, as a Conservative Contrarian Counter-Culture
pp. 241-278

Chapter 5:
The Enduring Ties that Bind, Cantonese Style
pp. 279-366

Chapter 6:
Seeking *Tong-Shaan*, while encountering *Gum-Shaan*
pp. 367-434

Conclusion
pp. 435-446

Bibliography
pp. 447-468

# FOREWORD

Much has changed in the four-plus decades since I first became friends with Douglas W. Lee. When we met at the University of Washington, most Chinese Americans were descendants of immigrants who came from Gwongdung to the West Coast between the 1850s and the 1920s. They spoke some variety or other of Cantonese, or at least the older generations still did. They lived mostly in Chinatowns, confined by redlining and restrictive covenants. They had branched out from their original "ethnic niche" of small businesses into educated professions, and had just begun to join forces with immigrants and their descendants from Japan, Korea, and the Philippines to advocate for civil rights under the umbrella term "Asian American." They might or might not have much contact with relatives left behind in the "old country." The remittances that had earlier tied them to their relatives in China had been cut off by China's revolution.

Few ever returned to China, and for the younger generations at least, these short visits were a kind of root-seeking, a distant emotional connection that did not distract them from their 100% Americanness. Some of the professionals among them had begun to form a scholarly field of Asian American studies, which drew its identity mainly from the idea that Asian Americans were Americans, just like Black, Brown, and Native Americans. The field was dedicated to fighting the "Sojourner Myth" perpetrated by White scholars, as an attempt to exclude Asian Americans from full membership in the American nation. Asian American studies, as a branch of American Studies or American Ethnic Studies, was and remains a field entirely separate from Asian Studies. The field was small, dedicated, isolated, and struggling. Doug was, as he states in his preface, among the early advocates for the professional development of Asian American Studies, as an academic field of study in higher education.

In the past, academic publishing was not much of a commercial enterprise. A scholar who dedicated his/her life to a single quest (a "hedgehog" in Isaiah

Berlin's terminology) could possibly look forward, decades down the road, to publication of a long (often multi-volume), detailed, and specialized work incorporating a lifetime of research, writing, and thinking about a single theme, often a broad one. Today, it is nearly impossible to do this.

Now, more than 40 years later, the world has changed. Recent immigrants from all over China (and from Taiwan) have made Mandarin the dominant "home language" of growing numbers of Chinese Americans, with sizable numbers speaking other varieties. Only recent poor immigrants live in Chinatowns, and Asian American is an established identity in US politics. Thousands of scholars practice Asian American studies, and if they fight a myth, it is that of the "model minority." But perhaps the biggest change is what we now call "transnationalism" in scholarship, politics, and family and everyday life. Chinese Americans, Americans of Chinese descent, Chinese living in America, all are ways we can describe today's ethnic group, as are parallel terms that replace "Chinese" with "Asian." People fly back and forth all the time (or at least they did in the pre-COVID era), talk every day on WeChat, and send presents both directions. Asian American studies no longer strives to separate itself from either American Ethnic Studies or Asian Studies, but has regular and mostly friendly relations with both of these larger fields. And it is more and more difficult for the hedgehogs in any field to publish long, detailed, specialized works of scholarship.

Doug Lee has lived through this near half century of transformation, or better to say, he has lived the transformation. Nevertheless, he has remained the respected hedgehog, dedicated to chronicling the "Gum-Shaan experience" as he calls it, the saga of that hardy and resourceful group of immigrants from Gwongdung and their descendants. And he has now composed a throwback piece of scholarship, *The Gum-Shaan Chronicles*, that will take six or more volumes to tell the story in sufficient detail and with appropriate precision.

In keeping with the reconciliation of Asian American studies and Asian studies, *The Gum-Shann Chronicles* documents the story of the Cantonese on both sides of the Pacific from the origins of overseas emigration and American immigration, to the early twentieth century. The first volume, *Seeking Tong-Shaan,* which I'm proud to introduce here, goes back to the homeland, beginning with the questions of "who are/were the 'Cantonese,' anyway?" and "where is this place they call *Tong-Shaan*?" which less careful scholars have simply called Guangdong or, in Lee's idiosyncratic but phonetically more intuitive spelling, Gwongdung?

Lee carefully differentiates the homeland of the Cantonese immigrant from the surrounding areas, as well as delineating the specific linguistic varieties they spoke both in *Tong-Shaan* and in *Gum-Shaan*. He then goes on to ask questions that have less precise and thus even more interesting answers: What distinguished *Tong-Shaan* culture from Chinese culture in general; how did it shape and how was it shaped by the immigrant experience? Finally, setting the stage for the next several volumes, Lee traces the effect of the immigrant experience on the view of *Tong-Shaan* from *Gum-Shaan*—how sojourners (no longer a dirty word, even though most of their descendants did turn out, in fact, to be Asian Americans) in *Gum-Shaan* looked upon and romanticized *Tong-Shaan* from a distance.

In former days, *The Gum-Shaan Chronicles* probably would have been attacked for its refusal to draw a firm line between Asia and America or between Asian American Studies and Asian Studies, but we can be thankful that that water has long flowed under the bridge of understanding. But also in former days, some academic press, somewhere, would have seen an economically feasible way of publishing what might have been a boxed set. Robert Caro got in under the wire and Barack Obama is well-known enough to defy the rules, but multivolume works on topics less hot than the US presidency are probably a thing of the past. Hence Doug has made the pragmatic and wise decision to publish his multivolume work himself.

I'm delighted and honored that Doug called me a few years ago to ask for advice on *The Gum-Shaan Chronicles,* and I'm happy to have been of some slight service in bringing at least the first volume to fruition. This product of a lifetime of hedgehoggian digging is work of great scholarly and public significance, and it is great news that it will soon be available to the reading public.

Steven Harrell, PhD, Professor Emeritus, University of Washington, and Editor of the University of Washington Press' <u>Ethnic Groups in China Series</u>

# PREFACE

### The "history" of how "this history" came about

This investigation has followed a long and circuitous path over the course of more than half a century, which has a significant bearing on its conceptualization, research, writing, and publication.

This effort began when I was a graduate student at the University of Michigan in 1968, where I did a research project on the Cantonese in Modern Chinese History. As a second-generation Cantonese-Chinese American, I was curious about the topic. My research paper lacked quality in its research and writing, but it did raise some interesting threshold questions. This experience served as the starting point of a lifelong quest. A decade later in 1979, I wrote my doctoral dissertation on "Political development in Chinese America, 1850–1900," which gave me a glimpse into the enormous possibilities of researching Cantonese-Chinese experience within a transnational context, in both China and America.

During the next several years 1979–1984, I chose to integrate my training in Modern Chinese History, with my interest in Chinese American History. My good intentions and naivete were dead on arrival at my first appointment in the Asian American Studies program at the University of Washington (1979–1984). After five years of teaching, research-writing, local Asian American community service, helping to found the Chinese Historical Society of the Pacific Northwest, and advocating the professional development of Asian American Studies, (helping to found the national Association for Asian American Studies and serving as its first national president,) I resigned my position. I was exhausted and frustrated by the incessant political intrigue and infighting in the Asian American Studies program at the University of Washington. By nature, I am not an activist, and try to avoid political contests. I was unaware that I had naively chosen to start my professional career at a time and place, where mutual distrust and indifference obstructed efforts at bridging the senseless gulf between Asian Studies and Asian American Studies.

Thereafter, for the next thirty years, until I retired in 2014, I resumed teaching in East Asian History, specializing in Modern China. At about the same time, I committed myself to investigating the origin and early chapters of Chinese American history and culture, with particular interest in the construction, representation, and reproduction of mid-to-late nineteenth-century Cantonese identity. I wanted to learn about how these matters were related to Cantonese co-contemporary experiences in China and elsewhere in distant overseas locations. I was intrigued with the question of how and why these vexing questions might be historically meaningful and significant in both Chinese History and Chinese American History.

Thus, began a solitary quest of nearly four decades, (1984–2022) where I purposefully avoided professional contacts with colleagues in both Asian American Studies and Asian Studies, which might involve mention my research activities. I did so because I believed that such revelations would be futile and frustrating, because of the earlier mentioned mutual distrust and social distancing between specialists in both fields. I had learned that there existed little interest or support for the kind of research that I had committed myself to. Asian American Studies specialists, with few exceptions, were primarily focused on contemporary Asian American issues, e.g., immigration, acculturation, assimilation, ethnic identity (e.g., the model minority dilemma,) race relations, ethnic community issues, bilingual education, and more recently Asian American LGBTQ issues. Consequently, most Asian Americanists only gave passing lip service to the study of nineteenth-century precedents. Similarly, Modern China historians maintained a persistent indifference and/or disdain for the study of the Chinese in America. My own doctoral advisor thought that there was little to be gained in the study of Chinese American History, beyond referencing restaurants, laundries, Chinatowns, and railroad building. He cautioned that I should limit my sojourn in Asian American Studies to as short a period as possible, because he believed that to linger too long would be the "kiss of death" to my professional career.

My secretive life as a reclusive researcher/writer was underscored, when I was invited to attend the Association for Asian American Studies'

2009 annual meeting, on the occasion of the 30th anniversary of the founding of the association. I was recognized as one of the association's founders, and its first national president. To my surprise, upon encountering several former colleagues, some exclaimed, "We thought that you had died!" Fortunately, during the elapsing thirty-odd years, the association had grown from a small membership of about forty people to several thousand, with multiple generations of new scholars, researchers, teachers, and advocates. The field is now robust and full of many new bright, smart, and energetic young minds, resulting in many new and wonderful scholarly developments. These experiences have greatly influenced my thinking, research, and writing. During my solitary quest of nearly four decades, (1984–2022) I strongly believed that the subject of my investigation had merit and value.

In this context, I want to acknowledge my great debt, deep respect, and lasting gratitude to H. Mark Lai. My long-time association and interaction with Mark was the sole exception to avoiding contact and sharing of my research with other researchers and scholars in Chinese American Studies. Mark is universally regarded as "the Dean of Chinese American History," having pioneered the teaching of Chinese American Studies at UC Berkeley. He also continuously produced groundbreaking scholarly research (using primary Chinese-language materials) in Chinese American History. The high quality of his thinking, research, and writing, belied the fact that he was a mechanical engineer by training. During, these many years, (1984–2009) we maintained regular contact, where he demonstrated a keen interest in my work. He was one of the founders, and a prominent leader of the Chinese Historical Society of America in San Francisco. I followed his example and helped to found the Chinese Historical Society of the Pacific Northwest, in Seattle (1986), where I served as the editor of its annual journal, and President of the society (1987–88). Mark served as a much needed, highly respected, and greatly appreciated mentor. Unfortunately, his death in 2009, robbed me of the benefit of his much-valued friendship and wise counsel. His careful eye for accuracy, for both the small details and the big picture, benefitted me greatly. I cherish his unwavering encouragement and generous support.

Starting around 1986, I committed myself to writing a narrative history of the Cantonese in the nineteenth century, beginning with their origin and experience back home in China, and then extending it to cover the Cantonese experience in Nineteenth-Century America. I had originally planned to revise my dissertation for publication. Quickly, my revision pivoted, while re-writing the introduction. As I worked, my introduction began to change focus. What had been an introduction to one work, soon became an introduction to another entirely different work. Quickly, this introduction began to have "babies" in the form of new chapters, and these chapters in turn became a whole new book project. Over the years, my book also "had babies," where one book became two, then three, four, five, and more. After thirty-five years, my project has become a nine-volume study, of which this book is the first volume. I hope that by sharing this book's long gestation, from a distant preliminary inquiry of fifty-two years ago, to its current publication, helps to contextualize the long and challenging process of its creation. Appreciating this background can help readers to more easily navigate this book and also to better grasp its message.

In 2015, I belatedly started to think about publication. I submitted various volumes to different university presses, which all seemed initially interested and supportive, but for various reasons eventually decided not to offer a contract to publish. The common denominator centered on increasingly shrinking budgets and new restrictive criteria governing acceptability of submitted manuscripts, such as total word counts, and the changing needs, interests, and expectations of various communities of readers. Today, academic presses can only afford to publish small, slim monographic works of about 200–250 pages, with about 100,000–125,000 words in paperback editions. Economically, logistically, and within a shorter period of time, these kinds of works can be moved quickly and easily. I subsequently realized that my project(s) did not fit these changing academic publishing standards and expectations.

In 2017, I was diagnosed with cancer, which then metastasized to become stage 4 cancer in later 2018. Fortunately, my treatment has enabled me to continue to pursue my publishing goals. I realize however, that my time is uncertain, as it is for all of us, as especially underscored by the COVID-19 pandemic of 2019–2022. I realize that if my work remains unpublished when I pass on, then it will also die with me. In this context, I have decided that the most effective, efficient, and timely way to publish my work is to self-publish. While it would have been nice to have an academic press publish my work, however, the lengthy effort, extended time frame, and technicalities involved are clearly unrealistic in my case.

Limited time however, is not my only consideration. My work has resulted in a series of several volumes, which merit being published together as a series, rather than as separate individual books. Beyond financial constraints and changing editorial standards, it is a given that no academic nor commercial press, would ever consider publishing a multivolume series by an unknown author. In today's publishing world, book series are common among popular fiction writers. Three better-known examples include: C.S. Lewis' *Narnia Chronicles*, J.K Rowling's *Harry Potter* series, and James Clavell's Asian historical adventure series, (*Taipan*, *Shogun*, and *Noble House*.)

There existed a time, when multivolume works in history were acceptable and appreciated. Three notable examples include: Edward Gibbon's six volume work, *Decline and Fall of the Roman Empire*, Winston Churchill's four volume, *A History of the English-Speaking Peoples*, and Hubert H. Bancroft's multi volumed histories of Central America, Mexico, California, and the Pacific Northwest respectively.

In Asian History, the most notable multi-volume works are the Cambridge Histories of China and Japan, which howeever, are not authored by an individual, but instead are usually edited by different individuals, with each chapter written by a well-established specialist of a particular period or subject area. There have been a few recent multi volume series in Chinese History. Two of the better known are the Free Press (1970s) three-volume series on the *Transformation of Modern China*; and the more recent (2010) Belknap Press, six-volume series on the *History of Imperial China*. In both of these cases, each volume has been authored by a different individual. More typically, some authors write and publish a major work, followed by a sequel, e.g., William T. Rowe's two books on the history of the city of Hankow.

In Asian American History, Judy Young's two volume study on Chinese women in San Francisco, and Pei Chi Liu's *History of the Chinese in the United States of America* (published in Chinese, 1976) are similar examples of two-volume works. I am unaware of any individual solo-authoring a multivolume series, in either Modern Chinese History or Chinese American History.

When I started working on this project, I certainly did not envision writing a multi volume study. In looking back, I see that my project simply evolved on its own, to become a multi volume series. This fact has been decisive in determining which publishing route my work can be published to its best advantage. These factors, have led me to choose to self-publish. Here, I inaugurate a nine-volume series, entitled, *The Gum-Shaan Chronicles: The Early History of Cantonese-Chinese America, 1850–1900*.The present book, *Seeking Tong-Shaan, Encountering Gum-Shaan: What it Meant to Be Cantonese in China and America, 1850-1900,* investigates the antecedent pre-emigrant Cantonese experience in Central Gwongdung, where "old world" thinking, experience, traditions, and practices became a template for constructing and contextualizing "new world" experiences and expectations.

It may be helpful to know why I choose to use the dates 1850-1900, in both the titles of the *Gum-Shaan* Chronicles series, and also for this first volume. I had originally chosen to use the term "nineteenth-century," but then I realized that this term was too ambiguous, and imprecise, because much of my attention is focused on the later nineteenth-century. Additionally, in both this volume, and the series of volumes to follow, I have occasion to refer to events and developments that occurred before 1850 (such as in the 1840s) and also after 1900 (such as in the 1920s). Such references are typically contextual, to demonstrate a pattern of development, or a chain of events, which may have occurred either before 1850 or after 1900. These references may also have intrinsic historical significance of their own. In this regard, my use of the dates 1850-1900 is not intended to be absolute nor precise, but rather to merely serve as a general frame of reference. They are purposefully intended to be flexible enough to expand, to include events and developments before 1850 and after 1900, while also serving as concrete and useful chronological bookends to my investigation.

In writing this book, I am mindful of four underlying concerns that have shaped this project. Appreciating these matters will facilitate a more productive and rewarding reading of this book.

Preface

**The challenge of using "Cantonese" and using "Chinese," as identifying labels**

I seek greater accuracy, authenticity, and specificity in my research and writing. This begins with how I categorize, and distinguish, between different, but related group identity labels. I intentionally use labels, such as "Cantonese," "Cantonese-Chinese," or "Cantonese-Chinese American," in place of "Chinese," "Han Chinese," or "Chinese American." Similarly in the Chinese language, I use the term *Yuet mei-wah Q* (Cantonese form) instead of either *Yue mei huaqiao*, (Pinyin mandarin form) or *Yueh-mei hua-ch'iao*, (Wade-Giles mandarin form). These changes on both sides of the English-Chinese language divide affirm my goal to use "Cantonese" or "*Yuet*" in place of "Chinese" or "Han Chinese," when making reference to things "Cantonese."

This revisionist distinction applies to things "Cantonese" in both China and America. I only use terms like "China" and "Chinese," when I refer explicitly to things "Chinese," as clearly evident in such references as, "Chinese History," "Chinese language," and "Chinese society." When I refer to things "Cantonese," I choose to be as accurate and authentic as possible, and to avoid ambiguity, such as choosing to use terms like "Cantonese-Chinese American History," instead of "Chinese American History," or "Cantonese sojourners," in place of "Chinese sojourners." These choices reflect my revisionist agenda, to be accurate and authentic, in regards to what I investigate.

**How I approach the task of Cantonese Romanization**

The manner of how I Romanize Chinese language items begins with how I reproduce and represent names, terms, and labels, as they were actually used in both Modern Cantonese-Chinese History and early Cantonese-Chinese American History. During the nineteenth century, and beyond, Cantonese language/speech and *Yuet* culture formed the basis of a distinctive ethnic identity and experience. It only seems natural to use terms that accurately reflect past speech/language conventions associated with this historical identity, and which also authentically replicate how they were actually pronounced, when spoken. In support of this goal, I choose first to Romanize/transliterate relevant Chinese language items by using their Cantonese forms, when required or appropriate. I avoid using whenever possible

Mandarin Chinese Romanization and transliteration, (both the contemporary *Pinyin* and the older Wade-Giles systems,) when using or referencing Cantonese names and terms.

In the initial use of a Cantonese term, I provide a Romanization of the Cantonese form (see clarification below), then for the benefit of those knowledgeable with Mandarin Chinese, I also supply the Mandarin *Pinyin* romanization in parenthesis. In some cases, I also provide the older Wade-Giles Romanization, which may be more familiar to "more experienced and knowledgeable" readers. This is also put into parenthesis. These Romanized terms are followed by the English translation, which is also in parenthesis. I typically follow this pattern, when a particular word, term or label, is introduced and used for the first time. Thereafter, I only provide the Cantonese form. An exception exists, when a subsequent use/reference can benefit from also repeating its Pinyin Romanization form as well, such as in the case of *Gwongdung* (*Guangdong*).

Regrettably for economic and logistical reasons associated with self-publishing, I am unable to provide Chinese characters for the Chinese terms I reference in this book. I make an exception in one case, to avoid confusion and error, as in the case of the term *Yuet* (*Yue*) (*Yueh*), (see Chapter 3).

While the decision to use Cantonese terms, and labels is natural and easy, its manner of application is complicated and problematic. There exist a variety of Cantonese Romanization systems. Four are commonly used in teaching Cantonese to non-Chinese speakers. They include: 1) Yale Romanization, 2) IPA (International Phonetic Alphabet) Romanization, 3) Sidney Lau Romanization, and 4) Meyer-Wempe Romanization. Other additional Romanization systems include: 5) Cantonese *Pinyin* Romanization, 6) *Jyutping* Romanization, 7) Guangdong Romanization, 8) Barnett-Chao Romanization, 9) New French Latinization of Cantonese Romanization, and 10) Standard Cantonese Romanization (first developed in 1888 by missionary John Morrison Chalmers, which in 1914 became the basis of modern Cantonese Romanization systems, in Canton and Hong Kong. It is no longer in use.) All of these systems use complicated series of vowels and consonants, together with numbers to indicate tones (one of six standard tones, and three other shifting tones). The choice of which system to use in this book has been very challenging, with each having its own distinctive symbols, forms, and combinations thereof.

Because I want to avoid needless confusion and frustration for non-Cantonese speakers/readers, while making it possible for them to achieve as authentic and accurate (Standard Cantonese) Cantonese pronunciations as possible, I adopt/utilize my own transliteration/ Romanization scheme. I have steadfastly rejected urgings of many colleagues to adopt one of the standard Cantonese Romanization systems for use in this book. e.g., the *Jyutping* Cantonese Romanization system used in Hong Kong, to achieve a requisite level of compatibility and authenticity expected of scholarly works in the field. I, again, reject this admonition because the overwhelming majority of non-Cantonese readers of this book will only need to pronounce Cantonese names, titles, words, and labels, as they are used in the context of this book. In most instances, readers will only need to know how to properly pronounce one word/term at a time within a specific context. This will not require readers to engage in actual Cantonese conversation. Thus, I believe adopting a formal Cantonese Romanization system would be counterproductive, even though it would be regarded by most as a desirable sign of authenticity and legitimacy.

Consequently, I choose to approach the task of Cantonese Romanization in three practical ways. First, whenever possible I adopt standardized well-known and commonly-used Cantonese pronunciations, (e.g., *Hakka*, and *Hoiping*) to replace Mandarin Chinese forms, (e.g., *Gejia* and *Kaiping* respectively.) Second, as a concession to practicality and ease for non-Cantonese (i.e., English) speakers, I often retain well-known names and terms in their established forms, rather than change them, (e.g., Hong Kong, Canton, and Sun Yat-sen). Third, I adopt my own idiosyncratic spelling/form for commonly used selected terms and labels, to reflect correct standard Cantonese pronunciations that are more "user friendly," (e.g., I use *Gum-Shaan* instead of the standard Cantonese speech form of *Gam-saan*.) In the case of common everyday speech, involving ordinary terms, (see chart below) I avoid using any of the recognized systems for Cantonese Romanization, because of their complexity of form, organization, and difficulty of application and use. These systems utilize an array of signs, symbols, and "tone" identifying numbers, which only serve to distract and confuse the non-Cantonese (i.e., Western) readers/speakers. The situation would be different if one were actually learning Cantonese, to be able to converse fluently, where standardized Cantonese Romanization is an essential linguistic tool. In the present situation, where one merely needs to know how to easily pronounce a single Cantonese word or term, such Romanization schemes needlessly impose a burden on the non-Cantonese speaker. For example, in the earlier referenced *Jyutping* Romanization system, the term for the *Yuet* language is Romanized as *Jyut6/yu5* (*Yueyu* in *Pinyin* Mandarin). I choose to simply Romanize this term as *Yuet-yu*. This different spelling (I drop the silent "J") and my omitting the tone indicators is much simpler and less confusing, which helps non-Cantonese speakers (especially Westerners) to more easily grasp a word's pronunciation.

While I regret that this approach does not indicate tonal variations, it is a decision not taken lightly and without reason. While tones are critically important, because of the existence of numerous Cantonese homophones, (e.g., as in English, "rose" (a flower) "rose" (arising), or "reign" and "rain," or "dear" and "deer.") Because the non-Cantonese speaker is concerned with only reading and pronouncing individual Romanized Cantonese words, the concern is with just one word or term at a time, in the context of its immediate reference or use in a particular situation. Most readers of this book, are not concerned with actually using any of the terms/words, in the course of conversing, where misconstruing a word's tone would likely be a problem in communicating the right word or term, because there are so many Cantonese homophones. While Cantonese language specialists and linguists, and others, may find this approach to be imprecise, somewhat inaccurate, and even ridiculous, I believe that within the context of this study, it is an approach that best supports the purpose of this book, because it offers practical common-sense help to the non-Cantonese speaker/reader. The following table offers some useful examples.

## Selected comparison of two approaches to Romanization of Cantonese

| English word/term | Standard Cantonese Romanization format [1](ref: Standard Cantonese) (*Kwong-chau-wa*) | My own adopted practical phonetic Romanization of standardized Cantonese (*Gwong-chau wah*) |
|---|---|---|
| vegetable | tsoi[5] | choy |
| to die | sei[3] | say |
| to blow | tsh/oy[1] | churi |
| again | tsoi[5] | joy |
| snack, light lunch | tim[3] sam[1] | dim-sum |
| cough | kat [7a] | cut |
| moon or month | yut [7b] | yuet |
| to enter | yap [8] | yup |
| to see | kinn[5] | ghyean or geean |
| hundred | pa:k [7b] | bok |
| female | noi[4] | nuri |
| paper | tsi [3] | gee |
| word | tsi [6] | gee |
| polite | ha:k[7b] hei[5] | hak-hay |
| north | pak[7a] | buck |
| liquor | tsau[3] | jow |
| fetch | tsip[7b] | jup |

In the following table, I cite examples of commonly referenced names, terms, and labels, frequently used in this book. Here, again, I adopt and use my own Romanization forms, as a matter of simplicity and practicality, for the benefit of non-Cantonese speakers.

Preface

## Comparative chart of the Cantonese Romanization of selected key terms and labels

| English term | *Pinyin* Mandarin Chinese form | Wade-Giles Mandarin Chinese form[2] | Standard Cantonese form | My own adopted alternative forms are in boldface |
|---|---|---|---|---|
| Home province Cantonese homeland | *Guangdong* | Kwang-tung | Kwong-tung | **Gwongdung**[3] |
| Canton (City of) | *Guangzhou* | Kwang-chou | Kwong-chau | **Gwong-chau** |
| Cantonese speech (General & specific) | *Guangdong hua-Guangzhou hua* | Kwang-tung hua Kwang-chou hua | Kwong-tung wa Kwong-jau wa | **Gwongdung wah** **Gwongchau wah** |
| Cantonese person/people | *Guangdong ren* | Kwang-tung jen | Kwong-tung yahn | **Gwongdung yan** |
| District Association | *Huiguan* | Hui-kuan | Ooi-kun | **Wooi-koon** or **Wui-kun** |
| Three District speech group | *Sanyi* | San-i | Saam-yap | **Saam-Yup** |
| Four District speech group | *Siyi* | Sze-i | Sze-yap | **Say-yup** |
| Toi-Shaan district (Hoisaan) | *Taishan* | T'ai-shan | T'oi-shaan | **Toi-shaan** |
| Chung-Shan district | *Zhongshan* | Chung-Shan | Chung-shaan | **Chung-Shaan** |
| Tang Mountain A colloquial term for the Cantonese homeland in Central Gwongdung | *Tangshan* | T'ang-shan | T'ong-shaan | **Tong-Shaan** |
| Gold Mountain A Cantonese colloquial term for Chinese America | *Jinshan* | Chin-shan | Kam-shaan | **Gum-Shaan** |
| Gold Mountain [supply] firm | *jinshanzhuang* | Chin-shan chuang | Kam shaan chung | **Gum-Shaan chong** |
| Chinese "natives" Chinese settlers in Fujian and Gwongdung before the 12th century CE | *Bendi* | Pen-ti (or Punti) | Poon-tei | **Bundae** |
| "Guest peoples" Chinese migrant/settlers (non-*Bundae peoples*), who settled in Gwongdung & Fujian after the 12th century CE | *Gejia* | Ke-chia | Hakka | Hakka |

## The challenge of accessing, reproducing, representing, and interpreting statistical data

A brief word is in order about how I handle quantitative/ statistical data, because while my purpose is irreproachable, my methods are not. I recognize the inherent difficulties of working with inadequate or missing historical statistical data. This is especially evident in chapter one, where I have reconstructed and realigned Cantonese demographic data, because of encountering incomplete, missing, or the challenge of non-existent data. Consequently, it should be understood that the observations I make in this investigation, regarding the use of quantitative data, are intended only for discussion purposes within the context of this book. They merely illustrate a "demonstrated pattern, an observable sequence, or an order of magnitude." I make no claim of any precise accounting based on the data presented. I readily admit that some of my mathematical computations are clearly suspect, because they are often unorthodox, and in some instances lack a credible basis. This latter point is especially evident in instances where I extrapolate statistical data applicable to one location for a particular point in time, and then apply it sequentially elsewhere over a longer period of time, e.g., using data on the population growth rate for one rural district in 1850, based on one set of computations, and then applying the same approach or rationale to other rural districts in the same manner, during the same period. Clearly what is applicable to one location, at one point in time, is not equally applicable in the same manner elsewhere. Again, because of unavoidable limitations, my intent is to merely offer a "demonstrated pattern," or "an order of magnitude." I hope that my good intentions are persuasive enough to help mitigate flaws in my methodology, by way of offering: 1) a new conceptualization about nineteenth-century Cantonese demographics, 2) a useful approach for how historical demographic data can be better organized and evaluated, and 3) a novel comprehensive comparative analysis of aggregate Cantonese demographics, during the period 1840–1900. In this manner, I see my approach to handing statistical data as a useful "place marker," where others in the future, armed with more accurate reliable data, and improved data analysis skills, can correct my errors to improve and expand upon my preliminary observations.

**Revisionist based conceptualizations and research strategies**

Throughout this book, I adopt and use a variety of theories and research strategies to facilitate advancing fresh interpretations about the past. Many are these are historiographic in nature, but others are borrowed from other disciplines and fields of study, e.g., geography, linguistics, economics, anthropology, sociology, environmental studies, ethnology, Chinese History, and Cantonese-Chinese American History, to name a few. These multi-sourced conceptualizations are helpful in better explaining a wide variety of complex topics, e.g., the structural composition and operational patterns of institutions and systems, collective identities and group interrelationships, changing processes, and the evolutionary relationship between *Yuet* language, Cantonese speech, and ethnic group identity in Central Gwongdung and in America.

**A wise admonition regarding how to conduct beneficial and significant historical research**

I follow the wise admonition to "say little, where others have already discussed extensively, and to elaborate more fully and carefully, where others have been silent or have said little." [3] In this context, much has been said about Chinese American identity and experience in *Gum-Shaan* (America,) from a Chinese American historical perspective; and also about pre-emigrant Cantonese-Chinese identity and experience back home in *Tong-Shaan* in Central Gwongdung, from a Chinese historical perspective. Unfortunately, however, little has been said about the critically important nexus between these two chapters of experience. The important relevance of pre-emigrant identity/experience is that, it not only represented an enduring ethno-linguistic and socio-cultural standard back home, but also provided a critical construct for their replication overseas in America and elsewhere. This critical relationship links together two closely related, but distinctly separate and equally vital portraits of later nineteenth-century Cantonese identity and experience.

**What this book represents, and why it matters**

The chief purpose of this book is to provide a remedy for the longstanding neglect of the subject of traditional Cantonese identity and experience, first in

*Tong-Shaan* in China, and then in *Gum-Shaan* in America. The organizational format of this book is indicative of this approach, with each chapter covering a key component of nineteenth-century Cantonese language, ethnicity, history, geography, demography, society, and culture. I offer a caveat, regarding the particular organizational format adopted here, because its relevance and practicality may not be so obvious, as one navigates the text. In this book, I have tried to balance two contradictory, often antagonistic imperatives, regarding how I frame issues both conceptually and organizationally.

Specifically, I have tried to balance the need to manage a large quantity of diverse material facts, while framing them within useful conceptual categories of analysis. These different tasks should be kept in mind, as my discussion navigates through a wide variety of topics and issues, which are only now amenable to fruitful conceptualization, discussion and interpretation. Each chapter represents an effort to construct a coherent and credible narrative in support of this book's stated theme, "What it meant to be Cantonese in the later nineteenth century."

The publication of this inaugural volume of the *Gum-Shaan Chronicles* underscores the great responsibility that I bear. I often ask myself, "How many people have the opportunity, honor, simple good luck, and good timing to undertake such a task?" I am humbled and grateful to undertake this enterprise, knowing that I am only a pioneer, with many others to follow, who will undoubtedly further expand and improve on what I have been fortunate to accomplish. My intent at the outset of working on this project over four decades ago, was to merely offer a new thoughtful "revisionist" perspective of early Cantonese-Chinese American History (1850–1900). I now realize that very few people get the rare opportunity to write the history of their own people. In publishing this work, I am mindful of the heavy responsibilities which I bear. I can only hope that my work does justice to this critical chapter of history.

**Some encouragement and support for others facing the challenge of publishing their work**

I want to take the opportunity to speak briefly to those individuals, who may have had, or who are encountering, difficult and frustrating publishing challenges. My message to you, is to never give up on your quest. This word of encouragement and support is directed especially towards those in academia. The struggle for tenure, for collegial understanding and support, and for recognition and publication of your work are indeed formidable and ongoing. You may not get tenure, collegial acceptance/support, or publication by a university press. This does not mean however, that your work lacks merit, or that it is unworthy of publication. First, openly accept and learn from valid criticisms and positive constructive suggestions of others. Always be mindful of your own shortcomings and inadequacies. In the alternative, you should also be confident in your abilities, proud of your work, and remain committed to your vision. Believe in yourself, and the fact that what you have to offer has value. With hard work, a deep commitment, and proper timing, your quest will be ultimately successful.

**Sacrifices made to facilitate a timely and economical publication of this book**

During this book's production, I have had to make a number of difficult decisions, which might normally compromise the quality and credibility of this work, as a scholarly publication. These decisions have not been taken lightly. As a practical matter, they reflect the pressing need to be pragmatic and realistic, regarding logistical and financial constraints with a private publication.

The sacrifices mentioned here, only relate to "things that would be nice to have," and which when eliminated, do not materially adversely affect the book's integrity, presentation, and ultimately its value. Again, it would have been nice to have had everything that one might have wanted in a scholarly work, to enhance the attractiveness and quality of its presentation. I believe however, despite these matters, the book's research, writing, and messaging remains uncompromised.

In the final analysis however, the sacrifices made, have reaped solid benefits for the book and its potential readership, without compromising its usefulness and value. The sacrifices of which I speak, include the following four items:

1) Eliminate having a book index
2) Eliminate the reproduction or printing of any Chinese characters, with the exception of a few Chinese characters in chapters 2 and 3, as they pertain to Cantonese speech and Yuet language (粵)
3) Reproduction of all maps, photos, and artwork only in black and white
4) Limit the sourcing of all photos and maps used in this book to only internet sources, which are identified as "public domain" sources, which clearly state that any and all such materials can be used and modified in any way, for any use, none of which require any permission to use, or license for use by other parties

It should be noted that because of these sacrifices, both the author and the reading public will benefit greatly. First, this book, and its successive companion volumes, will be published more quickly over the course of the next year or two, rather than over several years. Second, these books will be more affordable for the average consumer. Each paperback will cost somewhere between about $25.00 and $30.00, instead of between about $65.00 and $70.00. Similarly, each hardback copy will cost somewhere between about $35.00 and $40.00, instead of between about $80.00 and $85.00.

An awareness of these considerations, and the benefits that they helped to bring about, helps to explain and justify why they are deemed prudent and necessary.

---

[1] See following two works, S. Robert Ramsey, The Languages of China, (Princeton, New Jersey: Princeton University Press, 1989), pp.100–105; Jerry Norman, Chinese, (New York: Cambridge University Press, 1993, (originally published 1988) (Cambridge Language Surveys), p. 217.

## Preface

[2] Most people under age 60 have very little familiarity with, or may be entirely uninformed and ignorant about the Wade-Giles Romanization of Mandarin Chinese. Consequently, I have been advised to drop references to it. I have not done so, because on occasion such Romanized forms are helpful, because they were used exclusively in the secondary literature before the late 1970s. More importantly, such references, such as here, underscore the complexity of Romanization and its convoluted evolution, made more complex by the existence and use of other Han Chinese dialects. By demonstrating the various diverse Romanization forms, I underscore the difficulties inherent in adopting suitable Romanization for Chinese terms/phrases, and labels. I believe context, as well as content, are both critical elements, relative to what form of Romanization is adopted in any given situation.

3 Per a 1987 suggestion of Mark Lai, I have adopted the term "Gwongdung," for rendering the name of the home province of Cantonese people. This new atypical phonetic form replicates as accurately and authentically as possible the correct standard Cantonese pronunciation, for non-Cantonese speakers. This suggestion, was made in response to voicing my discomfort and frustration with various existing romanization forms, e.g., (Guangdong, mandarin Pinyin form) (Kwangtung, mandarin Wade-Giles form) and (Kwong-tung, the standard Cantonese form).

[4] This admonition is from Dr. Immanuel C.Y. Hsu, my doctoral advisor in Modern Chinese History at the University of California at Santa Barbara, (January 1976.)

# ACKNOWLEDGMENTS

This book mirrors an ongoing maturation and refinement in my thinking during the last few years, which allows me to be more confident in having my work published. In doing so, I want to acknowledge the wise advice and support of several individuals over the course of many decades. They include: Dr. Immanuel C.Y. Hsu, (my PhD advisor at UCSB); Mr. Him Mark Lai, (my mentor, colleague, and friend in Chinese American History); Dr. Alan P. Liu, (my professor and friend at both the University of Michigan and UCSB); Dr. Rhoads Murphey, (my advisor and mentor at the University of Michigan); and Dr. Robert Cruden, (my advisor/mentor at Lewis and Clark College.)

More recently, I have benefitted enormously from the encouragement and expert counsel of Dr. Stevan Harrell, former chair of the Anthropology Department at the University of Washington, and editor of the University of Washington Press' Ethnic Groups in China Series. I deeply appreciate his infinite patience, vast expertise in all things Chinese, especially southern Chinese, and his sharp eye for even the most miniscule detail, none of which have escaped his attention. He, more than any other person, has been instrumental in helping me to refine my thinking, and to be more mindful of the complexities involved in academic writing and publishing.

I also want to express my gratitude to three individuals, who have always been ready to offer help and support 24/7. Dr. Linda Walton, a much-esteemed colleague, and long-time friend, patiently edited versions of this manuscript, while providing many helpful constructive comments and suggestions on how to improve my thinking and writing. Her wise and patient advice has been decisive in helping me to improve on my very rudimentary editing skills. My son George Lee has been my "go-to-person," for questions about computer hardware & software issues, and for investigating a myriad of other technical issues and problems. Finally, I appreciate the tremendous help and constant support of my husband, Don Dickenson. His infinite patience, vast experience with computers, the internet, expert quantitative analytical skills, un-common common sense, and steadfast calmness in the face of unforeseen chaos, have helped me navigate a long complicated and often frustrating production process.

I have accepted most of the advice of these many individuals, while rejecting some of it. Whatever is significant and positive in this book, is due to

## Acknowledgments

their individual and collective efforts. Ultimately, however, whatever shortcomings and errors that may still exist in this book, I must claim as my own responsibility, without exception.

# INTRODUCTION

Cantonese people have been historically well-known in both China, and beyond, for the distinctiveness of their identity and their atypical experience(s), in comparison with other Han Chinese people. This is clearly evident in popularly ascribed characterizations, regarding their speech, shrewdness in business, obsession with fine cuisine, passion for social engagement, abiding belief in good luck, often via gambling, an unwavering commitment to hard work, with extreme patience in deferring consumption/gratification for future gain, and an uncompromising loyalty to and enduring love of one's family and native place.

Despite their prominence as a well-known subject in Modern Chinese History, Cantonese people remain paradoxically an inexplicitly enigmatic and provocative subject to discuss, notwithstanding numerous, albeit superficial, characterizations, which easily invite a sense of familiarity.

An improved understanding of this ascribed sense of Cantonese distinctiveness is possible, when we properly identify the basis and meaning of what constitutes this sense of Cantonese distinctiveness. The cross between an ascribed notoriety and unusual persona underscores a longstanding mixed tradition of indifference and bias against Cantonese people, both in China and beyond. The chief purpose of this book is to remedy this situation by inquiring into the nature of traditional Cantonese identity, as constructed and contextualized in the period 1850–1900, both at home in Central Gwongdung (Guangdong) and elsewhere in the expansive transnational overseas Cantonese-speaking world. This sense of traditional Cantonese distinctiveness materialized historically within the larger framework of an enigmatic and nuanced relationship between the "national" and the "ethnic" in China, as they have been represented in Modern Chinese History.

**The contemporary challenge of "national" versus "ethnic"**

The universal coin of the realm in today's world of ongoing struggles for collective social identity and national security is that of the "heads," of resurgent populist-nationalism, and "tails" of persistent advocacy for the rights of racial and ethno-linguistic minorities. No corner of the world is free of this powerful challenge in contemporary life. It manifests itself in the advanced post-industrial world and also in the underdeveloped world. Typically, this "Janus-headed" dilemma of struggle versus security, war versus peace, closure versus new beginnings plays itself out in a growing number of national/domestic conflicts with complex international implications. Some of the better-known examples include: the Kurds and Armenians in Turkey, the Basque and Catalan in Spain, the Rohingya in Myanmar/Burma, and the Tibetans and Uyghur[1] in China. It is a phenomenon that has deep historical roots and expansive socio-cultural branches that drive competition/conflict along many fronts in a transnational context, where "domestic issues" can produce progeny well beyond national borders and across cultural divides in distant locations.

While these matters are formidable, the binary formula of either peaceful co-existence or violent conflict is not necessarily applicable in every case. Beyond these extremes, there exist possible "middle ground" relationships and patterns of engagement, where there can be acceptance, fruitful cooperation, and even genuine good will. This not only underscores the complexity of national/ethnic relations, but also the diversity of their representation. There exist some ethno-speech minority groups, who have been well-positioned in the middle ground between the extremes of conflict and co-existence. They offer some useful clues about how to preserve, protect, and promote ethnic identity/experience, as a sustainable enterprise, which does not threaten, nor is threatened by, the "national." In this context, what we identify as "ethnic" has identifiably different connotations about what it means, and what it represents in a variety of contexts. Certainly, questions about how ethnicity is defined, how it is understood to function, and the manner of its application, significantly shapes how any particular national-ethnic paradigm is viewed and understood. We should remember that where religious, historical, and cultural issues are involved, they complicate national/ethnic competition and conflict, whereby they can reduce the chances for compromise and consensus.

**China and the conundrum of "national" versus "ethnic"**

The diversity of which I speak, and the complexities it mirrors in negotiating ethnic/national relations, is especially interesting in the Chinese environment. This is evident in the important distinction regarding how ethnic minority groups in China are grouped into two broad categories. First, there are non-Han Chinese "National Autonomous Minorities," such as the Tibetans, Mongols, Uyghurs, and various aboriginal tribal people, e.g., Miao, Han, Yao and Li. Second, there are Han Chinese ethno-speech minorities, within the dominant Han Chinese majority, e.g., the *Yuet* (*Yue*) Cantonese, the *Min* speaking people in *Hokkien* (Fujian) (Fukien), the *Hakka* in the *Lingnam* region, and the *Gan* in South-Central China.

The term "Han" has a well-known double connotation. First, it is the name of one of China's earliest and greatest imperial dynasties in remote antiquity, i.e., the highly esteemed Han Dynasty (202 BCE–220 CE). Second, the ascribed high pedigree of the term "Han" was later adopted as a generic ethnic label for identifying and distinguishing Chinese people from non-Chinese peoples, who were located on the periphery of what was historically known as "China Proper," (i.e., the homeland of the Chinese people, minus subsequently added areas of Tibet, Mongolia, the *Dongbei* (formerly known as Manchuria), and Xinjiang.) In other words, in China, there are "Han Chinese" and "other Chinese" (e.g., Mongols, Tibetans, Uyghurs, Turkic speaking Islamic peoples, Koreans, and various aboriginal peoples).

The two categories of Chinese ethno-speech minorities differ not only in their respective histories and socio-cultural constructs, but also in the matter of how they fit into China's ongoing "National versus minority ethnic-speech" debate. The National Autonomous Minorities encounter the "national" in the Han Chinese majority, where as highly visible and continually vulnerable minorities, the question of their mere existence has always been under close scrutiny. The situation may range from benign working relationships, laced with good intentions, e.g., with the Mongolians,[2] and various aboriginal tribal peoples, to hostile opposition and oppression, e.g., in the case of the Tibetans in Tibet, and the Uyghurs in Xinjiang.

In contrast, Han Chinese ethnic minorities, because they are Han Chinese first, and ethno-speech minorities second, they encounter the "national" from a very different perspective, with markedly different expectations and divergent experiences. While the lines separating the "national" from the "ethnic" are less pronounced and less volatile for Han Chinese ethno-speech minorities, this requires greater effort and understanding to grasp the challenge of Han Chinese ethnic preservation and promotion, within the national. While Han Chinese ethno-speech minorities embody inherent advantages over non-Han Chinese ethno-speech minorities, e.g., physical security and socio-cultural creditability, they also encounter challenges which non-Han minorities have not had to address. Certainly, high on this list is the ability and need to preserve, what are obviously more subtle and nuanced layers of ethnic identity and shades of experience, as they are intertwined within the voluminous folds of Han Chinese history and culture.

Membership within the Han Chinese majority has been a double-edged sword. On one hand there has been the comforting reassurance of being identified as part of the majority, and on the other hand, there has also been the disconcerting never-ending struggle to prevent the erosion of distinctiveness, and social distance or separation, associated with minority identity and experience. Among Mongols, Tibetans, Uyghurs, and other Autonomous National Minorities, there has undoubtedly long existed troubled relationships with the "national," i.e., the Han Chinese majority, where there has never been any doubt or confusion about the distinct and separate identities of these minority groups. In contrast, among Han Chinese ethno-speech minority communities, there has been a long-standing problematic relationship between being Han Chinese, and simultaneously also being a member of a Han Chinese ethnic/speech minority.

Among non-Han Chinese minorities, engagement between the "national" and the "ethnic" has always been predicated on obvious enduring ethno-speech distinctions and cultural/historical distances. In contrast, among Han Chinese minorities, the basis on which the "ethnic" has been predicated has been more subtle and abstract. Significantly, the lines that distinguished and separated the "ethnic" from the "national" were not as distinct, nor as clear, because their boundaries periodically shifted and changed in their ascribed identifications and meanings.

Consequently, ethnic identity and experience, in the context of encountering the "national," has meant entirely different things for these two categories of ethnic minority groups in China. While both groups are technically "ethnic minorities," they differ on how members of each category have viewed the National-Ethnic minority divide, relative to tactical positioning and strategic engagement in China's evolving constructs for National-Ethnic minority relations.

**"Han-ness" and "Chinese-ness" distinguished**

Uncertainty about the problematic relationship of the "national" and the "ethnic" in China, among Han Chinese ethnic minority groups and speech communities, is rooted to the vexing question of Han Chinese group identity formation and social engagement. Quite simply, how can we relate the two sides of the coin, "heads national and tails ethnic" in China, when we lack an appreciation of the delicate complexity of how the various Han Chinese (such as the *Yuet*/Cantonese) identities were constructed and how they related to each other? If we can clearly see the lines that divide and distinguish ethnic identity/experience between non-Han Chinese ethnic minority groups and the Han Chinese majority, then we should be open to the fact that such clear-cut distinctions may not be as true among Han Chinese ethnic minorities. Herein lies the underlying purpose of this investigation, which is to identify where and how Han Chinese ethnic minority groups illustrate various ambiguities and nuances, which complicate our understanding of the ethnic/national debate in its (Han) Chinese context.

The central theme of this book is the proposition that *Yuet* (*Yue*) Cantonese ethnicity/language in Central Gwongdung (*Guangdong*) (*Kwangtung*)[3] represents a critically important and useful case study for the re-examination of Chinese ethnicity within the collective Han Chinese identity. As a major regionally-based Han Chinese ethnic minority group and speech community, the Cantonese are historically unique because they dominated a well-defined geo-territorial space, established a distinct ethno-linguistic zone, and spawned their own enduring socio-cultural-historical tradition. This creative process evolved and replicated itself over time, under different material conditions, at many different locations. It began at the original Cantonese fountainhead in Central Gwongdung, which is often identified in this investigation as *Tong-Shaan* (*Tang-Shan*) or *Tong* (*Tang*) Mountain. Over time, it was later resurrected and replicated elsewhere in China, and then in many distant overseas locations.

In this manner, the Cantonese successfully established a historically significant and socio-culturally distinct persona, with an enduring presence in many different and distant locations. In doing so, they mirrored the constructs of Cantonese thinking and conduct, while at the same time they embodied Han Chinese social and cultural imperatives. Cantonese people undertook formidable challenges in the task of representing and replicating different layers of their identity. This reconstructed identity ensemble included both a sense of *Chinese-ness*, as well as an ethno-linguistically inspired sense of *Han-ness* (or *Tong-ness*, in the Cantonese case).[4]

In recent years, there have developed two fruitful avenues of scholarly inquiry about the construction of Chinese identity, involving macro/cultural-historical and micro/ethno-linguistic perspectives. The macro/cultural-historical perspective begins with the idea that,

> Chinese-ness entails common ancestry, homeland, mother tongue, and basic value orientation…the emergence of a cultural space (a symbolic universe) that both encompasses and transcends the ethnic, territorial, linguistic …boundaries that normally define Chinese-ness …we are critically aware of and deeply intrigued by its fluidity…These primordial ties- ethnic, territorial, linguistic- are…almost never present themselves simply as unambiguous conditions of human life…[thus] the fluidity of Chinese-ness [is] a layered and contested discourse.[5]

This notion of *Chinese-ness* intellectually embraces the totality of a self-ascribed, socio-historically crafted, and culturally authenticated collective

Chinese identity. It embodies a proportional calculus of inclusiveness and exclusiveness, relative to who are Chinese, as viewed among themselves, and in their relationships with other people. In this context, the particulars of who are considered to be Chinese is set within a familiar "we-they" binary, where language, culture, and history distinguish and separate Chinese people from non-Chinese people. While these considerations help explain the "us" among the Chinese, relative to the "them" of non-Chinese peoples, they do not however necessarily help us to better understand the inherent complexity that defines and sculptures the sense of *Chinese-ness* within the Chinese collective identity.

*Chinese-ness* is an arbitrary and artificially contrived abstraction, where Chinese people are represented respectively, as a legal definition, a political expediency, and an administrative convenience. It is a crafted identity resulting from an amalgamation of many different racial and ethno-linguistic groups, combining the dominant Han majority of about 1.2 billion, of a total population of 1.4 billion (2017), with fifty-five other ethno-linguistic minority groups, of about 200–250 million people.[6] This does not include the many millions of Chinese living elsewhere beyond China.

In this sense, *Chinese-ness* works well, when talking about aggregate numbers, involving the sum total of "us." Conversely however, it fails to meaningfully identify the material constructs of what constitutes the aggregate sum total that is embraced by this sense of *Chinese-ness*. This ambiguity results in large part because the term "Chinese" (as in Chinese people) translates from two separate and different terms, *Zhongguoren* (a Middle Kingdom/country person) and *Hanren* (a "Han" Chinese person). These two labels overlap, but bear different connotations. If the sense of *Chinese-ness* is too broad, and too amorphous, to be useful for seeking an improved reexamination of Chinese identity, then what, if any, other available options exist? It may be that a micro/ethno-linguistic perspective may help us to understand the construction of identity among ethnic groups in Han Chinese society.

Among the many layers which make up the Chinese identity, or the sense of *Chinese-ness*, none are more important than those of ethnicity and speech, as they have formed the essential building blocks of Chinese identity over many millennia. Specifically, anthropologists and historians have long utilized the "Han Chinese" ethnic label to study Chinese society and research Chinese History, relative to the idea of "others," as it specifically relates to various groups subsumed under the Chinese identity label. It is well to remember that while "all Han Chinese are Chinese, not all Chinese are Han Chinese." While there is clarity in the obvious, there remains however key threshold questions about "Who are the Han Chinese?" "What are the applicable distinctions among and between them?" and "Why do they matter?"

More recently, researchers have re-examined the Han Chinese identity label, with greater attention to the sense of *Han-ness*, relative to the notion of "Han China's diverse majority,"[7] In this context, *Han-ness* not only further helps differentiate between *Chinese-ness* and non-*Chinese-ness* (i.e., between those who are Chinese and those who are not), equally important it also identifies and clarifies which people make up the core constituency of the Han Chinese majority. In doing so, there is clearly the expectation that an improved understanding of Han Chinese identity will also mean an improved understanding of *Chinese-ness* in general. This is possible, because while the respective senses of *Chinese-ness* and *Han-ness* are closely related concentric identity labels, they differ in their individual focus, and in what each one embraces and excludes.

*Han-ness* represents an organically rooted authentic Chinese cultural label/expression. In Chinese history and culture, it is concrete and certain, without ambiguity or compromise. It has been enduring and constant, as a unifier and catalyst for the homogenous blending of diverse identities and experiences into a unified whole. Again, the vast majority of China's population is identified as "Han Chinese," as are nearly all of the Chinese living outside mainland China.[8] *Han-ness* has historically evidenced qualities of coherence and consistency- which are lacking in the sense of *Chinese-ness*. We can say that because *Han-ness* chronologically proceeds and culturally supersedes *Chinese-ness*, as the basis for the historical Chinese identity label, it has a presumed degree of enhanced credibility and authenticity in its representation of that identity.

We should remember however, that the Han Chinese identity was an expansive and evolving identity label, which absorbed others via intermarriage and acculturation for over two millennia. This pattern is significant, despite the fact that "Han," as an ethnic label, has only been used in the last few centuries. Over time many people were ascriptively regarded as "Han," but who themselves did not use the term nor identify with it.[9]

In today's discourse about the "diverse majority" within Han Chinese society and culture, it is less an expression of a bias against or an effort to exclude non-Han Chinese minorities from the sense of *Chinese-ness*, and more an effort to better appreciate the essence of *Han-ness*, as it enhances the meaning of *Chinese-ness* in today's world. This is not to say that the sense of *Han-ness* is not without its own challenges in deciphering the enigma of what legitimately constitutes the collective Han Chinese identity.

The categorial construction of *Han-ness* has been expertly mapped out in two recent studies,[10] which highlight both the centrality and complexity of *Han-ness* via a re-examination of the dynamic interplay of ethnicity and local speech communities, against the broader rubric of Chinese culture and history. As a practical matter, ethnicity and speech offer a useful litmus test for analyzing the label's working components, i.e., ethno-linguistic constructs and their socio-cultural and historical contextualization. This reveals various ways in which the Han Chinese identity has been constructed, utilized, and reproduced by diverse groups of people, who claim to identify with and represent alternative vintage editions of the sense of *Han-ness* within the larger context of the sense of *Chinese-ness*. These groups represent considerable diversity within an ascribed unity/uniformity that is commonly identified with the sense of *Han-ness*, even as they paradoxically contribute to the sense of *Chinese-ness* via their shared investment is things Chinese, e.g., culture, history, and the written language. They also enhance our understanding of where and how these groups balance contradictory tensions, regarding the advocacy of each one's own needs/imperatives, while supporting the broader requirements of a Han Chinese collective identity. This improves our understanding of what the Han Chinese identity means, to whom it applies, and the determinants shaping its representation and ongoing reproduction in both China and beyond.

Two approaches can help us to better understand the mechanics of *Han-ness*. One approach investigates regionally based Han Chinese ethnic minority groups and speech communities within China, as they have been traditionally subsumed under the Han Chinese identity label. Notable cases in South China include: 1) *Min*-speaking people in *Hokkien* (Fujian,) 2) the *Hakka* and *Pengmin* in the *Lingnan* region of S.E. China, and 3) both Cantonese *bendi* (*punti*) (hereafter referred to as *bundae*) or "natives" and the *Hakka* (or "guest") people in Central Gwongdung (Guangdong.) Various Han Chinese ethnic and/or sub-ethnic minorities and speech groups offer a variety of cases involving efforts at "negotiating ethnicities" within Han Chinese society.[11] Consequently, these groups underscore the critical importance of ethnicity and local speech community identifications, as major constructs of the broader Han Chinese identity label, especially in southern China. They help sort out and categorize diverse Han Chinese ethnic minorities and speech communities into key functional components of Han Chinese society and culture. Additionally, they act in contradictory fashion to unify them, because such distinctions have historically operated under an all-embracing Han Chinese cultural umbrella, where such groups have always shared a common high culture, historical tradition, and written language/literature.

The totality of the Han Chinese identity label, as the sum of its many constituent parts, mirrors a variety of interesting perspectives about how the Han Chinese identity has been constructed, both as a composite whole (i.e., The Han Chinese majority) and as a collection of distinct individual regional/local components (e.g., the *Yuet* Cantonese community) of a truly diverse majority. These perspectives help refine our understanding of how the Han Chinese identity mechanism operates, relative to its representation and reproduction.

There also exists an additional analytical model concerning Han Chinese ethnic minority groups and speech communities, with an alternative application and different goal in mind. In this approach, these groups are viewed as migrant communities located elsewhere in China, beyond their native places, e.g., the *Subei* community in Shanghai, or the *Teochiu* of East-Gwongdung in Hong Kong,[12] or as emigrant communities located overseas in diverse and distant locations, e.g., in the Americas, or Southeast Asia.[13] This investigative strategy is evident in several studies of later Nineteenth-Century and early Twentieth-Century China, e.g., in Beijing, Chinese Treaty Ports (e.g., Shanghai and Hankow) or British Hong Kong, and Taiwan. Other research has focused elsewhere overseas, such as in Japan, Hawaii, the US, Canada, Central and South America, and the Caribbean.[14]

These works have contributed significantly to a new understanding of the enduring relationship between Chinese migrants/emigrants and their former home base in various parts of China. More importantly, they provide a useful new mechanism for re-examining the material constructs of the Han Chinese identity, by offering a prism for separating and better understanding the place and role of key minority ethnic-linguistic components, as they contribute to Han Chinese identity formation and representation. They also contribute to an enhanced appreciation of the sense of *Chinese-ness*, which encompasses the sense of *Han-ness* in the construction of Chinese identity. The sense of *Han-ness* unified and homogenized externally evidenced divisive ethno-linguistic elements, while the sense of *Chinese-ness* reinforced and substantiated, what existed internally, e.g., values, beliefs, and attitudes, as they were authenticated by Chinese history and culture.

**The case of the Cantonese, regarding the sense of Han-ness and Chinese-ness**

Significantly, the chief focus of my investigation in this book is to provide a revisionist reappraisal of the material constructs of traditional Cantonese identity/experience, in its later nineteenth-century transnational context, as it arose from and revolved around communal, cultural, ethnic, and speech considerations. In Cantonese experience, *Tong-ness*[15] (Cantonese speech form) or *Tang-ness* (Mandarin speech form) is a much-esteemed Cantonese surrogate for *Han-ness*, where *Yuet*/Cantonese ethnicity, language, and culture served as a critical deciphering tool to help educate us about the challenge/response of ethnic-national relations among the Han Chinese "diverse majority."

These new perspectives about Han Chinese identity provide a useful reverse mirror image of that identity, as it has been relocated and reproduced in distant geographical locations, often within resentful, prejudicial, and hostile alien societies and cultures. To the extent possible, whether elsewhere in China or overseas in distant locations, the elements of social bias, ethnic prejudice, racial discrimination, and cultural marginalization associated with the process of removal, relocation, and reproduction of ethnic identity away from home, can be viewed as beneficially reaffirming the correlates of Han Chinese identity. They do so by reaffirming Han Chinese ethnic minority group and speech community imperatives, as they embrace the Han Chinese identity label. In doing so, they confirm the loyalty and commitment of these groups to the sense of *Chinese-ness*.

When viewed from the context of distant settings, involving prejudicial host societies (either in China or elsewhere overseas,) the particulars of any given Han Chinese ethnic minority or speech community's ethnic-speech identifications, to say nothing of its persona and psychology, are balanced precariously on the horns of a dilemma between the concrete sense of *Han-ness* (or *Tong-ness* in the Cantonese case) and the contrasting abstract sense of *Chinese-ness* respectively. The former might have taken a back-seat back home in one's native home, but in new distant alien settings, it drove the engine of nineteenth-century transnational Han Chinese group identity formation elsewhere beyond one's native place, either elsewhere in China or overseas.

## Nineteenth-Century Diasporic Movements and Transnationalism, a Conceptual Framework for Contextualizing the Cantonese Sense of "Han-ness" and "Chinese-ness"

A number of other conceptualizations have also been utilized to integrate and systemize the earlier mentioned focus on Han Chinese ethnic minority groups and local speech communities, regarding both their original native locations in China and their subsequent relocation elsewhere in China and overseas. Two deserve mention.

The first integrative conceptualization revolves around the idea of diasporic movements. There have been two types of historical diasporic movements. First, diaspora has resulted from collective trauma, involving a brutally forced exile or banishment from a homeland by others, e.g., the Jews, Armenians, the Kurds, and the Rohingya. Second, diaspora has existed as economically motivated migration and settlement, or colonization, as in the case of the ancient Greeks, Asian Indians (19th century), and the Chinese (15th through early 20th centuries). Beyond removal from one's homeland and experiencing a sowing or scattering of their people, people associated with diasporic movements also share an enduring memory of and loyalty to their former homeland, from which they have been removed and have become more-or-less permanently separated from. This separation is not just physical in nature, but also embodies psychological/emotional elements as well. It is above all else historical, to the extent that it defines and conditions the mindset, outlook, and thinking of those associated with the experience of diaspora. This happens across many generations, despite degrees of local socio-cultural acculturation, assimilation, and sociopolitical integration elsewhere. One's memory of and loyalty to one's origins, to one's roots back home somewhere else, however diluted by time and unavoidable change, is an unmistakable and persistent core value of groups identified with diasporic movements.

Both domestic Chinese migrants and overseas Chinese emigrants have been associated with diasporic movements. In this context, both groups mirrored their *Han-ness* via their respective regionally based Han Chinese ethnic minority group and speech community identifications, e.g., *Tong-ness* or *Cantonese-ness* among the *Yuet*/Cantonese, and also by their strong sense of *Chinese-ness*, via how host communities in China, and host societies in distant alien overseas locations, have viewed and responded to them. This use of diasporic movements, as a conceptual template to integrate and synchronize *Chinese-ness* and *Han-ness* among various Han Chinese ethnic minority groups and speech communities, has become an increasingly common analytical tool.[16]

"Transnationalism" is another widely used integrative theoretical construct for investigating elements of ethnic identity in a multiplicity of locations and relationships.

> [Transnationalism is] the emergence of a social process in which migrants establish social fields that cross geographic, cultural, and political borders. Immigrants are understood to be transmigrants when they develop and maintain multiple relations—familial, economic, social, organizational, religious, and political—that span borders… The multiplicity of migrants' [simultaneous and ongoing] involvements in both the home and host societies is a central element of transnationalism.[17]

For about half a century, 1850–1900, overseas Chinese history revolved around the polar issue of phenomenal largescale overseas migrations, which involved a wide variety of ongoing technological, logistical, economic, institutional, socio-cultural, and geopolitical changes on a global scale.[18] In this context, "transnationalism" provides a unifying analytical framework that enables us to capture, connect, and integrate the varied and disparate elements of the overseas Chinese emigrant experience. It does so by providing a unifying perspective that helps to tie together many different elements of that experience, as they were manifested in multiple locations, relationships, and processes that transcend time and space. In this way transnational perspectives have helped to create a multidimensional narrative that is open-ended, not only in its forward movement across time, but also in its ability to recapture and readjust relationships and perspectives previously neglected or unknown. It also empowers us to become more observant about our past, via a multi-facetted lens that enables us to see previously invisible, or seemingly disconnected and otherwise unrelated elements. This means viewing the past as a collection of discrete components evolving through time, where each one can be better understood via its evolving relationship with other elements, as they either operated together or worked independently.

**Distinguishing between "Han-ness," and "Tong-ness," or "Cantonese-ness"**

Among Cantonese overseas emigrants/immigrants, there existed ample evidence of pro-active decision-making, regarding their capability and willingness to engage in different types of activities simultaneously at various locations, and under changing material conditions, relative to a variety of persistent adversities and new opportunities. We should see them as empowered actors in their own historical narrative, rather than passive victims, where they made conscious decisions and sought out viable alternatives to their economic and situational dilemmas. Their many changing locations, evolving relationships, and shifting priorities underscored "the multiplicity of migrants' involvement in both their home and host societies," such that they were not constrained in their thinking and unable to think "outside the box." They were agile in their movements, as they were resourceful in their strategies, which suggest elements of free agency and rational thinking. They were not inextricably bound by traditional concerns about uniform-unified cultural zones-whether it involved traditional universalized Han Chinese ideas about the "Middle Kingdom," or time-honored distinctions regarding prevailing regional, ethno-linguistic identifications and communal loyalties (e.g., the South China of *Yuet*/Cantonese *Bundae* dominated Central Gwongdung.)

Interestingly, Cantonese-Chinese people, both as migrants in China, and as overseas emigrants elsewhere, represented this situation in an especially forceful way, where the sense of *Tong-ness* was considered among the Cantonese to be more authentic, cogent, and meaningful than the sense of *Han-ness*, not only in China, but also in America and elsewhere in the Cantonese-speaking world.[19] Simply stated, *Tong-ness* represented the traditional ongoing Cantonese obsession with historical legitimacy, cultural authenticity, and language/speech purity. This obsession materialized by way of an intellectually crafted and subjectively felt identification with Tang (*Tong* in Cantonese) dynasty (618–906 CE) models and standards, which pre-dated Mongol (Yuan) fourteenth-century contamination and Manchu (Qing) seventeenth-century compromising of *Han-ness*, which also unavoidably complicated and undermined the sense of *Chinese-ness*.

The Cantonese sense of *Tong-ness* served essentially the same function, which *Han-ness* served elsewhere in China, by underscoring the need to scale down *Chinese-ness* to a more concrete and manageable indicator of identity. In this way *Tong-ness* for the Cantonese, and *Han-ness* for other Chinese, embraced scaled-down lofty abstractions of history and culture, so that they could help service regional identity constructs, relative to the broader rubric of *Chinese-ness*. This agile, but largely sub-conscious, realignment of the image and reality of Cantonese group identity persisted in many distant locations, and remained relevant for future applications. Significantly, these actions contributed to the ongoing task of fashioning an evolving Cantonese-Chinese identity in China, America, and elsewhere.

Cantonese trans-migrants encountered difficult logistical and financial challenges, where they crossed exclusive national boundaries (e.g., China, the US, Australia, and Hawaii) to encounter alien and hostile societies, amid physical and economic hardship, often compounded by extreme prejudice and a deep-seated animus. In the process, they were not deterred by externally imposed racial categories (e.g., Chinese as an alien and undesirable race in the US,) nor were they compromised by conflicting ethno-linguistic loyalties and antagonisms (e.g., *Min, Yuet, Bundae, Hakka, Say-Yup,* and *Saam-Yup* etc.) Indeed, as these categories and layers of Cantonese identity were confronted, they were synchronized and incorporated into new chapters of experience, within a distinctly transnational context. They might be negotiated, compromised, and re-adjusted, but they always endured.

Transnationalism can be considered in a variety of ways, to help us better understand Han Chinese identity formation and composition in a multiplicity of locations and relationships. First, as a general theoretical approach, attention centers on a wide-spectrum view of the transnational experience and its relevance for reassessing the creation, or re-creation, of a socio-culturally rooted identity (e.g., *Tong-ness*) with prominent ethno-linguistic elements in a distinctly transnational context.[20] Second, there have also been specific case studies of emigrant Chinese in America and elsewhere, which document where and how extended communities of overseas Cantonese emigrants have addressed the challenge of Chinese identity (e.g., *Chinese-ness*) re-creation and representation at diverse overseas locations, and also as it has been exported for return to a variety of locations back home in China. Recent works about such efforts in America and Cuba, to name a few, are representative of this important work.[21]

This conceptualization of the transnational narrative has not lost sight of, nor become detached from, the "home front." More succinctly, overseas emigrant experiences and expectations were not regarded as irrelevant, but came to be viewed as critical constructs of the ongoing reconsideration of Han Chinese identity representation and reproduction back home in China, as well as overseas.[22]

In a transnational context, via the device of the diasporic movement(s), Cantonese emigrants/immigrants demonstrated the vitality and relevancy of their replicated Cantonese identity for use overseas. In the US, this occurred externally, (the sense of *Chinese-ness*) for use in dealing with American society, and with various other racial and ethnic minorities. It also materialized internally among Cantonese emigrants themselves, (the sense of *Tong-ness*) as a means of relating with fellow Cantonese., and other Chinese (the sense of *Han-ness*).

Over time, the Cantonese overseas emigrant community fashioned a layered identity which embodied elements of *Chinese-ness* and *Tong-ness* or "*Cantonese-ness"* in creative ways. It demonstrated great dexterity of mood and movement, where similar to their kin folk back home in *Tong-Shaan*, they were able to skillfully change, manipulate, and substitute these many elements of identity to alternately disguise and display their collective identity to others. Similar to the famous "rapid face changing" theatrics of Sichuan opera in Chengdu, this dazzling, but largely covert and unconscious action-response mechanism underscored the enduring influence of a "conservative contrarian counter-cultural" component of traditional Cantonese culture, as in the sense of *Tong-ness* or "Cantonese-ness." [23] Each layer of identity served a useful purpose for a particular occasion, need, or mood.

### Rethinking the Chinese National-Ethnic conundrum

It is useful to remember that Cantonese experience traditionally exhibited an antagonistic spirit, evident in its stubborn, often compulsive, obsession with historical legitimacy, cultural authenticity, and ethno-linguistic purity.[24] Significantly, this stance has not evidenced any overt opposition to Han Chinese supremacy or conflicted with *Chinese-ness*, (as in national-ethnic conflicts.) The Cantonese persona has not resulted from protracted violent conflict, but rather it has flowed organically from a slow, steady, and prolonged evolution, where continuity and maturation, and not rupture and separation, have been esteemed.

If the Cantonese have not pursued violent conflict to achieve sustainability for their community and culture, neither have they been content to merely passively co-exist within the envelope of the national interest. Instead, Cantonese society has been historically pro-active in taking the initiative to protect, preserve, and advance its own socio-cultural agenda and ethno-linguistic traditions. If we understand that Cantonese culture has been a "conservative contrarian counter-cultural" tradition in its temperament and outlook, (see chapter 4) then we can appreciate its ability and willingness to accommodate, to be malleable, and syncretic in its interactive strategies with the "national" interest. Again, the Han-Chinese identity, and the sense of *Chinese-ness*, are constructive rather than destructive in influencing how the "ethnic" (i.e., Cantonese) and the "national" (i.e., Chinese) are juxtaposed in the Chinese setting- as opposed to how such matters are addressed elsewhere.

The basis for most of the world's national-ethnic violent conflicts has revolved around political issues, such as separatist movements seeking revolutionary independence, whereby some ethnic minority groups see full separation and complete independence as the only solution to ensuring their survival. To be sure religious, historical, and cultural issues confuse and complicate the regionally-based ethnic minority agenda, to the extent that what distances the "ethnic" and separates it from the "national" often outweighs that which draws them closer, and which could potentially bind them together.

In the Cantonese case, there has never been a clear and convincing argument for physical separation and political independence, on the basis of an ethnic imperative. It may be that the Cantonese socio-cultural matrix, in conjunction with an intimate and enduring historical Chinese-Cantonese relationship, may have made such an option moot. This lack of violent conflict in the service of political independence is not merely a reflection of a pragmatic strategy for the sustainability of Cantonese identity and experience, but more significantly it also underscores the complex nuanced self-image of Cantonese society/culture as a vital, authentic, and enduring regionally-based historical, socio-cultural, and ethno-linguistic Han Chinese tradition.

The strong sense of the uniqueness of Cantonese identity and experience flows from the belief that Cantonese language/speech and culture is more "Chinese" than Mongol compromised and Manchu tainted Northern Chinese (Mandarin) speech and culture. Such a view mirrors more of an integrative frame of reference, rather than a separatist agenda, in the context of a "conservative contrarian counter-cultural" tradition. Put another way, the Cantonese have seen value in being part of the "whole," that is Han Chinese society and culture, and have preferred it instead of being alone in a "hole," where the trappings of socio-cultural separation and political independence would be of little solace, when compared to the benefit of being part of the larger grander sense of "Chinese-ness."

If we accept the proposition that the Cantonese, as an atypical regionally-based Han Chinese ethnic minority group and speech community, represents a reliable vehicle for exploring the complexities of Han Chinese identity formation, then the notion of *Tong-Shaan*, as a Cantonese fountainhead, is not only relevant, but also has practical value. As a revisionist conceptualization, it can serve as a useful investigative tool in which to represent and synchronize elements of Cantonese identity formation and reproduction, relative to both the broad categories of geography, history, language, and culture, as well as the specifics of ethnic minority and local speech community needs and interests.

This imperative presents a double challenge, with possible double benefits. First, there is inherent interest and intrinsic value in searching for the constructs of Cantonese identity and experience. Second, there is the expectation that these constructs will also further shed light on the nature of *Tong-ness*, and why it mattered. This in turn can help us refine our understanding of the broader sense of *Chinese-ness*, because the sense of *Tong-ness* (or *Cantonese-ness*) can be used as a template for better understanding it.

While Chinese identity construction and representation provides a thoughtful subject, as well as a useful context, in which to structure this investigation, it is not however, the only purpose of this inquiry. I also investigate another equally important, but historically neglected related topic. I do so within a different theoretical framework, where traditional parameters of historical inquiry are expanded, even as they are more narrowly construed. I begin at a familiar starting place, by surveying the constructs of Cantonese identity and experience. Specifically, I examine ethnicity, society, and culture at the Cantonese fountainhead in Central Gwongdung in the period 1850–1900. This task is also framed within a transnationally-orientated inquiry, which facilitates the adoption of a complementary integrative perspective, whereby important insights can be gained from both Modern Chinese social history and early Cantonese-Chinese American history.

In this sense, my focus is less one of myopically re-examining the nexus between *Chinese-ness* and *Tong-ness (*or *Cantonese-ness*) back home in Gwongdung, and more one of developing a litmus test to demonstrate how these variables materialized and functioned elsewhere overseas, and why they have been important. This investigative strategy underscores the benefit of cross fertilization between researching Modern Chinese Social History and Chinese American History, which can contribute significantly to a more accurate and complete understanding of the Cantonese transnational identity and experience in the later nineteenth and early twentieth century. My advocacy of this integrated analytical approach demonstrates a willingness to cross over intellectual divides and socio-cultural boundaries, evident in my earlier reference to diasporic movements and transnationalism.

This syncretic strategy not only distinguishes my plan of action, but also conveniently reveals my ongoing concern about the persistence of an unwarranted reluctance to cultivate constructive working relationships between Asian Studies and Asian American Studies. While the need to urgently consider these matters seems abundantly clear, the reasons why we have failed to do so remains obscure. This view is not new, but needs to be kept in mind, because it underscores a chronic dilemma that we need to be constantly aware of, if we are to overcome it.

> Since the 1960s, the desire to emphasize the "American" qualities of Asian Americans has led Asian American Studies scholars to distance themselves from Asian Studies specialists. This self-conscious separation continues to the present despite current celebrations of globalization and transnationalism.... Asian American scholars must not succumb to ... separating Asian and Asian American Studies, especially when studying one might cast light on the other.[25]

We need to link the "Asian" perspective with the "Asian American" experience in mutually rewarding ways, where the former educates and the latter elaborates on what has been an organic flow of history and culture from its Old-World roots to its New-World branches.

I offer this book as a step in the right direction. I seek to beneficially link together the mission of Chinese American historical investigation with the fruits of recent advances in Modern Chinese History and social science research. In this way Cantonese pre-emigrant identity/experience back home in Gwongdung, can inform us about Cantonese immigrant identity/experience in distant locations. Both perspectives can help us solve thorny problems of re-examination and re-interpretation. This task begins with an inquiry into the distinctiveness of the Cantonese in Chinese History, as a baseline for investigating their distinct collective identity, as a major Han Chinese ethno-speech minority group, in China and beyond.

**The atypical character of the Cantonese place and role in Chinese History**

Since remote antiquity through the later nineteenth and early twentieth centuries, Cantonese people distinguished themselves collectively, as a community with a distinctive evolving identity and set of unique experiences, different from other Han Chinese groups. While some other Chinese groups, such as the *Min* people of Fujian, might also have shared similar experiences (e.g., migration/settlement patterns in South China and elsewhere overseas), the particulars of Cantonese ethno-speech identity, socio-cultural engineering, and historical engagement however, clearly set them apart from other Han Chinese. In this regard, a brief review about the distinctiveness of Cantonese in Chinese History can serve as a useful Segway to this book's central theme of "What it meant to be Cantonese in the nineteenth century."

*The Cantonese, as the vanguard of ancient China's advancing southern frontier*

Commencing in the Qin-Han period (221 BCE to 220 CE), a growing Han Chinese presence established itself along the southeast Chinese coast in parts of present-day Gwongdung and Fujian Provinces, in the form of strategically located riverine military outposts and colonies.

In the succeeding millennium (first to tenth century CE), Chinese periodically migrated from various parts of North and Central China to settle in portions of Central and East Gwongdung, as part of "China's march to the tropics,"[26] a process somewhat similar to America's "Manifest Destiny." In both cases, scores of pioneer settlers trekked long distances across an immense and challenging landscape.[27] Each case involved technologically advanced settlers encountering tribal societies, with alternating episodes of indifference and conflict. The settlement process typically involved bypassing some areas in preference for other more attractive places, setting down in one place for a few generations, followed by succeeding generations picking up and moving on elsewhere, with the process repeated again and again.

In Gwongdung, migrants settled chiefly in Central Gwongdung's Pearl Delta Region, and in East Gwongdung's Han and Mei Rivers' alluvial plains. As the Han Chinese frontier advanced southwards, soldiers, refugees, exiled scholar-officials, and merchants, as well as pioneer settlers, all helped to establish a thriving Chinese presence in the vicinity of the rich Pearl River Delta in Central Gwongdung. Over the course of several centuries, the Canton region became over time a well-known oasis of Han Chinese society and culture[28] in a virtual sea of non-Chinese peoples and cultures. In this context, nineteenth-century Cantonese global migrations and settlement in distant places beyond China have a well-established precedent in the ancient Han Chinese settlement of Central Gwongdung. The early establishment of the Canton area, as a favorite destination for pioneers trekking from North China across Central and South China to China's southernmost coastal area, served as the origin of a well-defined Cantonese society and its distinctive *Yuet* regional culture.

While Han Chinese migrants played the chief determinative role in the forging of a distinctive Cantonese identity and experience, they did not act alone. In the *Lingnam* region of present day Gwongdung and Gwongsai (Guangxi) provinces, they encountered various pre-existing tribal societies. Over time there evolved a pattern of interaction between Chinese migrant-settlers and these tribal groups, which involved elements of tension and conflict, toleration and cooperation. In the following centuries, mutual tolerance, acceptance, and cooperation, led to a pattern of co-dependence and degrees of cultural and structural assimilation between Chinese and local non-Chinese communities. Cantonese pioneer-settlers in Central Gwongdung not only steadily transformed the region, but were themselves also transformed by the region. This resulted in a hybrid blending of *Tai* and Han Chinese languages, societies, and cultures. Over time, this amalgamation served as the origin of, and formed the basis for a distinctive *Yuet*/Cantonese ethnic identity, language(s) and culture.[29]

## *The Cantonese as a vital link with the outside maritime world (10$^{th}$–17$^{th}$ centuries)*

By the end of the Tang Dynasty in the tenth century CE, Canton represented itself less as an advance outpost of Han Chinese society and culture, and more as an integral part of it. Indeed, by this time, the Cantonese had shed their role as the pioneering wedge of Chinese culture, to metamorphosize into a key atypical socio-cultural variant within that culture. It did so by playing a new role in China's relationship with non-Chinese peoples and cultures along China's southeastern periphery. Canton, the chief city and provincial capital of Gwongdung province, became China's major link with the outside maritime world of Southeast and South Asia. In this sense, the Cantonese became a filter by which foreigners came to know China, and how Chinese society came to know about and interact with foreigners, at China's "back door," the immensely long coast of China. Over the course of a millennium (700 BCE to 1800 CE), most of China's knowledge and contact with foreigners came by way of Cantonese specialized knowledge and cultivated familiarity with the peoples and cultures of Southeast Asia. This later expanded to include trade with India, the Middle East, and eventually the West (Europe).

The Cantonese became legendary for their experience and expertise in dealing with foreigners, where they became the all-important "eyes and ears" of Chinese society for things foreign. This special expertise and unique experience, formed the basis of a contradictory traditional Chinese perspective about Cantonese people. If they were renowned for their expertise and skill in dealing with foreigners, they were also criticized and ridiculed for their obsession with profits and market shares, as well as their interest in foreign things, and their delight in the new and novel. These attributes were regarded as undesirable characteristics, because they were viewed as "un-Chinese" traits. In traditional Chinese society, scholarship, not making money, and Chinese culture, not foreign products, were the proper concerns of Chinese people. Obviously, the location and concentration of foreign commercial/trade activities associated with Canton, gave the region a unique persona, underscoring its special place and role in China's foreign trade and contacts with the outside world.

Introduction

***The pivotal Cantonese role in China's early modern foreign trade (1760–1860 CE)***

In the later eighteenth century, Canton leapt again to the forefront of China's foreign trade. Significantly, this time, the focus shifted from Southeast and South Asia, to contacts with the West (i.e., Europeans and Americans.) In the aftermath of the Manchu conquest of China (1644–1680), the new Qing regime adopted a policy designed to uphold both Manchu strategic geopolitical goals and traditional Han Chinese socio-cultural imperatives through the continued use of the Ming Tributary System. In this highly ritualized system of controlling contacts with outsiders, foreigners were only allowed minimal access to China. Such visits were tightly controlled, from the time foreign missions entered China until the time they left. By the eighteenth century, several Western countries, such as Spain, Portugal, Great Britain, Holland, and the papacy, joined traditional Asian states, such as Korea, Vietnam, Siam, and Burma, as tributary states in China's tributary system. By the early nineteenth century, the United States also joined this system. Between 1790 and 1820, the British, on behalf of all the Western tributary states, tried several times to seek changes in the conduct of Sino-Western relations, which included: 1) seeking full (Western style) diplomatic relations with the Qing government, 2) seeking unrestricted Sino-Western trade, and 3) seeking the resumption of Christian missionary activity in China.[30] In each case, these requests were rebuffed by the Qing court.

On the question of limited foreign trade however, the Qing court finally relented. In 1759, the *Qianglong* (*Chien-lung*) Emperor (r.1736–1795), reversed the ban on foreign trade and established a new system of limited foreign trade between China and the West, which lasted for almost a century, before it was dismantled in 1842. This new system of trade, commonly known as the "Canton System," officially recognized Sino-foreign trade, but also severely restricted it.[31]

Under the Canton System of trade, Western traders could no longer engage in illegal, but unenforced, trade at several southern Chinese ports (e.g., Ningpo, Fuzhou, and Amoy), instead they were limited to trading only at Canton. Canton, unlike other Chinese seaports, was located about 90 miles up the Pearl River from the coast. Under this new system, traders assembled in Macau (Macao) and then journeyed upriver to Canton. All Westerners were subject to tight regulations, where any non-compliance or breech could result in the denial of trading privileges.[32]

From the outset, westerners were denied entry into Canton, instead they were confined to *Shameen* Island, just outside the southwestern corner of the city's western suburbs. Western traders were only allowed to have dealings with their pre-assigned Cantonese merchant/broker, who were part of a merchant guild, known as the Cantonese Co-Hong.[33] Both Qing officials and Westerners were unhappy with the trade system, where the former constantly fretted over what they perceived to be widespread corruption and endless violations of trade regulations, and the latter resented the trade imbalance, the highhanded oppressive manipulations of the Cantonese merchants, and the deplorable living and working conditions associated with the enforced sequestering of foreign traders on *Shameen* Island.

All Western orders had to be paid for in silver. This further complicated trade, because Westerners purchased huge consignments of tea, silk, and porcelain, while Cantonese merchants purchased little, if anything in return. Consequently, Cantonese merchants enjoyed a growing surplus, while Westerners experienced growing trade deficits. The British and other foreign traders, in an effort to address the series of trade deficits, began to import raw opium, to meet what they thought might be a new market for the Chinese recreational use of Opium. Opium ultimately proved to be very marketable, commencing with the introduction of a few chests. By the 1820s, tens of thousands of chests were imported annually from British controlled India. Quickly, the British and other Western traders earned huge surpluses, while the Cantonese encountered growing trading deficits.

The Canton System was abolished after the Sino-British War of 1839–1842, better known as the "First" Opium War. This war resulted when Qing authorities tried to stamp out the nefarious opium trade at Canton, by confiscating and destroying inventories of Western owned opium at Canton. The British sent a naval force from India in response to these developments at Canton and quickly defeated the Chinese, resulting in the Treaty of Nanking in 1842.

The Canton System produced two important results for the Cantonese. First, it re-established Canton as the all-important center for China's foreign trade in the late eighteenth and early nineteenth centuries. Second, it underscored again the critical role and ascribed identity of the Cantonese (both the merchant princes and the population in general) in China's evolving relationship with the outside world, especially in the area of foreign trade. Qing officials viewed the Cantonese as being opportunistic, greedy, selfish, and shameless in their dealings with Westerners, to the point where they were often identified as *Hanjian* (Chinese traitors).[34] Others thought that despite their many faults, they were the best people to carry on the "business of business."

With the end of their monopoly over China's foreign trade in 1842, Cantonese merchants again, as in the post Tang period (tenth to seventeenth centuries CE), found themselves as just one of many groups in a crowded field. Still, they persisted and prospered. In the middle decades of the nineteenth century (1845–1870s), Cantonese flocked to newly opened treaty ports distributed along the Chinese coast (e.g., Shanghai) and at the confluence of major rivers (e.g., Hankow). They became the critical cornerstone of commerce and trade in British Hong Kong, conveniently located down river from Canton. In this sense, they became indispensable middlemen, as much valued and relied upon service providers to Westerners living and working among non-Cantonese Chinese in scores of newly opened treaty ports (e.g., *Shantou (Swatow), Fuzhou, Xiamen (Amoy), Ningbo, Hankow, Shanghai, and Tianjin (Tientsin.)*[35] Thus, Canton (together with Hong Kong) continued to play a leading role in Chinese commerce and foreign trade, and among rapidly expanding Cantonese overseas communities.[36]

### *The unconventional Cantonese anti-status quo role in Chinese politics*

While Cantonese merchants had exercised leadership in China's foreign trade for over a millennium, politically speaking however, traditional Cantonese influence in China's "national" political life paled in comparison. This is not to say that prior to the later nineteenth-century Cantonese people lacked occasions, when they were active in Chinese politics. There existed a significant Cantonese tradition of "loyalist inspired political resistance," where Cantonese were involved in peripatetic loyalist inspired political resistance, on the behalf of fallen regimes.

Commencing with the end of the Southern Song (Sung) in 1279, continuing with the end of the Ming Dynasty in 1644, and the end of the Nationalist regime in 1949, Gwongdung often became closely associated with the politics of resistance against newly installed Chinese regimes in the North. The scope of such activity ranged from a minor secondary passive role, typically involving token offerings of succor to various claimants to a fallen regime's claim to the *Mandate of Heaven*, to active leadership in nurturing anti-status quo opposition.

Gwongdung province emerged center stage of empire-wide "national" politics at the end of the Southern Song (Sung). During the quarter of a century (1250–1279 CE) of the Mongol conquest of Southern China, Gwongdung became one of the major centers for Song resistance. In advance of the fall of the Southern Song capital at Hangzhou in March 1276, two of the emperor's younger brothers were sent south to Fujian and Gwongdung respectively for their safety, and as a means of safeguarding the future of the dynasty. During the next three years (1276–1279) the Song cause survived in Central Gwongdung, and elsewhere, in the form of a campaign of resistance against the Mongols and their Chinese collaborators.[37] In addition to refugees from the Song court at Hangzhou, the exiled courts in Gwongdung also had many local Cantonese loyalists, who were vital to the Song cause. Certainly, local Cantonese intelligence capabilities, such as knowledge of local material conditions, and human and material resources helped keep the Song cause alive.[38]

Cantonese Song resistance in Central Gwongdung replicated itself again at the end of the Ming Dynasty in the middle of the seventeenth century. The Ming, like the Song before it, had also fallen to alien invaders from beyond the Great Wall. In an effort to quell a major rebellion that threatened Beijing, the Ming leadership hired a mercenary army of Manchus from their tribal homeland in Manchuria. After helping the Ming regime to put down a rebellion in the 1640s, the Manchus took over Beijing and declared themselves the new rulers of China. This initial "conquest" of China appeared quick and easy, but it subsequently turned into a long- protracted pacification campaign, where the actual conquest took four decades (1644–1683). During this period,

Gwongdung figured prominently as a site of Ming resistance and prolonged anti-Qing military operations and political opposition. The period of Ming loyalist resistance is known historically as the "Southern Ming" (1644–1662.) During this time, successive Ming pretenders established exiled Ming courts at various sites in southern China, with many in Central Gwongdung.[39]

With the establishment of the Qing Dynasty in 1644, the Manchu leadership rewarded three Han Chinese Ming generals, who had been instrumental in helping the Manchus to initially rise to power in China. They were known collectively as the "Three Feudatories." After two decades, however, the Qing court decided to reduce their autonomy, as a means of saving the high cost of subsidizing them. Consequently, the leaders of the Three Feudatories rose up in revolt against the Qing Dynasty (1673–1681.) During the course of several decades, segments of local Cantonese society were actively involved in promoting Ming loyalist aspirations, and pro (Gwongdung) feudatory anti-Qing resistance.

After the Qing consolidated its control over China in 1683, anti-Qing sentiment remained strong among segments of Cantonese society. The legacy of loyalist inspired resistance, so prominent at the end of the Song and Ming dynasties did not die with the end of Imperial China in 1911.

It manifested itself again in similar, albeit less dramatic and less colorful circumstances. During the last few years of Nationalist (Guomintang) (Kuomintang) rule on the Chinese mainland, amid the second Communist-Nationalist (CCP-KMT) civil war (1945–1949), Nationalist loyalist insurrectionary activity occurred. Although most of this activity took place chiefly among the Chinese Muslim communities in China's Northwest and Southwest,[40] some Nationalist related insurrectionary activities also occurred in Gwongdung, as well as Gwongsai and Tibet.

Recognition of the limited scope and role of Cantonese loyalist inspired efforts does not diminish their historical significance for Cantonese experience. While they might appear to be only incidental and superficial, they were in fact historically significant in their representation of the unconventional role of the Cantonese in Chinese politics and political change. While Gwongdung never became a new center stage for Chinese politics, it did on several occasions emerge temporarily as the center stage of China's political theatre. In this way, while Cantonese experience with political resistance often reflected more the serendipity of location, and the expediency of emergency measures in desperate times, it also evidenced how the Cantonese occasionally served as champions of "lost causes."

## *Cantonese anti-status quo opposition and the emergence of modern Han Chinese patriotism*

Modern Chinese nationalism in the early twentieth century had its origin, and a direct line of memory linking seventeenth-century Ming Dynasty loyalism and later nineteenth-century anti-Qing (i.e., anti-Manchu) sentiment. This was clearly evident in Dr. Sun Yat-sen's famous revolutionary slogan of "*fan Qing fu Ming*" ("Oppose the Qing and revive the Ming"). Significantly, Dr. Sun's adoption of the Ming loyalist rhetoric helped transform a mere historical reference into a useful early building block for modern Han Chinese patriotism.

In the early- to mid-nineteenth century, anti-Manchu sentiment became more covert, becoming largely a monopoly of Chinese secret societies, which were endemic throughout southeast China. Among the overseas Cantonese in both China and America, these secret societies and their anti-Qing rhetoric served as a useful Segway for Cantonese society to become actively involved in the 1911 Chinese Revolution.[41] During this time, political resistance in Central Gwongdung took on greater urgency and significance. This resulted from the timely confluence of burdensome old conditions and outdated logistics, with new technical advances and new opportunities. Gwongdung, because it remained very distant from the center of political power in Beijing, served as a place where it was easier to organize and conspire, without being noticed, or to more easily fight, when noticed. The appearance of new foreign inspired technology, such as the telegraph, newspapers, and trains, made it easier to engage quickly in an unprecedented way.

By the later nineteenth and early twentieth-century, political resistance no longer focused on supporting pretenders to a fallen dynasty or secret society operations, but embraced a new set of ideas and vision of the future. This revolved around new notions about what constituted the "national interest,"[42] via contradictory imperatives of a universalized "proto-Han Chinese nationalism" and a refashioned sense of Cantonese ethnic identity and experience. The former embodied a high idealism identified with future possibilities, while the later provided a comforting confidence, associated with an especially unique and enduring collective socio-cultural identity and historical experience. This new anti-status quo political opposition not only focused with laser-like precision on the moribund Qing regime, but also reconfigured the parameters of the struggle between East and West.[43] These matters invariably helped to redefine what it meant to be Cantonese (i.e., *Tong-ness*), and by extension what it also meant to be Chinese (i.e., *Chinese-ness*) in the modern world. This new wave of thinking centered on ideas about radical reform and political revolution. Cantonese inspiration came from the West, and thus re-enforced preexisting popular views of the Cantonese as *Hanjian* (Chinese traitors).[44]

The first notable individual representing this new wave of Cantonese political leadership was Hong Yau-wei (Kang Youwei) of Namhoi (Nanhai) County, one of Qing China's last great classical scholars. Hong, together with his close associate Leung Kai-chew (Liang Qichao) of Sunwui (Hsinhui) County, as members of the elite Cantonese Gentry class, they led the Cantonese inspired Radical Reform Movement of 1898. Hong and his group advocated "radical" reform, in marked contrast to the well-intentioned, but halfway measures of the earlier *Self-Strengthening Movement* (1860–1895). Hong's movement only lasted for about 100 days, from June through September, in 1898. After the failure of the *Hundred Days Reform Movement*, some reformers were arrested and summarily executed. Hong and Leung were fortunate to escape China, with foreign assistance. Hong and Leung subsequently embarked on "second careers" as emergent political leaders among treaty port Chinese and Overseas Chinese in Southeast Asia, the Americas, Japan, and in Europe.[45] Hong established China's first modern political party, the *Pao Huang-hui* or "Protect the Emperor Society" at Victoria, British Columbia, Canada on July 20, 1899[46] (more commonly known in English as "The Chinese Empire Reform Association, which became the Constitutional Party in 1909).

In the context of late Qing politics at the imperial court in Beijing, Hong and Leung stood out as unconventional political leaders, not only because they espoused a new agenda for radical reform and modernization, but also because of their Cantonese identities. While not all of the radical reformers in Beijing were Cantonese, the fact that the top leaders were, was enough to color the movement with a decided Cantonese taint. This arrival of a few avant-garde Cantonese political thinkers at the apex of Chinese national politics represented a seminal event, unprecedented in Chinese History and Cantonese experience. As the leader of the Radical Reform Movement of 1898, Hong came to personify the greater visibility, enhanced prestige, and unprecedented leverage of Cantonese political activists in the ongoing debate about Chinese modernity at the end of the Qing period.

At about the same time that Hong and his associates were active, Sun Yat-sen, another emerging Cantonese political leader, offered his own alternative game plan, in opposition to both the Qing regime and Hong's radical reform agenda. Sun's profile contrasted with that of his rival Hong. Sun, born into a peasant farmer family, in Chung-Shaan district, lacked the benefit of a classical education. Unlike Hong, an erudite and gifted classical scholar, Sun did not identify with Chinese society's social elites and their sophisticated culture. Not only was Sun's background socio-economically disadvantaged, it was also burdened with elements of communal ethno-cultural marginality. Hong, a member of the elitist Cantonese Gentry social class, identified himself as a member of the dominant *bundae* (*bendi*) or "natives" segment of Cantonese society. In marked contrast, Sun, as a *Chung-Shaan* local, is alleged to have had *Hakka* (*Gejia*) or "Guest peoples" blood in his family- which identified him with a suspect ethno-speech community minority in *Bundae* dominated Central Gwongdung.[47] Sun's home district of *Chung-Shaan*, with its Portuguese enclave of Macau (Macao) not only had a sizable *Hakka* minority community,[48] and also included other minority ethnic/speech communities.[49] In contrast, Hong's native Namhoi district lie at the center of the *Saam-yup* (three districts' speech group,) commonly identified with the more sophisticated urban scene of Canton, and its standardized "Cantonese" Cantonese speech community. Additionally, while Hong was securely positioned at the top of elitist mainstream Cantonese society, and had momentarily dominated center stage of China's national politics, Sun's experiences, identified him with the social and spatial periphery of Hong's world.

Sun, as an adolescent, was sent to live with his elder brother on Maui, in Hawaii. He later received an Anglican missionary education in Honolulu. He eventually became a Christian and earned a MD degree in Hong Kong, where he set up a private medical practice. By the late 1890s, Dr. Sun read and wrote English better than Chinese. While he spoke fluent Cantonese, his Mandarin remained rudimentary, only improving when he lived in Shanghai after 1912. In contrast, he demonstrated real world experience and had intimate knowledge of the modern Western world beyond China. His scientific expertise in medicine helped him cultivate an interest in Western thinking about modernization and political change. By the early 1900s, he became a dedicated disciple of revolutionary change. He was a co-contemporary of other revolutionary luminaries such as Lenin of Russia, Gandhi of India, and Atatürk of Turkey. While his knowledge of modern political thinking remained rudimentary, he nevertheless served as the vanguard of a new wave of Chinese political leaders dedicated to political revolution.[50]

During the decade 1895–1905, Hong and Sun became political rivals, as each in turn became an exiled political activist with a hefty price on his head. Sun quickly eclipsed Hong as the foremost emergent political leader of modern China. Hong's political cause of reform lost credibility, when its titular head, the *Guangxu* (Kuang-Hsu) Emperor died in 1908, to be succeeded by the boy emperor ("Henry" Pu-yi), which only a few reformers accepted as viable alternative symbol of reform. Hong also lost personal credibility among his followers, because of his implicated involvement in the mismanagement of the Chinese Empire Association's finances/investments, as well as his perceived egotistical and antagonistic behavior towards his associates and others in his party.[51]

In 1911, Sun finally succeeded in launching a campaign to overthrow the Qing regime. He served briefly as the provisional president of the Republic of China (December 1911). In his effort to hasten the fall of the Manchu government, Sun made a fatal strategic compromise with Yuan Shikai, the most powerful official of the late Qing period, after the failure of the Radical Reform Movement in 1898. In exchange for the Qing emperor's abdication and the surrender of the

Qing government, Yuan successfully negotiated a deal with Sun, whereby Yuan was inaugurated as the first president of the Republic of China in January 1912. Before his death in 1916, Yuan proclaimed himself "president for life," and was in the process of preparing to be proclaimed Emperor of China. Widespread and forceful opposition forced Yuan to shelve his plans to become emperor. During this time, Sun was branded an outlaw, with a price on his head. His Nationalist Party (*Guomintang*) (*Kuo-min tang*) had also been outlawed. He spent the remaining years of his life (1913–1925) dedicated to promoting China's "Second Revolution," to start anew with a "new" Republic of China.

By the early 1920s, both Hong and Sun seemed destined for the dustbin of history, as events quickly brushed them both aside. If Cantonese political thinking and leadership had successfully captured Chinese society's interest just before and after 1900, after 1912 however, it seems to have imploded and disintegrated. Sun died in 1925 and Hong in 1927. Neither of them realized their dreams in their own life time, despite their "moments in the sun," where they decisively shaped and redirected Chinese political discourse. Together, they left an enduring legacy of new ideas, ideals, and values regarding politics and political change. No one in the Chinese speaking world was unaware of and unaffected by their agendas, activities, and achievements, despite their many private setbacks and public failures.[52]

In talking about the transformative changes associated with an unorthodox Cantonese style of leadership, first in China's early modern foreign commerce and trade in the early nineteenth century, and then during the later nineteenth century with the radicalization of Chinese political discourse and political culture, it is too easy to be mesmerized by the daring activities of a handful of colorful mavericks. We should remember that there also existed other Cantonese, who while not as visible, nor as charismatic and famous, were also active agents in the historical narratives in both Modern Chinese History and early Chinese American History.

## *Transnationalism and Nineteenth-Century Cantonese Overseas Emigration to the Americas*

The golden age of large-scale Cantonese Chinese overseas migration occurred between the end of the Opium War and the deaths of Hong and Sun

(1841–1927). Unlike the handful of Cantonese merchant elites and political activists, who attracted attention with their celebrity status, Cantonese emigrants were typically without "faces" and lacked both financial resources and sociopolitical leverage, to the extent that no one cared about their plight. Ostensibly their exit from their home base in Central Gwongdung only impacted their families and local communities, but in fact they ultimately impacted much more. Over time, they also contributed significantly to the development of an expansive Cantonese overseas presence in diverse and distant locations, via a profoundly transformative Cantonese transnationalism. This transnationalism mirrored a wide variety of technological, logistical, financial, commercial, psychological, geopolitical, and socio-cultural changes in a complex grid of ongoing transformations all across the trans-Pacific region. It occurred simultaneously in Gwongdung, Southeast Asia, in North America, Central-America, the Caribbean, South America, all across the Pacific Rim, and beyond.

The Cantonese emigrant in 1850 initially represented extremes of poverty, hopelessness, marginalization, and victimization, by 1900 however, he came to represent varying degrees of material success, pride in overcoming difficult material and psychological challenges, and an optimism for not only surviving, but rising above marginalization and victimization. Through hard work, an uncompromising commitment, self-discipline, rational decision-making, and the courage to move out into an unknown and uncertain world, the highly vulnerable and uninformed Cantonese emigrant not only went on to address his own sense of dilemma, but in the process helped to reshape his world.

Cantonese transnationalism significantly contributed to the development of a wide array of economic enterprises and material developments all across the Pacific Rim, such as ethnic Chinese newspaper publishing, banking and credit, financial investments, (venture capitalism) commercial and corporate development, real estate, maritime communications and transportation, the professions (e.g., medicine, law, journalism, architecture, business & banking, education, engineering, and social services.) In this manner, Cantonese transmigrants took on new and different roles beyond their original ones, as poor emigrant-immigrants, to become sojourner/settlers, investors, educators, consumers, promoters, builders, negotiators, and brokers. The accumulated experience and expertise of living overseas helped transform succeeding generations of Chinese transmigrants from the status of poor, anxious, victimized aliens, into highly motivated, experienced, resourceful, and productive transmitters of new ideas, values, and expectations about personal well-being, and future individual and collective material success.

Over time, via international banking in Hong Kong, San Francisco, Vancouver, Hawaii, Lima, and Cuba, Cantonese-Chinese transmigrants pumped vast sums of wealth back into *Tong Shaan*, in the form of remittances, care packages, investments, voluntary contributions/ donations for schools and other charitable enterprises.[53] They lent their skills and expertise to modernizing their home villages and towns with new larger, better constructed homes, indoor plumbing, electricity, canned food, and other material benefits.

Chin Gee Hee (1844–1930) used skills he acquired in America, as a merchant, labor contractor and railroad entrepreneur, to finance and build the *Sunning* Railroad in his native *Toi-Shaan* County in 1906. This was the first operational commercial railroad in the Pearl River Delta. It was later torn up in 1938 (WWII,) to prevent the invading Japanese from using it.[54] Over time Cantonese emigrant/sojourners helped educate people back home about cars, radios, refrigeration, cameras, and alternative modern medical treatment therapies. Many also contributed to the building of schools, hospitals, and businesses.

In a manner of speaking, these many injections of ideas, technologies, and values from beyond *Tong Shaan*, helped reshape its image and understanding of the world beyond. With Hong Kong as a useful doorway to the outside world, in late Republican, and later Communist China (1927–1950, and 1980–2020), the Cantonese community became once again, the eyes and ears of Chinese society. Masses of Cantonese transmigrants offered themselves as a critical transformative link between their community, Chinese society, and the world beyond. This is especially inspiring because they did so under extraordinarily difficult conditions. They did so despite neglect and indifference of several Chinese regimes, and opposition and exploitation by foreign enterprises and governments. Despite pervasive exploitation and ongoing fear all across the trans-Pacific region, Cantonese transnational migrants, via a massive diaspora, settled as pioneering sojourners in scores of distant locations, where they ultimately blossomed into affirmatively experienced and expert agents. They ably demonstrated many material and non-material benefits of a new transnationalism. This development became all the more inspiring, because it was neither anticipated nor easy in its materialization. It confirmed the new role of Cantonese overseas emigrants in the later nineteenth and early twentieth centuries. In this way, Cantonese emigrant pioneer settlers bridged the tremendous distance between tradition and modernity, between the Cantonese community and an increasingly globalized transnational world beyond.

The several chapters of Cantonese experience in Chinese History, as outlined above, beneficially inform our understanding of the critical role of the Cantonese, as a major Han Chinese ethnic/speech minority, in the ongoing challenge of the national-ethnic debate in its Chinese context. More relevant, they help contextualize, "what it meant to be Cantonese in the nineteenth century," the subject of this book.

---

[1] "Uyghur" is also spelled in English in other ways, among the most common alternative spellings are: (Uighur) (Uigur) (Uygur).

[2] In 2020, protests occurred in Inner Mongolia regarding new curriculum changes in local education, where Chinese Putonghua (Mandarin) has become mandatory for use in classroom instruction and also where Chinese language textbooks replaced Mongol script-language written texts. This mirrors a pattern where Han Chinese officials have undermined the language/culture of various national autonomous ethnic minorities, not only in Tibet and Xinjiang (Uyghurs), but also in Inner Mongolia.

[3] In cases of transliterated Chinese terms, I will initially reference them in the officially recognized and widely used Pinyin in parenthesis, followed by the older Wade-Giles Roman-

ization, also in parenthesis. Third, whenever appropriate, in cases where Cantonese terms and their proper pronunciation are required for clarity and precision, I adopt recognized Cantonese-based Romanization in place of Mandarin Chinese (either the Pinyin or Wade-Giles) Romanization. In some cases, I adopt a more practical and user-friendly form of Cantonese transliteration in place of formal/official Cantonese Romanization, e.g., *Gum-Shaan* (Gold[en] mountain, instead of *kam shaan* or *Say-Yup* (Four district speech group) in place of *Sze-yap*, or the term *Bundae* (native) in place of *Poon-tei*, or its earlier Mandarin renditions of (*bendi*) and (*punti*) respectively. Consequently, hereafter I will use Cantonese Romanization in place of Mandarin Romanization when referencing Cantonese words, terms, and phrases. This starts with the use of *Yuet* in place of *Yue* and *Gwongdung* in place of *Guangdong*.

[4] See, The Gum-Shaan Chronicles: The Early History of Cantonese-Chinese America, 1850–1900, volume 4, Departing Tong-Shaan: The Organization and Operation of Cantonese Overseas Emigration (1850–1900), (Pittsburgh, Pa: Dorrance Publishing, 2022), see especially chapter 3, "The Cantonese Overseas Emigrant Reconsidered,"

[5] The Living Tree, The Changing Meaning of Being Chinese Today, edited by Tu Wei-Ming, (Stanford, California: Stanford University Press, 1994), (Preface to Stanford edition), pp. v, vi, & vii.; also see Richard W. Wilson, Learning to be Chinese, The Political Socialization of Children in Taiwan, (Cambridge, Mass: MIT Press, 1970).

[6] *Wikipedia,* "List of ethnic groups in China," The several largest of these 55 minority groups consists of the *Zhuang* with 19.9 million, *Hui* 10.58 million, *Manchu* 10.38 million, *Uyghur* 10 million, *Hmong/Miao* 9.4 million, *Yi* 8.7 million, *Tojia* 8.3 million, *Tibetans* 6.2 million, *Mongols* 5.9 million, *Dong* 2.8 million, *Buyei* 2.8 million, *Yao* 2.7 million, *Bai* 1.9 million, *Koreans* 1.8 million, *Hani* 1.6 million, *Li* 1.4 million, *Kazakh* 1.4 million, and the *Jai* 1.2 million. (2010 census figures)

[7] See, Agnieszka Joniak-Luthi, The Han, China's Diverse Majority, (Seattle: University of Washington Press, 2017 (Studies on Ethnic Groups in China, edited by Stevan Harrell, University of Washington Press)

[8] Wikipedia entry on "Han Chinese" the figures of 91.6% of 1.35 billion in 2014 is cited from the CIA (Central Intelligence Agency) Handbook. This Wikipedia article also cites alternative figure of 92% of 1.24 billion people for 2016. Among the total of 1.3 billion Han Chinese in the world, significant numbers live outside China. This includes: 22.5 million in Taiwan, 9.4 million in Thailand, 6.7 million in Hong Kong (See Wikipedia "Demographics of Hong Kong) 6.6 million in Malaysia, 3.8 million in the United States, 2.8 million in Indonesia, 2.5 million in Singapore, 1.6 million in Myanmar (Burma), 1.4 million in Canada, 1.3 million each in the Philippines and Peru, 1.2 million in Cambodia, 998,000 in Russia, 900,000 in South Korea, 866,000 in Australia, 823,000 in Vietnam, 700,000 in France, 655,000 in Japan, 400,000 in Venezuela, 350,000 in South Africa, 334,000 in Italy, 212,000 in Germany, 171,000 in Spain, 189,000 in India, 151,000 in Brazil, 147,000 in New Zealand, 144,000 in the Netherlands, and 135,000 in Panama.

[9] See Francis L.K. Hsu, Under the Ancestors' Shadow, Kinship, Personality, and Social Mobility in China, (Stanford, Ca: Stanford University Press, 1971), pp. 17–19.

[10] See the following two works: Joniak-Luthi, The Han, China's Diverse Majority; also see Thomas Mullaney and James Leibold, et. al. co-editors of Critical Han Studies: The History, Representation, and Identity of China's Majority (New Perspectives on Chinese Culture and Society) (Berkeley: University of California Press, 2012).

[11] See the following: Johanna Menzel Meskill, A Chinese Pioneering Family, the Lins of Wu-feng, Taiwan, 1729–1895, (Princeton, New Jersey: Princeton University Press, 1979); Sow-Theng Leong, Migration and Ethnicity in Chinese History, Hakkas, Pengmin, and Their Neighbors, (Stanford, California: Stanford University Press, 1997); Negotiating Ethnicities in China and Taiwan, edited by Melissa J. Brown, (Berkeley: University of California Press, 1996) (Institute of East Asian Studies, China Research Monograph 46); Down to Earth, The Territorial Bond in South China, edited by David Faure and Helen F. Siu, (Stanford, California: Stanford University Press, 1995).

[12] See the following: Emily Honig, Creating Chinese Ethnicity: Subei People in Shanghai, 1850–1980, (New Haven: Yale University Press, 1992); Bryna Goodman, Native Place, City and Nation, Regional Networks and Identities in Shanghai, 1853–1937, (Berkeley, California: University of California Press, 1995); Richard Belsky, Localities at the Center, Native Place, Space, and Power in Late Imperial Beijing, (Cambridge, Mass: Harvard University Press, 2005) (Harvard East Asian Monographs 258); Douglas Wesley Sparks, Unity is Power: The Teochiu of Hong Kong, (unknown binding) University Microfilms International (1975) ASSIN B00073D1LU.

[13] See generally, Andrea Louie, Chineseness Across Borders, Renegotiating Chinese Identities in China and the United States, (Durham, North Carolina: Duke University Press, 2004).

[14] See the following works: The Chinese City Between Two Worlds, edited by Mark Elvin and G. William Skinner, (Stanford, California: Stanford University Press, 1974), see especially following two essays/chapters in this work, "The Ningpo Pang and Financial Power in Shanghai," by Susan Mann Jones, pp.73–96; and "Merchant Association in Canton, 1895–1911," by Edward J. M. Rhoads, pp. 97–117; also see John King Fairbank, Trade and Diplomacy on the China Coast, The Opening of the Treaty Ports, 1842–1854, (Cambridge, Mass: Harvard University Press, 1964), regarding various Han Chinese ethnic minority groups and speech communities at Treaty Ports (e.g., Ningpo, Fujian's Min-speaking people, and the Cantonese) see especially the following: Chapter XII, "Problems in the Application of the Treaties at the New Ports," see especially section on the Cantonese as British allies, pp. 219–225; also see chapter XXI, "Wu Chien-Chang and the "Cantonization" of Shanghai 1852–53; also see, two volume work on Hankow, William T. Rowe, Hankow, Commerce and Society in a Chinese City, 1796–1889, (Stanford, Ca: Stanford University Press, 1984); William T. Rowe, Hankow, Conflict and Community in a Chinese City, 1796–1895, (Stanford, Ca: Stanford University Press, 1989); also see John M. Carroll, Edge of Empires, Chinese Elites and British Colonials in Hong Kong, (Cambridge, Mass: Harvard University Press, 2015); also see Elizabeth Sinn, Pacific Crossing, California Gold, Chinese Migration, and the Making of Hong Kong, (Hong Kong: Hong Kong University Press, 2013); also see, Noriko Kamachi, "The Chinese in Meiji Japan: Their Interaction with the Japanese Before the Sino-Japanese War," in The Chinese and Japanese, Essays in Political and Cultural Interactions, edited by Akira Iriye, (Princeton, New Jersey: Princeton University, 1980), as Chapter III, pp. 58–73; also see Philip A. Kuhn, Chinese Among Others, Emigration in Modern Times, (Boulder, Colorado: Rowman & Littlefield Publishers, Inc, 2008); Clarence E. Glick, Sojourners and Settlers, Chinese Migrants in Hawaii, (Honolulu, Hawaii: University of Hawaii Press, 1980); Elliott Young, Alien Nation, Chinese Migration in the Americas from the Coolie Era Through World War II, (Chapel Hill: University of North Carolina, 2014); also see From China to Canada, A History of the Chinese Communities in Canada,

edited by Edgar Wickberg et. al, (Toronto: McClelland and Stewart publishers, 1982); also see (James Morton, In the Sea of Sterile Mountains, The Chinese in British Columbia (Vancouver B.C.: J.J. Douglas Ltd, 1974); also see Adam McKeown, Chinese Migrant Networks and Cultural Change, Peru, Chicago, Hawaii, 1900–1936, (Chicago: University of Chicago Press, 2001); also see Jason Oliver Chang, Chino, Anti-Chinese Racism in Mexico, 1880–1940, (Urbana: University of Illinois Press, 2017); also see, Jeffrey Lesser, Negotiating National Identity, Immigrants, Minorities, and Struggle for Ethnicity in Brazil, (Durham, North Carolina: Duke University Press, 1999); also see Walton Look Lai, The Chinese in the West Indies, 1806–1995, A Documentary History, (Barbados: The Press of the University of the West Indies, 1998); The Chinese in the Caribbean, edited by Andrew Wilson, (Princeton, New Jersey: Markus Wiener Publishers, 2004); also consult a wide variety of books, monographs, and studies on the Chinese in America.

[15] This book adopts standard Cantonese romanization/transliteration, e.g., *Gwongchau-wah* in place of Pinyin Mandarin Chinese (*Guangzhouhua*) for Cantonese terms and labels. (In some cases, I adopt Cantonese phonetic forms that are more user friendly for English speakers (e.g., *Gwongchau-wah*). (see conversion table in introduction).

[16] See the following works: Andrea Louie, Chineseness Across Borders, Renegotiating Chinese Identities in China and the United States, (Durham, North Carolina: Duke University Press, 2004); Asian Diasporas, Cultures, Identities, Representations, edited by Robbie B.H. Goh and Shawn Wong, (Hong Kong: Hong Kong University Press, 2004); Asian Diasporas, New Formations, New Conceptions, edited by Rhacel S. Parreñas and Lok C.D. Siu, (Stanford, Ca: Stanford University Press, 2007); Displacements and Diasporas, Asians in the Americas, edited by Wanni W. Anderson and Robert G. Lee, (New Brunswick, New Jersey: Rutgers University Press, 2005).

[17] Madeline Y. Hsu, Dreaming of Gold, Dreaming of Home, Transnationalism, and Migration Between the United States and South China, 1882–1943, (Stanford, Ca: Stanford University Press, 2000) p.7, note 14, as cited from, Towards a Transnational Perspective on Migration: Race, Class, Ethnicity, and Nationalism Reconsidered, edited by Schiller, Nina Glick, Linda Basch, and Cristina Blanc-Szanton, eds. (New York: New York Academy of Sciences, 1992), p.ix

[18] See Kuhn, Chinese Among Others; also see McKeown, Chinese Migrant Networks and Cultural Change.

[19] See chapter 4 of this book, "Cantonese culture as a conservative contrarian counter culture."

[20] See Evelyn Hu-DeHart, Across the Pacific, Asian Americans and Globalization, (Philadelphia: Temple University Press, 2000).

[21] See Hsu, Dreaming of Gold, also see Chinese American Transnationalism, The Flow of People, Resources, and Ideas between China and America in the Exclusion Era, edited by Sucheng Chan, (Philadelphia: Temple University Press, 2006); also see Kathleen Lopez, Chinese Cubans, A Transnational History, (Chapel Hill: University of North Carolina Press, 2013).

[22] See Cities in Motion, Interior, Coast, and Diaspora in Transnational China, edited by Sherman Cochran, David Strand, and Wen-hsin Yeh, as General Editor, (Berkeley: University of California, 2007) (China Research Monograph, no. 62, Center for Chinese Studies, Institute for East Asian Studies, UC Berkeley)

[23] See chapter 4 of this book, "Cantonese culture as a "conservative contrarian counterculture,"

[24] This has been especially evident in Cantonese language, poetry, literature, Cantonese

opera, and popular culture. See the following: Roy T. Cowles, A Pocket Dictionary of Cantonese (Hong Kong: Hong Kong University Press, 1992 paperback edition); Marlon K. Hom, Songs of Gold Mountain, Cantonese Rhymes from San Francisco Chinatown, (Berkeley, California: University of California Press, 1987); Island: Poetry and History of Chinese Immigrants on Angel Island, 1910–1940 (Naomi B. Pascal Editor's Endowment- Second Edition) edited by Him Mark Lai, Genny Lim, and Judy Yung, (Seattle, Washington: University of Washington Press, 2014); Wing Chung Ng, The Rise of Cantonese Opera, (Urbana, Illinois: University of Illinois, 2015); Virgil K.Y. Ho, Understanding Canton, Rethinking Popular Culture in the Republican Period, (New York: Oxford University Press, 2005).

[25] Madeline Y. Hsu, "Unwrapping Orientalist: Restoring Homosocial Normativity to Chinese American History," Amerasia Journal 29:2 (2003): 230–253, see pp. 241. & 242.

[26] See generally, Herold J. Wiens, China's March to the Tropics, (New Jersey: Shoe String Press, 1954); also see, later edition with a different title, Herold J. Wiens, Han Chinese Expansion in South China, (New Jersey: Shoe String Press: 1967), pp. 55–129; also see, The Cambridge History of China, vol. 1; The Ch'in (Qin) and Han Empires, 221 BC-AD 220,(New York: Cambridge University Press 1986); also see Mark Edward Lewis, The Early Chinese Empires, Qin and Han, (first volume in series on the History of Imperial China), (Cambridge, Mass: Belknap Press of Harvard University Press, 2007), p. 151.

[27] See generally, Lee, Departing Tong-Shaan: The Organization and Operation of Cantonese Overseas Emigration (1850-1900), see especially chapter 3, The Cantonese Overseas Emigrant Reconsidered," A Cantonese frontier materialized in the American West at about the same time as the (White) American frontier advanced from East to West. The Cantonese frontier moved from northern California to the Pacific Northwest, then to the Great Basin, into the Rocky Mountain region, the American Southwest, the northern Great Plains, and western part of Texas. regarding Chinese in the American West, see the following: Rose Hum Lee, The Growth and Decline of Chinese Communities in the Rocky Mountain Region, (originally PhD dissertation Sociology, University of Chicago, 1947), (New York: Arno Press, 1978); The Chinese in Arizona, 1870–1950, A Context for Historic Preservation Planning, prepared by Melissa Keane, A.E. Rogerset. Al, for the Arizona State Historic Office and the City of Phoenix Planning Department (May 1992); Chris Friday, Organizing Asian American Labor, The Pacific Coast Canned Salmon Industry, 1970–1942, (Philadelphia: Temple University Press, 1994); Liping Zhu, A Chinaman's Chance, The Chinese on the Rocky Mountain Mining Frontier, (Niwot, Colorado: University of Colorado Press, 1997); Chinese on the American Frontier, Edited by Arif Dirlik, (with the assistance of Malcolm Yeung), (New York: Rowman & Littlefield Publishers, 2003) (Pacific Formations series); Liping Zhu and Rose Estep Fosha, Thenic Oasis, The Chinese in the Black Hills, (Pierre: South Dakota State Historical Society Press, 2004);Jean Pfaelzer, Driven Out, The Forgotten War Against Chinese Americans, (New York: Random House, 2007); Sue Fawn Chung, In Pursuit of Gold, Chinese American Miners and Merchants in the American West, (Urbana: University of Illinois Press, 2011); Sue Fawn Chung, Chinese in the Woods, Logging and Lumbering in the American West, (Urbana: University of Illinois Press, 2015); William Wei, Asians in Colorado, A History of Persecution and Perseverance in the Centennial State, (Seattle: University of Washington Press, 2016). Re: Chinese settlement in Mississippi and Louisiana, see following: James W. Loewen, The Mississippi Chinese, Between Black and White, (Cambridge, Mass: Harvard University Press, 1971); also see Rob-

ert Seto Quan, Lotus Among the Magnolias, The Mississippi Chinese,(Jackson, Mississippi: University Press of Mississippi: 2007)(originally published 1982); also see, Lucy M. Cohen, Chinese in Post-Civil War South, A People Without A History, (Baton Rouge: Louisiana State University Press, 1984); John Jung, Chopsticks in the Land of Cotton, Lives of Mississippi Delta Chinese Grocers, (2nd edition) (Yin-Yang Press, 2011).

[28] Note the distinction between "Han," as in the Han dynasty or Han period (202 BCE and 220 CE), and "Han," as an ethnic label, as in "Han" Chinese people and society. The same Chinese character is used in both cases, but each use represents a specific meaning/reference and separate, different connotation.

[29] See generally, Erica Brindley, Ancient China and the Yue: Perceptions and Identities on the Southern Frontier, c 400 BCE-50 CE, (Cambridge UK: Cambridge University Press, 2015); also see S. Robert Ramsey, The Languages of China, (Princeton, New Jersey: Princeton University Press, 1989), p. 102. (re: nexus between Tai and Cantonese languages)

[30] For general overview, see following: Immanuel C.Y. Hsu, The Rise of Modern China, (New York: Oxford University Press, 1990) (Fourth Edition), pp. 100-103; for more specialized discussion, see following: Paul, Rule, "The Chinese Rites Controversy: A Long Lasting Controversy in Sino-Western Cultural History," Pacific Rim Report 32 (Feb. 2004), pp. 2-8; also see, George Minamiki, The Chinese Rites: From its Beginning to Modern Times, (Loyola University Press, 1985); also see, The Chinese Rites Controversy: Its History and Meaning, edited by David E. Mungello, (Nettetal, Germany: Steyler, 1994); also see David E. Mungello, The Great Encounter of China and the West, 1500-1800, (Rowman & Littlefield, 2012) Catholic missionary activity had been allowed in the later Ming period, but had been banned in the early Qing as a result of the Rites Controversy (1742), where the issue of who headed the Catholic Church in China, either the Emperor of China or the Pope in Rome, was resolved. Pope Benedict XIV in Rome underscored his claim by excommunicating Chinese Catholics. The Kangxi (K'ang-hsi) Emperor banned Christian missionaries from China.

[31] The best description of this system of trade is provided in Hsu, Rise of Modern China, pp. 139-166.

[32] Ibid.,

[33] Ibid., pp.142–145, This guild had a government sanctioned monopoly over China's foreign trade and Southeast China's interregional trade in the period 1760–1842. It had a fluctuating number of merchant house members, ranging from 9 to 13, which were divided into three sub-groups, relative to a designated specialized area of trade expertise. They were: 1) the Southeast Asia (i.e., *Nam-yeung*) group, 2) the Fujian-East Gwongdung (*Teochiu* speaking areas of Chaozhou and Swatow) group, and 3) the group that supervised trade with Westerners at Canton, on Shameen Island. Individual Hong merchants were assigned to handle a few foreign traders in particular. One might take responsibility for dealing with the British and the Americans, while another would deal with the French, Spanish, and Portuguese. These merchants provided daily supplies of potable water, fresh produce, meat, and kerosene, as well as building materials, laborers, interpreters, and domestic service providers. They also took consignment orders for tea, porcelain, silk and other purchase orders from their assigned Western traders.

[34] Frederick Wakeman Jr., Strangers at the Gate, Social Disorder in South China, 1839–1861, (Berkeley: University of California Press, 1966), ref: *han-chien* (Chinese traitors,) p.49.

35 John K. Fairbank, Trade and Diplomacy on the China Coast, The Opening of the Treaty Ports, 1842–1854, (Cambridge, Mass: Harvard University Press, 1964), pp. 219–225; 393–409

36 See, Hsu, Dreaming of Gold, Dreaming of Home; also see Migration Between the United States and South China, 1882–1943, (Stanford: Stanford University Press, 2000); also see by the same author, "Trading with Gold Mountain: Jinshanzhuang and the Networks of Kinship and Native Places," in Chinese American Transnationalism, The Flow of People, Resources, and Ideas between China and America during the Exclusion Era, edited by Sucheng Chan, (Philadelphia: Temple University Press, 2006), see pp. 22–33.

37 The older prince was appointed Prince-Governor of Fuzhou, i.e., governor of Fujian Province, while the younger brother was appointed Prince-Governor of Canton, i.e., Governor of Gwongdung Province. With the fall of the capital at Hangzhou, the pretenders had to flee and relocate in advance of the Mongol invaders. In June 1276, Chao Shih (The elder brother) became enthroned as the Ti-Shih Emperor at Fuzhou. After the Mongols overran Fujian, the exiled Song court next fled into Gwongdung, relocating first at Ch'ao-chou (Chaozhou) in East Gwongdung, and then at Hui-chou (Huizhou) in Central Gwongdung. From February through November 1277, the exiled Song court relocated several times in the vicinity of Canton. By early 1278, it had re-established itself in Chung-Shaan (Zhongshan), not too far from present day Macao. By March 1278, it again relocated itself on Lantao Island, near Hong Kong, where in May of that year Chao Ping, the younger brother, became enthroned as the Ti-Ping Emperor. Shortly thereafter, the exiled court fled again, this time to a small island off the coast of Sunwui (Hsin-hui), located west of Chung-Shaan. In early 1279, the Mongols finally took over most of Central and Western Gwongdung, whereby they prepared for the final annihilation of the last remnant of the Song Dynasty. On March 19, 1279 the last Song emperor, the Ti-Ping Emperor, a mere boy of six, perished at sea. Rumors that he had in fact survived inspired Song loyalists in the Canton area to organize further resistance against the Mongols. see Herbert Franke (ed), Sung Biographies, (Wiesbaden: Franz Steiner Uerlaz, 1976), pp. 1011–1016.

38 See generally, Paul D. Buell, "The Sung Resistance Movement, 1276–1279: An Episode in Chinese Regional History," in The Annals of the Chinese Historical Society of the Pacific Northwest, vol 3: 1985–1986 (Bellingham, Washington: Western Washington University, Center for East Asian Studies)

39 See generally, Lynn Struve, The Southern Ming, 1644–1662, (New Haven: Yale University Press, 1984); also see The Cambridge History of China, Vol 7 The Ming Dynasty 1368–1644, Part I (Cambridge: UK, Cambridge University Press, 1988), see Chapter 11, Lynn A Struve, "The Southern Ming, 1644–1662," pp. 641–725.

40 See Wikipedia.org/wiki/Kuomintang_Islamic_Insurgency

41 See following works, L. Eve Armentrout Ma, Revolutionaries, Monarchists, and Chinatowns, Chinese Politics in the Americas and the 1911 Revolution, (Honolulu: University of Hawaii Press, 1990); also see "Political Development in Chinese America, 1850–1911," (PhD dissertation in Modern Chinese History, University of California, Santa Barbara, 1979), by Douglas W. Lee, see chapter 4, pp. 199–275, chapter 5, pp. 305–388, chapter 6, pp. 389–471, and chapter 7, pp. 472–542.

42 See D. Lee, "Political Development in Chinese America," see especially, Part II: The Politics of Idealism," pp.305–542.

43 See Douglas W. Lee, The Gum-Shaan Chronicles: The Early History of Cantonese-Chinese America, 1850-1900, volume 3, Facing Cantonese Adversity, Fleeing Tong-Shaan:

Cantonese Society and the Root Causes of Nineteenth-Century Overseas Emigration, (Pittsburgh, Pa: Dorrance Publishing, 2022), see especially, Chapter 8, "Bad Joss of Local Cantonese Fan-Kwai inspired *Luen* (chaos),

[44] Wakeman, Strangers at the Gate, ref: *han-chien* (Chinese traitors,) see p. 49

[45] See generally, Robert Worden, "A Chinese Reformer in Exile: The North American Phase of the Travels of K'ang Yu-wei, 1899–1909, "PhD dissertation (Georgetown University, 1972).

[46] Ibid., pp. 73, 75.

[47] See chapter 3 of this book, "Cantonese Ethnicity, as a series of ethnic group and speech community labels," re: definition and explanations of the terms *Bundae* and *Hakka*; also see, Lee, Departing Tong-Shaan, The Organization and Operation of Cantonese Overseas Emigration to America, 1850-1900, see chapter 2, "Moving from Bad Joss to Good Joss," re: *Bundae-Hakka* conflicts in Central Gwongdung and in America in the middle decades of the nineteenth-century.

[48] Ibid., re: ethno-linguistic make-up of Chung Shaan District in Central Gwongdung. The noted *Hakka* authority Luo Xianglin has argued that Sun was in fact a *Hakka*. See Luo's following works: *Kechia yanjiu daolun* (Introduction to the Study of the *Hakkas*) Xinning (Toishan) (Taishan): *Xishan shucang*, 1933); also see, *Kechiashiliao huipian* (Historical Sources for the Study of the *Hakkas*) (Hong Kong: *Zhongguo xushe*, 1965).

[49] Ibid., re: ethno-linguistic make-up of Chung-Shan District in Central Gwongdung.

[50] See the following biographies of Dr. Sun Yat-sen, Lyon Sharman, Sun Yat-Sen, His life and Its Meaning, A Critical Biography, (Stanford: Stanford University Press 1934, 1973 printing); Harold Z. Schiffrin, Sun Yat-sen and the Origins of the Chinese Revolution, (Berkeley: University of California Press, 1970); and C. Martin Wilbur, Sun Yat-sen, Frustrated Patriot, (New York: Columbia University Press, 1974); Marie-Claire Bergere,(French edition) (Paris: Fayard, 1994); (Marie- Claire Bergere, Sun Yat-sen, Janet Lloyd, translator) (Stanford, Ca: Stanford University Press, 2000);Memoirs of a Chinese Revolutionary, (autobiography) (no place cited: Silver Street Media, 2012); Charles Sheridan Jones & James Cantile, Sun Yat-Sen and the Awakening of China, (no place cited: Andesite Press, 2017); Tjio Kayloe, The Unfinished Revolution: Sun Yat-sen and the Struggle for Modern China, (no place cited: Marshall Cavendish International (Asia) pte ltd, 2018).

[51] L. Eve Armentrout-Ma, Revolutionaries, Monarchists, and Chinatowns, Chinese Politics in the Americas and the 1911 Revolution, (Honolulu: University of Hawaii Press, 1990), pp. 87–94; 112–117; 125–131; 143–146; and154–155.

[52] Ibid., see this work generally, also see "Political Development in Chinese America, 1850–1911," by Douglas W. Lee

[53] See following two works previously mentioned by Madeline Hsu, "Trading with Gold Mountain," and Dreaming of Gold Dreaming of Home; also see, Elizabeth Sinn, Pacific Crossing, California Gold, Chinese Migration, and the Making of Hong Kong, (Hong Kong: Hong Kong University Press, 2013).

[54] Willard G. Jue, "Chin Gee-Hee, Chinese Pioneer Entrepreneur in Seattle and Toishan," in The Annals of the Chinese Historical Society of the Pacific Northwest, (1983), pp31. 38; also see Chin Gee Hee, "Letter asking for support to build the Sunning Railroad," (1911), in Judy Young, Gordon H Chang, and Him Mark Lai (compilers and editors), Chinese American Voices, (Berkeley: University of California Press, 2006), pp. 125–128.

# CHAPTER 1
Central Gwongdung, The Cantonese Homeland and Fountainhead

**Introduction**

Central Gwongdung (Guangdong) (Kwangtung,)[1] the chief micro-region of Gwongdung province, is where key geo-demographic and socio-cultural constructs contextualized the historical development of a unique Cantonese group identity and history over the course of two millennia, from the third century BCE to the twentieth century CE. This narrative helped produce a set of "conceptual bookends," buttressing the construction of an historically distinct Cantonese persona. The first bookend is the reality of a "Cantonese homeland," where Cantonese society and culture originated and evolved. The other bookend is the idea of a "Cantonese fountainhead," from which Cantonese group identity and collective experiences emanated from to spread throughout Gwongdung province, then elsewhere in China, and ultimately globally in many distant overseas locations. The idea of a "Cantonese homeland," with its geo-demographic constructs and historical identifications, is easy enough to grasp, because it is unambiguous and concrete in its representation. In marked contrast, the notion of a Cantonese fountainhead is abstract and nuanced, and thus unclear by way of its conceptualization. This means that the latter requires some prefatory clarification, while the former does not.

In making reference to a Cantonese fountainhead, I utilize the traditional Cantonese metaphor of *Tong-Shaan*, (*Tang*) (i.e., *Tong* Mountain,) to formulate a conceptual nexus between the geo-historical development of Central Gwongdung, as a particular place, i.e., the home of the Cantonese people, and the idea of a "Cantonese fountainhead." *Tong-Shaan* serves as an ascribed iconic representation of the enduring and enigmatic relationship between Cantonese people and their ancestral homeland. In this manner, I hypothesize that Central Gwongdung, as a specific place, provided a material basis for the abstract construction of the notion of *Tong-Shaan*. This conceptual link between a particular place and how people mentally constructed and emotionally embraced it, via an abstraction, is what I mean when I use the term "Cantonese fountainhead." Beyond the technicalities of geography, demography, and history, it may seem unclear as to why we should take the quantum leap from viewing Central Gwongdung as a particular place, to theorizing about it, in the guise of *Tong-Shaan*, as a subjectively imagined Cantonese fountainhead. The answer, quite simply, is that a re-examination of the organic relationship between a people and their ancestral homeland, in terms of how it has been ascriptively remembered and iconographically represented over time, can help us to truly understand, "What it meant to be Cantonese in the nineteenth century."

It should be noted, that while I introduce and contextualize this idea here, I defer a full discussion of its manner of operation until chapter 6, at the end of this book. In support of these perspectives, the following five topics are discussed: 1) Gwongdung Province, as an ensemble of three micro-regions; 2) Central Gwongdung, as a regional conceptualization for the Cantonese homeland; 3) Central Gwongdung's five key ethno-speech micro-regions; 4) A demographic profile of nineteenth-century Central Gwongdung; 5) The Cantonese Heartland: A series of interlocking concentric forms in Central Gwongdung.

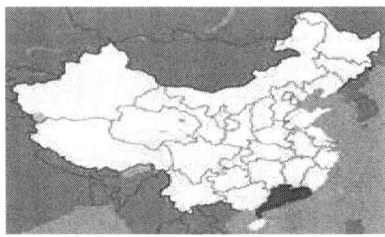

Map of China, with Gwongdung province located in the southeast corner (lower right)

**Gwongdung Province, as an ensemble of three micro-regions**

Gwongdung province is located in the southeast corner of China Proper.[2] Located near the Tropic of Cancer, parallel with the Hawaiian Islands, and northwest of the Philippines. It enjoys a semi-tropical to a tropical climate. The climate is influenced by topological features of mountain ranges along the province's northern borders and a long coastline along its southern flank. The result has been a well-protected and relatively insulated, historically semi-isolated geophysical unit, with marked climatic conditions. The area has been characterized by high levels of rainfall and moisture. High humidity in the spring-summer period is matched by seasonal monsoon winds, which bring heavy rains from the southwest in the late spring and summer. These features have enhanced agricultural productivity, especially in key river basins and deltas. However, typhoons are common and have often resulted in widespread destruction.

The most significant geographical feature setting Gwongdung off from the rest of Southern China is the *Nanling* Mountain range. The *Nanling* range forms a natural divide between Central and South China. It stretches from west to east for about 400 miles and north to south for about 130 miles.[3] It also acts as the major watershed, dividing the Yangtze River system of Central China from Gwongdung's *Sai-gong (Xijiang)* or West River system. The *Nanling* straddles Gwongdung's northern borders with neighboring Jiangxi (Kiangsi) and Hunan provinces. Although the *Nanling* separates Central and South China, it is nonetheless "comparatively low and discontinuous (with) many "breaks" where both cold [air] waves and human traffic may pass through conveniently.[4] South of the *Nanling*, in a wide arch from west to east, lies the *Dung-nam (Dongnan)* hills, which serve as an additional topological feature that further distinguishes and separates Gwongdung from Central China. Generally speaking, the mountainous regions of Gwongdung's northern borders, together with a long 1,500-mile southern coastline, provided Gwongdung with a well-defined and separate geographical identity, a situation similar to that of California in the western United States.

Nineteenth-Century Gwongdung was geographically larger than it is today, because at that time, it also included Hainan Island and coastal areas of neighboring Gwongsai province.[5]

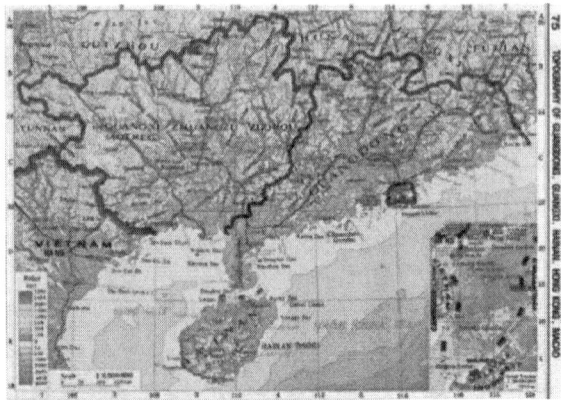

Map of Gwongdung province (on right) and Gwongsai province (on left), known collectively as The Lingnam Region

Nineteenth-Century Gwongdung had an area of about 82,000 square miles, (about the size of the state of Kansas (82,277 square miles),[6] with a relatively stable population of about 29–30 million people.[7] Its internal geographical composition was divided by a series of mountain ranges and river systems. This resulted in an ensemble of three well-defined micro-regions: 1) East Gwongdung, 2) West Gwongdung, and 3) Central Gwongdung.[8] Each micro-region was defined by a major river drainage system, as in the case of both East and Central Gwongdung, or the lack thereof, as in the case of West Gwongdung. In turn, each of these three micro-regions had its own series of sub-regions, outlined by a series of hills and valleys, with smaller rivers lacing alluvial flatlands. Each micro-region also comprised a series of well-defined separate ethnic groups and local speech communities.

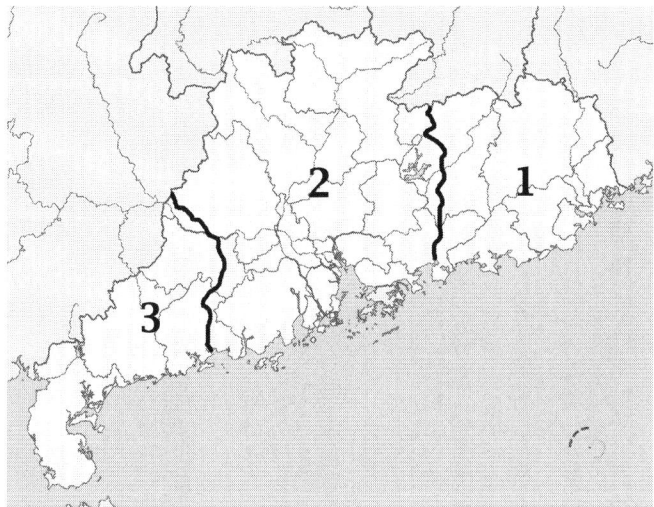

**The three micro-regions of Gwongdung province.** #1 is East Gwongdung, #2 is Central Gwongdung, #3 is West Gwongdung.

## *East Gwongdung*

East Gwongdung is the area between the Fujian-Gwongdung border and Central Gwongdung. This area is defined by the Han River drainage basin, which has its head waters in neighboring Fujian Province to the east. Its major tributary is the Mei River, which flows east-northeast to join the Han River about 150 miles upriver from the sea. There is also the Rong River, a short distance east of the Han River. It is the second longest river in the region, Typographically, East Gwongdung is an extension of the low coastal ranges that run along the southeastern Chinese coast, starting in Zhejiang, running through Fujian and ending in Gwongdung. The dividing line between East and Central Gwongdung is a small spur of mountains that thrust out from the *Nanling* Mountains to the sea, near the city of *Hoi-fung* (*Haifeng*) about 150 miles east of Hong Kong. These mountains also form the rain-shed divide between East Gwongdung's Han River and East-Central Gwongdung's East River.[9]

While "East Gwongdung" is well-known, its exact size and shape has never been clearly established.[10] What I identify here as East Gwongdung, represents a general description, rather than a specific technical reference. East Gwongdung was a sizable integrated and well-defined micro-region in Gwongdung, with its own distinct geo-typological features, demographics, socio-cultural distinctions, and ethno-linguistic technicalities. Historically speaking, East Gwongdung comprised an area, anywhere from a quarter to a third of Gwongdung's total area of an estimated 82,000 square miles, which is about 20,500 to around 27,060 square miles.[11] In the later nineteenth century, it had a population of about 2.5 million people.[12] East Gwongdung had two major urban centers. First, *Chaozhou* (identified locally as *Teochiu*),[13] the largest urban center of the region, located on the northern edge of the Han River Delta. Second, *Shantou* (formerly identified by Westerners as *Swatow*,) located on the coast about forty miles south of *Chaozhou*. It was the second largest city in East Gwongdung and the micro-region's chief seaport. The location and relationship of East Gwongdung's *Chaozhou* and *Shantou* mirrored that of Canton and Hong Kong in Central Gwongdung, where each micro-region had a dominant urban center located inland on the edge of a major river delta, flanked by a major seaport strategically situated nearby on the coast.

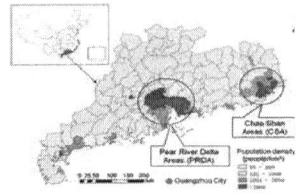 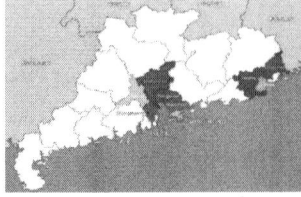

Canton-Hong Kong in Central Gwongdung
Chaozhou-Shantou in East Gwongdung

By the mid-nineteenth century, both Hong Kong and *Shantou* had become major seaports during the golden age of China's Treaty Ports (1850–1930), and both became major embarkation centers for Overseas Chinese emigration. Hong Kong serviced Cantonese overseas emigration to the Western Hemisphere, while *Shantou* serviced *Teochiu*[14] emigration to SE Asia. East Gwongdung had its own ethno-culturally distinct persona, commonly identified by the *Teochiu* label, which originated from, and evolved as an extension of southern Fujian's southern *Min* speech (*Min-nan hua.*) Consequently, these two micro-regions of East and Central

Gwongdung, while both were located in the same province, were not only distinctly separate geographic entities, but also remained historically separated from each other, as socio-culturally distant and ethno-linguistically distinct communities. This sense of separateness was also evident in the development of two major economic rivals within Gwongdung. First, with East Gwongdung's Han-Mei River complex, and its key urban centers of *Chaozhou* and *Shantou*, and second, the West-Pearl River complex, with its urban centers of Canton and Hong Kong.

## *West Gwongdung*

West Gwongdung is a second key micro-region of Gwongdung Province. Unlike both East and Central Gwongdung, West Gwongdung did not have either a major river drainage system, with a supporting rich delta ecosystem, nor a large demographic base. In this regard, the region lacked a history of dynamic economic development, as a robust commercialized agrarian-based economy. Significantly, West Gwongdung's total population numbered somewhere from several hundred thousand to nearly a million people, including both the Han Chinese and various local aboriginal peoples. In contrast, East Gwongdung's population, in just the core *Chaozhou-Shantou* (*Chaoshan*) region averaged about 2.5 million people in the nineteenth century.

Similar to East Gwongdung, West Gwongdung also defied exact definition and explicit delineation. The reason for this situation is, however, altogether different. In the case of East Gwongdung, the inherent difficulty in distinguishing its shape and size results from the problematic task of distinguishing and separating it from adjacent administrative units and peoples elsewhere, such as neighboring Central Gwongdung. In the case of West Gwongdung, the opposite is the case, where well-defined and clearly separate geophysical components more easily indicate a series of separate entities. Thus, West Gwongdung is the sum of many sub-parts that are only loosely bound (administratively) together to form the artificial entity of "West Gwongdung." The *Yun-Wu* (Misty) Mountain range divides West and Central Gwongdung, some 180–200 miles west of Hong Kong.[15] West Gwongdung was divided into four subunits: a) interior mountainous areas in the north and northwest, b) the coastal lowlands, c) the *Lei-chau* Peninsula, and d) Hainan Island.

West Gwongdung's major urban centers were smaller in number and size, than those in East and Central Gwongdung. They were limited to a few strategically located seaports, chiefly along the northeast coast of the *Lei-chau (Leizhou)* Peninsula, and on the northern and southern ends of Hainan Island. In the nineteenth century, urban development in West Gwongdung remained weaker here than elsewhere in Gwongdung. This lack of significant urban development resulted from the fact that Han Chinese settlement in West Gwongdung, in contrast to Chinese settlement of East and Central Gwongdung, occurred rather late, and within a much shorter time period, mainly in the seventeenth to nineteenth centuries CE. In contrast Chinese settlement in East and Central Gwongdung started nearly two millennia previously.

By the mid-Qing period (1750–1850 CE) local Chinese communities in West Gwongdung, especially in more remote areas, such as on Hainan Island and in mountainous areas north of the coastal lowlands, were typically viewed as the embodiment of a "pioneer society," similar to the situation on Taiwan in the same period of time.[16] In both cases, Han Chinese people migrated from Central China, settled down, then re-migrated, and then re-settled again in areas that had been previously been regarded as marginal, because of either adverse material conditions (e.g., dense forests, thick jungles) or the presence/opposition of pre-existing aboriginal peoples, e.g., the *Li* and *Miao* on Hainan Island.[17] The prevailing general impression of West Gwongdung, by others outside the region, was that it was remote and logistically difficult to travel about, because of its rudimentary communications and transportation. This resulted in the popular view that it was a forbidding place, i.e., the "backwater," or "outback" of Gwongdung. This perspective also applied to neighboring Gwongsai Province, whereby the two areas were frequently identified together as a vast frontier wilderness. This view persisted for over a thousand years, from Tang times through the mid-Qing period (8th to 18th centuries CE). Hainan Island in specific, became an infamous place of exile, for once highly placed and powerful officials from the capital in the Tang and Song (Sung) Dynasties, because it was deemed too harsh, inhospitable, as well as remote.[18]

West Gwongdung's coastal lowlands, both west and east of the *Lei-chau* Peninsula, resembled other areas of Gwongdung's long sea coast, where Han Chinese had settled and farmed for many centuries. This commonality of experience and intensive farming in coastal lowlands manifest itself in similar agricultural and commercial activity, typically organized on a traditional grid around various central places, associated with administrative and commercial (market) functions. The two chief urban centers in this area were *Pakhoi* (*Beihai*) (now in Gwongsai (Guangxi), located on the coast due west of the northernmost part of the *Lei-chau* Peninsula, and *Chin-kong* (*Zhanjiang*) located on the opposite northeast side of the *Lei-chau* Peninsula. As one moves north from the coastal lowlands, the landscape changes into low lying foothills, to become mountainous terrain.

The vast majority of the Chinese settlers in West Gwongdung originally came from *Min* speaking areas of East Gwongdung, while some came directly from Southern Fujian Province. This resulted in a predominantly Southern *Min* (*Min-nan hua*) ethnic speech community in West Gwongdung. While this speech was similar to the *Teochiu* dialect of East Gwongdung, however, it had its own distinct characteristics and identifying label. It was commonly known as the *Hainan* dialect or *Hoinam-wah*, (in Cantonese speech) or *Hainanhua, (in Mandarin)*) This group formed the majority of the people of West Gwongdung. There were however, some small pockets of *Yuet*/Cantonese people in West Gwongdung, but they only formed a minority in West Gwongdung.

During the nineteenth century, aboriginal peoples in the region also maintained a viable presence, with their own languages and cultures. The two most prominent aboriginal groups were the *Li* people, who speak a *Tai-Kedai* language, and the *Miao* people, who speak a *Hmong-Mien* language.[19] In the later nineteenth century, however, many people in southwestern Gwongdung and Gwongsai, including some aboriginal people, also spoke and understood standard Cantonese, in addition to their own speech.[20] This underscored the reality of the widespread use of Cantonese speech throughout the *Lingnam* (Gwongdung and Gwongsai) region in the nineteenth century.

In the early nineteenth century, most of the Han Chinese population consisted of peasant farmers, located chiefly in the *Lei-chau* peninsula itself, and along the coastal lowlands to the northeast and northwest. On Hainan Island, peasant farmers were most common on the northern side of the island, especially the northeast quadrant. In these areas, there also existed small numbers of merchants, and an even smaller number of gentry-types. One could also find a variety of "social strangers," i.e., forest people, outlaws, and peripatetic Buddhist monks, traveling tradesmen, and various service providers. Each area, i.e., coastal lowlands, the *Lei-chau* Peninsula, and Hainan Island, had its own respective historical, geophysical, and ethno-social identity.

The *Lei-chau* Peninsula and Hainan Island, however, have been more well known, and thus attracted greater attention than the coastal lowlands. If the coastal lowlands were unremarkable in both their demographics and socioeconomic conditions, in marked contrast, the *Lei-chau* Peninsula and Hainan Island were atypical in their material conditions and patterns of historical development. During the mid-late nineteenth century, both Chinese and Western interests rivaled each other for local control.

The *Lei-chau* Peninsula was the third largest peninsula in China, after the *Shandong* and *Liaodong* peninsulas in northeast China. It encompassed a land mass of some 3,300 square miles or 8,500 sq. km. The Gulf of *Tongking* lies to the west, the South China Sea lies to the east, and Hainan Island lies to the south. In the nineteenth century, *Chin-kong* served as the chief urban center, located on the northeast corner of the peninsula. In the later 1880s, after the Sino-French War 1884–1885, the French began to expand their activities and influence in the area, relative to their expansion in nearby *Tongking* (northern Vietnam). By 1898, the French obtained a ninety-nine years lease for the region around *Chin-kong*, which was re-named Fort Bayard.[21] A larger French enclave took shape in the northern *Lei-chau* Peninsula, known as *Kouang-Tcheou-wan*, more commonly known as "Kwangchow Bay." Its population in 1911 was about 189,000.[22]

Hainan Island, the third component of West Gwongdung, is the second largest island off the Chinese coat, after Taiwan. It is located about 200 miles east of North Vietnam and about 300 miles southwest of Hong Kong. It lies just off the coast from the *Lei-Chau* Peninsula, separated by the narrow *Qiongzhou* Strait (also commonly called the *Hainan* Strait,) which is about 19 miles wide (30 km.) Similar to Taiwan, Hainan served as the homeland of several aboriginal groups. Large numbers of Chinese settlers arrived in the mid-later Qing period in the latter eighteenth and early nineteenth centuries.

Aggressive settlement resulted in Han Chinese dominance of both Hainan's and Taiwan's coastal lowlands. This resulted in the ejection of the pre-existing aboriginal peoples, who subsequently retreated into the mountainous interiors of both islands that had not been initially attractive to Chinese farmer/settlers. *Haikou*, also known as *Kiung-chow,* was the largest city and administrative center on Hainan during the Qing period.[23] Another older name for *Haikou* had been *Qionshan*. Today, Hainan Island is also known simply as *Qiong*. Han Chinese settlement on Hainan occurred chiefly on the northeastern coastal lowlands. This left mainly the central and southern parts of the island, as an area dominated by communities of aboriginal peoples.

The Li people form the largest aboriginal group on Hainan Island, with about 1.3 million people, who occupy about 55% of the southern part of Hainan. The *Hmong* people form the second largest aboriginal group. They are known locally on Hainan as the *Miao* people. There are also significant numbers of *Hui* or Moslem peoples, i.e., about 20,000 descendants of sixteenth-century Arab merchants, who settled on Hainan and intermarried with local Han Chinese. Additionally, some descendants of the ancient Cham peoples from Champa (in what is now Vietnam,) also settled on Hainan Island. They are identified with the *Hui* group.[24]

In the nineteenth-century, Hainan Island was the southernmost frontier of Chinese society. The economy was decidedly agrarian, with local commercial activity and limited trade with some Southeast Asian neighbors. During this period, overseas Chinese emigration from West Gwongdung grew in size and scope, most notably in the case of Chinese emigrating from Hainan Island to Southeast Asia (Thailand, Singapore, Malaya, and Vietnam.) Interestingly, hardly any people migrated from Hainan to Hawaii and North America. This seems to have been generally the case of most of Chinese emigrating from West Gwongdung. Migration patterns reflected the strong influence of chain migration, where Hainan emigrants followed the lead of their own people and settled in the same previously chosen areas, e.g., in the *Nam-yeung* (*Nanyang*) or SE Asia.

**Central Gwongdung**

Central Gwongdung has been notable for four important reasons. First, it has been the largest, richest, and most heavily populated micro-region of

Gwongdung province. Second, it is the ancestral homeland of the Cantonese people, and the fountainhead of their *Yuet* (*Yue*) ethnicity, language, and culture. Third, it is the homeland from which the Cantonese diaspora originated, resulting in a globalized Cantonese-speaking world. Fourth, it provided a blueprint for the replication of early Cantonese overseas community life. Thus, Central Gwongdung deserves special attention regarding the distinctiveness of the Cantonese people in the nineteenth century, as well as the geographical source of their traditional identity and experience.

Geographically, Central Gwongdung consisted of four sub-micro-regions, which in the aggregate appears in the shape of an inverted triangle, i.e., wide at the top, and narrow at the bottom.[25] First, there existed a long narrow mountainous zone along the fringe of Gwongdung's northern borders with the neighboring provinces of Jiangxi, Hunan, and Gwongsai (Guangxi) respectively. Second, there existed a broad area located south of the outer mountainous zone, consisting of a series of up-river hills and valleys. These distinctive typographical features resulted from the long-term environmental impact of Central Gwongdung's three major rivers, the West, North, and East Rivers. Third, there existed the compact area the Pearl River Delta Region, where the micro-region's aforementioned river systems converged and overlapped. Fourth, and last, Metropolitan Canton (*Gwong-Chau*) (*Guangzhou*) strategically positioned itself on the northern portion of the Pearl River Delta, where the West, East, and North Rivers converged, as they also joined with the Pearl River at different locations. Canton, geo-territorially speaking, remained the smallest of Central Gwongdung's four micro-regions.[26] Significantly, however, because Canton served concurrently as the Capital of Gwongdung province, the central hub of Central Gwongdung's socio-economic and civic-political life, and the epicenter of Cantonese cultural life, its diminutive geo-territorial extent belied its historical significance in Central Gwongdung.

*Mountainous zone along Central Gwongdung's border with Jiangxi, Hunan, and Gwongsai*

Gwongdung's mountainous border sub micro-region has not been significant in the history of the Cantonese people, because it has traditionally lacked the degree of centrality, sizable population, and economic leverage more commonly associated with the other Cantonese zones, such as the Pearl River Delta region and Metropolitan Canton respectively. Demographically speaking, this area has traditionally hosted a smaller, more widely distributed population, consisting of Chinese settlers from Gwongdung (both Cantonese and non-Cantonese), Hunan, Jiangxi, and Gwongsai respectively. Local Han Chinese settlers share this micro-region with a variety of non-Han Chinese people, most of whom are members of designated national autonomous aboriginal minorities. This sub micro-region has few urban centers, none of which are large They are: *Lechang*, near the border with Hunan, and *Lianzhou, Yangshan, Huaji, Guangning, Fengkai,* and *Luoding* respectively, which are all located near the Gwongdung-Gwongsai border. This area served as the point of origin for Central Gwongdung's three major river systems, the West, North, and East Rivers.[27] In this way, geographically speaking, the outer mountainous region played a distant, but useful supporting role for Central Gwongdung's other micro-regions.

*The up-river hills and valleys sub micro-region*

The second key micro-region of Central Gwongdung consisted of up-river hills and valleys, which linked the outer mountainous micro-region with the alluvial plains further down river. It had a demographically larger and more uniform population, i.e., overwhelmingly Cantonese-speaking Han Chinese, as well as more urban centers and traditional rural communities, than did the outer mountainous zone.[28] The chief urban centers were *Shaoguan*, some distance south of the Gwongdung-Hunan border, and *Wenyuan, Yingde, Qingyuan*, and *Yunfu* respectively, all located some distance from the Gwongdung-Gwongsai border.

Contextually speaking, this zone was a transitional one, where its traditional role was to provide a nurturing geophysical context, with adequate spatial, ecological, and topographic features to support the development of Central Gwongdung's formidable river system. Four rivers formed the life line of Central Gwongdung, holding it together, even as they also divided it. This four-river complex has been alternately identified as: 1) the "West River system,"

Chapter 1

2) the "Pearl River system," or 3) the "West-Pearl River system." Currently, the term "Pearl River System" is a catch-all term linking together the West, North, East, and Pearl Rivers respectively. Consequently, the term "Pearl River" can mean alternately, either a complex river system consisting of four major rivers, as they were linked together, or it could alternately refer to just the Pearl River itself.[29]

Each of these four rivers is clearly identifiable as a separate entity, relative to its point of origin, and the route each individually charted across the countryside. As these rivers connected with each other, and entered into the Pearl River Delta, they become a complex web of "distributaries" i.e., waterways that flowed from larger rivers to form smaller ones, as opposed to "tributaries," i.e., where smaller rivers flow into larger rivers. Central Gwongdung's many rivers formed a complex and widely dispersed system of interconnected waterways, streams, and canals, which connected, disconnected, disappeared, and then reappeared in different configurations.

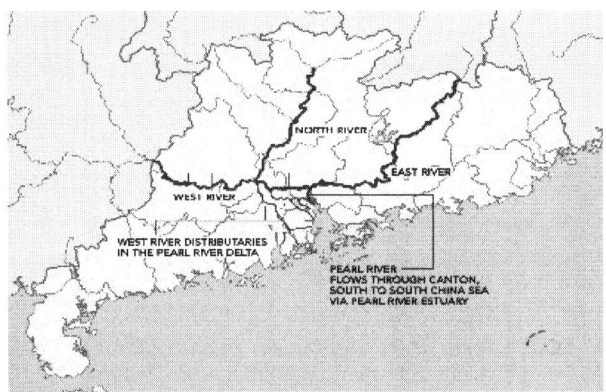

Central Gwongdung's four major rivers:
The West, North, East and Pearl Rivers

In the aggregate, they provided the vital energy that drove economic life in Central Gwongdung. This included: 1) supplying an essential and reliable source of potable water, to meet the needs of both rural and urban society, 2) materially supporting a highly commercialized agriculture, 3) providing relatively inexpensive, efficient, and convenient inland transportation linkages and routes, 4) procuring a wealth of fresh water marine resources (e.g., seafood, flora, and fauna), and 5) providing a bountiful ecosystem to support regional agrarian-based and commercially enhanced, economic development over an immensely long period of time. The transitional nature of this zone was underscored by the fact that these major river systems connected the outer mountainous zone with the pivotal micro-regions of the Pearl River Delta Region and Metropolitan Canton.

Gwongdung Province's largest and longest river is Central Gwongdung's West River (*Sai-gong*) (*Xijiang*). It flows east/southeast from the Yunnan-Guizhou (Kweichow) plateau for about 1,650 kms. It then crosses the Gwongsai-Gwongdung border and enters Gwongdung just below *Wu-chau* (*Wuzhou*) about 200 miles upstream from the sea. This river is famous for two reasons. First it is the largest and longest river in southern China, south of the Yangtze River. Like the Yangtze River, the West River flows west to east, and covers about one-fifth to one- quarter of southern China's land mass. It is commonly assumed that the West River joins up with and contributes significantly to the total volume of the Pearl River, the chief river flowing through Canton, and that they flow together as "the" Pearl River into the South China Sea near Hong Kong. This is actually technically incorrect. The situation is much more complicated, because the West River itself is so long and large, in advance of its arrival in the vicinity of the Pearl River delta.

Significantly, the West River delivers its large volume of water in two main, but separate ways, at two different locations, in the vicinity of Canton and the Pearl River Delta. First, the West River is joined by the North River *Pakk-kong* [*gong*] (*Beijiang*),[30] near the city of *Sam-shui*,) about 30 miles west of Canton. The North River has its headwaters in the *Dung-nam* (*Dong-nan*) Hills region, some 250 miles north of Canton. Second, the combined West and North Rivers, still commonly identified as "the" West River, then flows southeast, where it splits into two main distributaries. One distributary flows south-southwest through the western portion of the Pearl River Delta. This distributary itself then splits into two subsidiary distributaries. One flows south-southwest and empties in the South China Sea near *Kong-mun*

(*Jiangmen*) in *Toi-shaan*, (identified locally in *Say-Yup* speech as *Hoishan*), and the other flows south-southeast, eventually emptying into the South China Sea immediately west of *Chung-Shaan* (*Zhongshan*) district/peninsula, near *Zhuhai*, northwest of Macau. Third, the other major distributary of the West-North River confluence is one that flows further east, where it eventually empties into the Pearl River estuary, through a series of smaller streams or waterway outlets along the northwestern side of the Pearl River Estuary.[31]

Thus, the West River has four destinations. Three are key distributaries that flow across both the western and eastern portions of the Pearl River Delta, where each one links up with progressively smaller distributaries, which crisscross the Pearl River Delta. The main concourse of each of these distributaries eventually flows directly into the South China Sea. There is another West River destination via another series of smaller distributaries, which eventually form numerous outlets along the west side of the Pearl River Estuary, *Tanchau suri-dow* (*Tanzhou shuidao*) and the *Shuntak suri-dow* (*Sunde shuidao*.)[32]

The Pearl River or *Chu-Kong* (*Zhu Jiang*) is named after colorful pearl-colored shells found along the bottom of the river in Canton. The importance of this river arises from its intimate identification with Canton (*Gwong-chau*) (*Guangzhou*,) the capital of Gwongdung province. It flows through the city and connects it directly with the sea, some 90 miles downriver. Among the four major rivers of Central Gwongdung, the Pearl River is neither large nor very long, consequently the facts of its pivotal location, i.e., flowing through the heart of Canton and having a direct connection with the sea are what have historically distinguished it. The point of origin, contrary to what many believe, is not via a direct link with the West River. There are, however, some minor distributaries of the West River that do link up at some point(s) with the Pearl River.

The chief origin of the Pearl River however, has been two distributaries of the North River, i.e., the *Lubao yong* and the *Xinan yong*, which then converge with the *Liuxi* River. It is this *Liuxi* River which becomes the main concourse of the Pearl River immediately north of Canton.[33] The Pearl River then flows southeast of Canton for some twenty miles, where it is then joined by the *Dungkong* (*Dongjiang*) East River at the port of *Whampoa* (*Huangpu*). The East

River itself originates in the mountainous region of the *Dung-nam* area in northeast Gwongdung and neighboring southwestern Jiangxi province. The enlarged Pearl River finally empties about 20–25 miles downstream from Whampoa into the Pearl River Estuary, which then empties into the South China Sea, midway between Macau to the west and Hong Kong to the east. This occurs about ninety miles downstream from Canton.

## *The Pearl River Delta Micro-Region*

Central Gwongdung's two major integrated river systems, the West-North Rivers and the Pearl-East Rivers never actually merge to become one mighty river flowing into the sea, like Central China's Yangtze River. Instead, they both ultimately feed into the rich Pearl River Delta Region (PRDR) ecosystem. Eventually they drain out of the Pearl River Delta via the already mentioned series of distributaries. This delta lies south/southwest of Canton. While it is essentially a very large and broad alluvial plain, studded with hills and laced with a very expansive, complex, and constantly changing maze of waterways, it is actually not one, but two separate alluvial deltas, bifurcated by the central core branch of the Pearl River. The western Pearl River Delta, is fed by the combined North-West Rivers; and the eastern Pearl River Delta, is fed by the Pearl-East Rivers. Because of the abundant water and ideal climatic conditions, the PRDR micro-region has been the richest agricultural region not only in Central Gwongdung, but in all of Gwongdung Province.

The PRDR possessed the "very best of the best" of Central Gwongdung's cultivated lands. While other micro-regions may have had larger expanses of land and equally large rival concentrations of people, none rivaled the PRDR's productive capabilities, prominent status, and its many positive natural assets. It possessed in abundance some of the largest and most fertile contiguous tracts of level land in the province,[34] which were complemented with excellent abundant of water resources, (i.e., with the notable exception of the *Say-Yup/Ng-Yup* areas in the S.W. quadrant of the PRDR.) Additionally, in the PRDR, farmland came in manageable parcels, which were relatively easy to access and work. This micro-region, both literally and figuratively sat at the apex of Cantonese wealth and prosperity. Indeed, it long remained one of the richest and most intensely farmed regions in China. It was renowned for its ability to grow two rice crops per year, with the first harvest in June or early July, and a second one between mid-October and mid-November.[35]

In the nineteenth century, the PRDR supported a very rich commercialized agriculture, with a wide variety of other cash crops, such as rice, fruits, vegetables, sugar cane, silk, cotton, and tea. It was also one of the most densely populated areas, hosting a population of about five million people, crowded into twelve rural counties/districts, in an area of about 7,768 square miles.[36] Conservatively speaking, it is possible that as much as 50% or 12,000 square miles of the province's total amount of arable land was located in Central Gwongdung.[37] Put another way, in a much less favorable light, of the approximate 41,000–49,000 (or about 50,000 square miles of land in Central Gwongdung, only about 25% or about 12,000 square miles was ideally suited to commercialized agriculture, e.g., rice cultivation.[38] Recall that 70% of all Gwongdung, or almost 58,000 of its 82,000 square miles, was either hilly or mountainous, and therefore not suitable for commercialized rice farming.[39] It is quite possible that while the delta only comprised 10.76% of Gwongdung Province's area, it likely embraced somewhere between 40% and 50% of the province's available arable land for farming.

*The Metropolitan Canton Sub Micro-Region*

The fourth key sub micro-region of Central Gwongdung is Metropolitan Canton, known as *Gwong-chau.* (Guangzhou). [40]Canton has been the capital of Gwongdung for over two millennia. Historically, at least since Ming times (14th–17th centuries CE), Canton materialized as a bifurcated entity, consisting on one hand the province's largest urban center and capital; and on the other hand, it also included, as an enlarged entity, parts of two adjacent semi-rural/rural counties. They were *Namhoi* (*Nanhai*) and *Punyu* (*Pan-yu*), for an area of about 1,470.55 Square miles.[41]Historically, the size and shape of Metropolitan Canton changed over time, where administrative/bureaucratic and economic/ commercial interests converged and overlapped. In the nineteenth century, metropolitan Canton comprised an area of about 800 square miles, which included both an urban core area and adjacent portions of the aforementioned neighboring counties. [42] The population of early Nineteenth-Century Canton was about 500,000 people. [43]

The core area of Canton city proper consisted of two distinct separate, but connected entities. Both components lie along the north bank of the Pearl River.

The larger, and more influential, part consisted of the old walled city to the east. This section of Canton, because of its well-established location and history was regarded the more important and prestigious part of Canton. It had a strong sense of purpose, primarily because it hosted all of the major governmental institutions (offices of the Governor-general, the Governor, the Prefects, district magistrates, the Gwongdung provincial Imperial Examination compound, major city temples, shrines, as well as the provincial capital's execution grounds.) This part of the city also housed the city's major educational, civic, and philanthropic organizations as well, such as libraries, book shops, academies, hospitals, orphanages).

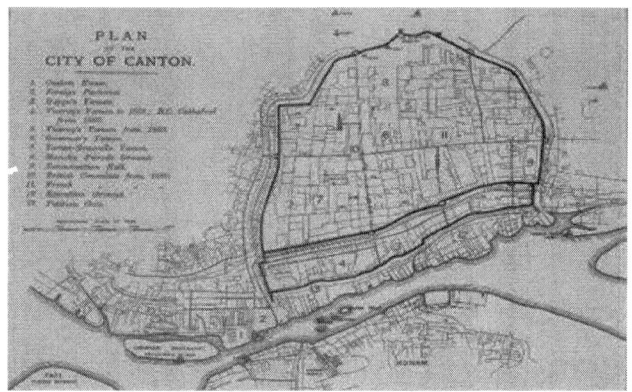

Map of Gwong-chau (Guangzhou) (Canton)
in the mid-late nineteenth-century

The other part of Canton consisted of the "western suburbs," located immediately outside the old city's western wall. This part of Canton lacked the orderly and precise grid-like north-south, east-west pattern of the government dominated eastern part of the city. Instead, this section materialized as a patchwork of narrow, congested, winding streets, lanes (*hongs*), and alleys.

It extended west along the northern bank of the Pearl River, and then north, north-west, bounded on the west by the northward (upstream) portion of the Pearl River. This area of Canton expanded in a seemingly random and haphazard manner, where commercial needs and business interests determined the pattern of the landscape. This urban landscape contrasted with the eastern part of the city, where officialdom required order and symmetry. If the eastern part of the city was enclosed within an imposing ancient wall, under the control of government officials and scholar/academic types, the western section had no city wall around it. It was managed by the city's merchants, through their numerous merchant guilds and associations. The western section hosted a proliferation of business and merchant enterprises. Here retail, wholesale, broker, comprador, credit, accounting, commercial facilities (warehouses, shops, stores, manufacturing operations), guild houses, theaters, temples, and both public and private gardens proliferated.

The commercially dominated western suburbs over time also expanded across the Pearl River to include *Honam* Island, which formed most of the opposite shore for both Canton's eastern and western sections. In the early nineteenth century, *Honam* Island hosted some of the most sumptuous palatial homes of Canton's merchant princes (e.g., *Howqua* (*Wu Kuo-ying*) had a fortune of about US $26 million (modern value of US $52 million) and a palatial home and gardens (famous throughout China) with about 500 servants).[44] *Honam* Island offered an area to expand business and merchant activities southward, away from the already crowded western section of the north bank of the Pearl River.

## Central Gwongdung, as micro-regional identity marker for the Cantonese Community

My theorizing about *Yuet*/Cantonese Central Gwongdung, as an ethno-cultural regional unit is not limited to merely distinguishing it from the larger context of Gwongdung's historical, geophysical, and administrative dimensions, as referenced above. It is rather an attempt to better define and distinguish the Cantonese community, by also contextualizing it as one of several pre-existing ethno-speech micro-regional units within Gwongdung.[45]

## Central Gwongdung

Gwongdung has often served as a useful prototype in Chinese regional studies.[46] In this regard, I am especially indebted to Skinner's pioneering work, in which he applied a social science systems' analytical approach to the Cantonese "rural marketing system," [47] where Nineteenth-Century Central Gwongdung can be viewed as a region of discrete complementary functional units.[48]

First, Central Gwongdung is a unit, in which there has been a long historical tradition of complementary dependence and economic exchange(s) between maximal hinterlands (The Pearl River Delta and up-river areas), and strategically located central places, such as Canton, *Whampoa, and Fat-Shaan.* Second, Central Gwongdung has served as a functionally integrated urban-rural system, with network lines connecting trade flow patterns between "cores" and "peripheries," as in the cases, of Canton or Hong Kong, and sub-regional administrative and/or commercial urban centers, such as *Hui-chou,* and *Shao-kuan.* Third, Central Gwongdung provided for the distribution of economic resources within a well-defined area, such as between the Pearl River Delta and areas elsewhere in Central Gwongdung, characterized by the concentration of critical resources, and measured against population density (e.g., *Saam-Yup* versus *Say-Yup* sub-regions within the Pearl River Delta sub micro-region.) Fourth and finally, Central Gwongdung easily serves as a basic physical unit, centering on river basins/watersheds, relative to the mechanics of transportation and communication within an agrarian-based society.

In regards to a geographical profile of Nineteenth-Century Central Gwongdung, it is relatively easy to delineate boundaries and mark off areas, because historically speaking, spatial and administrative signposts have marked the way. In contrast, it is more difficult to arbitrarily establish boundaries via their demographic and ethno-linguistic constructs. It should be remembered that while the *Yuet*/Cantonese identity clearly dominated, and otherwise shaped the distinctiveness of Gwongdung generally, it would be quite wrong to assume that *Cantonese* and *Gwongdung* were in fact synonymous. It would be more correct to say that "Cantonese" and "Central Gwongdung" enjoy such a close nexus, but clarification is needed to avoid over simplification.

Chapter 1

**Central Gwongdung's five ethno-speech micro-regions**

Beyond visualizing Nineteenth-Century Central Gwongdung, as a series of geophysical sub-divisions, we can also envision it alternately, as a series of key ethno-speech micro-regions. This perspective squares well with both my earlier geophysical sub micro-regions and with Skinner's idea of four mutually complementary regional approaches discussed earlier.[49] While these ethno-speech micro-region designations share some similarities with earlier referenced geophysical microregional units, relative to their location, shape, and size, such similarities are coincidental and superficial.

Ethno-speech sub micro-regions arise within another conceptual framework, which focuses on different identifying characteristics, contextualized by dissimilar criteria and concerns. This is readily apparent in my choice of different identifying labels such as "*Baak-wah* zones," and "non-*Yuet*/Cantonese Peripheral areas," in place of previously used identifying labels, such as "up-river hills and valleys," and "outer mountainous zone." I view these other elements as additional evidence of a material basis for conceptualizing about *Tong-Shaan*. Here I specifically identify five ethno-speech sub micro-regions in Nineteenth-Century Central Gwongdung. They are: 1) Metropolitan Canton, which included portions of neighboring rural counties; 2) The Pearl River Delta region (PRDR); [50] 3) The "Inner" *Baak-wah* zone; 4) The "Outer" *Baak-wah* zone; and 5) Non-*Yuet*/Cantonese Peripheral areas.[51]

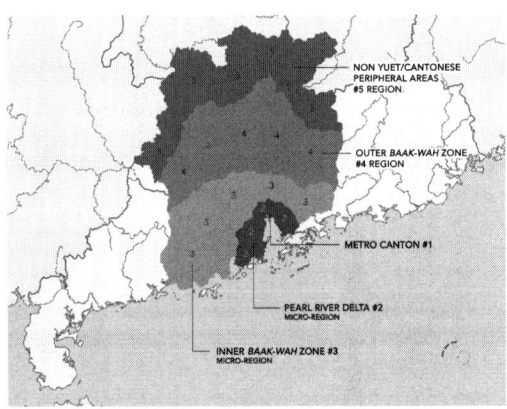

Central Gwongdung's five major ethno-speech micro-regions

## *The Metropolitan Canton ethno-speech Micro-region*

Ethno-linguistically speaking, the population of Metropolitan Canton was quite homogenous, with the vast majority of people identified as Cantonese (*Gwongchau-yan*) (*Guangzhouren,*) who all spoke standard Cantonese, i.e., *Gwongchau-wah* (*Guangzhouhua*). In nineteenth-century metropolitan Canton, and elsewhere in Central Gwongdung, Cantonese speech, as *Gwongchau-wah* was the most widely spoken form of Cantonese. It was not however, always identified as such.

In the area just outside Canton, Cantonese speech was identified as *Saam-Yup wah* (*sanyihua*) or the "Three districts' (or counties') speech". The distinction between *Gwongchau-wah* and *Saam-Yup wah* mirrored spatial and social boundaries, between Canton and its three adjacent suburban counties *Namhoi*, *Panyu*, and *Shuntak*. but it existed merely as a formal distinction of little consequence. This no doubt reflected the fact that *Gwongchau-wah* and *Saam-Yup wah* were basically identical. This distinction was more the exception, rather than the rule, because elsewhere in Central Gwongdung, standard Cantonese was simply identified as *Gwongdung wah*, (the speech of Gwongdung) in which case neither *Gwongchau wah* nor *Saam-Yup Wah* was applied or deemed to be relevant, as an ethno-speech group identifying label.[52]

Metropolitan Canton possessed unparallel resources that enabled it to prosper as the wealthy and influential hub of Central Gwongdung, and more generally for all of Gwongdung Province. During the nineteenth century, Canton dominated Central Gwongdung's financial markets, credit systems, wholesale and retail trade, and it also controlled Gwongdung's regional commerce, trade with other parts of China, and China's international maritime trade. This pivotal economic position helped fuel the commercialization of Cantonese agriculture in Central Gwongdung, facilitated by easy access to commercial loans, extensions of credit, and an extensive networking system throughout Central Gwongdung, and beyond. Economic prosperity, or at least the likely expectation of it, together with a large population and a common ethno-speech community lent solidarity to Cantonese endeavors in Metropolitan Canton and beyond. This highly advantageous situation helped *bankroll* Metropolitan Canton's role as the Cantonese speaking world's socio-cultural epicenter. It confirmed on the city, and its population, an undisputed position of leadership in nurturing and promoting a dynamic and unique Cantonese socio-cultural and ethno-speech persona.[53] In this context, Cantonese speech became the *linga franca* of Gwongdung, and by extension for the entire *Lingnam* region as well. Similarly, *Yuet* (*Yue*) culture became the cultural standard for the entire *Lingnam* as well.

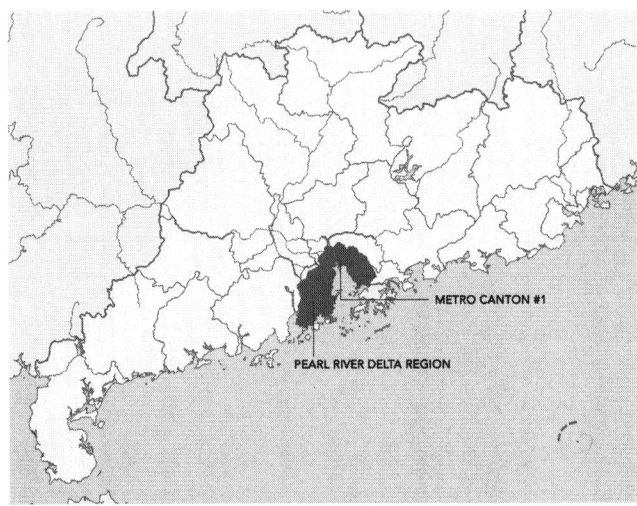

The Pearl River Delta Region (PRDR)
Ethno-Speech Micro-region (similar in size and location
as the geographical PRDR)

### *The Pearl River Delta ethno-speech Micro-region*

Geographically speaking, the Pearl River Delta Region (PRDR) micro-region is perhaps the most important component of Central Gwongdung's several ethno-speech micro-regions, by virtue of its location, size, natural and human resources. These features helped make it a critically important and unique central core area for Central Gwongdung. The PRDR supported a demographically large, stable, fairly uniform, and significantly unified ethno-speech community. The vast majority of this micro-region's population were identified as *Yuet/Bundae* people, the descendants of original Han Chinese migrants, who settled in Gwongdung between the Qin and Tang dynasties (2nd century BCE and 10th century CE). (See this book, chapters 2 and 3.) Additionally, nearly all of them and their progeny spoke a variety of Cantonese speech/dialect. Most spoke *Gwongchau-wah* or standard Cantonese (also known as *Saam-Yup wah*), or known more euphemistically as *Gwongdung-wah* or "*Gwongdungese.*" The chief exception to this was the *Say-Yup wah (Siyihua)* (or *Ng-Yup wah*) (i.e., four or five districts' speech.) (Also see this book chapters 2 and 3.) In a word, the PRDR served as the *Yuet*/Cantonese ethno-speech central core unit, and together with Metropolitan Canton, it represented the heartland of the Cantonese community in Central Gwongdung.

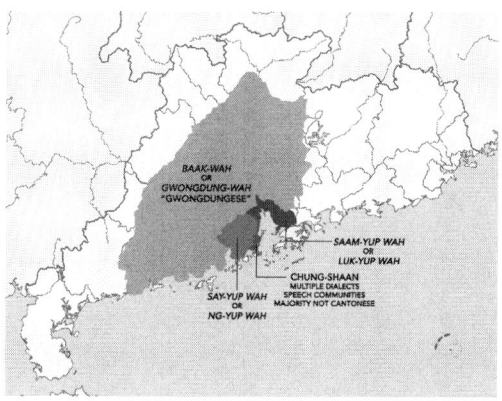

Key Cantonese speech communities in Central Gwongdung.
Note: the Chung-Shaan exception with several local
non-Cantonese speech communities

### Table 1.1 The 12 Rural Counties of the Nineteenth-Century Pearl River Delta Micro-Region #2 of Central Gwongdung[54]

| District Name | Total Area in Sq. Kilometers | Total Area in Sq. Miles | Percentage of the total area of Gwongdung Province |
|---|---|---|---|
| Namhoi | 1,263.75 | 487.8 | .67% |
| Punyu | 1,794.25 | 692.58 | .96% |
| Shuntak | 751.75 | 290.17 | .4% |
| Tungkun | 2,720.5 | 1,050. | 1.46% |
| Pao-on | 1,298.25 | 501. | .69% |

| | | | |
|---|---|---|---|
| Sun-wui | 1,922.5 | 742. | 1.03% |
| Toi-Shaan | 2,991. | 1,154.52 | 1.6% |
| Hoiping | 1,173.25 | 452.87 | .63% |
| Yanping | 2,034.75 | 785.4 | 1.09% |
| Hok-Shaan | 1,076. | 415.33 | .57% |
| Chung-Shaan | 2,876.75 | 1,110.4 | 1.54% |
| Chikkai | 224.25 | 86.56 | .12% |
| **Total (12)** | **20, 127** | **7,768.63** | **10.76%** |

The PRDR ethno-speech micro-region itself consisted of four regional sub-components, each comprising a set of rural counties/counties. Most of these, except unit #1, were somewhat triangular shaped units. As they each radiated out and away from Metropolitan Canton, they became wider and more elongated. They stretched southeast, south, and southwest respectively towards the South China Sea. These components included: 1) *Namhoi* and *Punyu,* two previously mentioned rural counties/counties immediately adjacent to Canton. Because of their immediate location and distribution on west-southwest and northeast sides of Canton respectively, these two counties did not form an elongated triangular stretch of land; 2) *Tungkun* and *Pao-on*, two rural counties, formed a stretch of land southeast of Canton, connecting Canton with British Hong Kong. These two counties, strictly speaking did not lie in the Pearl River Delta, because they were located on the eastern periphery of the Pearl River Delta estuary; 3) *Shuntak* and *Chung-Shaan* (formerly identified as *Heung-shaan*, until 1925) were two rural counties directly south and southeast of Canton. They connected Canton with the *Chung-Shaan* peninsula (the location of the Portuguese colony of Macau (Macao); and 4) four rural counties, commonly known as the *Say-Yup,* or "Four speech counties," (*Sunwui, Toi-shaan* (commonly spelled *Toishan* or *Hoishan*) (formerly identified as *Sunning*), *Hoiping*, and *Yanping*). It was common to often include *Hokshaan* among this group. When this occurred, the combined five rural counties, known as the *Ng-Yup* of "Five speech counties;" [55]

## *The Inner and Outer Baak-wah ethno-speech micro-regions*

These two closely related ethno-speech micro-regions consist of those rural counties located in Central Gwongdung's interior hinterland, arranged in an arc-like pattern from east to west. They were situated midway between the Canton-Pearl River Delta micro-region and the northern tier of counties strung along the border with neighboring *Gwongsai* (*Guangxi*) and *Hunan* provinces. Skinner identifies this area as the West Peripheral, Northwest, and North *Hakka* areas of Gwongdung.[56] I identify them as the "Outer" and "Inner" *Baak-wah* zones.

The term *Baak-wah* is derived from the colloquial Cantonese form of speech spoken in these two micro-regions. [*Baak-wah* (my own romanization) is better known in standardized Cantonese Romanization, as *baahk wá* [*pà:k wǎ:*] (in Chinese characters, 白話]. The Cantonese term *Baak-wah,* is pronounced in Mandarin Chinese as *Baihua* (*Pai-hua*). Although both the Cantonese and Mandarin forms are written with the same Chinese characters, their respective connotations are quite different. The mandarin Chinese form represents the idea of a Chinese vernacular written language, as opposed to the traditional classical written literary language, i.e., *wenyan*. In pre-modern times, before the end of the nineteenth century, *Baihua* referenced Chinese popular literary forms of writing, e.g., various genres of fiction. After the May Fourth Movement in 1919, it came to represent the ordinary everyday written form of Chinese. In this context, the Mandarin Chinese term *Baihua* refers primarily to written Chinese, and not to spoken Chinese, unlike the Cantonese case.[57]

In Cantonese, *Baak-wah* means "common speech," which means "Cantonese" speech, similar to the case where *Gwongdung-wah*, (*Gwongdungese*) has served as a widely used euphemism for *Gwongchau-wah* (i.e., the speech of Canton or "Cantonese.") The *Baak-wah* label is used to identify those forms of Cantonese spoken in the hinterland, located between the non-*Yuet*/Cantonese peripheral micro-region and the centrally located areas of Metropolitan Canton and the Pearl River Delta micro-regions.

In neighboring Gwongsai province, the term *Baak-wah* became over time a common label for identifying areas in which Cantonese speech was widespread.[58] The manner in which the term *Baak-wah* has been used in Gwongsai has influenced my own adoption and use of the term. I use the term as a "short-hand" device for referencing Cantonese speaking people located in Central Gwongdung's interior hinterland, located beyond Canton and the Pearl River Delta region. In short, the people of the interior hinterland were Cantonese (i.e., *Gwongdung-yan*) and they spoke a form of Cantonese very similar to the Cantonese (*Gwongchau-wah*) spoken down river in Canton and the Pearl River Delta region. It is however, identified locally by the Cantonese colloquial term *Baak-wah*, in place of *Gwong-dung-wah* ("*Gwongdungese*") or more correctly *Gwong-chau wah* or "Cantonese."

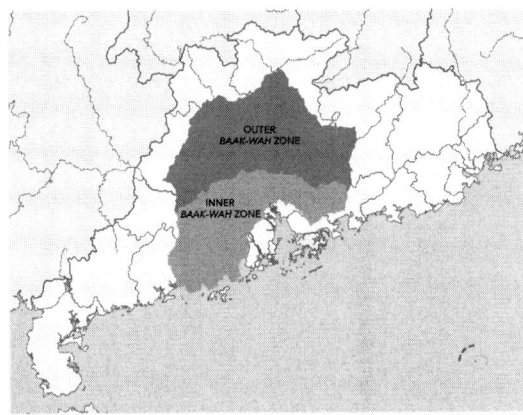

Map showing Central Gwongdung's "Inner" and "Outer" *Baak-wah* zones

The *Baak-wah* zones together spatially comprised the largest expanse of territory in Central Gwongdung. From east to west, it included the following county units of *Wuichau* (Huizhou), east of Canton; parts of *Heyuan* Northeast of Canton; parts of *Tsingyuan* (*Qingyuan*) north- northeast of Canton; parts of *Chao-Ch'ing* (*Zhaoqing*) northwest of Canton; and portions of *Yeungkong* and *Maoming* near western Gwongdung.[59]

There are two distinct and separate parts of the *Baak-wah* zone, which are identified respectively as the *Inner* and *Outer Baak-wah* Zones. Each part has its own distinctive set of geographical features. Significantly, although both units share similar demographic and ethno-speech characteristics, however, they did so within a dissimilar logistical (transportation, land utilization, arable/non-arable land ratios,) and socio-economic (local marketing systems and community infrastructures,) frameworks.

## Table 1.2 The 14 Rural Counties of the nineteenth-century Inner *Baak-wah* Micro-Region #3 of Central Gwongdung [60]

| District Name | Total Area in Sq. Kilometers | Total Area in Sq. Miles | Percentage of the total area of Gwongdung Province |
|---|---|---|---|
| Tseng-shing | 1,739.5 | 671.44 | .93% |
| Fayuen | 864. | 333.5 | .46% |
| Sam-shui | 851. | 328.48 | .45% |
| Say-wui | 967. | 373.26 | .51% |
| Ch'ing-yuan | 4,093.25 | 1,579.99 | 2.1% |
| Tsung-fa | 1809. | 698.27 | .96% |
| Pok-lo | 2,925. | 1,129. | 1.57% |
| Lung-men | 2,200.25 | 849.29 | 1.18% |
| Hui-chou | 5,517 | 2,129.56 | 2.96% |
| Ko-yiu | 2,784.25 | 1,074.72 | 1.49% |
| Ko-ming | 1,030.25 | 397.67 | .55% |
| Yeung-chun | 3,059.75 | 1,181.06 | 1.64% |
| Yeung-kong | 3,788.75 | 1,462.45 | 2.3% |
| Sun-hing | 1,373.25 | 530. | .73% |
| **Total (14)** | **33,002.25** | **12,738.74** | **17.89%** |

*The Inner Baak-wah Zone*

The *Inner Baak-wah* zone consisted of wide expanses of level alluvial plains. Its northern portion was characterized by a hilly transitional area between the Inner and Outer *Baak-wah* zones. The *Inner Baak-wah* zone itself radiated in an arc-like pattern, extending from the core area of the Pearl River Delta in an outward pattern, in the direction of distant mountainous areas to the northeast, north, and northwest. The "Inner" *Baak-wah* zone ended, and the "Outer" *Baak-wah* zone began, as the landscape changed topographically, becoming increasingly hilly. Here major rivers, such as the East, North, and West Rivers respectively, carved the land into valleys and ravines, interlaced with rolling foothills. This defined it, ecologically and economically, relative to how communities were distributed, and how they operated within local marketing systems.

Inner *Baak-wah* zone residents generally lived in what may be regarded as distant and somewhat marginal areas of Central Gwongdung, especially in the outer northern portions of the Inner *Baak-wah* zone, as one moved towards the Outer *Baak-wah* zone. The rare exception to this general condition included those rural counties located in the inner most part of the Inner *Baak-wah* zone, i.e., those immediately adjacent to the Pearl River Delta. This included *Fayuan, Samshui, Saywui, Tsingyuan, Tsengshing*, and *Poklo*. However, even in these counties, there existed various communities which had more in common with those elsewhere in the Inner *Baak-wah* zone, by way of a common identity and experience. It may be that because Inner *Baak-wah* zone daily life revolved around traditions and tensions rooted in local rural life in the interior, that over time this resulted in a sense of separateness from Cantonese society further downstream. This separateness reflected itself in an orientation towards and preoccupation with life in the interior. In this regard, people in the Inner *Baak-wah* zone did not identify themselves with the densely populated, economically well-leveraged down-river cosmopolitan urban centers and seaports of the coastal areas. As one moved away from the Canton-PRDR, and moved up-stream passing through the Inner *Baak-wah* zone, this orientation became more pronounced. It was evident in how local communities identified themselves and how they related to outsiders from communities further downstream. Interestingly, the overwhelming majority of Cantonese overseas emigrants to the Americas came from the Pearl River Delta region, conversely few came from the Inner *Baak-wah* zone, and likely hardly any came from the Outer *Baak-wah* zone.

*The Outer Baak-wah Zone*

Life in the Outer *Baak-wah* zone during the nineteenth century differed considerably from that in the Inner *Baak-wah* zone. This resulted chiefly from radically different prevailing material conditions in the two neighboring micro-regions. Outer *Baak-wah* communities, were isolated by significant distances from even small local urban centers. This may have been due to the fact that large portions of the "outer" *Baak-wah* zone ranged from hilly to mountainous terrain. In this sense, Outer *Baak-wah* zone people lived in a kind of "frontier society," more identifiable with conditions in the neighboring the non-*Yuet*/Cantonese Peripheral areas' micro-region to the North, and Northwest, rather than with those in neighboring Inner *Baak-wah* communities to the South. Rough terrain and challenging local conditions elsewhere in Central Gwongdung, e.g., the *Say-Yup* (or *Ng-Yup*) southwest quadrant of the Pearl River Delta, paled in comparison with those in the Outer *Baak-wah* zone and those in non-*Yuet*/Cantonese Peripheral areas. The Outer *Baak-wah* zone, especially its northern outer sections, historically lacked good farming terrain/soil to support economically profitable and ecologically sustainable farmland in comparison with most of the Inner *Baak-wah* zone. In the alternative, people in the Outer *Baak-wah* zone engaged in a wider variety of occupations and economic activities, than people in the Inner *Baak-wah* zone. This included mining, metallurgy, lumber, hill country farming (specialized local fruits, herbs, and forest products,) and livestock (e.g., horses, mules, and oxen,) local trade, and transport/ communication between and among the three areas of the Inner *Baak-wah* zone, non-*Yuet*/Cantonese Peripheral areas, and Gwongdung's norther border routes into neighboring Jiangxi, Hunan and Gwongsai.

Historically, the Outer *Baak-wah* zone, had a smaller, less concentrated local population, distributed over a significantly larger area with rougher terrain, consisting of 19.3 thousand square miles, in comparison with the smaller expanse of 12.7 thousand square miles in the Inner *Baak-wah* zone. See tables below) Because Outer *Baak-wah* zone people were distributed over a larger expanse of territory, local population density concentration ratios were likely among the lowest in Central Gwongdung. Significantly, given their remote location, Outer *Baak-wah* zone people had limited contact/interaction with Cantonese communities downstream in the Inner *Baak-wah* zone, to say nothing of contact/relations with distant communities even further downriver in the Pearl River Delta region. There material conditions fostered a greater sense of autonomy and self-reliance among Outer *Baak-wah* zone people. These matters were no doubt reflected in a variety of ways regarding how local marketing systems were organized and operated.

## Table 1.3 The 21 Rural Counties in the Nineteenth-Century Outer *Baak-wah* Micro-Region #4 of Central Gwongdung[61]

| District Name | Total Area in Sq. Kilometers | Total Area in Sq. Miles | Percentage of the total area of Gwongdung Province |
|---|---|---|---|
| Shaan-wei[62] | 4,204.5 | 1,622.9 | 2.25% |
| Hoi-feng | 2,080.25 | 802.97 | 1.11% |
| Chiu-tsim[63] | 4,000. | 1,544. | 2.5% |
| Ho-yuan | 4,037. | 1,558.28 | 2.7% |
| Sun-feng | 2,518.7 | 972.23 | 1.35% |
| Ying-tak | 5,554.5 | 2,144. | 2.97% |
| Ku-kong (Hsiao-kuan) | 2,971. | 1,146.80 | 1.59% |
| Kwong-ning | 2,443.25 | 943. | 1.31% |
| Tak-hing | 2,256.75 | 871.1 | 1.21% |
| Yun-fou | 3,424.25 | 1,321.76 | 1.83% |
| Yu-nam | 2,384.75 | 920.51 | 1.28% |
| Hoi-kien | 978. | 377.5 | .52% |
| Feng-chuen | 1,386.75 | 535.28 | .74% |
| Low-ding | 1,560. | 602.16 | .83% |
| Sun-yi | 3,534.25 | 1,364.22 | 1.89% |
| Mao-ming | 3,695.25 | 1,426.36 | 1.98% |
| Wah-heung (Hua-hsien) | 2,077.25 | 801.81 | 1.11% |
| Lim-kong | 2,405.25 | 928.42 | 1.39% |
| Wu-chu'an | 1,067.75 | 412.15 | .57% |
| **Total (19)** | **49,526.** | **19,323.2** | **29.10%** |

The distinction between Inner and Outer *Baak-wah* zones respectively, is an arbitrary and artificial one, indicative of the relative positioning of each micro-region with those of Metropolitan Canton and the Pearl River Delta respectively.[64] The Inner *Baak-wah* zone micro-region is geo-territorially closer to the Pearl River Delta, and in some cases also close to Metropolitan Canton, such that the people living there have a close geographical and socio-economic relationship with these areas. In much of the two *Baak-wah* zones, beyond distinguishing geographical and typographic considerations, there existed many geographic and demographic similarities. Both units of the *Baak-wah* zone effectively occupied the same general area as the previously referred to the "up-river hills-valleys micro-region," an area sandwiched in between the non-*Yuet*/Cantonese peripheral micro-region and the Pearl River Delta micro-region. In this position, the two *Baak-wah* micro-regions have played a similar key supporting role, by serving as a useful rear area or hinterland supporting the more dynamic, prosperous, and better positioned down-river Metropolitan Canton and the Pearl River Delta micro-regions.

The two *Baak-wah* zones also had different geophysical, and economic features. The Outer *Baak-wah* zone occupied the upper-most portions of the West, North, and East Rivers, which ranged from mountainous to hilly areas. Here, agricultural activities centered on non-rice production, e.g., forest products, charcoal, and various hill crops, such as tea, tree fruits (e.g., peaches), tobacco, and other crops. The Inner *Baak-wah* zone, because of its transitional upstream/downstream environment, closely resembled rural agricultural and urban economic life elsewhere. The *Baak-wah* zones also served as a conduit for moving people, goods, finances, and information all across Central Gwongdung, thus enhancing their full logistical integration.

Outer *Baak-wah* zone people were Cantonese speakers and also closely identified with *Yuet* culture. Despite these facts, over the course of time some modifications in local ethno-speech elements and socio-cultural sensibilities occurred in response to local needs, preferences, and interests. These changes were reflected in local traditions and practices, which no doubt require field investigation in order confirm to what extent such changes took place, and how they significantly differed from Cantonese speech and *Yuet* ethno-cultural identifications elsewhere, downstream in the Inner *Baak-wah* zone and the Pearl River Delta micro-region.

I would argue that whatever differences in Cantonese speech and *Yuet* ethno-cultural identifications existed between both groups of *Baak-wah* zone people and the people of the PRDR, typically reflected incremental degrees of change. They ranged from 1) virtually insignificant, hardly noticeable, minor changes/differences, such as word/phrase pronunciation; 2) noticeable, but unimportant modifications, such as new vocabulary associated with local speech changes; to 3) very obvious significant changes, such as "pseudo-dialect" identifications, different representation and reproduction of *Yuet* ethno-cultural characteristics, traditions, and practices.) [65]

### *The Non-Yuet/Cantonese peripheral areas' ethno-speech micro-region*

The last demographic/ethno-speech micro-region in Central Gwongdung is identified as the non-*Yuet*/Cantonese peripheral areas' micro-region. This region occupied roughly the same area as the outer mountainous geographical micro-region referenced earlier in this chapter. This ethno-speech micro-region is technically speaking not part of *Yuet*/Cantonese Central Gwongdung. While the area is geographically part of Central Gwongdung, significant portions of the resident population were neither Cantonese speaking, nor closely identified with the *Yuet* community of Central Gwongdung. Indeed, many locals were not *Yuet*/Cantonese, or even Han Chinese. To the east and far west there were concentrations of *Min/Hoklo* people, and to the Northeast and North there existed the heartland of the province's *Hakka* community. Additionally, along the northern tier of counties, to the North and Northwest, blending into neighboring Gwongsai province, there existed large numbers of non-Han Chinese aboriginal hill/mountain tribal peoples, such as the *Zhuang, Yao* and *Miao* peoples, with most located in neighboring Gwongsai, Province.[66]

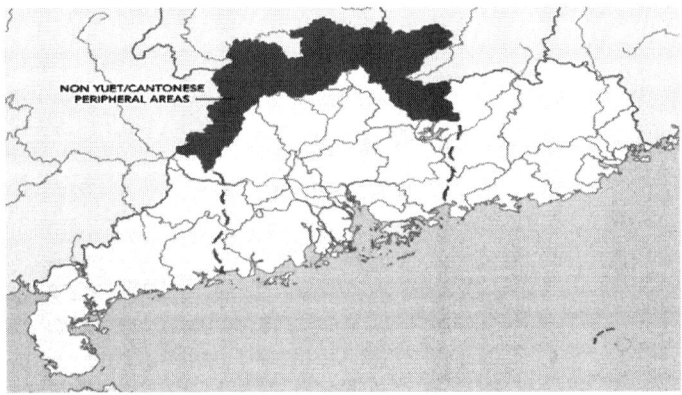

Map of Non Yuet/Cantonese Peripheral Areas' Ethno-Speech Micro-Region

The geography, ecology/environmental conditions, and resulting material living conditions were somewhat similar to those in the outermost portion of the Outer *Baak-wah* zone, resulting again in a frontier-like society/economy in the nineteenth century. I suspect that material conditions here, and perhaps also in the outer portions of the adjacent Outer *Baak-wah* zone, might not have been as uniform as suggested, to the extent that variations may have existed among and between various areas, as distinguished by mountain ridges and valleys, forests and farmlands. This likely reflected itself in a range of living conditions, economic activities, and distribution/settlement patterns of various local ethno-speech groups in this micro-region. While this was obvious, regarding distinctions between Han Chinese and non-Han Chinese resident groups, it may have been less obvious among Han Chinese locals, such as the *Yuet/Bundae*, *Min/Bundae*, and *Hakka* peoples, (see this book, chapters 2 and 3.) Such distinctions were even less obvious among groups in the *Baak-wah* zones, especially those which identified with *Yuet*/Cantonese speech and culture. Given these variables, we can surmise that local ethno-speech characteristics qualitatively distinguished this micro-region, because of the presence of both Han Chinese and non-Han Chinese local ethno-speech communities; but not necessarily so quantitatively speaking, because the local population was more widely distributed and less concentrated than elsewhere.[67]

In a sense, the non-*Yuet* peripheral areas' ethno-speech micro-region not only clearly delineated Gwongdung's provincial borders and those of a major ethno-speech micro-region, it also served as a "buffer zone," underscoring the critical place and role of geophysical, demographic, and ethno-speech identified peripheries in the larger scheme of what constitutes Central Gwongdung. While interesting, the atypical nature of these identifying features underscores the fact that they remained largely marginal, relative to the question of their influence on material conditions and socioeconomic developments elsewhere in Central Gwongdung's other micro-regions. This resulted from the fact that, this micro-region was neither centrally located, nor heavily populated, even though it was significantly ethno-linguistically diverse. It also lacked the dynamic socio-economic profile of Cantonese community life elsewhere in Central Gwongdung.

## Table 1.4 The 15 Rural Districts in the Nineteenth-Century Non-*Yuet*/Cantonese Peripheral Areas Micro-Region #5 of Central Gwongdung[68]

| District Name | Total Area in Sq. Kilometers | Total Area in Sq. Miles | Percentage of the total area of Gwongdung Province |
|---|---|---|---|
| Lu-feng | 3,103.75 | 1,198. | 1.66% |
| Ng-wah | 3,194. | 1,232.88 | 1.66% |
| Hing-ning | 1,700.5 | 656.39 | .91% |
| Lung-chun | 3,073.25 | 1,186.27 | 1.64% |
| Wo-ping | 2,334.75 | 901.2 | 1.79% |
| Lien-ping | 2,259.5 | 872.16 | 1.21% |
| Weng-yuan | 2,239. | 864.25 | 1.2% |
| Gee-hing | 2,003. | 773.15 | 1.06% |
| Nam-yung | 2,539.5 | 980.24 | 1.36% |
| Yen-fa | 1,460.25 | 563.65 | .77% |
| Lok-chong | 1,936.75 | 747.58 | 1.03% |
| Ju-yuan | 1,768.75 | 682.73 | .94% |
| Lien-heung | 1,800.25 | 694.89 | .96% |
| Lien-shan | 1,686. | 650.79 | .90% |
| Yeung-shan | 3,357.25 | 1,295.89 | 1.71% |
| **Total (15)** | **34,456.5** | **13,300.** | **18.80%** |

The fact that the Cantonese *Baak-wah* speech medium prevailed widely in both parts of the *Baak-wah* zone, leads me to conclude that a significant number of Han Chinese living in the Non-*Yuet*/Cantonese Peripheral areas micro-region were most likely also Cantonese speakers, who identified with *Yuet* society/culture, in its *Baak-wah* format. This occurred despite the fact that the Non-*Yuet*/Cantonese Peripheral areas' micro-region hosted significant concentrations of non-Han Chinese peoples and other non-Cantonese Han Chinese peoples (i.e., *Min/Hoklo* and *Hakka*), some, and perhaps many of whom also spoke a form of *Baak-wah* speech, in addition to their own non-Han Chinese, and/or non-*Yuet*/Cantonese speech forms.

## Table 1.5 Nineteenth-Century Central Gwongdung, a Micro-Regional Geographical Profile

| Micro-Region | Total Area in Square Kilometers (km) | Total Area in Square Miles (sq mil) | Percentage of total area of Central Gwongdung (estimated average total of 50,000 sq.mil)[69] | Percentage of the total area of Gwongdung (estimated total 82,000 sqm)[70] |
|---|---|---|---|---|
| Metropolitan Canton[71] | 2,071.99 sq km | 800 sq mil. | .016% | 1% |
| Pearl River Delta Region (12 rural counties) | 20,127 sq km | 7,768.63 sq mil | 15.5% | 10.76% |
| Inner *Baak-wah* zone (14 rural counties) | 33,002.25 sq km | 12,738.74 sq mil | 25.4% | 17.89% |
| Outer *Baak-wah* Zone (21 rural counties) | 49,526 sq km | 19,323.22 sq mil | 38.6% | 29.1% |
| Inner and Outer *Baak-wah* zones had a total of 35 rural counties | 82,528.25 sq km | 32,061.96 sq mil | 79.6% | 58.75% |
| Non-*Yuet* Cantonese Peripheral areas (15 rural counties) | 34,456.5 sq km | 13,300 sq mil | 26% | 18.8% |
| **Total** (62 rural counties) | 139,183.74 sq km | 53,930.59 sq miles[72] | 100% (actual total sq. miles is 105.5%[73]) | 77.55% |

The Non-*Yuet*/Cantonese Peripheral areas' micro-region had a mature and long-standing material nexus with the more preponderant and heavily populated *Yuet*/Cantonese downriver areas of the Outer and Inner *Baak-wah* zones. This was demonstrated, again, in the widespread use of the *Baak-wah* speech in this outermost ethno-speech micro-region of Central Gwongdung. The important point not to be missed here is that while this micro-region embodied characteristically atypical elements in its geo-demographic and ethno-speech profile, it nevertheless remained undeniably an integral component of Nineteenth-Century Central Gwongdung's composite profile.

## A demographic profile of Nineteenth-Century Central Gwongdung

Gwongdung province in the seventeenth and eighteenth centuries produced a prosperous society, with a rapidly growing population in the early to mid-nineteenth century. In 1786, Gwongdung had a population of around 15.9 million people. This figure nearly doubled to 29.75 million a century later in 1886.[74]

Behind this somewhat simplistic profile of a large and growing population, exists an interesting pattern of development that mirrored changing material conditions of Gwongdung. Specifically, in the half century from 1839–1889, when large-scale emigration overseas occurred, Gwongdung's population figures indicate two distinct patterns of development. Between 1839 and 1859, the population grew from around 25 million to about 29 million. This amounted to an increase of about two million per decade, or a growth rate of about 8% per decade. In contrast, during the following period, 1859–1889, population totals remained relatively stable, in contrast to the dynamic growth pattern of earlier decades. In this later period, the population only grew from 29.1 million to 29.78 million, this averaged a smaller increase of about 200,000 per decade. Consequently, the growth rate for Gwongdung dropped from 8% per decade before 1859, to a mere .7% per decade after 1859. This squares well with the fact that during this latter period a significant portion of the population had either been eliminated through several deadly ongoing civil conflicts (e.g., lineage, village turf wars, ethnic warfare (i.e., *Hakka-Bundae [Bendi]* wars), secret society conflict (i.e., the Red Turban revolt,) and local conflicts related to the Opium War and the expanded presence of Westerners.[75] Given these series of hardships associated with natural adversity, civil strife, and dire economic conditions during the later nineteenth century, Gwongdung's population in fact remained stable, even demonstrating a small degree of growth.

### Table 1.6 Gwongdung Total Population Estimates 1786–1900[76]

| Year | Total | Year | Total | Year | Total |
| --- | --- | --- | --- | --- | --- |
| 1786 | 15,923,000 | 1848 | 27,707,000 | 1874 | 29,558,000 |
| 1787 | 16,014,000 | 1849 | 27,899,000 | 1875 | 29,572,000 |
| 1788 | 16,112,000 | 1850 | 28,182,000 | 1876 | 29,592,000 |
| 1789 | 16,218,000 | 1851 | 28,389,000 | 1877 | 29,614,000 |

## Central Gwongdung

| | | | | | |
|---|---|---|---|---|---|
| 1790 | 16,337,000 | 1852 | 28,581,000 | 1878 | 29,632,000 |
| 1791 | 16,450,000 | 1853 | 28,732,000 | 1879 | 29,651,000 |
| 1819 | 21,392,000 | 1854 | 28,890,000 | 1880 | 29,672,000 |
| 1820 | 21,558,000 | 1855 | 29,034,000 | 1881 | 29,695,000 |
| 1830 | 22,662,000 | 1856 | 29,102,000 | 1882 | 29,706,000 |
| 1831 | 22,778,000 | 1857 | 29,139,000 | 1883 | 29,717,000 |
| 1832 | 22,895,000 | 1858 | 29,108,000 | 1884 | 29,717,000 |
| 1833 | 23,019,000 | 1859 | 29,178,000 | 1885 | 29,740,000 |
| 1834 | 23,306,000 | 1860 | 29,204,000 | 1886 | 29,751,000 |
| 1835 | 23,604,000 | 1861 | 29,228,000 | 1887 | 29,763,000 |
| 1836 | 23,904,000 | 1862 | 29,242,000 | 1888 | 29,774,000 |
| 1837 | 24,297,000 | 1863 | 29,261,000 | 1889 | 29,786,000 |
| 1838 | 24,763,000 | 1864 | 29,286,000 | 1890 | 29,800,000 |
| 1839 | 25,203,000 | 1865 | 29,295,000 | 1891 | 29,811,000 |
| 1840 | 25,744,000 | 1866 | 29,301,000 | 1892 | 29,826,000 |
| 1841 | 26,287,000 | 1867 | 29,311,000 | 1893 | 29,839,000 |
| 1842 | 26,415,000 | 1868 | 29,322,000 | 1894 | 29,852,000 |
| 1843 | 26,613,000 | 1869 | 29,338,000 | 1895 | 29,866,000 |
| 1844 | 26,802,000 | 1870 | 29,489,000 | 1896 | 29,881,000 |
| 1845 | 27,072,000 | 1871 | 29,507,000 | 1897 | 29,897,000 |
| 1846 | 27,312,000 | 1872 | 29,523,000 | 1900 | c30,000,000[77] |

The lower .7% growth rate for the decades after 1859 took place not only in a troubled era, but also during a time of large-scale overseas emigration. During this time, the vast majority of emigrants from Gwongdung to the Western Hemisphere came almost exclusively from *Cantonese* communities in Central Gwongdung, especially from those in the Pearl River Delta micro-region.[78]

The total population in Gwongdung Province most likely grew from an estimated 29.89 million in 1897 to just over 30 million around 1900.[79] These aggregate population estimates for Nineteenth-Century Gwongdung, while helpful in throwing light on a general demographic overview of Gwongdung, are nonetheless misleading because they represent only province-wide total estimates. Because non-*Yuet*/Cantonese communities, (e.g., *Min/Hoklo* of East and West Gwongdung, and the *Hakka* of Northeast Gwongdung) are also included, the resulting picture is skewed. Undoubtedly, various demographic changes occurred in East, Central, and West Gwongdung, relative to uneven population growth-decline ratios. This situation also materialized within Central Gwongdung's several geophysical and ethno-speech micro-regions.

Given the historical reality of a complex and changing Cantonese society in its many local variations, how can we fail to account for demographic changes on the local scene with greater specificity, which a province-wide perspective certainly cannot provide? Without the benefit of representative local *xian* (*Pinyin* mandarin form) (*hsien*) (Wade-Giles mandarin form) *yuen* (Cantonese form) (district or county) population figures, there is the danger of compromising the goal of a comprehensive, balanced, and documented local record of pre-emigrant Cantonese experience.

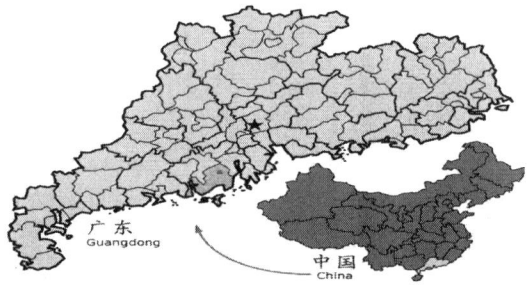

**In Nineteenth-Century Gwongdung, there were about 99 *xian* (districts/counties), as represented in the above map. About 62 of these *xian* were located in Central Gwongdung. Note: my theoretical models about Central Gwongdung's four geographical micro-regions and it's five ethno-speech micro-regions are independent of this scheme.**

Quantitative research on Nineteenth-Century Gwongdung is at best selective, regarding time and place covered; and highly fragmentary and piecemeal, regarding the manner and occasion of its reporting. In this regard, attention to data regarding sub-provincial levels is even more problematic. Province-wide population figures, remain suspect not only because of uncertainty regarding how and on what basis they were compiled; but because they tell us nothing about local population figures. Consequently, they are of only marginal interest concerning the case of pre-emigrant *Yuet*/Cantonese society.

Generally speaking, there does not seem to be any comprehensive population data available for various regional units of Gwongdung, e.g., West, Central, or East Gwongdung, much less for the micro-regions within Central Gwongdung itself. Traditionally, the compilation process reflected the interests and needs of the administrative structures of government responsible for producing such data, rather than any appreciation of regional or local communal expectations/interests, e.g., the Cantonese community.

In the Qing period, this meant that population statistics were initially compiled at the local level in the *xian* (district/county) or *fu* (prefecture) unit. The data was then used to compile province-wide totals, which were subsequently forwarded to Beijing. There were additions, exceptions, and modifications. The *tao* (circuit) unlike the *fu* and *xian* did not constitute a formal element of provincial administration, but rather functioned as an "arm" of the central government in Beijing.[80] Gwongdung was divided into six *tao*, each with an administrative center in an already designated major *fu* or urban prefectural centers.[81] This may explain in part why there was no effort to compile any regional sub-totals, above the district/prefecture level, and below the provincial level. Understandably, the Qing administrative system did not recognize or concern itself with ethno-linguistic categories, e.g., the Cantonese or the *Hakka*.

Central Gwongdung, unlike sub-regions of most other provinces in Qing China, had the distinction of serving as the geo-territorial homeland of a major ethno-linguistic community. In this regard, the Cantonese community was both historically distinct and demographically unique. This uniqueness lacked adequate historical documentation, by way of distinct and separate population figures, such as in the case of the *Cantonese* community. If this was true in the case of such a large and distinct ethno-linguistic segment, then it must have certainly been the case with other smaller ethno-linguistic communities. While Qing population data serves as an enduring testament to the integrative strength of late imperial China's governmental system, it also underscores inherent shortcomings in the system's record keeping and the limited usefulness of such records. Given historical omissions, it is not surprising that we lack population estimates specific for Central Gwongdung, or any of its micro-regions, e.g., the Pearl River Delta area or the *Baak-wah* zone. As a practical matter, it has been difficult to address this historical omission. Most researchers have been content with provided provincial total estimates and some random local district/county estimates. Data for local population estimates chiefly refer to *xian* (county) and *fu* (prefectural) population estimates, most are mainly from the Nationalist period during the 1930s.

This serious omission clouds any discussion of Nineteenth-Century Central Gwongdung. It is an issue that needs to be addressed, before any fruitful discussion can take place about the idea of a Cantonese fountainhead. In some instances, a desired set of population figures might be calculated, but this would depend on whether or not, in advance, other certain pieces of information could be accessed, formulated, computed, and properly evaluated, so that all the pieces can fit together. In many instances, I have discovered that the data I seek is only available in a roundabout way. Consequently, I have tried to piece together bits and pieces of quantitative data, based in part on informed estimates and in part on educated guesses, rather than on (unavailable) precise facts and figures, to obtain conceptually helpful and concretely useful representative estimates.

The resultant data provided below for Nineteenth-Century Central Gwongdung, its several ethno-speech micro-regions and their respective counties, is largely the product of this kind of detective work. The different formulas which I mention in the following paragraphs range from simple computations, based on available data, to somewhat complicated re-formulations, based on piecing together different sets of figures. Each approach is problematic, regarding relative degrees of accuracy and the degree of specificity of their respective results. Each one has its advantage, relative to the degree of simplicity and ease of use, and ascribed relevance. Each method also yields different figures, which require further explanation and integration. Ultimately, these resulting sets of varied statistical data can be used only to establish a "range of figures." Within this range, I have arbitrarily selected certain figures, which I believe can serve (for discussion purposes only) as credible, representative working figures for nineteenth-century Cantonese population estimates. In support of these concerns, I recognize three specific alternative methods.

1. I define and circumscribe what geographically constitutes later Nineteenth-Century Central Gwongdung and its component sub-units. I distinguish these sub-units by applying a hybrid set of criteria in contrast to those utilized by others. My designations utilize geographical categories, as they mirror socio-cultural, communal, and ethno-speech identifications, e.g., the *Baak-wah* zone.

2. I establish a "rough" estimation of the population for Central Gwongdung, based on Hsiao's method of multiplying what constitutes an average *xian* (county or district) population figure, i.e., 250,000, by the number of *xian* in Central Gwongdung, to obtain an estimated total for Central Gwongdung, and its several ethno-speech micro-regions.[82]

3. I compute a set of estimates "specific" and "representative" for all Central Gwongdung, its several sub-regions, and all their rural *xian*, based on demographic data and research strategies pioneered by Kuan and Skinner respectively.[83]

Skinner offers one of the most creative and constructive approaches for conceptualizing geo-territorial correlates, for how we might better visualize Gwongdung's major ethno-linguistic communities. Unfortunately, while he clearly delineates *Hakka* and *Teochiu* (*Min/Hoklo*) areas of Gwongdung, he does not break down and detail *Yuet*/Cantonese areas. Consequently, we can only assume that much or most of the remaining portions of Central Gwongdung was, by way of inference solidly *Cantonese*.[84] In my initial search for a graphic representation of the shape and structural components of what constituted the *Yuet*/Cantonese community of Central Gwongdung, I was drawn to Skinner's conceptualization. His designated areas of "Central, East Central, West Central," and parts of the areas he designates as "Northwest and West Peripheral" seem to conform to my own notion of what constituted Cantonese Central Gwongdung.[85] The attractiveness of this scheme is enhanced by the fact that he conveniently supplied rural population density figures for each of these regional units for the 1890s. The chart below summarizes this data. Note that I have highlighted those sub-regions, (boldfaced and underlined) which I regard as constituting Central Gwongdung. His "Central" sub-region consists of the Pearl River Delta region, which had the highest population density, with about 137 people per square mile.

### Table 1.7 Skinner's Rural Population Density in late Nineteenth-Century Gwongdung[86]

| Region Name | Rural Population densities per designated region | |
|---|---|---|
| | Per Square Kilometer | Per Square mile |
| Hainan Island | 63 | 24.3 |
| North Hakka | 64 | 24.7 |
| Northeast Hakka | 90 | 34.74 |
| **West Peripheral** | 116 | 44.78 |
| **Northwest** | 123 | 47.5 |
| **West Central** | 187 | 72.18 |
| **East Central** | 213 | 82.2 |
| *Teochiu* | 261 | 100.7 |
| **Central** | 356 | 137.4 |

On the basis of Skinner's data, it should be relatively easy to compute rough population estimates for Central Gwongdung in the late 1890s, but for a few technical problems. First, Skinner did not provide the total area of each of his designated nine regions, in either square kilometers or square miles. Second, my scheme for what constitutes Central Gwongdung embraces a different micro-regional scheme, than his designated "Central, West Central, and East Central" subregions. My notion of a Central Gwongdung would also include part of what he labels "Northwest and West Peripheral" areas. In the case of the former, I could not complete the equation of density per region, times the area for that region, to yield an estimated total population for that region. [e.g., If, hypothetically speaking, *Central* had an area of 2,300 square miles and a population density of 137.4, which forms the basis for a rough estimated population for "Central" of about 178,620, i.e., 137.4 times 2,300. In the case of the latter, I would have to arbitrarily delineate a boundary line across Skinner's "Northwest and West Peripheral," to separate *Yuet*/Cantonese from non-*Yuet*/Cantonese areas within these two regions, which is complicated by the additional problem of effectively distinguishing and separating what ordinarily must have been more densely populated *Yuet*/Cantonese areas of the Northwest region from this region's less densely populated *Hakka* areas. This problem also exists in trying to distinguish between *Yuet*/Cantonese and *Min/Hoklo* areas of Skinner's *West Peripheral* region. It is also a case, where I suspect that Skinner's density figures appear too low for this period of time, e.g., 356 per square kilometer or 137.4 per square mile for "Central." This was clearly a very heavily populated, high density concentration area, consisting of the *Saam-Yup* counties, (*Namhoi, Punyu, Shuntak*) and *Chung-shaan*, and a part of the *Say-Yup* counties (i.e., *Sunwui, Toi-shaan, Hoiping,* and *Yanping*).

K.C. Hsiao offers a contrasting, relatively easier, and faster, alternative to using Skinner's data for arriving at a rough estimate of Central Gwongdung's nineteenth-century population. Hsiao suggests that around the early nineteenth century (c1819) there was on average about 250,000 people per *xian* (county.) [87] For the purposes of discussion only, if we discount the following two points: 1) the real possibilities that Central Gwongdung's population aggregate totals and concentration patterns both increased significantly by the late 1850s; and 2) that average *xian* totals of 250,000 are unrealistic, when measured against material conditions of likely smaller concentration of populations in such areas as the Outer *Baak-wah* zone and the non-*Yuet* Peripheral areas, or larger population concentrations in the Pearl River Delta region. Despite these two points, let us assume that the figure 250,000 is a workable, albeit conservative, average estimate of the population for each district in mid-Nineteenth-Century Central Gwongdung (1850–1870). This seems consistent with other independent observations. *Ho Ping-ti* mentions that *Sun-ning* (in 1914, renamed *Toi-Shaan*) district's *Bojia* (*Pao-chia*) (official surveillance system registers) returns in 1828 were ridiculously low, with only 128,863 males and just 68,109 females, for a total of 196,972 or almost 197,000 adults.

## Table 1.8 Population Estimates for Central Gwongdung in the late 1830s (based on K.C. Hsiao's Formula)[88]

| micro-region | number of counties | average district total population | micro-region total population estimates |
|---|---|---|---|
| Metropolitan Canton | 02 | 250,000 | .5 million |
| Pearl River Delta micro-region | 12 | 250,000 | 3 million |
| Both *Baak-wah* zones | 35 | 250,000 | 8.75 million |
| Non *Yuet* Peripheral areas' micro-region | 15 | 250,000 | 3.75 million |
| Total Estimates for Central Gwongdung | 62 [89] | 250,000 | 15.5 million |

Ho's above cited figures (196,972) seem consistent in light of the fact that Nineteenth-Century Gwongdung had an unusually high amount of under-reporting of certain categories and widespread bribery to evade the *Bojia* registration altogether.[90] In this light, it seems entirely possible that the actual total for *Toi-Shaan*, and other Cantonese counties could very well have been closer to, or even above, Hsiao's estimated figure of 250,000. In all probability, by the later nineteenth century, the figure was most likely even greater. In this manner, minus the roundabout method of calculating using Skinner's earlier mentioned population density and area size figures, it should be easier to arrive at an estimate of district population totals by multiplying 250,000 times the number of *xian* (*hsien*) (counties) in Central Gwongdung.

There were about ninety-nine rural counties in Gwongdung at this time, and when this number is multiplied by 250,000, then the total population for Gwongdung, by this method, was about 24.75 million. This rough estimate is in line with the estimated 23.9 million figures provided by Yen, which shows that this rough estimation approach can be helpful in demonstrating "an order of magnitude."[91] In this manner, if we say that there were about 62 counties located in Central Gwongdung alone, then it is possible to say that the population of this area (i.e., 62 x 250,000) in the early decades of the nineteenth century was about 15.5 million. This effectively constitutes about 50% of Gwongdung's total population during the forty-year period 1855–1895 (see table 1.6 above, i.e., ranging from about 29 million in 1855 to about 29.8 million in 1895). On the basis of this approach, I have estimated the total population for each of Central Gwongdung's five ethno-speech micro-regions, based on the totals for each *xian* within a given micro-region, times the total number of *xian* in the micro-region. (see table 1.8 above)

A third approach for obtaining estimated population figures for Nineteenth-Century Central Gwongdung, relative to its four ethno-speech micro-regions (hereafter, as a practical matter, I do not include Metropolitan Canton) and their respective rural counties, is to definitively establish the geo-territorial context of what constitutes Central Gwongdung. First, I compile a comprehensive list of all of Central Gwongdung's counties. Second, I place groups of these counties into one of four ethno-speech micro-regions in Central Gwongdung, (again I do not include Metropolitan Canton) using the same scheme I used earlier above to calculate the total area for each of ethno-speech micro-regions of Central Gwongdung, i.e., the Pearl River Delta, the Inner *Baak-wah* zone, the Outer *Baak-wah* zone, and Non-*Yuet* Cantonese Peripheral areas.

On the basis of this scheme, I utilize Kuan's data on the population of each district in each of my several micro-regions of Central Gwongdung, where he provides data on the population of each district at some point in time during the early 1940s. Skinner suggests that Kuan's figures are unrealistic, in light of the 1953 Communist Chinese census. Skinner further believes that if we take the 1953 census, as the first reliable modern census, then we would have to conclude, relative to Kuan's data, that much of Gwongdung's population doubled in the decade before the 1953 census, which of course is highly unlikely because of the disruptions and destruction resulting from years of warfare associated with the Japanese invasion and occupation during WW II, followed by the protracted second Chinese Civil War between the Communists and the Nationalists (1945–1949). Skinner suggests alternately, that Kuan's figures are much more representative for 1900, rather than for the early 1940s.[92] He also suggests that, if 5% were deducted from what he believes are really 1900 figures, then one could arrive at a set of figures really representative for 1890.[93]

I accept Skinner's view and have adopted it as a starting point for my own investigation. I adopt his strategy for arriving at population figures (by district) for 1900 and 1890 respectively. For the period 1840–1880, I have relied on the growth rate pattern demonstrated in Yen's data. As noted earlier, two distinct growth rate patterns are discernable, first an 8% growth rate for the period 1839–1859, followed by a .7% growth rate for the following period 1859–1889.[94] By taking .7% of the 1890 figures, I arrive at the figures for 1880. I then repeated the formula for both the 1870 and 1860 figures. For 1850 and 1840 respectively, I changed the rate of growth from .7% to 8%., which is consistent with Yen's data. In this way, I was able to *reverse engineer* population figures to provide rough estimates for each district in Nineteenth-Century Central Gwongdung during the period 1840–1900.

I readily admit that the application of the growth rate of an entire province to individual counties is quite problematic, and likely statistically impossible. When so applied, it will certainly result in skewed figures. First there is the fact that growth rates varied in each county/district, because of different material conditions, e.g., the changing degree of population concentration and patterns of distribution. This most likely meant that there existed different growth rates for different localities, in different periods of time. Statistically it normally makes no sense to apply the statistical data for an entire province over the course of a century to each of its rural counties.

I suggest in the alternative, that rather than not making any effort at all to establish a general overview of Central Gwongdung's demographic patterns of development, it is more responsible to at least make the effort to construct "a general frame of reference," despite technical irregularities and inadequacies. In this context, I choose to establish a plausible demographic profile via a re-constructed quantitative analytical framework. I do so fully aware of the inherent methodological flaws involved. Despite these inherent problems, it would be well to remember that the resultant data is useful only for "general discussion purposes, within the context of this study." My intent is to arrive at a fairly reasonable set of aggregate estimates, to provide a basis for some informed inferences, that can represent "a general picture, rather than a set of precise figures." In short, the value of the possibility of a useful, although somewhat faulty, general picture outweighs the impossibility of having accurate and precise figures, given the limited availability of piece-meal information. In this manner it has been possible to estimate the population of each individual district in Nineteenth-Century Central Gwongdung by decade, which in turn provides a basis for estimating the totals for each key ethno-speech micro-regions which embraced them.

There are no existent reliable accurate, continuous sequential, and comprehensive population statistics for any individual counties in Central Gwongdung during the later Qing period (1800–1900). Until now, this has meant that any reference to such matters has only meant citing a few isolated figures from available statistical data, or alternately an ominous silence that loudly announces "we just don't know." By making a series of calculated, rational, and objective choices in regards to what we think is likely to be the case, or what can be deduced from what is likely the case, it may be possible to develop a somewhat helpful quantitative profile of Central Gwongdung's later nineteenth-century demographics. In this way, by reverse engineering it is possible to develop a number of quantitative local demographic "models" that can help educate us about prevailing socio-economic conditions. The following four tables are the product of this "reverse engineering" effort. My intent is to only suggest credible inferences, regarding "an order of magnitude" or a "discernable pattern of development."

## Table 1.9 Population Estimates for the Nineteenth-Century Pearl River Delta Region (PRDR) in Central Gwongdung, 1840–1900

| District Name | 1840[95] | 1850[96] | 1860[97] | 1870[98] | 1880[99] | 1890[100] | 1900[101] |
|---|---|---|---|---|---|---|---|
| Namhoi | 510,745 | 555,157 | 603,431 | 607,684 | 611,968 | 616,282 | 648,718 |
| Punyu | 471,923 | 512,959 | 557,564 | 561,494 | 565,452 | 569,438 | 599,409 |
| Shuntak | 299,761 | 325,827 | 354,159 | 356,655 | 359,169 | 361,701 | 380,738 |
| Tungkun | 523,275 | 568,777 | 618,235 | 622,593 | 626,981 | 631,401 | 662,528 |
| Pao-on | 137,113 | 149,035 | 161,994 | 163,135 | 164,284 | 165,442 | 174,150 |
| Sunwui | 497,626 | 540,898 | 587,932 | 592,076 | 596,249 | 600,452 | 632,055 |
| Toi-shaan | 586,423 | 637,416 | 692,843 | 697,727 | 702,645 | 707,598 | 744,840 |
| Hoiping | 392,861 | 427,022 | 464,154 | 467,425 | 470,720 | 474,038 | 498,988 |
| Yanping | 185,825 | 201,983 | 219,546 | 221,093 | 222,651 | 224,220 | 236,021 |
| Hok-shaan | 162,008 | 176,095 | 191,407 | 192,756 | 194,114 | 195,482 | 205,771 |
| Chung-shaan | 591,049 | 642,444 | 698,308 | 703,230 | 708,187 | 713,179 | 750,715 |
| Chikkai | 13,267 | 14,420 | 15,674 | 15,784 | 15,895 | 16,007 | 16,849 |
| Total | 4,371,876 | 4,752,033 | 5,165,247 | 5,201,652 | 5,238,315 | 5,275,240 | 5,550,782 |
| | 4.4 mil. | 4.7 mil | 5.1 mil | 5.2 mil | 5.2 mil | 5.3 mil | 5.6 mil |

## Table 1.10 Population Estimates for the Nineteenth-Century Inner *Baak-wah* Zone Population in Central Gwongdung, 1840–1900

| District Name | 1840[102] | 1850[103] | 1860[104] | 1870[105] | 1880[106] | 1890[107] | 1900[108] |
|---|---|---|---|---|---|---|---|
| Tseng-shing | 219,726 | 238,832 | 259,599 | 261,428 | 263,271 | 265,127 | 279,081 |
| Fayuan | 163,214 | 177,406 | 192,832 | 194,191 | 195,559 | 196,937 | 207,302 |
| Samshui | 122,639 | 133,303 | 144,894 | 145,915 | 146,943 | 147,978 | 155,766 |
| Saywui | 119,741 | 130,153 | 141,470 | 142,467 | 143,471 | 144,482 | 152,086 |
| Ch'ing-yuan | 438,222 | 476,328 | 517,747 | 521,396 | 525,071 | 528,772 | 556,602 |
| Tsung-fa | 108,028 | 117,421 | 127,631 | 128,530 | 129,436 | 130,349 | 137,209 |
| Poklo | 174,858 | 190,062 | 206,589 | 208,045 | 209,511 | 210,987 | 222,091 |
| Lung-men | 83,605 | 90,875 | 98,777 | 99,473 | 100,174 | 100,880 | 106,189 |
| Huichau | 446,245 | 485,048 | 527,226 | 530,942 | 534,684 | 538,453 | 566,792 |
| Ko-yiu | 367,095 | 399,016 | 433,713 | 436,770 | 439,848 | 442,948 | 466,261 |
| Ko-ming | 77,474 | 84,210 | 91,532 | 92,177 | 92,827 | 93,481 | 98,401 |
| Yung-chun | 255,555 | 277,777 | 301,925 | 304,053 | 306,196 | 308,354 | 324,583 |
| Yung-kong | 395,293 | 429,666 | 467,028 | 470,320 | 473,635 | 476,973 | 502,076 |
| Sun-hing | 181,893 | 197,709 | 214,901 | 216,415 | 217,940 | 219,476 | 231,027 |
| Total | 3,153,588 | 3,427,806 | 3,725,864 | 3,752,122 | 3,778,566 | 3,805,197 | 4,005,466 |
|  | 3.15 mil. | 3.4 mil. | 3.7 mil. | 3.75 mil. | 3.77 mil. | 3.8 mil. | 4 mil. |

## Table 1.11 Population Estimates for the Nineteenth-Century Population Outer *Baak-wah* Zone in Central Gwongdung, 1840–1900

| District Name | 1840[109] | 1850[110] | 1860[111] | 1870[112] | 1880[113] | 1890[114] | 1900[115] |
|---|---|---|---|---|---|---|---|
| Cho-yeung | 631,369 | 686,270 | 745,945 | 751,203 | 756,498 | 761,832 | 801,927 |
| Yin-ning | 432,481 | 470,087 | 510,964 | 514,565 | 518,192 | 521,844 | 549,309 |
| Wui-loy | 226,100 | 245,760 | 267,130 | 269,013 | 270,909 | 272,818 | 287,176 |
| Hoi-feng | 280,256 | 304,626 | 331,115 | 333,449 | 335,799 | 338,166 | 355,964 |
| Chiu-tsim | 80,376 | 87,365 | 94,961 | 95,630 | 96,304 | 96,983 | 102,087 |
| Wo-yuen | 159,742 | 173,632 | 188,730 | 190,060 | 191,400 | 192,749 | 202,893 |
| Sun-fung | 68,247 | 74,181 | 80,631 | 81,199 | 81,771 | 82,347 | 86,681 |
| Ying-tak | 236,101 | 256,631 | 278,946 | 280,912 | 282,892 | 284,886 | 299,880 |
| Ku-kong (Shao-kuan) | 170,992 | 185,860 | 202,021 | 203,445 | 204,879 | 206,323 | 217,182 |
| Kwong-ning | 200,454 | 218,428 | 236,878 | 238,547 | 240,228 | 241,921 | 254,653 |
| Tak-hing | 131,057 | 142,453 | 154,840 | 155,931 | 157,030 | 158,136 | 166,458 |
| Yun-fou | 215,661 | 234,414 | 254,797 | 256,593 | 258,401 | 260,222 | 273,917 |
| Yu-nam | 192,813 | 209,579 | 227,803 | 229,408 | 231,025 | 232,653 | 244,897 |
| Hoi-kien | 58,360 | 63,434 | 68,950 | 69,436 | 69,925 | 70,418 | 74,124 |
| Feng-chuen | 79,579 | 86,498 | 94,019 | 94,681 | 95,349 | 96,021 | 101,074 |
| Low-ding | 242,971 | 264,098 | 287,063 | 289,086 | 291,124 | 293,176 | 308,606 |
| Sun-yi | 323,721 | 351,870 | 382,467 | 385,163 | 387,878 | 390,612 | 411,170 |
| Maoming | 466,825 | 507,418 | 551,541 | 555,429 | 559,344 | 563,287 | 592,933 |
| Wah-heung | 317,654 | 345,276 | 375,300 | 377,945 | 380,609 | 383,292 | 403,465 |
| Lim-kong | 332,873 | 361,818 | 393,280 | 396,052 | 398,843 | 401,654 | 422,793 |
| Ng-keun | 92,570 | 100,619 | 109,368 | 110,138 | 110,914 | 111,695 | 117,573 |
| Totals[116] | 4,940,202 | 5,370,317 | 5,836,749 | 5,837,885 | 5,919,314 | 5,961,034 | 6,274,762 |
| | 4.94 mil. | 5.37 mil. | 5.83 mil. | 5.83 mil. | 5.91 mil. | 5.96 mil. | 6.27 mil. |

Central Gwongdung

## Table 1.12 Population Estimates for Non *Yuet*-Cantonese Peripheral Areas' in Central Gwongdung, 1840–1900

| District Name | 1840[117] | 1850[118] | 1860[119] | 1870[120] | 1880[121] | 1890[122] | 1900[123] |
|---|---|---|---|---|---|---|---|
| Lu-feng | 280,957 | 305,387 | 331,942 | 334,281 | 336,637 | 339,010 | 356,852 |
| Ng-wah | 256,836 | 279,169 | 303,444 | 305,583 | 307,737 | 309,906 | 326,216 |
| Hing-ning | 359,395 | 390,646 | 424,615 | 427,608 | 430,622 | 433,657 | 456,481 |
| Lung-chun | 246,301 | 267,918 | 290,997 | 293,048 | 295,113 | 297,193 | 312,834 |
| Wo-ping | 127,039 | 138,079 | 150,085 | 151,143 | 152,208 | 153,280 | 161,347 |
| Lian-ping | 70,962 | 77,132 | 83,839 | 84,430 | 85,025 | 86,624 | 90,130 |
| Weng-yuan | 111,157 | 120,822 | 131,328 | 132,253 | 133,185 | 134,124 | 141,183 |
| Gee-hing | 73,905 | 80,331 | 87,316 | 87,931 | 88,551 | 89,175 | 93,868 |
| Nam-yung | 157,204 | 170,873 | 185,731 | 187,040 | 188,359 | 189,686 | 199,669 |
| Yen-fa | 36,885 | 40,092 | 43,578 | 43,885 | 44,194 | 44,505 | 46,847 |
| Lok-chong | 71,698 | 77,932 | 84,708 | 85,305 | 85,906 | 86,512 | 91,065 |
| Ju-yuan | 64,759 | 70,390 | 76,510 | 77,049 | 77,592 | 78,139 | 82,251 |
| Lian-heung | 170,390 | 185,206 | 201,310 | 202,729 | 204,158 | 205,597 | 216,417 |
| Lian-shaan | 37,243 | 40,481 | 44,001 | 44,311 | 44,623 | 44,937 | 47,302 |
| Yeung-shan | 160,901 | 174,892 | 190,100 | 191,440 | 192,789 | 194,148 | 204,366 |
| Total | 2,225,632 | 2,419,150 | 2,629,504 | 2,648,036 | 2,666,699 | 2,685,493 | 2,826,858 |
|  | 2.2 mil. | 2.4 mil. | 2.62 mil. | 2.64 mil. | 2.66 mil. | 2.68 mil. | 2.8 mil. |

## Table 1.13 Aggregate Population Estimates for Nineteenth-Century Central Gwongdung, by Micro-Region, 1840–1900[124]

| Region | 1840 | 1850 | 1860 | 1870 | 1880 | 1890 | 1900 |
|---|---|---|---|---|---|---|---|
| Pearl Delta Region[125] | 4,371,876 / 4.37 mil. | 4,752,033 / 4.75 mil. | 5,165,247 / 5.16 mil. | 5,201,652 / 5.2 mil. | 5,238,315 / 5.23 mil. | 5,275,240 / 5.27 mil. | 5,550,762 / 5.5 mil. |
| Inner Baak-wah Zone[126] | 3,153,588 / 3.1 mil. | 3,427,806 / 3.4 mil. | 3,725,864 / 3.72 mil. | 3,752,122 / 3.75 mil. | 3,778,566 / 3.77 mil. | 3,805,197 / 3.8 mil. | 4,005,466 / 4 mil. |
| Outer Baak-wah Zone[127] | 4,940,202 / 4.9 mil. | 5,370,317 / 5.37 mil. | 5,836,749 / 5.8 mil. | 5,837,885 / 5.8 mil. | 5,919,314 / 5.9 mil. | 5,961,034 / 5.96 mil. | 6,274,762 / 6.27 mil. |
| Sub-Total for Cantonese Core area | 12.37 mil | 13.52 mil | 14.68 mil | 14.75 mil | 14.9 mil | 15.03 mil | 15.77 mil |
| Non-Yuet Cantonese Peripheral Areas[128] | 2,225,632 / 2.2 mil. | 2,419,150 / 2.4 mil. | 2,629,504 / 2.6 mil. | 2,648,036 / 2.64 mil. | 2,666,699 / 2.66 mil. | 2,685,493 / 2.68 mil. | 2,826,858 / 2.8 mil. |
| Total | 14,691,298 / 14.7 mil. | 15,969,306 / 15.96 mil. | 17,357,364 / 17.3 mil. | 17,439,695 / 17.4 mil. | 17,602,894 / 17.6 mil. | 17,726,964 / 17.7 mil. | 18,657,848 / 18.6 mil |
| Central-Gwongdung Total[129] | 25,744,000 / 25.74 mil. | 28,182,000 / 28.1 mil. | 29,204,000 / 29.2 mil. | 29,489,000 / 29.49 mil. | 29,672,000 / 29.67 mil. | 29,800,000 / 29.8 mil. | 29,900,000 / 29.9 mil. |

The above data can be useful in better visualizing the broad contours of demographic change in Nineteenth-Century Central Gwongdung. In better appreciating these matters, we can begin to understand where and how the changing relationship between the limited, and rapidly diminishing, availability of arable land, especially for commercialized rice production, and concentrated high-density population growth underscored the adversity facing the Cantonese community in Central Gwongdung. These material facts further support the proposition that Central Gwongdung serves as a workable material basis for conceptualizing about *Tong-Shaan*.

## Cantonese overseas emigration and the dilemma of Cantonese over-population in Central Gwongdung

In any assessment of the issues of later nineteenth-century Cantonese high-density population concentration and over-population, we must also consider the matter of co-contemporary Cantonese overseas emigration and its relationship with, and impact on these adverse demographic issues back home in *Tong-Shaan*.

In the period 1840-1900, about 3,176,673 people emigrated from Central Gwongdung, which made up about 22% of the aggregate total (14,261,806) of all Chinese overseas emigrants in this period. About 1.4 million (1,371,406) of these emigrants settled chiefly in Hawaii and the Americas. We can further surmise that approximately anywhere from 90% to 95% of the estimated 3.2 million (3,176,673) Cantonese who emigrated overseas world-wide in the period 1840-1900 or about 2.86 million (2,859,005) came from the Pearl River Delta Region alone.

During this period, 1840-1900, there was on average about 5 million people living in the Pearl River Delta Region. This effectively means that the 2.86 million (2,859,005) people who emigrated overseas in this period constituted about 57% of the 5 million people back home. Simplifying matters, we can tentatively say that just over 50% of the local population, in the Cantonese core area of the Pearl River Delta Region, emigrated overseas in the period 1840-1900.[130]

An awareness of these material facts about Cantonese overseas emigration further underscores the critical nature of high-density population concentration and population over-growth in Central Gwongdung, but especially so in the Pearl River Delta Region in the period under discussion. In short, what if the approximately 2.86 million people who emigrated overseas had not left home? When these Cantonese overseas emigrants are factored into the demographic totals for Central Gwongdung for the period 1840-1900, then the issues of high-density population concentration and over-population growth take on an added complexity and significance.

My reference here to the significant place and role of Cantonese overseas emigrants for later nineteenth-century Cantonese demographic issues, however brief, is intended to draw attention to their vital role in the present discussion.

For a more comprehensive and detailed discussion of these matters, see <u>Facing Cantonese Adversity, Fleeing Tong-Shaan, Cantonese Society and the Root Causes of Nineteenth- Century Overseas Emigration</u>, as volume 3 of the <u>Gum-Shaan Chronicles</u>, see especially Chapter 5, "Bad Joss of High-density Population Concentration and Over-Population.

**The Cantonese Heartland: A series of concentric forms in Central Gwongdung**

Central Gwongdung, as the fountainhead of Cantonese identity and experience, and the source of legions of Overseas Cantonese progeny, represents much more than a simplistic geographical reference point. While we know that the overwhelming majority of the Chinese in America from 1850–1900 were from Central Gwongdung, and have been identified with the Cantonese label, we remain uninformed about the material basis of the idea of a "Cantonese fountainhead," both as a geographic expression and as a socio-cultural designation. In this regard, I suggest it may be helpful to first inquire further into the meaning of the label "Cantonese Heartland," relative to its material constructs, before theorizing about the idea of a Cantonese fountainhead.

As noted at the outset of this chapter, the idea of a "Cantonese Heartland," both as a geo-territorial reference and as a socio-cultural label, can have greater meaning and relevance when demographic and territorial elements are examined more closely, as related components of inter-locking concentric relationships. Moving from larger encompassing units downward to smaller internally positioned compact ones, it may be possible to see subtleties between the extremes of ethnic speech distinctions and communal divisions within Cantonese society. In this context, I advance three conceptual categories, as tools for better understanding the "Cantonese heartland."

First, there is the notion of Central Gwongdung itself, as the great arena where the epic of Cantonese history and culture played out for two millennia. It was both geographically distant and culturally distinct from neighboring *Min*-speaking East and West Gwongdung respectively. Historically, Central Gwongdung sat impressively astride the wide expanse of the choicest middle portion of Gwongdung, embracing within its folds not only the largest portion of the province's total land mass, including some of its richest agricultural components, but also a majority of its total population. Again, Cantonese-speaking Central Gwongdung, has historically dominated the whole province, and more generally the whole *Lingnam* region.[131]

Second, within Central Gwongdung, there existed a smaller, more compact, and more concentrated *Cantonese* geo-territorial and ethno-linguistic entity. This, I identify as a "*Yuet*- Cantonese core area," which is a convenient way to group together exclusively *Cantonese* populated areas of Central Gwongdung. This includes: 1) the "outer" *Baak-wah* zone, 2) the "inner" *Baak-wah* zone, and 3) the Pearl River Delta Region, which also includes Metropolitan Canton. This means that the outer tier of counties, which were identified earlier as the Non-*Yuet* Cantonese Peripheral areas, are deleted and thus excluded from this more narrowly constructed and sharply focused view of what constitutes the Cantonese heartland in Central Gwongdung. Comparative quantitative data relating to the *Yuet*-Cantonese core area, Central Gwongdung, and Gwongdung province respectively is provided below in table 1.14.

Third, there existed another smaller, even more geographically compact and demographically condensed representation of the *Cantonese* community in the shape of the Pearl River Delta Region (PRDR). This compact micro-region, consisting of a dozen rural counties, which also embraced metropolitan Canton. The fact that for at least a century, 1850–1950, the vast majority of Chinese immigrants that journeyed to North America, generation after generation, came from the PRDR. This emigration pattern underscored the basic fact that this smallest and most concentrated expression of the Cantonese community, historically constituted the inner-most core of the "Cantonese homeland."

Interestingly, there developed a curious anomaly in Central Gwongdung, relative to the diminishing ratio between the availability of material resources (e.g., arable farmland) and the growing need/demand for opportunities to emigrate overseas. Historically speaking, those counties closest to Canton, and those micro-regions closer to the Pearl River Delta, were generally among the most productive and prosperous in Central Gwongdung. In this context, one would normally expect that a larger number of *Cantonese* overseas emigrants would come from those rural counties in micro-regions located further away from the kind of prosperity historically associated with Canton and the Pearl River Delta micro-region. This however, seems not to have been the case. This anomaly was due in large part to the fact that while the Metropolitan Canton and Pearl River Delta micro-regions were among the most prosperous in Central Gwongdung, they were also among the most heavily populated, with high density concentrations and over population, that made them among the most over-crowded areas in Central Gwongdung.[132] Significantly, most of the *Cantonese* Overseas emigrants came from these two heavily over populated micro-regions.

**The Pearl River Delta Region and the *Baak-wah* zone(s) distinguished: People, land, economics, and the option of overseas emigration**

The marked differences between the Pearl River Delta Region (PRDR) and the *Baak-wah* zone(s), relative to their respective territorial expanse, population size, and density concentration ratios (people per sq. mile [ppsm]), are important considerations that can further help to explain the discrepancy between the responses of the people of these two micro-regions to the challenge of overseas emigration alluded to above. We should remember however, that the distinguishing characteristics between the people of these two key micro-regions of Cantonese Central Gwongdung involve much more than contrasting differences in their respective degrees of economic productivity and material affluence. In this context, basic differences also reflected their contrasting geo-demographic profiles, relative to various immutable advantages and disadvantages associated with them.

The *Baak-wah* zone(s) embraced a huge expanse of land, as already shown earlier. In table 1.2, the Inner *Baak-wah* zone, with 14 districts/counties occupied about 12,738.74 sq. miles of land, which amounted to about 17.89% of Gwongdung. Similarly, in table 1.3, the Outer *Baak-wah* zone, with 21 districts/counties occupied about 19,323.2 sq. miles of land, which amounted to about 29.1% of Gwongdung. In the aggregate the two *Baak-wah* zones representing 35 districts/counties, occupied about 32,061.94 sq. miles or 47% (46.99%) of Gwongdung. In contrast, as shown in table 1.1, the rich Pearl River Delta Region with only 12 districts/counties, occupied just 7,768.63 sq.

miles or a mere 10.76% of Gwongdung. (Note: much of this data is also presented in table 1.5) Effectively the *Baak-wah* zone(s) occupied about four times (4.13) more land than the PRDR. Additionally, it had a much larger population distributed across a larger territorial expanse, with about 10 million (9.58 million) people in 1870, as shown in table 1.13. In contrast the PRDR which only had about 5 million (5.2 million) people at the same time (1870).

Distinguishing contrasting characteristics between the PRDR and the *Baak-wah* zone(s) are also evident in the critical matter of population density (people per sq. mile or ppsm), as it relates to the ratio between the respective populations and the availability of land for agricultural purposes. These matters underscored the local sense of, (or the lack thereof of) "crowdedness and congestion". Again, in 1870, the PRDR had about 5 million (5.2 million) people, who were crowded into an area of about 7,769 (7,768.63) miles, in marked contrast to the *Baak-wah* zone(s), where about 10 million (9.58 million) people occupied the large area of about 32,061.94 sq. miles (i.e., double the population of the PRDR, in an area four times larger than the PRDR). Thus, the total population of the *Baak-wah* zone(s) was much larger and more widely distributed over a wider expanse of land, than in the case of the people in the PRDR. In this light, it is reasonable to think that *Baak-wah* zone(s) population density was much lower than that of the PRDR.

Significantly, in 1870, the population concentration density of the PRDR was about 644 (643.5) ppsm. During the same time period (1870) the population density of the Inner *Baak-wah* zone was about 294 ppsm, and that of the Outer *Baak-wah* zone was about 302 (301.7) ppsm. In the aggregate, the population density of both *Baak-wah* zones was about 311 ppsm, which amounted to less than half of the 644 ppsm population density of the PRDR.

This contrasting geo-demographic profile served as a significant factor contributing to the marked difference between PRDR's enhanced material prosperity (i.e., both urban mercantile affluence and rural commercialized agriculture) and the co-contemporary less dynamic, but stable, if somewhat less prosperous *Baak-wah* material conditions. This contrasting profile also helps to explain the contradiction between evidence of economic adversity in some segments of rural society in PRDR (e.g., in *Say-Yup* areas), despite urban affluence and routine rural material prosperity in other areas, (e.g., in *Saam-Yup* areas), whereby overseas emigration became especially attractive and widespread. In contrast, the parallel lack of marked dynamic and sustained economic affluence in the *Baak-wah* zone(s) was in large measure beneficially mitigated by the regions' social and economic stability, such that the option of overseas emigration lacked the kind of appeal and urgency, so pervasive among the people of the PRDR.

In marked contrast, moving away from the Pearl River Delta, upriver into the Inner *Baak-wah* and Outer *Baak-wah* zones, and finally into the non-*Yuet*/Cantonese Peripheral areas' micro-region, the opposite seems to have been the case, where less and less people opted to emigrate overseas. In examining the records of local *Wooi-kun* (*huiguan*) (district associations) in Nineteenth-Century San Francisco, the preponderance of a monopoly of Pearl River Delta region rural counties representation stands in marked contrast to the paucity, near absence of representation among rural counties of the Inner and Outer *Baak-wah* zones, to say nothing of those of the Non-*Yuet*/Cantonese Peripheral areas' micro-region.[133] This can be partly explained in light of Chain migration theory, whereby people emigrate to areas where others from their native places have already established an initial presence, where "birds of a feather flock together."

**The "central core area" of the Cantonese homeland in Central Gwongdung**

As noted earlier, Central Gwongdung, with about 53,000 square miles,[134] comprises about 64% of the province's 82,000 square miles. This impressive set of figures underscores the magnitude of Cantonese controlled areas' dominance of Gwongdung province. We should, remember however, that this 64% included a substantial area inhabited by non-*Yuet*/*Bundae* Cantonese groups, e.g., the *Hakka*. When this area is deleted, then a smaller, even more concentrated and "pure" Cantonese *Yuet*/*Bundae* community remained. The resultant smaller, but clearly more exclusive Cantonese *Yuet*/*Bundae* dominated area, is still statistically significant at 46%, which means that the Cantonese core area of Central Gwongdung constituted nearly 50% of the province's total land mass. Put another way, this Cantonese core area constituted about 75% of Central

Gwongdung itself. These decisive ratios underscored the dominant position of the Cantonese in Nineteenth-Century Gwongdung, and more particularly Central Gwongdung, and the earlier described Cantonese core area(s) respectively.

The changing pattern of nineteenth-century Cantonese demographic data mirrors how we might see and better understand the shifting dimensions of what constitutes a Cantonese heartland, relative to the location, distribution, and concentration of the Cantonese population. Again, as stated earlier, Central Gwongdung contained about 57% of the province's total population in 1840, which subsequently increased to a significantly higher proportion of 62% by 1900. It can be observed, however, that the Cantonese component of the province's total population for most of the nineteenth century averaged around 60%. Similarly, the Cantonese core area's population made up about 48% or nearly one-half of the province's total population. Even more impressive is the fact that the Cantonese core area's population, which was exclusively Cantonese in composition, made up about 85% of Central Gwongdung's total population during the nineteenth century. Put another way, nearly 9 out of every 10 people (90%) in Central Gwongdung were located in this key Cantonese core area.

Finally, during most of the nineteenth century, it can also be seen that the smallest and most concentrated locus for the Cantonese community, the PRDR, hosted a minority of the Cantonese population in Central Gwongdung. The PRDR only had about 30% of Central Gwongdung's population, which also constituted about 35% of the Cantonese Core area. These last two figures are quite significant, because not only do they shed new light on the location, distribution, and concentration of the Cantonese community in *Tong-Shaan*, they also help us to understand underlying demographic data of nineteenth-century Cantonese overseas emigration.

We do know that the vast majority of Chinese immigrants to North America, Hawaii, Latin America, and the Caribbean were from the small compact area of the PRDR, such that during the course of the mid-late nineteenth century, the Western Hemisphere became essentially a Cantonese immigrant monopoly, via chain migration. In short, during the mid-late nineteenth century the PRDR, with only 30% share of the Cantonese community of Central

Gwongdung, effectively supplied almost all, or an estimated +90% of all Chinese immigrants in North America. Put another way, it seems clear that very, very few Cantonese going to America, or elsewhere in the Western Hemisphere, came from other parts of the Cantonese core area, or from elsewhere in the larger micro-region of Central Gwongdung, in contrast with those emigrants from the PRDR.

In this manner, while the PRDR hosted the smallest percentage share of the Cantonese community in Central Gwongdung, or the Cantonese core area respectively—it nonetheless supplied the overwhelming majority of all mid-late nineteenth-century Cantonese overseas emigrants going to America and elsewhere in the Western Hemisphere. This can help us to better understand the basis for the development of especially close ties that bound Cantonese overseas emigrants together with their native places in Central Gwongdung. It also re-enforces the idea that such emigrants held sharply focused views and deeply held beliefs about their relationship with the "Cantonese homeland," which shaped their understanding of the meaning/value of that relationship.

This simplistic, but integrated vision of the Cantonese homeland, commonly referred to as *Tong-Shaan*, had an enduring command of the loyalty and affection of the vast majority of the Cantonese in America and elsewhere in the New World, precisely because nearly all of them came from this smallest, richest, most concentrated, but also ethno-linguistically diverse portion of the "Cantonese homeland" in Central Gwongdung. As a means of better visualizing these three different expressions of what constitutes the "Cantonese Homeland," i.e., Central Gwongdung, the *Yuet*-Cantonese core area, and the Pearl River Delta Region (PRDR), see Table 1.14 below, which provides an overview of the representative quantitative data discussed above in a convenient comparative format.

## Table 1.14 Comparative geographical and demographic data for Gwongdung Province, Central Gwongdung, *Yuet*-Cantonese core area, and The Pearl River Delta Region[135]

| Field-Category | 1840 | 1860 | 1880 | 1900 | Average |
|---|---|---|---|---|---|
| 1)Gwongdung Province total area (in square miles) (200 rural counties)[136] | 82,000 | same | same | same | same |
| 2)Central Gwongdung total area (in square miles) (105 rural counties)[137] | 53,000 | same | same | same | same |
| 3)*Cantonese* core area total area (in square miles) (44 rural counties)[138] | 39,830 | same | same | same | same |
| 4)Pearl River Delta Region total area (in square miles) (12 rural counties)[139] | 8,568 | same | same | same | same |
| 5)#2 as a percentage of #1 | 64% | same | same | same | same |
| 6)#3 as a percentage of #1 | 46% | same | same | same | same |
| 7)#3 as a percentage of #2 | 75% | same | same | same | same |
| 8)#4 as a percentage of #1 | 10% | same | same | same | same |
| 9)#4 as a percentage of #2 | 16% | same | same | same | same |
| 10)#4 as a percentage of #3 | 21.5% | same | same | same | same |
| 11)Gwongdung Province estimated total population (in millions)[140] | 25.7 | 29.2 | 29.7 | 29.9 | 28.6 |
| 12)Central Gwongdung estimated total population (in millions)[141] | 14.7 | 17.3 | 17.6 | 18.6 | 17.0 |
| 13)*Cantonese* core area estimated total population (in millions)[142] | 12.37 | 14.68 | 14.9 | 15.77 | 14.4 |
| 14)Pearl River Delta Region estimated total population (in millions)[143] | 4.37 | 5.16 | 5.23 | 5.5 | 5.0 |
| 15)#12 as a percentage of #11 | 57% | 59% | 59% | 62% | 60% |
| 16)#13 as a percentage of #11 | 48% | 50% | 50% | 53% | 50% |
| 17)#13 as a percentage of #12 | 84% | 85% | 85% | 85% | 85% |
| 18)#14 as a percentage of #11 | 17% | 18% | 18% | 18% | 18% |
| 19)#14 as a percentage of #12 | 30% | 30% | 30% | 30% | 30% |
| 20)#14 as a percentage of #13 | 35% | 35% | 35% | 35% | 35% |

## Conclusion

My chief line of inquiry in this chapter has been to contextualize the proposition that the physical place of Central Gwongdung offers a useful material basis for conceptualizing the idea of *Tong-Shaan*, as the traditional Cantonese fountainhead. The wealth of historical, geographical, demographic, socio-economic, and ethno-linguistic information surveyed in this chapter underscores the fact that, Central Gwongdung is both objectively and subjectively well-suited to the task at hand. It is objectively useful, by way of the material facts and quantitative data that it offers, to support claims made about its significance and distinctiveness, as a particular place, with its own history, society, culture, and set of ethno-speech identifications. It is also subjectively beneficial, in the underlying perspectives it provides, regarding various representations and expectations of Cantonese emigrants, relative to their group identity and collective sense of history. Available objective data enables us to understand the material constructs of identity and experience, as they arise within the specific context of a particular physical location, as it has evolved through time. In contrast, subjective perspectives educate us about the critical nexus between a people and a place, where people embrace evocative ideas about a place, they called "home," and their evolving relationship with it. Central Gwongdung, as *Tong-Shaan*, became over time the focal point of their loyalties, their longing, and an iconic inspiration that shaped their group identity and informed their collective experience.

Simply stated, the notion of *Tong-Shaan*, as the fountainhead of Cantonese identity and experience, helps us to better grasp objective facts, and subtle subjective nuances, concerning, "What it meant to be Cantonese in Nineteenth-Century China and America."

---

[1] "*Gwongdung*" is my own romanization of the Cantonese form of the Pinyin (Mandarin Chinese) form of "*Guangdong*" and "*Kwangtung*" (the earlier Wade-Giles English Romanization form). (see my earlier comments in this book's preface).
[2] "China proper" refers to the geographical area populated by the dominant "Han" Chinese ethnic majority in China. It consists of contiguous administrative units known as provinces. In the Qing period of the nineteenth century there were 18 provinces, today there are about 22 provinces. Beyond China

proper there are autonomous regions, where non-Han Chinese people live, e.g., Tibet, Mongolia, Xinjiang, and the *Dongbei* (Northeast) (formerly known as Manchuria).

[3] Songqiao Zhao, Physical Geography of China, Beijing: Science Press, 1986,) p. 134.

[4] Ibid., p. 134.

[5] In 1952, a small section of western Gwongdung's coastline (now identified as *Qinzhou, Fangcheng gang,* and *Beihai* counties in Gwongsai) was re-assigned to Gwongsai (Guangxi), so that it could have direct access to the sea. Additionally, in 1988, Hainan was awarded the status of a new independent province.

[6] Gwongdung's total area in the nineteenth century was actually 81,834 square miles, this figure has been calculated from 212,005 square kilometers, with one kilometer equal to .386 square mile, thus 212,005 square kilometers equals about 81,834 square miles or almost 82,000 square miles.(see Ezra F. Vogel, One Step Ahead in China, Guangdong Under Reform, (Cambridge, Mass: Harvard University Press, 1989,) p.3; also see Cressy, Land of 500 Million, p. 38, re: Gwongdung size as 84,443 square miles; also see Companion to Chinese History, (New York: Facts on File, 1987,) p.153, re: Gwongdung has an area of 210,000 square kilometers or 81,000 square miles; also see Edward J.M. Rhoads, China's Republican Revolution, The Case of Kuangtung, 1895–1913, (Cambridge, Mass: Harvard University Press, 1975), p.8,re: Gwongdung's total area is given as 85,000 square miles. Finally, also see http://www.citypopulation.de/China-Guangdong.html, re: Figure for total area of Guangdong (Gwongdung) in 2013 given as 197,100 kilometers (this does not include Hainan Island, because it became an independent province in 1988), thus Gwongdung now constitutes about 76,080 square miles.

[7] See Table 1.6 Gwongdung Total Population Estimates 1786-1900.

[8] In the second map below, my designated micro-regions are mis-represented. Only West Gwongdung is clearly indicated. I do not accept nor use the designation of "Northern Guangdong" (Gwongdung,) as indicated. Instead, I would take portions of this "Northern Guangdong" and add them as natural extensions of Central and East Gwongdung respectively, as each one extends north to Gwongdung's northern border with neighboring Jiangxi, Hunan, and Gwongsai (Guangxi) provinces respectively. The first map above does not offer as much detail, but it does simply and clearly indicate the approximate division of Gwongdung into the three micro-regions of East, Central, and West Gwongdung.

[9] Rhoads, China's Republican Revolution, pp.10–11.

[10] Inquiries about East Guangdong (Gwongdung) typically yield nothing. The closest one gets to the subject is to focus on the major urban centers of *Chaozhou* (often known as *Chao-chow, Chiu-chow,* or *Teochiiu* in the local min-based dialect) and *Shantou* (formerly *Swatow.*) They are often cited collectively as "*Chaoshan*" which is a contraction for *Chaozhou* and *Shantou.*

[11] This is my own rough estimate, based on a simple visual observation of a nineteenth-century map of Gwongdung province.

[12] See Kung-Chuan Hsiao, Rural China, Imperial Control in the Nineteenth Century, (Seattle: University of Washington Press, 1960), p.5, see note #5. My figure for the population of East Gwongdung in the early nineteenth century is based on a simple formula of multiplying the number of districts (*xian*) (*hsien*) in East Gwongdung, which I calculate at about ten urban and rural districts, by the number 250,000, (the average *xian* population in the early nineteenth century (c1819), as suggested by Hsiao. Thus 10x250,000 equals about 2.5 million; Also see this chapter, pages 85-92, re: use of this and other alternative formulas for determining nineteenth century population figures for Central Gwongdung.

[13] *Chaozhou* is the Pinyin Mandarin Chinese form. *Ch'ao-chou* is the Wade-Giles Mandarin Chinese form. *Teochiu* is the local southern *min* dialect form of East Gwongdung. *Chiu-chau* or *Chiu-chow* are the Cantonese forms.

[14] Here I use *Teochiu* as an identifying label for the people and speech of East Gwongdung, in contrast to using *Chaozhou* for identifying the city, and more generally the core area of *Chaozhou-Shantou* (now identified as *Chaoshan*)

[15] Times Atlas of China, ed. J.M. Geelaw & T.C. Twichett, (N.Y. Times Books, 1974), pp. 77, 79.

[16] Re: Taiwan, see generally, Johanna Menzel Meskill, A Chinese Pioneer Family, The Lins of Wufeng, Taiwan 1729–1895, (Princeton, New Jersey: Princeton University Press, 1979).

[17] re: Hainan Island, see Edward H. Schafer, Shore of Pearls, (Berkeley: University of California Press,

## Chapter 1

1970)

[18] See Edward Schafer, <u>Shore of Pearls, Hainan Island in Early Times</u>, (Floating World edition: 2009), see chapter five, "Exiles," pp. 85–101

[19] See, S. Robert Ramsey, <u>The Languages of China</u>, (Princeton, New Jersey: Princeton University Press, 1989), Chapter 11, "The Minorities of South China," pp. 230–248.

[20] See, Jerry Norman, <u>Chinese</u>, New York: Cambridge University Press, 1988) (Cambridge Language Surveys Series), p. 215

[21] (The older name of *Chin-kong* was restored in 1946, at the end of WW II, when the French returned the city to China.)

[22] See <u>Wikipedia</u> entries for Leizhou Peninsula, *Guangzhou-Wan* Bay (*Kouamg-Tcheou-Wan*) (*Kwang-chow-Wan* Bay).

[23] See <u>Wikipedia</u> entries for China and South China Sea disputes. Hainan Island was re-organized in 1988, to form a new and separate Chinese province. In addition to Hainan Island, the new province also included about 200–250 neighboring islands arranged in three archipelagos: 1) the Spratly Islands, known in Chinese as *Nansha qundao*, 2) the Paracel Islands, known in Chinese as *Xisha qundao*, and 3) the Macclesfield Bank, known in Chinese as *Zhongsha qundao*. The province took the name of "Hainan" as its official name, because Hainan Island comprises about 97% of the new province's territory. The other 3%, consisting of the earlier mentioned islands of the three archipelagos, has been subject to various sovereignty disputes between China, Taiwan, Vietnam, the Philippines, Malaysia, and Bruni.

[24] See <u>Wikipedia</u> entry for Hainan Island and Hainan Province

[25] Each of these micro-regions is covered at greater length and in more detail later in this chapter.

[26] Canton has been Romanized several different ways. In Cantonese, 1) *Kwong-chau,* (standard Cantonese), 2) *Gwong-chau,* (my own adopted form), 3) *Kwong-chow,* (earlier western romanization of the Cantonese form), 4) *Guangzhou*, (Pinyin Mandarin Chinese romanization), and 5) *Kwang-chou*, (Wade-Giles Mandarin Chinese romanization).

[27] The name of the province of "Gwongdung" literally means, (the) "broad" or "wide" expanse (i.e., "*Gwong")*"in" or "to" the "East.(i.e., "*dung.*")

[28] See demographic data in table 1.13 "Aggregate Population Estimates for Nineteenth-Century Central Gwongdung, by micro-region, 1840–1900." See especially lines/rows labeled as Inner and Outer *Baak-wah* zone respectively, e.g., for year 1870, Inner *Baak-wah* zone estimated total population of 3.75 Million, and Outer *Baak-wah* zone estimated population of 5.8 million, for a total *Baak-wah* zone estimated population of 9.55 million. For that same year, the estimated population for the outer mountainous or non-*yuet* Cantonese peripheral areas was about 2.64 million. This illustrates that the estimated population of the outer mountainous areas was about 27% or just over 25% of that of the *Baak-wah* zone. This pattern remained generally consistent for the period 1840–1900.

[29] See <u>Wikipedia</u> entries for "Pearl River (China) Zhu Jiang" and "Xi River" respectively. Interestingly, the "Pearl River system" seems to be used more commonly, whereas traditionally in the past, in the West, the West River system was more widely recognized. In the XI (West) River entry, the West River is identified as "a tributary of the Pearl River." This is technically true to the extent that a portion of the West River flows into parts of the Pearl River. However, the West River is the larger of the two rivers. Technically speaking, the West River is actually a "distributary" (where a larger river flows into a smaller river). of the Pearl River.

[30] *Buck-Gong (*my own Romanization format*) (Pak-kong)* (standard Cantonese format*). Beijiang* is the *Pinyin* Mandarin Chinese format.

[31] See, Frederic Wakeman, Jr, <u>Strangers at the Gate, Social Disorder in South China, 1839–1861</u>, (Berkeley: University of California Press, 1966), see map of "Kuang-chou delta" [i.e., Pearl River Delta], located just opposite the book's title page at the front of the book. (no page number indicated)

[32] See <u>Wikipedia</u> entry for "Pearl River"

[33] Ibid., also see Wikipedia entry for "Pearl River Delta"

[34] The only other major areas for such productive widespread agricultural activity were: 1) East Gwongdung's Han River valley; 2) The coastal plains of West Gwongdung's Leichou (Leizhou) peninsula;

and 3) The coastal areas of Hainan Island.

[35] T.R Tregear, Geography of China, (Aldine Publishing co., 1966), p.258.

[36] See Table 1.9 "Population Estimates for Nineteenth-Century Pearl River Delta Region in Central Gwongdung, 1840–1900," also see Table 1.1, "The 12 rural districts of the nineteenth-century Pearl River Delta Region Micro-Region #2 of Central Gwongdung."

[37] My 50% figure is conservative. It is more likely that Central Gwongdung in fact had more than 50% of the province's arable land, perhaps as much as 60%. Calculations regarding what part of Gwongdung is represented by Central Gwongdung vary, depending on where one draws the line between Central Gwongdung and its adjacent areas of East Gwongdung, the northern tier of mountainous counties along the northern border with neighboring provinces, and those counties located in westernmost Gwongdung.

[38] The only other major areas for such agricultural activity in Gwongdung province were: 1) East Gwongdung's Han River valley; 2) the coastal plains of West Gwongdung and its Leizhou peninsula; and 3) coastal areas of Hainan Island.

[39] See Vogel, One Step Ahead in China, p. 252 (the 70% figure is Volgel's, and the 57,283.8 figure is mine, i.e., 70%of the 81, 834 square miles for all of Gwongdung.

[40] *Guangzhou*, (Pinyin Mandarin Chinese form); *Kwang-chou*, (Wade-Giles Mandarin Chinese form); *Gwong-chau*, (my own adopted form, see introduction comments on how I approach Cantonese romanization); *Kwong-chau*, (Standard Cantonese form); also see See Wikipedia entry for Canton (Guangzhou), where the name "Canton" is said to have been derived from the Portuguese word "*Cantao*." In the alternative there also existed the popular co-contemporary Japanese term of "Kanton." In the later eighteenth and early nineteenth centuries, the term "Canton" was commonly used interchangeably to refer to both the "city" of Canton, and the "province" of Canton (i.e., *Gwongdung* (*Guangdong*) Province. In much of the western literature of the period, most westerners frequently confused "Canton the city" with "Canton the province"- using the same name for both entities, which of course was incorrect. Canton was the city and *Kwangtung* (the proper spelling at the time) (*Guangdong*, spelling today) was the province. Historically speaking, Canton has been known as "The City of Rams," (*Yang-ch'eng*), see Frederic Wakeman Jr., Strangers at the Gate, p.14.

[41] Wei-lan Kuan, *Chung-hua min-kuo hsing cheng ch'u hua chi t'u ti jen k'ou tsung chi piao*, (Administrative Units and Local Population Statistical Tables for Republican China) (Taipei, Taiwan: 1955), p. 46. (Hereafter cited as Local Population Statistical Tables) (re: one square kilometer=.386 square mile). Traditionally, it has been common to list all three of the *Saam-yup* (Three speech districts) of *Namhoi, Panyu*, and *Shuntak* as key rural districts/counties located adjacent to and contributing parts of their respective land areas and populations to help form Metropolitan Canton. This source suggests that only *Namhoi* and *Panyu* were so positioned. I tend to agree with this view. While *Shuntak* was one of the *Saam-Yup* districts/counties, it was not however, directly physically attached to the city of Canton, as were *Namhoi* and *Panyu*. A portion of *Namhoi's* southern/southeastern area effectively cut *Shuntak* off from any direct physical link with Canton. This does not mean that *Shuntak* did not enjoy substantial links with Canton, but simply that it was not literally adjacent to it, as were *Namhoi* and *Panyu*. Looking at a map of the area reveals that *Shuntak* was located directly north of *Chung-Shaan*, whereby they shared a substantial border between them. In this context, *Shuntak* had important links with other neighbors, beyond those with Canton. In this regard, *Shuntak* differed from *Namhoi* and *Panyu*.

[42] The estimated figure of 800 square miles represents the observation that, in recent years, many think that the third district/county of Shuntak should also be included with Namhoi and Punyu as key components of Metropolitan Canton. Nineteenth-Century metropolitan Canton occupied an estimated 1% or about 800 square miles of Gwongdung's approximate 82,000 square miles.

[43] See, Table 1.8, the population estimate for Cantonese Central Gwongdung in the late 1830s is based on K.C. Hsiao's Formula

[44] Wakeman, Strangers at the Gate, p. 44.

[45] see generally the following, re Chinese regionalism: G. William Skinner, "Regional Urbanization in Nineteenth-Century China, in The City in Late Imperial China, ed. G. William Skinner (Stanford, Ca: Stanford University Press, 1977), pp.211–249 (hereafter referred to as "Regional Urbanization,"); also

see <u>The Living Tree, The Changing Meaning of Being Chinese Today</u>, ed. Wei-ming Tu, (Stanford, Ca: Stanford University Press, 1994, especially Myron L. Cohen, "Being Chinese: The Peripheralization of Traditional Identity," Chapter. 4, pp. 88–108; also see <u>Down to Earth, The Territorial Bond in South China</u>, edited by David Faure and Helen F. Siu, (Stanford Ca: Stanford University Press, 1995); also see, <u>Remapping China, Fissures in Historical Terrain</u>, edited by Gail Hershatter, Emily Honig Jonathan N. Lipman, et. al., (Stanford, Ca: Stanford University Press, 1996), see especially following three chapters: Emily Honig, "Native Place and the Making of Chinese Ethnicity," pp. 143–155; James H. Cole, "Competition and Cooperation in Late Imperial China as Reflected in Native Place and Ethnicity," pp.156–163; and Kwan Man Bun, "Mapping the Hinterland: Treaty Ports and Regional Analysis in Modern China," pp. 181–193; and Ming K. Chan, "A Turning Point in the Modern Chinese Revolution: The Historical Significance of the Canton Decade, 1917–27," pp. 224–241.

[46] Maurice Freedman pioneered research on traditional Cantonese society, among other subjects. See the following: Maurice Freedman, <u>Lineage Organization in Southeastern China</u>, (London, UK: Athlone Press, University of London, 1958); also see Maurice Freedman, <u>Chinese Lineage and Society: Fukien and Kwangtung</u>, (New York: Humanities Press, 1966); More recent studies on the Cantonese, as part of the recent renaissance in Chinese regional studies, include the following: Yuen-fong Woon, <u>Social Organization in South China, 1911–1949: The Case of the Kuan Lineage in K'ai-p'ing [Hoiping] County</u>, (Ann Arbor, Michigan: University of Michigan, 1984); also see, Janice E. Stockard, <u>Daughters of the Canton Delta, Marriage Patterns and Economic Strategies in South China, 1860–1930</u>, (Stanford, Ca: Stanford University Press, 1989); also see, <u>Down to Earth, the Territorial Bond in South China</u>, edited by David Faure and Helen F. Siu, (Stanford, Ca: Stanford University Press, 1995).Also see, Ezra Vogel, <u>Canton Under Communism, Programs and Politics in a Provincial Capital, 1949–1968,</u> (New York, Harper Torchbooks, 1969; (also issued by Harvard University Press, as part of the Harvard East Asian Series #41, 1969); also reprinted by Harvard University Press 1980), see ch. 1, pp. 12–37. Also see Vogel's more recent work on Guangdong, <u>One Step Ahead in China, Guangdong Under Reform</u>, (Cambridge, Mass., Harvard University Press, 1989.)

[47] See G. William Skinner, "Marketing and Social Structure in Rural China," in three parts. Part I, <u>Journal of Asian Studies</u>, 24:1, November 1964, pp. 3–43; part II, <u>Journal of Asian Studies</u>, 24:2, February, 1965, pp. 195–228; and Part III, <u>Journal of Asian Studies</u>, 24:3, May 1965, pp. 363–399; also see Skinner, <u>City in Late Imperial China</u>, In researching Nineteenth-Century Gwongdung population data, Skinner's citations for his analysis of *Kwangtung* (*Gwongdung*) were especially helpful. See, note #4, p.708, note # 13, p.709; and note #17, p.710.; also see Skinner, "Marketing and Social Structure," part II, pp. 207–208. (see map on p. 209). See especially p.216 re: the following quote. "... (a) region refers to any partition of activity-space made according to one of two criteria: (1) the homogeneity of things to be considered, producing a set of *formal* or *uniform* regions; or (2) the interrelatedness of things to be considered, producing a set of *functional* or *nodal* regions. I am also personally indebted to Professor Skinner for helpful research hints. Initially via a conversation with him on 5/6/1997. (e.g., his referring me to John S. Aird, "Population Growth," in <u>Economic Trends in Communist China</u>, edited by Alexander Eckstein, Walter Galenson, and Ta-chung Liu, (Chicago: Aldine Publishing Company, 1968), pp. 247–266. I also received a detailed letter dated June 4, 1997, in which Professor Skinner explained his understanding of Chinese population figures for the late nineteenth and early twentieth centuries. He believes that the early Communist Chinese census of the early 1950s mirrored more the demographic realities of half a century earlier around 1900, and as such, they best serve as a bench mark for the "reconstruction" of late Qing nineteenth-century Chinese demographics.

[48] 1] Regions as units involving "maximal hinterlands and high-level central places" in a functional relationship of complementary dependence and economic exchange(s); 2] Regions as units that serve as a, "functionally integrated urban [-rural] system," relative to network lines connecting trade flow patterns between "cores" and "peripheries;" 3] Regions as units which provide for the differential distribution of economic resources within a well-defined area, characterized by the concentration of critical resources, measured against population density; 4] Regions as physiographic units, centering on river basins and watersheds relative to logistical and economic mechanics of transportation in an agrarian based society. See Skinner, <u>City in Late Imperial China</u>, "Cities and the Hierarchy of Local Systems,

pp. 281–282.

[49] See Skinner's scheme first mentioned earlier in note #47 above, as related to the idea that Central Gwongdung provides a basis for conceptualizing about both the context and constructs of Cantonese community development.

[50] Note here I distinguish the Metropolitan area of Canton and its three adjacent rural counties/counties (Xian) from the surrounding Pearl River Delta micro-region for the purposes of discussion. Later in this chapter, I combine Metro Canton's three adjacent counties to include them within the larger micro-regional unit of the Pearl River Delta Region. Generally speaking, the latter is historically more accurate and relevant, then the former, when referring to the Pearl River Delta Region as the "heartland" of a "Cantonese fountainhead" in *Tong-Shaan*.

[51] Skinner also divides Central Gwongdung into three sections, his scheme provides for a smaller triangular Central unit, with two larger units on each side, i.e., West Central and East Central Gwongdung. In contrast, I have divided Central Gwongdung into a pattern of concentric areas. First the Canton metropolitan area, then the Pearl River Delta area, and finally the interior hinterland which embraced both Metropolitan Canton and the Pearl River Delta in an arc-like pattern, I identify as the *Baak-wah* zone. A full circle encircled Canton and the Delta area, with the sea on one side and the *Baak-wah* zone on the other. Additionally, I have included some areas north of Skinner's West Central and Central into my designated area of the *Baak-wah* zone. My configuration of Central Gwongdung revolves around culturally rooted communal criteria, whereas Skinner's revolves around spatial territorial criteria, relative to economic and marketing institutional considerations.

[52] See chapter 2, "The cornerstone of Cantonese identity, *Yuet* language and Cantonese speech," see especially section, "Distinguishing between "*Yuet*" (*Yue*) and "Cantonese"

[53] Note in the remainder of this chapter, I do not pursue any expansive inquiry about Metropolitan Canton, because it was a relatively small area (i.e., about 800 square miles) and has been both qualitatively and quantitatively different from the other designated micro-regions, relative to its unique status and role as the its largest urban center and provincial capital of Gwongdung province.

[54] Re: data on each district's area by square kilometers and percentage of Gwongdung's total area, see Kuan, Local Population Statistical Tables, p.46. Re: data on each district's square miles, computed on basis of 1 square kilometer equals about .386 square mile.

[55] Chikkai, a tiny rural district located on the eastern coast of Toi-Shaan, while located immediately adjacent to the *Say-Yup* area, has not been traditionally identified as part of the *Say-Yup* or *Ng-Yup* groups. Undoubtedly, despite this fact, because of its location, it has been an integral part of the Pearl River Delta micro-region.

[56] Skinner, "Marketing and Rural Structure," p.208 Skinner labels these areas as "Northwest" and "North Hakka," respectively.

[57] See, Jerry Norman, Chinese, (New York: Cambridge University Press, 1993), (Cambridge Language Surveys) p. 136.

[58] Gwongsai is bisected into two distinct speech communities, with a diagonal line drawn from the southwest to the northeast. North of that line, Mandarin Chinese (*Putonghua*) is the chief speech form, and South of that line Cantonese speech prevails. The *Baak-wah* label in Gwongsai identified Cantonese-speaking people/areas.

[59] Note the *Baak-wah* zone is divided into Inner and Outer zones; See Vogel, One Step Ahead, p. 249 (re: Guangdong's new administrative Metropolitan Regions after 1988, which now occupy much of what I label as the two *Baak-wah* zones.)

[60] Re: data on each district's area by square kilometers and percentage of Gwongdung's total area see, Kuan, Local Population Statistical Tables, p.46–49. Re: data on each district's square miles, I computed on basis of 1 square kilometer=.386 square mile, (see note #41 above.)

[61] Ibid., pp. 46-49. Note that here I only list 19 counties, however in the nineteenth-century there were 21 counties.

[62] Shaan-wei formed in 1935 from three pre-existing counties, Ch'ao-ying, Yin-ning, and Hui-lai, see Kuan, Local Population Statistical Tables, p. 48.

[63] Chiu-tsim (Tsu-chin), see Kuan, Local Population Statistical Tables, p. 49. Kuan's data states that

the total area for this district as 946.50 square kilometers, or 365.34 square miles appears unrealistically low. In observing the size and shape of this district, relative to Ho-yuan district just north of Chiu-tsim, the two seem similar in size, with the latter a bit smaller. The figures of 4,000 square kilometers, or 1,544 square miles is my own rough estimation reflecting this concern.

[64] The interior hinterland, which embraced both Metropolitan Canton and the Pearl River Delta in an arc-like pattern, I identify as the *Baak-wah* zone. It embraced Canton and the Delta area, with the sea on one side to the south, and the *Baak-wah* zone on the other to the north. Additionally, I have included some areas north of Skinner's West Central and Central into my designated area of the *Baak-wah* zone.

[65] Much of what I have to say here is intended to suggest avenues of thinking about possible ethno-speech and socio-cultural differences. My observations should not be regarded as the product of any field work or investigation of the work of others. I readily admit that my research interests and focus lie elsewhere, i.e., the Pearl River Delta region. My comments are based on my own thinking and are in most cases reflective of a rational inference based on my own reading of general conditions and are intended to merely provide a general, "most likely" descriptive frame of reference for discussion purposes only.

[66] Edward J.M. Rhoads, China's Republican Revolution, the Case of Kwangtung, 1895–1913, (Cambridge, Mass: Harvard University Press, 1975), p. 12; also see the following works, Hsiang-lin Lo, Ke-chia yen-chiu tao-lun (Introductory Research on the Hakkas) (Toishan: Shi shan Library, 1933);Wolfram Eberhard, The Local Cultures of South and East China, (Leiden: E.J. Brill, 1968);also see, Weiwen Zhang and Qingnan, In Search of China's Minorities, (Beijing: New World Press, 1993), pp. 282–296, 313–319; also see Chinese Historical Micro-Demography, edited by Stevan Harrell, (Berkeley: University of California Press, 1995).

[67] See demographic, table 1.13 "Aggregate Population Estimates for Nineteenth-Century Central Gwongdung, by micro-region, 1840–1900." See especially lines/rows labeled as Inner and Outer *Baak-wah* zone respectively, e.g., for year 1870, Inner *Baak-wah* zone estimated total population of 3.75 Million, and Outer *Baak-wah* zone estimated population of 5.8 million, for a total *Baak-wah* zone estimated population of 9.55 million. For that same year, the estimated population for the outer mountainous or non-*yuet* Cantonese peripheral areas was about 2.64 million. This illustrates that the estimated population of the outer mountainous areas was about 27% or just over 25% of that of the *Baak-wah* zone. This pattern remained generally consistent for the period 1840–1900

[68] Kuan, Local Population Statistical Tables, pp.46–49.

[69] Note: The aggregate totals offered here are the result of a "re-construction" of estimated figures, based on the statistical approaches formulated at the start of my investigation of both geographic and demographic data. There is an obvious discrepancy between these aggregate totals (i.e., 53,130.59 square miles) and the earlier aggregate figures of 41,00–49,200 square miles, based on the estimate that Nineteenth-Century Central Gwongdung was about 50%-60% of total square miles of the whole province of Gwongdung (i.e., 82,000 square miles). Again, the former is a "rough estimate" for illustrative purposes, and the latter is a "rough estimate" based on my own calculations, relative to a micro-regional investigation. In this context, I believe the latter estimates to be more demonstrative of "a pattern or sequence" that is more relevant, if not more accurate, to the discussion at hand. Both estimates underscore the inherent challenge of estimating both total and sub-total population estimates for nineteenth-century Chinese population figures. I accept the general estimate that Central Gwongdung constituted about roughly 50,000 square miles of Gwongdung's total land mass. Given a possible range from about 49,200 for my earlier estimates to the current estimated total of 53.130 sq. miles, then the general figure of about 50,000 is not an unreasonable estimated average.

[70] Gwongdung's total area in the nineteenth-century was actually 81,834 square miles, this figure has been calculated from 212,005 square kilometers, with one kilometer equal to .386 square mile, thus 212,005 square kilometers equals about 81,834 square miles or almost 82,000 square miles.(see Ezra F. Vogel, One Step Ahead in China, Guangdong Under Reform, (Cambridge, Mass: Harvard University Press, 1989,) p.3; also see Cressy, Land of 500 Million, p. 38, re: Gwongdung size as 84,443 square miles; also see Companion to Chinese History, (New York: Facts on File, 1987,) p.153, re: Gwongdung has an area of 210,000 square kilometers or 81,000 square miles; also see Edward J.M. Rhoads, China's

Republican Revolution, The Case of Kuangtung, 1895–1913, (Cambridge, Mass: Harvard University Press, 1975), p.8,re: Gwongdung's total area is given as 85,000 square miles. Finally, also see http://www.citypopulation.de/China-Guangdong.html, re: Figure for total area of Guangdong (Gwongdung) in 2013 given as 197,100 kilometers (this does not include Hainan Island, because it became an independent province in 1988), thus Gwongdung now constitutes about 76,080 square miles.

[71] These figures are my own rough estimates

[72] Note two different estimated total square miles for Central Gwongdung, one a general estimate based on average estimated 40% to 60% of Gwongdung's total of 82,000 sq. miles (which ranges from 41,000 to 49,200 sq. miles)- which I round off for practical purposes, to represent a scale of magnitude, i.e., 50,000 sq. miles. The other figure here of 53,130 sq. miles is a total based on working estimates in tables 1.1 through 1.4. This total would equal about 106.26 % (given an estimated total average of 50,000 sq. miles= 100%)

[73] This 100% refers to the general estimate total of 50,000 sq. miles, while the other estimated total of 51,130 sq. miles is greater than 50,000, actually equals 106.26%). We can safely assume that it also fulfills the 100% criteria of 50,000 sq. miles

[74] *Chung-kuo chin-tai ching-chi shih t'ung-chi tzu-liao hsuan-chi* (Selected Compilation of Statistical Data of Modern Chinese Economic History), [hereafter cited as CSDMC] compiled by Yen Chung-p'ing, et. al., (Taipei, Taiwan: Ko Hsueh Publishing House, 1955), p. 362, p. 372. (note: most of Yen's data was obtained from *Hu pu* (Board of Revenue) records in successive reign periods from the *Qianlong (Chien-Lung)* period of the 1780's through the *Guangxu (Kuang-Hsu)* period of the late 1890's.

[75] See Douglas Lee, Facing Cantonese Adversity, Fleeing Tong-Shaan: Cantonese Society and the Root Causes of Nineteenth- Century Overseas emigration, as volume 3 of The Gum-Shaan Chronicles: The Early History of Cantonese-Chinese America, 1850-1900, (Pittsburgh, Pa: Dorrance Publishing, 2023), see chapter 7, "Bad Joss of communal conflict and social chaos"; also see chapter 8, "Bad joss of local Cantonese-Fan-Kwai conflicts."

[76] CSDMC., compiled by Yen, pp. 362-374.

[77] 30,000,000 is my own estimate, the actual aggregate figure was more likely over 30,000,000, e.g., 31,000,000– 32,000,000. My estimate is not intended to be accurate or precise, but merely to indicate an "order of magnitude" or "demonstrated pattern of development," consistent with other referenced population data in this table. See CSDMC, compiled by Yen, p. 374. The last entry for Gwongdung's population is for 1897 with 29.89 million. If the population grew at the rate of .7%, as it did since 1859, then the population most certainly reached 30 million in the last years of the nineteenth-century, and most likely slightly exceeded that figure in 1900.

[78] The Chaozhou community, also known as *Teochiu*, consisted of East Gwongdung's Min speaking communities in the Han River region around both Chaozhou and its adjacent port city of Shantou (Swatow,) supplied Teochiu emigrants to primarily Southeast Asian Overseas Chinese communities. Conversely, very few *Teochiu* migrated to North America. Small numbers did appear in Hawaii and elsewhere. In Canada and the United States, their numbers were so few as to be statistically insignificant, i.e., less than .1%.

[79] CSDMC., compiled by Yen, p. 374, the last entry for Gwongdung's population is 1897 with 29.89 million. If the population grew at the rate of .7%, as it did since 1859, then the population most certainly reached 30 million in the last years of the nineteenth-century, and most likely exceeded that figure slightly by 1900. Note, some authorities disagree with the 28.4 million for 1851, because it was essentially a bureaucratically inflated total. Given some adjustments, some would argue that the figure should be around 21.7 million. See, Dwight H. Perkins, Agricultural Development in China, 1368–1968, (Chicago: Aldine Publishing Company, 1969), p.214. For discussion purposes and consistency with figures for the rest of the nineteenth-century, I have chosen to rely on the earlier figure of 28.4 million. Perkins' observation, however is well taken and should be kept in mind.

[80] Van Der Sprenkel, Sybille, Legal Institutions in Manchu China, (London: University of London, Athlone Press, 1962), p. 41.

[81] Zhongguo Lishi ti tu ji, (Historical Atlas of China), edited by Tan Qixiang, vol. #8 The Qing Dynasty, (Shanghai: Cartographic Publishing House, 1987), pp.44–45 (Map of Qing period Gwongdung's tao

divisions, with table on back of p. 45; also see, Van Der Sprenkel, Legal Institutions in Manchu China, p. 40,(regarding the fact that the matter is complicated because some of both the larger *hsien* and smaller *fu* were (often) called *chou* or *ting* [municipalities], and thus while some *chou* and *ting* were independent of *fu*, and [some] *chou* might have [a] *hsien* dependent on them, other *chou* and *ting* were themselves dependent on *fu* and co-ordinate [or parallel] with *hsien*... For certain purposes another grouping of two or more *fu*, [formed] the *tao* (often translated as 'circuit') [which] was [sometimes] interposed between the *fu* and the province....). Note: in regards to how I label traditional districts/counties in Gwongdung, I adopt and use the term *xian* (*Pinyin* mandarin form), instead of *Yuen*, (the Cantonese form). This may appear to contradict my earlier expressed desire (see book preface) to be authentic and specific in the choice of how I Romanize Chinese terms which refer to Cantonese terms. In this case, the *Pinyin* form of *xian* is universally recognized and used in Chinese historical and social science literature as the common reference for district or county This of course includes Cantonese districts/counties. Consequently, for the sake of practicality, uniformity and consistency, I adhere to this common practice to avoid unnecessary confusion.

[82] Kung-Chuan Hsiao, Rural China, Imperial Control in the Nineteenth-Century, (Seattle: University of Washington Press, 1960), p. 5.

[83] See generally, G. William Skinner, "Regional Urbanization in Nineteenth-Century China, in The City in Late Imperial China, edited by G. William Skinner, (Stanford, Ca: Stanford University Press, 1977), pp.211–249, see especially note #4, p.708; also see Kuan, Local Population Statistical Tables ; also see John S. Aird, "Population Growth," in Economic Trends in Communist China, edited by Alexander Eckstein, (re: population 1851–1953, see pp. 247–265; also see, G. William Skinner, "Marketing and Social Structure in Rural China," in three parts. Part I, Journal of Asian Studies, 24:1, November 1964, pp. 3–43; part II, Journal of Asian Studies, 24:2, February, 1965, pp. 195–228; and Part III, Journal of Asian Studies, 24:3, May 1965, pp. 363–399.

[84] Skinner, "Marketing and Social Structure in Rural China," Part II, p. 208.

[85] Ibid., p.208.

[86] Ibid., p. 207 (note Skinner uses *Kwangtung* Wade-Giles, Mandarin transliteration, whereas I use *Gwongdung,* the Cantonese transliteration. I have also provided density per square mile figures, in addition to Skinner's density per square kilometer data, (1 kilometer=.386 square mile) and deleted Skinner's data on average village-to-market ratios. Note those areas which I include as part of my notion of "Central Gwongdung"

[87] Hsiao, Rural China, Imperial Control, p. 5., see note 5.

[88] In regards to the number of counties/districts in Nineteenth-Century Central Gwongdung, there have been other alternative estimations. In the case of metropolitan Canton, some say there were two (Namhoi and Punyu), others say there were three (Namhoi, Punyu, and Shunak). Another view is that there were 19 counties/districts in the Pearl River Delta and part of the Inner *Baak-wah* zone. See Chinn, Lai &. Choy, Chinese in California, p. 24; for most of the *Baak-wah* zone, about 28 counties, see Volgel, One Step Ahead, p.4, Map of Guangdong's counties in 1984. The number 28 is an estimate, it is less precise than those given for Metropolitan Canton and the Pearl River Delta, because of changes in the number of counties, their borders/designations since the nineteenth-century, and also because my conceptualization of the *Baak-wah* zone, and what it embraces, is somewhat arbitrary for discussion purposes.

[89] While I mention the two adjacent rural counties (Namhoi and Panyu) as part of Metropolitan Canton, I do not include them in the total number of counties for Central Gwongdung, because they are already accounted for in the Pearl River Delta regional totals. In the aggregate population totals for Central Gwongdung, I purposely do not include any computations for Metropolitan Canton. I only include the other four micro-region's rural counties.

[90] Ping-ti Ho, Studies on the Population of China,1368–1953, (Cambridge, Mass: 1959), p. 52.

[91] CSDMC, compiled by Yen, pp. 362–374.

[92] Re: telephone conversation with Skinner 5-6-1997. Skinner did not explain why he believed that the 1940 figures should be viewed as being more realistically reflective of the period around 1900.

[93] Letter from Skinner, 4 June 1997.

⁹⁴ CSDMC, compiled by Yen, pp. 362–374.
⁹⁵ The 1840 figures are 8% (or.08) of the 1850 figures, this rate of growth is also demonstrated in data found in CSDMC, compiled by Yen, pp. 362–374.
⁹⁶ The 1850 figures are 8% (or.08) of the 1860 figures, this rate of growth is demonstrated in data found in CSDMC, compiled by Yen, pp. 362–374.
⁹⁷ The 1860 figures are .7% (or.007) of the 1870 figures, this rate of growth is demonstrated in data found in CSDMC, compiled by Yen, pp. 362–374.
⁹⁸ The 1870 figures are .7% (or.007) of the 1880 figures, this rate of growth is demonstrated in data found in CSDMC, compiled by Yen, pp. 362–374.
⁹⁹ The 1880 figures are .7% (or.007) of the 1890 figures, this rate of growth is demonstrated in data found in CSDMC, compiled by Yen, pp. 362–374.
¹⁰⁰ The 1890 figures are 5% (or.05)of the 1900 figures, as per suggestion of Skinner. (letter from G.W. Skinner, Anthropology Dept. UC Davis, dated June 4, 1997)
¹⁰¹ Kuan, Statistical Tables, pp.46–50. Skinner suggests that while these figures are for the early 1940s, they are most likely too inflated, given the reliability of the 1953 Communist Chinese census, then one would have to conclude that the population doubled in the decade or less between 1944–1953, which was/is not possible. Skinner further hypothesizes that these figures are more representative of the period around 1900. I have used these figures as a "baseline" for my analysis of nineteenth-century figures, where I have worked backwards, using known or plausible rates of growth by decade, and subtracting the difference. (letter from G.W. Skinner, Anthropology Dept. UC Davis, dated June 4, 1997)
¹⁰² See note #95.
¹⁰³ See note #96.
¹⁰⁴ See note #97.
¹⁰⁵ See note #98.
¹⁰⁶ See note #99.
¹⁰⁷ See note #100.
¹⁰⁸ See note #101.
¹⁰⁹ See note #95.
¹¹⁰ See note #96.
¹¹¹ See note #97.
¹¹² See note #98.
¹¹³ See note #99.
¹¹⁴ See note #100.
¹¹⁵ See note #101.
¹¹⁶ Note the following discrepancy between two tables referencing the Outer *Baak-wah* zone. This discrepancy involves the lack of identical listings of rural counties in table 1.3 and table 1.11 respectively. In table 1.3 the first district listed is Shaan-wei, but it is not listed subsequently in table 1.11. Additionally, table 1.11 first lists the three countiesof Cho-yeung, Yin-ning, and Wui-loy respectively, but these counties are not listed in table 1.3. In table 1.11, these 3 counties have been indicated with an asterisk*.This discrepancy exists because Shaan-wei was formed in 1935 by combining the three pre-existing counties of Ch'ao-ying, Yin-ning, and Hui-lai, see Kuan, Local Population Statistical Tables, p. 48.
¹¹⁷ See note #95.
¹¹⁸ See note #96.
¹¹⁹ See note #97.
¹²⁰ See note #98.
¹²¹ See note #99.
¹²² See note #100.
¹²³ See note #101.
¹²⁴ Totals are taken from tables 1.9 through 1.12
¹²⁵ See Table 1.9, line 13, bottom line, table on "Estimate of nineteenth-century Pearl River Delta Region Population in Central Gwongdung, 1840–1900."

126 See Table 1.10, line 15, bottom line, table on "Estimate of nineteenth-century Inner *Baak-wah* Zone Population in Central Gwongdung, 1840–1900."

127 See Table, 1.11, line 22, bottom line, table on "Estimate of nineteenth-century Outer *Baak-wah* Zone Population in Central Gwongdung, 1840–1900."

128 See Table 1.12, line 16, bottom line, table on "Estimate of Nineteenth-Century Non-*Yuet*/Cantonese Peripheral area Population in Central Gwongdung, 1840–1900."

129 See, CSDMC compiled by Yen, pp. 362–374.

130 My reference here to the significant place and role of Cantonese overseas emigrants for later nineteenth-century Cantonese demographic issues, however brief, is intended to draw attention to their vital role in the present discussion. For a more comprehensive and detailed discussion of these matters, see Facing Cantonese Adversity, Fleeing Tong-Shaan, Cantonese society and the Root Causes of 19th century Overseas Emigration, as volume 3 of the Gum-Shaan Chronicles, see especially Chapter 5, "Bad Joss of High-density Population Concentration and Over-Population, i.e., section entitled, "Cantonese overseas emigration and its relationship with the problem of rural high-density population concentration and over-population, see especially Table 1.12 and Table 1.13.

131 The *Lingnnam* region refers to an historical area which has traditionally included both Gwongdung and neighboring Gwongsai (Guangxi) province. In the Qing period this was also known as the *Liang-Kwang*. The former denotes a classical ascriptive historical and cultural label, whereas the latter denotes a historical administrative term.

132 See Lee, Facing Cantonese Adversity, Fleeing Tong-Shaan: Cantonese Society and the Root Causes of Nineteenth-Century Overseas Emigration, see especially chapter 5, "Bad Joss in High Density Population Concentration and Over-Population."

133 See the following, History of the Chinese in California, eds. Chinn, Lai, and. Choy, see table V, "Chinese in California by District of Origin, page. 20. It is most likely that the Hakka in 19th century America came from *bundae* (*bendi*)(*punti*) area of the Pearl River Delta region and not from *Hakka* homelands in N.E. Gwongdung, as a result of *Hakka* defeat in the *Hakka-B*undae wars of the mid-19th century, see, J.A.G. Roberts, "The Hakka-Punti [*bundae*,] [*bendi*] War," PhD dissertation., Oxford University, Queen's College, 1968, pp.104–122, 212–225.; also see "Political Development in Chinese America, 1850–1900," by Douglas W. Lee, (PhD dissertation in History University of California, Santa Barbara, 1989), see pp.154–179.

134 Earlier cited figure range 41,000–49,200 square miles suggested a relative size. This figure of 53,000 square miles represents the aggregate total of square miles derived from totaling sub-totals of my earlier calculations.

135 Note: data for this table has been taken from earlier referenced tables 1.9 through 1.13 in this chapter, computations as percent values are my own, based on data drawn from these several tables.

136 Note: Land mass totals (in square miles) for Gwongdung Province, Central Gwongdung, the Cantonese core area, and the Pearl River Delta Region remained generally consistent in the nineteenth-century.

137 See table 1.5, The figure of 53,000 is derived by adding the total area in square miles of Metropolitan Canton, The Pearl River Delta, the Inner and Outer *Baak-wah* zones, and the non-*Yuet* Cantonese peripheral area. Earlier in this chapter, the area for Central Gwongdung was stated as ranging between 41,000 to 49,200 square miles, this range is only approximate. Earlier, I advocated using the 50,000 sq. miles figure as a practical representation for the total sq. miles of Central Gwongdung. Here, for discussion purposes however, I have chosen the larger figure (53,000), to reflect the sum of all the micro-sub regions of Central Gwongdung.

138 See table 1.5.

139 Ibid.,

140 figure for 1900 is my own estimate, see table 1.6

141 See table 1.13

142 Ibid.,

143 Ibid.,

# CHAPTER 2
## The Cornerstone of Cantonese Identity:
## Y*uet* Language and Cantonese Speech

**Introduction**

The most distinctive identifying feature of nineteenth-century Cantonese society/culture was its *Yuet* (*Yue*) (*Yueh*) language, and Cantonese dialect/speech component.[1] It represented the strongest and most durable bonding agent supporting Cantonese solidarity and unity. Whenever and wherever Cantonese people gathered, whether at home in *Tong-Shaan* (Central Gwongdung) or overseas in *Gum-Shaan* (America) and elsewhere, one of the most cherished self-identifications, which they cared most about, was their language and speech. Cantonese people always relished conversing with fellow Cantonese, because their shared speech not only allowed them to talk freely, it also provided an effective protective barrier against compromising exposure and unwarranted intrusion by non-Cantonese speakers, such as other Chinese, and especially foreigners.

Beyond the immediate benefit of easy communication, Cantonese speakers delighted in using their speech in creative ways to express a multitude of interests and wide range of concerns. In this manner, only another Cantonese speaker could fully understand, truly appreciate, and enjoy the speech of a fellow Cantonese. Behind mere words and phrases, there existed a rich store of loaded references, veiled connotations, nuanced commentary, and multiple meanings. Additionally, apart from the immediate challenge of being unintelligible for other Chinese, to say nothing of foreigners, Cantonese speech required a complicated navigation through a communication minefield littered with Cantonese idiomatic words and phrases, puns, esoteric euphemisms, cultural signposts, historical references, local vernacular speech forms, and "insider" jokes and riddles. All of these elements underscored a deep love and great respect for Cantonese speech, to the extent that it functioned more than a mere medium for conversation. It also served as an empowering means of showcasing one's ethno-cultural identity, by underscoring a fundamental and enduring commonality among Cantonese people. In this sense, Cantonese speech, more than any other collective identifying characteristic, represented the very essence of what it meant to be Cantonese in Nineteenth-Century China and America.

**Distinguishing "language," "dialect," and "speech"**

My use of the terms "Cantonese language," "Cantonese dialect," and "Cantonese speech," is intended, as a practical matter, to simplify discussing the complex technical subject of Cantonese speech. Using these terms interchangeably, and in multiple combinations (e.g., language/dialect,) mirrors two immediate concerns. First, there is the effort to "cover all bases," relative to flexibly using composite terms (e.g., language/speech) to represent a full range of applicability to various references, situations, and relationships respectively. Second, the terms "language," "dialect," and "speech" do not function alone in an isolated linguistic bubble. They often operate within expanded frames of reference e.g., historical, political, social, cultural, geographic and ethnic contexts.

While their interchangeability represents an effort to "tidy up loose ends," by adopting a series of paired terms, we should not however, forget that each of these terms has its own technical meaning and specific use. Consequently, when these terms are used individually, their meaning and reference should be clear and unambiguous. In this manner, "language" technically means,

> a system that consists of the development, acquisition, maintenance and use of complex systems of communication, particularly the human ability to do so; a language is any specific example of such a system…[it]…refers to the cognitive ability to learn and use systems of complex communication… language also has many social and cultural uses, such as signifying group identity, social stratification… [and group solidarity and unity.][2]

The term "dialect," can be altogether different in meaning and use from "language." The distinctions about how it is defined, used, and understood are complex and convoluted, when considered in the broader context of "language." There are two different views about "dialects."

> One usage refers to a variety of a language that is a characteristic of a particular group of the language's speakers... dialects or varieties of a particular language are closely related and, despite their differences, are...close to one another on the dialect continuum. The term is applied most often to regional speech patterns, but a dialect may also be defined by other factors, such as social class or ethnicity... dialects... [are] often arbitrary and based on social, political, cultural, or historical considerations... A dialect is distinguished by its vocabulary, grammar, and pronunciation (phonology, including prosody). Where a distinction can be made only in terms of pronunciation... the term accent may be preferred over dialect. [3]

> The other usage of the term "dialect," specific to colloquial settings in [some] countries like Italy [or China] carries a pejorative undertone and underlines the socially subordinated status of a language [i.e., dialect] ... to the standard language but not actually derived *from* the standard language. In other words, it is not an actual variety of the "standard language" or dominant language, but rather a separate, independently evolved but often related language... under this usage, the "dialects" subordinate to the standard language are generally not variations on the standard language but rather separate languages in and of themselves. [4]

In the context of this book, reference to a "Cantonese dialect" can mean either one of the two explanations offered above. Clarification as to which meaning/use is referenced in any part of this book is contextual, which makes clear whether "dialect" is used to either represent a sub-unit of a language, (i.e., Cantonese as a regional dialect of Chinese) or an independent language (i.e., *Yuet*/Cantonese as an identifiable separate, but related language to Chinese.)

Similarly, the term "speech" has a distinct and separate connotation from both "language" and "dialect."

> "Speech" is human vocal communication using language. Each language uses phonetic combinations of vowel and consonant sounds that form the sound of its words ... and [then] using those words in ... a sentence. In speaking, speakers... use enunciation, intonation, degrees of loudness, tempo, and other non-representational or paralinguistic aspects of vocalization to convey meaning. In their speech, speakers also unintentionally communicate many aspects of their social position such as [their] sex, age, place of origin [and ethnicity] (through accent) ...Speech compares with written language which may differ in its vocabulary, syntax, and phonetics from the spoken language...[5]

Again, I often use these terms as paired items, e.g., language/dialect, or dialect/speech, which underscores their interchangeability in a general frame of reference. When I use any of these terms alone, they are used in the context of their technical meanings/connotations, relative to a particular meaning and precise representation, as just noted above. When I use them interchangeably, however, I refer to the common communication system, by which Cantonese people communicated with each other, either in speaking or writing. In the context of this chapter, and more generally in this book, my use of these terms, typically references primarily Cantonese speech, and only secondarily references Cantonese writing, e.g., anachronistic Medieval Tang Chinese characters, or Cantonese Chinese characters found nowhere else in written Chinese.

## Chinese dialects/speech in the historical development of the (Han) Chinese language

Two separate historical patterns of language development occurred in ancient China. First, there developed a national literary standard (e.g., literary or classical Chinese;) and common spoken medium or *koine* (i.e., the common dialect.) [6] Second, regional vernacular speech forms persisted, and further evolved into regional languages/dialects.[7]

> Dialect fulfilled additional functions in southern China. Beyond serving as an indicator of variance in language it helped balance such diverse tensions as cultural iconoclasm, ethnic chauvinism, and speech-territorial exclusiveness. The dialect brought together…diverse elements, thereby reducing… societal tensions, which sprang from the contradictory need to adhere to universal constructs of Chinese culture, while at the same time provide for its localized expression.[8]

Increasingly from the Tang period (7th–10th centuries CE) onwards, there developed a high degree of diversity among local vernacular speech forms, in contrast to an earlier established uniformity and unity of the Chinese written language. The nature and relationship between a *koine*, i.e., common speech medium, and regional vernacular speech has been difficult to decipher. One way to better grasp this problem is to recognize that there were degrees of commonality, as well as differences, within Han Chinese languages, and between Han Chinese dialects. The constructs of *Yuet*/Cantonese language/dialects serve as a useful case study, with regard to these matters.

The Han Chinese language exhibits a number of common typological features, which are evident among its several regional dialects, such as *Yuet*/Cantonese. These include: 1) a monosyllabic speech construction, where the great majority of words are typically represented by a single syllable, but which are usually used in a paired/two-character (term) format, as in the case of English, e.g., "in" and "to" when combined to form "into"; 2) a tonal based speech system, where each syllable is characterized by a fixed pitch pattern. A pitch movement may be level (neither rising nor falling), or it may be a contour (rising or falling, or a combination of the two). Additionally, tone(s) also include references to length and loudness, as well as pitch and contour. The use of Chinese tones serves to differentiate meaning, e.g., the same monosyllabic item, such as "ma" can represent different things, as indicated by the tone used, e.g., "horse," or "mother" (both are pronounced as "ma" but in different tones); 3) an isolating or analytic language, where Chinese words are usually closely linked with its morpheme (a word or partial word,) as in an affix. Chinese dialects have very few quasi-suffixes that function as grammatical determinatives. Instead, grammatical relationships are indicated by either word order or independent grammatical particles, rather than by affixes or internal changes in the word itself. Only a single consonant is allowed at the beginning of a syllable (which is purely a phonetic characteristic and not related to morphology);[9] 4) a common syntactic device using measures (or classifiers of things) with numbers and determinatives, e.g., *saam-ko-yan* (*san-ge ren)*, (i.e., three measure(s) of people/men, instead in English, "three people/men"; 5) an established grammatical word order of SOV (subject, object, verb.) Languages to the south and southeast of China predominantly follow the SOV pattern. In contrast, Northern Chinese speakers and Altaic language speakers, e.g., Korean, Japanese, Mongolian, typically place the adjective before the noun it refers to.[10]

> Few language names are as all-encompassing as that of Chinese. It is made to serve at once [many purposes] …This creates a certain awkwardness when one wants to speak about one of the varieties of Chinese; if ambiguity is to be avoided, it is necessary to employ a complex designation of some sort…(e.g.) in the case of a modern dialect, a geographical designation like Shanghai or Fuzhou dialect… After all, the modern Chinese dialects are really more like a family of languages… [11]

## The Developmental pattern of *Yuet* (*Yue*) dialect(s)/speech forms[12]

The most common understanding of what constitutes a dialect is that linguistically speaking, it is not a separate language, but rather an integral sub-component of an existing language, (i.e., see above, the first of two definitions of "dialect.") Its chief characteristic, which distinguishes it from others within a given language, is one of phonology, or pronunciation of the spoken word. The Chinese language is world renowned for its many dialects and regional/local speech forms, largely because many are mutually unintelligible, whereby the same written Chinese characters are often pronounced so differently, that speakers of different dialects sound as though they are speaking entirely different languages. Again, the fact that the written medium for nearly all Han Chinese dialects is identical, (with exceptions in both *Yuet* and *Min* dialects,) has helped to preserve the integrity of the Chinese language for thousands of years, while providing for the maintenance of scores of separate major speech communities in China, most of which are located in Southern China. [13]

> Traditionally, the accepted classification of the Chinese language ... [is its division] into dialect groups, which can be further subdivided, is based on phonological distinctions as the fundamental criterion. The pattern revealed by modem reflexes of the various dialects in comparison to ancient phonological categories serves as the principal means of delineating the major dialect groups. Other distinctions based on grammatical and lexical differences complement the primary one of phonology.[14]

Chinese dialects and local speech communities have come to be identified, over the course of time, with a particular geographical region and group of people. This results from the historic patterns of migration and settlement of Chinese settlers from North China to South China over the course of thousands of years. This has resulted in a highly diverse "dialect geography" in southern China, where Chinese dialects have been especially numerous and diverse.

Chapter 2

Historically and mechanically speaking, the origin and development of Han Chinese dialects/speech variants has resulted from the juxtaposition of key geo-historical and geo-demographic determinants. In South China, such geophysical/typological features as rugged terrain, with "pockets" of nestled valleys, cradled by mountainous spurs, together with interspersed sequential movement of groups of people, who migrated vast distances, then settled down for several generations, with later generations subsequently migrating elsewhere and relocating again. This prolonged process sculptured a fractured landscape of fragmented speech groups distributed all across South China, as regional dialects and local speech communities.[15]

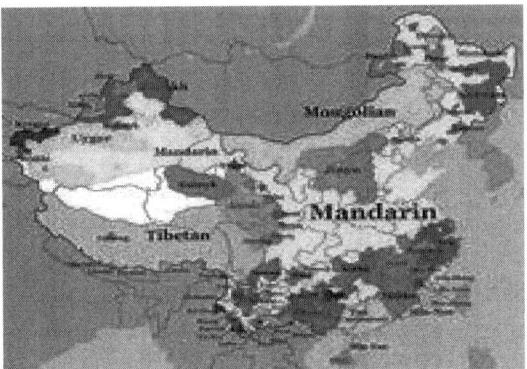

**Map of languages and Dialects spoken in China**

Historically, the *Yuet* linguistic pattern in Gwongdung resulted from changes associated with the settlement of successive waves of Han Chinese migrants from northern and central China, and their subsequent linguistic accommodation/synthesis with pre-existing local speech units.[16] In this context, during the millennium between the Han and Tang, (second century BCE to the tenth century CE,) non-Chinese language/culture influenced the nature of Han Chinese discourse in the *Lingnam* region.[17]

Y*uet*/Cantonese language/speech likely originated in very remote antiquity (around the third-second millennium BCE.) Specifically, the distant origin of *Yuet*/Cantonese language/speech can be traced back to local *Tai* peoples and their language, who were among the earliest people to inhabit significant portions of southern China and peninsular Southeast Asia. Today, *Tai* people form the majority of non-Chinese people in South China. Many millions are nearly invisible (with four exceptions, i.e., the *Dai* in Yunnan and the *Li* on Hainan Island, and the *Zhuang* and *Buyi* in Southwest China) because most have been culturally assimilated over time into Han Chinese society and culture. Most are bilingual in both the *Tai* language(s) and local Chinese dialects.

The major feature distinguishing and separating *Tai* people from local Han Chinese people is their language, which while similar sounding with southern Chinese speech/dialects, is in fact a distinct and separate language. Interestingly, it is estimated that about 60% of the Cantonese population is descended from an original aboriginal *Tai*-speaking population.[18] This results in an interesting historical pre-condition, where Cantonese people/speech are identifiably distinct from other Han Chinese and their speech.

The *Tai* base of the *Yuet*/Cantonese language did not survive in tact over the course of two millennia. While it began like a small isolated stream from remote non-Han Chinese origins, it subsequently flowed along as a tributary, where it further evolved by merging with other rivers of different varieties of the Chinese language. This process involved the juxtaposition of local *Yuet* speech with other Chinese speech communities, in the context of Chinese migrations and settlement. The trajectory of this process took place over the course of two millennia (Han-Qing periods 200 BCE-1800 C,) where Chinese migrations and settlement occurred in a generally southern direction, moving from North and Central China southwards, ending either at the sea or at the borders of Southeast Asia.[19]

The influence of the earlier *Tai* peoples and culture was especially critical in laying the foundations of the *Yuet* dialect(s) and culture Gwongdung. In the next millennium, between the Tang and Qing dynasties (10th-19th centuries CE,) Chinese language in Central Gwongdung became increasingly distinct, as different linguistic elements were deleted and others added. This process involved the blending of archaic Chinese of the pre-Tang period, with previously incorporated non-Han Chinese elements (e.g., *Tai*), together with newer forms of Chinese brought south to Gwongdung by successive waves of Chinese from North and Central China over the course of several centuries.

Gwongdung's Cantonese, *Hakka,* and Chaozhou dialects, all reflect Chinese speech forms from different periods in Chinese History, from different parts of China, as they have taken root and flourished in different parts of Gwongdung. They also reflect a shared experience in an evolving ancient southern Chinese experience.

> To sum up…present-day dialects spoken south of the Yangtze are the result of successive accretions of Northern elements over an old Southern Chinese base … in the mountainous regions of Fujian and Guangdong (Gwongdung), the Old Southern Chinese element has survived to a greater degree….[20]

This resulted in a rich mosaic of different and diverse speech communities, widely distributed across the southern Chinese landscape, with each one dating its arrival and settlement in a given locality at different points in time. Significantly, settlement patterns, in conjunction with the specificity of a particular geophysical setting, helped to nurture the development of regional languages/dialects, which in turn fostered the development of many different local speech communities. The common denominator of these regional languages/dialects is that they were all identifiably Han Chinese in their historical development and structural components, although each arrived, and developed as a regional language in different time periods. Each one also embodied different variants of the Chinese language, many with infusions of local non-Han Chinese (e.g., aboriginal peoples) language(s). In this manner, *Yuet* dialect/speech emerged as a major unified autonomous language in Gwongdung, on a par with the *Min* in Fujian, and the *Wu* in Jiangsu and Zhejiang. Interestingly, three of South China's seven major dialects, i.e., *Yuet* (*Yue*), *Hakka*, and *Min* (e.g., *Chaozho*u or *Teochiu*) became well-established and widespread within Gwongdung.[21]

Since Tang times, the *Yuet*/Cantonese language monopolized most of Gwongdung, to the extent that it was widely regarded as being the speech of Gwongdung, i.e., *Gwongdung wah,* or "*Gwongdungese.*" "Th[is] mixture of native and immigrant in Guangdong [Gwongdung] must have reached a critical mass of acculturation during the Tang dynasty." [22] In the millennium from the Tang to the later Qing (800–1800 CE) *Yuet*/Cantonese speech continued to evolve further.

> Cantonese is…more than a widely spoken dialect. It is a genuine regional standard. In Guangdong [Gwongdung] province, even people whose home language is not Yue [*Yuet*], including some national minorities, whose home language is not even Han Chinese, use it and respect it as a model for speech. No other Southern dialect…has this kind of stature.[23]

In this sense, *Yuet*/Cantonese speech became like a distributary, flowing off on its own from the main concourse of Chinese language, as a separate, but related, component of Han Chinese speech/language, in the form of a regional language/dialect and speech community. This ability of Cantonese society to preserve and maintain *Yuet*/Cantonese speech for over a millennium, (8th- 21st centuries), as a separate major regional language/dialect has been the chief determinant of the enduring distinctiveness of *Yuet*/Cantonese language and culture. *Yuet*/Cantonese speech, so much beloved by Cantonese people, stood out because of its atypical linguistic structural elements, which in turn bolstered *Yuet*/Cantonese ethnic group identity.

Prior to the Han Dynasty (2nd century BCE to 2nd century CE) there was little distinction between speech and written forms, but from the Han period onwards, there developed a schism between the written literary standard and a variety of vernacular speech forms- which became quite varied and extreme by the Qing period (1644–1911 CE).[24] In this light, one of the chief characteristics of the *Yuet* language(s)/dialects is that it has conservatively maintained a consistency in both its speech and written forms via its adherence to the distant constructs of "Middle Chinese" of the Tang period (618–907 CE). [25]

## Distinguishing between "*Yuet*" (*Yue*) and "Cantonese"

A source of confusion about how Cantonese people are identified, and the ambiguity about how their language is categorized, results from unfamiliarity with the identifying labels used to accomplish this task. Even among linguists, there exists a lack of clarity because of degrees of uncertainty, as to how these labels might apply.[26] This is especially so in the case of the two terms "Cantonese" and "*Yuet*" (*Yue*) (*Yueh*).

The term "Cantonese" is the better-known of the two terms, although no less confusing in its usage. The term *Gwong-chau* (*Guangzhou*) (廣州) is the Chinese name for the capital of Gwongdung (Guangdong) province, which in its anglicized form is "Canton."[27] In both the popular mind and linguistically-speaking, the term "Cantonese" refers specifically to the speech of the city of Canton (*Gwong-chau wah*) (廣州話) (or Cantonese speech.) "Cantonese," which is sometimes used interchangeably with *Yuet*, should be reserved for the dialect of the city of *Guangzhou* (Canton), and not be regarded as a general categorical term.[28]

In this regard, Cantonese speech (the speech of Canton) has long been recognized as the preeminent variety of the *Yuet* languages/dialects. In this more limited context, Cantonese, as the speech of Canton, has been described variously as: the "prestige or standard [Cantonese] language," the "standard dialect," or simply as "standard Cantonese."[29] It has also been referred to as "Cantonese-Cantonese," "regular Cantonese," or "Cantonese proper." It has been recognized as the primary variant of Cantonese, within the recognized varieties or categories of the *Yuet* languages/dialects. It is the most widely spoken *Yuet* dialect.[30] "Among the *Yuet* people, the dialect of Canton has enjoyed prestige for centuries…[it] has no local rivals."[31] The term *Gwong-foo wah* (*Guangfuhua*) (i.e. speech of the Canton prefecture, or in modern terms, the speech of Metropolitan or Municipal Canton) represents the idea that the speech of Canton has been regarded as the "core standard Cantonese."[32] Identified as "Cantonese proper," it is spoken throughout the Cantonese heartland, which includes Canton, Hong Kong, Macau, the Pearl River Delta Region, Chung-Shaan (Zhongshan), Fatshaan (Foshan), Dongguan, Zhuhai, Shenzhen, in the southern parts of Zhaoqing, Qingyuan, and in parts of Guangxi (Gwongsai), e.g., Wuzhou.[33]

We should remember that while the phrase *Gwongdung wah* (廣東話) (i.e., "*Gwongdungese*") is well-known and has served as a common surrogate for "Cantonese," there is actually no such thing as *Gwongdung-wah* or "*Gwongdungese*," i.e., the "speech of Gwongdung province." In this context, *Gwongdung wah* (廣東話) (i.e., the speech of Gwongdung Province) is meant to represent, to refer to, or be synonymous with *Gwong-chau wah* (which again literally means "Cantonese" speech, or the speech of Canton.) The singular importance of "Cantonese speech" or *Gwong-chau wah* (廣州話) is not confined exclusively to matters of speech or dialect, but is also evident in other culturally related areas, such as in the development of Gwongdung's traditional regional opera.

Historically, Cantonese regional opera was known as *yueh-chu* (*yuezhu*), not to be confused with *shao-hsing* opera, also known as *yueh-chu* (*yuezhu*), but written with different characters.[34] Generally speaking, Cantonese regional opera was performed in the "Cantonese dialect," i.e., *Gwong-chau wah* in most areas of Gwongdung, but in especially Central Gwongdung.[35] There existed, however, two other forms of regional Cantonese opera, where other speech forms/dialects were used instead of standard Cantonese. Indeed, the speech forms utilized were not even *Yuet* (*Yue*) dialects at all. These two other varieties of Cantonese regional opera included: 1) *Teochiu* (in the *Min* dialect of East Gwongdung) (*Ch'ao Chou* in standard Cantonese) (*Chaozhou* in Mandarin Chinese) opera, which originated in Swatow (Shantou) in East Gwongdung. The second example of non-Cantonese Cantonese regional opera is that of *Wai Chow* (*Wai-chau*) (*Waizhou*) opera, referred to in Hong Kong as "*Hoklo*" opera, because it was performed in the *Hokiken* dialect, the chief Southern *Min* dialect of Fukien (Fujian) province.[36]

This historical development mirrored a mixed picture regarding traditional Cantonese regional opera, where there co-existed non-Cantonese variant speech forms (i.e., *Swatow* and *Hoklo,* both of which were *Min* based speech/dialects) in the performance of what is broadly described as traditional "Cantonese regional opera." This anomaly can be explained, again, by appreciating the fact that "Cantonese" and "Gwongdung" have often been confused in their use and ascribed meanings. Here the general collective label of a "Cantonese regional opera" presumably refers to the general entity of a regional opera "in" and "for" Gwongdung, especially Central Gwongdung- where the

Cantonese speech/dialect is the largest and most widespread *Yuet* (*Yue*) speech form or dialect. Thus, the fact that non-Cantonese speech forms, indeed non-*Yuet* (*Yue*) forms, are used in the performance of both Swatow opera and Wai Chow opera is of little significance, and even less consequence. Because both of these varieties of "Cantonese regional opera" were performed in Gwongdung, and have been regarded as bona fide varieties of "Cantonese regional opera."

We should remember that there existed an important difference between Gwongdung's "Cantonese sense of linguistic exclusiveness," and its contrasting sense of "Cantonese ethno-cultural inclusiveness." Cantonese speech, by its nature, excluded non-*Yuet* Cantonese dialects and speech communities; but as an ethnolinguistic based cultural entity, it was inclusive, by way of embracing non-*Yuet* non-Cantonese speech communities within Gwongdung, as referenced above in regarding Swatow (Shantou) and Wai Chow (Waizhou).[37] These distinctions and anomalies underscore the complex and nuanced relationship among dialects and variant speech forms in *Yuet*/Cantonese Gwongdung.

There is some logic behind this confusion, regarding the use of the provincial name of "Gwongdung" (Guangdong) to serve as a surrogate for *Gwong-chau wah* or the speech of Canton. First, there is the obvious centrality of Canton, and by extension the prominence of its people and speech, as being the dominant linguistic, ethnic, and cultural force throughout Gwongdung (with the exception of *Min* speaking portions of both East and West Gwongdung). Second, Because Canton has been the social and cultural epicenter of *Yuet* (*Yue*) dominated Gwongdung province, as well as its geopolitical and economic center, it is not unreasonable to think and talk about it ascriptively, as the epitome (i.e., linguistically, culturally, and ethnically) of all things "Cantonese" in Gwongdung, especially in Central Gwongdung. Third, the use of "Gwongdung," as in *Gwongdung-wah* (*Guangdonghua*) (i.e., *Gwongdungese* or *Guangdongese)* underscores both the theoretical and geo-linguistic nexus between Canton, i.e., things Cantonese (such as speech and culture) and Gwongdung. Thus, there is a kind of rational basis for the somewhat confusing use of *Gwongdung wah* (speech of Gwongdung or "Gwongdungese") to actually mean "Cantonese" (or *Gwong-chau wah*, the speech of Canton.) Consequently, it is always understood, both among Cantonese speakers and non-Cantonese speakers (e.g., other Chinese) that when one is asked whether or not one speaks *Gwongdung wah* ("*Gwongdungese*") or the speech of Gwongdung, one is very clearly asking whether or not one speaks the Cantonese dialect (i.e., the speech of Canton).

The term "*Yuet*" (*Yue*) (*Yueh*) (粵) is most visible and commonly used in public as a graphic symbol for things Cantonese. The *Yuet* character (粵) is a common indicator for things Cantonese, e.g., in newspaper section headings, regarding news items pertaining to Gwongdung, Canton, Cantonese people, and Cantonese news, in social media, in entertainment (e.g., Cantonese films, Cantonese DVDs, Cantonese CDs, and videos) and cultural matters (e.g., Cantonese opera, drama, TV serials, Cantonese pop music and pop culture, history, language, ethnicity, and culture). In Chinese restaurants, menus with this character for *Yuet* (粵) indicate Cantonese dishes.

As a linguistic term, "*Yuet*" (粵) identifies a major regional language or related regional dialects in Southeast China. Li Fang-kuei was the first Chinese linguist to identify and classify major Chinese regional dialects in 1937. His scheme has been widely accepted, and became one of the main foundations on which Chinese dialectal research has been based.[38] Linguistically, the term "*Yuet*" has been used to identify the regional language/dialect of the *Lingnam* (*lingnan*) region, composed of the two nineteenth-century provinces of Gwongdung (Guangdong) and Gwongsai (Guangxi). In this regard, *Yuet* is a general category denoting a major Chinese regional language/dialect, whereby "Cantonese," as dialect/speech, is a sub-set of the larger *Yuet* language category. In this sense, we can say that *Yuet* is both a linguistic and ethnic identifying label,[39] whereas Cantonese speech, as a sub-component of the *Yuet* language, usually only connotes a form of speech within the Yuet language.

A fundamental reason why we should not confuse or conflate "*Yuet*" and "Cantonese" is that *Yuet* is a broad collective category, which includes several sub-groups in the form of varieties of speech, or related dialects, of which "Cantonese" is the best-known and most-widespread speech form. Thus, "Cantonese" (i.e., the speech of Canton or *Gwong-chau wah*) is but a single variety of speech or dialect, albeit the most important, within the larger category of *Yuet* dialects. The *Yuet* dialects or speech forms are spoken widely. In most of Gwongdung, and parts of neighboring Gwongsai province, *Yuet* speech coexists with other dialects, e.g., *Hakka* and *Min*, and even Mandarin (*Putonghua.*) In Central Gwongdung, however, *Yuet* language/speech in its several varieties is the dominant language or major regional dialect(s.) Again, Cantonese, i.e., the speech of Canton, while relatively widespread, remains, but a single a specific dialect or speech form of the *Yuet* language/ dialects. Evidence of this collective categorial role of "*Yuet"* is unmistakable in three well-known authoritative compiled lists of the *Yuet* dialects. (See chart 2.1 below).

**Distinguishing between "*Yuet*/Cantonese" and "*Yuet*-Cantonese"**

In this investigation, I frequently use the paired terms, of "*Yuet"* and *"*Cantonese,*"* as practical short-hand terms. I do this to connotate the idea of a "single word expression," consisting of a hybrid form of two pre-existing separate and independent terms. In this way, I graphically represent a close relationship, regarding what they represent. This is evident in how I refer to and use the terms "*Yuet* languages/dialects," and "Cantonese" dialect(s)/speech. In order to avoid earlier mentioned causes of ambiguity and confusion, I adopt two different ways to express alternative meanings, regarding the conceptual relationship between "*Yuet*" and "Cantonese."

In a manner of speaking, these linked terms embrace different categories of meaning, which can be a source of confusion. The manner of how I graphically link these two terms together signals their different alternative meanings, when they are linked together. The purpose of this conscious differentiation is to graphically represent their combination together, to form a specific composite term, with its own distinct meaning and usage. This is evidenced in the respective positioning of the two terms, where "*Yuet"* proceeds and "Cantonese" follows, with both resulting combined forms joined together by either a slash mark or a hyphen.

When I use the term ***Yuet*/Cantonese,** (note the slash mark) the intent is to use a term or label, in which "*Yuet*" and "Cantonese" are joined together, to function as a single composite entity. Here they can be viewed as being synonymous or possessing a mutuality of character, so that they can function together as a single term. The slash mark represents a unifier function, as in the use of such words "as" or "like," Thus, the hybrid term *Yuet*/Cantonese mirrors a relationship, where "*Yuet*" can be regarded "as" or "like" "Cantonese," in the sense that when so paired, they can be regarded as being synonymous in how we think of them and use them in the context of their placement and use in a particular context (e.g., in a specific sentence or frame of reference.)

In contrast, my use of the hybrid term **ized*Yuet*-Cantonese**, (note the hyphen mark) is intended to convey a different contextual relationship and meaning. Despite my also structurally joining together the same two terms, "*Yuet*" and "Cantonese," the intent here is to project and represent an altogether different connotation. Unlike the above referenced term "*Yuet*/Cantonese," the term "*Yuet*-Cantonese" cannot, as indicated with a hyphen, be regarded as being synonymous or possessing a mutuality of character. Instead, the hyphenated term represents a joint construction, where the two components of "*Yuet*" and "Cantonese" retain their individual sense of distinctiveness and separate connotations, even as they work together in tandem. The hybrid character of *Yuet*-Cantonese suggests a duality of construction, such that the hyphen in *Yuet*-Cantonese can mean or represent the conjunction "and*,*" as in *Yuet* "and" Cantonese.

The need to mechanically distinguish and differentiate between different ways of conceptually combining "*Yuet*" and "Cantonese" is rooted to the vexing question of how these two identifying labels represent different categories of meaning, even as they have been closely linked together as key signposts of a major Han Chinese regional language/dialect. This distinction can best be understood in light of how they are rendered in written Chinese, as a means of clarifying their respective positions and relationships, relative to what they may mean and represent.

In ancient times (pre-Han China, before the 2nd century BCE,) the Chinese character for *Yuet* (*Yue*) (越) referred ascriptively to a variety of barbarian peoples, collectively identified as the *Nam-Yuet* (南越), (i.e., *Nanyue* (Pinyin) or *Nan-yueh (*Wade-Giles), who were distributed in a wide area from the Yangtze River south to parts of present-day Jiangxi, Hunan, Fujian, Gwongdung, Gwongsai, and Northern Vietnam. In Vietnamese *Yuet* is pronounced as "*Viet*" as in "Vietnam" (pronounced in Cantonese *Yuet-Nam*) Yuenan (Pinyin) or Yueh-nan *(*Wade-Giles). After Vietnam achieved independence from China

Chapter 2

in the tenth century CE, this form for the character Yuet (越) was no longer associated with South China and its people, and instead became associated exclusively with Vietnam.

Over time, another different term, also pronounced nearly identical as *Yuet* (越), but written with a different Chinese character (粵), became a common synonymous reference for Gwongdung, its people and culture. When using the term *Yuet* (粵) in regards to "language," it is written as part of a compound term, *Yuet-yuh* (*Yueyu*) (粵語)." In this usage, the term "*Yuet*" (粵) refers to the *Yuet* (粵) people and their regional culture in Gwongdung, especially in Central Gwongdung. The term *yuh* (*yu*) (語) means language. Hence, *Yuet-yuh* (*Yueyu*) (粵語) simply means "the *Yuet* language." In contrast, the term "Cantonese" (as in Cantonese speech) in Chinese is rendered as *Gwongdung wah* (*Guangdonghua*) (廣東話) or "Gwongdungese", the speech of Gwongdung, which again, actually means the speech of Canton, or *Gwong-chau wah* (廣州話) or simply "Cantonese."

I purposefully draw attention to the two second characters of these two paired compound characters, which are "*yuh*" (yu) (語) for "language" and "*wah*" (*hua*) (話) for "speech." The significance of these two second characters is that they explicitly position and categorize the terms they follow. Specifically, again when we reference "*Yuet*," (粵) we use it with the paired term "*yuh*" (*yu*), i.e., *Yuet yuh*, (粵語) which means the *Yuet* "language(s)/dialect(s)." In contrast, *Gwongdung wah*, (廣東話) (again, synonymous with *Gwong-chau wah*) (廣州話) explicitly refers to the "speech" of Canton.

## Table 2.1 Major Han Chinese languages and dialects in Nineteenth-Century Gwongdung [40]

| Han Chinese *Bundae* (*Bendi*) "Native" language-Speech Groups in Gwongdung<br>All Han Chinese and their progeny, who migrated to and settled in Gwongdung between the Han and Tang periods (2nd Century BCE to the 10th Century CE) | | *Hakka* "Guest" speech Groups in Gwongdung as Han Chinese migrant/settlers after 12th century CE | Han Chinese Non-*Yuet* Non-Cantonese Speech groups in Gwongdung, after 14th Century CE |
|---|---|---|---|
| *Yuet (Yue)Bundae* language and dialect groups:<br>1st list of 5 *Yuet* dialects[41] 1.*Yuehai*, Pearl River Delta, West River valley; 2. *Siyi* (*Say-Yup*) *Kong-mon*) *Jiangmen* (formerly 4 district speech area); 3. *Gao-lei*, in SW Gwongdung; 4. *Qin-lian*, south Gwongsai (Guangxi); 5) *Gui-Nan* SW Gwongsai.<br>2nd list of 7 *Yuet* dialects, divided into 3 groups[42]<br>I) The Metropolitan Canton group, (1, *Guang fu* (Metro Canton,) Pearl River Delta, *Foshan, Zhongshan, Dongguan, Zhuhai, Shenzhen, Qingyuan*, Southern *Zhaoqing*;<br>II) The Interior Gwongdung/ Gwongsai group, 2) *Gou-lou* inland areas of West Gwongdung and East Gwongsai (*Yulin*), 3)*Yong-xun*, in *Yong-yu-yun* valley in Gwongsai, and *Nanning* (capital of Gwongsai);<br>III) The Coastal Gwongdung/Gwongsai group, 4) *Siyi* (*Say-Yup*) in *Kong mon* (*Jiangmen*), 5) *Gao-yang* SW Gwongdung, *Yangjiang* & *Lianjiang*, 6) *Wu-Hua*, in West Gwongdung, *Wuchuan, Huazhou*, and 7) *Qin-Lian*, southern Gwongsai, *Beihai, Qinzou, Fangcheng*.<br>3rd list of 5 *Yuet* dialects,[43] divided into 2 groups, with are further sub-divided into 5 sub-groups **The Pearl River Delta group**, 1. *Northern group*, 1a. *Sanyi* (*Saam-yup*) in *Foshan*, i.e. *Namhoi, Panyu, Shuntak*, & SE *Zhaoqing*, 1b *interior (Gou-lou) group*, the western Pearl River catchment, inland parts of western Gwongdung and Eastern Gwongsai,2. *Guang-Fu group*, (Metropolitan Canton), 2a *Gwong-Chau* (Guangzhou), Hong Kong , Macao, 2b *interior counties*, *Maoming,Yeung-chun,Yong-xun*),Nanning,& *Guiping* in Gwongsai, 3 *Southern group*, 3a, *Zhongshan* (*Chung-Shaan*), including *Saam-Yup* , *Say-Yup*, and *Sam-Heung-wah*, 3b *Kuan-Lan*, the East side of Pearl River estuary, including *Dongguan* (Tungkun), Boan (Pao-on), Hong Kong's New Territories, also included *Qin-lian*, a southern Gwongsai dialect, **The Non-Pearl River Delta *Yuet* group,** 4) *Wu-yi (Ng-Yup)* Five speech group)(former *Say-Yup* group (4 districts' group included *Toi-Shaan, Hoiping, Yanping*, and *Sunwui*) with *Hokshan* (*Hok-Shaan*) added, 5) *Liangyang* group, Eastern part of Gao-yang in Yangjiang (Yeungkong) and Yangchun (Yeungchun) | *Min Bundae* language & dialect groups:<br>1/ *Min Hoklo* Bundae of East Gwongdung, in *Chaozhou* (*Teochiu*), and Shantou (Swatow).<br>*Teochiu speech*<br>2/*Min Hoi-NamBundae* of West Gwongdung, *Liu-chau* (*Leizhou*) peninsula, Hainan Island<br>*Hoinam speech*<br>3/ NE *Min* in *Chung-Shaan* district | *Hakka* community's 4 *dialect* groups [44]<br>1.*Meixian* (The standard *Hakka* dialect)<br>2. Hailu<br>3. Huayang<br>4. Shatoujiao<br>Major Gwongdung distribution sites<br>1/ *Hakka* in Meixian county in East Gwongdung<br>2/*Hakka* in West Gwongdung, onthe *Liu-chau* (*Leizhou*) Peninsula and Hainan Island<br>3/ *Hakka* located in typically peripheral-marginal areas Central Gwongdung Pearl River Delta Region, e.g., in *Say-Yup* areas, and Chung-Shaan | (*Kuan-wah*) (*Guanhua*) "speech of the officials" or the Beijing dialect, as the precursor of modern "Mandarin" Chinese<br>*Min* speakers from Fujian<br>*Wu* speakers from (*Jiangnan*) Shanghai, Suzhou, Hangzhou<br>*Gan* speakers from Jiangxi<br>*Xiang* speakersfrom Hunan<br>Some random speakers from other provinces, e.g., Shandong Hubei. Sichuan and Yunnan |

Chapter 2

## Table 2.2 Major Yuet-Cantonese dialects spoken in Nineteenth-Century Central Gwongdung and North America[45]

| Saam-Yup wah (3 district speech) Cantonese speech community group identity label (i.e., Gwong-chau wah) 3 counties around the Metro Canton area (commonly identified as standard Cantonese) Distribution/location *Namhoi* *Panyu* *Shuntak* (also unofficially known as **Luk-yup wah**, when 3 other districts S.E. of Canton are also included) *Tungkun* *Pao-an* *Poklo* | Say-Yup wah (4 district speech) Cantonese speech community group identity label SW Pearl Delta *Sunwui* *Hoiping* *Toi-shaan (Toishan) (Hoishan) (Sunning)* *Yanping* **Ng-Yup wah** (when also Including *Hokshaan*) | Baak-wah[46] (or Gwongdung-wah) Cantonese speech community group identity label Inner and Outer *Baak-wah* zone people were *identified Gwongdung-wah*[47]*speakers* **Inner Baak-wah zone** Areas in interior of Central Gwongdung, NE, N, NW, & W of Pearl River Delta **Outer Baak-wah zone,** Area located beyond Inner zone, between it and the non-*Yuet* peripheral areas next to Gwongdung's borders | Chung-Shaan wah (Heung-Shaan) Cantonese speech community group identity label[48] Yuet/Cantonese speech *Saam-Yup* *Say-Yup* **Min** speech *Lung Doo (Loong doo)* (Lungtu) *Namlong (Namlau)* *Saam Heung wah* **Hakka speech** spoken within Chung-Shaan |
|---|---|---|---|
| Location/distribution of *Yuet* dialects (taken from lists in table 2.1) **1st list of 5 *Yuet* dialects**[49] 1.*Yuehai*, Pearl River Delta, West River valley **2nd list of 7 *Yuet* dialects,**[50] 1) **The Metropolitan Canton group**, (1, *Guang fu* (Metro Canton,) Pearl River Delta, Foshan, Dongguan, Zhuhai, Shenzhen, Qingyuan, Southern Zhaoqing, (but minus Zhongshan, (Chung-Shaan) **3rd list of 5 *Yuet* dialects,**[51] **The Pearl River Delta group**, 1. **Northern group**, 1a. *Sanyi* (*Saam-yup*) in Foshan, i.e.,*Namhoi, Panyu, Shuntak,* & SE Zhaoqing | Location/distribution of *Yuet* dialects (taken from lists in table 2.1) **1st list of 5 *Yuet* dialects**[52] 2. *Siyi* (*Say-Yup*)Kong-mon (Jiangmen) **2nd list of 7 *Yuet* dialects,**[53]**The Coastal Gwongdung/ Gwongsai group,** 4) *Siyi* (*Say-Yup*) in Kong-mon (*Jiangmen*), **3rd list of 5 *Yuet* dialects,**[54]**The Non-Pearl River Delta Yuet dialects,** *Wu-yi* (*Ng-Yup*) Five speech group, when *Hokshaan* is added to the *Say-Yup* group | Location/distribution of *Yuet* dialects (taken from lists in table 2.1) **1st list of 5 *Yuet* dialects**[55]1. *Yuehai*, West River valley; 3. *Gao-lei*, in SW Gwongdung; 1b *interior (Gou-lou)* group, the western Pearl River catchment, inland parts of West Gwongdung, **2nd list 7***Yuet* dialects, [56]**Interior Gwongdung,** 2) *Gou-lou* inland areas of West Gwongdung, 3) **The Coastal Gwongdung group,** 5) *Gao-yang* SW Gwongdung, *Yangjiang* &*Lianjiang*, 6) **Wu-Hua**, in W. Gwongdung, Huazhou and Wuchuan, **3rd list of 5 *Yuet* dialects,**[57]***Guang-Fu group**, interior counties*, Maoming, *Yeung-chun,interior (Gou-lou) group*, W. Pearl River area | Location/distribution *Yuet* dialects in Chung—Shaan district [58] (Taken from lists in table 2.1) *Chung-Shaan was divided into wards or county subunits, as 9 qu , also identified alternatively as 10 Doo (Du) of min speaking groups.* *Namlong (Namlau)* Min speech group a NE Min speech group dominant in Lung Doo and See Dai Doo *Saam-Heung-wah Min-speech group* was dominantin Gook Doo, NW of Macao *Lung Doo (Lungtu) min speech group* was the largest *Min* speaking group in *Chung-Shaan*- it was distributed widelyin the remaining 7 Doo units. **Yuet/Cantonese speech groups in Chung-Shaan,** *Saam-Yup*, in *Chung-Shaan*, area south of *Shuntak*; *Say-Yup* in Chung-Shaan, area east of Sunwui **Hakka speech group, in** *Chung-Shaan* |

138

It should be noted that in recent years, among some specialists, the *Say-Yup* (*Siyi*) or commonly identified in Chinese America as *Toi-Shaan* (*Hoishan*) (*Toishan*) (*T'aishan*) speech, is not regarded as properly speaking a "Cantonese dialect." This is because such speech is viewed as having markedly different "speech forms," especially its distinctive phonology, as to exclude it from what constitutes bonafide Cantonese dialects.[59] This exclusion of the *Say-Yup* is evident in the following table. While this development is noteworthy, because it is somewhat novel in its assessment, it should be regarded merely as a minority view, in the form of a provocative interpretation, which forms the basis for an interesting counterpoint, but not a definitive one.

## The Distribution/Location of Cantonese Dialects by Area and Cities[60]

| Area | Cities (Examples) |
|---|---|
| Central Guangdong (Gwongdung) Group | Guangzhou (Canton), Conghua, Fogang (Shijiao), Longmen, Zhengcheng, Huaxian |
| Northern Guangdong (Gwongdung) Group | Shaoguan, Qijiang, Lian Xian, Liannan, Yangshan, Yingde, Taiping |
| Northern Pearl River Delta Group | Nanhai (Nomhoi), Gaoya, Sanshui, Shunde (Shuntak), Foshan, Wuchan, Huazhou |
| Southern Pearl River Delta Group | Shenzhen, Dongguan, Boan, Zhongshan |
| Guangxi (Gwongsai) and Western Guangdong (Gwongdung) | Guangxi (Gwongsai) cities, Zhanjiang, Maoming, Lianjiang, Guazhou |

When we reference "*wah*" (*hua*) (話) or speech/dialect, it is usually paired with a location indicator, to indicate the locale where such speech exists, e.g., *Gwongdung wah,* (literally, the speech of Gwongdung province, but more correctly *Gwong-chau wah*, the speech of "Canton.") In this larger context, we can readily see that *Yuet-yuh* (*Yuet* language(s) is the broader category/classification, while Cantonese speech, i.e., *Gwongdung-wah* (i.e., *Gwong-chau-wah*) is a sub-component of larger category of the *Yuet* language(s). This helps to explain my use of the compound composite terms of "*Yuet*/Cantonese" and "*Yuet*-Cantonese."

**Cantonese speech**

Cantonese speech, similar to other southern Chinese dialects and speech forms, is a rich and complicated mosaic of several components. It is the chief beneficiary of the *Yuet* language/dialects group, because it is the best known and most widely utilized speech form in the *Lingnam* region of southeastern China. Again, when we refer to *Gwongdung-wah* or "*Gwongdungese*," as the language/speech of Gwongdung, i.e., Central Gwongdung, we really mean *Gwong-chau wah* or "Cantonese," i.e., the speech of Canton.[61] Considerable confusion arises whenever discussion probes into what Cantonese speech embraces and what it does not. Perhaps, one can better understand this situation by thinking of the *Yuet* languages/dialects, as consisting of one major dialect, i.e., Cantonese, with several variants or related speech forms, all co-existing under the *Yuet* language label. While *Yuet*/Cantonese speech groups are a relatively homogeneous group, they are in fact widely distributed geo-territorially, within a linguistically heterogeneous context. This means that the *Yuet* language, and related Cantonese dialects/speech forms (e.g., *Baak-wah*) represent a well-defined unified group, where commonalties outweigh differences.

Cantonese speech has clearly distinguished *Yuet*/Cantonese culture, and separated the people of Central Gwongdung from the rest of Han Chinese society, by integrating the distinctive elements of *Yuet* cultural identity and Cantonese speech, as they have simultaneously contributed to and represented the uniqueness of Cantonese ethno-linguistic identifications and socio-cultural traditions. It also linguistically embodies, and historically links, Central Gwongdung with impeccable Tang standards, via historical legitimacy, cultural authenticity and language purity.

> In general, the *Yue* [*Yuet*] dialects give the impression of being a well differentiated sub-variety of southern Chinese with a strong overlay of northern Chinese elements. These elements, however, are clearly not of recent origin; rather,

> they point in many ways to the late Tang as their source. The strongest indication of this is that the phonological categories of *Yue* [*Yuet* speech] can almost all be viewed as deriving from late middle Chinese which...was the variety of literary Chinese current in the middle to late Tang dynasty.[62]

This Cantonese identification with Tang standards/models has greatly influenced the construction of an historically integrated *Yuet*/Cantonese persona. This is nowhere more evident than in the establishment and evolution of Cantonese dialects/speech communities/groups, which are covered in greater detail in chapter three, regarding Cantonese ethnic group and speech community labels. The data in the above tables integrate various linguistic sub-categories of Cantonese speech, i.e., dialects and speech communities, and contextually synchronizes them with key geophysical and demographic variables. Interestingly, this starts with the generalized amorphous category of "Cantonese," which is further conflated by associating it with the nebulous catch-all parallel term "*Gwongdung-wah*" (*Guangdonghua*) or (*Gwongdungese*) or (speech of Gwongdung.)

Historically, using these terms only made sense, and were used primarily beyond Gwongdung- i.e., outside the Cantonese speaking community, because they were clearly ascriptive in nature. Cantonese speaking people in Central Gwongdung, in referencing themselves, with other Cantonese speakers, never referred to themselves as speaking *Gwongdung wah* (*Gwongdungese*). Instead, they usually identified their speech by more specific and concrete identifying labels, easily recognized by other Cantonese people, such as *Gwong-chau wah, Saam-Yup wah, Say-Yup wah,* or *Baak-wah.* A Cantonese individual would only refer to his/her speaking *Gwongdung-wah*, only when speaking to a non-Cantonese speaker, e.g., "Yes I am also Chinese, but I do not speak *Putonghua*, I speak *Gwongdung-wah*," (meaning, "I speak Cantonese.") There existed the presumption that there ascriptively existed a single oral speech medium in Gwongdung, and it was Cantonese speech. This claim was not tenable, because it was simply false. However, because of its well-established use and widespread familiarity, any questioning of its validity became moot. Despite this conundrum, this initial threshold form of Cantonese (speech,) i.e., *Gwong-chau wah* (廣州話) serves as a useful starting place for surveying major speech forms of Cantonese speech.

Cantonese speech forms can best be visualized, whereby each is positioned along a "Cantonese speech continuum." In Table 2.1 above, seven Cantonese speech forms are so positioned. The list starts with the most finite, narrowly construed speech form, and then the listed items move in ascending order to progressively larger, more widely distributed speech forms. The order of sequence starts with *Gwong-chau wah* (*Guangzhouhua*), the speech of Canton. Historically speaking, this "speech of Canton" (or *Gwongchau-wah*) has been widely recognized as the embodiment of Cantonese speech via its several already mentioned ascribed synonymous identifications, e.g., "Standard Cantonese," "primary Cantonese," "core Cantonese," and my own coined label, "Cantonese/Cantonese."

The remaining speech forms represent, in successive order, additional speech forms located in progressively larger, and more numerous local spatial configurations, (e.g., a series of groups of neighboring contiguous rural districts/counties.) The *Baak-wah* speech form/community, as the last Cantonese speech form of this list, is geographically and demographically the largest Cantonese speech form/group/community in Central Gwongdung, but also the least visible, least known, least distinguished, and thus least influential of all the Cantonese speech forms/dialects. The specifics of each Cantonese speech form will be covered elsewhere (see chapter three.) The purpose of this cursory review of Cantonese speech, has been to offer a reliable composite profile of the important place of Cantonese speech in Nineteenth-Century Central Gwongdung, and by extension elsewhere in both the *Lingnam* and the Cantonese wah-Q (overseas Chinese) world.

## Technical components of Cantonese speech[63]

The enduring distinctiveness, indeed uniqueness, of *Yuet*/Cantonese language and speech is nowhere more clearly evidenced than in its technically complex structural composition, relative to its historically diverse and distant sourced pedigree, difficult and diverse linguistic constructs, and authentic ethno-cultural persona. This has been evidenced in many interesting ways, as referenced below.

## *Yuet* Language and Cantonese Speech

1) The *Yuet* dialects have eight or more tones (level, contour and mixed), Mandarin only has four tones.[64] Because Cantonese exhibits greater variety in its tonal nuances, via their enhanced functionality, it has the capability of expressing a greater variety of meanings within established categories. This is especially marked in the tonal structure of Cantonese, as compared with other major Chinese dialects. The singular importance of "tones" in Chinese is legendary, and long the bane of novice students of Mandarin Chinese. Again, modern Mandarin Chinese has four well-defined tones, whereas Cantonese has nine fixed-tones, together with two additional special tones, known as "changed tones." These two latter tones have the ability to reflect antecedent word relationships, relative to the development of new vocabulary items that have historically evolved from earlier terms.

This is evident in the case of such words as *yeen* and *t'oi*. The word *yeen* for "tobacco" is related to the word, *yeen*, meaning "smoke." The two are written with different characters. In pronunciation, they sound almost identical, with the chief difference being one of tonal variation. Thus, *yeen* as "tobacco" is spoken in a changed tone, and *yeen* as "smoke" is not spoken in a changed tone. Similarly, *toi* for "table" is derived from *t'oi* for "terrace." [65] In this manner tonal variation, via changed tones, provides Cantonese speech with an expanded lexicon that has incorporated new words, relative to antecedent conceptually related terms or ideas. In this way, Cantonese serves as an authentic replication of the classical Tang standard, because it reflects a vitality and elasticity of that distant speech tradition. These are qualities which modern Mandarin, (and other Han Chinese dialects) with its limited four tones, cannot easily duplicate, nor benefit from.

2) Cantonese is both a formal and informal speech medium. Its pronounced tonal variation has resulted in an extremely rich store of colloquial expressions, which have remained quite separate from the formal body of the dialect, relative to morphology and usage. These colloquial expressions, which when written in Chinese characters often appear as archaic/anachronistic. In some cases, they are not even recognized outside of *Yuet*/Cantonese communities."… Cantonese… is the only Chinese dialect with widely recognized (by both Cantonese and non-Cantonese Chinese people),

nontraditional graphs for colloquial words and expressions.'"[66] Additionally, in Cantonese colloquial writing, vernacular literature, (but not in formal composition,[67]) as well as in everyday speech, Cantonese people use nontraditional characters/graphs for colloquial words and expressions, found nowhere else in contemporary Chinese language or speech.

While Beijing discourages the use of Cantonese idiomatic and colloquial writings, with its use of Middle Chinese terms, words, expressions, and phrases, it has persisted in Canton and more so in Hong Kong, as clearly evident in local Hong Kong Cantonese language newspapers and other types of media.[68] Cantonese written forms exhibit atypical features associated with colloquial expressions in speech, whereby many Cantonese written forms mirror forms of an earlier age, i.e., Tang period. Cantonese is one of a few major dialects which uses written characters that are unconventional, seldom used, or unfamiliar to most other Chinese. Many of these characters reflect pre-modern (Middle Chinese literary) forms and usages, and thus often represent archaic Chinese connotations.[69] Some of these characters are well-known throughout China, and are closely identified by non-Cantonese Chinese, as having a distinctly unique and often exclusive Cantonese identification and usage.

> Cantonese vocabulary is noted for a certain kind of conservatism. Some of its everyday words, especially monosyllables, correspond in Mandarin [Chinese] to very archaic lexical items used only in literary expressions; such words...as *min* [*mien*] [for]"face," *keng* [*gang*][for] "neck," *hang* [meaning]"to go, [or] [to] "walk"; *sik*,[ meaning] "to eat"; and *wah*, [meaning] "to say."[70]

Some examples of this are quite simple and obvious in everyday usage. As earlier noted, the most obvious case is the Cantonese preference for *mo* (in mandarin <u>wu</u>) as a standard negative prefix, over the more commonly used Cantonese form of *but*, pronounced in mandarin as *bu*). Many of the specialized Chinese characters used, in either writing everyday common Cantonese colloquial terms, or in writing the more refined and esoteric Cantonese "classical" literary tradition, often appear as archaic terms and anachronistic forms, which most Chinese either do not recognize or have no practical familiarity with. In this regard, the Cantonese literary tradition has scores of characters used in poetry and prose, drama and novels, and other genre of literary writing, which are found only in the Cantonese literary tradition, and only rarely, if at all, elsewhere in Chinese writings.[71] Similarly, in colloquial writing, vernacular literature, and in everyday speech, but not in formal composition,[72] Cantonese people use non-traditional characters/ graphs for colloquial words and expressions, which are not found anywhere else in contemporary Chinese language or speech, again, they nonetheless persist in Canton and especially Hong Kong.[73] A few key examples of such forms demonstrate the persistent use of such older speech forms.

**Table 2.3 Idiomatic Cantonese phrases, some of which use older (archaic) Chinese characters[74]**

| English text | Cantonese text (using my own Romanization) | English text | Cantonese text (using my own Romanization) |
|---|---|---|---|
| bragging, boasting | *chieh dai pow* | risking one's life | *bok maing* |
| "that is crazy" or "that is ridiculous!" | *ho chee seen* | To marry a man | *ga (nam yen)* |
| unreasonable | *mow gai* | To wed a woman | *choe (nueri yen)* |
| To read or study | *dook shee* | To eat something | *sick yeah* |
| "Are you serious?" "Are you for real?" "Are you kidding me!" | *yao mo gow chaw?* | "Even if," or "No matter what" | *"fam bok see"* *"sai but gee"* *"mow lean haw"* |

3) As a conservative dialect, Cantonese speech preserves the tonal categories of the Tang dynasty literary standard. When a Tang period poem is read or recited in Cantonese, it accurately retains its original rhyme pattern more so than in any other Chinese dialect.[75]

> In general [,] the *Yue* (*Yuet*)) dialects give the impression of being a well differentiated sub [-] variety of Southern Chinese with a strong overlay of Northern Chinese elements. These elements, however, are clearly not of recent origin; rather they point in many ways to the late Tang as their source. The strongest indication of this is that the phonological categories of Yue can almost all be viewed as deriving from Late Middle Chinese which…was the variety of literary Chinese current in the middle to late Tang dynasty.[76]

4) Some *Yuet* dialects have so-called "changed" tones. e.g., in both *Gwong-chau-wah* (standard Cantonese) and the Toi-Shaan (Hoi-Shaan) and other (*Say-Yup*) (*siyi*) dialects, the tones of certain words, chiefly nouns, have a tonal contour different from their etymological category when used in everyday speech. This change is morphological, the meaning of which is "everyday familiarity with the object in question." [77]

5) In Cantonese, there occurred a weakening of the 'k' sound to become an "h" sound in most words. In other cases, some of the "k" sounds have changed into "f" sounds. [78]

**Table 2.4 Examples of Chinese "k" sounds, rendered as Cantonese "h" or "f" sounds**

| English | Mandarin (Putonghua) | Cantonese (*Yuet-wah*) |
|---|---|---|
| Look | kan | hon |
| polite | keqi | Hak hei |
| bitter | Ku | fu |
| quick | kuai | fai |

6) In the *Yuet* dialects, the most common way to form plural pronouns is by using the suffix tei6, [pronounced as "*tei*" or "*tey*"] or its dialectal cognate, as in Standard Cantonese, [and in the various] *Chung-Shaan*, and *Tengxian* dialects. Other *Yuet* dialects, such as *Toi-Shaan* (*Hoisaan*) (*Taishan*) [and

other *Say-Yup* speech forms] and *Yeungkong* (*Yangjiang*) make plural forms by a process of tonal change(s). [79] In standard Cantonese speech "the sign of the plural," as in the first- second- or third- person plural is indicated by using the colloquial Cantonese term *k'ui-tei*, (or "*kueri-dae*") ("they" or "them,") is normally written using archaic Chinese characters. Note that the term *tei* is actually a modification of the character/word for *tei* (*dae*) meaning "earth" or "land," with a "mouth" radical next to the "earth" radical. Thus, this strange hybrid character has two radicals in an unusual combination. Most Chinese, including many Cantonese speakers, would not know about it, much less be able to recognize this combination. Again, while every Cantonese speaker uses the term *k'ui-tei* in everyday Cantonese vernacular speech to denote the "third person plural," few if any, would know the characters, or be ale to write them down. This exemplifies, again, an "insider's Cantonese," whereby everyone knows the phrase and uses it every day, but not everyone knows the exact characters for it. Instead, when writing the Cantonese-Chinese character for the "third person plural," most Cantonese speakers would use instead standard modern Chinese characters, which are indicative of "formal Cantonese" in their use and pronunciation, i.e., in written form, Cantonese speakers would use the familiar Mandarin form, i.e., (*ta-men*).

7) Pronominal possession in the *Yuet* languages is usually shown by placing the specific noun measure between the pronoun and the thing possessed, e.g., in Standard Cantonese hhey4 *pun*3 *sy*1 (*keruy bun shee*) (my own transliterated form), i.e., which literally means "he-measure-book," or alternately, "his volume book." In English, we would simply say, "his book." This appears to be peculiar to the *Yuet* language(s).[80]

8) Cantonese speech has a distinct nasal quality, reminiscent of Vietnamese and other SE Asian speech forms, in contrast to Mandarin Chinese forms. First of all, there is the nasal consonant "ng," an initial sound that has completely disappeared in most of Northern China. Some Cantonese speakers place this nasal consonant in front of words, where it did not originally belong. Second, there is an initial "m-" nasal consonant in Cantonese speech, where Mandarin has historically lost it.[81]

Chapter 2

## Table 2.5 Examples where nasal consonants exist in Cantonese, but not in Mandarin

| English | Cantonese | Mandarin (Putonghua) |
|---|---|---|
| tooth | *nga* | *ya* |
| "I" or "me" | *ngo* | *wo* |
| bank | *ngan hong* | *yinhang* |
| tail | *mei* | *wei* |
| (to) ask | *man* ("mun," my own Romanization) | *wen* |
| literature | *man hok* ("mun-hawk" my own Romanization) | *wenxue* |

Cantonese is the unit/form of Chinese speech that has been geographically, geo-historically and linguistically most closely related to Southeast Asia, and therefore exhibits a special affinity with other speech groups near or in Southeast Asia, e.g., non-Chinese peoples and cultures, (e.g., Tai peoples) who speak with a distinct nasal quality. One example is the fact that Cantonese speakers have more in common with speakers of Vietnamese and Southern Min, than with speakers of Mandarin Chinese.[82] While this affinity for nasal consonants, producing distinct nasal sounds, had its distant origins in Southeast Asian related speech forms, its more immediate association dates from the several centuries of integrated Chinese political/military control and cultural hegemony of both the Lingnam and North Vietnam's Red River region. By the end of the Tang period, Vietnamese and Cantonese communities went their separate ways.[83] However, in many ways the two neighbors continued to retain and preserve many commonalties in their respective speech communities, of which the nasal affinity is the best example. We should remember however, that Cantonese speech does not have nasalized vowels, as do many *Min* (Fujian) dialects. The point to remember here is that Cantonese has structurally preserved in its speech forms, some distinct features of the past, which represent both pre-Tang non-Chinese and Tang Chinese linguistic characteristics.

9) Syntactically, in Cantonese certain adverbs follow, rather than precede the verbs they refer to, which is common in other Chinese dialects. (see following chart) [84]

**Table 2.6 Cases where adverbs follow the verbs they refer to, often opposite in Mandarin**

| Cantonese[85] (my own Romanization) | Mandarin (Putonghua) | Sequence order in English |
|---|---|---|
| *Kueri bei saam-bun su ngo*<br>He gives 3 volume book to me | *Ta ba san-ben shu gei wo*<br>He 3 volume book, gave to me | He gave me three books |
| *Ngo seen mai-ye hai gai-see*<br>I go buy things first at the market | *Wo xian shangjie mai dongxi*<br>I first go-market buy things | First, I am going to the market to buy some things |
| *Kueri kou-gaw ngo*<br>He tall more (then) me | *Ta bi wo gao*<br>He compare(d) (to) me (is) tall(er) | He is taller than I |

10) Generally speaking, the more colloquial a Cantonese expression and syntax is, then the greater the degree of dialectical variation with other Chinese dialects. This in turn underscores, again, the uniqueness of the Cantonese medium and its capacity to express varied sentiments and values. Some common examples include the following: 1) The Cantonese preference in colloquial speech for *mo* (*wu* in Mandarin) as the primary negative prefix, over the more widespread and conventional use of *bu* in Mandarin Chinese, ("*but*" in Cantonese.) This is similar to a variety of French forms utilized to express the negative form of a word or words, e.g., *ne* [verb] *pas* for "not" or *ne* [verb] *jamais* for "never;" 2) The Cantonese colloquial term *jai* is a common suffix attached to noun forms, to indicate a relationship of "smallness" or status of "youthfulness" or "subordinate position." Examples include: *mui-jai* (or "*mooi-jai*") for "maid

servant girl/maiden"; *nam-jai* for "boy"; *bo-jai* for "small pot"; *jun-jai* for "small bottle"; *to'i-jai*, for "small table"; *ch'e-jai* for "cart" or "small car/vehicle"; and *ook-jai* for a "small house" or a "hut."

Another such example is the Cantonese terms *tsip* (meaning to fetch or pick up) which can be written in an older "Classical form," but which is however, usually written instead in its more well-known "modern" Chinese forms, i.e. *dai* or *na*, e.g., *dai dongxi* (bring or take something) or *na dongxi* (pick-up or bring something).

Among Cantonese in America, the term *fow* is used to indicate a "town" "city" or "urban area." The original meaning of this term is "seaport." In Nineteenth-Century America, it replaced the more conventional term(s) for "city" or "town," i.e., *chau* (*zhou*) or *sheng*, (*cheng*). San Francisco, the earliest and largest Chinese community in the United States became known colloquially as *Dai-fow* or "Great [seaport] town." Similarly, Sacramento was called *Yee-fow* or "Number 2 [seaport] town." Stockton was called *Saam-fow* or "Number 3 [seaport] town." Similarly, Japanese town, known among the Japanese as *nihon machi*, was called by the Cantonese *Yat-bun-fow* or "Japan(ese) [seaport] town." Americans called the section of town where Chinese people lived, "Chinatown." The Cantonese called it *Tong-yan fow* or "Tang peoples' [seaport] town." In smaller Chinese communities, the term *Tong-yan gai* or "street of the Tang people "served as a substitute for *Tong yan fow* (Chinatown). In addition to proper nouns for names of places, the term *fow* (meaning "town") was also used in reference to movement into or away from "town(s)." In this context, *yup-fow* meant, "to go to town" or "to enter the city." Conversely, *chut-fow* meant, "to leave town," or "to go out of town." To go elsewhere, e.g., to another town, was termed *gwo-fow*, or to pass through to another town. Small towns were known as *fow-jai* (note the suffix jai for "smallness.") Curiously, the term *fow* remained, relative to its use, as part of proper nouns for names of places, confined to the West coast, and especially California in the nineteenth-century. When Chinese migrated and settled in the Midwest and East Coast, the practice of transliterating established American names (e.g., New York or Chicago) into Chinese was more common, in place of standardized references concerning the term *fow*.[86] These are common terms found in everyday Cantonese speech that are in fact remnants of older forms, which are no longer used in current standard *Putonghua* or *Guoyu* forms of Chinese, and also in most other Chinese dialects/speech forms.[87]

11) Colloquial Cantonese, as an informal speech medium for use with family and friends, has served as a kind of "insider's Cantonese speech." This is analogous with formal and informal aspects of Japanese, and distinctions between formal and informal/personal French expressions. In Cantonese, the situation is more complex and extreme. Cantonese speech makes a sharper distinction between colloquial expressions and formal or literary expressions, by way of a sophisticated mastery of the complex nuances of shifting tones.

> ...While a basic tone is not associated with a particular meaning any more than a consonant or a vowel is, (however) a changed tone has a morphological meaning something like: "that familiar thing one often speaks of," Thus a word with a change tone is a colloquial, everyday expression. It is never used in a literary combination or context.[88]

Changing tones in Cantonese are also used as a tool for expanding vocabulary by means of transliterating and incorporating foreign (especially western) loanwords.[89]

### Table 2.7 Examples of the use of shifting tones to differentiate between different words [90]

| Word with "basic tone" | Corresponding word with "changed tone" |
|---|---|
| *mui* (younger sister) | *mui* (girl) |
| *yat-ko yan* (a person, individual) | *yat-ko-yan* (alone) |
| *t'ong* (sugar) | *t'ong* (candy) |
| *wong* (yellow) | *wong* (egg yok) |
| *ma t'ai* (horse's hoof) | *ma t'ai* (water chestnut) |

## Table 2.8 Using shifting tones for transliterating foreign terms/words [91]

| English term | Transliterated Cantonese term, using a changed tone |
|---|---|
| downtown | *dang-tang* |
| Reno | *Li-noh* |
| gas stove, | *ge-sih* luh |
| apartment | *paak-muhn* (pronounced as "park-men" ("t" in apartment in Cantonese is silent) |
| cake | *kik* (meaning a western style cake)[92] |
| ball | *Po* |
| guitar | *kit t'a* |
| fashion | *fa-san* |
| tire | *ta:i* |
| chocolate | *tsu ku lik* |
| saxophone | *sek si fung* |
| vaseline | *fa si ling* |

12) In the *Yuet* dialects, the Middle Chinese voiced obstruent's (obstructing elements) appear as voiceless aspirates in the *ping* (level) tone, and in a smaller number of words in the *shang* (rising) tone, but as voiceless non-aspirates in the remaining tones. This applies to the *Gwong-chau-wah* (Guangzhou) dialect, but not all other *Yuet* dialects[93]

13) The *Yuet* language retains all Middle Chinese final consonants. This is (not unique to just the *Yuet* language, but is also found in other southern Chinese dialects.[94]

14) In the *Yuet* language, the *ru* (contour) tone, (i.e., those that ended in "p," "t" and "k" in Middle Chinese) [95] can be split into three, or even four categories conditioned by vowel length, which seem to be peculiar to the *Yuet* language(s).[96]

15) Speakers of Standard Cantonese (*Gwong-chau-wah*) vary considerably in their pronunciation of the sibilant (hissing sound) initials, some use a dental articulation, while others employ a palatal pronunciation; most speakers palatize the sibilants to some degree before high front vowels.[97]

16) *Yuet* dialects vary greatly in the number of vocalic (having many vowels, or ability to affect a vowel) contrasts. They can possess, from a high of nine or ten vowel phonemes (a family or class of related sounds, regarded as a single sound) e.g., in *Tengxian Yuet* speech [98] to a low of five in *Toishaan* (*Hoishaan*) (*Say-Yup wah*) (*siyi hua*) *Yuet* speech.[99]

17) In Cantonese (*Gwong-chau-wah*) (*Guangzhouhua*) (speech) finals, there is a distinction between long and short vowels[100] This length distinction is closely related to the development of the *ru* (contour) tone in all *Yuet* dialects... showing clearly that a long/short contrast was a feature of proto-*Yuet* speech. [101]

18) The *Yuet* dialects are the most conservative speech group in their preservation of the Middle Chinese final consonants. Although a number of *Min* and *Hakka* dialects retain all six of the old ending consonants, they do not always do so with the same words, in contrast, the *Yuet* dialects faithfully preserve the final consonants, with few exceptions. [102]

19) A distinctive feature of the *Yuet* dialects is the split of the upper *ru* (contour) tone into two subtypes conditioned by phonetic vowel length. Such a development is found nowhere outside the *Yuet* language(s).[103]

20) In the *Yuet* dialects, there exists a curious anomaly in regards to the demonstrative *ko* (expressed in various tones), which in Standard Cantonese means "that," but in other *Yuet* dialects it means "this." This resulted from different patterns of development, where there developed a contrast between near and far demonstratives among different *Yuet* speech groups, where "ko" meant "this" in some *Yuet* dialects and meant "that" in others.[104]

21) *Yuet* use of negatives (e.g., the Cantonese preference/use of *m1* (or "*mow*") (my own transliteration) versus the mandarin "*bu*") generally resemble those in *Min* and *Hakka* forms. The *Yuet* existential negative is distinguished from other Southern and Central Chinese dialects by being in the *shang* (rising) tone. The tones used in the *Yuet* forms are likely influenced by the tone of the existential verb *jau*4 ("*yow*") (my own transliteration), meaning "There is" or "there are."[105]

22) The *Yuet* dialects differ syntactically from Mandarin and other Chinese dialects, as in the case of using measures alone (without numerals or

demonstratives) as definite determiners exists throughout the *Yuet* dialects and seem to be limited to them, e.g., in Standard Cantonese, *tsek*7b *kai*1 (*jeurk gai*) (my own transliteration) "The chicken" as opposed to *jat*7a *tsek*7b *kai*1 (*yat jeurk gai*) (my own transliteration), "a chicken" or "one chicken." [106]

23) *Yuet* dialects share syntactically with the *Wu* dialects the order direct object-indirect object, e.g., in Standard Cantonese, *pei*3 *sy*1 *no*4 (*bay-shee-ngo*) (my own transliteration), means "give book me," i.e., give me [the] book. In Mandarin Chinese, it would be *gei wo shu* (give me book). [107]

**Contextualizing the nature and meaning of the technical aspects of Canonese speech**

*Yuet*/Cantonese, as a written form of older, archaic or "Middle" Chinese, and its closely related Cantonese speech, is not yet a "dead language." In the past it has had, and today it continues to provide, lasting symbolic value and historical meaning for Cantonese-speaking people. It is representative of a rich tradition which incorporates many atypical, archaic written forms of Chinese, as colloquial terms/phrases. In this way Cantonese embraces a wide range of older classical literary forms, many from "medieval (or middle) Chinese" of the Tang period. We should remember that most Cantonese words and phrases might be pronounced differently in Mandarin and other Han Chinese dialects, but the written character(s) are usually identical. This commonality of the written script underscores the fact that Cantonese is a Han Chinese dialect, and not a non-Han Chinese language. The notable exception to this is, again, the incorporation of older, "classical" or "anachronistic" items into everyday Cantonese by way of colloquial terms and phrases. This means that the different pronunciation of words in Cantonese speech arises not only from differences in oral/speech pronunciation, but may also be due to the fact that an entirely different (e.g., Middle Chinese) word or phrase is being used.

Given the many technicalities cited above regarding Cantonese speech, it should be abundantly clear why it has been so difficult for other Chinese to become familiar with it, and even more onerous, to learn to speak it, even in a rudimentary way. It is far easier for a Cantonese speaker to learn to speak standard mandarin, then for a mandarin speaker to learn to speak Cantonese, despite the old adage, "*Tian bu pa, di bu pa, tsui pa Guangdongren jiang kuanhua.*" (meaning, "one is unafraid of heaven, one is unafraid of the world, but one fears (it) when a Cantonese (tries to) speak mandarin (i.e, old officials language, now mandarin). Similarly, because of these demanding technicalities, the Cantonese have been legendary in their obsession, love, and respect for their speech. If the structural technicalities of Cantonese speech have made it elusive and enigmatic for others, these very qualities have engendered deep affection, great respect, and widespread enjoyment among Cantonese people, who consider it easy and natural to engage in conversing in Cantonese. These positive qualities associated with engaging in Cantonese speech are similar to the enjoyment of fine Cantonese cuisine, both were highly subjective in nature.

Beyond the technical aspects of Cantonese speech, there remains the equally important and difficult task of deciphering the social context of engaging in Cantonese conversation.

## The important distinction between formal and colloquial forms of Cantonese speech

A major characteristic distinguishing Cantonese speech, among speakers of standard Cantonese, is the marked difference between its colloquial and formal forms. While there are well-defined variations among the various *Yuet*/Cantonese dialects or speech forms, relative to their colloquial and formal forms, the distinction however, has been especially prominent in standard Cantonese- the best known and most widely form of Cantonese speech. This distinction results from the intersection and overlapping of the purpose for which a speech form is adopted/used, and the vocabulary utilized to communicate ideas and information. In the case of colloquial or everyday speech, a limited simple unambiguous vocabulary, together with an easy straightforward communication delivery vehicle is a practical necessity. In contrast, formal speech typically involves an extended, intellectually rigorous and explicitly technical vocabulary, which offers greater precision of expression and clarity of meaning. Additionally, formal speech serves to communicate a wide-spectrum of complex, often abstract ideas and technical terms, which are not relevant, nor normally used in daily speech.

I myself only learned to speak Cantonese, when I was sent to boarding school in Hong Kong at age ten, in 1955–1956. I subsequently undertook an extended "refresher course," after I married into a Hong Kong family in the late 1960's. Prior to that time, I only spoke English, and could only vaguely understand short simple Cantonese phrases, such as *loi sick faan* (come eat dinner), or *kwai-kwai dae, mo choe*! (be good and be quiet!) In a short period of several months, given my total immersion in an all Cantonese-speaking environment, I learned to speak reasonably well and understand colloquial speech (everyday speech). I soon noticed however, that there existed a big difference between the "everyday" (colloquial) Cantonese speech that I could speak and understand, and the kind of Cantonese (formal) speech that I heard on the radio or elsewhere. In regards to the latter, I was only able to catch a few nouns, verbs, and colloquial phrases here and there. Generally, I could not understand what was being said.

A similar situation exists today, in the case of a foreigner learning to speak Cantonese, where he/she would be comfortable and confident in conversing at a rudimentary level, in a simple conversation. However, in watching a newscast on TV, or hearing a speech or lecture, he/she would not be able to understand the vast majority of what would be said. As a means of demonstrating this critical distinction between colloquial and formal forms of speech. See following chart with equivalent terms in English.

| Colloquial English text | Formal English text |
|---|---|
| Today, an official reported that people for the two sides were talking again, and that there was no problem. Both sides promised to keep talking, to find an answer to their problems, despite the exchange of angry hostile words between them. | Today, an official spokesman for the two warring factions reported that negotiations had resumed, and that remaining issues were in fact quite inconsequential, without any ramifications. Both sides pledged to seek a meaningful and pragmatic solution to their respective concerns, notwithstanding the acrimonious and belligerent pronouncements of the two combatants. |

## Distinguishing between "spoken" and "written" Cantonese

In written Cantonese there has historically existed some ambiguity and confusion regarding what differences exist and how these differences contextualize how we can better understand how Cantonese speech and Cantonese writing are related. The value in appreciating such distinctions can help us move beyond their obvious differences to better grasp how they are related and what they each represent.

> It is generally agreed[108] that Cantonese speech is different from Mandarin not only in the pronunciation of written words, but also in the extent to which the spoken register diverges from the standard written register. The differences between the spoken and written varieties of Cantonese apply not only to the syntax but also to the lexicon, phonology, and graphology. In other words, Cantonese can be regarded as having two "realization systems": one typically used in spoken or informal contexts[109] and the other in written or formal contexts. Note however, that the former also has a written and the latter also has a Cantonese spoken realization! For simplicity's sake, we use the term "spoken form" for the informal variety, and the "written form" for the formal variety.[110]

## The social context of engaging in Cantonese speech, and why it matters

The *Yuet* language, and especially its Cantonese speech forms, have added meaning and value, when the social context of engaging in Cantonese speech is factored in. In this context, the traditional Cantonese preoccupation with, and affection for, Cantonese speech is a major distinguishing characteristic of traditional Cantonese society and culture. Beyond the technicalities of speech, as just discussed above, there existed the critically important social context which framed and motivated how Cantonese people engaged in Cantonese speech/conversation. Any discussion about Cantonese speech would be incomplete, without mention of the social context surrounding Cantonese speech.

The significance of a socially contextualized Cantonese conversation is much more complicated and nuanced, then merely just being a case where two people meet and share common ideas, values, and interests. The mutuality of which I speak, revolves around an implicitly shared loyalty, pride, and affection for the actual speech form, such as standard Cantonese speech, which the parties mutually admire, enjoy, and demonstrate a shared proficiency in speaking. In this manner, Cantonese speech itself, is both a means and an end to mutually satisfying and productive Cantonese social engagement. Thus, it is the speech form itself, around which a mutually shared interest and proficiency revolves around, and not the subject matter or context of the conversation. Quite simply, speaking Cantonese with other Cantonese people is an intuitively sensed, but not overtly articulated, shared confidence and comfort in conversing in a much admired and beloved speech form. Shared Cantonese speech automatically extends to embrace a shared identification and pride in a common Cantonese ethnic persona, socio-cultural tradition, and historical legacy. It is this social context that has made Cantonese speech such a powerful and enduring element of what it meant to be Cantonese in the nineteenth century and beyond. This important social role of engaging in Cantonese speech reflected itself in a number of interesting ways.

### *Astonishment, when encountering non-Cantonese people speaking fluent Cantonese*

Most Cantonese people have traditionally expressed astonishment over the ability of non-Cantonese (i.e., other Chinese and foreigners alike) to fluently converse in Cantonese. Cantonese people, like many other Chinese today, are not surprised to meet non-Chinese who speak fluent *Putonghua* (Mandarin Chinese.) It is however, less common to meet foreigners who are exceptionally fluent in speaking *Putonghua*. In marked contrast, many, indeed most, Cantonese speakers are very surprised to hear a non-Cantonese Chinese individual, much less a foreigner, speak reasonably good Cantonese. Needless to say, they are utterly astonished and fascinated, when encountering a foreigner who is exceptionally proficient in conversing in Cantonese, to the extent that such individuals can easily use Cantonese puns, idiomatic phrases, insider jokes and riddles, and draw upon esoteric socio-historical references and enigmatic inferences. This reminds me of how Japanese people were mesmerized by Americans on Japanese TV during the 1970s–1990s, who could ramble on, in both formal and idiomatic Japanese, as easily and naturally, as any Japanese person would do. Japanese audiences were amazed and baffled that a *gaijin* (foreigner) could speak Japanese so proficiently. This mirrors a deeply held conviction that while Cantonese speech is easy and simple for Cantonese people, it clearly remains inherently difficult, if not impossible, for non-Cantonese people to learn to speak, much less to speak it well. Because Cantonese speech is recognized as having a special intrinsic meaning and value for Cantonese people, it naturally follows that if others (e.g., foreigners) find it difficult, or more likely impossible, to learn to fluently speak Cantonese, and even more unlikely that foreigners could, or would, appreciate the inherent value and intrinsic meaning of speaking Cantonese. This quandary arises, when encountering a non-Cantonese person speaking fluent Cantonese speech, because besides an obvious proficiency in speech, there is also the implication that such an individual also has an appreciation and understanding of the complex socio-cultural nuances of Cantonese conversation, so implicit in Cantonese social engagement. This makes encountering a non-Cantonese Chinese or foreigner speaking exceptionally fluent standard Cantonese a truly astonishing experience for most Cantonese people.

### *The problem of being Cantonese, but not speaking proper Cantonese*

Among Cantonese people, there has evolved an unmistakable pride, even arrogance, about Cantonese speech. On one level, as intimated earlier, there is a defensiveness about engaging in Cantonese speech. In this regard, the speech medium itself serves as a "password" for gaining access to the inner sanctum of Cantonese society and culture. In a manner of speaking, it is not enough to speak Cantonese, or even to speak it well. It is perhaps more important to speak it properly, rather than embarrass yourself and others by speaking it improperly. This has been especially true in sophisticated urban centers like Canton and Hong Kong, where Cantonese conversation is engaged in a sophisticated and nuanced manner. Proficiency in Cantonese speech has meant, among other things, being aware of Cantonese social conventions, and how they have been used and represented in speech.

One example concerns masculine versus feminine alternative verb forms, which while they also exist in Mandarin and Taiwanese, as well as in classical and modern Chinese forms, however in Cantonese, their use and the manner of their representation are perhaps more exaggerated. Generally speaking, in Chinese there are no feminine and masculine word forms, which are so common in French and other European languages. However, certain verbs are designated for use by either a male or a female speaker. Consequently, it would be incorrect and socially embarrassing for an individual conversing in Cantonese, to use the wrong verb form with regards to him/herself. A good example of this is the correct verb form meaning "to marry." In Cantonese, men "*choe*" (my own Romanization) a wife, while women "*ga*" (my own Romanization) a husband. An equivalent distinction in English might be, men "get married" when they take a wife; but women "get wedded" when they are taken as a wife. Note here the man is active, i.e., he "takes." In contrast, a woman is passive, i.e., she is "taken." It appears that this gendered biased perspective is operational in how the Cantonese verbs regarding "to get married" and "to get wedded" are used. The urbanized sophistication of Cantonese speech in Canton, Hong Kong, and elsewhere demonstrated that among Cantonese, there existed great respect, affection, and enjoyment in conversing in Cantonese, but that there also existed a critical social context, in which Cantonese speech takes place, which one needs to be constantly mindful of.

This situation reveals a dark side to Cantonese speech, via an unmistakable self-indulgent intolerance and even insolence. This regrettably produced varying degrees of arrogance, conceit, snobbishness, and elitism among many Cantonese speakers, which historically characterized Cantonese speakers and tainted their speech. This revelation underscores a common stance among many, if not most, Cantonese speakers, that while their speech is highly respected and much beloved, it is also very nuanced, complicated, and demanding in its use. It is a treasured legacy, which requires cultivation and demands loyalty and respect. If you are Cantonese, but cannot speak it, it is truly unfortunate, because, you are not "whole" nor "all that you should be." On the other hand, if you can speak Cantonese, you must do so properly, or not at all. This means being mindful of the many conventions, rules, traditions, standards, and customary practices, regarding how to properly speak Cantonese. Because as a speaker of Cantonese, one is an heir to a grand legacy. In speaking Cantonese, one must be worthy of such a gift, which requires not only proficiency, but also discipline and responsibility. This is why it is all the more surprising, even astonishing, when a non-Cantonese, especially a foreigner, speaks fluent Cantonese. In doing so, such an individual is obviously proficient, however, there is also the sense that he/she has also become informed or sensitized about the social context of engaging in Cantonese speech. In knowing something about the social context of speaking Cantonese, one can better appreciate its many technicalities. These matters, again, help underscore what it meant to be Cantonese in the nineteenth century.

---

[1] Generally speaking, in the context of this investigation, I often use the terms "language," "dialect," and "speech" interchangeably, as a convenient shorthand means for talking about the medium through which Cantonese people communicated with each other, both orally and through writing. Contextually and Linguistically each of these terms has a specific technical meaning and application, which I explain below in the following text. Traditionally, the term *Yuet* [Cantonese form](*Yue*) (Pinyin Mandarin form], similar to the term "Cantonese" referred to a "dialect" of the Chinese language. Today, most authorities regard *Yuet* (*Yue*) as a Chinese language, and "Cantonese" as a dialect of the *Yuet* (*Yue*) language
[2] See internet, language-Wikipedia, https://en.wikipedia.org/wiki/Language
[3] See internet, dialect-Wikipedia, https://en.wikipedia,org/wiki/Dialect
[4] Ibid.,
[5] See internet, speech-Wikipedia, https://en.wikipedia.org/wiki/Speech
[6] See, Webster's New world Dictionary of the American Language, (2nd edition) (Cleveland, Ohio:

World Publishing Company, 1964), p.810.
[7] Jerry Norman, Chinese, (Cambridge Language Surveys) (New York: Cambridge University Press, 1988 (1993 paperback edition), p.5.
[8] Marjorie K.M. Chan and Douglas W. Lee, "Chinatown Chinese: A Linguistic and Historical Re-evaluation," p. 122, in Amerasia Journal, 8:11, 1981, pp. 111–131; also see, Marjorie K.M. Chan, "Cantonese opera and the growth and spread of vernacular written Cantonese in the twentieth century," pp. 1–18, in Preceedings of the Seventeenth North American Conference on Chinese Linguistics (NAC 11-17) edited by Qain Gao (Los Angeles: GSIL Publications, University of Southern California, 2005).
[9] Norman, Chinese, pp. 10, 11.
[10] Ibid., p. 11.
[11] Ibid., see Introduction, p.1
[12] There exists a difference of opinion regarding the term "dialect." Among linguists, it is an accepted technical term of well-established meaning and use, but among anthropologists there has developed a preference for alternative terms, e.g., "variations of speech, speech variants, and speech communities," as they can better represent other concerns beyond the technicalities of language study. My own position is that when talking about the technical aspects of language, relative to sub-structural components of a language, I use the term "dialect." When referring to local speech in regards to social, anthropological, and historical matters, then I often use "speech variants," "speech forms," and/or "speech communities." When both terms are equally applicable, and not contradictory, I use the hybrid term(s) "dialect/speech."
[13] See generally, Hong Yuan Dong, A History of the Chinese Language, (New Jersey: Routledge University Press, 2014); also see Chao Fen Sun, Chinese, A Linguistic Introduction, (Cambridge UK: Cambridge University Press, 2006).
[14] Chan and Lee, "Chinatown Chinese", p. 117.
[15] Norman, Chinese, p.210.
[16] Ibid., pp. 183–187.
[17] See generally, Herold J. Wiens, Han Chinese Expansion in South China, (New Jersey: Shoe String Press: 1967), pp. 55–129; also see Norman, Chinese, p. 186.
[18] S. Robert Ramsey, The Languages of China, (Princeton, New Jersey: Princeton University Press, 1989), pp. 232–233.
[19] See Herold J. Wiens, China's March to the Tropics, (New York: Shoe String Press, 1954).
[20] Norman, Chinese, pp.210–214.
[21] Ramsey, The Languages of China, (Princeton, New Jersey: Princeton University Press,1989), p.87. In 1989, there were approximately 950 million Han Chinese speaking *Han-yu* (Chinese). This included: 679,250,000 or 71.5% speaking [exclusively or primarily] *Putonghua* or Mandarin Chinese; 80,750,000 or 8.5% speaking one of the *Wu* dialects; 38,950,000 or 4.1% speaking one of the *Min* dialects; 35,150,000 or 3.7% speaking *Hakka*; and 47,500,000 or 5.%speaking *Yue* (*Yuet*) dialect(s) (i.e., Cantonese) in central Gwongdung and southern Gwongsai (i.e., *Baak-wah*).
[22] Ramsey, The Languages of China, pp. 98–99.
[23] Ibid., p. 99.
[24] Norman, Chinese, p.4
[25] Evidence of this conservatively managed consistency of *Yuet/Cantonese* speech/language is discussed at length and in considerable detail in last part of chapter 6 of this study.
[26] See generally Norman, Chinese, pp.214–221; and Ramsey, The Languages of China, pp. 98–107; Maria Kurpaska, Chinese language(s): A Look Through the Prism of "The Great Dictionary of Modern Chinese Dialects," (Walter de Gruyter: 2010).
[27] In regards to romanization, I follow my earlier established format, 1) the [standard] Cantonese form, 2) the Pinyin Mandarin form (in parenthesis), followed by the English equivalent term.
[28] Norman, Chinese, pp. 214–215.
[29] Ibid., p. 215. 216.
[30] See internet, *Yue* Chinese, Wikipedia https://en.wikipedia.org/wiki/yue_chinese
[31] Ramsey, The Languages of China, p.99.
[32] See Ann Oi-kan yue, Hashimoto, Studies in Yue Dialects 1: Phonology of Cantonese, (New York:

Cambridge University Press, 1972), also see works by Robert S. Bauer and Paul Benedict, <u>Modern Cantonese Phonology</u>, (Berlin/New York: Mouton de Gruyter, 1997); Stephen Matthews and Virgina Yip, <u>Cantonese: A Comprehensive Grammar</u>, (London/ New York: Routledge, 1994); Anne Yue-Hashimoto, "The Yue Dialect," in <u>Languages and Dialects of China</u>, in <u>Journal of Chinese Linguistics Monograph Series,</u> edited by William S.Y. Wang, (Berkeley: University of California Press) Number 3:1991.

[33] See <u>Zhongguo yuyan dituji (di 2 bn) Han yu fangyan juan</u> (Language Atlas of China) (2nd edition) Chinese Dialect(s) volume (Beijing: The Commercial Press, 2012), p. 125. (A joint work by the Australian Academy of the Humanities and the Chinese Academy of Social Sciences, 1987–1989).

[34] See Barbara E. Ward, "Regional Operas and their Audiences: Evidence from Hong Kong," in <u>Popular Culture in Later Imperial China,</u> edited by David Johnson, Andrew J. Nathan, and Evelyn S. Rawski, (Berkeley: University of California Press, 1985, see especially chapter 6, pp.161–187; see especially p. 163

[35] Chan, "Cantonese opera and the growth and spread of vernacular written Cantonese in the Twentieth Century," pp. 1–18

[36] Ibid., p. 163, also see, Colin Mackerras, <u>The Chinese Theatre in Modern Times</u>, (London: Thames and Hudson, 1975), especially part II.

[37] Gregory E. Guldin, "Seven Veiled Ethnicity: A Hong Kong Chinese Folk Model," in <u>Journal of Chinese Studies</u>, 1:1 (June 1984), pp. 139–156, see p. 144; also see chapter 3, of this book.

[38] See, Li Fang-kuei, "Languages and Dialects," in <u>The Chinese Yearbook</u>. (Shanghai: Commercial Press, 1937); Li mentions 7 major Chinese dialect groups. They are: 1) Mandarin (*Beifanghua*), 2) *Wu*, 3) *Xiang*, 4) *Gan*, 5) *Kejia* (*Hakka*), 6 *Yue* (Gwongdung/Cantonese) and 7) *Min* (Fujian); also see subsequent major work, Yuan, <u>*Hanyu fangyan gaiyao*</u> (*An Outline of the Chinese Dialects*).

[39] Regarding *Yuet* (*Yue*) as an identifying ethnic label, see chapter 3 of this book, "Cantonese Ethnicity, as a Series of Ethnic & Speech Community Labels."

[40] In cases of representing key Chinese terms, I use the Cantonese form when referencing Cantonese items, then I also supply the *Pinyin* (standard "Mandarin" Chinese form) in parenthesis, e.g., Gwongdung (Guangdong).

[41] See Jiahua Yuan, <u>*Hanyu Fangyan gaiyao*</u> (*An Outline of Chinese Dialects*) (hereafter cited as HYFYGY) (Beijing: Wenzi Gaige Chubanshe, 1960).

[42] Reference work of joint Australian-Chinese research project on *Yuet* (*Yue*) dialects, <u>*Zhongguo Yuyan Dituji (di 2 ban) Han Yu Fangyan juan*</u> (Language Atlas of China) (2nd edition) (Beijing: Commercial Press, 2012)

[43] Ann Yue-Hashimoto, <u>Pathology of Cantonese</u>, (Cambridge UK: Cambridge University Press, 1972)

[44] Norman, p.266

[45] I use the term "North America," when I include Canada as well as the United States, regarding the distribution and settlement of overseas Cantonese communities.

[46] The *Baak-wah* label was not commonly used by Cantonese people in either Central Gwongdung or North America, instead people reverted to the more familiar traditional identification by native district/county. Its use was confined to local use among people at home in their native districts/counties of the *Baak-wah* zone and in the southern part of neighboring Gwongsai province, as a general "catch-all" identifying label. In the context of this investigation, I use *Baak-wah* as a unifying speech community identity label, indicative of a geo-demographic category, with common ethno-speech characteristics, as to permit such ad hoc labeling.

[47] Note: In both the Inner and Outer *Baak-wah* zones or ethno-speech micro-regions, *Yuet* dialects are prominent. While there are no specific designations, e.g., Say-Yup, there may exist local variations/forms, which await field research to verify. I use the general term *Gwongdung-wah* ("Gwongdungese" or "Gwongdung speech") to represent the *Yuet* speech forms commonly used throughout the *Baak-wah* zone. It is perhaps this historically widespread use of *Yuet*/Cantonese speech in this large area that gave rise to the practical application of the term "Gwongdung-wah" (*Guangdonghua*) in Gwongdung province. This helps to explain the enigma of the use of this figure of speech.

[48] Note: Here I apply the *Yuet*/Cantonese ethnic group and speech community label to all the people of

Chung-Shaan district/county, despite fact that there existed significant and sizable non *Yuet*/Cantonese groups, such as the *Min* speaking *Lung Doo* and *Nam Long* communities, as well as the *Hakka* community. See, Gregory E. Guldin, "Seven Veiled Ethnicity: A Hong Kong Chinese Folk Model," in Journal of Chinese Studies, 1:1 (June 1984), pp. 139-156, see p. 144; also see chapter 3 of this book. regarding linguistic exclusion and ethnic inclusion aspects of the *Yuet*/Cantonese identity label in Nineteenth-Century Central Gwongdung.

[49] See generally, Yuan, HYFYGY.
[50] See generally, Language Atlas of China.
[51] Ann Hashimoto or Oi-kan yue or Hashimoto-Yue, Pathology of Cantonese, (Cambridge UK: Cambridge University Press, 1972)
[52] See Yuan, HYFYGY.
[53] See generally, Language Atlas of China.
[54] Ann Hashimoto or Oi-kan yue or Hashimoto-Yue, Pathology of Cantonese, (Cambridge UK: Cambridge University Press, 1972)
[55] See Yuan, HYFYGY.
[56] See generally, Language Atlas of China.
[57] Ann Hashimoto or Oi-kan yue or Hashimoto-Yue, Pathology of Cantonese, (Cambridge UK: Cambridge University Press, 1972)
[58] Note: Here I apply the *Yuet*/Cantonese ethnic group and speech community label to all the people of Chung-Shaan district/county, despite fact that there existed significant and sizable non *Yuet*/Cantonese groups, such as the *Min* speaking *Lung Doo* and *Nam Long* communities, as well as the *Hakka* community. See text in chapter four, regarding linguistic exclusion and ethnic inclusion aspects of the *Yuet*/Cantonese identity label in Nineteenth-Century Central Gwongdung.
[59] See, Yue-Hashimoto, "The Yue Dialect," in Languages and Dialects of China, in Journal of Chinese Linguistics Monograph Series, Number 3:1991, pp.294-324.
[60] See, Andrus, Tony, et. al. Language Specific Peculiarities Document for Cantonese as Spoken in Guangdong and Guangxi Provinces of China, (developed by Appen Butler Hill), pp. 1-9, see especially page 1. This text is part of IARPA (Intelligence Advanced Research Projects Activity) Babel Cantonese Language Pack IARPA-babel 101b-v0.4c, LDC2016S02 web download Philadelphia Linguistic Data Consortium, 2015 (copyright now held by the US government) (developed by Appen Butler Hill for IARPA Babel Program, containing 215 hours of Cantonese conversational and scripted telephone speech collected in 2011.
[61] Norman, Chinese, p. 215.
[62] Ibid., p.221.
[63] In this section I offer key examples to illustrate examples of the unique distinctiveness of Cantonese dialect/speech. There are numerous other examples, many of which are quite technical in nature.
[64] Norman, Chinese, p. 216
[65] Ibid., p.103.
[66] Ramsey, The Languages of China, p.99.
[67] Norman, Chinese, P. 215.
[68] Ramsey, The Languages of China, p. 99.
[69] See generally, Michael A. Fuller, An Introduction to Literary Chinese, (Cambridge, Mass: Harvard East Asian Monographs # 176,) (Harvard University Asia Center, 2004); also see Paul W., Kroll, A Student's Dictionary of Classical and Medieval Chinese, (Leiden, The Netherlands: Brill Publication, 2017) (Revised edition).
[70] Ibid., p.104
[71] See Marlow Hom, Songs of Gold Mountain, Cantonese Rhymes from San Francisco Chinatown, (Berkeley: University of California Press, 1987); also see Peter T. Morris, Cantonese Love Songs, An English Translation of Jiu Ji-yung's Cantonese songs of the early 19th Century, (Hong Kong: Hong Kong University Press, 1992).
[72] Norman, Chinese, p. 215.; also see *Ming-Ch'ing Kwangtung she-hui ching-chi yuan-chiu* (Research on Kwangtung Society and Economy in the Ming-Ch'ing (Qing) period), compiled by the Society for

research on Kwangtung Society and Economy in the Ming and Ch'ing Period) (Kuangchou: Kwangtung [Guangzhou: Guangdong] People's Press, 1987) (hereafter referred to as RKSEMC), p. 215.

[73] Ramsey, The Languages of China, p. 99.

[74] This information is based on my own recollection of familiar Cantonese idiomatic terms/phrases. The English transliterations/romanizations are also my own. They do not conform to standard Cantonese. They are intended to be easily and accurately pronounced by English speakers. Standard Cantonese transliteration utilizes various symbols and notations which are unfamiliar to English speakers, which only serve to confuse and distract from efforts to easily and quickly pronounce Cantonese sounds.

[75] Ramsey, The Languages of China, p. 99.

[76] Norman, Chinese, p. 221.

[77] Ibid., P. 219

[78] Ramsey, The Languages of China, p. 100.

[79] Norman, Chinese, P. 219.

[80] Ibid., P. 220

[81] Ramsey, The Languages of China, p. 101.

[82] Note: in southwestern Mandarin speech, spoken in Sichuan and Yunnan, has retained use of the "*ng*" and Southern *Min* speech has more nasal qualities than *Yuet/Cantonese*, per conversations with Professor Stevan Harrell.

[83] The Vietnamese achieved their final independence from a millennium of Chinese rule in a series of campaigns between 906–939 CE

[84] Ramsey, The Languages of China, pp. 104–105.

[85] Note: I have dropped all numerical indicators (expressed as exponents) of tones for the Cantonese romanizations,

[86] Original Chinese translations/transliterations of nineteenth-century American place names were done in Cantonese, thus the characters for "New York" transliterated in Cantonese sounds similar to the English words "New York," but not so when pronounced in Mandarin Chinese. Similarly, the early, older Cantonese term for "Seattle" was pronounced as "*Sea-at-lo.*" After WWII, this form changed to *Sai-nga-too*

[87] Ramsey, The Languages of China, p.100; Norman, Chinese, pp. 217, 220.

[88] Ramsey, The Languages of China, p. 103; also see, Norman, Chinese, p. 219.

[89] While transliteration is often used in other Chinese dialects, and in many foreign languages, to incorporate essentially alien words and speech forms, in the case of Cantonese speech, simply changing the tone of a mono-syllabic term or word easily accomplishes the task, without resorting to cumbersome whole word or whole phrase transliterations.

[90] Ramsey, Languages of China, p. 103.

[91] Ibid., P. 104; also see Chan &. Lee, "Chinatown Chinese," pp. 112–113.

[92] See, Chan &. Lee, "Chinatown Chinese," pp. 112–113.

[93] Jerry Norman, Chinese, (Cambridge Language Surveys) (New York: Cambridge University Press, 1988 (1993 paperback edition), P. 215.

[94] Ibid., p. 216.

[95] S. Robert Ramsey, The Languages of China, (Princeton, New Jersey: Princeton University Press, 1989), p. 43.

[96] Norman, Chinese, p. 216.

[97] Ibid., p. 216, as cited from HYFYGY, p. 183.

[98] Ibid., P.217, as cited from Anne Hashimoto Yue, Phonology of Cantonese, (Cambridge, UK: Cambridge University Press, 1972) (author cites 1979, but there is no entry for that year, the year 1972 is the logical choice)

[99] Ibid. P. 217, as cited from Yuen Ren Chao, "*Taishan yuliao,*" (*Taishan* [*Toi-Shaan*] Language materials) Bulletin of the Institute of History and Philology of the Academia Sinica (Taipei, Taiwan, 1951) (no page given)

[100] Ibid., P. 217, as cited from Anne Hashimoto Yue, Phonology of Cantonese, (Cambridge, UK: Cambridge University Press, 1972), p. 152ff

[101] Ibid., p. 217.
[102] Ibid., p. 216.
[103] Ibid., pp.217–218.
[104] Ibid., p. 220
[105] Ibid., p. 220.
[106] Ibid., p. 221
[107] Ibid., p. 221.
[108] See following, Robert S. Bauer and Paul Benedict, <u>Modern Cantonese Phonology</u>, (Berlin/New York: Mouton de Gruyter, 1997); Stephen Matthews and Virgina Yip, <u>Cantonese: A Comprehensive Grammar</u>, (London/ New York: Routledge, 1994); Anne Yue-Hashimoto, "The Yue Dialect," in <u>Languages and Dialects of China,</u> in <u>Journal of Chinese Linguistics</u> Monograph Series, Number 3:1991.
[109] Yue-Hashimoto, "The Yue Dialect," pp.294-324.
[110] Andrus, Tony, et. al. Language Specific Peculiarities Document for Cantonese as Spoken in Guangdong and Guangxi Provinces of China, (developed by Appen Butler Hill), pp. 1-9, see especially page 8.

# CHAPTER 3
## Cantonese Ethnicity: A Series of Ethnic Group and Local Speech Community Identity Labels

**Introduction**

Chinese cultural labels, as indicators of group identity, have historically possessed meaning and value, when used to distinguish between Chinese and non-Chinese people. In time, this tradition influenced the choice of identifying categories, regarding "we" and "they" relationships within Han Chinese society itself.[1] Interestingly, while these labels have been a persistent concern among Chinese people, they have been challenging for outsiders to identify and understand. In this regard, nineteenth-century Chinese views about "Han Chinese ethnicity" have been especially perplexing, because there exists considerable ambiguity and confusion, as to what they actually represented and how they were used. A better way to understand traditional Han Chinese ethnicity, is to view it as a series of more sharply focused and narrowly constructed identification labels. This situation was especially evident in Nineteenth-Century Gwongdung.

Gwongdung's several ethno-speech group identity labels helped to delineate with greater accuracy and specificity various key ethno-speech sub-units of Han Chinese society in Gwongdung. They did so by clearly distinguishing between what they excluded and what they embraced, which emphasizes again the traditional concern for properly identifying *insiders* and *outsiders*. This use of narrowly constructed ethno-speech group identity labels has been historically significant in Gwongdung, especially within Central Gwongdung's *Yuet*/Cantonese society and culture, to the extent that it can be argued that the enigmatic distinctiveness of nineteenth-century Cantonese identity and experience resulted in large part from their historical maintenance and use. It is no exaggeration to say that these labels were among the most fundamental and powerful determinants of what it meant to be Cantonese in the nineteenth century. These matters merit discussion not only because of their intrinsic value, but also because they help clarify earlier remarks about the nuanced relationship between "Chinese-ness" and "Han-ness," within China's "diverse majority."[2]

Chapter 3

**Distinguishing between "ethnic group" and "speech community" Identity labels**

While traditional Han Chinese ethnic and speech community identity labels in Gwongdung were closely related, regarding what they represented and how they were used, they were however, quite distinct and separate entities.

By way of "ethnic group labels," I mean those objective criteria which were used to identify a group of people of a region or locality, by way of mutually shared identifiable traits. The signposts for distinct ethnic group identities have been: 1) shared biological links with past generations, 2) shared understanding about local community socio-cultural foundations, 3) shared affinity for popular and folk cultures, 4) shared beliefs/values as shaped by shared local institutions/traditions, 5) common communication tools, in both speech and the written mediums, and finally, 6) shared cultural customs, practices, and traditions regarding thinking and behavior, e.g., gender roles and relationships, apparel and accessories, hair styles, and social taboos.

"Ethnicity" and "race" have often been confused with each other, because some people mistakenly think that the two terms are synonymous, when they are not. Significantly, "race" denotes unalterable human distinguishing physical traits, such as skin color, whereas "ethnicity" denotes cultural distinguishing characteristics, such as language, religion, and social customs and practices. Ethnic characteristics can be adopted altered, and discarded, but racial traits cannot.

Various local ethnic groups stood out, each by way of a well-defined and distinct persona, as located within a particular communal context. In this way, ethnic group identity labels served to highlight shared aspects of daily life, as they materially distinguished, and socially distanced, various ethnic groups from one another. Common stock in an ethnic group's history, present endeavors, and future expectations, promoted strong ethnic group identifications, validated by well-defined ethnic group labels.

The local speech community identity label, in contrast, served as a simple and practical way to underscore the critical role of local speech, in the construction of community identity labels. In Gwongdung, Chinese dialects, distinguished and separated different groups in an especially powerful and fundamental way. They did so chronologically, across an immensely long period of time (i.e., two millennia,) and both spatially and socially, across a wide and varied geo-social landscape. In this way, local speech was an especially effective device for directing where "birds of a feather flock together." Local speech communities in Gwongdung historically presented themselves in one of two different polar opposites, relative to their socio-demographic construction. At one extreme, there were entire rural districts, or even a cluster of them, where everyone spoke the same local Han Chinese dialect, or sub-dialect (speech form). At the other extreme, there existed some rural districts, where within their borders, several dialects or speech forms were spoken, where neighboring wards, and even some villages had different mutually unintelligible speech forms.

The existence of different local speech groups within a single district, or cluster of districts, was especially problematic, because verbal communication remained onerous, if not impossible. In such cases, local communication between different local speech communities was only possible by either writing in Chinese characters, or resorting to a mutually understandable third dialect (e.g., standard Cantonese.) Interestingly, this dilemma of seeking viable oral communications among different speech communities also materialized within overseas Cantonese communities. In Latin America, there were instances where Chinese speaking different dialects, often communicated with each other in Spanish.[3] Similarly, in Hawaii some Chinese resorted to using either the Hawaiian language or pidgin English to communicate across dialect/speech differences with other Chinese immigrants.[4] In America in the early twentieth century, some local Chinese immigrants, either wrote in Chinese or used pidgin English to overcome dialectal differences. In this manner, local speech community identity labels strengthened local speech community solidarity, while also protecting and promoting their ongoing use. In doing so, these labels also, distinguished and separated speech groups from each other.

Because ethnic and speech identity labels each addressed a particular dimension of group identity, i.e., ethnic affiliation or speech identification, each one needs to be adequately defined and properly understood, to avoid confusion. While mindful of these distinctions, I often utilize both "ethnic group" and "local speech community" identity labels together, because they function best, when used together, where they complement and strengthen each other in an especially cogent and useful way. In this manner, they jointly contribute to a more complete and robust construction of communal group identity in Nineteenth-Century Central Gwongdung.

We should remember that nineteenth-century local institutional and situational variables contextually complicate how we view and understand, or misunderstand, Gwongdung's ethnic group and local speech community identities, to the extent that where and how these two identity markers meet and overlap has often resulted in considerable uncertainty and confusion. This problem most often arises when these two identification categories overlap in what they ascriptively represent, e.g., when they are commonly viewed as being synonymous in their connotations. Despite these challenges, these identity labels remained critically important expressions of localized ideas about "we-they" and "insider-outsider" relations in Gwongdung. Together, they underscored the distinctiveness of the nineteenth-century Cantonese persona and experience, in their transnational application in both *Tong-Shaan* (Central Gwongdung) and *Gum-Shaan* (America). On one hand, they projected an ascribed image of simplicity and spontaneity, because they were so natural and easy to use, as to defy any need to define or explain. On the other hand, they often appeared so confusing, as to require a guidebook for deciphering their enigmatic meanings and tangled relationships. Today, considerable confusion still exists, because they have often been carelessly used and indiscriminately applied, or worst yet, viewed merely as enigmatic anachronisms of limited use and value.

## The development of ethnic group and speech community identity labels in Gwongdung

The origin and early development of Gwongdung's ethnic group and local speech community identity labels is closely related to the migration and distribution pattern of Han Chinese settlers in Gwongdung over the course of two millennia. Initially, a particular group's close association with a specific place identified it, and set it apart from others. In this way, an intimate and historic relationship often evolved between a place and a particular group. By the late nineteenth century, most of the local Chinese communities in South China, most notably in Gwongdung and Fujian, consisted of descendants of migrant groups from other parts of China. Most involving many generations, with on-going and overlapping movements, over many centuries and a vast landscape. Scores of Han Chinese migrant groups had their local identities forged at different points in time and at different locations.

The identity of these groups, relative to spatial and historical labels might often embrace not one, but several reference points. It was not uncommon in Gwongdung and elsewhere in southern China, to find communities which identified, via genealogical records, with not just one, but with several key progenitors, each identified with a particular time and place, e.g., the Han Dynasty in Shaanxi, the Tang Dynasty in Henan, the Southern Song Dynasty in Fujian, and finally during the Ming dynasty in Gwongdung.[5] One Lee family genealogy, from *Nam Tseun* Village in Toi-shaan district in Central Gwongdung, goes back some twenty-six generations to the *Song* (*Sung*) period (960-1279 CE). It mentions that the progenitor of this lineage had originally lived somewhere in Shaanxi province, in northwest China. The more immediate progenitor migrated to Gwongdung in the *Song* period.[6] This far-reaching link with earlier times and distant places lent authenticity to a group's genealogy and provided legitimacy to the status of successive generations, even as they became located in different places. In Gwongdung, a particular locale associated with the "most recent" settlement, e.g., Central Gwongdung, was paramount to a group's sense of its position in time and space. History and culture might work together to delineate from where and how a particular group came to be in Gwongdung, ultimately, however, the specifics of a particular place in Gwongdung itself bound members of a community together and underscored its unique sense of identity.

The sense of community in Gwongdung could be circumscribed by many criteria. The most immediate was geo-territorial, where spatial, typographical, and ecological elements defined physical boundaries, A group's core area typically had clearly identifiable boundaries and characteristics, e.g., a river basin, alluvial plain, or a small valley between mountain ranges. These considerations also helped distinguish sub-groupings within larger units. One dominant group might occupy most of the delta region of a major river, and other sub-groups might occupy adjacent areas in pockets, nestled in small inlets, or at the foot of a range of hills. In time, through successive generations, over the course of many centuries, specific settler groups dominated particular areas. This seems to have been especially the case regarding the settlement patterns of migrant Han Chinese ethnic groups. The resultant distribution and settlement pattern in Gwongdung, in which the people of a given region, or even within a single district, typically became the basis for how ethnic group labels were constructed and applied. By the nineteenth century, geography, folklore, history, and tradition had rooted successive generations to specific locales, where local ethnic identities were paramount in linking groups of people to specific locations for extremely long periods of time. This settlement pattern lent support to the establishment of socio-cultural boundaries among and between different local ethnic groups.

Speech divisions also functioned as another important factor influencing the evolution of ethnic group labels in Gwongdung among Han Chinese settlers and their successive descendants. The result was the development of a complex ethno-linguistic mosaic in Gwongdung. Each Han Chinese ethnic group brought its own speech from a particular distant part of China, in a particular time period, and then rooted it to a specific geo-territorial context in Gwongdung. Over the course of several centuries, each speech community reproduced and extended its speech tradition through successive generations. In the process of replicating original speech patterns, there also occurred inevitable mutations of the original speech forms. These changes may have involved any or all of the following:1) a modification of older forms, once divorced form their original setting and transplanted in a new setting, via possible changes in pronunciation, syntax, grammar, and vocabulary; 2) linkages with other pre-existing local speech communities in various areas settled in Gwongdung, via incorporation of elements of pre-existing language/speech forms; 3) linkages with other co-existing (e.g., dominant) local speech communities, via mutual transfer of speech forms between and among co-existing speech communities; and 4) linkages with subsequent Chinese migrant speech communities, via mutual transfer of speech forms with the newer speech communities. The singular importance of the evolution of "local" speech in Gwongdung should not be interpreted to mean that literacy and standardized (i.e., written) languages were either absent or without influence, which certainly was not the case. It is rather a case, where local speech variables were more instrumental in developing the nexus between a given a place and its local ethnic-speech identifications.

The changes associated with language modification, i.e., local speech forms, resulted in the development and maintenance of various segmented speech communities. By way of segmentation, I specifically refer to the rise and persistence of various local speech communities, many of which embodied various gradations within them, which can be identified as sub-dialects or sub-speech groups. Again, in almost every case, local speech communities became closely identified with a particular geo-territorial location. This in turn, underscored in explicit terms the "we" and "they" boundaries associated with the rise and maintenance of local speech community identity labels in Gwongdung. If geo- historical determinants directed settlement patterns of Chinese migrations in Gwongdung, ethno-linguistic and socio-cultural considerations helped to maintain and reproduce them.

Social imperatives were also a key factor in the development of ethno-speech group labels in Gwongdung, as exemplified in the prominence of lineage/clan groups. The evolution of group labels not only meant that a particular ethnic group and speech community often became closely identified with a particular locale or region, it also meant that a complex web of group affiliation networks existed to help re-enforce group identity and solidarity. It is well known that the lineage system is strongest and most developed in southeast China, and especially in Gwongdung.[7] In this sense, ethno-speech group identity labels were not only historically rooted to a specific geo-territorial locale, they also benefited from the perpetuation of an ethno-speech community via a highly supportive social system. In Gwongdung, lineage organizations provided order and meaning, to what otherwise would have been merely a proliferation of people. Lineage systems promoted group solidarity in two ways. First, they did so vertically, via generational units. Secondly, they did so horizontally, via segmented sub-lineage units, or branches known as *fongs* "fangs." "The Chinese lineage did not operate on a stationary time-scale. Not only biologically [vertically] but also socially [horizontally] it added new generations to its system...."[8]

In Gwongdung, the centripetal pattern of shared historical migration and settlement pattern of a speech community, as rooted to a specific area and perpetuated by a complex extended lineage system, resulted in closely-knit and deeply rooted ethno-linguistic based communities. Paradoxically, they enhanced solidarity within, and also stimulated competition among and conflict between them. The most extreme manifestation of this phenomenon at the local level was the emergence of the mono-clan village, where common place of origin often became synonymous with a particular lineage or clan unit. In this situation, one surname bound every member of the local community,[9] where, everyone also spoke the same dialect/speech form. The maintenance of different, often conflicting, clan units within complex lineage systems in rural Gwongdung was complicated by the persistence of different speech communities, which re-enforced the sense of "we" against "they." Again, these developments were closely tied to particular places. It was often a case where a sub-dialect spoken within a single district or regional marketing area, did not exist anywhere else.[10]

**Gwongdung's major ethnic group identity labels**

In considering Nineteenth-Century Gwongdung's major ethnic and speech community identity labels, we should be aware of their respective composition, structuring, and functional characteristics in support of this task, see tables 3.1 and 3.3 below, regarding the nomenclature and categorization of Gwongdung's various ethnic group and local speech community labels respectively.

***Han Chinese Bundae (Bendi) (Punti) ethnic group identity labels***

The dominant Han Chinese component in Gwongdung, both chronologically and ethnographically speaking, was the *Bundae (Bendi) (Punti)* group, commonly known as the "natives" or the "original early settlers/residents" group(s).[11] This group formed the oldest, largest and most influential segment of Han Chinese society in Gwongdung, and by extension in the entire *Ling-Nam* region in late imperial China, during the Ming and Qing periods (1368–1911 CE).

Confusion about the meaning and use of the term *Bundae* arises from a misunderstanding of what the term actually means, and what it represented by way of ascribed associations. Originally *Bundae* meant "this place," relative to migrating and settling at a particular destination. Over time, its meaning evolved further. Certainly, by the *Tang-Song* (*Sung*) periods (8th-13th centuries CE) it came to mean "native(s)," or "original/early" settler(s), where groups of people became identified with a place in which they settled. This newer meaning was intended to differentiate between two different groups of early Han Chinese migrants/settlers in Gwongdung, and in neighboring Fujian and Gwongsai. Technically speaking, those migrant/settlers, and their progeny, who arrived before the twelfth century CE[12] were identified as *Bundae* Han Chinese people. In contrast, those Han Chinese migrating and settling in Gwongdung after the twelfth century CE came to be identified as *Hakka* ("guest") people(s).

In this manner, "*Bundae*" evolved further as an identity label, whereby its ascribed meaning and application criteria changed over time. It had originally served as a spatial reference point, as in "this place." Subsequently, over the course of several centuries, it became a chronological place marker, indicating whether a group of migrants had originally settled in Gwongdung, and elsewhere, either before or after the twelfth century CE. Unintentionally, over time this benign chronological indicator took on an expanded role, with greater complexity and nuanced meanings. Sequentially speaking, the term *Bundae* evolved from serving as a spatial locator, to a chronological indicator, and finally became an ethno-speech identity label. Significantly, *Bundae* and *Hakka* migrant/settler groups, not only arrived and settled in Gwongdung in two different periods, but also embodied markedly different ethnic identifications and speech forms. This complex lengthy transformative process took place in three phases.

First, there developed a long gestation period, where an embryonic Han Chinese society and culture was transplanted from Northern China to the *Lingnam* region in the eight centuries from Han to Sui times (202 BCE-600 CE). During this long period, many generations of Han Chinese settlers were engaged in the long onerous process of transforming the *Lingnam* region, e.g., absorbing and assimilating indigenous Pre-Han Dynasty *Tai*, *Yao*, and *Miao* cultures, using Han-Chinese standards and institutions.

Second, during the later Tang period (9th-10th centuries CE,) there occurred a significant transformation of the ascribed status and role of the Han Chinese in Gwongdung, relative to their relationship with Han Chinese society and culture.

This involved the full socio-cultural integration of Gwongdung's Han Chinese residents with "mainstream" Han Chinese society and culture, such that they were no longer viewed by others, nor by themselves, as marginalized Chinese people living on the periphery of Chinese society and culture.

Third, in the five centuries (1127–1644 CE) between the end of the Northern Song (Sung) and the establishment of Qing, Gwongdung, and more generally the *Lingnam* region, experienced tremendous growth of its population and economic prosperity, which confirmed the significant shift of China's socio-economic and cultural center from northern to southern China.[13] During this time, Gwongdung's Han Chinese *Bundae* established and enhanced their own "brand," as a key component of an ascendant southern Chinese society/culture. In this respect, they constructed, embraced, and personified a separate and distinct *Yuet/Bundae* regional socio-cultural tradition. This tradition had deeply buried ethno-linguistic roots, which supported the trunk and expansive branches of *Bundae* experience in Gwongdung. Over many centuries, shared *Bundae* ethnic and speech identifications sprouted anew, generation by generation, giving expression and meaning to *Bundae* identity and experience.

In Gwongdung however, the Chinese *Bundae* group did not materialize as a single uniform and unified entity. It materialized in the form of two co-contemporary, yet clearly different and separate groups, who differed chiefly in their geographical deployment in Gwongdung and their respective ethno-speech identity constructs. Each group successfully established an enduring monopoly over a sizable micro-region of Gwongdung, where their ethnic-speech identifications dominated local society and culture within a particular micro-region.

These two groups were the *Min Bundae* group located in East and West Gwongdung, and the *Yuet Bundae* located in Central Gwongdung respectively. In a matter of speaking, both groups were reluctant partners in the settlement of Gwongdung, in a process lasting several centuries. They each shared in their co-contemporary experiences in the settlement of Gwongdung, but in separate areas, with each mirroring an unusual and perplexing linguistic situation. In both standard Cantonese and in Southern *Min* speech, the term "*Bundae*" is pronounced virtually the same, however, the term for "person" is not the same at all. Consequently, in Cantonese a "native person" is a *Bundae yan*, and in

Southern Min speech, it is *Bundae lang*. Technically, they were rivals in their quest for a new homeland in Gwongdung. Geographical, chronological, demographic, and logistical determinants orchestrated where each group migrated and settled, how much territory each gained control over, and the extent of each group's ethno-speech identifications' spatial distribution and socio-cultural dominance.

**Table 3.1 Han Chinese Ethnic Groups & their Dialects in Nineteenth-Century Gwongdung[14]**

| Han Chinese *Bundae (Bendi) (Punti)* "Native" Ethnic-Speech Groups in Gwongdung all Han Chinese and their progeny, who migrated to and settled in Gwongdung between the Han and Tang periods (2nd Century BCE to the 10th Century CE) | | *Hakka (Kejia) (K'o-chia)* "Guest" ethnic-speech groups in Gwongdung as migrant/settlers in the post 12th century CE | Other Han Chinese Non-*Yuet* (Non-Cantonese Speech) groups in Gwongdung, after 14th Century CE |
|---|---|---|---|
| *Yuet (Yue) Bundae* language and dialect groups: 1st list of 5 *Yuet* dialects[15] 1. *Yuehai*, Pearl River Delta, West River valley; 2. *Siyi (Say-Yup)* Kong-mon) Jiangmen (formerly 4 district speech area); 3. *Gaolei*, in SW Gwongdung; 4. *Qin-lian*, south Gwongsai (Guangxi); 5) *Gui-Nan* SW Gwongsai. 2nd list of 7 *Yuet* dialects, divided into 3 groups[16] I) **The Metropolitan Canton** group, (1, *Guang fu* (Metro Canton,) Pearl River Delta, Foshan, Zhongshan, Dongguan, Zhuhai, Shenzhen, Qingyuan, Southern Zhaoqing; II) **The Interior Gwongdung/ Gwongsai group**, 2) *Gou-lou* inland areas of West Gwongdung and East Gwongsai (Yulin), 3) *Yong-xun*, in Yong-yu-yun valley in Gwongsai, and Nanning (capital of Gwongsai); II) **The Coastal Gwongdung/Gwongsai group**, 4) *Siyi (Say-Yup)* in Jiangmen (Kong mon), 5) *Gao-yang* SW Gwongdung, Yangjiang & Lianjiang, 6) *Wu-Hua*, in West Gwongdung, Wuchuan, Huazhou, and 7) *Qin-Lian*, southern Gwongdung, Beihai, Qinzou, Fangcheng. 3rd list of 5 *Yuet* dialects,[17] divided into 2 groups, with are further sub-divided into 5 sub-groups I) **The Pearl River Delta group**, 1. *Northern* group, 1a. *Sanyi (Saam-yup)* in Foshan, i.e. Namhoi, Panyu, Shuntak, & SE Zhaoqing, 1b *interior (Gou-lou) group*, the western Pearl River catchment, inland parts of western Gwongdung and Eastern Gwongsai, 2. **Guang-Fu group**, (Metropolitan Canton), 2a *Gwong-Chau* (Guangzhou), Hong Kong, Macao, 2b *interior counties*, Maoming,Yeung-chun,Yong-xun) ,Nanning,& Guiping in Gwongsai, 3 **Southern group**, 3a, *Zhongshan*(Chung-Shaan), including *Saam-Yup*, *Say-Yup*, and *Sam-Heung-wah*, 3b *Kuan-Lan*, the East side of Pearl River estuary, including Dongguan (Tungkun), Boan (Pao-on), Hong Kong's New Territories, also included *Qin-lian*, a southern Gwongsai dialect, II) **The Non-Pearl River Delta group**, 4) *Wu-yi (Ng-Yup)* Five speech group)(former *Say-Yup* group (4 districts' group included Toi-shaan, Hoiping, Yanping, and Sunwui) with Hok-Shaan (Hok-Shaan) added, 5) *Liangyang* group, Eastern part of Gaoyang in Yangjiang (Yeungkong) and Yangchun (Yeungchun) | *Min Bundae* language & dialect groups: 1/ *Min Hoklo* Bundae of East Gwong-dung, in Chaozhou (Teochiu), and Shantou (Swatow) *Teochiu speech* 2/*Min Hoi-Nam Bundae* of West Gwongdung, Luichau (Leizhou) peninsula, Hainan Island *Hoinam speech* 3/ NE *Min* in *Chung-Shaan* district | *Hakka* community's 4 dialect groups[18] 1.*Meixian* (The standard *Hakka* dialect) 2. Hailu 3.Huayang 4. Shatoujiao  Major Gwongdung distribution sites 1/ *Hakka* in Meixian county in East Gwongdung 2/*Hakka* in West Gwongdung, on the Luichau Peninsula and Hainan Island 3/ *Hakka* located in typically peripheral-marginal areas Central Gwongdung Pearl River Delta Region, e.g., in *Say-Yup* areas, and Chung-Shaan | *(Kuan-wah)(Guanhua)* "speech of the officials" or the Beijing dialect, as the precursor of modern "Mandarin" Chinese. *Min* speakers from Fujian. *Wu* speakers from (Jiangnan) Shanghai, Suzhou, Hangzhou. *Gan* speakers from Jiangxi. *Xiang* speakers from Hunan. There were also some random speakers from other provinces, e.g. Shandong, Hubei, Sichuan, Yunnan. |

### *The Min-Bundae ethnic group identity label*

One of the earliest and most distinct Han Chinese *Bundae* groups to enter and settle in NE Gwongdung were the *Min*-speaking people from neighboring Fujian province, located northeast of Gwongdung. The initial migration/settlement of the *Min/Bundae* group in Gwongdung occurred at about the same time, (Qin-Han periods, 2nd century BCE to 2nd century CE), when other Han Chinese *Bundae* groups, such as the *Yuet/Bundae* group settled in Central Gwongdung. Similar to the larger *Bundae* category, the *Min Bundae* group itself was also sub-divided into two distinctly separate sub-groups.[19]

### *The Min/Hoklo Bundae (Teochiu) group in East Gwongdung*[20]

Early Han Chinese migrant/settlers in East Gwongdung were from neighboring Fujian province, hence the dominance of Southern *Min* ethno-speech identifications (e.g., *Min-nan hua*) in East Gwongdung. Consequently, *Min* language and culture distinguished the *Teochiu* community in East Gwongdung by socially distancing it from Central Gwongdung's Cantonese community and its *Yuet* culture. This social distance complemented the physical/spatial separation of *Min* and *Yuet* speech communities. Consequently, these two micro-regions, in the same province, were not only distinct geographic entities, but also historically separate, socio-culturally and ethno-linguistically distant communities. In this regard, *Teochiu* people in East Gwongdung have a closer historical relationship and ethno-cultural identification with the *Min*-speaking people of neighboring Fujian province, than they do with the *Yuet*-Cantonese in Central Gwongdung. In this regard, historically speaking, East Gwongdung has maintained its sense of separateness from Central Gwongdung, not only geographically, economically, but also ethno-linguistically, as a major rival ethnic/speech micro-region within Gwongdung.[21]

### *The Min/Hoinam (Hainan) Bundae group in West Gwongdung*

*Min/Hoinam Bundae* migrant/settlers in West Gwongdung encountered a very different geographical and ecological environment in West Gwongdung, than did other *Bundae* settlers in both Central and East Gwongdung. *Both*

*Min/Bundae* settlers in East Gwongdung and *Yuet/Bundae* settlers in Central Gwongdung discovered very fertile agricultural land, nestled within large expansive river deltas, fed by numerous tributaries, distributaries, with numerous lakes, bays, and estuaries lending further environmental support. In contrast, West Gwongdung conspicuously lacked these critically important resources and a nurturing environment.

As a micro-region, West Gwongdung was less uniform and less united in its geography. In this regard, *Min/Bundae* settlers had less options for settlement, because most of the land was mountainous, with limited resources and opportunities to develop both extensive agricultural enterprises and large urban centers like Central Gwongdung's Canton and Hong Kong, and East Gwongdung's Chaozhou and Shantou (Swatow). Indeed, *Min/Bundae* settlement in West Gwongdung occurred more slowly, and on a smaller scale than in *Min/Bundae* settlement in East Gwongdung and *Yuet/Bundae* settlement in Central Gwongdung. Additionally, while *Bundae* settlement in both East and Central Gwongdung occurred in the millennium long interim, between the Han and Tang periods (2nd century BCE to 8th century CE), *Bundae* settlement in West Gwongdung occurred at a much later point in time, several centuries later, and within a shorter time frame- chiefly in mid-late Qing period (17th-19th centuries CE). West Gwongdung's nineteenth-century demographic profile also paled in comparison with East and Central Gwongdung. Nineteenth-Century East Gwongdung had about 2.5 million people, and Central Gwongdung had 7.6 times as many people, with an estimated population of about 19 million people.[22] In marked contrast, West Gwongdung only had between several hundred thousand to nearly a million people. Notably, this smaller population included not only the Han Chinese *Bundae* people, and a Hakka community,[23] it also included a sizable aboriginal tribal population, i.e., the *Li* and *Miao* tribes, which were located on Hainan Island and the mountainous areas in the Gwongsai (Guangxi) Gwongdung border areas.

Unlike earlier Han Chinese *Bundae* settlers in East and Central Gwongdung, the vast majority of Han Chinese *Bundae* settlers in West Gwongdung did not come from Northern and Central China. While some came from Fujian, most came from the earlier referenced *Min/Hoklo* (*Teochiu*) area of East Gwongdung. Consequently, *Min* speech variations or sub-dialects in West Gwongdung reflect this dual source (i.e., East Gwongdung and Southern Fujian) of the Min/*Bundae* community in West Gwongdung.

While there is little to distinguish and separate the two *Min/ Bundae* groups in East and West Gwongdung respectively, despite the fact that their respective speech forms (dialects) are quite distinct and often difficult to understand, because they remained separate ethno-speech identities. This no doubt reflected the fact that the two communities were historically distinct and separate components of the *Min/Bundae* presence in Gwongdung. First, they were both spatially separated by the wide expanse of Central Gwongdung. Second, they were also chronologically separated, because *Min/Bundae* settlement in West Gwongdung occurred later, and even then only during a brief period of time. Third, and perhaps most importantly, each group embodied a different set of *Min/Bundae* speech constructs, with *Min/Hoklo* speech in East Gwongdung and *Min/Hoinam* speech in West Gwongdung. The chief tie binding them together however, was the unified *Min/Bundae* ethnic group identity label.

### *The Yuet (Yue)(Yueh) Bundae group in Central Gwongdung*

Historically, the term *Yuet (Yue)* (粤) has been widely regarded as a synonym for (all of) Gwongdung, its people and culture. Even today, the term is a much-recognized colloquial label used throughout China to represent both the people and province of Gwongdung. Technically, the term "Yuet," properly speaking refers exclusively to only Central Gwongdung. Traditionally, its use has been restricted to general references regarding the Gwongdung region in a formal third-person context, usually by non-Gwongdung Chinese people. The term remains a convenient group label, as a useful "short-hand" reference for things related to "Cantonese" (Central) Gwongdung. Some of the more common examples include: 1) headlines or section headings in Chinese newspapers to indicate news items relating to the Gwongdung area; 2) section headings on restaurant menus, to distinguish Gwongdung's regional cuisine (Cantonese food) from other Chinese regional cuisines,[24] and 3) labels on commercial compact discs, movie videos, and DVD's, to distinguish Cantonese (Hong Kong) from Mandarin (Chinese mainland and Taiwan) pop music, videos, and films.

Historically *Yuet* is but one of several terms associated with South China, and more specifically with the *Lingnam* area of Gwongdung and Gwongsai (Guangxi). Because of the ambiguity of multiple meanings and imprecise application, confusion and uncertainty has resulted. As already mentioned in chapter 2, but which bears repeating here, two key terms, long historically associated with Gwongdung and its people, are easily confused, because they are both pronounced in approximately the same way, in both Cantonese (*Yuet*) and Mandarin (*Yue*) (*Yueh*), but written with two different Chinese characters.

The first term (越) *Yuet (Yue)* was widely used in remote antiquity, during the later Zhou, Qin and early Han periods (fourth century BCE to first century CE). This form of *Yuet* referred to the people and culture of a vast region, stretching from the area of the lower Yangtze provinces of Zhejiang and Jiangsu, through Fujian, and Gwongdung provinces, all the way into north Vietnam's Red River valley.[25] There existed a hybrid state/society of *Nam Yuet* (*Nanyue*) (南越) (Vietnamese form, *Nam Viet*) in the period, 204–111 BCE).

By the Tang period (618–907 CE), this form of *Yuet* (越), as an ascribed hybrid identity label no longer applied to Gwongdung and its people, and more generally the *Lingnam* region.[26] When the Vietnamese achieved their independence from China in 938–944 CE, people in Gwongdung began to distance themselves from, and eventually no longer identified with the older hybrid *Yuet* cultural identity label (越). With an end of a Sino-Vietnamese nexus, Han Chinese people in Gwongdung and Gwongsai, developed their own distinct, separate ethnic identification, by using a different Chinese character for *Yuet* (*Yue*) (粵), but which was pronounced in the same way as the older term *Yuet* (*Yue*) (越).

This new *Yuet* (粵) group identity label for the *Yuet/Bundae* Chinese in Central Gwongdung emphasized the sense of one's "ethnic" identity, as opposed to one's "cultural" identity. This was evident in the change-over from the earlier *Yuet* label (越) to the newer more specific and practical ethno-linguistic *Yuet* (粵) label. At the same time, (in the Tang period), the words "*Gwong-chau*" (Canton) and "*Gwongdung*," came into widespread use, as official geo-administrative terms. It then became common to view the *Lingnam* area as a key component of an increasingly integrated and maturing Southern China, rather than merely as the site of a distant Sino-barbarian frontier, where local rulers, "…made the most contributions(s) of any…rulers toward the development of the present-day special ethnic character of the Ling-nan [*Lingnam*] peoples…."[27]

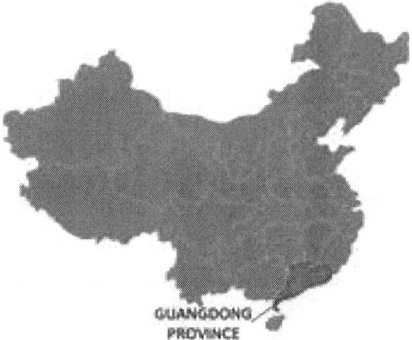

"***Yuet***"(Yue) (粵) used when referring to people and things identified with Gwongdung (Guangdong) province, (or more correctly and specifically to Central Gwongdung) from late Tang times onwards (800–1900 CE)

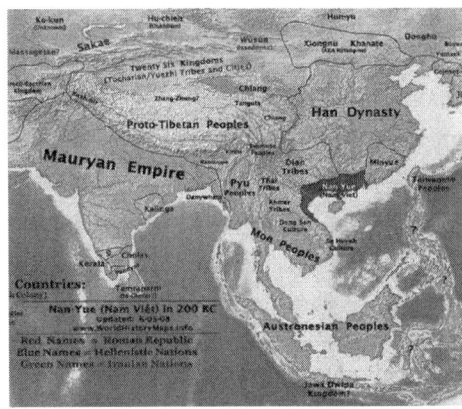

"***Yuet***"(Yue)( 越 ) in reference to the ancient *Yuet* (Yue) cultural zone, in SE China and N. Vietnam or the ancient Sino-Vietnamese kingdom of *Nan Yue*(*Nam-Yuet*) (Cantonese form) or (Vietnamese form) (Nam-Viet) (214–111 BCE)

## Cantonese Ethnicity

The net result of this adoption of *Yuet* (粵) to replace an earlier, anachronistic *Yuet* (越), was the growing importance of the underlying ethno-speech constructs of Han Chinese *Yuet/Bundae* identity and experience in Gwongdung, but especially in Central Gwongdung, and more generally in the *Lingnam*. Viewed in this light, the wide expanse of territory occupied by *Yuet/Bundae* people underscored the prominence of *Yuet* (粵) language, culture, and ethno-speech identities in Central Gwongdung. This dominant position was borne out in the distribution pattern of *Yuet* (粵) people and language in Central Gwongdung. This in turn underscores the proposition that Central Gwongdung is the ancestral homeland of the *Yuet* (粵) people and their culture. Nineteenth-Century Central Gwongdung was the largest, most densely populated, economically advanced, and socio-culturally advantaged micro-region in Gwongdung.[28] This large expansive area consisted of several key *Yuet/Bundae* controlled areas, which I identify as five key sub-regions, based on Vogel's 1989 administrative/geo-territorial configurations of Gwongdung.[29]

**Table 3.2 Five major *Yuet/Bundae* areas in Nineteenth-Century Central Gwongdung**

| *Yuet/Bundae* designated areas | Description of the general location and areas embraced within a specific *Yuet/Bundae* area |
| --- | --- |
| *Yuet/Bundae* area #1 | The southern two-thirds of the northern tier of 31 rural counties and urban districts of Northern Gwongdung, including the present Metropolitan Regions, from east to west, of *Heyuan, Shaoguan, Qingyuan,* and *Zhaoqing*. |
| *Yuet/Bundae* area #2 | The provincial capital of Canton and a number of adjacent Metropolitan region counties, (which includes the three *Saam-Yup* counties) |
| *Yuet/Bundae* area #3 | The block of counties located to the east and southeast of Canton, Which included: *Huizhou, Dongguan* county, the *Shenzhen-Boan* areaand (British) Hong Kong |

| | |
|---|---|
| *Yuet/Bundae* area #4 | The counties of the southern, western, and southwestern areas of the Pearl River Delta Region, which include: *Jiangmen* (*Kongmen*) the former *Say-Yup* areas), *Zhongshan* (*Chung-Shaan*), and some of the counties of the *Foshan* region. |
| *Yuet/Bundae* area #5 | The block of counties to the west-southwest of Canton, which include: *Zhanjiang, Maoming*, and *Yangjiang*. |

In the aggregate, the *Yuet*/Cantonese *Bundae* community occupied nearly all of Central Gwongdung, which was about 53,130 square miles. Realistically speaking, however, one should delete the non-*Yuet*/Cantonese peripheral areas, consisting of fifteen rural districts in an area of about 13,300 square miles, where few *Yuet*/Cantonese *Bundae* people lived.

Three characteristics underscore *Yuet*/*Bundae* prominence in Central Gwongdung. First, this group occupied and controlled the largest amount of territory in Central Gwongdung, which embraced the widest expanse of fertile farmland in all of Gwongdung. This territory of about 39,830 square miles constituted about 75% (i.e., 74.96%) of Central Gwongdung's total 53,130 square miles, or an estimated 48.5% of Gwongdung's total area of about 82,000 square miles.[30] Second, in the later nineteenth century the *Yuet*/Cantonese *Bundae* total population averaged an estimated 16.6 million. This represented the single largest aggregate high density population concentration in Gwongdung, which means that it represented about 57% of late Nineteenth-Century Gwongdung's total population of about 29 million.[31] Third, *Yuet*/ *Bundae* Central Gwongdung dominated and effectively monopolized Gwongdung's economy, and by extension that of the entire *Lingnam*. Specifically, *Yuet*/*Bundae* Cantonese merchants effectively controlled Gwongdung's commercialized agricultural enterprises and markets, financial/banking systems, retail and wholesale sectors, venture capital investments, and communications/ transportation systems. In the period 1850–1900, they also masterminded the monopoly of Cantonese overseas emigration, first out of Canton, Whampoa, and Macau, and then later in Hong Kong, which although a British colony after 1842, provided ample opportunities for the local Cantonese merchant community to thrive.[32]

Dating from at least the early Ming period (14th Century CE,) *Yuet/Bundae* Cantonese speakers in Central Gwongdung commonly identified themselves by using a more concrete and specific identity label, instead of using the somewhat abstract generic ethno-cultural *Yuet* (粵) identity label. In this regard, *Yuet/Bundae* Cantonese speakers typically referred to themselves as *Gwongdung-yan (Guangdong-ren)*, i.e., "a Gwongdung person." Again, all of the people of Gwongdung, both *Yuet/Bundae* and *Min/Bundae*, as well as the *Hakka*, were technically speaking all "Gwongdung people," because they all lived in Gwongdung.

Significantly, if oddly, only one segment of Gwongdung society actually made such a claim. Not everyone could identify with this proposition in the same manner, relative to its degree of accuracy, and whether or not one felt comfortable with such an identity label. It would be more correct to say, that while everyone in Gwongdung could say that they were "from" Gwongdung, however not everyone described him/herself as a *Gwongdung-yan* or "Gwongdung-person." Only the *Yuet/Bundae* Cantonese majority claimed to be both "from" Gwongdung, and "being" a *Gwongdung-yan* or "Gwongdung person." Indeed, over time, *Gwondung yan* and Cantonese in fact, came to be regarded as being synonymous.

Other Han Chinese *Bundae* groups, such as *the Min/Hoklo,* and *Min/Hoinam,* as well as the *Hakka*, have traditionally preferred to identify themselves by their respective ethnic/speech identity labels. These identifications omit any reference to Gwongdung. For these people, it is enough to merely identify themselves with *Chaozhou, (Teochiu)*, *Shantou, Hoinam (Hainan)*, or as a *Hakka* person, because everyone knows that such references unmistakably identify the speaker, as a person from somewhere in Gwongdung, such as Eastern or Western Gwongdung, even though there is no claim of being a *Gwongdung-yan* (Gwongdung person). While they were "also from Gwongdung," they did not identify themselves as a *Gwongdung-yan*, because this would convey the mistaken impression that they were *Yuet*/Cantonese, which they emphatically were not. Among *Yuet*/Cantonese people, however, this identification was easy, natural, and automatic.

Ultimately, the term *Gwongdung-yan i.e., a.* "Gwongdung person" became an enduring, if somewhat enigmatic, synonymous nineteenth-century identification for a Cantonese person.³³ In Gwongdung, and everywhere else in the Chinese speaking world, there was the unmistakable fact that when one referenced a *Gwongdung-yan* or "Gwongdung person," one expected other Chinese to automatically understand that such a reference did not allow for any ambiguity, because it could only refer to Cantonese people. This understanding and expectation represented one of the fundamental and enduring features of the nineteenth-century *Yuet/Bundae* Cantonese identity, which in turn served as one of the chief constructs of "what it meant to be Cantonese in the nineteenth century."

### *Gwongdung's Hakka (Kejia) (K'o-chia) ("guest") ethnic group identity label*

The *Hakka* presence in Nineteenth-Century Gwongdung offered a counter-balance to *Bundae* dominance, (i.e., to both *Min* and *Yuet Bundae* groups) by way of a persistent reminder that while *Bundae* interests and needs were paramount, they were never absolute nor uncontested. In this context, *Hakka* experience predicated itself on the proposition that, while not always sustainable, *Hakka* needs and interests mattered, and by extension *Hakka* identity mattered.

*Hakka (Kejia)(K'o-chia)* (*Khei-ka lang* in the Chaozhou/Teochiu dialect,)³⁴ ancestors migrated from northern China, most likely from parts of the central plain region of the Middle and Lower Yangtze regions, (*Hunan, Anhui, Jiangsu*) to two major regions in southern China, i.e., the Southeast coast (in *Zhejiang* and *Fujian*) and the *Lingnam* region (in Gwongdung and Gwongsai.) Generally speaking, *Hakka* southward migrations occurred in five general periods between the third and nineteenth-centuries.³⁵ When referencing *Hakka* migrations and settlement in Gwongdung, primary attention usually focuses on the post-twelfth-century CE period. In this light, *Hakka* migration/settlement experience contextualizes how we might understand the range of meanings associated with this label, particularly when viewed alternately as either a cultural label or as an ethnic label. I choose to emphasize the "ethnic" over the "cultural," because it better informs us about *Hakka* ethnic/speech group identity, relative to its material construction and historical contextualization.

> A group that shares, consciously or unconsciously, a common culture and tradition can only be designated as a "cultural" [group]. It becomes [an] "ethnic" [group]... when, in competition with another, these shared markers are consciously chosen to promote solidarity and mobilization, with a view to enhancing the group's share of societal resources or simply minimizing the threats to its survival. [36]

This perspective lends strong support to how I view the *Hakka,* as a key ethnic identity label, which contrasted with the co-contemporary Han Chinese *Bundae* identity and experience in nineteenth-century Gwongdung. Thus, while they formed a marginalized and maligned ethno-speech minority in Gwongdung, and elsewhere, they were not by any means marginalized in terms of their shared identities and experiences. Significantly, the *Hakka* ethnic label resulted from the timely confluence of three key elements: 1) ethnicity, 2) migration, and 3) re-settlement within key micro-regional systems.[37] The most distinctive features of *Hakka* experience have to do with the intricate relationship between their historical migrations and how these movements have contributed to the formation of a self-empowering and enduring *Hakka* ethnicity. In this way, *Hakka* ethnic identity resulted from the dynamics of spatial changes and ethnic conflict, arising from episodic migrations in different periods.

The most critical period seems to be in the early-mid Qing Dynasty. After a prolonged period of incubation, (1500–1800 CE) the *Hakka* pushed down from their core area in *Meixian* (*Mei* County/district), (commonly identified as the "*Hakka* homeland" in Northeast Gwongdung,) into various *Bundae* settled core areas of Central Gwongdung, such as the Pearl River Delta area, which ignited ethnic competition and conflict with the *Yuet/Bundae*. Indeed, the term "*Hakka*" is believed to have been first used in official literature chronicling *Hakka-Bundae* conflicts in the 1860s.[38]

By the time of large-scale Chinese overseas emigration in the nineteenth century, the *Hakka* were spatially well distributed in many parts of Gwongdung. They were solidly entrenched in the peripheral areas of the upper reaches of the West River, North River, East River, and the Han River. They had also become a common demographic feature in heavily populated *Bundae* areas of both Central and East Gwongdung. As the *Hakka* became interspersed with local *Bundae* people, they were not however, even partially integrated with them.[39]

As "late arrivals," the *Hakka* had to be content with settling in marginal areas not already taken, nor heavily populated, by *Bundae* people. This migratory pattern involved moving into what are described as the peripheral areas of a core area in several key macro-regions.[40] In Gwongdung, this meant that the earliest *Hakka* migrants to the *Lingnan* region initially settled in the upper reaches of major river systems, such as the Han River, the East River, and West River. These areas were not as easy to farm, nor as productive as the lowlands, already occupied by *Bundae* people. Due to prolonged adversity in these marginal areas, the *Hakka* subsequently resumed their migrations, moving from the peripheral areas into some key down-river core areas. During the 17th-19th centuries CE, this meant moving from the upper reaches of the Han River into the *Teochiu* area of Eastern Gwongdung, and from the upper parts of the West River into *Yuet/Bundae* occupied areas of the Pearl River Delta in Central Gwongdung.

In Skinnerian terms, the *Hakka* moved from "the core of a periphery," in *Hakka* controlled *Meixian,* to "the periphery of a core," in *Yuet/Bundae* controlled areas of the Pearl River Delta region. This movement from the *Yuet/Bundae* peripheral to a *Yuet/Bundae* core area nurtured *Hakka* ethnicity, via initial contact and subsequent conflict with pre-existing Yuet/*Bundae* inhabitants.[41] It should be noted that the "late arrival persona" of the *Hakka* reflects more the adverse distribution and settlement patterns of this group, relative to the *Bundae* peoples, rather than the mere historical sequence of their arrival in Gwongdung. It seems that the bias historically directed against them related more to their recent migrations, i.e., post seventeenth-century, with specific reference to core-peripheral areas within Gwongdung. In this manner, adversity and ascription worked together to preserve a separate and distinct *Hakka* ethno-speech identity.

In the nineteenth century, socio-ethnic bias, discrimination, and hostile conflict often characterized *Hakka–Yuet/Bundae* relations. By this time, the *Hakka* in Central Gwongdung emerged as a major ethnic minority group, when it transitioned from being merely a cultural group, with its own distinctive social system, to become a mobilized ethnic community fighting for its survival against its *Yuet/Bundae* neighbors. Only in the *Meixian* area in northern East Gwongdung, were the *Hakka* able to maintain themselves as the dominant group in their own "homeland." In the Qing period, this area was known as *Jiaying* District. It was renamed *Meixian* (*Mei-hsien*) during the Double Ten Revolution in 1911. While generally a backward area, *Meixian*, about the same size as the neighboring *Min/Hoklo* dominated *Chaozhou/Swatow* (*Shantou*) region, it nonetheless provided long-term stable economic/logistical support to its resident *Hakka* population. In this manner, the *Hakka* of the *Meixian* area were able to stand their own ground.

It could be argued that because the *Min/Hoklo* in the Chaozhou region, understood what it meant to be excluded from, i.e., independent of, the *Yuet*/Cantonese cultural scene, that they could possibly appreciate the *Hakka* position, even though they themselves technically possessed *Bundae* status and encountered conflicts with their *Hakka* neighbors. Thus, the *Hoklo-Hakka* status quo, in which the *Min/Hoklo-Hakka* relationship manifested itself in East Gwongdung, differed markedly from the *Yuet/Bundae-Hakka* relationship of Central Gwongdung.

It is significant, that as the *Hakka* migrated, settled, and then again re-migrated and re-settled, they were never able, nor willing, to unite in solidarity with each other into a single mobilized, consolidated, and unified ethnic community.[42] This lack of social cohesion and ethnic solidarity across geographical boundaries prevented the *Hakka* in the *Ling-Nam,* and other S.E. China coastal micro-regions respectively, from acting in unison across provincial/regional boundaries. Consequently, *Hakka* struggles in *Yuet/Bundae* Cantonese Central Gwongdung remained from the outset quite separate and independent from *Hakka* struggles elsewhere. In this regard, the dynamics of *Hakka* ethnicity, migrations, and micro-regional re-settlement coalesced in an especially troublesome way, precisely because of the atypical nature of how these components orchestrated *Hakka* experience.

The topic of *Hakka* speech is especially revealing, regarding the constructs of *Hakka* ethnic identity. There existed an interesting paradox about *Hakka* speech, as viewed from two different extremes. First, it has been viewed as a potent antagonistic sign of *Hakka* uniqueness, which emphasized distinctiveness and separation, as the basis for the establishment and maintenance of *Hakka* ethnic group identity. Second, it has also been viewed as playing an ascribed, but discretely benign role, where *Hakka* ethno-speech identity, while distinct, has actually been remarkably flexible and readily adaptative to changing circumstances, relative to the various places/people it came into contact with.

> …while the ancestors of the Hakka may have indeed come from the north, it is unlikely that they brought their language with them.[43] Rather migrants from the north adopted (but also influenced) the language of the area of settlement, which predated their migration… many…who came south at the same time, and then became Hakkas, Yue Speakers, or Min speakers, depending on the language of the area in which they settled…[where] they adopted a dialect depending on their destination.[44]

In short, while the *Hakka*, like the *Min/Hoklo*, continued to form a distinct, and in many ways unique, ethno-speech minority in Gwongdung, by the late nineteenth and early twentieth centuries, they had culturally, and especially linguistically, become part of the dominant *Yuet* culture of Central Gwongdung, just as they had become, spatially-speaking, part of the Gwongdung scene. In the *Hakka* case, the line separating and distinguishing the *Hakka* from the *Yuet/Bundae* Cantonese majority, outside of those areas where the *Hakka* formed the dominant majority (i.e., *Meixian*) eroded over time. In many cases the *Hakka became* bi-lingual in both *Hakka* and Cantonese. This was especially true in areas where the *Hakka* were located in smaller concentrations, in chiefly *Yuet/Bundae* Cantonese populated areas, where they developed symbiotic relationships with the dominant Cantonese majority, e.g., in the New Territories of British Hong Kong. In large urban areas such as *Fatshan (Foshan)*, Canton, and Hong Kong, resident *Hakka*, in their local speech, were in many cases virtually indistinguishable from the resident *Yuet/Bundae* Cantonese majority.

> ...there is the unresolved ambiguity over what the term "Cantonese" actually embraces. In language, it is one of the *Yue* *[Yuet]* dialects, but in reference to circumscribing the people or society of a specific region, it is understood often to include non-*Yue*-speaking peoples, e.g., *Hakka*.[45]

The ascribed *Hakka* persona and the *Hakka-Bundae* relationship aside, in the mid-nineteenth century, *Hakka-Bundae* relations descended into a cascading spiral of violent conflicts, where many thousands of both *Hakka* and Yuet/*Bundae* people were killed, and many more suffered injury and property damage/loss. In this light, distinctions about the evolution and socio-cultural positioning of *Hakka* speech, relative to *Hakka* identity and experience, while interesting, seem moot. They remained of little interest, and even less consequence, amidst the reality of ongoing *Hakka-Yuet/Bundae* conflicts. Still, they matter because they help us to better understand *Hakka* ethnicity.

We should remember that while ethnic identity, via ethnic communal mobilization, drove the engine of *Hakka-Yuet/Bundae* conflict- ultimately however, the fundamental basis for such conflict remained essentially geo-economic in nature. The *Hakka* in Gwongdung, and more generally elsewhere in the *Lingnam*, were distinguished by their long-standing economic disabilities, relative to the *Bundae* majority. In *Yuet/Bundae* controlled areas, the *Hakka* typically were tenant farmers of Yuet/*Bundae* landlords. This dependent relationship, and not the mere presence of the *Hakka*, served to fuel *Hakka-Yuet/Bundae* conflicts.

Between 1855–1868, for thirteen years, violent warfare raged between the *Hakka* and *Yuet/Bundae* in the Cantonese heartland of the Pearl River Delta region of Central Gwongdung.[46] This conflict spilled over elsewhere in the expanding overseas Cantonese-speaking world, including in America. The best-known case in America was the 1854 Weaverville War in northern California. There were also other local episodes elsewhere in Northern California at Oroville and Marysville.[47]

Ultimately, *Yuet/Bundae-Hakka* relations stabilized, because of: 1) the overwhelming final 1868 victory of the *Yuet/Bundae* over the *Hakka* in the heartland of the Pearl River Delta region of Central Gwongdung, and 2) the insignificant numbers of *Hakka* people in the Americas, who lived only in small scattered, concentrated pockets in widely separated locations, with the marked absence or a severely reduced *Yuet/Bundae* presence, e.g., in Hawaii and Jamaica.[48]

Significantly, towards the end of the nineteenth century, *Yuet/ Bundae-Hakka* distinctions became increasingly blurred, and ethnic conflict a thing of the past. As noted earlier, the evolving *Hakka* group, via its settlement patterns over several centuries, had made itself an integral, if not integrated, part of Gwongdung society. This does not mean that bias and discrimination disappeared, because it did not. It is to say however, that the *Hakka* might have their own dialect and live in their own communities, but by the late nineteenth century, many actually lived close to, or in the midst of areas dominated by various *Yuet/Bundae* groups. Over time, those *Hakka* who remained behind in *Yuet/Bundae* dominated areas of Central Gwongdung, who had not been eliminated by death, deportation, and relocation beyond *Yuet/Bundae* areas, very often lived near or within key urban areas, such as Canton and Hong Kong. In this context, many *Hakka*, out of necessity, became bi-dialectal, speaking both *Hakka* and Cantonese. Over time, they were assimilated into Cantonese society, whereby only their speech, spoken chiefly within the family and local *Hakka* community, distinguished, but did not separate them from Cantonese society, which spatially and socially enveloped them. This situation underscores the complex nuanced relationship between ethnicity and speech in its Cantonese speech community historical context.

**Cantonese local speech community group identity labels**

While the *Yuet/Bundae* group constituted the largest, most dominant, and economically advantaged ethnic group in Nineteenth-Century Gwongdung, it did not materialize as a uniform and unified group. The label served as a convenient, but somewhat dysfunctional, ethnic group label, by way of its construction and operation. Behind this general categorial ethnic group label, there existed a series of ethno-speech sub-groups, whose identity labels frequently obscured, and often took the place of, the *Yuet/Bundae* ethnic group identity label in identifying various local speech communities.

## Table 3.3 Geo-demographic profiles of the Seven Major Cantonese speech communities in Nineteenth-Century Central Gwongdung[49]

| Name of local Cantonese Speech community | Area description and location in Central Gwongdung | Names of administrative sub-units | Estimated total area in square miles | Estimated average population per sub-unit 1840–1900[50] | Estimated total average population 1840–1900[51] |
|---|---|---|---|---|---|
| Cantonese[52] widely identified as *Gwongdung-wah* (*Guangdonghua*) | Generally widespread in most of Central Gwongdung and the *Lingnam* region | Chiefly in Central Gwongdung | (none) | (none) | (none) |
| 1. *Gwong-chau wah* (speech of Canton) | Capital of Gwongdung | Urban Canton | 800[53] | 500,000 | 500,000[54] |
| 2. *Saam-yup wah*[55] (*San-Yap wa*) (*Sanyihua*) (*San-i hua*) | 3 rural districts adjacent to Canton, *Namhoi*, *Panyu*, & *Shuntak* | Namhoi Punyu Shuntak | 488[56] 693[57] 290[58] | 593,000 548,000 348,000 aggregate aver. (496,000) | 1,489,000 1.48 million |
| 3. *Luk-yup wah*[59] | An expansion of the *Saam-yup* speech group, with an additional 3 districts. | Tung-kun Pao-on Poklo | 1,050[60] 501[61] 1,129[62] | 159,000 189,000 aggregate aver. With *Saam-Yup* (608,000) | With additional 3 districts new Aggregate total 2,436,000 2.4 million |
| 4. *Say-yup wah*[63] (*Sze-Yap wa*) (*Siyihua*) (*Ssu-I hua*) 4 district speech community | 4 rural districts S.W. of Canton, also known as the *Kongmun* (*Jiangmen*) are, located in the S.W. portion of the Pearl River Delta region, southwest of the *Saam-yup wah* community. | Sunwui Toishaan[64] (*Toi-shaan or Hoi-shan*) Hoiping Yanping | 742[65] 1,155[66] 453[67] 785[68] | 578,000 681,000 456,000 216,000 aggregate aver. 482,750 | 1,931,000 1.9 million |
| 5. *Ng-Yup wah*[69] (*Ng-Yap wa*) (*Wuyihua*) (*Wu-I hua*) 5 district speech community | The combining of an additional rural district with the *Say-Yup* to form a "five districts" speech community. Hokshaan was located west of Yanping | Hokshaan[70] (*Hok-Shaan*) | 415[71] | 188,000 Ng-Yup aggregate aver. With *Saam-Yup* 423,800 | none Ng-Yup Aggregate average 2.1 million |
| 6. *Chung-Shaan wah*[72] (*Heung-Shaan-wah*) (*Zhongshan-hua*) *Chung-Shaan* is a nominal speech community label, actually no such speech community existed, *Chung-Shaan* actually had several local speech communities. | A district, south of *Shuntak*, occupying a peninsula with Macau located on its southern tip. | Chung-Shaan[73] | 1,110[74] | 686,500 | 4,800,000 4.8 million |

| 7. Baak-wah[75] Gwongdung wah) | Large area of Central Gwongdung between Pearl River Delta region and the mountainous region along Gwongdung border with Gwongsai (Guangxi) to the west, and with Hunan and Jiangxi to the north | The Inner Baak-wah zone[76] The Outer Baak-wah zone[77] | 12,700[78] total 19,323[79] total | 3.6 million total 5.7 million total | 25.5 million total 40 million total |

As a practical matter, these subordinate speech labels had added responsibilities and greater specificity in their identifications, because they represented the most commonly used, practical everyday group identity labels in the *Yuet/Bundae* ethnic community. The importance of these sub-group identities lies in their patterns of convergence/ divergence and emphasis on local "speech," as the chief means of distinguishing and differentiating among the various sub-components. Interestingly, the emphasis in Gwongdung on speech operated in two contradictory ways. First, it broke down the broader category of "ethnic" into discrete, but closely related speech groups, where local speech complemented and fine-tuned how ethnicity was represented and reproduced. Second, while "speech" has been closely identified with "ethnic," on its own, however, it enriched the hybrid meaning of "ethno-speech" by offering useful alternative, and yet complementary, perspectives, motivational constructs, and identification criteria, regarding local group identity. Various Cantonese speech forms were identified at different times and different locations, by different local speech group identity labels. In the nineteenth century there were seven Cantonese speech communities. (see table 3.3. above)

## *The Cantonese speech community group identity Label*

As observed earlier, "*Yuet*" (粵) has long been accepted as a micro-regional cultural reference and useful synonym for Central Gwongdung and its people. This use however, has generally been limited to referencing universalized abstractions in Central Gwongdung, such as serving as regional historical and cultural signposts. Beyond this larger purpose, it was seldom, if ever, utilized to reference and/or represent everyday local group identity labels in Central Gwongdung. In its place, the term "Cantonese" functioned as an important identity label, because it sharply focused attention on the character and construction of the dominant speech community in Gwongdung, especially in Central Gwongdung. Over time, because of its association with the Capital of Gwongdung, Cantonese speech came to be regarded as "standard Cantonese," when positioning it, relative to other varieties of Cantonese speech or dialects.

While it was widely spoken, it remained, but one of several *Yuet* dialects or speech communities in Central Gwongdung. (see table 3.1 above, re: 3 lists of officially recognized *Yuet* (*Yue*) dialects.) My technical reference to Cantonese speech here is deliberately brief, because the subject has already been discussed extensively in chapter two. My task here is to identify and differentiate between various Cantonese speech group identity labels, relative to how ethnicity was constructed and represented in Nineteenth-Century Central Gwongdung.

The subject of a Cantonese speech community may appear simple and straight forward, but in fact, it has been chronically problematic, because what normally pertained to just the city of Canton, e.g., Cantonese speech or *Gwongchau wah*, has over time come to be applied to the speech of the whole province of Gwongdung, i.e., *Gwongdung-wah (or "Gwongdungese")*. While this has been quite natural and easy for Cantonese people to intuitively understand and accept, it has however, been perplexing for outsiders (i.e., foreigners and other Chinese) to grasp, because it has been an enduring, but confusing and enigmatic practice.

I have already touched upon the vexing dilemma of the problematic relationship between "Cantonese" and "*Gwongdung-wah*" in chapter two, relative to technicalities of language and speech. In revisiting the subject again, however, my attention here is focused more narrowly on the subject of Cantonese speech community identification labels.

In the nineteenth and early twentieth century, (1800–1930) a high degree of ambiguity and confusion existed, regarding what the term "Cantonese" actually meant and what it represented, relative to its interchangeability with other commonly used pseudo-synonyms. During this time, (the situation continues to exist somewhat today) it was common nearly everywhere in China to refer to the dominant *Yuet* speech community in Gwongdung, and elsewhere in the

*Lingnam* region, with the term *Gwongdung-wah* (*Guangdonghua*), or literally "the speech of Gwongdung,"(or "Gwongdungese"). In this context, there existed the facile, if unwarranted, presumption that the two terms "Cantonese" and "*Gwongdung-wah*" were synonymous, when this clearly has not been the case. Cantonese speech existed as the best known and most widely spoken *Yuet* dialect, however in reality it was just one dialect and speech community, among many others in Central Gwongdung.

When people use "Cantonese" and "*Gwongdung-wah*" interchangeably, as if they were actually synonymous, they are unintentionally and unknowingly (perhaps among Cantonese people, it has been intentional) perpetrating and perpetuating an identity fraud. This problem reflected a discrepancy between accepting the common misperception that Cantonese speech served as "the representative speech" of Gwongdung, while in fact it was only "a widespread speech" in Gwongdung. What has not been clearly articulated, is the assumption that everyone knows about the true relationship between Cantonese speech and Gwongdung speech (if there was one, but in fact it has never existed). This has resulted in a well-known fiction between these two categories of speech in Central Gwongdung.

All Han Chinese people knew that while Cantonese speech was the dominant speech form in Central Gwongdung, it was not the only Han Chinese *Yuet* dialect spoken there. Despite this, there still persists the custom or tradition of acting as though Cantonese was in fact the only speech in Central Gwongdung, and more generally elsewhere in Gwongdung and the *Lingnam* region. Thus, as a habit, Chinese people still use the terms "Cantonese" and *Gwongdung-wah* (speech,) as if they were synonymous. Clearly this has never been the case, because many people in Gwongdung were non-Cantonese, who spoke other dialects, e.g., *Min* and *Hakka*. A case in point existed in the later nineteenth century, where *Teochiu* (Chaozhou) and *Hakka* people living in Sichuan were commonly identified as *Gwongdung yan* (*Guangdong ren*), merely because they or their ancestors were from Gwongdung, despite the fact that many of them did not speak any Cantonese.[80] *Gwongdung-wah* (Gwongdung speech) belies a commonality with Cantonese speech, which has never existed, but which nonetheless figuratively persists. In this context, there developed over time the common misperception, that when asking a person if he/she speaks *Gwongdung-wah*, (Gwongdung speech) that one is really asking if an individual speaks Cantonese (*Gwong-chau wah*). If a person did speak Cantonese, he/she would simply have replied, "Yes, I speak *Gwongdung-wah* (Gwongdung speech, i.e., Cantonese). If that individual did not speak Cantonese, but instead spoke another dialect spoken in Gwongdung, there would not be a denial, i.e. "No, I do not speak *Gwongdung-wah*." The individual would simply say affirmatively, "I speak *Teochiu,*" or "I speak *Hakka*." In other words, all of the people who live in Gwongdung are in fact people "from Gwongdung," but not all of them speak Cantonese.

Historically speaking, among the Cantonese, and most other Han Chinese as well, it became widely accepted that the two terms *Gwongdung-wah* (Gwongdung speech) and "Cantonese speech," (*Gwong-chau wah*) were to be regarded (figuratively speaking) as being synonymous speech community identifying labels, even though this was in fact factually incorrect. This view underscores the common recognition and acceptance by Han Chinese people, that the Cantonese people form the dominant majority, not only in Central Gwongdung, but throughout Gwongdung- and by extension the *Lingnam* region. This widely held perception underscores the singular dominance of the Cantonese, where *Yuet* ethnicity/culture and Cantonese speech has prevailed for over two millennia, as the "face, heart and voice" of Gwongdung. As a practical matter, any individual who identified him/herself as a speaker of *Gwongdung-wah* in effect identified him/herself as a member of the Cantonese speech community, while also embracing its ethnic group identity label.

As a convenience, the term "Cantonese" scales down the lofty abstractions of *Yuet/Bundae* identity and experience to a more concrete and intimate level of identification. It does so in much the same way that *Yuet* itself scales down the lofty abstractions of *Chung-wah* (*Zhonghua*), i.e., the quality or essence of "Chinese-ness." In a similar manner of speaking, as already referenced in the introduction, the sense of *Han-ness* scales down the abstraction of the sense of *Chinese-ness* in traditional Han Chinese identity label(s) to more concrete and manageable levels of understanding. I would argue that in Nineteenth-Century Central Gwongdung, the "Cantonese" label, conceptually served as a similarly useful speech community group identity label. It did so, because it reflected persistent concerns about reconciling symbolic cultural abstractions with paramount concerns for expressing local speech community group identities, as they related to local ties, needs, and interests.

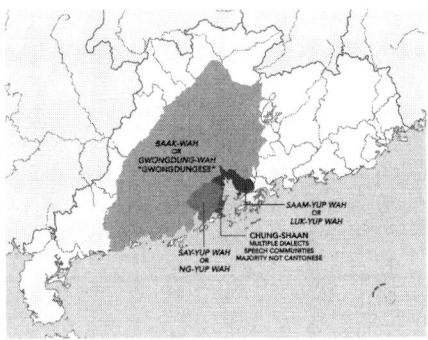

Cantonese speech communities in Central Gwongdung

## *Gwong-chau wah (Guangzhouhua) Cantonese speech community group identity label*

Traditionally, in metropolitan Canton, and throughout Central Gwongdung, Cantonese was literally known as *Gwong-chau wah*, (the speech Canton). This remained true even when spoken in British Hong Kong. Linguists have identified and classified the speech of Canton as "standard Cantonese," the chief dialect or speech community in Central Gwongdung. In imperial China, it was commonly identified as *Gwong-foo-wah* (*Guangfuhua*), the speech of the Canton prefecture. Other ways of identifying Canton's speech include: "Cantonese proper," and "core standard Cantonese."[81] The historical primacy of *Gwong-chau wah* is underscored by the fact that over time, it has come to be regarded as the *lingua franca* for much of Gwongdung and the *Lingnam*. In this sense, *Gwong-chau wah*, as standard Cantonese, has been widely recognized as the chief form of Cantonese speech in the Cantonese-speaking world. As noted earlier, the use of the term *Gwondung-wah* (*Guangdonghua*) (speech of Gwongdung province) has been universally regarded as being synonymous with *Gwong-chau wah* (*Guangzhouhua*) (the speech of Canton). It was common among speakers of different forms of Cantonese, some of which were mutually unintelligible with *Gwong-chau wah* (speech of Canton or standard Cantonese), to develop the ability to at least understand *Gwong-chau wah*, even though they could not speak it well, or not at all.

### *The Saam-Yup wah Cantonese speech community group identity label*

Interestingly, in *Namhoi*, *Punyu*, and *Shuntak*, a cluster of three rural districts adjacent to Canton,[82] the form of Cantonese spoken, while identical to *Gwong-chau wah* (Standard Cantonese,) has not however been identified as such. In this area, Cantonese speech is known as *Saam-Yup wah (Saam-Yap wa)* (*Sanyi hua*) or the "three districts' speech."[83] Historically, both *Gwong-chau wah* and *Saam-Yup wah* were virtually indistinguishable, and could thus be regarded as one in the same. It is clear, however, that their respective meanings and application represented distinct and different frames of reference. In this context, if *Gwong-chau wah* functioned as "Standard Cantonese," then *Saam-yup wah* existed as a 'shaded variant" with its own distinct characteristics and concerns, e.g., historical, geo-demographic, and communal speech identities.

The *Saam-yup wah* speech community coincidently embraced not only *Namhoi, Panyu*, and *Shuntak*, but also included three other neighboring districts, which also surrounded Canton. This included T*ungkun* and *Pao-on* (after 1866, large parts of *Pao-on* became part of Hong Kong's New Territories), both of which lie south-southeast of Canton, across the Pearl River estuary from *Shuntak* and *Chung-Shaan* districts. It also included *Poklo*, located directly north of Canton. Altogether, these six districts physically encircled Canton, providing for an extended contiguous Cantonese local speech community/zone. (see map above and also see table 3.3 above)

It is useful to know that some speech community labels often changed to accommodate additions or deletions of those districts, which combined to form such multi-unit designations, e.g., see the next section below regarding *Say-yup* and *Ng-yup* labels. In the present case, while the *Saam-yup wah* speech community actually embraced six, and not just three, rural districts surrounding Canton, one must ask "why wasn't this larger configuration called the *Luk-yup wah* or Six district speech group/community utilized, instead of continually being identified as the *Saam-yup wah* (three district) speech group/community?" Unfortunately, there is no factual basis or reasonable answer to this question. I surmise however, that the retention of the inaccurate, but highly meaningful, *Saam-yup wah* label reflected more the high pedigree/status and enhanced socio-economic leverage of the *Saam-yup* group over the other three districts. Again, the advantages of premier location, superior communication/transportation logistics, intimate long-time association with Canton, and unrivaled economic wealth paved the road for *Saam-yup* high status and socio-economic clout in the Pearl River Delta region, and elsewhere beyond in Central Gwongdung.

Since remote antiquity, *Saam-yup* people reflected a well-defined and highly effective communal persona, in partnership with the people of Canton. It is not unreasonable to accept the proposition that the people of *Tung-kun, Pao-on*, and *Poklo* did not identify with, much less, share in this legacy. Because of the long-established close ties between Canton and the *Saam-yup wah* community, *Saam-yup wah* people embodied ascribed elements of preeminence, pride, and even arrogance, about their place and role in the Cantonese heartland of Canton, and in adjacent parts of the Pearl River Delta region. This meant that while the people of *Tung-kun, Pao-on*, and *Poklo* were, as a practical matter, included in the *Saam-yup wah* speech community, they accepted such membership as "silent partners," without the benefit of explicit representation in the group identity label, i.e., the *Luk-yup wah* group label.[84] In all other respects, especially in the technicalities of local speech, the Cantonese speech in all six districts remained virtually identical with each other. Over time, the *Saam-Yup wah* community took on an ascribed (i.e., largely self-ascribed) position of leadership in the larger Cantonese speech community, (e.g., among the six districts surrounding Canton) which expanded to claim leadership over all of Central Gwongdung, and even the *Lingnam* region. Situational preeminence paralleled social prestige, economic leverage, and speech dominance- where *Saam-Yup wah* served as a credible extension of the pedigree and prestige of *Gwong-chau wah's* high status as "Standard Cantonese."

Since Song (Sung) times, the *Saam-Yup* counted among their numbers the most powerful and influential mercantile and gentry elites of the province. The famous Co-Hong monopoly that dominated the Canton Trade System (1759–1842,) was in fact a *Saam-Yup* monopoly. The *Saam-Yup* both monopolized and personified the very essence of the Cantonese speech community. It did so by virtue of its unchallenged control over Canton's commercial-economic resources, social life, and cultural scene, while embodying the essence of the Cantonese persona.

In the late eighteenth and early nineteenth century, newly established *Shu-yuan* (academies) proliferated all across South China. In Central Gwongdung, the *Saam-Yup* led the way with the establishment of the largest, and best endowed *Shu-yuan* in Gwongdung. This deep commitment and generous financial support of classical learning paid off rich dividends, whereby the *Saam-Yup* in the first part of the nineteenth century captured 40%-70% of all *Chu-jen* (provincial graduate) positions at the triennial imperial civil service provincial exams in Canton.[85] *Saam-yup* elites directed, and underwrote, Cantonese economic development (i.e. financial and commercial) and orchestrated Cantonese cultural activity in literary, artistic, musical-dramatic (i.e. Cantonese opera), civic/philanthropic, educational, and even architectural and landscaping achievements. The great Chin (Chen) lineage family compound, a popular tourist attraction in Canton, remains a vivid reminder of the opulent wealth and sophistication of *Saam-Yup* elites. *Saam-Yup* speech community elites served as self-appointed arbitrators of Cantonese taste, e.g., in the pursuit of wealth, quest for literary fame, and the insatiable quest for gourmet delights.

Similar to the *Bundae* v. *Hakka ethnic group identity labels*, the *Saam-Yup* speech community label makes little sense, when used alone. Its usefulness and value are only apparent, when used in conjunction with other corresponding Cantonese speech community identity labels, such as the *Say-Yup, Chung-Shaan, or Baak-wah*. In this sense, the *Saam-Yup* label functions best, when positioned on a local speech community continuum with other local Cantonese speech community labels. It does so by highlighting the evolution/maintenance of identity that, while initially only related to speech forms, over time also embraced ethno-cultural identity elements as well, such as place of origin and ethnic-speech communal solidarity.

In this context, there has traditionally existed a synchronization of concerns about the purity or exclusiveness of the *Saam-Yup wah* speech community, with a preoccupation for both preserving the geo-territorial integrity of the *Saam-Yup* community, as well as enhancing "turf-building" capabilities in service of *Saam-Yup* socio-economic interests. Over time, the *Saam-Yup* speech community embodied a strong sense of communal solidarity, whereby elements of speech and ethnic identity distinguished and separated it from other components of the larger *Yuet/Bundae* ethnic group, and more particularly the larger Cantonese speech community. The significant place and role of the *Saam-Yup wah* speech community was especially important, relative to its historical relationship with its arch-rival, the *Say-Yup wah* speech community.

### *The Say-Yup wah Cantonese speech community group identity label*

In contrast to the *Sam-yup wah* speech community, there also existed the *Say-yup wah* (*Sze-Yap wa*) (*Siyihua*) (*Ssu-I hua*) or the "Four Districts' speech group," (i.e., the speech of the districts of *Toi-shaan* (formerly known as *Sun-ning*,) *Hoiping, Sunwui,* and *Yanping.*) These four districts lay southwest of Canton, in the western part of the Pearl River Delta.

The *Say-Yup* speech community not only included the four rural districts of *Toi-shaan, Hoiping, Sunwui,* and *Yanping*, but also occasionally included neighboring *Hokshaan* district, located immediately west of *Sunwui* and north of *Hoiping*. When this occurred, the *Ng-Yup* (*Wu-i*) (or five district) speech group label replaced the *Say-yup* label. (see table 3.3) This alternative *Ng-Yup* label was used by the *Hokshaan* people to strategically associate themselves with the *Say-Yup* speech community. This only occurred when and where *Hokshaan* people were active in advancing their own needs and interests. In a sense, the *Hokshaan* people as *Ng Yup* speakers, in effect represented the unusual situation of a "periphery on a periphery," in contrast to the more normative scheme of a "periphery of a core area." This continued to occur overseas, e.g., in America, especially in Chinese neighborhoods in Philadelphia, where there existed a significant concentration of *Hokshaan* people.[86] Traditionally speaking, when only *Say-yup* people were involved, then only the *Say-yup wah* label applied. When *Hokshaan* people were added, then the *Ng Yup* label applied.

The *Saam-yup wah* and *Say-yup wah* speech communities, while mutually unintelligible in their respective speech forms, were in fact neighbors. The *Say-*

*yup* district of *Sunwui* lie to the west side of the *Saam-yup* districts of *Namhoi* and *Shuntak*. This close geophysical positioning of these two local Cantonese speech communities, each with radically different (mutually unintelligible) speech forms and rival socio-economic interests and needs, resulted in chronically troubled nineteenth century *Saam-yup/Say-yup* speech community relations.

The *Say-Yup* group label, similar to the *Saam-Yup* label, initially arose from purely linguistic criteria, regarding the classification of various *Cantonese* speech groups in Central Gwongdung. It represented a cohesive segment of Central Gwongdung's population in four (or five, if Hokshaan District is included) particular districts. My use of the term *Say-Yup* refers explicitly to the peoples of the four or five districts embraced by the label. Today, the whole area formerly known as the *Say-Yup wah* community, is now known as the *Kong-mun* (*Jiangmen*) Metropolitan Region.

It is important to note that while *Say-yup wah* was just another *Yuet/Cantonese* dialect in Central Gwongdung, its subsequent ascribed status and role elsewhere, e.g., in Chinese America changed significantly. In the half century 1850–1900, *Say-yup wah* became the *defacto lingua franca* of early Cantonese Chinese America, as a result of the effects of chain-migration. In the later nineteenth and early twentieth century, *Say-Yup* people achieved numerical superiority and ethno-speech communal hegemony in Nineteenth-Century Chinese America.[87] Back home in Central Gwongdung, *Say-Yup wah* people represented a disadvantaged and often marginalized speech community in the eyes of the dominant and more prestigious *Saam-Yup* speech community. In America, however, commencing in the 1860s, *Say-yup wah* had become the dominant Cantonese dialect throughout Chinese America, and by extension throughout the entire Western Hemisphere. This demonstrates the powerful precedent of *Yuet* ethnic and Cantonese speech community identifications back home in Central Gwongdung, and their long-term influence on the development of Cantonese ethnicity and speech in distant locations elsewhere.

The chief difference between *Saam-yup wah* and *Say-yup wah* is one of pronunciation, to the extent that the two Cantonese speech forms are mutually unintelligible. In other matters such as grammar, syntax, lexicon they are similar. Thus, *Say-up wah* is a bona fide Cantonese dialect. It remains the largest and best-known mutually unintelligible *Yuet* dialect or Cantonese speech form in Central Gwongdung's pivotal Pearl River Delta region.[88] This is significant for two important reasons. First, the existence of the *Saam-yup wah* and *Say-yup wah* speech communities represented the most distinctive and important dichotomy of Cantonese speech forms in the Pearl River Delta micro-region. This is to say that the *Saam-yup/Say-yup* bifurcation remained singularly unique, because while they were geophysically close neighbors, and both hosted demographically large communities, with high density population concentrations in rural settings, they also inexplicably represented the only two mutually unintelligible Cantonese dialects in the Pearl River Delta region, the heartland of the Cantonese speech community.[89]

Second, this situation was not duplicated elsewhere in Cantonese Central Gwongdung, or anywhere else in Gwongdung, and by extension elsewhere in the *Lingnam* region. In short only in this case, has there been such a radical difference in the socio-spatial positioning of two key local Cantonese speech forms or dialects.

## Table 3.4 Examples of different daily speech forms in *Saam-yup wah* and *Say-yup wah*

| English translation | *Saam-yup wah* or (*Gwong-chau wah*) or Standard Cantonese (all pronunciation/transliterations are my own) | *Say-Yup wah* (all pronunciation and transliterations are my own) |
|---|---|---|
| I don't know what you are talking about | Naw umm gee doe nay gong mut yeah | Naw umm ay tury nay gong moot yah |
| Right now, where are you going? | Yi ga, nay huri been she? | Koi see, nay oh nai huri? |
| Where am I going now? | Naw yi ga huri been she? | Naw koi see huri nai ah? |
| Right now, I don't know where he/she went (to) | Naw yi ga, dim gee doe, kuri huri been she. | Naw koi see umm a tueri kuri huri oh nai |
| Right now, I don't know what you are talking about | Naw yi ga umm gee doe nay gong mut yeah | Naw koi see umm a tueri nay gong moot yah |
| That man has never been here before, but I seem to recognize him from before, but I forgot where I saw him before | New ko yen tsung lai mai lai ko nee she, but ko naw ying duck kuri, haul nung naw yee chien guin ko kuri, donhi, naw yi ga umm gai duct hai been she guin ko kuri | Ko ko knien maing lai ko oh koi seck, ung hai naw knien ko kuri, ang hi naw umm gay ouck oh nai knien ko kuri. |

Historically speaking, this highly distinct and unique bifurcation between two mutually unintelligible neighboring Cantonese dialects, in the core area of the heartland of the Cantonese speaking world, has been critically important, less so because it highlights obvious speech differences, but more importantly it underscores the critical role that speech had in shaping nineteenth-century Cantonese ethnicity. In this regard, other critical elements at work in shaping Cantonese ethnicity beyond that of speech included the equally important elements of local socio-cultural, and ethno-speech bias.

*Saam-Yup wah and Say-Yup wah speech community traditional distrust, resentment, and rivalry*

Socio-culturally speaking, the *Saam-Yup* and *Say-yup* speech communities existed as rival counterpoints within the larger *Yuet*/Cantonese speech community in Central Gwongdung. While they were geographically close, their ascribed characters and identities were quite different and distant, with each set within its own self-contained world, often persistently at odds with each other. Historically, self-ascribed positive *Saam-Yup* characteristics contrasted with typically negatively ascribed characteristics and observations about the *Say-yup/Ng-Yup* communities.

The *Say-yup* community's ecology contrasted sharply with the *Saam-Yup*, which had abundant fertile land and water resources, whereas the *Say-Yup* did not. *Say-yup* areas were commonly identified with very rocky terrain, with farmland often located between hilly spurs and mountainous plateaus. Individual parcels were smaller and usually separated from each other by other parcels, making them more difficult to reach and to work. They usually required much more intensive work to produce, than what came so easily in *Saam-Yup* areas. Additionally, water for irrigation was difficult to obtain, and still harder to utilize, because of the arduous logistics involved in rough hilly or semi-mountainous terrain, high above major rivers, and the lack of abundant irrigation network systems. In some areas, like *Hokshaan*, major rivers bypassed, i.e., only encircled most of the district, depriving it of their benefits.

Generally, *Say-Yup* areas lacked the convenience of nearby medium or large urban centers, which again were so common in neighboring *Saam-yup* areas, (e.g., Canton, *Fatshan, Whampoa*) with their beneficial commercial, financial, transportation-communication logistical support systems. Indeed, the poor quality of much of the *Say-Yup* farmland and the lower standard of living in *Say-Yup* communities suggest that *Say-Yup* people had more in common with co-contemporary residents on the outer *Baak-wah* zone, traditionally among the poorest micro-regions of Central Gwongdung, than they did with their near-by more affluent *Saam-yup* neighbors in the heart of the Pearl River Delta. In good times, *Say-yup* farming was hard, and in bad times, it was all but impossible. Beyond poor or non-existent land and water resources, the *Say-*

*yup* also lacked the opportunity to develop significantly large-scale and widespread commercial enterprises. While the *Saam-yup* were able to easily and efficiently develop commercialized agriculture, *Say-yup* neighbors were hard pressed to do so.

A typical *Say-Yup* area landscape

*Say-yup* location in the southwest quadrant of the Pearl River Delta, considerable distance from the pivotal confluence of major river systems, meant a disadvantaged commercial position. In contrast, the *Saam-yup* community was conveniently positioned in and around Metropolitan Canton, with its rich complex of rivers and waterways. *Saam-Yup* farmlands were pivotally located in the area of the Pearl River, where the East River and major extensions of the West and North Rivers respectively fed into the Pearl River Delta. This rich waterway system not only benefited the agricultural base of the *Saam-yup*, but equally important it also provided both the basis and context for *Saam-yup* monopolization of Central Gwongdung's regional and international commercial opportunities. In contrast, the *Say-yup* community lacked such access. The *Say-yup* could only access the eastern and southeastern extensions of the West River, which mainly flowed through the eastern most parts of *Say-Yup* country, which in effect meant that the West

River distributaries by-passed, rather than flow through *Say-yup* lands. In this way, without major rivers coursing through the *Say-yup* countryside, and without key urban centers like *Fatshan, Whampoa*, to say nothing of the lack of major urban centers like Canton or Hong Kong, the *Say-yup* community did not have the material basis and opportunity to generate minimal degrees of prosperity, let alone surplus wealth, as did the *Saam-yup* speech community.

In this context, *Say-yup* central places, had a smaller volume of economic activity, smaller number of merchants, who were less dynamic, less influential, and less wealthy. The combined disadvantaged character of both agrarian and commercial activities in the *Say-yup* community invariably meant a community historically less affluent, less influential, less self-confident, and less secure. In the mid nineteenth century, this set of material conditions, when combined with a large concentrated high density *Say-yup* population, lower standards of living, reduced opportunities for economic growth (i.e., high consumption, little or no surplus) resulted in a speech community with a very different communal experience, outlook, and expectation than that of the *Saam-Yup* speech community.

The *Saam-yup* group, because of its location adjacent to Canton, and its possession and control over "the best of the best" farmland in the Pearl River Delta region, held an undisputed monopoly over Central Gwongdung's financial and commercial enterprises, and preeminent leadership in Cantonese society and culture. Consequently, as *Saam-yup* people identified with an ascribed sense of urbane sophistication, *Say-yup* people saw this as arrogant snobbishness. Similarly, because the *Saam-yup* had concentrated material wealth, others saw them as self-absorbed and greedy. If they claimed commercial expertise, others saw them as prone to exploitative manipulation. If they had a confident bravado, others saw this as self-indulgence and conceit. If they had financial shrewdness, others saw it as selfish duplicity. When the *Saam-yup* claimed cultural authenticity, the *Say-Yup* saw this as an unfounded chauvinistic arrogance.

The *Saam-yup* tended to view of the *Say-yup* people as ascriptively poor, parochial, coarse, crude, and provincial (uneducated, unsophisticated, and unattractive) in their bearing and conduct. They were frequently referred to as *heung-ha yan* (*xiangxia ren*) "country folk," or "country bumpkins." Their speech was regarded as being too loud and too coarse, making it hurtful to the ears; and their demeanor was viewed as rude and offensive, because it was awkward and crude. The *Say-yup*, were viewed as generally poor, ignorant dirty farmers and country people. For their part, *Say-yup* people were defensively proud and aggressive, unafraid to go out and to push hard to get ahead, in order to improve their lives. The *Say-yup* were self-ascriptively speaking, very frugal with their time and material resources. They did not waste time (or money) on the trivial, the unnecessary, the superficial and ornamental, but instead concentrated on what was really important, e.g., working hard, deferring consumption and gratification, while promoting priority one, family well-being, and communal solidarity.

Group tensions between the *Say-Yup* and *Saam-Yup* communities might have their roots in mutually unintelligible speech and mutually biased ascriptive "we/they" group traits, however, spatial separateness and discrepancy of economic opportunities helped fuel ethnic competition and conflict between these two communities. This mutual dislike and distrust at the fountainhead at *Tong-Shaan* resurrected itself in *Gum-Shaan*, where it continued to poison relations between the two speech communities all across Cantonese-Chinese America, from Mega-Chinatowns like those in San Francisco and New York City, to a myriad of smaller ones in Hawaii, Texas, Idaho, Oregon, to medium-sized Chinatowns widely scattered all across the American Midwest and along the Atlantic seaboard, e.g., Chicago, St. Louis, Philadelphia, Washington DC[90] and Boston. All of this flowed from the particular mechanics of *Saam-yup* and *Say-yup* speech community rivalry back home in the Cantonese heartland of the Pearl River Delta.

I believe that the development and maintenance of *Saam-Yup* and *Say-Yup* ascribed speech community group identity labels ultimately resulted, less from socio-economic criteria, and arose more directly and forcefully from the intersection of marked speech/dialectical differences and geo-territorial spatial separateness. Beyond physical-spatial separation and social distancing from the *Saam-Yup*, the *Say-Yup* group was characterized first and foremost by the distinctiveness of its speech.⁹¹ Quantitatively, it is the largest and most distinctive and unique Cantonese speech community within the dominant *Yuet/Bundae/* Cantonese complex. This distinctiveness arises from the fact that the *Say-Yup* is the largest, most clearly well-defined, and mutually unintelligible Cantonese dialect in the *Yuet/Bundae* Cantonese speech community.

The phonological differences distinguishing and separating *Say-Yup* wah from the *Saam-Yup* wah are so marked, that it is only with difficulty that individuals from the two speech groups can communicate with each other, without resorting to writing Chinese characters, or using another third-party speech medium, e.g., Mandarin, English, or even Spanish (as among Cantonese Chinese communities located in in Peru, Mexico, and Cuba). In this manner, the *Say-Yup* group, similar to the *Hakka, Min-Hoklo*, and other non-*Yuet* groups in Gwongdung, remained a well-defined speech medium, which the dominant Cantonese (*Gwong-chau wah* or *Saam-yup wah*) speaking majority in Gwongdung could not communicate with. However, unlike the *Hakka,* the *Min-Hoklo*, and other non-*Yuet* speech groups, there was no doubt that *Say-Yup wah* was indeed linguistically and culturally an integral and integrated part of the Cantonese community, and more generally its *Yuet/Bundae* cultural base. If there were marked differences in phonology, there were few, if any, in grammar, lexicon, syntax. In short, the physical placement of the *Say-Yup* in the heartland of Central Gwongdung's Yuet/*Bundae* Cantonese region historically validated the authenticity and distinctiveness of *Say-Yup wah* within the *Yuet*/Cantonese language family. Linguistic analysis of the *Yuet* (*Yue*) language underscores the unifying nexus of *Say-Yup* and *Saam-Yup* speech within the *Yuet* language, and it also highlighted the distinctiveness of both speech forms, as identifiably distinct and separate *Yuet*/Cantonese speech communities.⁹²

While there existed a concrete spatial and speech nexus between *Saam-yup* and *Say-yup* speech forms, it is also true that historically the qualities of distinctiveness and separateness resulted in the development of significant and enduring barriers between the two groups. This helps to explain the contradiction of *Saam-Yup*/*Say-Yup* similarities and differences, degrees of separation and closeness, and antagonistic tension alternating with tolerance/cooperation.

> "...the speech of each community...has tended to diverge from that of other...The amount of divergence depends largely on the degree to which it is isolated from its neighbors... the greater the barriers to travel and communication, the greater will be the differences in speech."[93]

In this context spatial separation underscored and reinforced the social distancing of speech community distinctiveness between the *SaamYup* and *Say-Yup* speech communities.

Because oral communication between the *Say-Yup* and *Saam-Yup* communities had been traditionally problematic, it tended to reinforce a reluctance to overcome basic speech differences. This speech factor in turn, while initially serving as a baseline for dividing and separating the *Saam-Yup* and *Say-Yup* speech communities, ultimately became a basis for (sub-) ethnic rivalry, and local speech community competition, and conflict. This development over time only reinforced the sense of separateness, complemented by ethnic group stereotyping. One should not forget legendary Cantonese concerns about the degree of authenticity of one's experience, the continuity of one's culture, the purity of one's speech tradition, and how they were less a reflection of social bias, and more a litmus test of ethnic group and local speech community identity.

### *The Chung-Shaan wah Cantonese speech community group identity label*[94]

*Chung-Shaan* (*Zhongshan*) district, (formerly known as *Heungshan* district before 1925), was one of the smaller districts in Central Gwongdung. It was one of only a few districts in Gwongdung to occupy an entire peninsula. *Chung-Shaan's* west coast faced the *Wong Mao Kong* (Yellow Rushes Harbor) and its east coast formed the west side of the Pearl River estuary. Macao (Macau) lay at the tip of the *Chung-Shaan* peninsula, directly due west of Hong Kong on the opposite side of the Pearl River estuary. *Chung-Shaan* district was centrally positioned, relative to several neighboring speech communities. *Saam-yup Shuntak* district bordered *Chung-Shaan* in the north, while *Saam-yup* (actually *Luk-yup*) *Pao-on* district lie due East on the other side of the Pearl River estuary (just north north-west of Hong Kong. Additionally, both *Say-yup Sunwui* and *Toi-*

*Shaan* districts lie due west across the *Wong Mao Kong* (Yellow Rushes Harbor.) In a sense, the combined distinctive geophysical setting and central positioning of *Chung-Shaan* contributed to its sense of distinctiveness, which historically distinguished it from other districts in the Pearl River Delta region. These factors contributed to a social distance between *Chung-Shaan* and its neighbors.

*Chung-Shaan* people represented a distinctively unique ethno-speech complex, unparalleled in all of Central Gwongdung. It was the only district, out of approximately 60 districts in Central Gwongdung that lacked a uniform and unified ethno-speech format, with a single dominant *Yuet/Bundae* ethnic group and Cantonese speech community within its borders. This resulted in a unique situation, where *Chung-Shaan* embraced within its borders several Han Chinese ethnic groups and a variety of local speech communities, which included representative elements of the *Yuet* and *Min Bundae*, and the *Hakka* ethnic groups and speech communities. (see tables 3.1, 3.2, and 3.3) In *Chung-Shaan*, no Han Chinese ethnic group or local speech community was able to achieve numerical demographic superiority, nor a clear ethno-speech majority, social dominance, or civic hegemony.[95] This resulted in one of the most diverse, complex, and nuanced pattern of an ethnic-speech community in Central Gwongdung, and more generally throughout Gwongdung province. In *Chung-Shaan* there existed not just one, but actually five separate speech communities located within its borders.

1) A *"Chung-Shaan"Chung-Shaan* group, a "true" Cantonese sub-dialect. This speech community centered in the administrative center of *Shekki*, and the first nine *qu* (sub-districts) of Chung-Shaan.
2) A northeastern *Min*-based *Chung-Shaan* group, which identified as two separate and distinct speech communities, the *Loong Doo (Lungtu)* and the *Nam long (Nan-lau)*.
3) A southern *Min* speaking related *Chung-Shaan* group, known as the *Saamheung-wah* (*Sanxianghua*) (or "Three rural speech group.")
4) A local *Chung-Shaan Hakka* community.[96]
5) A local contingent of *Yuet*/Cantonese people, consisting of a small *Saam-Yup* speech community located in northern *Chung-Shaan*, and a small *Say-Yup* speech community located in southwestern *Chung-Shaan*.

Map of Chung-Shaan district/county

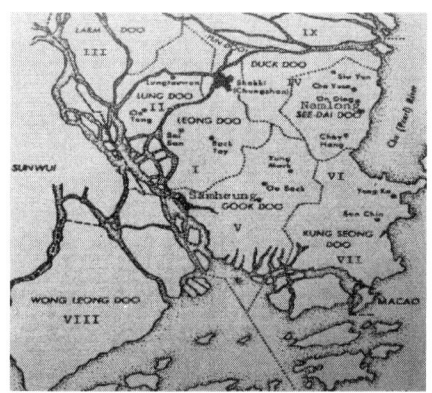

Map of Chung-Shaan Speech communities

(adapted from Char, 1975:17)

The sense of being linguistically distinct and separate among Chung-Shaan people, however, only applied to these several ethno-speech identities and relationships, as they were specifically located and contextualized within Chung-Shaan district itself. We should remember four important points, relative to these ethno-speech sub-units in Chung-Shaan society.

First, while we know there were five local speech communities in Chung-Shaan, it is not known what percentage each group represented, and which, if any, formed a clear majority in Chung-Shaan, or whether such a majority even existed.

Second, over time, membership in any one of these speech/ethnic groups was not always easy to determine, because many people were or became bi-dialectal, or even tri-dialectal in speech.[97]

Third, beyond Chung-Shaan district, local speech distinctiveness and separateness became irrelevant, such that they were often dropped, as if they had never existed, because formerly their maintenance in Chung-Shaan was accomplished by excluding others, who did not identify with any particular local Chung-Shaan speech community. In contrast, beyond Chung-Shaan, elsewhere there developed the sense of "inclusiveness" among Chung-Shaan people, regardless of their specific speech community identifications, whereby several ethno-speech groups joined together to represent themselves collectively as a single entity, i.e., the Chung-Shaan group or simply as Chung-Shaan people.

Fourth, Min speech communities of Chung-Shaan did not suffer the kind of social distancing and cultural exclusion from Central Gwongdung's dominant *Yuet-Bundae*/Cantonese group, as experienced by Min speech communities in East Gwongdung (Teochiu dialect/speech) and West Gwongdung (Hoinam [Hainan] dialect/speech) respectively. This situation also prevailed in Chinese America, as well as in Chung-Shaan. Again, this case suggests that the *Yuet*/Cantonese "Chung-Shaan" group label functioned more as an "inclusive" label, rather than an "exclusive" speech label, in both China and America.

Such a linguistic distinction was not similarly made with regard to the *Lungtu*, [Lung-Doo] *Nam Long*, and *Saamheung* people and their speech. Presumably they were treated simply as immigrants (to America) from the Chung-Shaan district, with no attempt by outsiders [i.e., *Yuet/Bundae*] to isolate the [southeast] *Min* speakers as a separate ...entity.[98]

In this light, the *Chung-Shaan* group label, as a geo-historical indicator, represented a greater emphasis on place of origin, rather than on speech/dialect among the Cantonese/*Bundae* majority in Central Gwongdung. Significantly, while *Chung-Shaan* district hosted one of the most unique ethno-linguistic configurations in Central Gwongdung, and more generally elsewhere in nineteenth-century Han Chinese society, its unique diverse distinctiveness was easily accommodated within the folds of a practical *Chung-Shaan* collective identity.[99]

## The Baak-wah (Gwongdung wah) Cantonese speech community group identity label

What I identify as a *Baak-wah* speech community represents the introduction of a new term and conceptualization, regarding a large amorphous segment of the *Yuet/Bundae Cantonese* community that has not been discussed by others. Generally speaking, this subject has been largely ignored by researchers in both Chinese and Chinese American studies. My use of such terms as *Baak-wah* zone, *Baak-wah* group, and *Baak-wah* speech community respectively, draw attention to a wide expanse of territory, a demographically large and widely disbursed component of the *Yuet/Bundae* ethnic group and Cantonese speech community- all of which are long overdue for investigation. This omission results, because in the study of Central Gwongdung's various ethnic groups and speech communities, attention has typically focused on Canton and the Pearl River Delta, with little focus elsewhere. This has also been the case in the study of nineteenth-century Cantonese-Chinese American society and culture.[100]

Historically speaking, both the *Baak-wah* area and its people have been conspicuously absent in the scholarly study of Central Gwongdung. As part of my effort to present an improved and more complete profile of Central Gwongdung's ethno-speech components, I want to address the persistence of this "black hole," regarding this neglected area and its people. Undeniably, Canton and the Pearl River Delta micro-region have traditionally snared the lion's share of attention, because of their ideal location, naturally endowed geophysical advantages, enhanced economic standing, dominant ethno-speech elements, and socio-cultural preeminence, to the extent that other remaining areas and peoples of Central Gwongdung, i.e., the *Baak-wah* community, have long been relegated to the role of a non-descript backdrop for Canton and the Pearl River Delta region. Here, I adopt the term "*Baak-wah*" to help better conceptualize this heretofore neglected micro-region of Central Gwongdung, via a much-needed appreciation of its material components.

My adoption of the term "*Baak-wah*," while easy to use, nonetheless has a complicated and nuanced history that can easily confuse, when not clearly explained. In this way it is likely to mislead, if not properly qualified. This is clearly the case when the Cantonese term "*Baak-wah*," is referenced in its mandarin form, *Baihua* (*Pai-hua*), as used in both mainland China (*Putonghua*) and Taiwan (*kuo-yu*). In its mandarin usage, the term means something entirely different from its Cantonese meaning/use. The term *Baihua* initially materialized with the advocacy for a modern Chinese written vernacular language, during the May Fourth Movement 1919–1920s.[101] In contrast, those who identify with the Cantonese term *Baak-wah,* and use it with reference to themselves, do so quite differently.

The Cantonese term *Baak-wah* does not refer to a Chinese "written" vernacular language, but instead refers to the "spoken" vernacular form of the speech component of language. I adopt the term *Baak-wah* to represent the common widespread Cantonese vernacular speech of a large region, which I identify as the *Baak-wah* zone, (see chapter one of this book).[102] Significantly, the *Baak-wah* zone, as the homeland of the *Baak-wah* speech community, embraced the largest extent of land, (26,000 square miles, or about 65%) of Central Gwongdung; and the largest number of people, about 9.36 million or about 62% of the population in Central Gwongdung. (see table 3.5)

Specifically, *Baak-wah* speech, is a form of Cantonese speech, spoken by the people who live in outlying areas of Central Gwongdung, beyond the pivotal

Pearl River Delta Region. In this larger area, local people speak a form of Cantonese that is similar to *Gwong-chau wah* or Standard Cantonese, with some minor local variations in different localities. In this large micro-region, locally spoken Cantonese has not been technically identified as either *Gwongchau wah* (Standard Cantonese) or *Saam-yup wah*, even though there existed many similarities between all three varieties of Cantonese. *Baak-wah* people are bona fide Cantonese speakers, but who have not identified with, nor have they been identified as speakers of *Gwong-chau wah* or *Saam-Yup wah.*

One useful approach to developing a new framework for thinking about the large expanse of territory and people beyond Canton and the Pearl River Delta region, is to revisit my earlier discussion about the term *Gwongdung-wah* (Speech of Gwongdung province), (or "*Gwongdungese*") the common synonym for Cantonese speech (i.e., *Gwong-chau wah*.) If we accept the proposition that *Gwongdung-wah* (i.e., the Speech of Gwongdung province) has in fact served, and continues to serve as a widespread surrogate for *Gwong-chau wah* (i.e., the speech of Canton,) then we can move forward to search for instances where it can have practical application and beneficial use. Such a move can serve as a useful step in formulating new terminology, to serve as a basis for theorizing about the nature of ethnicity and speech in the geographical area under discussion. In short, the idea of *Gwongdung-wah*, as a convenient synonym for "Cantonese speech," offers a creative and intriguing model for constructing a new categorial label for a micro-region, its people, and their speech community.

While the term *Gwongdung-wah* (the speech of *Gwongdung*) could serve as such an identification device, I choose instead to adopt and apply the term *Baak-wah*, as a more authentic technical term, which can be more practical and precise in properly identifying this micro-region, its people, and their speech. I first came across the term *Baak-wah* in 1991, on a trip to Gwongsai (Guangxi) province/autonomous region, which is adjacent to the north/northwestern side of Gwongdung. In Gwongsai, there were/are two major Han Chinese speech communities, as well as many (non-Han Chinese) ethnic minorities' speech communities. While a majority of the Han Chinese in Gwongsai speak a form of Mandarin Chinese, commonly identified as *Xinan Guanhua* (or south-west "officials' speech" (or SW Mandarin), which is similar to official Mandarin taught in schools and used in the media (i.e., *Putonghua.*) In contrast, a sizable segment of the Han Chinese in southern and southeastern Gwongsai speak Cantonese, which has been identified locally as *Baak-wah* (*baihua*), (also identified in *Pinyin* as *Yueyu* and in Cantonese as *Yuet-yuh*). In this context, *Baak-wah*, has been a technically precise and ethno-linguistically authentic Cantonese speech community identity label for Cantonese-speaking people in southern and south-eastern Gwongsai.

With this precedent in mind, it has been easy and natural to adopt the *Baak-wah* label for use in neighboring Gwongdung, more specifically for parts of Central Gwongdung. There exist two sound reasons for this choice. First, the term *Baak-wah* is already a well-known and widely used technical term, associated with *Yuet*/Cantonese speaking peoples. Second, the *Baak-wah* label, as a generic speech community label, from the outset, is specifically related to the subject of Cantonese speech (or the Cantonese dialect,) as applied to a wide geographical area and widely distributed population. In this context, I have adopted *Baak-wah* to identify that form of Cantonese speech spoken beyond Canton and the Pearl River Delta region. I expand upon this initial precise technical application, (in Gwongsai) by enlarging the frame of reference of where and how, I further use *Baak-wah* to identify other closely related phenomena. This has resulted in such designations as, *Baak-wah* zone (the area or micro-region where this Cantonese speech community has been located), *Baak-wah* people or group (those who live in an area, so identified), and finally *Baak-wah* speech and/or speech community (a group identity label.)

As previously discussed in great detail in chapter one, the *Baak-wah* zone consists of a wide fan or inverted triangular shaped region, covering the area between the Pearl River delta region and the mountainous areas of Gwongdung's northern frontiers. (see map below) It is useful to know that the boundaries delineating the *Baak-wah* zone here are ethno-linguistic, rather than geo-administrative, in their conceptualization. This means that this zone represents areas in which the *Baak-wah* community is located. Clearly, what distinguishes the *Baak-wah* zone is that it is a general region defined by ethno-linguistic criteria, relative to the *Yuet* Cantonese/*Bundae* majority.

The *Baak-wah* zone consists of a wide fan or inverted triangular shaped region, covering the area between the Pearl River delta region (PRDR) and the mountainous areas of Gwongdung's northern frontiers. (see map below) It is useful to know that the boundaries delineating the *Baak-wah* zone here are ethno-linguistic, rather than geo-administrative, in their conceptualization. This means that this zone represents areas in which the *Baak-wah* community is located. Clearly, what distinguishes the *Baak-wah* zone is that it is a general region defined by ethno-linguistic criteria, relative to the *Yuet* Cantonese/*Bundae* majority.

### Table 3.5 Nineteenth-Century *Baak-wah* zone: total area (in square miles) and estimated average aggregate population, in Central Gwongdung and all of Gwongdung[103]

| Category | Inner *Baak-wah* zone | Outer *Baak-wah* zone | *Baak-wah* zone totals | Central Gwongdung total area and population | Gwongdung province total area and population |
|---|---|---|---|---|---|
| Total area in square miles | 12,700 sq. mils.[104] | 19,300 sq. mils.[105] | 32,000 sq. mils | 39,830 sq. mils.[106] 53,130 sq. mils.[107] | 82,000 sq. mils.[108] |
| Estimated aggregate population | 3.65 Million[109] | 5.71 million[110] | 9.36 million | 15 million people[111] | 28 million people[112] |
| *Baak-wah* zone as a percentage of a total area and *Baak-wah* people as a percentage of the total aggregate population | | | | *Baak-wah* zone = about 65% of this total area. The *Baak-wah* population = about 62% of estimated total population | *Baak-wah* zone = about 31% of this total area. The *Baak-wah* population = about 33.4% of estimated total population |

The *Baak-wah* zone can be conceptually divided into two zones and three sub-components. The three sub-components are: 1) East Central Gwongdung, in the East River basin area; 2) North Central Gwongdung, in the North River basin between the Canton/Pearl River delta region and the *Doungan* hills to the north; and 3) West Central Gwongdung, centering in the West River basin, to the west and northwest of the Canton/Pearl River delta region, extending to embrace a portion of West Gwongdung (which itself extends to the Gwongdung border with Gwongsai and Vietnam. These three components conform conveniently to post-1988 administrative reforms.[113]

The *Baak-wah* zone also constitutes two broad ethno-culturally based units, relative to their positioning with: a) the core Cantonese/ *Yuet-Bundae* group (i.e., those Cantonese speech communities located in and around the Canton/Pearl River Delta Region; or b) *Hakka* dominated tier of districts along Gwongdung's northern borders.

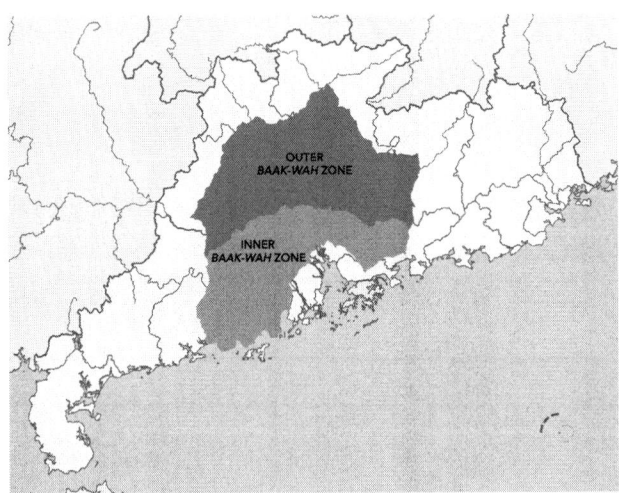

The "Inner" and "Outer" *Baak-wah* zones of Central Gwongdung

It is useful to know, that while the *Baak-wah* zone was not as agriculturally and commercially rich as the Canton/Pearl River delta region, neither did it experience the many socio-political disturbances around the Canton area in the nineteenth and early twentieth century.[114] Additionally, areas in the *Baak-wah* zone did not exhibit the kind of intense communal strife associated with the Pearl River delta's inequity of high-density population and a growing scarcity of arable land and water. The *Baak-wah* zone also remained largely untouched by the immediate volatile dangers of Sino-Western conflict, which engulfed the Canton area in the period 1839–1860s.[115] This is not to suggest that the region and its people did not face adversity, nor encounter conflict.

The people of this region were not on the "cutting edge" of change in the Cantonese world, relative to commercial enterprise, political activity, and socio-cultural trend setting. The important place and role of the *Baak-wah* zone, was that it both materially and psychologically served as a useful and all-important "rear guard area" that bolstered the *Yuet*/Cantonese identity and extended its experience. Thus, while the *Baak-wah* community might lack the color and excitement of the center of the Cantonese community in Canton and the Pearl River Delta Region, it did have the benefit of greater security and stability, associated with *Baak-wah* separateness and social distance. This may explain why relatively few *Baak-wah* Cantonese/*Bundae* people migrated overseas, in comparison with Pearl River delta area (both *Bundae* and *Hakka*) peoples. Only a small number of *Baak-wah* zone people emigrated from a handful of about 14 *Baak-wah* districts, (primarily those immediately adjacent to the Canton/Pearl River delta region,) in the inner *Baak-wah* zone. Additionally, two of these fourteen inner *Baak-wah* zone districts had significantly large *Hakka* populations. These fourteen districts were as follows:

1) Counties north of Canton, i.e., *Samshui (Sanshui), Saywui (Ssu-hui) (Sihui), Fayuan (Fahsien)* [now known as *Hua* County], and *Tsignyuan (Ch'ing-huan) (Qingyuan)*
2) Counties southeast of Canton, nominally *Saam-Yup* (or alternately *Luk*-Yup) related areas, i.e., *Poklo (Polo) (Boluo), Tsengshing (Zengcheng) (Tseng-cheng), Tungkun (Dongguan) (Tung-kuan), Pao-on (Baoan) (Pao-an)* [a district with a large *Hakka* population, bordering on and part of Hong Kong]
3) Counties northwest of the *Say-Yup* and west of the *Saam-Yup* districts, i.e., *Koyiu (Kao yao) (Gaoyao), Koming (Kao-ming) (Gaoming), Hokshaan (Hoshan) (Heshan)*.
4) Counties west and southwest of the *Say-Yup* area, i.e., *Chikkai (Ch'ih-ch'i)* (today no longer a separate district), [essentially a *Hakka* enclave]

*Yeunchun (Yang-chun) (Yangchun), Yeungkong (Yang-chiang)* [today known as *Yeungsai (Yangxi)*]

Materially and symbolically, speech and ethnicity within the widely disbursed *Baak-wah* community helped secure and maintain the *Yuet*-Cantonese/*Bundae* monopoly over the largest portion of Central Gwongdung. It did so by re-enforcing the high value and positive force of the *Yuet/Bundae* label itself. This was evident in the extended maintenance of the cultural authenticity and territorial integrity of the larger *Yuet/Cantonese* speech community. Finally, the *Baak-wah* people, by their sheer number and hard work, promoted Yuet/*Bundae* Cantonese power by perpetuating its control over key material resources, such as land and water. It seems certain, that but for the "invisible" and "silent" contributions of the *Baak-wah* group, the powerful hegemony of the Cantonese in Central Gwongdung would not have been possible. Finally, it could be argued that, but for the positive role of this group, the terms "*Yuet*" and "Cantonese," as an ascribed (often self-ascribed), synonymous ethno-linguistic and cultural group label for Central Gwongdung and its people, could never have been fully developed, let alone flourish both at home and overseas. The centrality of this proposition lies in the fact that *Baak-wah* and *Gwongdung-wah* are interchangeable, because they are in fact synonymous. Thus, there is a great deal of sense behind the *Gwongdung-wah* term/label ("G*wongdungese*") as a surrogate for the generic speech form known as "Cantonese."

## Speech label "exclusivity" and ethnic label "inclusiveness" in Cantonese identity formation

The ascribed homogeneous character of language and culture at the Cantonese fountainhead, has quite obviously not been as simple, nor as true, as has been traditionally assumed. Technically speaking, the *Yuet*/Cantonese group identity label, initially referred primarily to linguistic concerns, and only more broadly to cultural-historical matters.[116] Conceptually speaking, it is possible to discern that over time, *Yuet*/Cantonese speech and ethnic labels, relative to group identity formation and reproduction, came to represent different, but related, identity constructs.

The sense of distinctiveness and separateness among nineteenth-century Cantonese speech communities underscores the fact that in Central Gwongdung, but especially in the Pearl River Delta region, local speech communities have historically been exclusive, relative to excluding those who did not share the same speech. In this context, *Saam-yup wah* speech, as a speech variant of Cantonese speech, formed a distinctive and separate speech community. This distinctiveness of Cantonese speech communities arbitrarily and definitively divided up Cantonese society into several distinct, self-contained units, (see tables 3.2 and 3.3) where local inter-group communication was problematic, and often impossible.

In this context, I hypothesize that mid-late nineteenth century and early twentieth century *Yuet*/Cantonese speech identification labels arose from, and were bound to, a series of *Yuet* dialects or speech groups. On the basis of their technical construction and resultant uses, these dialects or speech groups remained "exclusive," by way of what they excluded. The converse seems to be true regarding the construction of "Cantonese ethnicity," where ethnic identity constructs were inclusive, because unrelated speech communities could be, and often were, included under the rubric of "Cantonese ethnicity." In this manner, we should remember to distinguish between Cantonese *as a dialect or speech community*, and Cantonese *as an ethnic community*. Again, the two are closely related, and overlap, but they are not by any means synonymous. In this way, speech can be viewed as having been *exclusive*, by way of what it excluded; and ethnicity has been *inclusive*, by way of what it included.

Significantly, the Cantonese ethnic group identity label was meant to be inclusive of many different subgroups, who, while they may be only marginally related, or even technically outside the *Yuet*/Cantonese speech group, they are nonetheless embraced by the *Yuet*/Cantonese ethnic group label. Inclusion is based on common denominators of a shared geo-historical pattern of development over a long time. In this perspective, "Ethnic boundaries can therefore both be drawn to "separate" groups speaking the "same" language...as well as to "include" groups speaking "differing" languages...."[117] This view of the development and persistence of ethnic group labels in Gwongdung can help explain the contradiction associated with the apparent arbitrary exclusion or inclusion of unrelated speech communities, relative to Cantonese society and *Yuet* culture.

> These tiers of identity- that of ethno-lingualism and of province do not necessarily contradict or work against each other, nor are most Chinese confused by them...either membership category may give rise to an identity which circumscribes an ethnic group.[118]

Historically speaking, the *Yuet*/Cantonese identity label originally had special meaning and specific uses at the Cantonese fountainhead in Central Gwongdung. Over time, this changed within the context of an expansive transnational Cantonese overseas Chinese world. Overseas, such distinctions had little meaning and less relevance, if any, in the case of Chinese immigration/settlement in the Americas, and elsewhere. Overseas, the distinction between Chinese immigrants and resident non-Chinese peoples was clear enough, without any need for explanation. Additionally, the overwhelming majority of the Chinese in the Americas were from *Yuet*/Cantonese Central Gwongdung, and undoubtedly most of them were Cantonese speaking.

This meant that the old *Yuet* (粵) group label had little meaning or relevance in America and elsewhere overseas. If there had been sizable non-*Yuet*/*Bundae* Cantonese blocs in America, then the *Yuet* label may have been relevant and useful, as in the case of extended *Hakka-Bundae* conflicts in mid-Nineteenth-Century California.[119] Such instances, however, were relatively rare. In this light, *Yuet* and *Bundae* labels had less meaning and value among the Chinese in the Americas. In short, the *Yuet* ethnic group label only existed as a general abstract, and increasingly anachronistic, symbolic reference. There remained, however, the critical need for concrete, specific group labels to distinguish sub-units within the *Yuet*/Cantonese ethno-speech community, e.g., *Saam-Yup*, and *Say-Yup*. This need formed the basis for a reassessment of how local speech labels and ethnic group labels functioned, relative to their realignment for use in sustaining Cantonese identity beyond Central Gwongdung, within an expanded global context.

In Cantonese-Chinese America, important internal distinctions existed within the *Yuet*/Cantonese ethnic group label (e.g., the *Saam-yup* and *Say-yup*.) These ancillary labels were important both back home in Central Gwongdung and elsewhere overseas. In Chinese America, however, they replaced the generalized *Yuet/Bundae* Cantonese group label, as a more meaningful and functional basis for group identity, in both the local ethnic community, and the series of speech community relationships embraced by it. This underscores the fundamental importance of the distinctiveness of ethnic groups, as they incorporated distinct and diverse speech community labels, relative to their transnationally contextualized meanings and applications.

Nearly all of the nineteenth-century inhabitants of the Pearl River Delta region, and more generally Central Gwongdung, were in fact geographically, demographically, and ethno-linguistically closely linked together, despite differences in local speech, as members of a single unified Cantonese society and *Yuet* culture. In this context, ethnic boundaries were distinguishable from speech community boundaries, despite the former being inclusive and the latter being exclusive, in their positioning of different speech groups of people within their respective socio-spatial boundaries. "Among the *Yuet* … language differences do not make inviolate ethnic boundaries. They merely draw clear lines of sub-ethnic distinctions."[120] This delicate balance of tensions between "ethnic inclusiveness" and "speech community exclusiveness," underscored the sense of distinctiveness of the *Yuet*/Cantonese persona in the mid-late nineteenth and early twentieth century, both back home in Gwongdung and in America.

> This de-emphasis on linguistic distinctiveness, furthermore, squares well with current anthropological thinking about ethnicity. Ethnicity can be seen as a status ascribed to a group of people who regard themselves and are regarded by others as descended from common ancestors. [In turn] Common cultural patterns are a prevalent but by no means necessary concomitant element of their status.[121]

In this context, Cantonese ethnic group identity formation consists of the transformation of any number of potential categories of identification, such as local speech communities, into a new ascribed basis for group interaction, from which Cantonese ethnic group labels actually emerge. Over time, those Han Chinese groups that the *Yuet*/Cantonese could not ethnically dominate, nor linguistically incorporate, it socio-culturally rejected and geo-territorially isolated, e.g., East Gwongdung's *Min Teochiu,* and West Gwongdung's *Min/Hoinam.*

## The challenge of Cantonese Ethnic identity and communal competition and conflict

Certainly, one of the most powerful and fundamental determinants of *Yuet*/Cantonese ethnicity was the Cantonese sense of communalism, whereby group relations distinguishing "we" and "they" often rested on ethnic considerations. In Cantonese community life, ethnic relations had a singularly unique and critical role. In the nineteenth century, the enigma of an alternating need for ethnic solidarity and the allowance of ethnic competition/conflict often perplexed outsiders, in both China and America.

The subject of ethnicity is lost in the unwarranted assumption that Cantonese group identity and experience in Central Gwongdung was bound to an exclusive polarity, where one had to choose between culture and ethnicity, as the only categorical imperatives regarding identity and experience. In this context, Cantonese ethnicity properly speaking, became a major force, and not just an inconsequential factor in the operation of community social organizations in *Yuet*/Cantonese society. Given the historical importance of ethnic group labels, as convenient and useful indicators of identity among Cantonese people, it is logical to expect that ethnic group relations have traditionally played a key role in the formation and operation of traditional social institutions. In short, local community leaders and institutions might differ little from elsewhere in traditional Chinese society, but the peculiar kind of coherence associated with alternating tensions of ethnic solidarity and ethnic conflict, between and among various ethnic/speech components in Cantonese society, resulted in an added dimension of community life, different from elsewhere.

Given the legendary eccentricities of *Yuet* culture, it is easy to see that Central Gwongdung offered a uniquely diverse social landscape, where ethnic and local speech community group relations lent color and a sense of urgency, regarding how key components of local community life were orchestrated. In this manner, as local leaders addressed local needs and promoted local interests, from within local community-based institutions, they were also advancing the interests of their respective ethnic groups and speech communities.

Certainly, high on the list of local priorities was the goal of communal autonomy, or more succinctly "ethnic/speech group autonomy." In this context, one can see that the 1857 *Yuet/Bundae* seizure of *Hakka* lands in *Hoiping* and *Yanping* by local *Say-Yup* people, as more than a violent expression of ethnic rivalry and conflict. It was also a clear manifestation of the high priority and potent force of an ethnic agenda of local ethnic community leaders, and the series of communal institutions they led. This is not to say that ethnicity served as the sole, or the most important, motivating force at work in community life, but it is to suggest that the pressures of ethnic solidarity and conflict were paramount concerns of local ethnic/speech community leaders, and the community institutions they led.

When I refer to "ethnic group solidarity," I mean those criteria which promoted socio-communal bonds among members of an ethnic/speech group, within a communal setting, relative to other groups located in the same general area. The development and persistence of ethnic group labels was essential not only to the formation of ethnic group identities, but also to maintaining them over immensely long periods of time. In this context, the ethnic group label, as the distillation of centuries of experience in association with geo-territorial referents, migratory settlement-distribution patterns, ethnic community socio-economic institutions, and speech community standards, represented the structural basis on which ethnic group solidarity rested in Central Gwongdung. Again, each label mirrored elements of speech community "exclusiveness," as well as ethnic community "inclusiveness," in the interests of both distinguishing and fortifying ethnic/speech group solidarity.[122] Thus, Cantonese ethnicity helped forge not only distinctive sub-sets of ethno-linguistic identities, but also promoted Cantonese ethnic group solidarity.

By the nineteenth century, ethnic solidarity meant first and foremost a shared identity, predicated on ascribed and self-ascribed commonalties of speech and experience. In Gwongdung, the locus of ethnic group solidarity was quite fluid, as it easily shifted from sub-sets within an ethnic group or speech community, to center on other progressively larger ethnic/speech group units. In this context, ethnic solidarity might mean on one hand solidarity within the *Toi-shaan* community, as a sub-set expression of ethnicity and speech affinities within the larger *Say-Yup* community. It is also true that ethnic group solidarity could also be exhibited in the *Say-Yup* group itself, as a component within the larger *Yuet/Bundae*/Cantonese ethnic community. Ultimately, ethnic solidarity might also be expressed in *Yuet/Bundae* Cantonese or *Hakka* ethnic groups, relative to each other. Ethnicity, together with speech, became supreme arbitrators of both the objective reality and subjective image of *Yuet*/Cantonese "we" and "they" communal inter-group relations, both in Central Gwongdung and elsewhere overseas. The singular importance of the "ethnic factor" in local community relations, relative to ethnic solidarity, is a point too often misunderstood and underestimated, by even the better informed.

> Ethnic differences were less significant in the formation of systems of social organization...In South China, ethnic differences were perceived as a matter of cultural rather than racial attributes, for, at least by the eighteenth century, inhabitants of South China were predominantly Han [Chinese].[123]

In this context, ethnicity, and local speech related considerations, provided a continuum on which to place one's own community in relationship with others. Additionally, while ethnic solidarity and conflict do in fact represent polar extremes of this continuum, it does not necessarily follow that they were mutually exclusive, as expressions of where a given ethnic community positioned itself, or how it related to others. Again, ethnic identity, as a matter of self-perception or how one sees others in relationship to oneself, was quite fluid in Cantonese society. The formula for ethnic solidarity appears on its face as a simplistic affirmation of the existence of easily observed material conditions, whereby "birds of a feather flock together."

Relative to the matter of ethnic group labels, it is easy to see that a group of people living in the same geophysical locality, sharing the same speech, and identifying with the same historically and culturally sculptured experience, would as a matter-of-fact, focus on the "mutuality" of common ethnic identity and experience. In this way, ethnic solidarity represented a group affirmation of mutual interests, needs, and expectations regarding community life. This perspective had social, economic, psycho-cultural (i.e., subjective), and local political-civic ramifications. In this way, each ethnic community, relative to its ethnic group label, e.g., *Yuet, Bundae,* and Cantonese mirrored mutually shared views and responses to community life related social, economic, cultural, and civic matters. Ethnic solidarity meant essentially a willingness to see the needs and interests of the ethnic group, as one of shared assets and shared liabilities.

The expression of ethnic solidarity in Nineteenth-Century Gwongdung usually manifested itself in the routine, the ordinary, and commonplace. This means that it centered on the mundane realities of everyday life, relative to living arrangements, marketing patterns, communal social life, and in such simple things as "bragging rights" over local achievements. In a manner of speaking, ethnic solidarity, whether in reference to large units as the *Yuet* and *Bundae*, or to smaller ones like *Say-Yup*, or *Chung-Shaan's Min* speaking community, simply meant the acceptance of "who" and "what" we are. As a "given," little time and effort was given to explaining or justifying it. It simply existed. Practically speaking, ethnic solidarity meant quite simply adhering to a cardinal principle of Chinese society and culture, where the primacy of the group always existed as a necessary basis for a stable, peaceful, and prosperous society.[124] Central Gwongdung's ethnic communities recognized ethnic solidarity's usefulness in promoting ethnic group needs/interests.

Ethnic solidarity in Cantonese society operated in two different, but closely related spheres. If we visualize ethnic group solidarity from an inward and outward perspective, then it is possible to see that the former focused on *intra-group relations*, while the latter on *inter-group relations.* The sense of togetherness and mutuality just alluded to above, regarding common needs and interests reflected an *inward perspective*. It found expression in already mentioned ascribed traits as the routine, ordinary, and mundane. This aspect of ethnic solidarity was unconscious in its motivation and unarticulated in its expression. Here we can appreciate the need and value for compromise, consensus, and deference, where individuals and groups within an ethnic/speech group achieved intra-ethnic group solidarity, under a set of common needs and shared expectations, which differed from those associated with inter-ethnic group relations.

In contrast, there also existed an *outward perspective* of ethnic solidarity, with its focus on inter-group relations. Here, ethnic group solidarity did not always express itself in compromise, deference, or mutual consideration, but rather in an assertive and combative response to imagined or real threats. The qualities of togetherness and mutuality did not arise from the routine and commonplace, but from the ad hoc, special, or expedient. This reflected a condition or mode of defensiveness and hypersensitivity, rather than confidence and tolerance. As noted earlier, the "inner group is aware of itself only when it faces an outer group."[125] Again, these categories serve to illustrate contrasting, but not necessarily mutually exclusive characteristics. The reality of the situation in Nineteenth-Century Gwongdung was most likely much more fluid and less polarized. As such, it provides additional useful evidence of what it meant to be Cantonese in Nineteenth-Century China and America.

[1] In this text, all subsequent references to Han Chinese are indicated by the simple term Chinese. All references to Chinese people, language and culture is assumed to be in reference to Han Chinese people, language, and culture. I have dropped the "Han" from Han Chinese, except when/where explicit reference to ethno-linguistic matters requires its use.

[2] See the following two works: Agnieszka Joniak-Luthi, The Han, China's Diverse Majority, (Seattle, Washington: University of Washington Press, 2017); also see Thomas Mullaney and James Leibold, et. al. co-editors of Critical Han Studies: The History, Representation, and Identity of China's Majority (New Perspectives on Chinese Culture and Society) (Berkeley: University of California Press, 2012).

[3] See generally following: Walton Look Lai, The Chinese in the West Indies, 1806–1995, A Documentary History, (Barbados: Press of the University of the West Indies, 1998); Jeffrey Lesser, Negotiating National Identity, Immigrants, Minorities, and the Struggle for Ethnicity in Brazil, (Durham: Duke University Press, 1999); The Chinese in the Caribbean, edited by Andrew R. Wilson (Princeton, New Jersey: Markus Wiener Publishers, 2004); Moon-Ho Jung, Coolies and Cane, Race, Labor, and Sugar in the Age of Emancipation, (Baltimore: John Hopkins University Press, 2006); Lisa Yun, The Coolie Speaks, Chinese Indentured Laborers and African Slaves in Cuba, (Philadelphia: Temple University Press, 2008); Arnold J. Meagher, The Coolie Trade: The Traffic in Chinese Laborers in Latin America, (Xlibris Corporation, 2008); The Chinese in Latin America and the Caribbean, edited by Walton Look Lai and Tan Chee-Beng (Leiden, the Netherlands: Brill, 2010); Kathleen Lopez, Chinese Cubans, A Transnational History, (Chapel Hill: University of North Carolina Press, 2013); Jason Oliver Chang, Chino, Anti-Chinese Racism in Mexico, 1880–1940, (Urbana: University of Illinois Press, 2017).

[4] Chinese immigrants were among the first outsiders to learn to speak in the Hawaiian language. See, Clarence E. Glick, Sojourners and Settlers, Chinese Migrants in Hawaii, (Honolulu: University Press of Hawaii and the Hawaii Chinese Historical Center, 1980), p. 13.

[5] *Taishan shang Nan-ts'un Li-shih Tsu-pu*, Genealogy of the Lee Clan of Nam Tsun Village of Toishan District (Gwongdung Province), compiled by Lee Fung-nam (1964) (Unpublished manuscript)(hereafter cited as *Taishan Tsu-pu*,) pp. 28–31.

[6] Ibid., The district of *Sunning* was renamed *Toi-shaan* (T'ai-shan) in 1914; also see Kaiwing Chow, The Rise of Confucian Ritualism in Late Imperial China, Ethics, Classics, and Lineage Discourse, (Stanford, CA.: Stanford University Press, 1994), p. 214 (re: genealogies, Chapter four, "Ancestral Rites and Lineage in Early Ch'ing Scholarship," pp. 98–99,100–103, 115–118. Also note: I have chosen to use the earlier Wade-Giles term "Sung" in place of the Pinyin term "Song" to help non-Chinese readers/speakers avoid certain confusion. (i.e., pronouncing *Sung* as "Song," as in the phrase "song and dance."

[7] Freedman, *Chinese Lineage and Society*, p. 5; also see Yuen-fong Woon, Social Organization in South China, 1911–1949, The Case of the Kuan Lineage in K'ai-p'ing County, Ann Arbor, Michigan: Center for Chinese Studies, 1984), pp. 1–19.

[8] Maurice Freedman, Lineage Organization, in Southeastern China, (London: University of London Athlone Press, 1958), pp. 46–50; also see Chow, Rise of Confucian Ritualism, ch.3, "Lineage Discourse: Gentry, Local Society, and the State," pp.71–97.

[9] Ibid., p. 2

[10] See generally, William Skinner, "Marketing and Social Structure in Rural China, Part II" Journal of Asian Studies, vol 24: no. 2, February, 1965, pp. 207–208, (reference to Kwangtung [Gwongdung]).

¹¹ In some of the literature, *Pen-ti* or *Punti* are the more familiar and most commonly used forms. I have avoided their use for two reasons. First, they represent older Mandarin forms of a distinctly Cantonese reference term, and secondly, non-Chinese speakers seeing "*Punti*" or *Pen-ti* would likely tend to mispronounce the term altogether as "Pun-tee," when it is actually pronounced in standard Cantonese as "Bun-day." In the case of Cantonese romanization/transliteration, I use *Bundae* (not *Bun-day*). I also avoid using standard Cantonese romanization, as in *Poon-tei*, as promoted in the Cowles/ Missionary Cantonese Romanization system, to represent more simply and easily the standard Cantonese pronunciation of the Mandarin term *Bundi* or *Punti*, in Pinyin and Wade-Giles respectively. It seems somewhat awkward to adopt the Yale Cantonese Romanization system, "*Bundeih*."Rather than drop the "h" from *Bundeih* to make it "*Bundei*," which is more accurate and easier for the English speaker to pronounce, I have chosen instead to use an entirely new, different, but similar transliteration approach. In this context, *Bunda*e is not only simpler and easier, but also as accurate and useful a reproduction of the standard Cantonese pronunciation, than the term "*Poon-tei."*

¹² The designation "CE" means the "Common Era," which has replaced the designation AD (which is Latin for "year of our lord."), similarly BCE "before the common era" has replaced BC (Before Christ). These changes mirror the effort to move beyond the Western/Christian bias in reference to how time periods are identified by adopting newer and more neutral, less culturally biased chronological designations and labels. This change over is somewhat compromised by the fact that both sets of identifications refer to essentially the same time periods. So much for being politically correct.

¹³ See generally the following, Chi Ch'ao-ting, Key Economic Areas in Chinese History, as Revealed in the Development of Public Works for Water Control (New York: Paragon Book Corp., 1963 reprint); also see, Mark Elvin, The Pattern of the Chinese Past, A Social and Economic Interpretation, (Stanford, California, Stanford University Press, 1973).

¹⁴ In cases of representing key Chinese terms, I use the Cantonese form when referencing Cantonese items, then I also supply the *Pinyin* (standard "Mandarin" Chinese form) in parenthesis, e.g., Gwongdung (Guangdong). In some instances, I also provide the older Wade-Giles Romanization, also in parenthesis.

¹⁵ See Jiahua Yuan, *Hanyu Fangyan gaiyao* (An Outline of Chinese Dialects) (hereafter cited as HYFYGY) (Beijing: *Wenzi Gaige Chubanshe*, 1960).

¹⁶ Reference work of joint Australian-Chinese research project on *Yuet* (*Yue*) dialects, *Zhongguo Yuyan Dituji* (*di 2 ban*) *Han Yu Fangyan juan* (Language Atlas of China) (2ⁿᵈ edition) (Beijing: Commercial Press, 2012)

¹⁷ Ann Hashimoto or Oi-kan yue or Hashimoto-Yue, Pathology of Cantonese, (Cambridge UK: Cambridge University Press, 1972)

¹⁸ Jerry Norman, Chinese, (Cambridge Language Surveys) (New York: Cambridge University Press, 1988 (1993 paperback edition), p.266

¹⁹ It is believed that the Min speaking community in East Gwongdung, (identified as the *Min/Hoklo Bundae*), consisted of descendants of settlers, who came from neighboring Fujian. Similarly, the Min speaking community of West Gwongdung, (identified as the *Min/Hoinam Bundae*), is also believed to have originated with migrants from Fujian to West Gwongdung, i.e., they were not Min Bundae migrants from East Gwongdung.

²⁰ See table 3.1 Flow chart of key Han Chinese ethnic group and local speech community identity labels in Nineteenth-Century Gwongdung province, see especially line items 1a &

1b. A word of clarification, regarding the various ethnic group categories profiled, especially in regards to the sequence of their discussion. Ostensibly, this study is about the *Yuet*-Cantonese people, the dominant ethnic group and speech community in Central Gwongdung. In this context, my discussion of other Han Chinese ethnic groups and local speech communities in Gwongdung, and more specifically in Central Gwongdung, is of only passing interest. Consequently, when non *Yuet*/Cantonese groups are referenced, I limit my discussion to comparisons and contrasts, e.g., *Min/Hoklo Bundae* and *Min/Hoinam Bundae* groups. However, when moving on to discuss various sub-ethnic groups, or sub-dialect local speech communities, I only discuss those associated with the *Yuet*/Cantonese *Bundae* group, while avoiding referencing those associated with other *Bundae* groups, e.g., the *Min/Hoklo* and *Min/Hoi-Nam*. When necessary, I cross-reference parallel groups within a broad category of ethnic identity labels, in order to fairly and fully represent all key groups in such a category, e.g., those within the *Bundae* group. However, as I move down vertically from broader categories (e.g., *Bundae*) to more narrowly framed sub-categories (e.g., *Yuet*/Cantonese *Bundae*) I shift my approach. I only cover those sub-categories relevant to the chief topic (i.e., the *Yuet*/Cantonese). Thus, I do not discuss the sub-categories of other groups, e.g., the *Min/Hoklo*, *Min/Hoi-Nam*, or the *Hakka*. In contrast, I go into considerable detail and depth in discussing the many sub-units of the Yuet/Cantonese *Bundae*, e.g., the *Baak-wah*, the *Saam-Yup*, *Say-Yup*, *Chung-Shaan*, e.g., the *Long Do*, *Nam lau*, *Saam-heung-wah* local identity labels.

[21] Overseas, today (2018) there are about 2 to 5 million *Teochiu* speakers, who are concentrated primarily in Thailand, Malaysia, and Singapore. *Teochiu* speaking people can be found in over twenty foreign countries. See Wikipedia entry for *Chaozhan*.

[22] For Central Gwongdung's aggregate total of 19 million people in the nineteenth century, I averaged the totals by decade (1840–1900) to arrive at 19 million. See chapter 1, table 1.13 "Aggregate Population Estimates for Nineteenth-Century Central Gwongdung, by micro-region, 1840–1900." For East Gwongdung's total population of 2.5 million, see chapter 1 of this book, see endnote #13,

[23] As a result of *Hakka* defeat in the *Hakka-Bundae* wars (1855–1868) Several hundred thousand *Hakka* survivors were deported from *Say-Yup* districts in the Pearl River Delta region of Central Gwongdung and relocated in portions of West Gwongdung in either the *Leizhou* (*Leichow*) peninsula or on Hainan Island. Others were deported to either neighboring Gwongsai (Guangxi) province further west, or returned to *Meixian* district in East Gwongdung. Large numbers also emigrated overseas to *Tongking* in North Vietnam, Borneo, Peru, Dutch Guiana, Jamaica, and Hawaii. See generally, J.A.G. Roberts, "The *Hakka-Punti* [*Bundae*] War," PhD dissertation Oxford University, Queen's College, 1968.

[24] The common, implied presumption here is that "Gwongdung" food actually means "Cantonese" food. Note that *Chaozhou* (*Chao-chou*) (*Teochiu*) or East Gwongdung cuisine, although also from Gwongdung, is never referred to as "Gwongdung cuisine"*per se*. It is rather, always referred to as *Chaozhou*, or*Teochiu*, or *Shantou* cuisine.

[25] The two terms have near identical pronunciations in Cantonese (*Yuet*) and Mandarin (*Yue*). In Vietnamese, the Cantonese term *Yuet* is pronounced as *Viet*. Thus, the Cantonese term "*Yuet-Nam*" is pronounced in Vietnamese as "Vietnam." Historically speaking, this particular form of *Yuet* (越) is understood to represent the rich cultural and historical traditions of southernmost China (the *Lingnam*) and northern Vietnam (*Tongking*) in remote antiquity, i.e., the Qin-Han period. It is a term which embraces the ancient peoples of both

Gwongdung and those of Northern Vietnam in the very distant past. When Vietnam gained its independence from China in 938 CE, after the fall of the Tang dynasty, this form of *Yuet* (越) ceased to have any relevance for the people and culture of Gwongdung. Instead, the character *Yuet* (粵) became the sole *Yuet* (粵) label regarding the Cantonese people and things Cantonese.

[26] The term *Yuet* (*Yue*) (*Yueh*) originally applied to pre-Han period geography and society for a vast region that spread from Zhejiang, through Fujian, and Gwongdung (Guangdong) in Southern China to North Vietnam's Tonking region, specifically the Red River Valley. This term is pronounced as "Viet" in Vietnamese. Thus Yuet-Nam (Cantonese form) is pronounced as "Vietnam" in Vietnamese. The connotation of this form of *Yuet* () underscores a shared Sino-Vietnamese embryonic experience in remote antiquity. When Vietnam gained its independence from China in the 10th century CE, after the fall of the Tang dynasty, another word emerged as a specific identifying group label for the dominant Han Chinese group in Gwongdung, and more specifically for Central Gwongdung. This term is *Yuet* (*Yue*) pronounced virtually the same, in both Cantonese and Mandarin, but written with a different Chinese character. This new term represents things that pertain exclusively to the people, who form the dominant ethnic majority in Gwongdung, and more generally the Lingnam region.

[27] Ibid., pp. 142, 143; also see Hsu Sung-shih, Yueh-chiang Liu-yu Jen-min (The Spread of People in the Yueh-Chiang), Shanghai, 1939, p. 176.

[28] See this book, chapter 1, section 2 on Central Gwongdung.

[29] See generally, Vogel, China One Step Ahead, chapters 5–8.

[30] See this book, chapter 1, endnote #6, with references to works by Vogel, Cressy, and Rhoads. I use the figure of 81,834 sq. miles, rounded off to 82,000, based on calculation from 212,005 sq kilometers, with one kilometer = to .386 sq. mil.

[31] See chapter 1, table 1.6

[32] See generally, Douglas W. Lee, The Gum-Shaan Chronicles, The Early History of Cantonese-Chinese America, 1850-1900, Volume 4, Departing Tong-Shaan, The Organization and Operation of Cantonese Overseas Emigration to America, 1850-1900, (Pittsburgh, Pa: Dorrance Publishing, 2022); also see in general the following works, John M. Carroll, Edge of Empires, Chinese Elites and British Colonials in Hong Kong, (Cambridge, Mass: Harvard University Press, 2005); Cities in Motion, Interior, Coast, and Diaspora in Transnational China, edited by David Strand and Sherman Cochran, General editor Wen-hsin Yeh, (Berkeley: University of California, Berkeley, 2007) (Center for Chinese Studies China Research Monograph #62 ); Christopher Munn, Anglo-China, Chinese People and British Rule in Hong Kong, 1841–1880, (Hong Kong: University of Hong Kong, 2009); Elizabeth Sinn, Pacific Crossing, California Gold, Chinese Migration, and the Making of Hong Kong, (Hong Kong: University of Hong Kong, 2013).

[33] Today this is less the case, e.g., a Chaozhou person (who speaks *Min* speech and who in the past (prior to 1980s) was identified as a Chaozhou (*Teochiu*) person, has been identified more recently (since 1980s) as a *Guangdong ren* or Guangdong (Gwongdung) person, in much the same way as have the *Yuet*/Cantonese people.

[34] Chan, Bitter-Sweet Soil, p. 8.

[35] These five migrations occurred: 1) 311–873 CE; 2) 874–1276 CE; 3) 1276–1682 CE; 4) 1682–1867 CE; and 5) 1867 CE to the present, see Hsiang-lin Lo, K'o-chia Yen-chiu Tao-

lun (An Introduction to the Study of the *Hakkas* in its Ethnic, Historical and Cultural Aspects) (Kwangtung, China: 1933) (Taipei, Taiwan: Ku-t'ing shu-wu, 1975 reprint), pp. 64b, 46–47.

[36] Orlando Patterson, "Context and Choice in Ethnic Allegiance: A Theoretical Framework and Caribbean Case Study," in Nathan Glazer and Daniel P. Moynihan, eds., Ethnicity and Experience, pp.305–349 (Cambridge, Mass: Harvard University Press, 1975), see p.306. As a result of *Hakka* defeat in the *Hakka-Bundae* wars (1855-1868) Several hundred thousand *Hakka* survivors were deported from *Say-Yup* districts in the Pearl River Delta region of Central Gwongdung and relocated in portions of West Gwongdung in either the *Leizhou* (*Leichow*) peninsula or on Hainan Island. Others were deported to either neighboring Gwongsai (Guangxi) province further west, or returned to *Meixian* district in East Gwongdung. Large numbers also emigrated overseas to *Tongking* in North Vietnam, Borneo, Peru, Dutch Guiana, Jamaica, and Hawaii. See generally, J.A.G. Roberts, "The *Hakka-Punti* [*Bundae*] War," PhD dissertation Oxford University, Queen's College, 1968.

[37] Sow-Theng Leong, (edited by Tim Wright), Migration and Ethnicity in Chinese History, Hakka, Pengmin,and Their Neighbors, (Stanford, Ca: Stanford University Press, 1997), (hereafter cited as ME/CH, pp. 97–175.*Hakka* migrations in Southern China occurred when an upturn in economic activity created economic opportunities within a core micro-region, resulting in the migration of the *Hakka* into that core area from the periphery of a micro-region embracing such a core area.

[38] Ibid., pp. 9–15, 19.

[39] Lo, K'o-chia yen-chiu, p. 46–47, also see, Rhoads, China's Republican Revolution, Case of Kwangtung, pp. 12–13; also see, Leong, "The Hakka Chinese," pp. 19–22, 14–17.

[40] G. William Skinner, "Regional Systems in Late Imperial China," paper given at the Second Annual Meeting of the Social Science History Association, Ann Arbor, Michigan, 1977.

[41] S.T. Leong, "The Hakka Chinese: Ethnicity and Migrations in Late Imperial China," unpublished paper, Annual Meeting of the Association for Asian Studies, Washington, DC 1980, pp. 3–4.

[42] Leong, ME/CH, p.14.

[43] Ibid., p 33, as cited from Jerry Norman, Chinese (Cambridge Language Surveys) (Cambridge, UK: Cambridge University Press, 1988 (1993 paperback edition), p. 222.

[44] Ibid., p. 33, as cited from Chen Zhiping, *Kejia yuanliu xinlun* (A New Discussion of the Origins of the Hakka), *Naning Gwangxi jiaoyu chubanshe*, 1995, chapters 4–6.

[45] Marjorie K.M. Chan and Douglas W. Lee, "Chinatown Chinese: A Linguistic and Historical Re-Evaluation,"Amerasia Journal 8:1 (1981) p. 121.

[46] The most comprehensive and detailed examination of the *Hakka-Bundae* war remains J.A.G. Roberts, "The *Hakka-Punti* [*Bundae*] War," PhD dissertation Oxford University, Queen's College, 1968.

[47] See generally, "Conflict and Web of Group Affiliation in San Francisco's Chinatown," by Stanford Lyman in Pacific Historical Review, 43:4 (1974), pp. 473–499; also see by same author, "Urban Change at the Sinitic Frontier: Social Organizations in the United States' Chinatowns, 1849–1898," Modern Asian Studies, (1983), vol. 17, pp.107–136.

[48] See generally the following: Clarence E. Glick, Sojourners and Settlers, Chinese Migrants in Hawaii, (Honolulu: University of Hawaii, 1980); also see Russell D. Lee, "The Perils of Ethnic Success: The Rise and Flight of the Chinese Traders in Jamaica," PhD dissertation (sociology) Harvard University, 1979.

Chapter 3

⁴⁹ Source of data for table 3.3, see chapter 1 of this book, tables 1.9, 1.10, and 1.11.
⁵⁰ These averages were obtained by averaging estimated aggregate population figures for each area, by decade, for the period 1840-1900. These figures are not intended to represent precise figures, but rather to demonstrate an order of magnitude. This data is based on initial data found in chapter 1, see tables 1.9, 1.10. & 1.11.
⁵¹ Ibid., tables 1.9, 1.10, & 1.11.
⁵² The term "Cantonese" or Gwongdung-wah (or "Gwongdungese") should not be regarded as a speech community category per se, but rather as a generic term or label, when referencing in the abstract Cantonese speech in Gwongdung, especially in Central Gwongdung, and among overseas Cantonese emigrants/migrants.
⁵³ See chapter 1 this book, table 1.5 (the figure of 800 square miles also included portions of Namhoi and Panyu districts, which formed the outlying suburbs of Canton's city center.)
⁵⁴ See chapter 1, table 1.8
⁵⁵ *Saam-Yup* (my own romanization), *San-Yap* (standard Cantonese form), *Sanyi* (Pinyin mandarin form), and *San-i* (Wade-Giles mandarin form).
⁵⁶ See chapter 1, table 1.1
⁵⁷ Ibid., table 1.1
⁵⁸ Ibid., table 1.1
⁵⁹ See Liang Ch'i-ch'ao (Wade-Giles mandarin form) (Liang Qichao, Pinyin form), (Leung Kai-chew, Cantonese form) Hsin Ta-lu yu-chi (Journey to the New World) as found in *Chin-tai chung-kuo shih liao tsung-kan* (Historical Materials in Modern Chinese History), edited by Shen Yun-lung (vol. 96-97), pp. 386-387. Liang cites that as late as 1903, the *Luk-Yup* speech community was well-known and widely used in Cantonese-Chinese America. In San Francisco, this term was used to identify a local Cantonese community organization, along with the *Saam-Yup* district association. It should be pointed out that the *LukYup* actually only formed an alliance group, and was not a bonafide district association (*wooi-kun*) (*huiguan*) (*hui-kuan*). At that time there was no Say-Yup district association, it had disbanded and divided itself into several rival *Say-Yup* district associations.
⁶⁰ See chapter 1, table 1.1
⁶¹ Ibid., table 1.1
⁶² Ibid., table 1.2
⁶³ *Say-Yup* (my own Romanization), *Sze-Yap* (standard Cantonese form), *Siyi* (Pinyin mandarin form), *Ssu-i* (Wade-Giles mandarin form).
⁶⁴ *Toi-Shaan* (my own Romanization), *Toishan* or *Hoishan*, (more familiar *Say-Yup* forms) (*Taishan*) (Pinyin form), (*T'ai-shan*) (Wade-Giles form).
⁶⁵ See chapter 1, table 1.1
⁶⁶ Ibid.,
⁶⁷ Ibid.,
⁶⁸ Ibid.,
⁶⁹ *Ng-Yup* (my own Romanization), *Ng-Yap* (standard Cantonese form), *Wuyi* (Pinyin mandarin form), and *Wu-i* (Wade-Giles form).
⁷⁰ *Hok-Shaan* or *Hokshaan* (my own Romanization).
⁷¹ See chapter 1, table 1.1
⁷² *Chung-Shaan (my own Romanization), Chung-Shan (more familiar form, which also happens to be the Wade-Giles mandarin form). Zhongshan (Pinyin mandarin form). Chung-Shaan*, pior to 1925 was known as *Heung-Shaan* or *Heung-shan*, (Cantonese forms) *Xi-*

*angshan* (pinyin mandarin form).

[73] Note, as discussed in greater detail in the following section of this chapter, the *Chung-Shaan* district hosted several speech communities, some of which were not *Yuet*, such as various *Min* and *Hakka* speech communities. Consequently, many *Chung-Shaan* speech communities cannot be technically identified as "Cantonese" speech communities per se. However, as noted in the text that follows, local *Min* and *Hakka* speech communities in *Chung-Shaan* have the distinction of being included, identified as part of the larger *Yuet*/Cantonese ethnic group, which means that while technically outside the Cantonese speech community, these groups have been traditionally included in the *Yuet*/Cantonese ethnic community. This situation only exists in *Chung-Shaan* district and nowhere else in Gwongdung.

[74] See chapter 1, table 1.1

[75] The term *Baak-wah* represents my own Romanization form. See introduction to this book.

[76] The Inner *Baak-wah* zone was populated almost exclusively by Han Chinese *Yuet/Bundae* peoples, most of whom were Cantonese speaking speech communities. There were also some *Hakka* people. Additionally, some non-Han Chinese, in the form of aboriginal tribal peoples, occupied extreme remote areas in the northern, northwestern, and northeastern outer parts of the Inner *Baak-wah* zone.

[77] The Outer *Baak-wah* zone, unlike the Inner *Baak-wah* zone, had a larger non-Han Chinese aboriginal population, and possibly more *Hakka* people as well. There was also a smaller number, i.e., smaller ratio, of *Yuet/Bundae* people who closely identified with the Cantonese speech community

[78] See chapter 1, table 1.5

[79] Ibid., table 1.5

[80] In the mid nineteenth-century, many *Teochiu* people migrated from East Gwongdung to settle in Chongqing (Chunking) Sichuan (Szechwan). At about the same time, many *Hakka* were also relocated in Sichuan , after their defeat and forced removal from parts of Central Gwongdung (such as the *Say-Yup* area of the Pearl River Delta), at the end of the *Hakka-Bundae* Wars in the 1860s.

[81] See Ann Oi-kan yue Hashimoto, Studies in *Yue* Dialects1: Phonology of Cantonese, (New York: Cambridge University Press, 1972); also see *Zhongguo yuyan dituji (di 2 ban) Han yu fangyan juan* (Language Atlas of China) (2nd edition) Chinese Dialects volume (Beijing: Commercial Press, 2012), p.125 (joint work of the Australian Academy of Humanities and the Chinese Academy of Social Sciences, 1987–1989.)

[82] *Namhoi, Panyu*, and *Shuntak* as "the three districts' group" have been traditionally grouped together for many reasons, beyond their common Cantonese speech community label. In recent years, however, there have been instances when *Namhoi* and *Panyu* have been identified together, without *Shuntak*. One example concerns where and how these rural districts help form greater Metropolitan Canton, relative to the inclusion of some of their respective territories within Metropolitan Canton's administrative boundaries. Namhoi is adjacent to Canton' south side, Pan Yu is adjacent to Canton's southwest side. This resulted in land being incorporated into Metropolitan Canton from both Namhoi and *Panyu*. Shuntak is not directly adjacent to Canton, but instead is adjacent to *Namhoi's* southern border. Consequently, Shuntak could not have contributed any land to help form Metropolitan Canton, because it was not adjacent to Canton, but instead lie one district removed from it. Consequently, when talking about *Saam-Yup* districts being adjacent to Canton, this is only true

Chapter 3

in the cases of *Namhoi* and *Panyu*, but not in the case of *Shuntak*. This technicality aside, there persists a popular consensus that in the nineteenth century, all three districts were regarded as close to and strongly identified with Metropolitan Canton.

[83] See table 4.3 below Re: Romanization method adopted for transliterating two Cantonese dialects. I have intentionally adopted a different Romanization method than that adopted more generally elsewhere, e.g., the Cowles/Missionary system of 1888). The "Three District(s) speech" in that system of Romanization of <u>Saam yap</u> and Sze-yap respectively. I have chosen to utilize instead what seems to me a simpler, easier to recognize and use system that more accurately reflects the way in which these terms were pronounced and transliterated by the Cantonese Chinese community in America. Thus, I have chosen different forms for "*Saam-yap*" and "*Sze- yap*" respectively. I use a new set of forms to replace the bewildering array of variations, e.g., we should use "***Saam-Yup***" in place of *Sam-yap*, and *Saam-yap*, and use "***Say-yup***" in place of the *Sze-yap*, and *Sei-yap* respectively. Please also note that I have made similar ad hoc changes in the Cantonese Romanization for *Chung-Shaann*, to replace *Chung-Shan(Zhongshan)*.

[84] The *Luk-yup* label may have actually been used among the people of *Tung-kun, Pao-on*, and *Poklo*. I have heard some references to such an identification in Hong Kong and elsewhere in the Pearl River Delta region.

[85] <u>The City in Late Imperial China</u>, ed. G. William Skinner (Stanford: Stanford University Press, 1977, pp.497–498.

[86] See generally, David Te-Chao, "Acculturation of the Chinese in the United States, A Philadelphia Study," (PhD dissertation, University of Pennsylvania, 1948).

[87] See, "Political Development in Chinese America, 1850–1900," by Douglas W. Lee, (PhD dissertation, (History) University of California, Santa Barbara, 1979, see specifically, Chapter 3, "Communal Development and Nascent Politics, 1880–1895," section on "Realignment of power: Part 2, The Rise of the *Say-Yup* people," pp. 151–178.

[88] Regarding the *Say-Yup Yuet* dialect/speech community, relative to other *Yuet* dialects/speech communities, see chapter 5 of this book, "The ties that bind, Cantonese Style," see especially the section on, "Distinguishing between "*Yuet*" (*Yue*) and "Cantonese."

[89] Note in the following map conventional Romanization is utilized, *Sam-Yap* and *Sze-Yap*, which I choose to Romanize as *Saam-Yup* and *Say-Yup* respectively.

[90] See following: Douglas W. Lee, "The Early Chinese Community in Washington D.C., 1880–1930," in <u>The Annals of the Chinese Historical Society of the Pacific Northwest</u>, 1:1 (1983), pp.86–120.

[91] See *Saam-Yup* and *Say-Yup* comparative speech tables in chapter 5, "The Ties that Bind, Cantonese Style," of this study, under section regarding the *Yuet*-Cantonese language.

[92] These observations have been documented by at least three separate and independent investigations. See the following, Jiahua Yuan, <u>Hanyu fangyan gaiyao</u> (<u>An Outline of Chinese Dialects</u>) (Beijing: Wenzi Gaige Chubanshe, 1960); also see, <u>Zhongguo yuyan dituji</u> (di 2 ban) <u>Han yu Fangyan juan</u>, (<u>Language Atlas of China</u>) (<u>Chinese dialects volume</u>) (2$^{nd}$ edition) (Beijing: The Commercial Press, 2012); also see, Ann Hashimoto, (also cited by her Chinese name, Oi-kan Yue, or Hashimoto-Yue) <u>Phonology of Cantonese</u>, (Cambridge UK: Cambridge University Press, 1972).

[93] Ramsey, <u>Languages of China</u>, p.23.

[94] Note: *Chung-Shaan* is a term with three different connotations. It can refer to either a di-

alect/speech community or an ethnic group label. It can also refer to a geo-territorial and administrative division, i.e. a county or district, as in *Chung-Shaan* district.

[95] See, Marjorie K.M. Chan, "Zhong-shan Phonology: A Synchronic and Diachronic Analysis of a Yue (Cantonese) Dialect," (M.A. thesis, University of British Columbia, 1980).

[96] Chan, "Chinese in North America," pp. 244–245.

[97] Chan, "Zhong-shan Phonology," p. 245, re: difficulty in determining what percentage each sub-group had of the total Chung-Shaan population in the nineteenth and early twentieth century; re: Chung-Shaan bidialectal speakers, e.g., *Hakka*-Chung-Shaan/Cantonese, *Nam Long* and Chung-Shaan/Cantonese, or *Loong Doo* and *Hakka*; also see Chan;" also see Marjorie K.M. Chan, "The Chinese in North America: A Preliminary Ethnolinguistic Study," in Annals of the Chinese Historical Society of the Pacific Northwest, (Seattle, Washington, (1984) (editor, Douglas W. Lee), pp. 233; also see Nicholas C. Bodman, "The *Nam Long* Dialect: A Northeastern Min Outlier in Zhongshan Xian and the Influence of Cantonese on its Lexicon and Phonology," in Tsing Hua Journal of Chinese Studies (New Series) (1982) 14.1 to 2:1–19, at p. 3.

[98] Chan, "Zhong-shan Phonology," p. 246.

[99] Ibid., p. 245; also see Chan, "The Chinese in North America," pp. 244–246

[100] See the following: Thomas Chinn, H. Mark Lai, and Philip Choy, A History of the Chinese in California, A Syllabus, (San Francisco, Chinese Historical Society of America, 1969). This small monograph is actually a seminal work, which laid down the early scholarly parameters of the study of the Cantonese Chinese in America, which nearly all subsequent studies (including the present one) have been based on and which owe an enormous debt to.

[101] In Mandarin speaking areas of North China and Taiwan, the term *Pai hua* was first popularized by progressive intellectuals in the May Fourth period of the 1920s. In this context, the term represents the adoption of the forms associated with standard Mandarin (the Beijing or old *Kuan-hua*), as the standard for China's modern vernacular language.

[102] Steven Harrell (in consultation 11/8/2020) states that *Baak-wah* is a label also used in the area of the Luichau (Leizhou) Peninsula, which lies outside what I consider to be the "Inner Baak-wah zone." This "wider application" underscores the expansive use/familiarity of this term or label in various parts of Gwongdung.

[103] See chapter 1, table 1.5 for the total area of the *Baak-wah* zone in square miles, for population of the *Baak-wah* zone, see chapter 1, tables 1.10, 1.11, and 1.13 respectively. For nineteenth-century aggregate population totals of the *Baak-wah* zone, the Cantonese core area, and all of Gwongdung province, see chapter 1, table 1.13

[104] See chapter 1, table 1.5

[105] Ibid., table 1.5

[106] Ibid., table 1.5 Here I subtracted the area of the non-*Yuet*/Cantonese peripheral areas (13,300 sq. mil.) from the total area of Central Gwongdung (53,130 sq. mil) to arrive at the total of 39,830 sq. mil. for Cantonese Central Gwongdung.

[107] Ibid., table 1.5, the figure of 53,130 sq miles for Central Gwongdung represents the inclusion of non-yuet peripheral areas (13,300 sq mils)

[108] See chapter 1, endnote #7.

[109] See chapter 1, table 1.10, this figure is an average for the period 1840-1890.

[110] Ibid., table 1.11, this figure is an average for the period 1840-1890.

[111] Ibid., table 1.13 this figure is an estimated average for the period 1840-1890

[112] Ibid., table 1.13 this figure is an estimated average for the period 1840-1890

[113] See generally Vogel, One Step Ahead, pp. 249, 461, 463-464. (Regarding contemporary counties and their respective populations), relative to my designation of which counties are in the *Baak-wah* zone and which are in *Hakka* dominated areas, I have relied on discussions with Professor Zhou Taming, a visiting anthropologist from Zhongsan University in Canton at Pacific Lutheran University in the 1993-94 academic year

[114] See, Douglas W. Lee, Facing Cantonese Adversity, Fleeing Tong-Shaan: Cantonese Society and the Root Causes of Nineteenth-Century overseas Emigration, volume 3 of The Gum-Shaan Chronicles, The Early History of Cantonese-Chinese America, 1850-1900, (Pittsburgh, Pa: Dorrance Publishing, 2023), see especially chapter 7, "Bad Joss in Communal Conflict and Social Chaos."

[115] Ibid., see chapter 4, "Bad Joss in Local Cantonese *Fan-Kwai* Conflicts."

[116] Chan and Lee, "Chinatown Chinese" pp. 111–131; see, 111–117, 121; also see H. Mark Lai, "The Guangdong Historical Background," p. 77.

[117] Gregory E. Guldin, "Seven Veiled Ethnicity: A Hong Kong Chinese Folk Model," in Journal of Chinese Studies, 1:1 (June 1984), pp. 139–156, at p. 144.

[118] Ibid., p. 146.

[119] 1854 Weaverville War in northern California, with other local episodes at Oroville and Marysville

[120] Guldin, "Seven Veiled Ethnicity, pp. 144, 146.

[121] S.R. Charsley, "The Formation of Ethnic Groups," in Urban Anthropology, ed. A. Cohen, (London: Tavistock Publications, 1974), pp. 337–368, at. 350; also see Fredrick Barth, Introduction to, Ethnic Groups and Boundaries, Ed. F. Barth, (Boston: Little Brown, Co., 1969), p. 12.

[122] See generally this book, chapter 3, "Cantonese Ethnicity as a Series of Ethnic and Speech Group Labels,"

[123] Woon, Social Organizaton in South China, p.7.

[124] Lucian W. Pye, The Spirit of Chinese Politics, A Psychocultural Study of the Authority Crisis in Political Development, (Cambridge, Mass: MIT Press, 1968), p. 86; also see, Richard H. Solomon, Mao's Revolution and the Chinese Political Culture, (Berkeley: University of California press, 1971) (originally published in the Michigan Studies on China series), p. 80.

[125] Wakeman, Strangers at the Gate, p. 58.

# CHAPTER 4
## Cantonese Culture, As a Conservative Contrarian Counter-Culture

**Introduction**

Beyond geo-historical, demographic, and ethno-linguistic considerations, Central Gwongdung's unique place in Chinese society and culture arises from an ascribed characterization of its dominant *Yuet*/Cantonese culture. In support of this contention, I offer a revisionist perspective, where I hypothesize that traditional Cantonese culture represented itself as a conservative contrarian counterculture (C4).[1] Over time this C4 tradition manifested a biased perspective about why and how Cantonese people were socio-culturally distinctive, and how this in turn influenced their relationships with others (i.e., with both other Chinese people and foreigners).

**The challenge of identifying and deciphering traditional Cantonese Culture**

Historically in Han Chinese society, certain groups identified with a given locality have earned a reputation, or have become identified in such a way as to highlight the uniqueness of their identity and experiences. There has never been any question of whether or not these groups are in fact Han Chinese, but rather a question of where these groups are positioned on the Han Chinese continuum. In this context, I suggest that the focus should be on where and how such groups reflect distinct varieties of Han Chinese socio-cultural standards. Some of the better-known cases include people from: 1) Sichuan, 2) Shandong, 3) the *Min* people in Fujian, 4) the Gan of the mid-Yangtze River region, 5) the *Subei* of Jiangsu,[2] 6) the *Hakka* of South China, 7) and the *Yuet*-Cantonese of Gwongdung. In this context, the Cantonese conspicuously stand out, because their collective identity evolved in such a way as to exhibit a persistent tension, whereby questions about identity and experience have been historically framed as a defensively oriented critique of mainstream Han Chinese society and culture.

The character of traditional Cantonese culture in late Imperial China has been a long-neglected topic, largely because it has lacked a suitable conceptualization. While some have called attention to its distinctiveness, none have grappled with formulating a rationale to explain it. Admittedly, concerns about this subject have been confined primarily to Cantonese scholars, because of an obvious vested interest and relevance. In contrast, other Chinese and foreigners have merely taken note of the distinctiveness of the *Yuet*/Cantonese people and have been content with this observation.[3] Beyond initial casual comments, there hasn't been any serious interest to explore further. As noted earlier in the preface, my original interest, over half a century ago, in studying Cantonese people revolved around the question of why and how they were distinctive, hence different from other Han Chinese people. As my thinking about these questions evolved over many decades, I adopted a number of alternative theoretical constructs to explain this sense of Cantonese distinctiveness.

At the outset some thirty years ago, I originally hypothesized that Cantonese culture represented itself as an "iconoclastic cultural tradition."[4] Today, I see that my earlier thinking was inadequate for deciphering traditional Cantonese culture. Specifically, the idea of an iconoclastic culture places too much emphasis on the idea of "destroying the heterodox" of an intervening established orthodoxy, to promote a more authentic and purer lost tradition. In this regard, my earlier conceptualization was premised on, and unnecessarily emphasized, an overly negative perspective, regarding how we might envision and understand traditional Cantonese motivation and engagement in cultural matters. This is especially so because my prior thinking tended to sensationalize Cantonese distinctiveness, without providing a reasonable rationale of its construction, and a realistic assessment of its contextualization. Clearly the historical narrative does not support such a view.

While Cantonese society did reject various elements of Han Chinese culture, identified with intervening Mongol and Manchu chapters of history, it did not however, actually seek to root out and destroy the heterodox. It sought instead to affirmatively remind others that Cantonese culture represented an orthodox embodiment of a pre-existent, more authentic and pure alternative branding of *Han-ness*, which Cantonese people identified as *Tong-ness*

*(Tang-ness.)* [5] Because Cantonese society long revered the glories of the *Tang* (Cantonese form "*Tong*") dynasty (7th-10th centuries CE), it readily adopted the *Tang* standard, which exempted Cantonese society and culture from *Yuan* and *Qing* period cultural norms and standards.

Over time, biased (non-Cantonese) Chinese perceptions of things Cantonese, via ascribed traits, such as "atypical," "unconventional," and "unorthodox," became synonymous with how other Chinese often viewed and thought about Cantonese people. We should be mindful however, that it is not enough to say that traditional *Yuet*/Cantonese culture has been atypical, unconventional, or unorthodox. We must ask how and why this has been so. Such an inquiry requires an improved definition, and demanding examination of its material elements, regarding what it meant and what it represented. In this regard, while elements of my earlier interpretation of Cantonese culture can still be identified within the traditional Cantonese mindset, I now realize that their role has been more symptomatic, rather than determinative, in how they have contextualized nineteenth-century Cantonese thinking and experience. In this manner, they exist more as secondary subjective views regarding how cultural matters were perceived and idealized.

Cantonese people embraced their ascribed image to their advantage, where they rationalized the meaning and value of their culture, via a kind of "reverse engineering," in an ongoing deliberate, albeit somewhat subconscious, disassembly and "retro-fitting" of the Han Chinese-Cantonese relationship. This involved a skillful distancing of the Cantonese persona from traditional "mainstream" Han Chinese culture, again, one largely perceived as Mongol contaminated and Manchu compromised, while also simultaneously repositioning it and closely identifying it with the Tang era, which had impeccable authentic classic Han Chinese credentials.

Traditional Cantonese society did not commit resources, energy, and effort to "force" other Han Chinese to follow their lead. It was enough that historical and cultural imperatives called attention to the issue, and thus put mainstream Han Chinese society on notice. In this regard, the Cantonese position has been less one of overt hostile opposition and blatant rejection, and more a case of critical self-re-examination. It emphasized less what other Han Chinese accepted or rejected, and more where and how Cantonese people over time represented a more authentic chapter of experience and cultural expression. Thereafter, Cantonese society moved on, quite content to "go it alone." Indeed, most Cantonese believed that other Han Chinese could not "be like us," because they had been (Mongol) contaminated and (Manchu) compromised.

Traditional Cantonese identity was durable, with no need to defend it, or to seek approval from others, because it existed, both existentially and materially. This perspective underscored Cantonese confidence in who they were, what they represented, and why it mattered. This outlook, borne out of a defensive pride in being historically distinctive and culturally authentic, is a cherished component of Cantonese thinking about "us" and "them." It separates and distinguishes Cantonese people from other Chinese, to the extent that others are aware of Cantonese group identity, even though they are often unable to identify it, much less understand and appreciate it. The Cantonese sense of a lack of empathy for other Han Chinese people, who cannot relate to, nor understand the Cantonese perspective, often makes them appear to be condescending and dismissive. It would be helpful to remember that this position is merely a defensive tactic in support of the sense of Cantonese distinctiveness. These realizations have led me to search for a new alternative conceptualization about traditional Cantonese culture.[6]

## Traditional Cantonese culture, as a conservative contrarian counter-culture (C4)[7]

The paradigm of a conservative contrarian counter-culture, (C4,) relative to traditional nineteenth-century Cantonese identity and experience, shares a commonality with my earlier notion of Cantonese culture as an "iconoclastic cultural tradition." This nexus revolves around traditional Cantonese pride in, and obsession with, questions about ethno-linguistic purity, cultural authenticity, and socio-political legitimacy. The C4 model is more positive in its construction and contextualization of Cantonese culture, as evident in the specific terms used, relative to what they mean, and how they work together to help explain a complex and nuanced subject.

In choosing the term "conservative" as an initial categorial identifying label regarding traditional Cantonese culture, I intentionally draw attention to the motivational element. By way of "conservative," I mean an attitude or mindset, where effort is exerted to protect, preserve, and promote a view or experience which is deemed to have historical meaning, cultural value, and which also embodies important identity associations. I do not use the term "conservative" in a political sense, as in "conservative versus liberal." Here the term "conservative," connotates the idea of protecting and nurturing something to be treasured. In the Cantonese case, such aspirations are directed at protecting and promoting a regionally-based cultural tradition, as a time-honored legacy, i.e., *Yuet* culture and Cantonese speech. This tradition has intrinsic value and meaning of its own, because within it are located the enduring constructs of group social and ethnic identity. My use of "conservative" highlights the traditional Cantonese concern for protecting and promoting a *Yuet*/Cantonese regional culture (folk, material, and high culture).

It will be recalled that the *Tang* period represents a special time in the history of Han Chinese experience in Gwongdung. First, it was only in the later *Tang* period (9th-10th centuries CE) that Gwongdung became fully integrated into Chinese society, whereby its people merged with mainstream Chinese society. As a result, Gwongdung made the transition from being a mere outpost of Han Chinese society on China's southernmost frontier, to become a critical component of a newly emergent and ascendant Southern Chinese cultural tradition in Chinese society. Over time, the Cantonese embodied this new identity, underscored by a heightened prestige and credibility, set within a blooming southern Chinese culture. Second, by the Tang era, a newer *Yuet* (粵) label had replaced the earlier, somewhat pejorative *Yuet* (越) label, as the definitive symbolic referent for things Cantonese in Chinese society. This newer *Yuet*/Cantonese persona represented a stubborn conservatism, constantly preoccupied with issues of historical legitimacy, cultural authenticity, and ethno-linguistic purity.

While this development reached full maturity by the *Song (Sung)* period (10th-13th centuries CE), the Cantonese chose to identify themselves with the earlier *Tang* period (8th-10th centuries CE), an era famous for its martial glory and cultural brilliance. In contrast, the *Song* period reflected an era of political weakness, as witnessed in the steady decline of China, with the loss of North China in 1127 CE, and the remainder of southern China in 1279 CE to barbarian conquest dynasties. Interestingly, the *Tang* period model provides an ironic twist of history, because similar to the *Yuan* and *Qing* periods, it also encountered significant cultural influences from Central Asia, via North China. Under the Tang imperium however, contacts with and influences from Central and Northeast Asia developed under the congruence of Han Chinese self-rule and a brilliant cosmopolitan cultural florescence, which produced a dynamic and enduring Medieval Chinese identity and experience.

One consequence of this *Tang* achievement was the initial construction and early development of a distinctly *Yuet*/Cantonese ethnic-speech persona, and authentic regional socio-cultural tradition. These elements became the building blocks of Cantonese group identity and experience. In this light, the *Yuet* ethnic and cultural group label came to represent a chronological indicator of both regional historical maturation and socio-cultural integration. Over time, it resonated as a vital symbolic representation of a self-ascribed authentic and conservative Cantonese cultural tradition.

The remembrance of the greatness and centrality of the *Tang* period in Cantonese experience is evident in numerous signs and symbols identified within traditional Cantonese culture. It is a concern deeply rooted in the Cantonese psyche, as evident in various colloquialisms in the Cantonese oral folk tradition, concerning identity at the fountainhead and beyond. This identification with the "Chinese Millstone of greatness" of the *Tang* Dynasty persisted, both at home and in distant overseas locations.[8]

Symbolic references to the *Tang* period were graphically represented in Cantonese-Chinese America, for over a century, until as late as the early 1960s. Cantonese-Chinese in nineteenth-century America routinely referred to themselves, among themselves, in colloquial terms. They did not call themselves Chinese (i.e., *Chung-Kwok Yan*) (*Zhongguo ren*) nor did they call themselves *Gwongdung yan* or "Gwongdung" people. Instead, they routinely referred to themselves as *Tong-yan* (Cantonese form) (*Tangren*) (*Pinyin* form), i.e., "Tang people" or "Men of Tang." As Americans coined the term "Chinatown" to identify where local Chinese were often located in American communities, the Cantonese called their part of town *Tong-yan gai* (*Tangrenjie*) or "Street of the Tang people." Another colloquial phrase frequently used among Cantonese in America, similar to how

Americans coined the term "Chinatown," was to identify their community as *Tong-yan fow* or literally, "Tang people's (seaport) town." Similarly references to Chinese food and clothing were *Tong-ts'aan*, meaning "Tang food," and *Tong-Saam*, meaning "Tang clothing or garments" respectively.

In colloquial Cantonese or "insider's Cantonese," routine references to home in China did not make mention of China, i.e., *Chung-kwok* (*Zhongguo*) or even refer to Gwongdung province. In this context, "home" did not mean merely a physical spatial reference, but rather a place with powerful historical and cultural associations. It was the all-important fountainhead, from which *Yuet*/Cantonese identity and experience flowed forth.[9] Consequently, nineteenth-century overseas Cantonese in America referred to their place of origin, i.e., their home, as *Tong-shaan* (*Tangshan*) or [land of the] *Tang* [peoples'] Mountain(s). This contextualizing of contemporary nineteenth-century Cantonese identity and experience with the cloak of 8th-10th century CE *Tang* Dynasty historical associations and cultural identifications, set the Cantonese apart from other Chinese. They were identifiably Han Chinese, but they did not think and behave like other Han Chinese.

Traditionally, the Cantonese have proudly claimed that their regional culture truly represented the essence of traditional Han Chinese culture, because it faithfully embodied the cultural coding of an earlier, purer Chinese (i.e., *Tang*) tradition. This claim of an experience historically more legitimate, and an identity culturally more authentic, underscored the persistence of a conservative cultural mindset in Gwongdung. Indeed, because Cantonese society reverently believed in the meaning and value of this proposition, it came over time to regard its conservative persona as a cultural icon in of itself.

"Contrarian," is the second categorial term that I use to re-evaluate the distinctiveness of traditional Cantonese culture, relative to both its descriptive features and its multi-faceted representations. When the evocative term "contrarian" is paired together with the adverbial prefix-label "conservative," as in "conservative contrarian," there is the greater possibility for a more reliably precise and accurate analysis of the material constructs of traditional Cantonese culture. Unlike the term "iconoclastic," which myopically focuses on the idea of destroying the heterodox, to promote an earlier orthodox view or condition, the term "contrarian" offers a more realistic way to examine Cantonese views about group identity. In this new theoretical construct, my focus shifts from a negative ascribed paradigm of rejection and destruction, to an affirmative one of positive self-examination and self-promotion of group identity. This also involves a concurrent re-configuration and re-positioning of that identity, by preserving and promoting it within the larger context of history and culture. This new view does not focus merely on the sense of the atypical, unorthodox, and unconventional, but rather on how such differentiation is constructed and contextualized, as icons of cultural authenticity, political legitimacy, and ethno-linguistic purity.

The contrarian imperative rejects conventional wisdom and opposes popular opinion, because they can obstruct the ability to visualize and to think about alternative ideas and views. Specifically, the Cantonese effort to protect and promote their own vision of who they were/are and their place in the Chinese scheme of things, mirrors a stubborn persistence to be "true" to their historical roots and cultural legacies, as in the case of *Tong-ness*, as a means of better understanding and representing the sense of *Han-ness* and *Chinese-ness* in Cantonese experience. A person with a contrarian position or mindset, is one who disagrees with an accepted perspective, and who proceeds against, current opinion, conventional thinking, or established practice, from a position typically opposed to that of the majority.[10]

I apply contrarian thinking to the task of addressing broad historical and cultural issues. In this context, contrarian opposition arises from an ability and a willingness, to see and think about a situation, a problem, or task from an alternative perspective. In this perspective, a contrarian can be viewed as a "trailblazer," one who because he/she is a visionary, can just as likely be labeled as "crazy" as well as "brilliant."[11] During the nineteenth century, others (other Chinese and non-Chinese alike) often thought of the Cantonese as "crazy," while doubtlessly, most Cantonese thought of themselves as being "brilliant." In this light, on opposite sides of the Cantonese-Chinese cultural divide, the Cantonese, as contrarian actors, can be regarded alternately as either "heroes" (the Cantonese view) or as "*Hanjian*"[12] (Chinese traitors) and "non-conformists," (the views of many other Chinese) relative to existing labels regarding *Han-ness* and *Chinese-ness* respectively.

My reference to "contrarian" is wide-spectrum in its conceptualization, and also case specific in its analytical application, whereby I draw attention to the key role of historical and cultural contextualization. In this context, I focus on those individuals and groups of people, who reject and oppose popular views and conventional thinking, regarding such critically important matters as the basis of culturally defined ethno-linguistic group identities, and the meaning of related collective experiences. I view traditional Cantonese contrarian thinking as a collective mindset, attitude, and outlook, which rejects and opposes popular opinions or conventional thinking about the meaning and representation of traditional Cantonese group identity and collective experiences, as they have emerged in Chinese History and evolved within Han Chinese culture. The C4 goal, again, is to protect Cantonese identity and promote/preserve *Yuet* culture.

The final component of my new conceptualization of traditional Cantonese culture embraces the term "counter-culture." Popular non-Cantonese Chinese views of Cantonese society and culture traditionally expressed themselves in the form of biased group stereotyping, e.g., the Cantonese represented a hearty, stubborn, independent provincialism, underscored by xenophobic fears and chauvinistic bias, renown throughout China for its unconventional character. As a "counter-culture," Cantonese culture identified with a wide spectrum of unusual inclinations and unorthodox interests, often resulting in the view by others, that it was typically bizarre.

> They were considered uncommonly bellicose ... often looked down upon as serpentine *Yeh-man* (savage southern barbarians) whose habits were bizarre and uncouth. [13] The corresponding Cantonese reaction is an intense, though defensive, pride in their origins .... (a) claim that their province is the most Chinese of all areas. While the rest or China was sullied by barbarian Mongol and Manchu invasions, Kwangtung [Gwongdung] remained "pure." Cantonese is also the dialect closest to archaic [Tang] Chinese. The family, which is the basis of Chinese culture, is stronger there than anywhere else.[14]

These contrasting misperceptions, served as the basis on which elites, and rank-and-file members of traditional Cantonese society alike, understood that their *Yuet* culture functioned as a "counter-culture," within the broader rubric of traditional Han Chinese culture, to the extent that Cantonese people collectively personified Cantonese regional cultural sensibilities and imperatives during the late Qing period, 1800–1911CE. This perceived "different" character of Cantonese group identity contributed greatly to the C4 tradition of traditional Cantonese society and culture. While these biased perceptions and resulting group stereotypes, based on (often superficial) subjective generalizations, are clearly suspect, they do however, reveal something of the meaning of widely held views and common beliefs, about who the Cantonese were and how they were unique in a society which traditionally valued unity and uniformity.

These negatively ascribed characterizations of the Cantonese, i.e., of both their society and culture, dovetail well with more positive self-ascribed self-identifications about Cantonese thinking and behavior. Together, they formed the basis of an operational counter-culture, where Cantonese views, thinking, and conduct represented a persistent contrasting reverse mirror image of nineteenth-century Han Chinese society and culture. This counter-culture did not threaten, detract from, nor compromise mainstream Han Chinese culture. Its pedigree, prestige, and forceful expression flowed from its persistence, less as just another variant of the Han Chinese culture, and more as a vibrant and enduring counter culture within it, but clearly distinct and separate from it.

Quantitatively, Cantonese language and culture represented one of several sub-variants of Han Chinese speech/culture in South China. Other examples include the *Min* of Fujian,[15] the *Wu* of the lower Yangtze (*Jiangnan*),[16] and the *Subei* just north of Shanghai.[17] Thus, quantitatively speaking, mere differentiation was of little consequence. Qualitatively, however, the Cantonese image and persona had considerable meaning. As a result of both ascribed and self-ascribed traits, the meaning of traditional Cantonese culture was based less on mere distinctiveness, and more on the atypical character of that differentiation. Such matters as Cantonese speech, lifestyle, sense-of-community, economic enterprise, and political culture represented not just an additional variation on a theme, but functioned as a significant counterpoint to that theme, via a formidable "counter-culture." This occurred on two separate, but related levels of experience. First, there was the unique cultural tradition represented by the *Yuet*/Cantonese community of Central Gwongdung in local speech, ethnic community and regional cultural sensibilities. Second, this C4 tradition projected over time a heightened self-consciousness, within a strong ethno-linguistic chauvinism. The result has been the persistence of a unique Cantonese persona involving alternately, elements of defensiveness and arrogance, relative to "mainstream" traditional Han Chinese society/culture.

Traditional Cantonese culture existed as a powerful and enduring counter-culture, guided by a decidedly conservative contrarian core value system. Over time, it provided both the basis on which Cantonese experience was predicated, and an enduring standard to which it traditionally adhered to. In this manner, Cantonese culture offered itself as a kind of "reverse image" of Han Chinese culture, which embraced it. This image evolved for over a thousand years, from the *Tang* to the *Qing*, and it is one which has been highly subjective in outlook and content. It is as much the result of how other Chinese view and respond to the Cantonese, as it is one shaped by Cantonese self-perceptions. Both perspectives have strongly influenced how the Cantonese relate to other Chinese in China, and with non-Chinese people elsewhere.

This situation is not to suggest that the Cantonese went out of their way to be unorthodox in their thinking and unconventional in their behavior, merely for its shock value. It underscores the view of many in traditional Chinese society, including the Cantonese themselves, that a different outlook and set of normative behavior standards prevailed among the Cantonese, in the form of a C4 tradition. These criteria harkened back to classical Tang models, as a means of providing authenticity to the *Yuet* cultural standard, and legitimacy to Cantonese socio-economic and political imperatives. By cloaking contemporary nineteenth-century actions with a ninth-century aura, Cantonese persona/conduct not only exempted itself from conformity with prevailing Chinese (Manchu manipulated) standards; but equally important, it liberated Cantonese creative energies to seek uniquely local (i.e., Cantonese) solutions to onerous and perplexing socio-economic and ethno-speech community problems in Gwongdung and elsewhere. This in turn, led to the advent of new ideas and values at the end of the nineteenth century.

**The historical-cultural context of Cantonese speech supporting a C4 tradition**

One of the most concrete and persuasive arguments in support of the notion that Cantonese speech embodied a C4 tradition, is the matter of Cantonese speech itself. In this context, I hypothesize that Cantonese linguistic technicalities, such as phonology, tonal variations, lexicon, and syntax demonstrated that the Cantonese oral tradition mirrored Cantonese conservative contrarian values, as they underscored Cantonese obsession with cultural authenticity and language purity. This fixation reflected itself in various structural technicalities inherent in Cantonese speech, (see chapter 2). These matters underscored traditional Cantonese claims about enduring, but often enigmatic, *Yuet*/Cantonese language/speech identifications with classical "Middle" Chinese *Tong* (*Tang*) forms. This formed the basis for Cantonese claims that their speech was "more Chinese" then that of other southern Chinese dialects, because it maintained greater fidelity with "Middle Chinese" (*Tong*) (*Tang*) authentic speech forms and literary traditions.

This claim of purity of form, by preserving *Tang* models, can be somewhat misleading, relative to what the claim actually embraces. It is certainly not a case where Chinese speech of the *Tang* period has been preserved, unchanged in full, since the ninth century; but rather a case where "a blend" of archaic Chinese of the pre-*Tang* period has been blended with elements of non-Han Chinese, i.e., *Tai* oral traditions, to form the basis of a *Tang* inspired and structured speech/language model. Evidence of this persists today in the case of Cantonese-Chinese characters found in Cantonese language newspapers, in Facebook pages in Hong Kong, and even in Cantonese opera.[18] Ultimately, *Tang* period Chinese models formed the essential core of Cantonese speech.

While it is misleading, to claim that Cantonese speech has preserved *Tang* speech fully in-tact, it is however, correct to say that among Han Chinese dialects, Cantonese speech remains the closest to *Tang* speech by way of where and how *Tang* forms have been preserved and retained. This has been reflected in a persistent concern about authenticating Cantonese speech, by continually associating it with *Tang* models of a thousand years ago. Quite simply, Cantonese, as a form of speech, with "Middle" Chinese identifications, has not been a "dead language," but rather a vibrant, living, and admired language/speech medium in Gwongdung, the *Lingnam*, and beyond.

Cantonese speech had, and continues to have, symbolic meaning and historical value for Cantonese-speaking people. In this regard, the term *Yuet* (粵) itself is representative of a larger lexicon that incorporates many atypical, archaic written forms of Chinese as colloquial terms/phrases. In this way, Cantonese embraces a wide range of older classical literary forms, many from "medieval Chinese" of the *Tang* period. These forms punctuate modern Cantonese writing in personal correspondence, sub-titles for Mandarin Chinese films, on Cantonese menus, in Cantonese language newspapers in Canton, Hong Kong, San Francisco, and elsewhere in the Cantonese-speaking world. Most Cantonese words and phrases might be pronounced differently than in Mandarin or any other Han Chinese dialect, but often written with the same Chinese character(s). This commonality of the written script underscores the fact that *Yuet*/Cantonese is a Han Chinese language/dialect. The exception to this, is again, the incorporation of older, "classical" or "anachronistic" colloquial terms and phrases. This means that the different pronunciation of words in Cantonese speech arises not only from differences in pronunciation, also because an entirely different (e.g., Middle Chinese) word/phrase is being used.

Traditional Cantonese loyalty and commitment to a revered speech tradition has not been a mere habit or blind obsession for its own sake. It has been rather, a keen and persistent (but largely unconscious and unarticulated) loyalty to a venerated tradition that has historically manifested itself in a variety of ethno-linguistic and cultural symbols. The fact that ethno-linguistic and cultural symbols arose from, and reflected the classical standard of an earlier era, again underscored traditional Cantonese concerns about socio-cultural authenticity and ethno-speech purity. This view further bolsters the idea that *Yuet*/Cantonese speech/language has played a key role in promoting and sustaining traditional Cantonese culture, one richly imbued with a C4 mindset.

**Cantonese speech, as a vehicle for expressing C4 values**[19]

Historically, Cantonese speech clearly identified Cantonese people, and distinguished their culture, which set Central Gwongdung apart from the rest of Gwongdung, and more generally the rest of Han Chinese society. It did so by concretely integrating elements of cultural identity and speech communication, which confirmed the distinctiveness of the Cantonese, and the uniqueness of their C4 tradition. Again, it did so by highlighting the claim that *Yuet* speech linguistically embodied, and historically linked, Cantonese Central Gwongdung with the *Tang* period. In this manner, *Yuet*/Cantonese dialect/speech forms emerged as a conservative orientated oral tradition, whereby the meaning of group identity, and the context of its related collective experiences, became the metric for measuring cultural authenticity and linguistic purity in the Cantonese speaking world.

*Cantonese speech developmental characteristics supporting a C4 spirit*

In reviewing briefly some of the developmental characteristics of Cantonese speech, it is possible to demonstrate where and how the intersection of language and culture support the notion of a Cantonese C4 tradition. Specifically, I identify four examples that support this line of thinking.

First, traditional Cantonese views about their language/speech underscored an essentially conservative attitude, whereby authenticity was regarded as a necessary prerequisite for any claim of purity of form and legitimacy of status, within the context of Chinese language and culture.

> Cantonese is said to be a conservative dialect, and to a certain extent this reputation is deserved. In its sound system it preserves with great fidelity the final consonants and tonal categories of the Tang dynasty literary standard. This means a Tang poem read in Cantonese keeps more of its original patterns of rhyme than when read in Mandarin- or any other [Chinese] dialect.[20]

In this manner, the Cantonese community boldly claimed that its dialect(s) and speech forms represented more faithfully classic *Tang* models and forms. This naturally placed Cantonese, and more generally *Yuet* culture, in a conflictive position relative to "mainstream" Han Chinese society, via its conservative contrarian agenda. This stance was viewed by others, as alternately defensive and arrogant. This resulted in a stubborn independent mindset. Flowing from this, there existed a willingness to stand firm, to be unafraid to stand out, or to stand alone, as a largely self-ascribed, representative of an earlier authentic and pure speech tradition. Previously mentioned factors, such as heavy involvement in commercial enterprise and political resistance[21] did not lack for a suitable empowering Cantonese oral and literary tradition.

Second, Cantonese traditionally embodied the ability to linguistically and conceptually bridge the wide gap between China and the outside world. In the pre-*Tang* era, this meant reconciling Chinese language and culture with non-Chinese speech and culture on China's southernmost frontier. This involved, again, traversing the great historical and cultural distance from *Yuet* (越) to *Yuet* (粵). From the Tang period onwards, it meant harmonizing the many disparate dimensions of medieval Sino-foreign relations in the South. Linguistically, this included such technical matters as: a) the expanded function of tonal variations, as a means of expanding vocabulary; b) the proliferation of colloquial terms to represent with greater specificity, new and different phenomena encountered; and c) the facile transliteration of foreign loan words into Chinese, e.g., Western terms during the late *Qing* period. These several developments underscored a pragmatic oral tradition, amid rapidly changing conditions in southeast China. This is not to ignore similar changes taking place elsewhere in southern China, but rather to reaffirm the material elements of Cantonese language development, in the context of its C4 tradition, as it squares with ascribed claims of *Yuet*/Cantonese cultural authenticity and language purity.

Third, Cantonese represented a strong, persistent oral tradition. Once a local Cantonese speech tradition became well-established and clearly defined by the *Tang* period, it remained fairly constant and resistant to change in the succeeding millennium, from the 9th through 20th centuries CE. Cantonese speech retained its original forms more authentically and more completely, than most other southern Chinese dialects. Geo-historical, ethno-linguistic, and material conditions combined to help provide an ideal setting in which to nurture and preserve Cantonese speech, both as an organic extension of classical models established in the *Tang* period; and as an atypical evolving variant of Han Chinese language and culture.

Historically, both Cantonese speech and *Yuet* culture had the benefit of double protection from external Chinese influences, which included: 1) relative protection of long distances from the upheaval of alien invasions and conquest of northern China, and 2) relative isolation/insulation from the influences of other major dialects/speech forms of the Chinese language, especially regarding other major southern Chinese dialects. This occurred despite the fact that the Canton area became China's premier seaport for over a millennium (9th-19th centuries CE), which dramatically undercut Cantonese geophysical remoteness and isolation. This fact did not, however, compromise the exclusivity and cocoon-like protective separation and social distancing of *Yuet*/Cantonese speech from other Chinese speech communities. Indeed, the greater the discrepancy between the Cantonese, and their authentic *Tang* modeled speech community and ethno-regional culture, and the diluted Han Chinese speech and culture of northern China, the stronger the force of the C4 tradition in Central Gwongdung. This development evidenced a deft balancing of Cantonese defensiveness and arrogance.

Fourth, Cantonese in its several forms, is not only widely spoken, but is also widely recognized as a major regional speech unit. While originally specific to the Canton area, and more generally the Pearl River Delta micro-region, over the course of time it became the *lingua franca* for an entire region. In time, Cantonese identity and experience closely associated with *Yuet* language and culture, not only predominated in Central Gwongdung, but throughout the *Lingnam* region beyond it. By the early twentieth century, a transnationally constructed Cantonese group identity, and its collective experience, drove the engine of an expansive overseas Cantonese speaking-world beyond it. The only exceptions were *Min*-speaking enclaves in East Gwongdung (e.g., Chaozhou-Shantou) and West Gwongdung (Hainan, i.e., *Hailam* speech), and in Chung-Shaan county/district in Central Gwongdung (e.g., *Nam-lau, Lung-doo,* as *Min* dialects.)

This supports the view that geography not only helped delineate the boundaries of Cantonese speech and culture, but also buffered and nourished its separate identity and experience. In this way, Cantonese speech and *Yuet* culture were unchallenged for over a thousand years. In this region both non-Han Chinese groups, e.g., aboriginal groups) and non-*Yuet* speaking Han Chinese (e.g., *Hakka*, *Teochiu* or *Chaozhou*) either spoke a form of Cantonese with varying degrees of fluency, or at the very least had some familiarity or understanding of it.[22]

Historically speaking, geo-demographic and ethno-linguistic distinctions aside, *Yuet*/Cantonese speech and culture remained unrivaled in Central Gwongdung, in large part due to the pattern of Cantonese speech development supporting a C4 spirit.

### *Yuet/Cantonese speech as southern China's only bona fide regional dialect*

My assertion that Cantonese is unique, because it is the only truly "regional dialect," is more tenable, when one looks more carefully at the character of South China's other two major dialects, i.e., the *Wu* and *Min* dialects, neither of which can be viewed as true regional dialects. There is in fact no standard *Wu* or *Min* dialect or variety of speech, but rather a proliferation of varieties of *Wu* and *Min* dialects/speech communities.

The *Wu* dialect is spoken by nearly twice as many people as the *Yuet* dialect(s), i.e., 80 million versus 40+ million, however, it has never been a uniform, or unified regional standard like the *Yuet* dialect. Specifically, the *Wu* dialects are divided into a "northern group" located primarily in *Jiangsu* and a "southern group" located primarily in *Zhejiang*.[23] Typically, a person from a *Wu*-speaking locality knows that he/she speaks one of the *Wu* dialects, but he/she does not identify with a *Wu* region or recognize a *Wu* culture.[24] While the term "*Jiangnan*" (*Kong-nam* in Cantonese) is commonly used to represent a unified, uniform regional standard for the lower Yangtze River Delta region, where the *Wu* dialects predominate, its connotation is cultural in its representation, rather than linguistic in its reference. Most speakers of *Wu* dialects instead relate to a sub-region, or a well-defined urban dominated area, e.g., Shanghai, Suzhou, or Hangzhou.

The *Min* dialect, so closely identified with Fujian Province, has often been regarded as a kind of regional standard, because of its widespread use in *Fujian*, in parts of Gwongdung, on *Taiwan*, and in *Min*-speaking overseas emigrant communities. In this light, "…despite the very considerable differences found among the [*Min*] dialects themselves, this group is, next to Mandarin, the most distinctive and easily characterized group of Chinese dialects,"[25] such that they can be viewed together as a "pseudo" regional standard. However, in regards to both its geo-historical development, and ethno-linguistic parameters as a speech community, the *Min* dialect has been both quantitatively and qualitatively problematic, as to preclude equating it on a par with *Yuet*-Cantonese, as a genuine regional standard. Within the *Min* dialects or speech communities, there existed greater diversity than within either the *Wu* or *Yuet* dialects.

The suggestion that the *Min* dialect(s) represent a regional standard is problematic, because of a decided lack of uniformity and unity of these dialect(s), relative to their northern, southern, and western forms, not-to-mention *Taiwan* extensions and East/West Gwongdung variants. Because of *Fujian's* unusually rough terrain, its mountainous region was one of the last regions of Southern China to be settled. This meant that migration and settlement-distribution patterns in *Fujian* have been more episodic, then elsewhere in South China. Migrant groups in *Fujian* became more isolated and insulated in various pockets of territory, making contacts and linkages with other migrants of the same speech community elsewhere more difficult and tenuous. The result has been the development of different major speech forms within the *Min* dialects, different in character and construction from those of the *Yuet* community. Only in *Taiwan* has there evolved, what can be regarded as a dialect or speech community standard since the re-establishment of the failed Nationalist (KMT) regime, following the second Chinese Communst-Nationalist civil war, 1945-1949.

There are two major *Min* speech groupings. First there are *Min* speech communities of the interior, versus those of the coastal area; and second, a more important distinction between the so-called northern *Min* (*Fuzhou*) and the southern *Min* (*Amoy/Xiamen*) groups. The Northern and Southern *Min* speech communities are the largest and most important *Min* speech communities in *Fujian*. As already observed earlier, *Min* speech communities also expanded to embrace *Taiwan*, Eastern Gwongdung (the *Chaozhou-Shantou* group,) and western Gwongdung (the *Hainan* and *Hailam* groups). Each of these *Min* speaking sub-units claimed a "market share" of the larger *Min* speech community. While there was only one Canton in Gwongdung, Fujian offered the reality of several "Cantons," as rivals for "market shares" in the larger *Min* speech community. The fact that the Northern and Southern *Min* dialects respectively, each have a large "market-share" of the larger *Min* speaking community, and that they were/are mutually unintelligible underscores the fact that in *Fujian* there is in fact no regional standard, but possibly two or more. Thus, a *Min* regional standard exists only in theory. As a practical matter, the *Min* situation does not provide an adequate basis to claim that the *Min* dialect is a regional standard, on a par with the *Yuet* of Gwongdung.

In marked contrast, speakers of the *Yuet* dialect(s) have a well-developed sense of group identity, tied to a particular region. In this manner, membership in a common Cantonese speech community implies concurrent membership in a shared *Yuet*-regional culture. This regional culture arises from, and is contained within, the specific geo-territorial framework of Central Gwongdung, and again, more generally for the entire *Lingnam* region.

We should remember the importance of differences between Gwongdung's linguistic exclusiveness and its ethno-cultural inclusiveness, because this further distinguishes Cantonese speaking (central) Gwongdung, from both *Min* speaking Fujian and *Wu* speaking *Jiangnan*. The *Yuet* dialect, by its nature, excluded non-*Yuet* dialects or speech communities; but as an ethno-linguistic-based cultural unit, it has been inclusive, by way of embracing non-*Yuet* speech communities within Gwongdung.[26] This certainly has been the case regarding *Min* speaking communities in *Chung-Shaan* county in the Pearl River Delta region, and to a less degree among some *Min* speaking communities in both East and West Gwongdung.[27] In this context, Cantonese, as a regional dialect, with its own distinct written form[s], reinforced regional solidarity for the people of Gwongdung, and more generally the entire *Lingnam* region.

> Cantonese is thus more than a widely spoken dialect. It is a genuine regional standard. In Guangdong [Gwongdung] Province, even people whose home language is not *Yue* [*Yuet*], including some of the national minorities whose home language is not even Han Chinese, use it and respect it as a model for speech. No other southern dialect, including Shanghainese [a *Wu* dialect], has this kind of a stature [in China] ... The *Yue* [Yuet] speaker, by contrast, will always identify himself as "Cantonese." He looks to Canton as the center of his local culture. He recognizes [the] Canton dialect as standard.[28]

Historically and linguistically, Cantonese (*Gwong-chau wah*, i.e., *Gwongdung wah* or "*Gwongdungese*") has never been challenged by any of its related dialects or speech communities for its leadership position in the *Lingnam*. It has been easily and widely recognized as the *lingua franca* for an entire region. Even beyond Gwongdung, it has been recognized as a regional standard. It may be that this widespread recognition has often led to the inaccurate view that "Cantonese" (*Gwongdung wah* or "*Gwongdungese*") is synonymous with all of the people and all of the speech units of Gwongdung, and the entire Lingnam region, which again, is of course not true. This discrepancy does not, however, undermine the notion of Cantonese as a regional dialect. It is one thing to say that it is incorrect to assume that everyone speaks or identifies with the Cantonese label; and it is quite another thing to say that the vast majority of the people in Gwongdung do not recognize nor accept the preeminence of Cantonese, as the chief dialect of Gwongdung, or that it does not serve as a *defacto* regional linguistic standard.

The value and meaning of Cantonese as a regional standard, is further supported by the notion of "dialect boundaries," whereby demarcation lines between dialects can be classified as either weak or strong. The boundaries between major dialect groups, e.g., *Min* and *Yuet* or between the *Min* and the *Wu*, are properly speaking "strong boundaries." The transition among and between these groups are sharp and well-defined. In contrast, there also existed "weak boundaries," e.g., *Yuet Saam-Yup* and *Yuet Say-Yup* speech, or between *Yuet* (Cantonese) and *Hakka*, or between *Min* and *Hakka*, which were often unclear and less well defined, i.e., demonstrating the presence of a transitional zone or area.[29]

I suggest that if strong dialect boundaries divide major Chinese dialects, then their presence is not only indicative of major dividing lines between and among various Chinese dialects, but are also helpful in determining whether a Chinese dialect is or is not a regional standard. Relative to the notion of a regional standard, it is possible to say that where there is a bona fide regional standard, as in the case of *Yuet*/Cantonese, it is characterized by strong dialect boundaries around its periphery. This clearly distinguishes and separates *Yuet*/Cantonese from other major dialects, e.g., the *Min* or the *Wu*. It is also true that there are weak boundary lines separating various *Yuet*/Cantonese dialects and related speech forms (e.g., *Saam-Yup, Say-Yup, Baak-wah*, or *Chung-shaan*.) Quite simply, it is possible to advance the notion of Cantonese as fulfilling a unique role as a regional speech and cultural standard. As such, over the course of several centuries, it served as an effective vehicle for expressing the C4 values of socio-cultural authenticity and ethno-speech purity.

## Cantonese communalism as a C4 bias regarding ethnic group solidarity and conflict

Given the strong sense of community in Gwongdung, relative to the pattern of its geo-historical development, the primacy of ethno-linguistic group identity labels,[30] and community spatial-situational configurations, it is easy to understand that the ethnic/speech element of rural communalism in the nineteenth century had an especially forceful place in Cantonese society and *Yuet* culture. This centrality of Cantonese communalism, by way of defining local needs and interests, expressed itself as a fundamental contradiction, concerning how ethnic group solidarity and conflict were managed in community life.

As a means of better understanding this critical aspect of Cantonese experience at the fountainhead, and its importance for community life in early Chinese America, I advance the idea that Cantonese communalism expressed itself as a conservative contrarian counter-culture C4 bias. This perspective both prefaced and infused efforts to address the challenges of maintaining Cantonese ethnic/speech group solidarity, while also collectively mitigating against ethnic/speech tensions and conflicts. This, often contradictory multi-tasked effort embodied mixed elements of an obsessive advocacy for cultural authenticity, ethno-speech purity, and communal/civic legitimacy. This C4 bias underscored the complex interplay between ethnic solidarity and ethnic conflict in the Cantonese-speaking world. It did so by orchestrating how these dichotomous elements might be played out, either alone, working together, or against each other.

My earlier discussion of ethnic group labels in Chapter 3 underscored the centrality of ethnicity in *Yuet* culture and Cantonese society. Given an enhanced awareness of the central role of ethnic relations in Cantonese community life, we still lack an adequate understanding about the manner of their operation. This inadequacy is especially evident during a particularly troublesome and volatile chapter of Cantonese ethnic communal strife in the middle of the nineteenth century (1850–1870).[31] It occurred under marked adverse conditions, arising from the intersection of foreign invasion, domestic socio-political unrest, and general widespread economic hardship. Against the dramatic backdrop of the first Anglo-Chinese Opium War (1839–1842) and the *Hakka-Bundae* (*Bendi*) (*Punti*) wars 1855–1867, the facade of a peaceful Cantonese communal order and economic prosperity easily crumpled, revealing basic contradictory tensions in Cantonese society's deft balancing act with ethnic solidarity and ethnic conflict. A closer look at local ethnic solidarity and conflict can help us to understand the enigmatic working relationship between Cantonese ethnic communal solidarity/conflict and the C4 imperative that guided that relationship.

In Central Gwongdung, Cantonese communalism existed as a tradition of long-standing, where it shaped daily life in the millennium from the Tang to the late Qing period, (9th-19th centuries). The established sense of community among the Cantonese paralleled Chinese views and practices regarding community life, commonly found elsewhere in traditional Han Chinese society. In this context, the Cantonese shared with other Chinese people four common concerns regarding community life. These included: 1) a well-defined sense of community, in which group solidarity revolved around common perceptions/responses to local issues and problems of an agrarian based society; 2) the sense of community, as being socially rooted to established community institutions of family and lineage, as they were physically circumscribed by fixed spatial and social boundaries of daily life; 3) the perception that local needs and interests were paramount in the larger context of a geo-territorially extended, culturally homogeneous, and demographically large society; and 4) a persistence of parochial attitudes of dislike/distrust of outsiders, from beyond the local community.

In this context, traditional Cantonese society differed little from other segments of pre-modern Chinese society, regarding the shape and meaning of communalism in daily life. We should note however, that despite this generalization, a significant difference existed in Cantonese society, where locals had to cope with the constant challenge of ethnic group solidarity and conflict. The Cantonese case was conflated by a complex mosaic of local rival ethnic groups and speech communities, as already surveyed in chapter 3, which were either absent in most other Han Chinese communities, or significantly less complicated and volatile in their manifestation.

The strong sense of community in *Yuet*/Cantonese Central Gwongdung manifested itself in both a physical and subjective sense. In the former, it usually embodied the hamlet /village and the family/lineage institutions, and in the case of the latter it embraced ethnic/speech community elements, relative to group identity issues and experiences. Mechanically speaking, the precise coordinates of each were neither uniform nor constant. Geo-territorially, the sense of community could alternately mean respectively a single hamlet, interconnected hamlets comprising a village, or even a compact group of villages within a rural marketing system, all depending on what particular frame of reference is referenced.[32]

Most commonly, the sense of community revolved around the nuclear village, with its associated hamlets. In mono-clan villages, not only did everyone share the same surname, they also typically spoke the same speech/dialect. In other situations, a cluster of villages, some with mono-clan lineages, and others having multiple surnames, formed a community linked by other mutually forged bonds. One such bond was the constant movement of brides back and forth between villages.[33] The structuring of how villages obtained brides illustrates the social basis of what constituted a local community, (see section on bridal transfers between mono clan villages in chapter 5.)

In one context, community might mean an agnatic-based lineage system. Alternately, in an expanded sense, community might mean larger units, such as marketing towns and urban centers, which presupposed an even more varied context for "community." It is safe to say that the most important constant in the Cantonese sense of community was its geophysical context, as a well-defined area, where limited contact, travel, and communication were relatively easy- e.g., travel by foot, making a round trip within half a day to a day. Socially speaking, community was subjectively viewed to mean a group of people who identified with each other on a regular basis, and where there was a strong historical sense of "we," relative to commonly shared needs and interests. In this context, anyone not belonging to this restrictive social sense of community was viewed as "them" as in the sense of being "outsiders."

The historical distinctiveness of Cantonese experience, regarding the nature of ethnic/ speech communal development in the nineteenth century, pivots on how these matters were influenced by C4 ideas and values. In this regard, it may be helpful to advance a number of propositions regarding the role of Cantonese ethnic/speech community constructs in *Yuet*-Cantonese society and culture.

First, Cantonese communalism manifested itself in a physical and subjective sense. The hamlet or village expressed the former, and the psycho-cultural projections of "we" and "they" expressed the latter. These two aspects of traditional Cantonese communalism sprung from a single ethos, and were bonded together, like two sides of a coin.

Second, ethnicity, while not the exclusive driving force behind Cantonese communalism, was nonetheless a major determinant shaping its configuration in *Yuet*/Cantonese Central Gwongdung. In this regard, Cantonese ethnicity, as the basis for local group identity and experience, set a uniquely Cantonese stamp on typically Chinese institutions, traditions, and frames of reference. In essence, a distinctively Cantonese color emerged from a prism of atypical Chinese passions and phobias, concerning community life, as it revolved around issues of local ethnic solidarity and conflict.

Third, considerations of a C4 bias in Cantonese communalism have less to do with drawing attention to the atypical and ascribed exotic qualities associated with Cantonese life, than it does with underscoring how a certain "perception" or "frame of mind" has historically predisposed Cantonese people in Central Gwongdung to see and think about their local communities in a very distinct and personal manner.

Fourth, if we accept the proposition that *Yuet*/Cantonese culture was essentially conservative in its outlook and contrarian in its mindset, then we can understand why there was always a compulsion to see the Cantonese persona as alternately defending and promoting itself, as an authentic counter-culture variant of traditional Chinese culture. This biased perspective heavily influenced Cantonese views about what "ethnicity" and "community" meant, especially when they were used together, relative to the particulars of Cantonese experience.

Fifth, Cantonese communalism typically expressed itself as a C4 bias, in terms of its compulsive preoccupation with matters of authenticity, purity, and continuity. This perspective embodied an ongoing tension between the Cantonese-speaking world and "mainstream" Han Chinese society. In this way, the Cantonese sense of "ethnic community" arose from, and revolved around considerations about the centrality of cultural authenticity and speech purity, relative to the construction of local ethnic group identity. This preoccupation with a well-defined self-ascribed separate ethnic character was constant and ongoing. Its most astute expression was the local ethnic community.

Sixth, the concrete elements of speech, geo-territorial positioning, ethnic folklore and folk culture scaled down the lofty abstractions of history and culture, and at the same time elevated the local ethnic community to a position of central importance. This C4 bias was, again, less a rejection of mainstream Han Chinese norms and values, and more an affirmation of Cantonese ideals, ideas, and expectations. It provided a grand, but functional, standard, whereby the idealized nature of *Yuet*-Cantonese ethnic and local speech components legitimized their place and authenticated their persona. It also offered useful strategies for coaching the intricate interplay of ethnic group relations on the

*Yuet*/Cantonese playing field, where local playbooks about Cantonese inner controls and outer limits preserved the essence of harmony and order, while protecting the ethnic community turf and advancing its strategic interests.

Significantly, these observations apply transnationally, as they embraced both antecedent experiences at the Fountainhead in *Tong-Shaan*, and co-contemporary ones in *Gum-Shaan* and elsewhere overseas.

## The Cantonese sojourner's dilemma, an expression of C4 values about tradition and change

The Cantonese-Chinese Diaspora from 1850–1900 was instrumental in the development of a distinct Cantonese *Wah-Q* (*Huaqiao*) (Overseas Chinese) tradition. This tradition had its roots in sojourning beyond Gwongdung, elsewhere in China. In the eyes of most Cantonese people, it was one thing to sojourn in another community in Gwongdung (e.g., *Swatow* in East Gwongdung, or *Haikou* on Hainan Island in West Gwongdung,) or to take up temporary residence in another Chinese province, such as in *Qingdao* in *Shandong*, *Hankow* in *Hubei*, *Shanghai* in *Jiangsu*, *Chongqing* in *Sichuan*, or nearby British Hong Kong or Portuguese Macau. It was however, quite another thing to make the long, and perilous, journey overseas to dwell among "barbarians" on a distant continent. Later nineteenth-century Cantonese overseas Chinese migrations to Southeast Asia, Japan, Hawaii, North America, Latin America and the Caribbean meant consciously sojourning beyond the nurturing embrace of Cantonese society and culture.[34] It also meant slipping beyond the pale of an emotionally supportive and psychologically sustaining community.

### *The Cantonese Sojourner's Myth: Purpose and Promise*

Every Cantonese emigrant venturing abroad shared a common purpose and promise, similar with those of other southern Chinese overseas emigrants. The "purpose" was to seek material gain, ideally by a stroke of good luck, and realistically by hard work. The "promise" was to return home with enough money to settle down to a life of comfort and security for oneself and one's family. This formula of "purpose" and "promise," formed the basis of a "Sojourner's Myth." Thus, Cantonese who migrated abroad, saw themselves as sojourners, because they understood their purpose in going, and expected to keep their promise of return. This meant that the journey abroad was only a temporary expediency. It was regarded by both the emigrant abroad, and the family left at home, as an inconvenient, uncomfortable, difficult, but temporary task. The bond with kith and kin left at home formed a long umbilical cord of interdependency, re-enforced by the abstractions of Chinese history and culture. During the period 1850–1900, it was unimaginable that any Cantonese emigrant would permanently settle down beyond Gwongdung.

Among Cantonese people, sojourning had a special meaning, whereby its problematic nature served as a major force shaping life in America. Mechanically speaking, the rigidity of attitude and outlook, regarding the purpose and promise of sojourning abroad, underscored the "myth" in the "Sojourner's Myth." It did so by juxtaposing benign, but highly speculative and subjective good intentions, grand visions, and happy dreams of financial success, against a backdrop of harsh objective realities involving difficult logistics, hard times, and the relentless challenge of the unforeseen and unpredictable. There emerged from this situation a contradiction between the "image" and "reality" of sojourner life overseas.

One way of dealing with this contradiction, for both the Cantonese emigrant/sojourner, and those left behind back home, was to mystify the sojourner experience. This took place in the fluid context of constant movement and endless change, where the fundamentals of *Wah-Q* (Overseas Chinese) identity and experience were constructed, and reconstructed, again and again, with all their ambiguities and contradictions. In this way, the myth carried forward the notion of "promise," however elusive and frustrating it might be. It did so by providing a widely accepted consensus about the standard by which one's experiences overseas was measured. For many *Wah-Q* in America, and elsewhere, the fact that one was late in returning home, or that one might never get back home, did not compromise one's identity and one's mission. The promise might not be kept, but that did not invalidate the promise itself. The promise endured and remained true.

This fervent belief is evident in the fact, that as late as the mid-1960s, various temples and storage facilities in San Francisco were crammed full of boxes of bones and spirit boxes (where there were no actual remains) of deceased *Wah-Q*, all awaiting return for burial in ancestral villages in Gwongdung.[35]

Only the US trade embargo with the Peoples' Republic of China after 1949 prevented fulfillment of the promise beyond the grave. While the perpetuation of this myth gave strength and courage to endure many hardships overseas, it also created a dilemma for those who identified with it.

If Cantonese *Wah-Q* shared a common purpose and promise, they also invariably shared in a common dilemma concerning life overseas. This Sojourner's dilemma centered on how to resolve the contradiction between making good on the promise to return home safely, within as short a period of time as possible, and with as much money as possible; and the reality of long-term, possibly permanent, residence abroad. The fantastic sojourner's dream was one that only a few ever realized. Many had to settle for just a safe return after years abroad, with only a modest sum of money. Most fared considerably worse, whereby at best they returned home with very little to show for their many years abroad, or worse yet, they never returned at all. Many would over time periodically visit home, but invariably return overseas to continue to chase their dreams. For some, as in the case of many of the Chinese in Southeast Asia, some sent for their wives and families and settled down permanently abroad. In America, before 1965, this seldom happened.[36]

Prior to 1882, the powerful magic of the Sojourner Myth, with its purpose and promise, made it impractical and imprudent to bring along or send for wives and children. In the period 1850–1880s, the Sojourner Myth had not yet become complicated, elusive, or so contradictory. Hundreds of thousands of Cantonese Chinese made the long voyage to America, where sojourning seemed so fresh, exciting, and promising. Even as months became years, and years became decades, the sojourners' promise seemed obtainable, because it remained so real. Periodic home visits, when time and money were available, lent credibility to the myth of eventual success.

After 1882, however, with the enactment of America's first federal Chinese Exclusion Laws, among Cantonese emigrants, the emphasis was less on "Sojourner" and more on "Myth." This meant that more and more Chinese in America were faced with an uncompromising harsh reality. The promise of return seemed increasingly faint, more elusive with the passage of time, because of the unfulfilled purpose. Financial success became more and more difficult, because the exclusion laws accompanied economically hard times. Additionally, anti-Chinese legislation at the local and state level and popular hysteria against the Chinese made life in America a risky venture.

During the 1880s, the shinning luster of *Wah-Q* hope and high expectations in America had become tarnished and corroded. By 1900, there emerged among the Cantonese in America, both individually and on a community-wide basis, a growing pessimistic outlook concerning the sojourner experience. In America, *sik-fu* (*chiku*), i.e., literally to "eat bitterness," became an enduring colloquial phrase symbolizing the unfolding reality of great hardship in the sojourner's dilemma. An earlier optimism and self-confidence had been replaced with a fatalistic passive acceptance of a very grim reality.

In America and elsewhere, the C4 mindset, with its inherent bias supporting Cantonese distinctiveness and durability, provided a positive and practical framework for dealing with an intractable dilemma. It did so by bolstering acceptance of one's difficulties and confidence in one's self, as fixed within a collective mindset, where the harsh realities of a difficult life were beneficially contextualized in an abstract frame of reference. Here filial piety, loyalty to one's community, pride in one's ethnic and speech identifications, the much-valued camaraderie of fellow sojourners, the courage to face the uncertain and to address the difficult, all underscored a hearty and persistent "can do" outlook. Over time, both individually and collectively, the Cantonese sojourner developed more realistic responses to this sense of dilemma, where as a practical matter, he focused his energy and effort on "survival," and less and less on "success." This formula for survival was neither consciously formulated nor publicly articulated, but nonetheless it became a well-known and widespread consensus among Cantonese sojourners in diverse distant locations.

## *Cantonese Sojourners' views of "Tradition" and "Change," as a reflection of C4 bias*

Cantonese immigrant/settlers in America were well positioned, by way of their experience, enterprise, and location, to reassess their dilemma within their own historical and cultural frame of reference. They did so in terms of what they perceived to be a proper perception of tradition and change, because their reassessment arose from within their own C4 mindset and outlook. Their views about tradition and change were rooted to an experience that had its origins in a self-proclaimed self-ascribed tradition of historical continuity, cultural authenticity and ethno-linguistic purity. Quite simply, in regards to the changing nature of "tradition" and "change," and the shifting equilibrium between the two, the Cantonese perspective represented an extraordinary response to an unusual set of circumstances.

This perspective mirrored an initially subtle change of attitude and outlook, regarding how one positions oneself regarding tradition and change. However, because of the changing meaning(s), and the complex shifting interrelationship between these categories in a new transnational context, Cantonese thinking about them underwent significant and timely change. In this light, as the Sojourner Myth seemed to fail because of its growing irrelevance and impracticability, the resulting sojourner dilemma, by its very nature, forced a redefinition of the *Wah-Q* experience, relative to "tradition" and "change."

Cantonese-Chinese identity and experience in America reflected divergent points of reference. On one level, consistent with antecedent experience at the Fountainhead in Central Gwongdung, Cantonese immigrants in America replicated and extended *Yuet*/Cantonese society and culture. In this regard, they personified the very essence of that tradition. Their C4 values and mindset, represented a conservative expression of their respect for "tradition." This tradition came in multiple layers, which when peeled away revealed yet another layer. At the very center lie the hyper-sensitive and hyper-active Cantonese psyche.

In the Cantonese view, "tradition" meant an almost intuitive and compulsive awe of established standards and precedents, but again, only those recognized within the Cantonese frame of reference, as represented by the sense of "*Tong-ness*." "Tradition" in this context was quite simply "The Cantonese Tradition," which is "A" Chinese Tradition, but not necessarily the same as "The" Chinese tradition. In America, the Cantonese sojourner viewed tradition two ways.

First, he saw it in an impersonal, formal, and abstract manner. Consequently, his response was equally formal, impersonal, often expressed through ritual, signs, and symbols. In this regard, he differed little from other

Chinese. Respect for elders, a preference for hierarchical relationships, the primacy of the group, over the individual, a need for order and harmony, the avoidance of *leun* (*luan*) (chaos or anarchy), esteem for learning and scholarship, a delight in the aesthetic beauty of nature, and a preoccupation with family and social engineering, all of which represented elements of a Cantonese inspired vision of "tradition." [37]

Second, the Cantonese sojourner saw tradition from a highly personal and subjective perspective, which flowed from his quintessentially C4 heritage. In this context, "tradition" revealed itself in personal, informal, and subjective-but concrete references. These included among other things, e.g., traditional Cantonese colloquial terms of speech, *Bundae* folklore, *Saam-Yup* customs, *Baak-wah* traditions, and *Say-Yup* ethnic community standards respectively.

In the first vision of "tradition," tradition was immobilized and frozen into a much venerated, but largely fossilized vision of how the past related to the present. It was intellectualized as a set of norms and values, to be jealously guarded against imprudent tampering or untimely compromise. In the second view of "tradition," tradition existed as an organic entity, fluid in nature and evolving in character. Its value lay precisely in its many expressions of the personal, the concrete, and the specific. Tradition was not something to be admired from a distance; but viewed as an article of daily life, to be fully experienced and utilized to address real life issues.

Traditional Chinese views of "change," e.g., modernity, have been often stereotyped as the converse of Chinese views of "tradition," suggesting that they were mutually exclusive, with each dependent on the other for meaning and value. "The pairing's implied exclusivity forces upon us a rigidly bipolar view of reality...[and] the assumption persists that all of the characteristics of culture will arrange themselves someplace along a tradition-[change] continuum..."[38]

The Cantonese sojourner's perception of change is better understood when viewed on two important, but different, co-existing levels of operation.

On one level, the Cantonese *Wah-Q's* view of change represented an extension of prevailing views of "tradition" in pre-modern Chinese society. In this context, "change," like "tradition," was viewed myopically through the rose-colored lens of a biased parochialized culturalism. In this light, "change" was highly suspect, when its parameters did not fall within well-established criteria. This view complemented and interfaced with the more formal, abstract, and intellectualized vision of tradition, as discussed earlier. It was essentially a conservative traditionalist view of "change," as the complement of the formalized, abstract view of "tradition." In this view, the Cantonese in America represented, again, an extension and reflection of prevailing views and values of traditional Chinese society.

On another level, the Cantonese sojourner's perception of change was progressive and distinctly modern in its orientation. This view squares well with the second, more personal and subjective view of tradition. Both reflected the essence of the Cantonese C4 tradition, which favored the ability to assert a position, and support an interpretation, or to accept a situation, based on self-proclaimed assertions of cultural authenticity and ethnic/speech purity.

In America, and elsewhere overseas, Cantonese views of tradition and change did not offer themselves as detached intellectualized critiques, because there was neither the time, ability, nor the opportunity for such a luxury. Given the difficulties associated with *Wah-Q* life in Nineteenth-Century America, it is easy to see that Cantonese views of tradition and change did not flow from an intellectual synthesis, but arose instead from the exegeses of practical field experiences.

Certainly, difficult socio-economic circumstances and harsh political conditions helped forge a tough, common-sense perception of "tradition" and practical understanding of "change." In short, Cantonese sojourners' views of "tradition" and "change" reflected a dichotomous line of thinking. On one hand there was a stubborn loyalty to established formulas and standards, as recognized within the *Yuet*/Cantonese experience. On the other hand, there was the perception that these elements were not bound to established traditions or preconceived ideas. Instead, they were regarded as flexible and functional assets in a strange new world. This opened the door to many potentially useful, pragmatic applications.

The Cantonese sojourner in America, as a true beneficiary of the *Yuet* tradition, was among its most skillful and dedicated practitioners. In the tradition of remote ancestors along the advancing Sinitic frontier in the *Lingnam* of remote antiquity, Cantonese migrants in later Nineteenth and early Twentieth-Century America demonstrated a facile skill in balancing the contradictory requirements of preserving a much-valued cultural tradition, while at the same time devising practical solutions for addressing complex and radical changes in daily life. In Cantonese overseas emigrant communities, without the comforts and constraints of family life, this balancing act produced, again, "a peculiar kind of coherence."[39] In this altered context, "form" preserved tradition, but "function" provided a practical means of embracing change. This was evident in communal institutions like the *Wooi-koon* (*Huiguan*), clan/lineage associations, where "old world" standards and symbols consistent with community life at the Fountainhead in the "Old World" were resurrected for duty in the very different context of a "Bachelor Society" in the "New World." This unique ability to alternately preserve tradition and to also embrace change, stemmed in large part from the C4 spirit of Cantonese culture. Specifically, as the Cantonese sojourner moved to better understand and possibly resolve his dilemma, his ideas and actions served as an expression of his C4 mindset, regarding "tradition" and "change" in early Chinese America.

## Conclusion

The notion of Cantonese culture as a C4 tradition represents a long-standing interest in the origins and development of the traditional Cantonese persona, by way of underscoring the complexity of its character and the long historical process which shaped it. This historical fact is important in two regards. First, antecedent Cantonese experience and values shaped the mindset and expectations of Chinese immigrant-sojourners in America. In this context, early Chinese community and culture in North America was not just Chinese, but a unique, atypical Cantonese variant form. Secondly, antecedent Cantonese culture helped orchestrate a wide spectrum of interpersonal relationships, both within the ethnic community and beyond it, which included: 1) the pattern of relations within the *Yuet*-Cantonese *Wah-Q* (Overseas Chinese) community, among various *Yuet*/Cantonese ethnic groups and speech communities; 2) relations with other Han Chinese, after 1890, e.g., relationships with Chinese foreign students, peripatetic politicians, entrepreneurs, professionals, and diplomats; 3) relations with other Asian immigrant communities, such as the Japanese, Koreans, and Filipinos; 4) relations with other "people of color" such as Blacks, Hispanics, Hawaiians, and Native Americans; [40] and finally 5) with White society.

The centrality of antecedent Cantonese culture has been advanced, via the premise that Cantonese culture has been quintessentially conservative in orientation and contrarian in spirit. This novel interpretation of Cantonese culture is intended as an introduction to the rich and complex "Old World" heritage of Cantonese-Chinese America, regarding both the function and form of its ethnic institutions, customs, and practices; and conceptual categories, as well as material facts. It also serves as a potentially useful analytical tool for re-examining established assumptions about the origins and developmental pattern of the early Cantonese-Chinese American identity and experience. The antecedent Cantonese foundation is critical to understanding early Chinese American history, and the subtle socio-cultural nuances underlying it.

My emphasis on this complex subjective dimension of identity formation, and the practical experiences identified with it, underscores the effort to "humanize" and otherwise de-mystify traditional stereotypical views of the early Chinese sojourner in America, and elsewhere. In this regard, there is the greater chance that we might be able to better understand the complexities of nineteenth-century Cantonese society and culture in both *Tong-Shaan* (Central Gwongdung) and *Gum-Shaan* (America.) This again offers another avenue for appreciating what it meant to be Cantonese in both China and America, in the later nineteenth and early twentieth-century.

[1] Regarding practical considerations of convenience and ease of use, when referencing "conservative contrarian counter-culture" in the context of this investigation, I often use the acronym C4 as a substitute reference. I do so especially when such references occur as a sequential series of references, e.g., within a given discussion section. Otherwise, when I refer to the term in an isolated context, after having not mentioned it for some time, then I use the term in its full form. In this context the full term "conservative contrarian counter-culture" and its acronym (C4) should be regarded as being synonymous.

[2] Emily Honig, Creating Chinese Ethnicity, Subei People in Shanghai, 1850–1980, (New Haven: Yale University Press, 1992).

[3] See generally, Frederick Wakeman Jr., Strangers at the Gate, Social Disorder in South China, 1839–1861, (Berkeley: University of California Press, 1966), Wakeman was among the first to draw attention to the historical, social, and cultural distinctiveness of the Cantonese, as they became sandwiched between Qing (Manchu) and foreign (Western) competition and conflict in the mid-nineteenth century.

[4] In an iconoclastic perspective, iconoclasts believe that they represent an earlier, more authentic, pure, and therefore more valid tradition- one untainted by what they believe to be intervening heterodox (i.e., deviant) thinking, behavior, traditions, and practices. This perspective justifies opposition to, rejection of, and destruction of an established intervening orthodoxy. In the Cantonese case, this involved the rejection of alien dominated interregnums in Chinese social and cultural history, i.e., the Mongol/*Yuan* (1279–1368 CE) and Manchu/*Qing* (1644–1911 CE) periods. The basis for this rejection is that these two eras were tainted chapters in Chinese history and culture, where Han Chinese socio-cultural standards of authenticity and purity were compromised by foreign military conquest, political domination, and alien cultural pollution. This idea focuses on the self-positioning of Cantonese identity and experience within traditional Han Chinese society and culture, relative to where and how it differs from mainstream Chinese socio-cultural standards, and why it matters. This perspective offers an alternative way of thinking about "Chinese-ness" and "Han-ness," as framed within a distinctly Cantonese historical/cultural perspective. See my earlier reference to "Chinese-ness" and "Han-ness" in the introduction to this book.

[5] *Tong-ness* is the Cantonese form)

[6] I am especially indebted to Dr. Stevan Harrell of the University of Washington for calling my attention to the notion of a "conservative contrarian" outlook and experience. His thinking and suggestions have been a very positive influence in my more recent thinking about the constructs of traditional Cantonese culture.

[7] The use of the acronym C4 represents an easier and more convenient way to refer to the otherwise longer technical term "conservative contrarian counter-culture."

[8] Lucien Pye, The Spirit of Chinese Politics, A Psycho-Cultural Study of the Authority Crisis in Political Development, (Cambridge, Mass: MIT Press, 1968), pp.50–66.

[9] See chapter six of this book for an expanded discussion of *"Tong-Shaan."*

[10] https://en.wikipedia.org>wiki>contrarian

[11] Ibid.,

[12] Regarding the term *Hanjian* (*Han-chien*) (Chinese traitor), see Wakeman ., Strangers at the Gate, p. 49.

[13] Edouard H. Schafer, The Vermilion Bird: Tang Images of the South (Berkeley: University of California Press,1967) chapter 12, as cited in Wakeman., Strangers at the Gate, p.57, note 23.

14 Ch'en Hsu-ching, "*Kuang-tung yu Chung-kuo*," (China and Kwangtung), Tung-fang tsa-chih, (Eastern Magazine) 36:2: pp. 41–45 (January 1939), also see Wakeman., Strangers at the Gate, p.57, note 24.

15 A situation similar to Cantonese settlement in Gwongdung in the post Han dynasty period occurred among *Min* speaking Han Chinese emigrants from Fujian in Taiwan during the 18th and 19th centuries, see Johanna Menzel Meskill, A Chinese Pioneer Family, The Lins of Wu-feng, Taiwan 1729–1895, (Princeton New Jersey: Princeton University Press, 1979).

16 Re; Wu dialects, see Jerry Norman, Chinese, (Cambridge Language Series, editor B. Comrie, CJ Filmore, et. al) (UK: Cambridge University Press, 1988), pp.199–204. Wu speech is found primarily in Jiangsu, south of the Yangtze River, with the exception of the area of Nanjing (Nanking), and in Zhejiang, and N.E. Jiangxi. There are two chief varieties of Wu speech, the northern (Jiangsu) and the southern (Zhejiang) groups.

17 Honig, Creating Chinese Ethnicity, pp. 6–11.

18 Marjorie K.M. Chan, "Cantonese Opera and the Growth and Spread of Vernacular Written Cantonese in the Twentieth Century," pp. 1–18 in The Proceedings of the Seventeenth North American Conference on Chinese Linguistics (NAC11-17), edited by Qain Gao, (Los Angeles: Gsil Publications, University of Southern California, 2005).

19 I discuss *Yuet*-Cantonese language/speech in considerable detail in chapters 2 and 3, and in the last section of Chapter five," The ties that bind, Cantonese style."

20 Ramsey, Languages of China, p.99.

21 See last part of the introduction to this book

22 Norman, Chinese, p.215.

23 Ibid., p. 199, as cited from Yuen Ren Chao, "Contrastive Aspects of the Wu Dialects," Language, 43, 92–101, see especially p.100.

24 Ramsey, Languages of China, p.98.

25 Norman, Chinese, p.228.

26 Gregory E. Guldin, "Seven Veiled Ethnicity: A Hong Kong Chinese Folk Model," in Journal of Chinese Studies, 1:1 (June 1984), pp. 139–156, at p. 144.

27 As previously noted in chapter 3 in the case of non-Cantonese speech used in the performance of both Swatow (Shantou) and Wai Chow (Waizhou) opera in traditional Cantonese regional opera.

28 Ramsey, Languages of China, p.99, and p. 98.

29 Norman, Chinese, pp.189–190.

30 See this book, chapter three, "Cantonese Ethnicity: A series of Ethnic and Speech Group Labels."

31 See Douglas W. Lee, Facing Cantonese Adversity, Fleeing Tong-Shaan; Cantonese Society and the Root Cause of Nineteenth-Century Overseas emigration, as volume 3 of The Gum-Shaan Chronicles: The Early History of Cantonese Chinese America, 1850-1900, (Pittsburgh, Pa: Dorrance Publishing, 2022), see especially chapter 7, "Bad Joss of Communal Conflict and Social Chaos."

32 See generally the following, G. William Skinner, "Marketing and Social Structure in Rural China, Part I," Journal of Asian Studies, 24:1 (November, 1964), pp. 3–43, see p.6; also see same author, "Marketing and Social Structure in Rural China, Part II," in Journal of Asian Studies, 24:2 (February, 1965), pp. 195–228; also see by same author, "Marketing and Social Structure in Rural China, Part III," in Journal of Asian Studies, 24:3 (May, 1965), pp. 363–399.

33 See section on mono-clan villages' intermarriage patterns in rural Cantonese society in

chapter 5 of this book

[34] See generally, Douglas W. Lee, Departing Tong-Shaan: The Organization and Operation of Cantonese Overseas Emigration to America (1850-1900), as volume 4, The Gum-Shaan Chronicles: The Early History of Cantonese- Chinese America, 1850-1900, (Pittsburgh, Pa: Dorrance Publishing, 2023).

[35] As a young boy growing up in San Francisco's Chinatown, I had heard stories about a repository for the bones of "Old timers" awaiting shipment back to China. As a practical matter, by the 1950s, most older sojourners who died in the states were buried in special Chinese cemeteries in their local communities. It is likely that only a few left instructions to have their remains shipped to Gwongdung for burial in their ancestral villages. In this regard, San Francisco served as the most obvious location for this service. After the U.S. Embargo on trade and contact with mainland China after the early 1950s, this practice was no longer possible. The embargo remained in effect until the late 1970s. Re: *Jianyun* (the collection and sending of bones [back home] to China, See, Elizabeth Sinn, Pacific Crossing, California Gold, Chinese Migration, and the Making of Hong Kong, (Hong Kong: Hong Kong University Press, 2013), see chapter 7, "Returning Bones," pp. 265–295. "Spirit boxes" consisted of boxes with ritual paperwork inside identifying a deceased individual, but the location of whose remains were unknown or unobtainable. This practice or returning remains among the Cantonese was common elsewhere overseas, and even in non-Cantonese Chinese communities in China. In regards to Cantonese practices in Shanghai, see, Guang-Zhao gongsuo zhengxinlu (Account-book of the Canton(ese) [Regional] Association),"*Lin-ian jinzhi shumu*" (record of yearly income and expenditures), 1873 and 1877, hand copied manuscript, courtesy of Du Li, Shanghai Museum; *Shanghai Siming Gongsuo si da jianzhu zhengxinlu* (Account-book for the four major construction projects of the Shanghai Siming Congsuo) (Shanghai, 1925),also see, Bryna Goodman, Native Place, City, and Nation, Regional Networks and Identities in Shanghai, 1853–1937, (Berkeley: University of California Press, 1995), note 12, p.90, also see pp.90–99; also see the following two essays in Cities in Motion, Interior, Coast, and Diaspora in Transnational China, edited by Sherman Cochran, and David Strand. Wen-hsin Yet, General Editor, (Berkeley, California: Institute for East Asian Studies, University of California, Berkeley: 2007), see chapter 9, by Elizabeth Sinn, "Moving Bones: Hong Kong's Role as an "In-between Place" in the Chinese Diaspora," pp. 247–271; also see chapter one, regarding more generally Chinese burial of the dead during the Republican Period (1911–1920s), Caroline Reeves, "Grave Concerns: Bodies, Burial, and Identity in Early Republican China," pp. 27–52; finally, see Hon-ming Yip, "Institutionalizing Charity, Hong Kong and Homebound Burial of Chinese Americans, 1900–1949, in Chinese America, History and Perspectives, 2018 (special dedicated volume, This Land is Our Land, Chinese Pluralities Through the Americas), pp. 1–11.

[36] Chinese Exclusion (1882–1943) officially ended in 1943, but as a practical matter Chinese immigration remained very limited under a quota system in the period 1954–1965. Consequently, only with the immigration act of 1965 (also known as the "Pan Asian Immigration Act") did Chinese (and other Asian) families become reunited and Chinese men could send for their wives and children. Starting in 1968, reunited Chinese families topped 20,000 per year. By 1980, there were about 80,000 Cantonese immigrants in the US (chiefly via Hong Kong); and by the year 2000, there were about 204,000, and by 2018 there were 233,000. By 2020 Cantonese immigrants via Hong Kong made up about 10% of all Chinese immigrants in the US. See www.migrationpolicy.org/article/chinese

37 See the following two works, Pye, The Spirit of Chinese Politics, and Richard Solomon, Mao's Revolution and the Chinese Political Culture, (Berkeley: University of California Press, 1971).

38 Paul A. Cohen, Discovering History in China, American Historical Writing on the Recent Chinese Past, (New York: Columbia University Press, 1984), p. 92.

39 Lyman, Chinese Americans, p.49

40 See Douglas W. Lee, Establishing *Gum-Shan* at Dai-Fow (Cantonese San Francisco): The Genesis of Chinese America (1845-1865), as volume 5 of The Gum-Shan Chronicles: The Early History of Cantonese-Chinese America, 1850-1900, (Pittsburgh, Pa: Dorrance Publishing, 2023), see specifically, Chapter 3, "Dai-Fow: A New Cantonese Fountainhead in Chinese-America," see section entitled, "Sandwiched in and Squeezed out," Cantonese spatial/social relations with other major ethnic neighbors and neighborhoods..

# CHAPTER 5
## The enduring ties that bind, Cantonese style

**Introduction**

A major contributing factor to the sense of distinctiveness of Cantonese people has been a steadfast collective bond of shared experiences and expectations, forged over the course of a millennium, from the Tang Dynasty to the later Qing period (7th-20th centuries CE.) I identify this development as "enduring ties that bind, Cantonese style." These ties were not unique to Cantonese society alone, because many of them also existed in other locations in traditional Chinese society, and elsewhere in the world. In the Cantonese case, however, otherwise ordinary factors contributing to Cantonese solidarity and unity played themselves out in an extraordinarily constructive and successful way, resulting in a uniquely distinctive Cantonese group identity and sensibility.

Among Cantonese people, there existed a set of material conditions, group experiences, socio-cultural constructs, and ethno-speech elements that helped to bridge divisions and manage tensions within society. In doing so, they helped foster Cantonese distinctiveness, by sustaining its cohesiveness over many centuries. This often resulted in unpredictable contradictory swings between the extremes of Cantonese hyper-sensitive defensiveness and arrogant condescension. Collectively speaking, the Cantonese were perceived as being unusually cliquish in their interactions with others. This occurred both within the Cantonese community, and with others beyond it. Among outsiders, ranging from non-Cantonese Chinese neighbors to the dreaded *Fan-kwai* or foreign devils, i.e., Westerners, this sense of "insider solidarity" among Cantonese people, regardless of location and social class, stood out as a distinguishing social trait.[1]

In Cantonese society, there existed concentric rings of loyalty and solidarity. It started with the nuclear family, and then embraced extended families via agnatic lineages, with parallel links among lineage related hamlets and villages in rural communities, and local neighborhoods in urban areas. Still further, it embraced ethnic groups, speech communities, rural counties, and micro-regions. These ties existed in tension with adverse conditions and counter forces that often sought to undermine them. Many of these ties were ordinary features of Cantonese daily life. What made them exceptional was the force of their collective power to build both intra-communal consensus and inter-communal cooperation. Over time, they became extraordinarily effective in their combined ability to marshal varied competing interests, to meet conflicting needs of diverse local groups, in support of a distinctive sense of Cantonese group solidarity and unity.

There existed many different kinds of ties that bound Cantonese people together. They can be divided into two broad categories. The first group consists of a number of material conditions, that nurtured Cantonese solidarity, even as they might also undermine it. The second group comprised several socio-cultural determinants. Each component contributed to the sense of Cantonese solidarity and unity, via the sense of "enduring ties that bind, Cantonese style." Understanding the meaning and value of these enduring ties underscores, "what it truly meant to be Cantonese in the nineteenth-century."

**Prevailing material conditions nurturing Cantonese solidarity and unity**

Material conditions affecting Cantonese group solidarity and unity lay beyond the ability of anyone to control or direct. However, when anticipated and carefully monitored, dangerous imminent threats could be minimized, and chronic adverse conditions could be mitigated.

*General geographical determinants, relative to socio-cultural integration*

Geographical matters promoted Cantonese solidarity and unity along two different fronts. First, externally there persisted the insurmountable reality of Gwongdung's geo-physical separation and great distance from other parts of China. Significantly, the existence of high rough mountainous terrain along Gwongdung's northern borders, separated Gwongdung from neighboring *Jiangxi*, *Hunan*, and *Gwongsai* (*Guangxi*) provinces. Additionally, a long southern coast-line, physically encapsulated Gwongdung, effectively separating and distancing it from other parts of Central and South China. This physical separation nurtured a separate geo-historical context and a distinct socio-cultural tradition, distinctively different from elsewhere in China. Second, internally within Gwongdung, local mountains, foothills, rivers, valleys, and peninsulas physically distinguished and separated geophysical micro-regions. While these elements initially separated and divided local communities, they also provided the means to integrate and unify them, via river and road linkages. These connections over and around geophysical barriers enhanced the ability to communicate, negotiate, and compromise.

Gwongdung's set of geophysical features nurtured a distinctive *Yuet*/Cantonese society, renowned throughout China for its ascribed image and colorful reputation. This sense of distinctiveness mirrored a delicate balancing of contradictory socio-cultural tensions, whereby degrees of differentiation and separation were balanced with degrees of cooperation and synchronization. Thus, despite differences in outlook and experience, different local groups were able to synchronize competing agendas and negotiate conflicting interests/needs, resulting in beneficial degrees of geo-demographic integration and rival ethno-speech acceptance.

Put simply, socio-cultural and ethno-speech boundaries, given changing circumstances, could become useful links, where diverse separate groups, which were identified as "we" and "they," could over time become consolidated into a new "we," encountering a new "they," (e.g., *Yuet*-Cantonese versus *Min-Teochiu*, or *Hakka*, became Cantonese *Tong-yan* (*Tangren*) versus the *Fan-kwai* (foreign devils, i.e., Westerners/ foreigners.) In this way, Gwongdung's objective geographical features played an instrumental, but invisible, role in shaping Cantonese society's socio-cultural and ethno-speech communal configurations and relationships, to the extent that they also became important enduring Cantonese binding ties.

## *Waterways as boundaries and linkages*

Central Gwongdung's many waterways served as an additional key element contributing to traditional Cantonese solidarity and unity. This situation was especially evident in the core area of the Pearl River Delta region (PRDR.) Because of this fact, and as a means of condensing my comments about the critical role of waterways in helping to forge ties among Cantonese people, my comments here focus on the case of the PRDR. It is historically significant, that the overwhelming majority of nineteenth-century Cantonese overseas emigrants to America originally emigrated from the PRDR. This fact underscores the critical role of waterways, as an enduring tie among Cantonese people in particular.

Waterways of the PRDR, depending on their location, size, and what areas they touched or served, juxtaposed two different frameworks for contextualizing life in Central Gwongdung. First, there is the purely environmental context, where a vast system of waterways supported a very rich ecological system, which in turn supported rich commercialized agricultural development for over two millennia. Second, there is the socio-economic and cultural context, where this richly endowed environment nurtured a material prosperity closely identified with: 1) widespread large-scale urban development; 2) profitable nineteenth-century regional and international commercial trading system; 3) a wealthy and prosperous Cantonese society, notorious for its conspicuous consumption, and 4) the epicenter of both an enduring rich folk culture, and a widely respected Cantonese aesthetic and intellectual tradition. All of these developments materialized as a result of the beneficial confluence of many local waterways.

The centrality of waterways as boundaries and linkages in the PRDR was most evident in its four major inter-connected river systems, i.e., the West, North, East, and Pearl Rivers. These waterways provided easy and relatively inexpensive water transportation. At the same time, they also distinguished various sub-units within the PRDR. They did so by carving out and separating key sub micro-regions. Commencing in the Outer *Baak-wah* zone, moving down stream through the Inner *Baak-wah* zone into the heartland of the PRDR, these vital waterways give definition and life to the PRDR. As these rivers flowed into the core area of the PRDR, they eventually concentrated and disgorged their waters either directly into the Pearl River estuary itself, or alternately via nearby inlets into the South China Sea. Within the PRDR, each river etched out a well-defined sub-area with its own defined space, identifiable with its own series of typographical markers, by way of foothills, mountainous spurs, valleys, and alluvial plains.

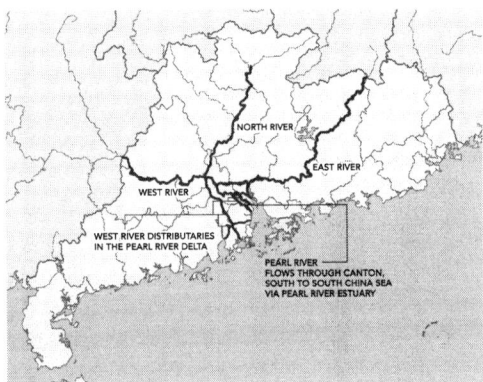

**Major rivers in the Pearl River Delta Region (PRDR)**

As these waterways flowed, they branched, joined, and separated again, whereby they functioned as established boundaries, which distinguished localities and separated communities. These communities mirrored concentrations of people, who identified with a host of different common denominators. Some mirrored specific local speech communities, others related to ethnic neighborhoods, and still other were distinguished by their specialized products, commodities, or commercial enterprises to name a few. In this manner, major waterways of the PRDR divided, separated, and distinguished population concentrations, relative to their number, density, size, and distribution. They also typically formed the basis for the location of "central places," in the shape of hamlets, villages, towns, and cities. This sense in which waterways formed boundaries, that distinguished and separated, was continually fine-turned, as major rivers, become smaller distributaries and tributaries, and eventually even smaller creeks and streams. In this way, *Saam-yup, Say-Yup, Chung-Shaan*, and *Hakka* speech communities were often distinguished and separated by rivers, channels, and inlets. Hamlets, villages, and small towns, as smaller central places, were also identified and separated by various creeks, streams, canals, and lakes.

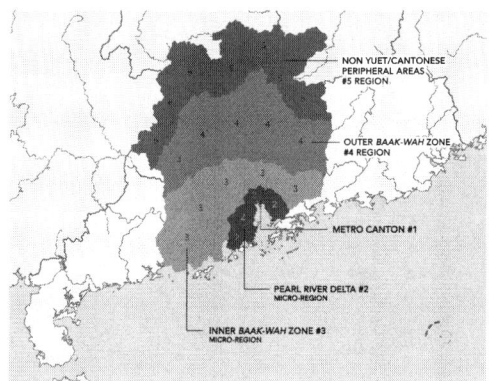

**Central Gwongdung's four major ethno-speech micro-regions mirror Gwongdung's four similarly constructed geo-physical micro-regions (see chapter one)**

Waterways also served as vital linkages, by way of easier and cheaper transportation routes, which connected upstream and downstream communities, thereby linking different locations with still other distant locations. Traversing great distances became easier, faster, and more economical via waterways. In this manner, rivers, canals, streams, and inlets linked together and integrated Central Gwongdung's various micro-regional units and economic zones. As distant places and diverse communities were connected, this development formed the material basis for the constant flow of people and goods between the urban and the rural, between the coast and the interior, and between remote mountainous outposts and the more densely populated areas scattered across the rolling countryside. In this manner, transportation and communication, relative to both social networking and economic development, effectively integrated various local, micro-regional, and province-wide network systems. Finally, waterways linked key central places, e.g., Canton, *Fat-shaan, Whampoa, Sam-shui, Hui-chau,* as vital nodules in Central Gwongdung's administrative, social, and economic infrastructures. As this complex network of waterways physically linked together and geographically integrated Central Gwongdung, it also provided the material basis for establishing Cantonese regional solidarity and unity, despite geophysical separation and ethno-linguistic differentiation of its constituent components.

### *Cantonese Central Places*

A central place is essentially the clustering of people together in one location, relative to their living and working arrangements. A "central place" also locates the position of a community, relative to the distribution and positioning of other similar communities across a well-defined geographical area. Technically speaking, "a Central place [is] the generic term for cities, towns, and other nucleated settlements with central service functions...[positioned] in interlocking spatial systems... [as in the] case of China..."[2] More practically, central places clearly established the physical location and logistical relationship between, what may be described as the "cores" and "peripheries" of community life, as mirrored in a variety of relationships and activities across spatial, socioeconomic, and ethno-speech boundaries.

Nineteenth-Century Central Gwongdung embraced a well-developed network of "central places," which shaped and directed Cantonese community development. In a landscape filled with scattered diverse central places, there existed mutual benefits associated with socio-economic integration and synchronized ethno-speech communal relations. In this manner even remote isolated areas were linked together, and in varying degrees integrated, with distant central places, and their higher density populations, within various micro-regions, such as the PRDR and others throughout Central Gwongdung. Cantonese Central places mirrored traditional administrative requirements, social relationships, and economic activities. In this manner, clustered groups of people, at various locations, and in various concentrations, maintained important ties with peoples/communities at other places, albeit on different levels, in different ways, and in different degrees.

In Central Gwongdung, central places took many physical forms. Scattered all across the Cantonese landscape, they differed in their size, shape, location, distribution, and function. In ascending order, by size, they included the: 1) hamlet, 2) village, 3) minor town, 4) standard market town, 5) intermediate market town, 6) central market town, 7) local city, and 8) regional city.[3] All of these central places, regardless of size, shape, or location fit into an integrated system, often characterized as a hierarchical network, in which they embraced either distinctly administrative or economic/market functions. Some mirrored elements of both, depending on how the two systems (administrative and economic) were structured, and where they may have overlapped.[4]

*Metropolitan Canton, Central Gwongdung's most "Central Place"*

Canton's critical importance derived from its historic role as the oldest and largest urban center in Gwongdung. This pivotal role expanded beyond Central Gwongdung to embrace, the *Lingnam* Region and a transnational overseas Cantonese community. This centrality of Canton flowed from its pivotal physical location and its linkages with critically important waterways connecting it with other strategically located central places throughout Gwongdung. These geographical determinants were historically framed as vial geopolitical and economic linkages.

An important reason for Canton's historic preeminence is that it served for two millennia, as the chief Han Chinese regional center for southeast China, between Fujian and North Vietnam. In the period from the Qin through the Tang, (221 BCE-907 CE,) Canton achieved renown as the largest, most prosperous, and celebrated Chinese urban center in South China.[5] A millennium later, in the nineteenth century, it fulfilled four critical roles, first as Gwongdung's capital, second as the chief economic center in the *Lingnam*, third as the epicenter of Cantonese society and culture, and fourth as China's "window to the outside world."

Canton, despite its historic role as late Imperial China's chief international trade center, was not, technically speaking, an oceanic seaport, which Hong Kong became in the later nineteenth century. Canton's preeminence in China's international trade, and the experience and expertise of its people in dealing with foreigners, resulted less from its proximity to the sea, and more from its pivotal location in the Pearl River Delta. This beneficial co-dependency defined and circumscribed Canton's critical role as Gwongdung's most central place.

The Pearl River and Metropolitan Canton historically mirrored a co-dependent relationship, where each helped establish and affirmed the centrality of the other. The river flowed through the city, while the city sat astride the river, each giving life and purpose to the other. The Pearl River, with its links with other major rivers, provided a critical linkage between Metropolitan Canton and its surrounding hinterland. In turn, Canton both attracted and managed the huge volume and high value flow of people and goods along the Pearl River. This centrality of Canton, via its critical positioning on the Pearl River, stemmed from two separate, but related dimensions of activity, relative to Metropolitan Canton's many links with the Pearl River Delta, and other parts of Gwongdung.[6]

First, and most importantly from the perspective of late Imperial Chinese governance, is the fact that as the capital of the region, Canton exercised civil jurisdiction and political control over both Gwongdung and Gwongsai provinces.[7] In this context, centrally located institutions of civil and military administration in Canton extended their control over all of Gwongdung, and the *Lingnam* region beyond it. The large collection of local officials, each assigned to a specific office, at a particular location, filled a vast administrative network, in a myriad of prefectural and district capitals, all controlled by Canton's administrative apparatus.

Second, Canton's paramount position in Central Gwongdung, and more specifically in the Pearl River Delta, underscored its role as the region's leading economic center. The basis for Canton's central position in the economic life of the province, and especially in Central Gwongdung, arose from its ability to manage the flow of people and goods both on the micro-region's major waterways and also among and between the region's several strategically located key central places.

By the nineteenth century, it exercised a monopoly over directing and regulating Gwongdung's communication, transportation, and commercial activities. It did so by monitoring the manner, and regulating the degree, in which the delta's many waterways functioned as boundaries, linkages, and thoroughfares within the region. In addition to controlling all major waterways, Canton also monitored and directed the flow of people and goods within a network of strategically located central places, including the roads connecting them.

Canton's logistical monopoly over both Gwongdung and Gwongsai was structurally in part administrative and in part economic. In the case of the former, as the capital of the province, Canton directed and controlled the movement of scores of officials, government agents, and support-personnel on official government business. Additionally, it also controlled the movement of troops, grain, tax revenues, state licensed monopoly agents, and *corvee* (forced) laborers. Finally, it coordinated the movement of students sitting for either the Chinese Imperial Civil Service Exam's qualifying exams in their home districts, or the regular triennial provincial exams held in Canton. Economically speaking, as the chief regional urban center for Central Gwongdung, and more generally for the *Ling-Nam* Region, Canton served as the hub of a huge wheel of Cantonese commerce and general economic activity, involving countless merchants, entrepreneurs, craftsmen, artisans, suppliers, and common laborers. This mass of people, constantly on the move, clogged rivers and roadways, as they moved from one central place to another, along a vast chain of strategically placed central places.

During the nineteenth century, Canton became one of a small select handful of "mega" urban centers supporting and guiding Qing China's vast domestic/regional trade system. It served as the chief southern terminus of trade with Central China. This pivotal role initially resulted from a well-established pattern of inter-regional overland commerce in the interior with Hankow in Hubei, dating from the late Ming and early Qing periods.[8] Since the mid-nineteenth century, with the establishment of Shanghai, as the premier Chinese treaty port and the British Crown Colony of Hong Kong, as major western controlled foreign entrepot trade centers, Canton continued as a major player in coastal and international trade- despite the demise of the Cantonese trading monopoly under the Canton Trade system (1760–1842).[9] Throughout the mid-late nineteenth century, Canton maintained its

Chapter 5

preeminent economic presence and dominant administrative role, as Gwongdung's "most central place."

*A network of major central places as urban satellites surrounding metropolitan Canton*

A network of key central places, in the form of well-positioned local cities and regional urban centers, surrounded Metropolitan Canton, as key nodules in a widening network of strategically positioned central places. Each provided Canton with needed logistical and material support, while extending the capital's influence and control to outlaying sections of the Pearl Delta, and beyond throughout Central Gwongdung. By virtue of their location at key places along major waterways of the Pearl River Delta, and beyond it in more remote areas of Central Gwongdung, this handful of key central places played a similar role to that of Canton itself, but on a smaller scale, within a smaller context. These additional subordinate key central places were strategically positioned within three concentric circles surrounding Canton, with each succeeding ring extending further away from Canton out into Central Gwongdung.

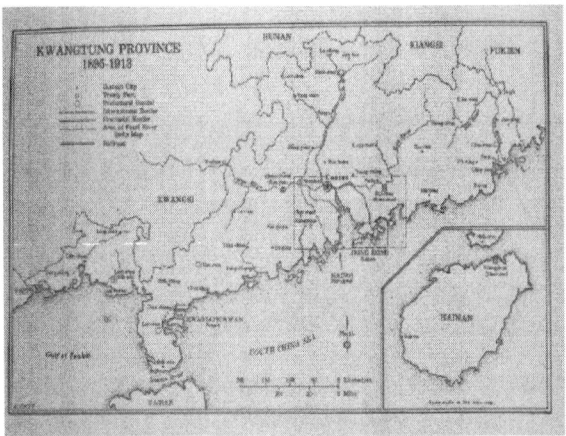

**Detailed Map of Central Gwongdung's Four Major River Systems** (adapted from Edward J.M. Rhoads, China's Republican Revolution, The Case of Kwangtung [Gwongdung], 1895-1913) (Cambridge, Mass: Harvard University press, 1975). (map is located on page after the table of contents page).

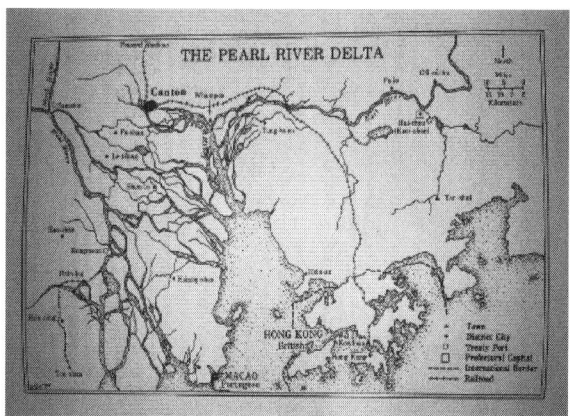

**Central Gwongdung's Four Major Rivers Converging Around Canton in the Pearl River Delta Region** (adapted from Edward J.M. Rhoads, <u>China's Republican Revolution, The case of Kwang-tung, 1895-1913,</u>) (Cambridge, Mass: Harvard University Press, 1975) (located after table of Contents page)

The first series of key satellite local urban centers consisted of key cities on the outlying fringe area of metropolitan Canton. This included: a) *Fat-Shaan (Foshan)*, located immediately to the West- Southwest of Canton; b) *Whampoa (Huang-pu)*, located East-Southeast of Canton, where the East River joins the Pearl River; and c) *Sai-chow (Xizhou) (Hsi-chou)*, which lies East of Canton. It should be noted that this inner-most tier of satellite urban centers immediately adjacent to Metropolitan Canton formed only the "bottom-half" of a concentric circle around Canton, because there were no similar satellite urban centers of similar size and importance to the northwest, North, or Northeast. This results from the fact that *Fat-Shaan, Sai-chow*, and especially *Whampoa* were located on/near major waterways to the Southwest, South, and Southeast of Canton. Areas to the Northeast, North, and Northwest lacked a similar abundance of waterways. Consequently, it seems safe to say that these key satellite urban centers immediately adjacent to Canton were ideally positioned to complement Metropolitan Canton's commercial, and transportation-communication needs/interests.

The second group of strategically located satellite urban centers embracing Canton, consisted of a wider ring of regional urban centers, which appear to have been more independent because of their greater distance away from Canton, and their greater autonomy in managing the logistics of Inner and Outer *Baak-wah* Zone commerce and transportation. Many of these second tier "outer" central places were located to the north of Canton, in contrast to the earlier mentioned fact that the area north of Canton lacked regional urban centers in the first ring/tier of concentric rings around Canton. This meant that in the first concentric ring of urban centers around Canton, regional urban centers were located chiefly southeast, south, and southwest of Canton, such as *Fat-Shaan* and *Whampoa*- but none were located to the north in this concentric ring. The opposite seems to have been the case, relative to the second concentric ring, where the situation was reversed, with regional urban centers located to the north of Canton, but few to none to the south.

These distribution patterns reflected the determinative influence of the physical geography of Central Gwongdung in the first and second concentric ring areas. In the first concentric ring, the PRDR, located to the southeast, south, and southwest of Canton provided ample sites for the development of major urban regional centers in the first concentric ring area. In recalling the "fan-shape" pattern of Central Gwongdung, the PRDR formed that part nearest the narrow point of this configuration. Consequently, it was never possible to have additional key regional urban centers south of Canton in a "second concentric ring," because the area south of Canton remained quite limited to a narrow stretch of land between Canton and the sea, such a second ring of urbanized central places was not physically possible. This clearly was not the case in regards to the areas north of Canton, where there existed nearly unlimited extended expanses of land.

Specifically, the upstream concourse(s) of the West, North, and East Rivers supplied an abundance of logistically ideal sites for the location of major regional urban centers in the second concentric ring area. Generally speaking, these northern satellite units were located more "upstream" from Canton, where they functioned as key nodes in a wider network grid that blanketed most of the Inner *Baak-wah* zone, and much of the Outer *Baak-wah* zone. These sizable, highly visible, and critically important "upriver" urban satellites functioned as vital key central places for the subregions in which they were located, again much in the same way that Canton served Central Gwongdung. In some cases, a single strategically located satellite urban center fulfilled this function; and in other cases, two related, but separate regional urban centers were logistically and economically bound together to service a key subregion.

Key urban satellite units in this second ring included: a) *Sam-shui*, located West of Canton, near where the North and West Rivers join together, resulting in the subsequent formation of the two largest waterways feeding the myriad of river channels, canals, and creeks that lace the Southern-southwestern portion of the PRDR; b) *Chao-Ch'ing*, located to the west of *Sam-shui* on the West river functioned as a smaller, but important western counterpart of *Sam-shui* on the middle reaches of the West River; c) To the North, *Ching-yuan* on the North River; and d) beyond *Ching-yuan*, *Ying-te* on the upper reaches of the North River in the "outer" *Baak-wah* zone. Both were critically important as the only satellite urban centers North of Canton in the *Baak-wah* zones; e) *Hui-chou*, east of Canton, was the most important strategically located urban satellite center for a large area east of Canton.

Given this pivotal position, *Hui-chou* had no rivals to its dominant position in the eastern portion of Central Gwongdung's Inner and Outer *Baak-wah* zones. It is significant to note that *Sam-Shui* to the west of Canton, and *Hui-Chou* to the east of Canton, both served as key urban centers on major rivers, as each river enters into the periphery of Central Gwongdung; and f) To the southwest, located in the *Say-yup* dominated southwestern part of the PRDR, the city of *Kong-men* (*Jiang-men*), located in *Sun-hui* (*Hsin-hui*) county, southwest of Canton, served the northern portion of the large *Say-Yup* or alternately *Ng-yup* area, when *Hokshaan* is included, southwest of Canton. In the later nineteenth century, *Toi-sing* or *Toi-shaan* City in *Toi-Shaan* county, (known before 1914 as *Sunning*,) also served as a vital satellite urban center among the strategically located key regional urban cities in the second concentric ring surrounding Canton. This group constitutes the largest number, and most autonomous and widely disbursed major satellite urban centers in both the Pearl River Delta, and the *Baak-wah* zones.

The third group of key regional satellite urban centers consisted of two atypical urban units located southeast and southwest of Canton, as major seaports servicing transoceanic regional and international commerce and trade for not only Central Gwongdung, but for the entire *Ling-nam* region, between Fujian, Gwongsai, and the Chinese-Vietnamese border. These two urban centers were Portuguese

Macao (Macau) and British Hong Kong. Because both Macao and Hong Kong were under western (Portuguese and British) leadership, investment, and control, they were atypical in comparison with other Cantonese urban centers in the PRDR, relative to their pattern of growth and development, in association with foreign/Western intervention and control. Still, given their physical location and their economic linkages and impact on the PRDR, they were inescapably part of the grid of regional satellite urban centers surrounding Canton in Central Gwongdung in the mid-later nineteenth century.[10] In the period 1890–1910, Hong Kong displaced Canton, as the most influential Central place of Central Gwongdung.

**Network of key regional central places surrounding Canton. The larger ones are located southwest and southeast of Canton. Other smaller, but more autonomous and independent regional central places are located to the north and northwest.**

*Hamlets and villages, as basic communal building blocks in the Cantonese heartland*

G.W. Skinner, the chief authority and pioneering researcher of traditional Chinese central places, was among the first to conceptualize and systemize the study of the socio-economic constructs of traditional Chinese central places. His work regarding Cantonese central places forms the basis of my own thinking about this subject, for which I am most indebted.[11]

Skinner's theory about traditional Chinese central places emphasizes economic considerations, where market activity is the chief construct. In his view, standard market towns existed as the basic unit of an ascending order of central places, which are configured and distributed systematically across a vast rural Chinese landscape. He specifically excludes villages and hamlets, because they lacked significant market activity. I disagree with this view, because while they lacked market activity of the size, volume, and influence associated with local standard market towns, it does not follow that all rural villages and hamlets were per se, totally deficient in such activity.

I myself, choose to identify villages, and some larger hamlets, as "pseudo-market" sites, where there existed some exchange of goods and services in a very limited context. This most likely took the form of a barter economy, where there was little or no cash involved. Such activity can be viewed as evidence of a type/degree of "market activity." Moreover, I look beyond the economics of market activity, to focus on the sociology of community life. I consider the factor of non-market activity, to be equally determinative of what constitutes a bona fide central place in Chinese society. Thus, I understand Cantonese villages and hamlets to function as organic clusters of people, structures, and activities, which are socially contextualized, as well as commercially interrelated.

Generally speaking, most people, especially outsiders have regarded the scores of villages that dot the rural landscape of Central Gwongdung as the smallest and most ubiquitous kind of central place in rural Cantonese society.[12] Technically speaking however, this is incorrect. Below the village there existed a smaller self-contained central place unit, commonly identified as a "hamlet." A hamlet is a small cluster of buildings, numbering anywhere from several to a few dozen or more. Typically, these small clusters of the local population consisted of small single unit dwellings, most as single-story structures, with a single large room, some with partitions to provide identifiable smaller room-like spaces, e.g., a sleeping area, a cooking area, a storage area, and a general main space for eating, and other household activities. Alternately, small one-story buildings may actually have interior walls, which formed actual rooms.

In the mid-late nineteenth century, those rural districts with villages and hamlets which sent their men overseas, often benefited from overseas remittances of cash, that allowed many families to construct modest new two, and even three or five story-structures, with many rooms on all levels.[13] Both *Saam-Yup* and *Say-Yup* areas of the PRDR evidenced a great deal of such construction activity in the later nineteenth century. Undoubtedly, such activity was more common in *Saam-Yup* areas in the earlier period 1860–1875, but reversed with more construction occurring in *Say-Yup* areas later during the period (1875–1900).[14] Other structures included sheds, out-buildings, communal halls, and even some commercial units by way of an occasional shop/store, or small public eating place.

Photo of larger multi-storied homes built
with Cantonese overseas remittances

The hamlet is often regarded as a sub-unit of a village, or as an insignificant independent entity on its own, neither of which has been identified as a "central place."[15] Hamlets were almost exclusively residential clusters, without any regard to any exchange of goods and services, even among local residents, most of whom journeyed to a neighboring larger village or the nearest marketing town. Additionally, most hamlets, because they were sub-units of villages, functioned less independently and more in unison with other hamlets, which together made up the larger village unit.

A typical hamlet consisted of a row of structures, attached or unattached, along a path or dirt road, numbering anywhere from half a dozen to a few dozen. They may have been located on just one side of the dirt path or rudimentary road, or alternately in the case of a few dozen or more structures, they may have occupied both sides of a dirt road. In larger hamlets, there may be as many as 2–3 dozen structures, along a series of dirt paths that intersected with other dirt paths or roads. There was often a duck pond, a small grove of trees or bamboo, amid additional scattered structures. The clustered structures and primitive grid of bisecting dirt paths, again easily invite the ascriptive image of what appears to most outsiders as a "typical village." The hamlet was distinguished by its "self-contained" image, sitting alone by the side of a duck pond, positioned some distance from a roadway, often appearing as an idyllic bucolic rural settlement.

In Gwongdung, villages were often large, but disassembled and fragmented central places, scattered randomly over a fairly large area. In many cases, a typical village may have had as many as a few hundred to perhaps several hundred, or even a thousand people, living in scattered, but interconnected hamlets. These hamlets were connected by miles of small dirt paths, which wound their way over and around hills, mountainous spurs, across ravines, around the bend of a river or stream. In this way, the hamlet was merely the smallest cluster of permanent groupings, that could be construed as a "central place," where there existed a routine of established social intercourse and in some minimal exchange of goods and services. In contrast, a village consisted of a single densely populated cluster of structures, with several dozen to several hundred people.

There were two kinds of villages, distinguished by their size, shape, and location. First, there were "single unit villages," where a concentrated cluster of structures at a single location, within a single configuration, constituted the whole village. Second, there were "segmented villages," where there existed a central core of what we normally visualize as "the" village, which was also linked to adjacent hamlets. These hamlets surrounded a village, located in different directions, and distributed by varying distances from the core village, and from each other. In some cases, dozens of interconnected hamlets, scattered over a wide area of a few square miles, were interconnected with each other to a core village.

Villages were distinguishable by the fact that locals identified with them as separate, well-defined entities, which may or may not have included interconnected hamlets. Villages, by their nature, represented basic social, economic, geographic, and demographic central place units. Locals generally viewed their village, and not their hamlet, as the basic geo-demographic socio-economic unit. The vast majority of Cantonese immigrants in Nineteenth-Century Chinese America came from rural parts of Central Gwongdung, and they invariably identified themselves first by their surname and second by their native place. In this context, native place meant first one's home district and speech community, e.g., *Toishan* county, in the *Say-Yup* speech community; or alternately *Namhoi* county, in the *Saam-yup* speech community. Second, it embraced one's native village or town. In my father's case, he identified himself as a *Toi-shaan* man, from *Nam-tsun* village, near the market town of *Say-Giu*, (town #49) outside *Toising*, the county-seat of *Toi-shaan* district. This need for, and interest in, one's local identification, relative to one's identified speech/county community and village/town established a basis for proper and meaningful social interaction among members of the Cantonese "Bachelor Society" in Chinese America for about a century (1850–1950). Only with the influx of "other" non-Cantonese-Chinese after 1970, did this basis for personal identification via native place group labels lose its importance, meaning, and value.

Cantonese villages typically hosted key local community social-cultural organizations and economic institutions, which included: local village temples, village schools, village lineage organizations, the *bo-ga* (*Baojia*) (*Pao-chia*) or local community surveillance and security system units. Additionally, a local market place might be located in some of the larger villages, which were surrounded by numerous hamlets. Two of the most fundamental local institutions of rural community life were commonly identified with larger villages. They included: 1) the local lineage group; and 2) local market systems. The former establishes the social identity of local rural communities, while the latter met their economic needs.

### *Environment and ecology*
#### *The traditional Cantonese natural environment*

Gwongdung's natural environment ranged from the uninviting, demanding, and difficult to deal with, to the very attractive, beneficial, and easy to work with- depending on what period and location are referenced. Natural calamities, in the form of droughts, earthquakes, floods, and typhoons were critical factors at work impacting prevailing environmental conditions in Nineteenth-Century Central Gwongdung. Generally speaking, however, positive natural environmental conditions far outweighed negative ones. Chronic adverse conditions, however, such as high-density population and over population, together with economic immiseration of peasant-farmers contributed to the destabilization of Cantonese society, by undermining its economic well-being.[16]

In the alternative, acute factors, such as natural calamities, endangered nineteenth-century Cantonese society, but in a different way. I do not consider natural calamities to be a chronic factor at work in the Cantonese natural environment, on a par with their occurrence elsewhere in China. In Cantonese society, they were not as costly, nor did they involve such dire consequences, as they did elsewhere in China. This is not to say that natural calamities were unimportant, and without dire consequences. Indeed, it was a material condition that factored heavily in how Cantonese people thought about and responded to their natural environment. This was evident in a particularly troublesome spate of natural calamities, which hit the Pearl River Delta region in the middle decades of the nineteenth-century.

> …a surprisingly bad harvest [in 1849] [17] [and]…a series of droughts in 1848, 1849, and 1850, rice riots…terrible inflation…[18] 1852 was a bad year for agriculture…summer floods had destroyed many villages …and almost completely ruined the rice harvest…[19] …after heavy flooding in the [Pearl River] Delta…[20] [In 1856] …[widespread] destruction caused by floods in the Canton area after 110 inches of rain had fallen in two months…[21]

The issue is not whether natural calamities were among Central Gwongdung's problematic environmental conditions adversely impacting nineteenth-century Cantonese society- because they were definitely important. I contend however, that while natural calamities were not uncommon, their adverse impact in Central Gwongdung were often mitigated by their comparatively short duration and limited adverse impact. Natural calamities in Central Gwongdung, relative to their environmental impact, economic effect, and the areas and populations affected, were, by comparison with those occurring elsewhere in China, not nearly as catastrophic- relative to the time and financial costs needed for recovery. Prevailing conditions in Central Gwongdung, both before and after natural calamities struck, tended over time to mitigate catastrophic natural disasters. Consequently, the great danger of natural calamities in

Central Gwongdung resulted less from a sense of their chronic plaguing the land, and more from their periodic acute occurrences with devastating effects.

> Guangdong [Gwongdung] was susceptible to the vagaries of nature, but disasters did not hit with nearly the same force [as elsewhere in China.] Droughts …were common, but tended to be local and less lasting, and the floods…did not match the intensity of… northern…floods… Famines were common in northern…China's famine region…[but] rare in… Guangdong.[22]

While natural calamities engendered social instability and exacerbated local economic hardship(s), they also enhanced local material conditions, such as in soil productivity and abundant potable water, which made recovery relatively quicker and easier than elsewhere. Thus, Cantonese natural calamities, while not as catastrophic as elsewhere, even while they contributed greatly to general confusion and communal instability, were generally manageable. As such, they also factored as key environmental considerations affecting Cantonese solidarity and unity. In responding to natural calamities, mutual needs generated the willingness to overcome differences, to cooperate and work together for the greater benefit of all parties. This served as further evidence of Cantonese binding ties that promoted group solidarity and unity in hard times.

In Central Gwongdung, prevailing environmental conditions fundamentally influenced Cantonese group cohesiveness and communal attachment. In this regard, the Cantonese were neither unique nor special, when compared with people elsewhere. What was distinctive about the Cantonese case however, was the beneficial link between generally positive environmental conditions, and how well local Cantonese people adapted to using them to mitigate adverse environmental conditions, e.g., natural calamities. Over the course of two millennia, this adaptation was capitalized on, with the efficient synchronization of Cantonese socio-economic resources to address existing environmental conditions. Local environmental conditions complemented and nurtured Cantonese socio-economic endeavors, to the extent that the former were useful as means of enhancing social organization and economic activities. This resulted in high rates of economic productivity, and a high degree of integrated socio-economic institutionalization, as in lineage affiliated villages and local market systems.

As already noted earlier in chapter 1, Central Gwongdung was blessed with well-endowed natural features and abundant natural resources. In urban areas, daily life benefitted greatly by effectively utilizing local waterways to enhance the logistics of transportation and communication, which helped produce both urban and regional economic prosperity. In rural areas, which constituted most of Central Gwongdung's vast landscape, abundant fresh water, rich soil, wide expanses of arable land, and an ideal climate, supported an unusually rich and agriculturally productive region. This was especially true in the PRDR, where such factors supported a long growing season, permitting double, and even triple cropping of commercial crops (rice). Given a favorable natural environment, ingenuity and hard work, farmers built extensive complex irrigation networks, some extending up hillsides. Interestingly, local Cantonese adaptation to the natural environment occurred simultaneously in three different, but related ways, which included, structural, physiological, and behavioral responses.

The Cantonese structural response involved establishing, building, and maintaining scores of local communities, ranging from large, complex, densely populated, urban centers, to small remote villages and hamlets. These pre-modern structural responses, when compared with modern approaches, seem parochial and ineffective, however, they were quite sufficient and productive in the context of the mid-later nineteenth century.

Cantonese people also demonstrated a physiological response to their natural environment, by developing various adaptative strategies. This often involved using natural resources, man-made materials, and technology, to bring about material changes to support and enhance human adaptation to physical surroundings and material conditions in the natural environment.

The best example of this kind of a response were traditional Cantonese rural communal hydraulic engineering projects. All across the Cantonese rural landscape, there existed ample evidence of well-developed hydraulic engineering projects. In both hilly terrain and in wide expanses of level alluvial plains, irrigation projects were common. This involved the use of pumping mechanisms, e.g., foot pumps, animal and water powered pumps, to transport water from waterways (rivers, streams, and creeks) across considerable distances, often from lower to higher elevations. Many different types of wooden, stone, and earthen structures were linked with vital rivers, streams, creeks, and canals. In upper elevations, water might be collected from streams and stored, or it might be pumped up, collected, and then funneled laterally across hilly terrain, via trenches or man-made raised troughs. Often times, individual farmers had to carry buckets of water on poles to water difficult-to-reach upper-level rice terraces. In areas where land had been recovered along the banks of rivers and coastal areas, which were situated at lower elevations with adjacent bodies of water, farmers had to build earth embankments, such as dikes and levees, in order to farm on adjacent recovered plots of land.

All of these hydraulic related projects required much time, effort, and hard work to build and maintain over long periods of time. They might serve individual farmers with specific plots of farmland, but invariably this physiological response was typically a collective one, involving whole communities, where the entire community benefitted. This collective physiological response also occurred in other ways, e.g., building small bridges, road and path construction, maintaining local volunteer firefighting units, providing for flood control, flood relief, local (rice) granaries for emergency food assistance, and local militias to provide for local security.

Local Cantonese communities also exhibited various behavioral responses to their natural environment. This, often involved adaptative strategies, where behavioral considerations figured prominently. In rural settings, behavioral changes typically occurred when local environmental conditions required it, or when a tangible material benefit could be realized. The former was evident in cases involving crop selection and management, relative to soil use during the course of a year. Farmers had to be adaptable in their behavior, conforming to changing climate, weather, and other environmental conditions, relative to making choices, adopting strategies, and utilizing natural resources. The latter evidenced itself in the use of "night soil" as a common fertilizer for crops. In every home, ranging from small huts in remote hamlets and villages, to multi-unit dwellings in towns and cities, people saved containers of human waste, i.e., feces. These containers were collected locally and then transported, usually without any processing, to be used for fertilizing crops in the fields. The use of night soil mirrors an adaptative behavioral response to the environment, where an easily available, but otherwise very offensive and noxious waste material, came to have practical use and material benefit as a natural fertilizer for farm crops. Unfortunately, lacking the benefits of modern science and technology, rural Cantonese people were ignorant about the dangers of parasitic infections, e.g., *Clonorchiasis*, caused by *Clonorchis sinensis*, more commonly known as the Chinese liver fluke disease.[23]

*Ecology and the Cantonese human ecosystem*

In Nineteenth-Century Central Gwongdung, Cantonese people were acutely aware of their natural environment, despite not knowing anything about the term "the natural environment." In this context, the natural environment serves as a useful introduction to discussing the traditional Cantonese awareness/responses to ecological issues. In this manner, it may be possible to gleam from the historical narrative some useful clues about Cantonese experience in addressing ecological matters. When referencing to what might be viewed as a traditional Cantonese approach to ecology, I refer to how Cantonese people related to biotic and abiotic components in their natural environment, with specific regards to three levels or areas of human ecological study: 1) population, 2) community, and 3) the Cantonese ecosystem, where people interacted with elements of their natural environment. The subject of population has already been covered in chapter 1, regarding Central Gwongdung's significant high-density population concentration and over-population growth, which placed an extraordinary strain on what might be regarded as the Cantonese human ecosystem. In this ecosystem, biotic natural resources, (i.e., flora and fauna) and abiotic natural resources (e.g., soil and water,) were subject to long-term exploitation. This impacted, in perhaps less obvious and less dramatic ways, an awareness of "universal" natural resources, (e.g., climate, weather, air, and energy.)

One example of how demographics affected the Cantonese ecosystem was the lack of sizable natural forests in Central Gwongdung. After millennia of deforestation, as a means of opening up more land to cultivation, Central Gwongdung, and many portions of Gwongdung more generally, lacked significantly large dense old-growth forests, with the exception of those in the non-*Yuet* peripheral areas region, and in the outer most parts of the outer *Baak-wah* zone. In the nineteenth century, there did not exist any awareness, much less any appreciation, of the dire consequences of deforestation. The adverse impact of Cantonese deforestation contrasted with Cantonese careful management of water resources, as evident in already noted extensive complex irrigation projects in rural communities. The re-planting of trees and other natural flora, remained quite limited in both effort and location, relative to the primary needs of farming. Such activity always remained sporadic, and on a small scale, such that it never ameliorated prior long-term deforestation's adverse impact.

The Cantonese rural community illustrated how locals related in varying ways to biotic and abiotic resources in their natural environment. In a manner of speaking, when we consider that Cantonese society placed a great strain on the natural environment, ironically it was Cantonese local communities which served as first responders in the effort to mitigate that strain. They did so by adopting a practical approach to the task of farming, utilizing technology, material natural resources, and hard work to maximize production, without undermining future expectations, by exhausting available natural resources. Such key matters as land ownership, land distribution, land classification, and land use were in a matter of speaking dependent upon successful farming activities. In this regard local rural communities were the pivotal mid-point between the burden of a large population and the onerous efforts of individual farmers. In this way, food production was maximized whenever and wherever possible, to the extent that it balanced precariously between the extremes of over exploitation and the practical conservation of natural resources.

The pre-modern Cantonese human ecosystem presented a contradictory situation regarding how local communities used and/or abused renewable and non-renewable resources. Renewable resources, such as water, fish, crops, and vegetation were exploited to the maximum, but in a relatively responsible manner. The idea of conservation did not exist as either public policy nor as tradition/custom among Cantonese people. As a practical matter however, it was consciously practiced in daily life. My earlier comments about the ubiquitous presence of hydraulic projects scattered across the Cantonese rural landscape exemplified the day-to-day practical application of conservation in the use of precious water resources. This occurred, despite the fact that Central Gwongdung, in comparison with many other parts of China, had a climate and weather pattern that produced abundant precipitation, especially with summer monsoons. The abundance of water, via precipitation, and a large complex system of rivers, did not mean that water could be wasted, or that conservation as a practical matter was unnecessary. Cantonese people valued water resources, even in areas where it was abundant. Fish and marine animals were farmed and harvested, but not exploited to the extent that they were materially endangered- even when commercially harvested.

The need to live and work within constraints, imposed by the natural environment, while maximizing the use of renewable natural resources, also applied to agricultural land use. Much of Gwongdung was hilly or mountainous, and only about a third of the province consisted of arable land. This meant that the encroachment of farmers on areas of natural vegetation, e.g., hill country meadows, was as a practical matter quite limited. Cantonese farming methods, systems of land ownership and land use, the use of credit, and reliance on local marketing systems, all underscored the premium value of farmland. In this respect, Cantonese farmers worked constantly to make the land, as a renewable resource, as productive as possible.

Questions about how Cantonese people viewed and addressed non-renewable resources is less clear. When we think about non-renewable natural resources, we often think of commercially valuable metal ores, exotic metals associated with high technology, and fossil fuels. In nineteenth-century Cantonese society these kinds of natural resources were virtually unknown, with the exception of coal, gold, silver, mercury, and lead, which were mined at select locations. Given the modest scale of mining operations for coal and a few precious metals, with pre-modern technology and restrained market conditions, we can surmise with a reasonable degree of certainty that non-renewable natural resources were not at risk in nineteenth-century Cantonese society.

As noted earlier, my interest in the Cantonese human ecosystem centers on where ecology intersects with economics, relative to access to and use of natural resources. In Central Gwongdung, as a practical matter, as discussed above, local rural communities focused their conservation efforts primarily on addressing the use of renewable natural resources. We can conclude that prevailing conditions, together with geography, climate, and abundant renewable resources, balanced the heavy burden of Cantonese high-density population concentration and population over-growth. This was especially evident in rural communities, where practical conservation measures helped to mitigate the adverse impact of a large population.

Profitability served as a kind of "prime directive," in the minds of wealthy merchants and poor peasant alike. This meant that financial investments, hard work, deferred consumption, mounting financial and credit obligations, and the sustainability of renewable natural resources, were all dependent on the profitability of farming activities. From planting to harvest, nearly every segment of Cantonese society was consciously aware of the valuable, but often precariously fickle process of agricultural production in the Cantonese economy. Certainly, what were essentially ecological concerns positioned within a traditional Cantonese ecosystem, evidenced a practical conservationist mindset and effort to maximize profit potential via the careful use of renewable natural resources. Nineteenth-Century Cantonese people may not have known about environmental conservation nor appreciated the importance of human ecology, but they were in their own way very mindful of environmental conditions and limitations, and did their practical best to work constructively with them. They did so while responding affirmatively to the requirements of their, as yet unknown, human ecosystem. In this way, they served as additional key elements contributing to the "enduring ties that bind, Cantonese style," because they helped secure a stable Cantonese society and prosperous economy.

## Key social, economic, and cultural constructs bolstering Cantonese solidarity and unity

A second group of ties that attracted Cantonese people to each other, which also easily and quickly bound them together, were Cantonese socio-cultural linkages. These ties were highly respected and deeply appreciated, since they were so easy to recognize and timeless in their appeal. Whenever Cantonese encountered fellow Cantonese, even if they were total strangers, these ties were frequently among the first to be identified and embraced, because they demonstrated unequivocally that one was indeed among one's own people. This often resulted in a robust, psycho-emotional sense of appreciation and well-being, even among strangers. This mutual sense of recognition and reliance evidenced unmistakable signposts of a shared appreciation of the past, understanding of the present, and expectations about the future.

### *Cantonese speech, as the critical nexus between ethnic group identity and social engagement*

As already noted in chapter 2, one of the most distinctive identifying features of nineteenth-century Cantonese society/culture was its *Yuet* (*Yue*) (*Yueh*) language, and Cantonese dialect/speech component.[24] It represented the strongest and most durable bonding agent supporting Cantonese solidarity and unity. Cantonese speech historically engineered Cantonese group solidarity and promoted communal unity, via social engagement. This occurred in a number of interesting ways.

First, as a technical matter, *Yuet*/Cantonese speech provided an "insiders' speech," which only the initiated, i.e., fellow Cantonese speakers, could use, understand, appreciate, and benefit from. Cantonese people were traditionally lampooned by others, such as mandarin (*Putonghua*) speaking Chinese, regarding their awkward attempts to speak Mandarin Chinese, "*tian bu pa, di bu pa, cui pa Guangdong ren jiang kuanhua*." "[one] is unafraid of heaven, [one] is unafraid of earth, but one really fears a Cantonese person speaking Mandarin." [25] If this situation was reversed, it would likely be even more awkward and stressful for a Mandarin speaker to try to speak Cantonese, and perhaps even more comical and painful for a Cantonese-speaking individual to witness such a spectacle. In short, while Cantonese speech flowed forth smoothly and naturally for Cantonese speakers, it was extraordinarily difficult for other Chinese, especially Mandarin speakers, to speak and understand it, due to the technicalities involved. This language barrier between *Yuet*/Cantonese speech and other Chinese dialects have remained quite formidable, even today. Cantonese people conveniently conversed among themselves in a smug fashion, where "We know who we are, because of our special language/speech, which you cannot even begin to understand or appreciate. This is something for us to know, and something for you to try to grasp, if you can?"

Second, Cantonese speech offers evidentiary clarification regarding how the sense of *Chinese-ness* can be made more concrete and relevant to regional (e.g., *Yuet* language and culture) needs and interests, by way of a re-fashioned sense of *Han-ness*. Among Cantonese people, the sense of *Cantonese-ness* or *Tong-ness,* has been historically utilized to distinguish and clarify, a regional/local *Yuet*/Cantonese perspective, as a more authentic and acceptable representation of this sense of *Han-ness*. This facile ability to apply a distinctive regional (Cantonese or *Tong-ness*) perspective to the reality of co-existing Chinese dialects and speech communities has been useful. In this manner, a distinctive regional experience and outlook unambiguously defined and promoted Cantonese speech and *Yuet* culture. In Cantonese social engagement, this sense of "Cantonese-ness" or *Tong-ness*, helped to decipher the complex construction and meaning of "Chinese-ness," in Central Gwongdung and elsewhere beyond.

Third, *Yuet* language/speech met two distinctly contradictory, but not mutually exclusive, imperatives. On one level, it mirrored and contributed to the local need for distinctions among, and differentiation between, different local speech communities in Central Gwongdung, and elsewhere in Gwongdung and the *Lingnam*. On another level, local speech needs were met, via effective social engagement, within the unifying framework of the *Yuet* languages. The variety of dialect/speech forms lent legitimacy and sustainability to diverse speech communities in Central Gwongdung. This diversity of Cantonese local speech communities never threatened nor compromised *Yuet*/Cantonese group solidarity and unity, to the extent that such competition and conflict could do irreparable harm. Established language/speech ties within the larger context of Cantonese speech and *Yuet* culture, promoted the sustainability of the various Cantonese speech communities and undermined barriers against social engagement, while also nurturing *Yuet*/Cantonese group identity. It did so by demonstrating what it included, and what it excluded, from the *Yuet*/Cantonese persona. In this regard, the centripetal force of *Yuet*/Cantonese language spun different varieties of Cantonese speech from the peripheries to the center of *Yuet*/Cantonese collective identity and experience, which helped neutralize the diametrical centrifugal force of *Yuet*/Cantonese speech diversity, which pulled speech groups from the center to the peripheries.

Fourth, *Yuet*/Cantonese language served as the critical bonding agent, which helped to bind together various factors promoting traditional *Yuet*/Cantonese group solidarity and unity. The commonality of Cantonese speech, widely recognized in the form of "standard Cantonese," e.g., *Gwongfu wah*, or *Gwong-chau wah*, evidenced the early development and usefulness of a *lingua franca* in Central Gwongdung, and more generally for the *Lingnam* region. Commonalities of speech and vernacular literature, by way of shared familiarity with colloquial terms and expressions, enhanced Cantonese social engagement. It also provided a concrete basis for the ability to communicate, to cooperate, and to meet common needs/interests, while protecting the *us* against the *them*, as *insiders* encountered *outsiders*. Contact with, and efforts at control by *outsiders*, e.g., Northern Chinese, Mongols, and Manchus respectively, were contextualized and minimalized, whereby *Yuet*/Cantonese thinking could concentrate on local needs and promote local interests, with relatively little concern for outsider influence and interference. Even in times when outsiders took control of Central Gwongdung, as in the Mongol/*Yuan* and Manchu/*Qing* periods, *Yuet* language and Cantonese speech successfully fortified Cantonese society and sustained its *Yuet* regional culture in Central Gwongdung, and elsewhere. In the process, *Yuet* language and Cantonese speech became the most powerful tie that bound Cantonese people together.

## *Ethnic groups and speech communities, as building blocks for Cantonese solidarity and unity*

As already referenced in chapter 3, among Cantonese people ethnic group and local speech community identifications were critically important to establishing and maintaining intra-group cohesiveness and unity, while also helping to mitigate ethnic inter-group competition and conflict. In this context, Cantonese ethnic group labels meant that a particular ethnic group/speech community, not only became closely identified with a particular locale, but also became identified with particular complex of web-group affiliation networks. These identifications could exacerbate ethnic/speech rivalry, and yet also paradoxically re-enforce ethnic/speech solidarity. These distinctions formed an important bonding mechanism among Cantonese people.

The push for ethnic/speech solidarity occurred simultaneously on two levels. First, there existed well-defined *intra-communal* spatial and social boundaries, which separated and insulated ethnic groups and speech communities from each other. In this manner, intra-ethnic/speech group interests and needs were jealously protected and actively pursued. Second, these boundaries also effectively separated and distanced different *inter-ethnic groups* and speech communities from each other, to the extent that when they encountered each other, they did so with biased mindsets and agendas, often resulting in episodic competition and conflict.

This bifurcated view of *intra-group* ethnic-speech community solidarity and *inter-group* ethnic-speech community competition/ conflict should not be viewed as two polar opposites, without any positive benefits. In a sense, communal *inter-group* tension and rivalry embraced within its folds the common denominator of a mutual appreciation of mutually shared Cantonese language/speech (as distinct from non-Cantonese speech) and *Yuet* culture (as distinguished from other varieties of Han Chinese regional cultures). The pervasiveness and fundamental character of *Yuet*/Cantonese culture and language, both proceeded and superseded local ethnic group and speech community identifications, because they were widely understood and greatly appreciated. This commonalty helped to neutralize natural tensions among various different *Yuet* ethnic groups and local Cantonese speech communities, where intra-communal cooperation and inter-communal competition/conflict could be reconciled and beneficially utilized to meet mutual needs/interests.

The particular, even peculiar, conflicting demands of localized ethnic and speech communal pride, together with local economic needs, and territorial/turf maintenance prerequisites, required as a matter of mutual survival, any number of negotiations, timely compromises, and long-term accommodations. These realities served as a critical determinant impacting inter-communal relations throughout the Cantonese heartland of Central Gwongdung, and also within distant overseas Cantonese communities. This contradiction helped mitigate communal divisiveness, by embracing useful linkages, whereby discrete entities managed to negotiate ways to work together. In this way, they could move forward to promote common interests and sustain mutual needs, to achieve a broader, more inclusive sense of ethnic-speech solidarity and unity. Recall, there existed a delicate balance between the "exclusiveness" of Cantonese speech communities and the "inclusiveness" of *Yuet*/Cantonese ethnic groups. (see chapter 2.) The former excluded those not conforming in their speech, while the latter embraced those with differences of speech.

> we should focus more on ethnic communities rather than on … mere boundaries of speech communities. Among the *Yuet* … Cantonese/*Bundae* group, [where] language differences do not make inviolate ethnic boundaries. They merely draw clear lines of sub-ethnic distinctions. [26]

The manner in which ethnic/speech identifications sliced and split up people in Central Gwongdung was never as simple as it might appear to have been. In this regard, it might be helpful to view such identifications, as pieces of a jigsaw puzzle, where each ethnic group and speech community appeared as individual pieces of a puzzle. Thus, when properly pieced together, they collectively formed a coherent and cohesive picture. In this manner, Central Gwongdung's ethnic groups and speech communities mirrored an unusual, but functional, solidarity and unity, despite differences in their technical construction and ascribed representations of their respective ethnic-speech identifications. This provides irrefutable evidence of additional important enduring binding ties among Cantonese people.

## *Marginalized homosocial relationships and the construction of Cantonese communal solidarity*

Traditional Chinese society and culture supported an especially active and versatile homosocial scene.[27] By way of "homosocial," I mean a broad range of activities and relationships, where men interacted with each other, via both private and public social engagement, to achieve a wide variety of personal and professional goals. Certainly, among the most important was the mitigation of social competition and conflict. This tradition dates from the Tang period (9th century CE), and became well-established during the Ming and Qing periods (14th–19th centuries CE.)

Significantly, homosocial engagement figured prominently as a key feature in nineteenth-century Cantonese society, both at home in Central Gwongdung, in America, and elsewhere overseas. In traditional Cantonese communal settings, homosocial engagement took place within a rich and prolific array of social organizations, where web group affiliation orchestrated homosocial activities and relationships.[28] Key institutions included: agnatic lineages, pseudo-kinship groups (e.g., fraternal orders), (*wooi-kun*) (*huiguan*) (*hui-kuan*),[29] also known as native place associations, village organizations, e.g., *Bow-ga* system (*Bojia*) (*Pao-chia,*) (for local surveillance,)[30] urban neighborhood groups, merchant guilds, worker's groups, tradesmen associations, secret societies, literary societies, music clubs, martial arts clubs, and temple associations, all of which proliferated all across the Cantonese landscape.

Generally speaking, traditional Cantonese homosocial activities/relationships helped cement interpersonal relations among men, which helped to mitigate social competition and conflict. Strong homosocial relations could lead to heightened socialization among social elites and commoners alike. By way of public and private homosocial relationships, I mean a variety of relationships ranging from purely platonic identifications, to fictive relationships, with ubiquitous "uncles" "cousins" and "brothers." Degrees of brotherly affection among friends, served to strengthen traditional Cantonese homosocial relationships across chronological, spatial, and social boundaries. Generations of Cantonese men folk took part in a hyper-active homosocial scene, where they exhibited a strong and continuous need for homosocial identification and engagement. Noticeably, women, as bona fide members of the community in which they lived, were conspicuously absent from public social engagement and local civic participation.

The goal of Cantonese homosocial engagement always centered on meeting one's needs, while also advancing one's interests. When such matters were allied with the interests of others, homosocial interaction became the tool of choice for advancing personal and professional goals. This often involved dealing with contradictory conditions of security and stability, alternating with that of insecurity and instability. This anomaly shaped the pattern of Cantonese homo-socialization.

Interestingly, traditional Cantonese homosocial engagement not only occurred in mainstream Cantonese society, it also figured prominently among socially marginalized groups, often located outside and beyond mainstream Cantonese society. The ranks of the socially marginalized included: bandits, pirates, boat people, charcoal producers, and lepers among others. This aspect of Cantonese homosocial engagement among the socially marginalized is especially interesting, because it reveals an important, but neglected dimension of the "ties that bind, Cantonese style." In examining Cantonese homosocial engagement among the socially marginalized and spatially distant, the meaning of traditional Cantonese homosocial engagement is confirmed and enhanced, because its usefulness and value was not confined to just its original pristine social context and spatial setting in Central Gwongdung, i.e., in *Tong-Shaan*, but also characterized and enriched the mid-late nineteenth-century transnational Cantonese diaspora.

When order and peace prevailed, established patterns and relationships worked reasonably well, but when instability and uncertainty became the norm, as in the mid-late nineteenth century, then established ways of doing things were questioned, as they became dysfunctional. When this happened, the pattern of homosocial interaction, and nature of homosocial relationships, became susceptible to change, relative to how they were used and valued. This seemed especially evident in the ambiguous area of homosocial relations under changing socio-economic conditions, at the shifting spatial-social peripheries of Cantonese society. This was best exemplified in the case of massive numbers of single young males associated with large-scale nineteenth-century Cantonese overseas emigration, during especially in hard times, [31]

By the mid-late nineteenth century, deteriorating conditions of disorder and instability ushered in especially troubling times involving intensified community conflict, social chaos, and foreign intervention.[32] Across different Cantonese social classes, various groups encountered different types of change and degrees of destabilization. While this development had an adverse impact on Cantonese society in general, it became especially troublesome for those men, who were identified with degrees of social marginalization and spatial separation. In essence, while we can visualize and understand, both the content and context of homosocial engagement in mainstream Cantonese society in "normal" times, it does not necessarily follow that we can do so, as easily and as well, in the case of the socially marginalized and geo-physically distant and isolated. Here I argue that the ascribed identities and shared experiences of the socially marginalized and spatially separated, provide another example of "the enduring ties that bind, Cantonese style."

During troubled times, there often existed various groups of Cantonese men, who for a variety of reasons were socially marginalized, to the extent that they were located at the social and spatial boundaries of Cantonese society. Homosocial relationships among these men involved living without the benefit of normal family life and the support of conventional community social organizations/institutions. This situation became more widespread in Central Gwongdung in the chaotic half century 1850–1900. During this period, Cantonese society encountered an extraordinary degree of instability, conflict, and violence.[33] The net effect of this prolonged period of tension and violent conflict resulted in the marked destabilization of Cantonese society.

Social destabilization occurred in both urban and rural communities in Central Gwongdung. It played itself out along the coast, in nestled valleys of the Pearl River Delta, and in upriver rural communities. It adversely affected poor peasant farmers and urban workers, as well as affluent rural gentry, and urban merchants alike. It created havoc especially among the very poor, and with the migrant population. Beyond the physical destruction of property, loss of life, people also experienced varying degrees of physical dislocation, material deprivation, and emotional distress. Under these adverse conditions, increasing numbers of the socially marginalized were challenged to maintain essential homosocial relationships, as a means of ensuring group solidarity and unity, even as they were socially/spatially separated from mainstream Cantonese society. This dire situation gave rise to a variety of atypical, ad hoc, "special shared-interests' groups" in Cantonese society, whose

Chapter 5

social constructs, collective experiences, special interests, needs, outlook, and priorities cut across Cantonese social class lines.

**Table 5.1 Socially Marginalized and Spatially Distant/Separated Segments of Nineteenth-Century Cantonese Society, each with its own Homosocial Communal sub-culture** [34]

| Socially marginalized groups within Cantonese society | Sub-groups within an identified socially marginalized group in Cantonese society | Negatively ascribed collective character and activities and their location |
|---|---|---|
| ***Miscellaneous Socially Marginalized People*** Consisted of groups of people, who were forced to live at the socio-spatial peripheries of Cantonese society. They were identified as undesirable people, because they bore negatively ascribed liabilities, deficiencies, disabilities.[35] | *Hakka*, as an ethnic minority, *Tanaka*, as alien boat people, Lepers, with a feared disease, charcoal makers, embalmers, and "night soil" collectors were viewed negatively as service providers in distasteful, marginal occupations, with discriminatory labels, social disabilities and economic burdens, | Discrimination based on negatively ascribed group traits and identifications regarding: historical origins, the nature and character of their occupations, lifestyles, and/or socio-ethno-linguistic identities. Most were forced by tradition, law, custom, to relocate in undesirable areas, e.g., in remote mountains. |
| ***Inner Social Strangers*** Consisted of groups, who because of situational, occupational, socio-economic traits became alienated from their peers, stemming from resentful feelings of being unappreciated, unfairly treated, or being forced to live life "under a cloud" of suspicion. | 1) dissatisfied peasant farmers, 2) disgruntled members of local lineages and villages, 3) members of alienated ethnic-speech groups, 4) marginalized members of low-level occupations (e.g., petty merchants, craftsmen, shopkeepers, yamen clerks, low level servants, runners.) | These people identified with mainstream Cantonese society, but moved on to develop their own separate communities and sub-cultures. in undesirable areas, e.g., in remote hill country, in the upper reaches of major rivers, or in isolated valleys, on island along the sea coast. |
| ***Outer Social Strangers*** This group included men whose identifications and activities reflected an anti-status quo bias and experience. | 1) members of secret societies, 2) rowdy elements, consisting of a variety of vagabonds, transients, peripatetic peddlers, con artists, migrant laborers, and homeless migrants, 3) criminal elements, including bandits, robbers, outlaws, pirates, smugglers, mercenaries, hill bandits, and 4) members of professional criminal gangs and syndicates. | These people were the chief purveyors of community conflict and violence. Because of their anti-status quo identity and actions, they became divorced from, and were often at war with mainstream society. They contested existing social values and community standards. They became powerful through physical intimidation and violence. |

| Migrants and overseas emigrant-sojourners Cantonese migrants and overseas-sojourners typically consisted adolescents and young men, ages 15–30, who were forced to leave home to search for work elsewhere, to reduce pressure on whatever limited resources remained available to one's family at home. | The great majority came from scores of poor rural villages and hamlets. Most were of the peasant-farmer class. Some also came from towns and major urban centers e.g., Canton, and Whampoa. Nearly all came from the Pearl River Delta region, with some from the Inner Baak-wah zone. Nearly all were *Yuet*/Cantonese, with the greatest number of *Say-Yup*, *Saam-Yup*, followed by smaller numbers of *Hakka* and *Chung-Shaan* groups. | The time frame typically ranged anywhere from several months to a few years, to many decades. Overseas they established their own ethnic communities, e.g., Chinatowns, in such distant overseas locations as: Hawaii, America, Canada, Mexico, Peru, Cuba, Southeast Asia, and Australia. |
|---|---|---|

In mid-late Nineteenth-Century Gwongdung, the number of the socially marginalized social strangers and migrant-sojourners grew dramatically, such that their experiences were no longer a rarity, but had instead become more common place and widespread. Given the growing transnational character of Cantonese life, as influenced by neighboring British Hong Kong, with its growing monopoly over Cantonese overseas migration, the number of socially marginalized men migrating overseas grew rapidly. This development engendered a new genesis of the social reality circumscribing Cantonese community life at *Tong Shaan*, and beyond, where changing material conditions helped forge a new chapter of experience for the socially marginalized, even as they became transplants in various distant places. Over time, new alternatives developed, where traditional Cantonese homosocial relationships could be used to address the challenge of truncated Cantonese family relationships, within a transplanted communal setting, set within a transnational framework. A critical factor at work was the timely mutation of the Cantonese homosocial basis for group solidarity.

In numerous distant locations, Cantonese emigrant sojourners responded creatively to the challenge of replicating traditional Cantonese community institutions and homosocial relationships, as a means to help foster meaningful social engagement within the transplanted ethnic (Cantonese) community. This occurred while local Cantonese encountered increasingly hostile host societies. Changing local conditions confirmed the usefulness and applicability of traditional homosocial constructs for rebuilding Cantonese group solidarity/unity, both overseas and at home. The historical significance of Cantonese socially marginalized homosocial relationships, and their contribution to the reconstruction of Cantonese communal solidarity in new distant overseas locations, lies in the relevance and resiliency of traditional Cantonese homosocial engagement, as yet another enduring binding tie, Cantonese style.

### *Enduring ties among Cantonese agnatic lineages[36] and their associated local villages*

Among both urban and rural communities in Nineteenth-Century Gwongdung, agnatic (i.e., common descent via the male line) lineages were among the most basic and influential social institutions of Cantonese society. Anthropologists have long recognized that lineages were especially large and abundant in Gwongdung.[37] They were ubiquitous in rural Cantonese communities scattered throughout Central Gwongdung. Beyond their large size and widespread proliferation, another critical feature of Cantonese agnatic lineages, especially in their rural setting, was their close partnership with local villages.

> ...the lineage and the village tended markedly to coincide, so that many villages consisted of single lineages. This coincidence of agnatic and local community was found in other parts of [China]... but in the south-east [Gwongdung] it appears to have been most pronounced.[38]

The intimate linkage between agnatic lineages and their associated local villages provided a common and unmistakable bond between individuals and their rural community. It did so in three very important ways. First, it provided a double bond between people and their local community, where blood ties reinforced communal ties and roots, which provided space to support the expansive branching of lineage generational units across time. Second, Lineages lent legitimacy to local villages, by providing a stake in a time-honored identity. Third, villages and hamlets served as a useful means for lineages to maintain a formidable geo-territorial presence, by way of control over allied villages and hamlets in concentrated localities, such as a portion of a rural district. One of the better-known cases is the

*Kuan* lineage in Hoiping district.³⁹ Local lineages formed the primary basis for social relations both within a village, and beyond it with neighboring villages. This configuration and connection were especially powerful in forging lineage-community ties among people in mono-clan villages.

Mono-clan villages were extraordinarily homogenous, because of the agnatic basis of organization, whereby everyone in the village shared a common descent from a single primogenitor (founding male ancestor.) Consequently, all the residents of a mono-clan village were blood related and shared the same surname.⁴⁰ This connection expanded exponentially, when a village's hamlets were also included. In many parts of Central Gwongdung, and especially in the Pearl River Delta region, mono-clan villages were very common and widespread features of rural community life.

The long-term perpetuation of mono-clan villages was only possible because of the extreme care taken in monitoring and restricting the sourcing of brides for adult single males, within each mono-clan village. Adult men in mono-clan villages could not marry women from their own village, because they were blood related. Consequently, all the married women in a mono-clan village formed the only exception to the fact that everyone else in the village were related by blood to a single remote ancestor. In this manner, all mothers and wives were technically speaking "outsiders" in every mono-clan village. Thus, all the brides for the male population of a mono-clan village were chosen from a limited number of pre-determined neighboring mono-clan villages, and some multi-clan villages. In the following diagram, a theoretical model of five mono-clan villages is used to demonstrate the manner in which mono-clan villages secured brides for their adult single males, while preserving the ongoing integrity of each of several neighboring mono-clan villages' "pool of bridal candidates."

In a theoretical scheme of five mono-clan villages (see figure 5.1 below), all of the men in Village #1 are all surnamed **Wong**, however all of the women were originally surnamed (i.e. *nee*- "maiden named" or "born as") either *nee* **Ng** or *nee* **Lee**, with a small number surnamed *nee* **Chin**, because the Wong men traditionally take their brides only from villages #2 or #3, and a few may take their brides from village #4 (most likely when there were not enough available brides during a given period of time from villages #2 and #3. In similar fashion, the **Lee** men from village

Chapter 5

#3 only took their brides from either the *Ma* clan in village #5 or the ***Chin*** clan in village #4. This explains why there were so many *nee* **Lee** women in the *Ng* clan village, but no *nee* **Ng** women in the ***Lee*** village. In this manner, mono-clan villages carefully regulated the source of new females into the mono-clan village, which helped perpetuate the mono-clan agnatic descent group, without "over-drawing" from any one "gene-pool" as a vital source for mono-clan village brides. This regulated marriage system benefited all of the participating mono-clan villages. In each mono-clan village, records were kept listing all males, generation by generation in the clan genealogy.

**Figure 5.1 Five mono-clan villages with pre-determined neighboring mono-clan villages, as pre-selected exclusive sources of brides/wives**

Village #1
**Wong** mono-clan village
**Wong** brides/wives only
taken in as *nee* **Ng**, *nee* [41]
**Lee**, or *nee* **Chin** women

| Village #2 | Village #3 | Village #4 |
|---|---|---|
| **Ng** mono-clan village | **Lee** mono-clan village | **Chin** mono-clan village |
| **Ng** brides/wives only | **Lee** brides/wives only | **Chin** brides/wives only |
| taken in as *nee* **Lee** or | taken in as *nee* **Ma** or | taken in as *nee* **Wong** or |
| *nee* **Ma** women | *nee* **Chin** women | *nee* **Ng** women |

Village #5
**Ma** mono-clan village
**Ma** brides/wives only
taken in as *nee* **Wong**,
or *nee* **Ng** women

Additionally, each family unit in each village kept records, or at least kept in mind within "living memory," the village-family source of brides over the generations in its mono-clan village, as a means of not "going to the same well too many times." These records and memories existed for practical reasons. However, in the all-important matter of family genealogies, or mono-clan village temple records, no mention was made of any female residents, either those born within the village (e.g., in a **Lee** village all *nee* **Lee** females), or those brought in as brides, who later became mothers of male members of the mono-clan village (e.g., in a **Lee** village, all the Mrs. **Lee's**, who were *nee* **Ma** or *nee* **Chin** brides.)

In many rural Cantonese communities, there also existed multi-clan villages, where two or more clans resided, e.g., a village composed of people identified with the ***Yee***, ***Louie***, and ***Wong*** clans respectively. While more than one clan might inhabit a particular village, each lineage group occupied a distinct section, and mixed neighborhoods were rare.[42] As in the case of mono-clan villages, women from multi-clan villages were routinely married out to men in pre-selected neighboring villages, and women from other pre-selected neighboring villages were brought into their multi-clan village. However, unlike the mono-clan village, the situation was more complicated because there were multiple clans residing in a single village. Quite naturally both "in-marriage" and "out-marriage" patterns had to be carefully orchestrated to ensure stability via continuity and consistency over time, in regards to the existence and operation of multiple clans in the same village. Neighboring villages also adhered to carefully constructed and purposefully maintained traditional selection options for their "in-marriage" and "out-marriage" patterns. In the case of multi-clan villages, the purpose of such careful pre-selection of neighboring villages, as proper sources for brides, did not result from the effort to perpetuate the solidarity of a single clan, but rather to assure a balanced and equitable flow of brides back and forth across a busy and crowded field of bridal exchanges. Presumably over time, **Yee**, **Louie**, and **Wong** clans in this village routinely supplied brides/wives to a set number of neighboring villages, and conversely those same villages also sent their brides via a similar predetermined parallel pattern. Bridal exchange patterns involving multi-clan villages (serving both as a source and a receiver of brides), for obvious reasons, were by their nature significantly more complicated than those involving mono-clan villages.

The intimate relationship between agnatic lineages and their associated local villages represented a powerful tradition of "the enduring ties that bind, Cantonese style." In traditional Cantonese society, after one's surname, the next most important personal identifying label was one's native place. Among the vast majority of Cantonese, in both Central Gwongdung and elsewhere overseas in distant locations, one's native place was first one's home county, e.g., Toi-shaan, (commonly spelled as Toishan, or locally as Hoishan) and after that it was typically one's native village. In the case of most Cantonese, the mention of one's surname and one's village often conveyed the idea of a unified single identity, because many, if not most, Cantonese (who formed the vast majority of Cantonese overseas emigrants) were from villages, of which most had strong lineage connections. In this context, there developed an especially intimate and enduring bond among rural Cantonese people, because of the intimate association between local lineages and their associated villages. This became an especially enduring tie that bound Cantonese men folk together in early Chinese America.

*Traditional Cantonese rural marketing systems, as essential hubs for local economic activity*

Beneath the arbitrary distinctions and orderliness of geographic labels, e.g., the Pearl River Delta Region, and the artificial formality of rural districts, e.g., *Toi-Shaan*, the traditional Cantonese village functioned as an invaluable resource to service rural community needs. Economically speaking, the most important function of the village, as the lowest level Cantonese central place, was its pivotal role as an entry level location for the local exchange of goods and services, again, often within a barter economy. I have already identified larger villages as "pseudo-market places," relative to the exchange of goods and services within a well-defined local communal economic area. The critical importance of the local village, as a pseudo- market place, and the standard market town, centered on their placement, as strategically located nodules, within a complex grid network or system that blanketed rural Central Gwongdung, and elsewhere beyond.

> central places are readily analyzed on the assumption that the economic function of a settlement is consistently associated with its position in marketing systems which are themselves arranged in a regular hierarchy.[43]

Among the ubiquitous Cantonese villages that dotted the rural landscape of Central Gwongdung, some functioned as strategically located endpoints for the exchange of goods and services in local communities. In this manner, no person in any village, and its adjunct hamlet(s), was ever more than one day's walk from a larger village, or standard market town, that served as a local market, where one could obtain needed services or commodities unavailable in one's own village.

As noted earlier, Skinner distinguished among scores of strategically located markets distributed widely across rural Gwongdung, and identified them as being of one of two prototypes, i.e., the "Standard market town," and the "Intermediate market town."[44]

### Table 5.2 Skinner's Conceptual Model of Hierarchy of Rural Chinese Central Places as Market Place Units[45]

| Type of central place | Type of market | Maximum dependent territory |
|---|---|---|
| Minor market[46] | Minor market | Minor marketing area |
| Standard market town[47] | Standard market | Standard marketing area |
| Intermediate market town | Intermediate market | Intermediate marketing area |
| Central market town | Central market | Central marketing area |
| Local city | Local markets distributed within a city | City trading area |
| Regional city | Local markets distributed within a city | Regional trading area |

My conceptualization of Cantonese central places, which also include villages and some hamlets, can be better understood, when viewed within the larger context of the traditional Cantonese rural marketing system. Generally speaking, the size of various market centers ranged from a fairly sizable large village, to a small town, to a mid-size town or small city, and finally to neighborhood markets distributed throughout large urban centers. Size was relative, but function was not. This was as true for rural (village and hamlet) markets, as it was for larger more urbanized markets. "On the whole…each market…has a definite and recognizable area, and looks upon the people of certain villages as its primary customers; and the villagers regard it as their town."[48]

The operational viability of rural market central places, was bound to a fixed calendar in which market activity occurred on regular schedules, varying from locality to locality. In this context, most rural markets were normally "periodic" rather than "continuous" in their scheduling of market activities. In other words, market activity took place periodically on a fixed schedule at predetermined locations or markets, rather than at places with markets that were in continuous operation, i.e., those open every day. Generally speaking, continuous markets, i.e., those open every day on a regular basis, were an urban phenomenon, confined to specific neighborhoods in large towns and major urban centers. As a practical matter, rural marketing activities were scheduled in tandem with neighboring markets elsewhere, in order to coordinate their respective schedules, thereby avoiding the problems of having either too many markets operating at the same time within the same area, or in the alternative not having an adequate number of operating markets to support a particular area.

In addition to providing adequate support of marketing activities within a micro-region or designated marketing area, scheduling also provided adequate opportunity and time for various producers, traders, and craftsmen to sufficiently make their rounds from one market place to another, within a well-defined circuit or territorial unit. In traditional Chinese society, the itinerant peddler (e.g., knife sharpeners, barbers, and pottery-ware sellers) toting his wares with his carrying pole, served as the mainstay of the mobile service firm in traditional rural Chinese society.[49] In this way, artisans, craftsmen, repairmen, salesmen, and small-time entrepreneurs were able to circulate from one market place to another, each within a pre-determined larger market area, confident of their own monopoly, without concern over whether or not someone else's market territory had been compromised. Both consumers and tradesmen benefitted from a well-ordered rural market system, in which

> The pulsations of economic activity which occur as both mobile firms and mobile consumers converge on rural markets define one of the basic life rhythms in all traditional agrarian societies…Thus, when markets are periodic rather than daily, market towns [and villages] may be distributed far more densely on

the landscape so that the most disadvantaged villagers can manage the trip to market in a reasonable period of time.[50]

In traditional Chinese society, Chinese notions of time were bound to the idea of periodic cycles. A number of traditional time cycles were used to identify rural market schedules. (see below table 5.3) Generally speaking, the lunar *hsun* or "decade" averaged 9.84 days, while the independent *hsun* averaged 10 days. The independent duodenary (fortnight) cycle averaged 12 days, while the lunar fortnight averaged 14.765 days, and the solar fortnight averaged 15.218 days per cycle. In Gwongdung, the duodenary schedules (averaging 12 days) seem to have been used primarily in the upper reaches of the West River (i.e. portions of the outer *Baak-wah* zone); whereas downstream in the "inner" *Baak-wah* zone and Pearl River Delta Region PRDR) rural market schedules generally followed the lunar *hsun* ("decade") cycle (averaging 9.84 days).[51]

An indication of the importance of market cycles, as the basis for the scheduling of market days, is evident in some of the names for strategically located villages. In the area where my father's village of Nam Tseun is located in rural Toi-Shaan District, there is a standard Market town known as *Say-giu* (in the *Say-yup* dialect) (in standard Cantonese *Say-gau*) or in English, "town #49." (located midway between my father's village and the county-seat of Toi-Shaan City (Toi-Sing). The name "Four-Nine" is well known in Toi-Shaan, indicating that the town has historically served as a standard market town, with scheduled market days held every 4th and 9th days, which is about once a week. As indicated by the name "Four-Nine," this schedule suggests a busier than normal schedule, with marketing occurring every five days, rather than the average nine to ten days, as suggested by Skinner. This is understandable because the larger higher density population concentration in the Pearl River Delta area, especially in the *Say-Yup* districts, where the terrain was hilly and marketing activity was both concentrated and in a high volume. Market activity occurred more frequently, in order to serve a larger, more concentrated rural population.

## Table 5.3 Traditional Chinese Rural Marketing Cycles[52]

| Cycle | Manner of Operation |
|---|---|
| *Hsun* ("decade") | Ten (10) days in duration, each day in the cycle is named after one of ten *kan* ("stems") which have a fixed sequence. |
| *Hsun* (non-decade) | Twelve days in duration, cycle is similarly defined by a fixed sequence of twelve *chih* ("branches"). The "stems" and "branches" day designations originated in the Shang period (2nd millennium BCE), and they are still used today for each day of the lunar calendar. |
| *Chieh-ch'i* or the 24 solar fortnights | The tropical year is divided into 24 fortnights. The onset of each fortnight is recorded for reference in popularly used traditional Chinese almanacs. These fortnight dates provide fixed points in the solar year, which regulate annual rural agricultural activities. |
| Lunar month | A number of short-term cycles are tied to the lunar month. The lunation or *synodic* month bears no function/relationship to the rotation of the earth- which averages about 29.53 days in length- the lunar month cannot recur indefinitely with precisely the same number of days. The traditional Chinese month alternated between 29- and 30-day months, with 30-day months occurring slightly more often. In this manner, marketing schedules tied to the lunar month could not reoccur regularly and are therefore irregular in their cycles. |
| The Lunar month as subdivided into a *lunar decade* | Here the *hsun* is also applied. The three lunar *hsun* begin respectively on the 1st, the 11th, and the 21st day of the 30 days lunar month. For 29 days lunar months, the third *hsun* lacks one day. |
| The Lunar month as subdivided into a *lunar fortnight* | The first lunar fortnight runs from the 1st through the 14th day of the lunar month, and it is always shorter than the second fortnight, which is either 15 or 16 days in duration. |

The ubiquitous nature of the traditional village in the mid-late nineteenth century, with its important role as the most basic and common "central place" unit of the Pearl River Delta, came about in large measure because of its pivotal role in providing for critically needed socio-economic standardization and geo-territorial integration of rural Cantonese society. As such, the local village, and the daily life it engendered, served as the common material basis with which the vast majority of Chinese immigrants in America both identified with, and greatly esteemed. It was an experience that they carried with them to the new world, where they tried to replicate it, whenever and wherever they could. In this regard, the real historical significance of the myriad of Cantonese villages and hamlets that dotted the rural landscape of the Pearl River Delta region was not in their great number, nor in their ascribed uniformity of structure and operation. It was rather in their critical function as a widely-shared common experience, which formed the basis for understanding the essential constructs of community life among Cantonese people back home in *Tong-Shaan*, which in turn formed the basis for replicating communal institutions and daily life in *Gum-Shaan*.

Early Cantonese communal experiences in *Dai-Fow* (San Francisco), the Sacramento River Delta, and the elsewhere in Northern California in the period 1845–1860s mirrored time-honored precedents of co-contemporary Cantonese society in Central Gwongdung. Cantonese traditional marketing schedules and patterns were replicated in early Chinese America. This material fact underscored a remarkable homogeneity of common identifying themes and shared experiences among fellow Cantonese immigrants in Nineteenth-Century *Gum-Shaan*.

### *The primacy of native place as a critical identification label among Cantonese people*

When I was growing up in various Chinatowns in Washington DC, New York, and San Francisco, I vividly recall meeting an endless stream of "uncles" and "cousins." In these encounters, I repeatedly heard animated expressions about home, by way of references to one's native place. I soon became aware, undoubtedly in a very superficial way, of the importance of one's native place, as a key identity label among Cantonese people. It seemed that people interacted more easily and quickly, once they knew that they came from the same place, or places that were closely linked with each other. There existed in ascending order, from the general to the specific, and from the less important to the really important, an underlying importance to "where one came from." When encountering another person, who might also be from Gwongdung, a series of rapid-fire questions would arise, to obtain a correct reading of an initial hazy intuition.

## Chapter 5

> Are you Chinese? Are you a *Gwongdung yan* (person)? Oh, you are! Me too! What part of Gwongdung are you from? Oh, Central Gwongdung! Me too! What is your district? Oh! We are both from *Toi-Shaan*! So, we both speak *Say-Yup wah*! What is your home town or village? Oh! that is next door to my village? Do you know so and so? You do! Well, he is my cousin on my father's side. Oh! I am so glad we met, we have so much to talk about! What is the latest news from home? Here is what I heard about…Really, you heard it too? [53]

Native place identifications were somewhat fluid, depending on what context framed references to one's native place. At one extreme, the locus of one's native place embraced the concrete specifics of a particular local place, from village/hamlet, to town, to home district. At the other extreme, an individual's native place entailed references, which were ambiguous, abstract, and amorphous in nature. These extremes of references to one's native place, were again quite fluid. One could use either one, and even use them interchangeably, and not confuse others, who identified with similar conceptual and concrete correlates of what could be construed as an individual's native place. Thus, one could identify one's native place with a precise concrete reference, e.g., *Nam-Tsuen* Village in *Toi-Shaan* district. In the alternative, when referencing one's native place with other Cantonese speakers, one could generalize with an imprecise and abstract, but commonly used, euphemistic metaphor, i.e., *Tong-Shaan* (see chapter 6). The choice of which reference to utilize, depended on pragmatic considerations, e.g., the prevailing social context, the number of persons in the conversation, who is asking for such information and why, and who is responding. Is the inquiry casual or formal, does the exchange of such information involve other social, economic, or legal matters?

Traditional Cantonese native place identifications attract my interest, because while they were undoubtedly significant and enduring, they have not been sufficiently assessed, relative to the nature of their historical contextualization among Cantonese people. In advancing a creditable claim about the widespread application of Cantonese native place identifications, I utilize a practical litmus test to demonstrate why such identification labels were so important, and that they represented, yet another key Cantonese binding tie.

This approach involves a more nuanced, expansive, and complex view about native place identifications, beyond my earlier comments about their place and role in traditional Cantonese homosocial engagement. This litmus test is rooted to the historical narrative of large-scale later nineteenth-century and early twentieth-century Cantonese overseas emigration. This nexus provides helpful material facts, e.g., chronology, demographics, and geography, which beneficially illustrate the historical basis and social reality, of why and how native place identifications were so important among Cantonese people, both at home and elsewhere in distant overseas locations.

In the mid-late nineteenth century, chain migration drove Overseas Chinese emigration to distant locations in Southeast Asia and the Western Hemisphere. Chain migration is a "movement in which prospective migrants learn of opportunities, are provided with transportation, and have initial accommodation and employment arranged by means of primary social relationships with previous migrants."[54] In this manner, chain migration theory underscores the close nexus between earlier emigrants, and those that follow later in time, relative to where emigrants emigrate from and the choice of what distant destination to migrate to, as well as how to get there, and what to do upon arrival. In this manner, both prior and subsequent social relationships among fellow emigrant/immigrants are critically important, by way of key web group affiliation relationships, as they are structured within emigrant/immigrant social organizations and institutions. This has been especially evident in the case of later nineteenth-century Cantonese Chinese overseas emigration to America.[55]

## Table 5.4 Cantonese-Chinese in California by select Cantonese and Non-Cantonese Speech communities from Central Gwongdung, 1855–1928 [56]

| Year/period | Say-Yup | Saam-Yup | Chung-Shaan | Hakka | Totals |
|---|---|---|---|---|---|
| 1855 | | | | | |
| Total[57] | 16,107 | 6,800 | 14,000 | 1,780 | 38,687 |
| percentage[58] | 41.6% | 17.6% | 36.2% | 4.6% | 100% |
| 1866 | | | | | |
| total | 32,500 | 10,500 | 11,500 | 3,800 | 58,300 |
| percentage | 55.8% | 18% | 19.7% | 6.5% | 100% |
| 1868 | | | | | |
| total | 35,900 | 10,000 | 11,800 | 3,300 | 61,000 |
| percentage | 58.8% | 16.4% | 19.4% | 5.4% | 100% |
| 1876 | | | | | |
| total | 124,000 | 11,000 | 12,000 | 4,300 | 151,300[59] |
| percentage | 82% | 7.3% | 7.9% | 2.8% | 100% |
| 1926-1928[60] | | | | | |
| total | 23,000 | 1,500 | 2,500 | 500 | 27,500 |
| percentage | 82.5% | 6% | 9.5% | 2% | 100% |
| Total per group | | | | | |
| and total | 231,507 | 39,800 | 51,800 | 13,680 | 336,787 |
| Percentage | 100% | 100% | 100% | 100% | 100% |

Evidence of hundreds of thousands of Cantonese in later Nineteenth-Century America, each distinguished by their native place identification, via affiliation with a specific *wooi-koon* (*huiguan*) native place social organization, concretely demonstrates the ubiquitous character and critical importance of native place identity labels. They do so by reinforcing the social reality that local identification labels represented useful and valued ID tags, regarding from where Cantonese emigrants originated from, as well as their aggregate numbers, and what percentage of the local immigrant ethnic community they constituted. Such native place identifications, by way of home district/county and speech community labels, provided a useful way to categorize and calculate the changing demographic profile of the Cantonese resident population in America, during various periods of time. It also provides a convenient and invaluable means for accounting for where Cantonese emigrants came from, by way of specific home districts/counties.

The data in table 5.4 above reveals that native place identifications mirrored, indirectly here by way of local speech community identification labels, e.g., *Saam-Yup* speakers, that Chinese immigrants were distinguished primarily by such identifications. The terms *Saam-Yup* (Three Districts' group," *Say-Yup* (Four Districts' group), *Chung-Shaan* (*Chung-Shaan* district group(s) all clearly represent native place identifications. The only possible exception is the *Hakka* label, which referred to just ethno-speech identification, without any reference to any native place. This scheme underscores the underlying primacy of native place identities.

In northern California during the period 1850–1860, all the people from the *Saam-Yup* group established and affiliated with a single native place association, identified as the *Saam-Yup Wooi-koon* (*Sanyi Huiguan*.) Thus, when we speak of *Saam-Yup* people, we are in effect talking about the people of the three districts around Canton, i.e., *Namhoi, Punyu*, and *Shuntak*. Their resident aggregate numbers never grew as large, nor as quickly over time, as to necessitate forming any additional *Saam-Yup* district associations. The rival *Say-Yup* group's case was markedly different, and decidedly more complicated.

In the early period 1845–1851, *Saam-Yup* people, led by *Saam-Yup* merchant elites, dominated San Francisco's Chinese community, both demographically and economically. This changed dramatically in the following decades, 1851–1870, when the number of *Say-Yup* people dramatically increased in both number and community power. In 1851, many *Say-Yup* members exited from the one of the first *wooi-koon* established in Chinese San Francisco, i.e., the *Kong Chow Wooi-koon*, to form their own *Say-Yup Wooi-koon*, which over time also stood in opposition to the *Saam Yup Wooi-koon*. Over the next few decades, numerous additional *Say-Yup* based *wooi-koon* were formed, as existing *Say-Yup wooi koon(s)* split, resulting in the formation of new rival *Say-Yup* related *wooi koon(s)*. By the 1890s, there only remained one *Saam-Yup Wooi-koon*, but in marked contrast there existed three to five *Say-Yup*-related *wooi-koon(s)*, depending on which year is referenced, because their total number changed in a short period of time, where some split, and formed new ones, and then recombined with others, and then split again.[61]

While the total number of *Saam-Yup* people in the California's Cantonese community grew in the decade 1860–1870, the *Saam-Yup* percentage or market-share of the total number of Cantonese in California steadily declined from 17.6% in 1855 to 7.3% in 1876 (see table 5.4). In this same period, however, the *Say-Yup* group experienced spectacular growth, in both its aggregate numbers and percentage or market-share of California's Cantonese community. In 1855 there were about 16,000 *Say-Yup* people, which formed about 42% (41.6%) of the Chinese population in California. By 1866, this number grew dramatically to about 32,500, which constituted about 55.8% of the Chinese in California. By 1876, the *Say-Yup* group reflected a predominant demographic and socio-political hegemony in California, with a population of 124,000, which formed a market-share of about 82%. (see table 5.4).

The value of the statistical data offered above, is that it clearly demonstrates that native place (and speech) identifications were extremely important, relative to how representative demographic profiles were categorized, and how they then served as the basis for important web group affiliation institutional relationships. Specifically, as demonstrated in the above table, native place identifications, when viewed collectively, illustrate how what might be initially perceived as a mere sentimental expression of loyalty to a place called home, was in reality something much more powerful and consequential, relative to contextualizing the social reality of Cantonese homosocial engagement in America, and elsewhere (e.g., Canada, and Latin America.)[62]

Native place identifications had an over-riding importance in Cantonese life, as best exemplified in the routine rhythm of daily homosocial engagement. At home in *Tong-Shaan*, in Central Gwongdung, one's native place identification was second only to one's surname. Indeed, as a practical matter, its important role actually took precedence over one's surname. In initial introductions among Cantonese speaking strangers, the first question asked is, "*Ni kwai sing?*" (What is your honorable surname?) This question represented a mere formality, a necessary courtesy. The fact that this question has been posed in Cantonese, already establishes the fact that the person being questioned, has already been identified as someone from Central Gwongdung. It only remains to definitively determine what this person's native place is, most commonly his home district (and local speech community). Thus, the second question posed was typically, "*Ni heung-ha, hi been she?*" (Your [native] country[side], where is it?" (i.e., "what is your home district?") This second inquiry about one's native place identification served as a critical prerequisite for potential positive social engagement, especially regarding interaction between Cantonese speaking strangers. This line of questioning underscored the challenging task of communicating information and negotiating competing interests and needs, which underscored the required apriorii anchoring of one's persona to a specific native place.

This critically important determination of one's native place (home district) remained an operational prerequisite in both Central Gwongdung, and elsewhere in Cantonese communities around the world. When encountering a Cantonese speaking individual, another Cantonese person could often easily guess his native place, in a general frame of reference, by recognizing and placing his particular Cantonese dialect or variant speech form, e.g., *Saam-Yup wah* or *Say-Yup wah*. In other cases, however, a Cantonese speech variant or dialect could not be determinative, in ascertaining an individual's native place identification. Two such examples include the *Luk-Yup* speech group, where one could be either from one of the original *Saam-Yup* group districts, i.e., *Namhoi, Punyu*, or *Shuntak*, or possibly from one of the other three additional districts, i.e., *Tungkun, Pao-an*, or *Poklo*. Similarly, in the *Ng Yup* group of districts, an individual could be from one of the traditional *Say-Yup* districts, such as *Toi-Shaan, Hoiping, Sunwui*, and *Yanping*, or possibly from the additional district of *Hok-shaan*. In these cases, in order to determine an individual's native home district, one had to simply ask, "what is your home district?"

In contrast, if one spoke *Nam-Lau, Long-Doo*, or *Samheung-wah*, then one would/could doubtlessly be identified as a *Chung-Shaan* person. The problem here is that, if one did not speak any of these dialects or variant forms, then one could not identify any of them, much less identify these speech forms with the *Chung-Shaan* District. Similarly, if an individual from *Chung-Shaan* spoke either *Saam-Yup wah*, or *Say-Yup wah*, Cantonese speakers could not possibly know that such an individual's native district was in fact *Chung-Shaan*, because such speakers could be very well (and most likely, even if mistakenly) identified with the *Saam-Yup*, or *Say-Yup* communities, located elsewhere beyond *Chung-Shaan*.

The situation with a *Hakka* speaker from Chung-Shaan mirrors a similar problem, regarding dialect/speech form and native place identification. In this light, knowing a Cantonese speech variant/dialect, can be of only limited help in identifying an individual's native district.

In traditional nineteenth-century Cantonese society, the singular importance of an individual's native place identification, typically in the form of one's home district, was underscored by the fact that it usually served as the all-important determination of a person's identification. In this context, both the question and the resulting answer about another person's native place affirmed in concrete and familiar terms, the importance of native place identifications among Cantonese people in the nineteenth century. In this manner, regardless of one's particular native place identification, "native place" fostered a pronounced sense of community, a sense of belonging, and familiarity- especially away from home. In distant overseas locations, such matters took on added importance and urgency, as they embraced a wide-spectrum of sentimental, emotional, and psychological characteristics. Individually and collectively, these factors underscored the primacy of native place identifications as an especially powerful and enduring additional "binding tie, Cantonese style."

### *Cantonese cuisine: The Cantonese obsession with food preparation and consumption*

There is an old Chinese saying, 生在苏州, 活在杭州, 吃在广州, 死在柳州. (i.e., one should be born in Suzhou, live in Hangzhou, eat in Guangzhou (Canton), and die in Liuzhou. This old saying reflects the common belief that in the 18th-19h centuries, a handful of southern Chinese cities embodied very special features or traits. Specifically, **Suzhou** had the most beautiful women and gardens, **Hangzhou** had the most beautiful scenery, **Guangzhou** (Canton) had the best quality and variety of food, and **Liuzhou** had the best wooden coffins in China.

The renowned distinctiveness of Cantonese cuisine revolved around a common traditional obsession with food preparation, presentation, and gastronomic enjoyment. This typically involved a constant critiquing of all aspects of food preparation and consumption. These matters invite closer scrutiny, as another means of showcasing traditional Cantonese group solidarity and unity.

Cantonese cuisine is well-known as one of China's several major regional cuisines.[63] Its chief identifying characteristics include:1) the subtle use of sauces and condiments, 2) emphasis on the freshness of ingredients (meat, seafood, vegetables, and fruits,) 3) diversity of ingredients, with particular concern about when, and how, they were combined together, to achieve subtle flavors and textures, and 4) the use of several diverse methods of preparation and cooking, i.e. stir-frying, steaming, and roasting (e.g., Cantonese BBQ.) Some preparation involved different sequential stages/combinations of cooking methods, e.g., stir-frying, followed by stewing.

Historically speaking, the Cantonese, like other southern Chinese, were famous for their regional tea culture.[64] In Cantonese tea culture, *Dim sum* figures prominently. *Dim sum*, (means "little touch[es] of [the] heart, or "the heart's little [delightful] treats") became especially well-known and greatly appreciated among Cantonese, non-Cantonese Chinese, and foreigners alike. The Cantonese *Dim sum* repertoire consisted of a wide variety of small bite-size dumplings, similar to hors' oeuvres or finger-food, each with different kinds of fillings, (e.g., different combinations of meat, seafood, and vegetables,) and different kinds of wrappings, (e.g., wheat flour, white rice paste, brown rice paste, or glutinous rice paste, fried eggs, vegetable leaves, fruit leaves, animal skin, and dried reconstituted bean curd.) Some items were also served without any wrapping. *Dim sum* came in a stunning variety of shapes, sizes, and forms, e.g., square, round, triangular, odd shaped, flat, humped, and amorphous.

Cantonese *Dim sum* also came in a variety of flavors, e.g., sweet, sour, bitter, salty, and spicy, or combinations thereof, e.g., sweet-sour, sweet-sour-spicy, and bitter-sweet. The manner of how the ingredients inside each kind of *Dim sum* were processed, in order to be stuffed into bite-size pieces, was also quite varied, e.g., ground, diced, shredded, minced, sliced, chopped, or left "whole." There also developed diverse cooking methods, e.g., steaming, sautéing, stewing, stir-frying, deep frying, baking, or roasting. *Dim sum* could be served cold, room temperature, or hot. It could appear as a soup in a bowl, as long items/pieces laid out on a plate, as little dumplings arranged in groups of three or four on small plates, or as large platters of noodles, pasta, or rice. Some *Dim sum* dishes were not small at all, but consisted of regular sized servings of either a half or whole cut-up, and neatly arranged, steamed chicken, roasted duck, or Cantonese roasted or BBQ pork. Some *Dim sum* were soft, Jell-O-like, others hard and brittle, or chewy. The key characteristic of *Dim sum* was its seemingly endless variety of color, texture, cooking method, manner of presentation, flavor, shape, size, and form. The bottom-line in Cantonese *Dim sum* was to create a diversity of quality, with an unlimited quantity of inviting tasteful portions.

In nineteenth-century Cantonese society, food preparation, cooking, presentation, and enjoyment, formed the basis of Cantonese obsession with food. Even among the poorest peasant-farmer families, family meals, especially dinners on special occasions, e.g., weddings, births of sons, or significant birthdays ($70^{th}$, $80^{th}$, $90^{th}$ or $100^{th}$) were occasions for conspicuous consumption of food. Undoubtedly, among the lower strata of society, among urban poor and rural peasant-farmers, there undoubtedly existed economic constraints, which limited food options to basic staples of rice, sweet potatoes, vegetables, and on rare occasion, some meat (chicken or pork) and seafood (fish). Among the affluent however, such as among the Gentry and merchant classes, surplus financial resources enabled the wealthy, and not so wealthy, to enjoy a wide-variety of foods, both at home and at commercial eating establishments, catering to any budget. In Cantonese society, there was always a new restaurant, a new dish, or a new food fad to try out. Rich merchants and modest shop keepers alike, expended much time, effort, and money into eating well. Wealthy Cantonese merchant types led the way, with Cantonese rank-and-file following closely behind, all in the constant pursuit of gastronomic delights. Over time a close relationship formed between an obsession with food and a conventional Cantonese consensus about its value.

By the mid-nineteenth century, in both *Tong-Shaan* (Canton, Whampoa*)* and in *Gum-Shaan* (San Francisco, Portland, and later in New York City, Chicago, and Boston) there were well-established and celebrated Cantonese restaurants that provided opulent well-appointed entertainment venues. In *Dai-fow* (Chinese San Francisco) Wealthy Cantonese merchants hosted lavish banquets in palatial settings, entertaining fellow Cantonese, as well as important Americans (local politicians, civic leaders, wealthy prominent American businessmen, and occasional celebrities). The following two later nineteenth-century photos illustrate these beautiful optics.

Late 19th Century photos of the Interior of palatial Cantonese restaurants, likely in *Dai Fow* (Chinatown San Francisco)

Cantonese people have had a well-established reputation regarding their traditional obsession with the selection, preparation, presentation, and gastronomic enjoyment of food.[65] In this context, the Cantonese were quite simply the "foodies" *par excellence* of traditional Chinese society. Over the course of several centuries, Cantonese food became famous for the diversity of its many subtle textures and delicate flavors. This stemmed in large part from the relative complexity of the preparation and cooking process. Cantonese food preparation involved a great variety of ingredients and many techniques on how to prepare them. Significantly, Cantonese dishes were legendary among other Han Chinese people for their exotic and often bizarre character.

> Chinese from other provinces often stressed the uniqueness of the Cantonese. …Northerners always [thought] of the Cantonese as eating something ungodly, such as newborn rats ("honey peepers"), raw monkey's brains, fried snake, or sauerkraut of buffalo curd.[66]

Over time, among many affluent Cantonese, there developed a vicious cycle of comment and debate, concerning the cutting-edge of the art of eating well. To some extent, this obsession with food and the need to comment on it, also existed among other less affluent people, albeit in different ways and different degrees. What one ate, and how it was prepared was always important to most Cantonese people, regardless of their financial status. Good food, in the context of one's material circumstances, was always enjoyed and much appreciated. In this context, one did not miss Beijing duck, if one had never eaten it. Thus, even poor people enjoyed what they were able to have on special occasions. Obviously, people of means, even modest means, invested considerable time and effort (commensurate with their income), to acquire the best ingredients possible (for the wealthy these were typically rare and expensive,) and finally in their proper preparation and cooking. Obsession with these matters lent fame to a particular dish, and the chef who created it.

This climate of constant critiquing of food preparation and food enjoyment, created a continuous demand for newer, more elaborate and more innovative ways to prepare and serve food. This was especially true in urban areas, where wealthy merchants were concentrated. It occurred routinely, in the case of fine Cantonese cuisine, at legendary sumptuous Cantonese multi-course banquets, which dazzled the eyes and heightened the senses of smell and taste, in great anticipation of a truly spectacular dining experience. Truly, no emperor of China could have enjoyed a better gourmet experience. Yet, many Cantonese demanded and expected no less.

## Enduring Ties that Bind, Cantonese Style

There always seemed to be a new "food fad" on the horizon. This could include any number of concerns e.g., the latest new flavor enhancement, the newest way to prepare duck, the best source for a particular kind of oil or soy-sauce, the best time of the year for a particular vegetable or fruit, or the discovery and perfection of a novel way to stew frogs. Cantonese cooks invested a great deal of their time, energies, and material resources to invent new creative ways to properly prepare and enjoy various kinds of food. Each dish had a fancy and exotic name.[67] Even steamed chicken feet bore the fancy name of *fung-jow* (*fengjiao*) or "Talons of the Phoenix."

Among wealthy merchant-types, no expense, no detail, and no inconvenience, concerning food preparation and cooking, was ever too much trouble to undertake. Obviously, poor peasant-farmers and urban poor were never in a position to enjoy this kind of a life-style. However, among many members of the merchant and Gentry classes, this seems to have been more the rule, rather than the exception. Within the merchant class, there were distinctions and divisions. Wealthier merchants could demand nothing but the best; and well-to-do merchants routinely enjoyed good food. Small "mom-and-pop" types could seldom, if ever, afford such indulgences- however even they ate relatively well, compared to the majority of the rural poor. Generally, merchants were never hungry, they ate often, and they usually ate very well. Wealthy Cantonese merchants were at the forefront of the legendary Cantonese obsession with food, because they had financial resources, trading opportunities, and commercial networks necessary to obtain on a routine basis the rich variety of expensive and rare ingredients, to prepare technically complex, routinely expensive, sufficiently exotic, increasingly rare, and gastronomically delightful dishes.[68] This might be Lychee nuts with stewed wild boar viscera, roasted lizard garnished with dragon fruit, and legendary birds' nest soup and shark's fin soup. Cantonese merchants were ascriptively among the best known and most demanding "foodies" in the Cantonese-speaking world. During the course of Cantonese banquets, conversation often centered on a critique of the food being served, e.g.,

1) the degree of freshness (fish and vegetables) or quality of the ingredients used (e.g., proper aging, proper texture, proper color, proper odor, proper weight, proper shape, and the correct quality and size),

2) the proper seasoning and the subtlety of flavor(s) appropriate for a particular dish,
3) the appropriateness of the dish for the time of the year, the particular month, and the specific occasion,
4) proper slicing or cutting, relative to size of the object to be cut, and direction of the cutting (e.g., with or against the meat grain),
5) the correctness of the cooking and serving temperature, whether an item is undercooked, overcooked, or just right,
6) the proper blending of ingredients (i.e. like-sized items with other like-sized items, each kind with others of the same likeness,)
7) observing the quantity of ingredients utilized, e.g., too little salt, or too much ginger.
8) the proper balancing and combining of flavors(i.e., salty, sour, spicy, sweet, bitter),
9) the quality and appropriateness of the accompanying sauces, condiments, and last minute- add-on-ingredients, e.g., cilantro or slivers of green onions;
10) critique of the presentation of food items, each dish's composition, the proper serving temperature, the proper order served, in conjunction with other dishes on the menu, with proper spacing in the serving order, selection of the proper container or dishware appropriate to the food item(s) served. Are the dish selections, individually in proper sequence and collectively appropriate to the occasion and the time of the year? Do they mirror appropriately, different food groups, categories, as they may represent symbolically certain ideas, ideals, or themes.
11) comments about the eating utensils, dishes, table settings, neatness, cleanliness, temperature of the room, lighting, and ventilation, and of course comments about the quality of the service, regardless whether the meal is at someone's home or at some restaurant,
12) A final critique typically assessed whether the host has been generous and creative, or stingy and unimaginative in his/her/their choices?[69]

The singular importance of food existed as a tangible concern, which all Cantonese people, regardless of class, economic standing, and location, could easily and readily identify with. Encountering Cantonese food was one of the surest signs that a Cantonese individual was among his/her own people. In this context, Cantonese cuisine served as a critically important component of Cantonese solidarity and unity. It did so in a manner that needed no rationale, no explanation, and no defense. It was among the most powerful, commonly understood, and universally appreciated "enduring ties that bind, Cantonese style." It was clearly among the most physically, emotionally, and aesthetically satisfying components of such Cantonese ties.

### *The Cantonese mania for gambling as a fast track for obtaining Fa-choy (Good fortune)*

Cantonese people, were commonly viewed by others, especially by Americans in America, as quiet, somber, self-effacing, docile, hard-working, thrifty, able to endure grueling schedules and physically exhausting work, willing to defer material gratification/consumption, capable of enormous feats of endurance, under physically difficult conditions, requiring little nourishment and rehydration. Nothing was too dirty, too onerous, too insignificant and mundane, or beneath one's dignity to do for an economic benefit or the expectation of future gain.

With the exception of a minority of wealthy Gentry and merchant types, most Cantonese exhibited a preference, often out of necessity, for a simple, plain, and thrifty style of life. With the exception of a few special occasions, such as a wedding, the birth of a child, or an unusual event like passing the imperial civil service exams, most people preferred quiet, non-descript, ordinary lives. Everyone had duties to perform and responsibilities to meet, there was little time or reason to waste time and precious material resources on needless displays of conspicuous consumption and frivolous activities. This outlook reflected itself in how people dressed, e.g., plain clothing, in dark somber monochromes of black, brown, blue, and grey; and the demeanor of their behavior, e.g., humble, self-effacing, somber, quiet, minding one's own business, avoiding interpersonal tension and conflict, keeping out of the lime light, and never "tooting one's own horn." This stereotypical perspective, while not true for everyone, served as a facade for how Cantonese people viewed and dealt with life's many challenges and hardships. This view, while certainly true, should not be construed to mean that Cantonese people lacked alternatives in their thinking and conduct.

Among Cantonese people, and more generally in traditional Chinese society, there existed a well-known and much appreciated "safety valve" for venting feelings of resentment, frustration, and unfairness about the harsh realities of daily life. In contrast to endless drudgery and toil, there existed the possibility and promise of a quick easy way to achieve material success, security and well-being. This required little beyond being alert and a willingness to take risks. This alternative centered on a well-established tradition of celebrating good luck and good fortune. Among most Cantonese people, this sentiment expressed itself with a special gusto, sustained effort, and great form. This was especially evident on special occasions, regardless of how limited one's financial resources were, e.g., a wedding, the birth of a child (especially a boy), a special birthday (e.g., 70$^{th}$ birthday), and most especially while celebrating the Chinese lunar new year, now known alternately as the Spring festival in contemporary mainland China.

Nineteenth-Century Cantonese took special joy in celebrating good luck and were obsessed with the quest for good fortune. They expressed freely their innermost hopes, dreams, expectations, and obsessions, when actively pursuing good luck and good fortune. When doing so, they revealed a very different side of their character and thinking. In this context, many Cantonese were anything but quiet and somber, thrifty and retiring. Instead, they typically became compulsive, and even impulsive. Quick nimble reflexes, amid a rush of adrenalin, and not serious prudent thinking were more prized and applicable. In place of passively accepting a demanding, often harsh reality, there materialized, even if just temporarily, a robust sense of euphoria, associated with the possibility that great expectations might, just might, come about. This is similar to when people today buy lottery tickets for huge multi-million dollar jackpots. This contrasting sense of optimism gave rise to an exciting celebration of good luck, as a possible life altering event/development.

In Cantonese society, the colors of choice for celebrating good fortune were always bright red and gold. These colors highlighted popular colorful visual symbols and signs, which were displayed to inspire hope and excite the senses. To celebrate good luck and good fortune was the great venting mechanism, to combat a fairly grim reality, where mere dreams of fantastic strokes of good luck opened the flood gates of great happiness, success, and security. On festive occasions, drawings, and replicas of gold coins and silver *taels* (ingots), paintings or print-outs of chubby, happy, adorable little toddlers, a wide array of symbolic representations of various animals, flowers, trees, and examples of Chinese calligraphy were ubiquitous, as colorful and auspicious decorations to decorate the walls and furniture, in every room, and various places that people frequented. Especially popular were printed images and statutes of the trinity, of the three auspicious figures of (Mr.) *Fook*, (Mr.) *Lok*, and (Mr.) *Shou*, (figures positioned in the center, right, and left respectively, representing good luck, prosperity, and longevity respectively.)

Photo of 3 porcelain figures of Fook (in the center),
Lok (on the right), and Shou (on the left)

In popular Cantonese folk culture, two contrasting views and responses to life formed the basis for how people could approach life's many challenges. On one hand, one had to commit oneself to hard work, make many sacrifices, deny material gratification, endure physical, emotional, and social hardship, experience setbacks, encounter varying degrees of embarrassment, harassment, condemnation, and rejection. Only with a laser-like focus on a set of practical goals, and a commitment to be disciplined, responsible, and dedicated, could one hope to be successful and happy, even in a very modest way. In the alternative, one had to always remember that life was always a risky venture, with no guarantees. The unsuspecting, unpredictable, and unimaginable were ever ready to wreak havoc on one's good intentions, wonderful plans and joyous dreams about the future.

One also needed an alternative contingency "Plan B," to circumvent and overcome life's possible disappointments and setbacks. Typically, many, if not most, Cantonese people chose to obsessively chase every opportunity to garnish good luck and enjoy good fortune, usually identified as *Fa-choy* (i.e., good fortune or prosperity.) Many deeply believed that, "In life not everyone can obtain *Fa-Choy*, but some do, and it could very well happen to anyone, even me!" Consequently, many, if not most, Cantonese people worked hard at trying to obtain *Fa-Choy*, as much as they worked hard in their daily life. For most Cantonese, the commonly agreed upon game-plan to obtain good fortune was to aggressively pursue good luck via the Cantonese mania for gambling, as a fast track for obtaining *Fa-choy*. Many Cantonese, in both urban and rural settings, across all class lines, among both young and old, men and women, among the rich and poor- all enjoyed gambling in varying degrees, in a wide variety of games of chance, in diverse and different settings.[70]

Cantonese gambling took many forms, in a variety of different social settings, governed by different logistics, ranging from petty, small stakes, to spectacular high rollers. As an activity, it could take place as part of a family social event, such as a friendly game of *mahjong*, or it could take place at a professional gambling establishment. It could take place as an infrequent, social event, or as part of a "vice trade," involving professional gambling, often associated with criminal organizations. One could gamble with family and friends, or with complete strangers. The common theme and shared expectation were always the same, gambling could change one's fate in an instant, hopefully for the better, and regretfully for the worst. One only had to be willing to take a risk. If one did not do so, then good luck and good fortune might never be obtained. One had to always try, and try again. In this sense the great expectation about the efficacy of gambling, as a means to obtain good luck and good fortune, while always elusive, as it was compulsive, was to always remember that, even if only remotely possible, it could be a real possibility! This perspective fueled the Cantonese mania for gambling at home in Central Gwongdung and in numerous distant overseas locations, e.g., in Chinese America.

Popular traditional Cantonese gambling included the following e.g., *Mahjong*, *Pai-gow*, *Ma-dow* (Dominoes), *Fantan*, *Keno*, lotteries, and betting on cock fights and martial arts competitions.

Chapter 5

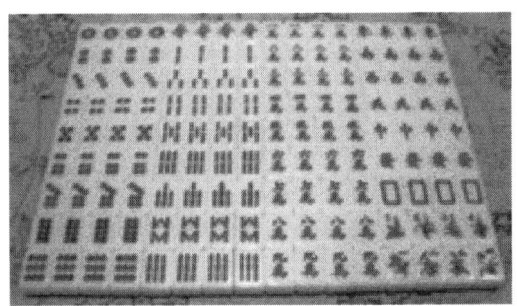

*Mahjong* tiles

Playing *Mahjong* involved four players

Playing *Mahjong* at a gambling venue

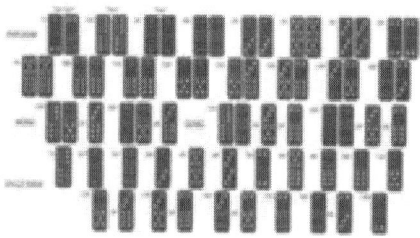

*Pai-gow* (domino-like) pieces/dominos

Mixing *Pai-gow* cards/dominos

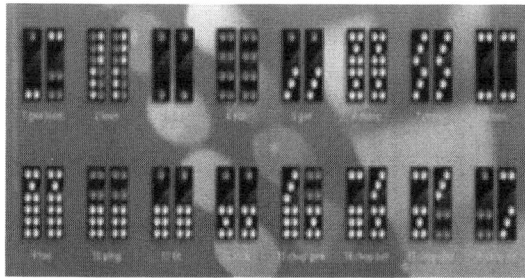

*Pai-gow* paired combinations

Chapter 5

Modern *Fantan* gambling

Traditional *Fantan* game

In the mid-nineteenth century, Cantonese gamblers were introduced to card playing in Hong Kong, and elsewhere in the New World (Hawaii, Canada, and America). Over time, in Canton and elsewhere, card playing became popular among many Cantonese gamblers. Gambling in its many forms attracted both amateur and professional gamblers.

One interesting form of betting, was the *weixing* lottery. It became over time one of the most popular nineteenth-century lottery games in Gwongdung.[71] This lottery centered on guessing the surnames of the most likely successful provincial Imperial Civil Service Exam candidates. In the Qing Dynasty (1644–1911 CE), once every three years, Imperial Civil Service Exams were held in each of China's 18 provinces, followed by the Metropolitan (or "National") exam held in Beijing in the fall. Only those individuals who passed the provincial exam were entitled to sit for the exam held in Beijing, where successful candidates received official appointments, as junior grade officials. Competition in the provincial exams was very stiff. In 1870, of the 9,000 individuals, who sat for the exam in Canton, only seventy-two passed. This only constituted about one successful candidate per every 125 candidates.[72]

In Chinese society there were several hundred common surnames, of which about a few dozen surnames were among the most common. Those who played this lottery gathered information on the surnames of the current candidates, (such as, which were the more common surnames of the current exam candidates, how many bore a certain surname, which surname was more common in those counties, known to have produced larger percentages of successful exam candidates in the past, and studying previous reports, about prior successful candidates' surnames.) The intent was to enable gamblers to successfully compete with other players in guessing the most likely surnames of successful exam candidates.[73]

While a few individual Cantonese gamblers became rich, most did not. Indeed, many became destitute, often also dragging down their families with them. Most however, typically lost modest sums of cash, and considered themselves lucky to be able to go back to their daily lives. Most invariably expected that there would always be future opportunities to gamble again. The "Cantonese mania for gambling, as a fast track for obtaining *Fa-choy*," while elusive as a means of obtaining financial success, remained an enduring expectation for many Cantonese people, and also a passionate obsession. This was especially common among the lonely hardworking *Wah-Q* (Overseas Chinese) immigrant sojourners in *Gum-Shaan* (America) and elsewhere. This mania for gambling was an especially strong and compelling example of another enduring tie that binds, Cantonese style."

## *Cantonese opera: communal engagement and the glittering centerpiece of popular culture*

Cantonese Opera evolved as a regional variant of Chinese opera during the Ming and early Qing periods (14th-18th centuries CE.) By the later nineteenth century, during the era of largescale Cantonese overseas emigration, it had become quite distinct from *Peking* (Beijing) opera and *Jiangnam* (South/Central China) opera forms. In Gwongdung, but especially in the Cantonese heartland of Central Gwongdung, Cantonese opera became enormously popular in both remote rural market centers and in major Cantonese urban centers. It became a very alluring entertainment attraction that cemented the sense of Cantonese solidarity and unity, both at home and elsewhere.

Historically speaking, the early development of what might be regarded as Cantonese opera in the early Qing period was only "Cantonese" because it was performed in "Cantonese speaking" Gwongdung, but in reality, at that time, it also represented other non-Cantonese Chinese opera traditions from beyond Gwongdung, e.g., *Peking* (Beijing) (or *Kunqu* theater), and *Jiangnam* forms, i.e., from Jiangsu and Zhejiang. In Gwongdung, these other non-Cantonese forms were collectively identified as *Waijiang Ban*, (i.e., outside or non-local non-Cantonese forms), as distinguished from *Bundae-baan (Bendi Ban)*[74] (i.e., Cantonese "native" or "local" forms). In the eighteenth century, local Cantonese traveling troupes *(Bundae-baan) (Bendi Ban)* became more popular and numerous, as the non-Cantonese traveling troupes (*Waijiang Ban*) declined in number and popularity, because of the ascendency of local Cantonese preferences and interests.[75]

In the mid-nineteenth century, three developments provided for the effective institutionalization of Cantonese *Bundae-baan* traveling opera troupes. They were: 1) the *Jiqing Gongsuo*, a clearing house for establishing business/professional contacts between patrons and traveling troupes; 2) the *Bahe Huiguan*, a guild organization to oversee the interests and needs of the Cantonese opera community at large; and 3) the *Hongchuan* or "red boats" system, to provide economical travel and efficient mobile living accommodations for traveling opera troupes across the wide expanse of the Pearl River Delta.[76]

"Red boats" were flat-bottomed red colored boats commonly used to ferry opera troupes across the Cantonese landscape, which was laced with a rich network of waterways, e.g., the Pearl River Delta region. These red boats and rural Cantonese opera traveling troupes became synonymous. The red boat era reached its zenith point just before the end of the Qing period (1900), when over thirty full-size opera troupes were reportedly active in Gwongdung.[77]

The performing season extended nearly all year round, starting in Canton, followed by extensive tours all across the countryside. The season was divided into two parts. Part I extended from the sixth month of the lunar calendar, through the winter solstice. Part II took place, after the winter break, for the lunar new year, and extended through the fifth lunar month.[78]

During the period, 1850–1930, Cantonese opera developed simultaneously on two separate, but related parallel paths of development, relative to their geophysical location and socio-cultural institutional environment, simultaneously both in Cantonese Central Gwongdung, and transnationally in the Cantonese diaspora.[79] True Cantonese (*Bundae-baan*) opera became over time enormously popular, among all Cantonese social classes, in both rural and urban society. This resulted from its enormous appeal, especially among the under-educated and uneducated. Cantonese opera provided a much sought after and deeply appreciated distraction from mundane and arduous lives of the poor, and those of modest resources. Cantonese opera, with its glittering color, stunning costumes, ingenious wigs and make-up, props and scenery, mechanical devices, aerobatics, orchestral music, singing, and story-telling attracted and delighted large loyal audiences.

Beyond Gwongdung, "…Cantonese opera had landed on distant shores across the South China Seas, and the Pacific by the mid-nineteenth century…in disparate locales, with San Francisco and Singapore leading the way in an emergent transnational theater…"[80]

Chapter 5

Enduring Ties that Bind, Cantonese Style

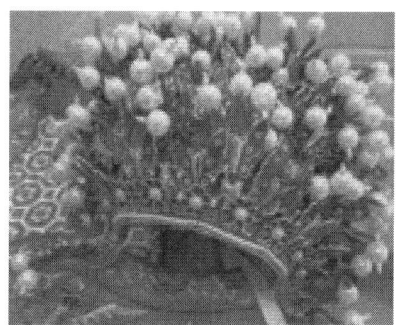

# Chapter 5

## Enduring Ties that Bind, Cantonese Style

Chapter 5

Enduring Ties that Bind, Cantonese Style

Chapter 5

After 1900, Cantonese opera not only provided much appreciated entertainment, it also complemented and enhanced local ethnic Cantonese community institutional development within many overseas Cantonese communities. This was especially notable among Cantonese communities in America and Canada. It served as a useful and profitable element of Cantonese transnational business enterprises, linking Canton, Hong Kong and Singapore with San Francisco, Vancouver, and New York City, with a steady stream of movement of people and investments.[81]

Cantonese opera, institutionally speaking, also helped enhance the development of a new local civic culture, where the immigrant/sojourner public interfaced with both traditional social organizations and new business and community philanthropic enterprises, as new avenues for civic engagement, especially after 1920.[82] Aside from an entertainment venue enjoyed by many, the immigrant theater was "….an important site for the negotiation and inscription of power relations, normative behaviors, and community politics in exclusion-era Chinatown."[83]

Undoubtedly, in both *Tong-Shaan* and *Gum-Shaan*, Cantonese opera bound Cantonese people together by providing a mutually understandable and rewarding consensus about popular Cantonese culture in the later nineteenth and early twentieth century. It did so by providing a context and means for sharing elements of Cantonese identity and experience, which only fellow Cantonese people could intuitively identify with and deeply appreciate. As a medium for showcasing Cantonese popular culture, Cantonese opera was especially effective in affirming and promoting, "What it meant to be Cantonese in the nineteenth century."

## *Cantonese popular culture, as a series of traditions, customs, and practices*

Cantonese popular culture, as reflected in local traditions, customs, and practices served as additional examples of "enduring ties that bind, Cantonese style." In many ways, traditional Cantonese popular culture mirrored elements of traditional Chinese popular culture, which has been covered extensively by others elsewhere.[84] Less has been done in investigating traditional Cantonese popular culture. Here I merely list some representative topics of traditional Cantonese popular culture, as additional examples of significant and enduring ties which bound Cantonese people together. They include: personal dress, adornment, hairstyles, personal hygiene, dietary options and realities, socialization process, weddings, child-bearing, managing sickness, traditional medicine, death rituals, funerals, ancestor worship, popular superstitions, fortune-telling, *feng-shui*, folkways, folklore, folk music, folk art, folk festivals, popular religion, homosocial activities and relationships, gender and gender relations, homosexuality, mental illness, education and literacy, local rural and urban institutions, peer-group relations, sports, recreation, anti-social behavior and its consequences, organized crime, social classes, special interest groups, dispute resolution mechanisms, and popular political culture- to name a few.

Collectively, these elements served as a powerful force for promoting "enduring ties that bind, Cantonese style." Whenever a Cantonese person encountered other Cantonese people, who either personified or who had shared encounters and experiences with any of these elements, there typically resulted an immediate sense of mutual empathy, a shared institutive understanding, and appreciation. This mutuality of which I speak, took many forms, ranging from quiet restrained empathy, to blusterous laughter, to exaggerated expressions of grief and despair, to searing moments of hostility and physical violence, or numbing, listlessness and lethargy. In this wide range of mental and emotional responses, relative to encountering other Cantonese people, there existed an immediate mutuality of thinking and outlook, which only other Cantonese people could identify with and deeply appreciate. This mutual recognition and appreciation of shared traditions, customs, and practices, were unmistakable signs that a Cantonese individual was indeed among his/her own people. These enduring ties provided a strong sense of security and well-being, that came with being with others, who both understood and shared, what it meant to be Cantonese.

## Chapter 5

### *The ties that bind, Cantonese style*

If we say that Cantonese people in the later nineteenth and early twentieth century were historically distinct in their group identity and shared experiences from other Han Chinese, we do so on the basis of recognizing that they both embodied and benefited from especially strong and "enduring ties that bind, Cantonese style." This is to say that Cantonese distinctiveness, while interesting, was not in of itself particularly unique. In truth, many of the elements that bound Cantonese people together, also existed elsewhere in Han Chinese society, and quite possibly elsewhere in the world. In this context, we need to better appreciate the nature, and understand the underlying constructs, of Cantonese distinctiveness, rather than merely extoll such distinctiveness for its own sake.

Cantonese people, as family and friends, enjoyed especially close ties arising out of a shared identification with, and appreciation of, Cantonese identity and experience. This enduring and intimate association even manifest itself among complete (fellow Cantonese) strangers. Interestingly, this social reality remained equally true, and perhaps even more compelling and stronger in Cantonese homosocial engagement beyond *Tong-Shaan*, in diverse and distant overseas locations. These matters greatly impacted what it meant to be Cantonese in the mid-late nineteenth and early twentieth century, in both China and America, and elsewhere in an expansive transnational Cantonese-speaking world.

[1] See Frederic Wakeman Jr. Strangers at the Gate, Social Disorder in South China, 1839–1861, (Berkeley: University of California Press, 1966), p.56

[2] "Marketing and Social Structure in Rural China- Part I," by G. William Skinner, Journal of Asian Studies, 24:1, November, 1964 (Association for Asian Studies Reprint (1980) Series No.1), p. 5, in part quoted from, Walter Christaller, *Die zentralen Orte in Suddeutschland* (Jena, 1933), August Losch, *Dieraumliche Ordnung derWirtschaft* (Jena, 1944); as cited from English translation, The Economics of Location (New Haven, 1954).

[3] Skinner, "Marketing and Social Structure in Rural China, Part I" Skinner only includes the following places as "central places," 1) the standard market town, 2) the intermediate market town, 3) the central market town, 4) the local city, and 5) the regional city. Specifically, he does not include smaller entities below the standard market town, which I do. These include the village and hamlet. Skinner's definition of a "central place" revolves primarily around economic activity, especially market functions of the entities which he identifies. My reference to "central places" refers more to socio-communal criteria, hence my inclusion of villages and hamlets as "central places."

[4] Ibid., pp. 7–9, Skinner briefly outlines two opposing views concerning the nature of Chinese "central places," as mirroring elements of either the *artificiality* of administrative centers or the *naturalness* of market centers in their structural organization and functions. Relative to the issue of whether they are separate or integrated, Skinner cites the proponents of two opposing views. Chang Sen-dou, who based his work on the pioneering theories of C.K. Yang, theorizes that the two are conjoined, whereby the *hsien* (*xian*) (i.e., district) capital in the administrative hierarchy is equated with the intermediate market town of the economic hierarchy. In contrast, Fei Hsiao-t'ung hypothesizes that the two are entirely separate, as exemplified in the models of the "garrison town" and the "market town." Skinner believes that both of these views are wrong. He instead advances the view that the two often coincide and overlap, depending on an analysis of the relationship of administrative-market activities and structural organization for a given central place.

[5] Michael Tsin, Nation, Governance, and Modernity in China, Canton 1900–1927, (Stanford: Stanford University Press, 1999), p. 17; also see generally works of Edward Schafer, The Vermillion Bird, Tang Images of the South, (Berkeley: University of California Press, 1967); and The Golden Peaches of Samarakand, (Berkeley: University of California Press, 1963), p. 15.

[6] Tsin, Nation, Governance, and Modernity in China, see "The Making of Nineteenth-Century Canton," pp. 19–23.

[7] See "Merchant Associations in Canton, 1895–1911," by Edward J. M. Rhoads, in The Chinese City Between Two Worlds, edited by Mark Elvin and G. William Skinner (Stanford, California: Stanford University Press, 1974), p. 99.This included other leading metropolitan centers in the region, (e.g., *ting, chou*), dozens of urban prefectures (*fu*), and hundreds of rural districts *xian* (*hsien*). Located in Metropolitan Canton itself, were the official offices (i.e., *Yamen*) of: 1) the Governor-General of the *Leung-Gwong*, 2) the Governor of Gwongdung (both offices were combined in 1905,)2) the *Hoppo* (official in charge of administering the Canton or Co-Hong Monopoly Trading System 1760–1842), 3) the seat of theGwongchau (Guangzhou) prefecture, which took in the surrounding fourteen (rural) districts or counties (*xian*), 4) the Prefect of metropolitan Canton,5) the district magistrates of two ad-

jacent rural districts, i.e., Nam-hoi and Pun-yu. Metropolitan Canton also housed the Office of the Tarter-General, the resident Manchu military commander of 47,000 Manchu and Chinese Bannermen, who were housed in the "Tarter Quarter."

[8] See generally, William T. Rowe, Hankow, Commerce and Society in A Chinese City, 1796–1889, (Stanford: Stanford University Press, 1984), see Chapter 2, "The Trade of Hankow," pp.52–89.

[9] See generally, John K. Fairbank, Trade and Diplomacy on the China Coast–The Opening of the Treaty Ports, 1842–1854, (Stanford: Stanford University Press, 1969), see following, Ch. 12, "Problems in the Application of the Treaties at the new Ports," re: Cantonese migrants, merchants at new Treaty Ports, pp. 219–225; also see, Ch. 14, "Reorganization of the Canton System," pp. 248–263; also see, Ch. 17, "The Foreign Invasion of the Coasting Trade," re. coastal "Junk Trade" see, pp. 311–328; finally, also see, Ch. 21, Wu Chien-Chang and the 'Cantonization" of Shanghai 1852–1853," pp. 393–409.

[10] Re; Macao and Hong Kong, see generally, Edward J.M. Rhoads, China's Republican Revolution, The Case of Kwangtung, 1895–1913, (Cambridge, Mass: Harvard University Press, 1975), pp. 14–15.

[11] Briefly between 1992–1994, when he was at UC Davis, I was fortunate to establish and maintain informal contact with him. His observations about the subject, and comments on work were invaluable. See, Skinner, "Marketing and Social Structure in Rural China- Part I,"; also see Part II, as originally printed in The Journal of Asian Studies, 24:2, February, 1965.

[12] Note: hereafter I define and describe villages and hamlets as "central places," within the context of my own scheme, as explained earlier.

[13] See generally, June Mei, "Researching Chinese-American History in Taishan: A Report," in The Chinese American Experience: Papers from the Second National Conference on Chinese American Studies, edited by Genny Lim, H. Mark Lai, Daniel Chu, and Ted Wong, ( San Francisco: Chinese Historical Society of America and the Chinese Cultural Foundation of San Francisco, 1984), pp. 57-60; also see, Madeline Hsu, Dreaming of Gold, Dreaming of Home: Transnationalism and Migration Between the United States and South China, 1882–1943, (Stanford, Ca: Stanford University Press, 2000),pp. 40–45; also see generally, Chinese American Transnationalism: The Flow of People, Resources, and Ideas Between China and America During the Exclusion Era, edited by Sucheng Chan, (Philadelphia,: Temple University Press, 2005),pp. 22–33; 156–173.

[14] See generally, "Political Development in Chinese America, 1850–1911," by Douglas W. Lee, PhD dissertation University of California, Santa Barbara (History) (1979), see chapter 3, "Communal Development and Nascent Politics, 1880–1895," section C, "Realignment of Power, the Rise of the *Say-Yup* People," pp. 151–179. The Cantonese community in America experienced a major demographic and economic shift, with the decline of the *Saam-Yup* portion of the Chinese community in America, and parallel increase of the *Say-Yup* people in the period 1870–1900. Consequently, *Say-Yup* remittances back home grew rapidly in volume and value between 1870–1900.

[15] If villages, in Skinner's scheme, were not viewed as "central places," it is because they did not embody nor conform to his notion of a location of market activity, then by extension the hamlet was even less of a candidate for inclusion in the category of "central places."

[16] See Douglas W. Lee, Facing Cantonese Adversity, Fleeing Tong-Shaan: Cantonese Society and the Root Causes of Nineteenth-Century Overseas Emigration, as volume 3 of The Gum-

Shaan Chronicles: The Early History of Cantonese-Chinese America, 1850-1900, (Pittsburgh, Pa: Dorrance Publishing, 2023), see especially chapter 5, "Bad joss of high-density population concentration and over-population; also see chapter 6, "Bad joss of peasant-farmer economic immiseration."

[17] Frederic Wakeman J–., "The Secret Societies of Kwangtung, 1800–1856," in Popular Movements and Secret Societies in China, 1840–1950, edited by Jean Chesneaux, (Stanford: Stanford University Press, 1972,) p.39.

[18] Wakeman, Strangers at the Gate, p. 127.

[19] Ibid., pp. 136, 135,

[20] "The Heaven and Earth Society and the Red Turban Rebellion in Late Qing China," by Jaeyoon Kim, Journal of Humanities and Social Sciences, 3:1 (2009), pp. 1–35, see p.6

[21] China Mail, 14 August 1856, as cited in "The Hakka-Punti War," PhD dissertation by J.A.G. Roberts, Queen's College, Oxford University (1968), p.44.

[22] David Faure, The Rural Economy of Pre-Liberation China, Trade Expansion and Peasant Livelihood in Jiangsu and Guangdong, 1870–1937, (Hong Kong: Oxford University Press, 1989), pp.57–58.

[23] See following internet sources: 1) Merck Manuals,https://www.merchmanuals.com/professional/infectious-diseases/...flukes/clonorchaisis ; 2) Center for Disease Control (CDC), https://www.cdc.gov/parasites/clonorchaisis/index.html

[24] Generally speaking, in the context of this investigation, I often use the terms "language" "dialect" and "speech" interchangeably, as a convenient shorthand means for talking about the medium through which Cantonese people communicated with each other, both orally and through writing. Contextually and Linguistically, each of these terms has a specific technical meaning and application, which I explain below in the following text. Traditionally, the term *Yuet* [Cantonese form](*Yue*) (Pinyin Mandarin form], similar to the term "Cantonese" referred to a "dialect" of the Chinese language. Today, most authorities regard *Yuet* (*Yue*) as a Chinese language, and "Cantonese" as a dialect of the *Yuet* (*Yue*) language

[25] Meaning the "language of the officials," (more commonly known as the *Beijing* dialect,] the predecessor of modern Mandarin Chinese.

[26] See, Gregory E. Guldin, "Seven Veiled Ethnicity: A Hong Kong Chinese Folk Model," in Journal of Chinese Studies, 1:1 (June 1984), pp. 139–156, see p. 144, 146.

[27] By "homosocial," I mean various types and degrees of socialization, among and between men, in both their private arrangements and public engagements.

[28] Stanford Lyman long ago observed how Cantonese immigrants replicated their homosocial world amid web group affiliations in a host of resurrected Chinese social organizations in America, e.g., clans and family associations, *wooi-kun* (*huiguan*) or district associations (or native place associations), guilds, and secret societies. See the following works: "The Structure of Chinese society in Nineteenth-Century America," by Stanford M. Lyman, PhD dissertation, University of California, Berkeley (Sociology), 1961; also see same author, The Asian in the West., (Social Science & Humanities publication No. 4, Western Studies Center, Desert Research Institute,) (University of Nevada, Reno, Nevada: University of Nevada Press, 1970; also see by same author, Chinese Americans, (Ethnic groups in comparative Perspective Series) (New York: Random House, 1974); ; also see "Conflict and Web Group Affiliation in San Francisco's Chinatown, 1850–1910," in Stanford M. Lyman, The Asian in North America, (Santa Barbara: ABC Clio Press, 1977), pp. 103–118; also see; also see, Chinatown and Little Tokyo: Power, Conflict, and Community Among

Chinese and Japanese Immigrants in America, (Minority Structures and Race and Ethnic Relations Series) (New York: Associated Faculty Press, Inc., 1986.)

[29] *Wooi-kun* (Cantonese form), *huiguan* (Pinyin mandarin form) *hui-kuan* (Wade-Giles mandarin form)

[30] *Bo-ga* (Cantonese form) *Bojia* (*Pinyin* mandarin form) *Pao-chia* (Wade-Giles mandarin form)

[31] See The Cambridge History of China, vol. 9, Part One: The Ch'ing Empire to 1800, edited by Willard J. Peterson, (Cambridge, UK: Cambridge University Press, 2002), Chapter 8, "Women, Families, and Gender Relations," by Susan Mann, p. 456, see note 111; also see Sow-Theng Leong, Migration and Ethnicity in Chinese History, *Hakkas, Pengmin,* and Their Neighbors, (Stanford: Stanford University Press, 1997) (author deceased, manuscript edited by Tim Wright), see introduction by G. William Skinner, pp.9–12.

[32] See Douglas W. Lee, Facing Cantonese Adversity, Fleeing Tong-Shaan: Cantonese Society and the Root Causes of Nineteenth-Century Overseas Emigration, as volume 3 of The Gum-Shaan Chronicles, The Early History of Cantonese Chinese America, 1850-1900, (Pittsburgh, Pa: Dorrance Publishing, 2023), see chapter 7, "Bad Joss of Communal Conflict and Social Chaos, and chapter 8, "Bad Joss of Local Cantonese-Fan Kwai Conflicts." Re: This narrative included: 1) the Opium War 1839–1842, 2) the Red Turban revolt, 1854–1856, 3) the *Hakka-Bundae* (*Bundi*) wars, 1855–1868, 4) endemic lineage conflict and inter-village turf wars, 1840–1870, 5) ongoing tension and conflicts engendered by Cantonese secret societies, 1800–1870), 6) the growing presence and ongoing conflicts with western/foreign missionaries, merchants, and maverick adventurers (i.e., the *fan-kwai*), 1839–1885, 7) Cantonese urban disorders, 1850–1900, 8) the Sino-French War, 1884–1885, and 9) the Cantonese boycott American goods 1905–1906.

[33] Ibid., also see chapter 8, "Bad joss of Local Cantonese-Fan Kwai Conflicts."

[34] Data in this table is a summary of my own thinking, there are no cited documentary sources.

[35] In our own society, similarly marginalized people include: the homeless, ex-convicts, sexual deviants and predators, immigrants, ethnic and racial minorities, drug addicts, and the mentally ill.

[36] Chinese lineages were agnatic in nature, because they were organized around direct patrilineal descent from a common remote progenitor. As a practical matter, members of a single lineage shared the same family surname, e.g., Li, Chin, or Wong. Literature on this subject has traditionally used the terms of lineage and clan interchangeably. See: Maurice Freedman, Lineage Organization in Southeastern China, (London: University of London, The Athlone Press, 1958), p. 1. Today, the generally preferred term in anthropology is "lineage." In this book, I may occasionally use both terms, but in most cases I use "lineage," to maintain consistency with the prevailing practice in the field of Chinese anthropology.

[37] Freedman, Lineage Organization, p.124.

[38] Ibid., p.1.

[39] Yuen-fong woon, Social Organization in South China, 1911–1949, The case of the Kuan Lineage in K'ai-p'ing County, (Ann Arbor, Michigan: University of Michigan Center for Chinese Studies, 1984). note: the author uses the older Wade-Giles romanization of "K'ai-p'ing," instead of the pinyin form "Kaiping," ("Hoiping" is the *"Say-Yup"* (*Siyi*) form). Inexplicability however, the author uses the pinyin form of "kuan" instead of the Wade-Giles form of "k'uan."

[40] Freedman, Lineage Organization, see chapter 1, "Village and Lineage in Fukien and Kwangtung," pp. 1–8; also see by same author, Chinese Lineage and Society in Fukien and Kwangtung, (New York; Humanities Press, 1966), chapter 1, "Village, Lineage, and Clan," pp. 1–42.

[41] *Nee* means "born as" or what we may identify as a female's "maiden name"

[42] Freedman, Lineage Organization, p.2, as cited from Chen Han-seng, Agrarian Problems in Southmost China, Shanghai, 1936 (also published as, Landlord and Peasant in China, New York, 1937), p.37.

[43] Skinner, "Marketing and Social Structure in Rural China- Part I," p. 5.

[44] Ibid., p. 1–15. I include villages (and hamlets) as "central places" in my own scheme, because I use social and geographical criteria, and do not rely exclusively on economic ones, as does Skinner in his scheme of what constitutes a "central place." I do, however, agree with Skinner that the standard market town is the central nodule of traditional Chinese marketing systems, which also was the case in Cantonese marketing systems. In this context, again, villages are below the grid of Skinner's central places, in terms of their economic function. In my own view, they still they remain "central places," even if subordinated to other such units arranged in a hierarchy above them.

[45] Ibid., p.9.

[46] In my own view, a "village" could serve as a "minor market." Skinner, however, does not make any such reference. He believes that the "town" is the smallest and natural endpoint of a series hierarchy of central places distributed all across the rural Chinese landscape.

[47] In my own view, a "very large village" could function as a "pseudo" standard market town. Skinner, however, does not make any such reference. He believes that only a bona-fide "town" can serve as a "standard market town."

[48] Skinner, "Marketing and Social Structure in Rural China Part I," p.17, see note 42, as cited from Yang Mou-Ch'un (Martin Yang) A Chinese Village: T'ai T'ou, Shantung Province, (New York, 1945), p. 190

[49] Skinner, "Marketing and Social Structure in Rural China- Part I," p. 10.

[50] Ibid., p. 11, see note #22, which provides, "The consumer by submitting to the discipline of time is able to free himself from the discipline of space."

[51] Ibid., p.13

[52] Ibid., p.12

[53] This is an imaginary conversation of my own creation, based on bits and pieces of what I recall hearing as a child.

[54] John S. MacDonald and Leatrice D. MacDonald (1964). "Chain Migration Ethnic Neighborhood Formation and Social Networks". *The Milbank Memorial Fund Quarterly.* 42 (1): 82–97.

[55] See the following works: "The Structure of Chinese society in Nineteenth-Century America," by Stanford M. Lyman, Ph.D dissertation, University of California, Berkeley (Sociology), 1961; also see same author, "Conflict and Web Group Affiliation in San Francisco's Chinatown, 1850-1910," in Stanford M. Lyman, The Asian in North America, (Santa Barbara: ABC Clio Press, 1977), pp. 103-118; also see ; also see, Chinatown and Little Tokyo: Power, Conflict, and Community Among Chinese and Japanese Immigrants in America, (Minority Structures and Race and Ethnic Relations Series) (New York: Associated Faculty Press, Inc., 1986.)

⁵⁶ Chinn, Lai, & Choy, History of the Chinese in California, A Syllabus, (San Francisco: Chinese Historical Society of America, 1984.) p.20, table 5. Note: instead of referring to data for the years 1850, 1860, 1870, and 1880 respectively, *Wooi-koon* based demographic totals are actually for the following years, 1855,1866, 1868, and 1876 respectively.
⁵⁷ Ibid.,
⁵⁸ Chinn. Lai, & Choy, History of the Chinese in California, P.20, Table 5
⁵⁹ Ibid.,
⁶⁰ Note the reduced aggregate totals resulted from the dual adverse impact of Chinese Exclusion (1882-1943) and the onset of the Great Depression, after 1928.
⁶¹ Chinn. Lai, & Choy, History of the Chinese in California, P.20, Table 5
⁶² Re: Chinese in Canada, see the following: Kay J. Anderson, Vancouver's Chinatown, Racial Discourse in Canada, 1875-1980, (McGill-Queens's University Press: Montreal, Canada, 1991); Lisa Rose Mar, Brokering Belonging: Chinese in Canada's Exclusion Era, 1885-1945, (London, UK: Oxford University Press, 2010); Re: Chinese in Latin America and the Caribbean, see the following: The Chinese in Latin America and the Caribbean, edited by Walton Look Lai and Tan Chee-Beng (Leiden, the Netherlands: Brill, 2010); Kathleen Lopez, Chinese Cubans, A Transnational History, (Chapel Hill: University of North Carolina Press, 2013); Jason Oliver Chang, Chino, Anti-Chinese Racism in Mexico, 1880-1940, (Urbana: University of Illinois Press, 2017).
⁶³ In China, there are four recognized major regional Han Chinese cuisines, Northern (e.g. Beijing), Eastern China (e.g. Jiangmen e.g. Shanghai or Suzhou), Western China (e.g. Sichuan), and Southern China, (e.g. Cantonese, Fujian, Hainam). These four types can be broken down into 8-9 sub-types (e.g. Hunan, as Southern Chinese. Regarding the distinctiveness and commonalty of Southern Chinese food generally, see the following: "The Complex Causation of South Chinese Foodways," by Eugene N. Anderson, Jr, in The Annals of the Chinese Historical Society of the Pacific Northwest (Seattle:1984), see pp. 147-158.
⁶⁴ Ling Wang, Tea and Chinese Culture, (San Francisco: Long River Press, 2005), Ch. 5, "Teahouse Culture," pp. 82-83.
⁶⁵ Jacqueline M. Newman, Food Culture in China, (Westport, Connecticut: Greenwood Press, 2004), pp. 93-94.
⁶⁶ Wakeman Jr., Strangers at the Gate, Social Disorder in South China, p. 57, as cited from E.H. Schafer, The Vermillion Bird: T'ang Images of the South, (Berkeley and Los Angeles: University of California Press, 1967), see ch. 12.
⁶⁷ See film, Eat, Drink, Man, Woman (1994) directed by Ang Lee. This film illustrates many of the complexities of Chinese cooking. While it focuses on non-Cantonese Chinese cooking, it mirrors many similar gastronomic concerns associated with Cantonese cooking.
⁶⁸ The Cantonese conservative contrarian counter-culture (C4) perspective regarding a positive image and prominent role of merchants in traditional society and culture also existed elsewhere in Chinese society, contrary to the well-entrenched Confucian bias of the time, especially in other parts of southern China. It was a pronounced feature of mid-to-late nineteenth-century daily life in *Wu* speech communities of the lower Yangzi, e.g.in Jiangsu, and Zhejiang provinces, and especially in Shanghai. It also existed among Min speech communities located throughout Fujian, at Fuzhou (Foochow) and Xiamen (Amoy), and East Guangdong (Gwongdung) at Chaozhou and Shantou (Swatow). Additional major strongholds with a strong and vibrant mercantile bias also existed in Hubei at Hankow, at Chongqing (Chungking) in Sichuan (Szechwan). It even existed at other distant locations in

northern China, e.g. among the famous Bankers of Shaanxi (Shensi) province, and among traders in Shandong (Shantung). The Cantonese mercantile elites in later Nineteenth and early Twentieth Century Chinese America were also conspicuous consumers of fine Cantonese cuisine.

[69] These observations are my own, based on my own experience and knowledge of how my Cantonese family, and that of my in-laws, together with a host of other Cantonese friends and associates, invariably critique food. I have observed that this critiquing of food is especially intense and refined in Hong Kong. In the middle-late nineteenth-century, this must surely have been the case in Canton and elsewhere throughout the Pearl River Delta in Central Gwongdung. It also materialized wherever Cantonese merchants settled in the mid-late nineteenth-century, e.g. Honolulu, San Francisco, Portland, New York, Chicago, Singapore, Manila, Saigon, Victoria, and Vancouver. My views are confirmed in Jacqueline M. Newman, Food Culture in China, (Westport, Connecticut: Greenwood Press, 2004), pp. 93-94

[70] See generally the subject of gambling in Canton from the late Qing through the Nationalist period (189-1940), in Virgil K.Y. Ho, Understanding Canton, Rethinking Popular Culture in the Republican Period (Oxford Studies on Contemporary China series), (UK: Oxford University Press, 2005), see Chapter IV, "Gambling in Canton: Myth and Reality of a Calamity," pp. 156-218, see especially section on "Black Hole of Impulsive and Compulsive Gambling," pp. 189-218."

[71] Ibid., pp. 47; also see Liu Heng, *Huahuxing* (Flower Lottery) *youyanggyu shanfang shichao* in QGB, vol. 124, p. 632.

[72] Benjamin A. Elman, A Cultural History of the Civil Examinations in Late Imperial China, (Berkeley: University of California Press, 2000), see "Provincial *Chu-jen* quotas during the Qing Dynasty, 1645-1900," p.664, as quoted from *Ch'in-ting k'o-ch'ang t'iao-li* (Imperially prescribed guidelines for the civil service examination grounds) 1832, 1887 editions, see specifically table 3.6 "Ming-Qing Dynasty Ratio of Graduates to Candidates in Other Provincial Examinations."

[73] See, "Betting on Empire: A Socio-Cultural History of Gambling in Late Qing China," by En Li, (Washington University, St. Louis Missouri, PhD dissertation, (History) December 2015), see especially Chapter 2, "Printed Hope: Lottery and Public Life in Nineteenth-Century Guangdong," pp. 64-134, Chapter 3, "Contradictory Men: Licensing the "Surname Guessing" Lottery in Guangdong, 1884-1886," pp. 135-179; and Chapter 4, "Across the Pacific: Betting Beyond the Empire," pp.180-238.

[74] *Bundae-baan* is the Cantonese form of *Bundi-ban* (*Pinyin* mandarin form)

[75] Wing Chung Ng, The Rise of Cantonese Opera. (Urbana: University of Illinois Press, 2015), pp12-20.

[76] Ibid., p. 25.

[77] Ibid., pp. 25, 26, 30.

[78] Ibid., pp. 25-26.

[79] Ibid., pp. 23-3; re development of Cantonese opera in transnational setting of Cantonese overseas communities, see pp. 133-151; also see Virgil K.Y. Ho, Understanding Canton, see chapter 6, "Cantonese Opera as a Mirror of Society," pp. 311-346. re: Cantonese opera development in Gwongdung, see pp. 25-43. 311-331.

[80] Ng, The Rise of Cantonese Opera, page 139, also see pp. 133-139.

[81] Ibid., Chapter 7, "Theater as Transnational Business," pp.152-169.

[82] Ho, Understanding Canton, see chapter 6, "Cantonese Opera as a Mirror of Society," re: Cantonese opera development in Gwongdung, see pp. 25-43. 311-331; re: development among overseas Cantonese, see pp. 132-151.

[83] Ng, The Rise of Cantonese Opera, p. 172.

[84] Generally, see the following: Margery Wolf, The House of Lim, A Study of a Chinese Farm Family, (New York: Appleton-Century-Crofts, 1968); Popular Culture in Late Imperial China, edited by David Johnson, Andrew J. Nathan, and Evelyn S. Rawski (Berkeley, California: University of California Press, 1983); Death Ritual in Late Imperial and Modern China, edited by James L. Watson and Evelyn S. Rawski Margery Wolf, (Berkeley: University of California Press, 1988); Violence in China, Essays in Culture and Counterculture, edited by Jonathan N. Lipman and Stevan Harrell, (Albany, New York: State University of New York Press, 1990); Janet M. Theiss, Disgraceful Matters, The Politics of Chastity in Eighteenth-Century China, (Berkeley: University of California, 2004); Yangwen Zheng, The Social Life of Opium in China, (UK: Cambridge University Press, 2005); Martin W. Huang, Negotiating Masculinities in Late Imperial China, (Honolulu: University of Hawaii Press, 2006); Avron Boretz, Gods, Ghosts, and Gangsters, Ritual Violence, Martial Arts, and Masculinity on the Margins of Chinese Society, (Honolulu: University of Hawaii Press, 2011); Giovanni Vitiello, The Libertine's Friend, Homosexuality and Masculinity in Late Imperial China, (Chicago: University of Chicago Press, 2011).

[85] See following three essays in, Studies in Chinese Society, edited by Arthur P. Wolf, (Stanford, California: Stanford University Press, 1978), "Peasant Insurrection and the Market Hierarchy in the Canton Delta, 1911-1912," by Winston Hsieh, in, pp. 79-101; also see "Marriage Resistance in Rural Kwangtung," by Marjorie Topley, pp. 247-268; also see "Cantonese Shamanism," by Jack M. Potter, pp.321-345. Also see following works: Janice E. Stockard, Daughters of the Canton Delta, Marriage Patterns and Economic Strategies in South China, 1860-1930, (Stanford, California: Stanford University Press, 1980); Yuenfong Woon, Social Organization in South China, 1911-1949, The Case of the Kuan Lineage in K'ai-p'ing County [in Guangdong], (Ann Arbor, Michigan: Center for Chinese Studies, Michigan Monographs in Chinese Studies, No. 48, 1984); Down to Earth, The Territorial Bond in South China, edited by David Faure and Helen Siu, (Stanford, California: Stanford University Press, 1995); Virgil K.Y. Ho, Understanding Canton, Rethinking Popular Culture in the Republican Period (Oxford Studies on Contemporary China series), (UK: Oxford University Press, 2005).

# CHAPTER 6
## Seeking *Tong-Shaan*, while encountering *Gum-Shaan*

**Introduction**

Historically, the Cantonese have been perceived as a people, who celebrate their distinctiveness and separateness from other Han Chinese, via their obsession with issues of historical legitimacy, socio-cultural authenticity, and ethno-linguistic purity. The search for a material basis on which these claims rest, has been a challenging assignment evolving in unsuspecting ways over a long period of time. It has remained elusive and resistant to fruitful study, largely because it has lacked a suitable analytical framework.[1] The purpose of this chapter is to construct and utilize such a framework.

In response to this challenge, I choose to focus on the important, and seemingly simple, elements of Cantonese group identity and the collective experience(s) associated with it, as they have evolved through time within an expanding transnational/diasporic context. In this new formulation, I visualize a vital nexus between group identity and the subjectively perceived experiences associated with it. Significantly, they worked together to weave a complex and much-nuanced historical narrative, which formed the basis of what it meant to be Cantonese in China and America.

During the period 1850-1900, a time of large-scale Cantonese overseas emigration, the task reconciling a harsh objective reality, with fluid subjective perceptions of that reality, constantly thrust itself to the forefront of Cantonese endeavors both at home in Central Gwongdung and in diverse distant overseas locations. In this manner, the act of leaving home, and the sense of loss and longing that followed in its wake represented a profound challenge to Cantonese overseas emigrants, and the families they left behind. How these elements interfaced and orchestrated Cantonese activities and relationships in distant and diverse locations invites closer examination.

I view Cantonese group identity as the result of two independent, but closely related socio-cultural engineering feats. First, there developed the collective identity of an antagonistic conservative contrarian counter-culture (C4), which clearly distinguished and set the Cantonese apart from other Han Chinese people (see chapter 4.) This tradition gave rise to an externally ascribed image and reputation for social cohesion, communal unity, and cultural uniformity, in the form of a *Yuet*/Cantonese regional culture, society, and language. Second, behind this outward façade of uniformity and unity, there also materialized chapters of local ethno-linguistic distinctiveness and diversity, via a series of ethnic group and local speech community identity labels, (see chapter 3.) These two co-existing constructs of Cantonese identity and experience promoted varying degrees of toleration and cooperation, alternating with periods of competition and conflict, which together formed the material basis of traditional Cantonese society and culture. In this way, Cantonese experience forged a separate chapter of history, with degrees of distinctiveness within Chinese History, and degrees of separation from mainstream Han Chinese society. In doing so, it also securely positioned traditional Cantonese identity and experience within both contexts.

This perspective draws heavily on, and benefits from, work in both Modern Chinese History and Chinese American History. It does so by underscoring a mutuality of common origins, core values, and experiences. This background of shared identity and common experiences provides important points of departure for discussion, where different material conditions, diverse experiences, and changing perceptions/responses in one location, e.g., back home in Central Gwongdung, complemented those in America and elsewhere.

As a means of linking together the many discrete elements referenced above, I choose to focus on the conceptual construct of "self, home, leaving home, sojourning, and the sense of loss and longing for home." I see these simple, easy to grasp, terms as a useful vehicle for discussing what are otherwise inherently complicated issues about the Cantonese and their collective transnational/diasporic experiences.

In a move to simplify matters, and to also enhance the attractiveness and usefulness of my discussion, I adopt metaphors to graphically represent key elements of my novel conceptual construct. Specifically, I utilize two metaphors to concretely represent the dilemma of "seeking home," with the simultaneous alternative experience of "encountering (another) home."

These metaphors are *Tong-Shaan* (*Tang-shan*) (or *Tong* mountain) and *Gum-Shaan* (*Jinshan*) (in standard Cantonese *Gaam-shaan*) (or Gold(en) mountain). *Tong-Shaan* is a metaphor for "home" in Central Gwongdung; and *Gum-Shaan* is a metaphor for "home" in America, or more expansively all of North America.

Cantonese overseas emigrants, from the moment of their departure from *Tong-Shaan* were constantly obsessed with the difficult task of "when and how" to return home to *Tong-Shaan*, thereby fulfilling both the purpose of leaving home and the promise of return. The problematic challenge to this simple proposition of returning home to *Tong-Shaan*, was the enigmatic quandary of sojourning in *Gum-Shaan*. This situation presented itself as a difficult to decipher and resolve contradiction, regarding how to reconcile the Cantonese emigrant/sojourner's shifting loyalty to his "temporary" home in *Gum-Shaan*, with his loyalty to his "permanent" home of *Tong-Shaan*.

These two metaphors may appear as a set of balanced bookends propping up the sojourner experience, whereby each conceptually complements the other in a symmetrical fashion. This oversimplification belies the fact that the two metaphors are not strictly speaking equal in their ascribed characteristics and function, as metaphors for home.

The *Gum-Shaan* metaphor projects a simple, straightforward, and easy to grasp construct. *Gum-Shaan*, as Gold(en) Mountain is exactly what it represented itself to be, a metaphor well-grounded in the concrete, the factual, and historical. Cantonese emigrants initially came to America in large numbers, because of the lure of gold during the California Gold Rush of 1849. For the next half century, successive gold and silver strikes in Oregon, Washington, Nevada, British Columbia, The Dakotas, and Alaska continued to fuel the *Gum-Shaan* dream of seeking wealth from gold and silver mining, despite the development of numerous other avenues to achieve material prosperity (e.g., commercial agriculture and railroad construction, etc.) Quite simply, gold strikes provided a convenient, accurate and authentic basis for the metaphor of *Gum-Shaan*, as a place with specific physical features and reliable representations that anyone and everyone could readily understand and relate to.

The case of the *Tong-Shaan* metaphor represents an entirely different matter. In addition to representing the notion of a Cantonese emigrant's permanent home in Central Gwongdung, *Tong-Shaan* also symbolized another abstraction with its own set of nuanced historical and cultural associations. In this regard, there exists the need to not only to distinguish between *Gum-Shaan* and *Tong-Shaan*, but to also examine more closely the more complicated *Tong-Shaan* metaphor.

*Tong-Shaan* embodies the notion of a "Cantonese Fountainhead," which facilitates the interweaving of discrete elements, such as history, geography, demography, ethnicity, language/speech, and culture, as they materialized within both a comparative historical context and transnational/diasporic environment. Consequently, the commonality of which I speak, relative to a shared sense of Cantonese identity and experience, is embodied in, and flows from, the notion of a "Cantonese Fountainhead." This proposition serves as a useful starting point, and much needed standard, for re-evaluating what it meant to be Cantonese in both China and America, in the period 1850-1900.

**Locating and giving form to the notion of a Cantonese Fountainhead**

In seeking to locate and give shape to the idea of a traditional Cantonese fountainhead, I utilize a two-part discussion. First, earlier I introduced the idea of Central Gwongdung, as a regional site and material basis for conceptualizing about the historical homeland of Cantonese society and its *Yuet* culture, (see chapter 1). In support of this view, I analyzed key geophysical, demographic, and ethno-speech components, as they constituted a material basis for thinking about the idea of a traditional Cantonese fountainhead. Second, here in this chapter, I formulate a much needed and useful theoretical construct, to explain the nature and meaning of the idea of a traditional Cantonese fountainhead, relative to why it mattered so much in traditional Cantonese society and culture. Simply put, here I move beyond examining the material basis for conceptualizing about a Cantonese fountainhead, to actually thinking about its practical application.

The Cantonese community historically formed a distinct regional community, with its own character, arising from inwardly common and outwardly distinct variables. These elements embraced a wide variety of geo-territorial, demographic, ecological, economic, socio-cultural, and ethno-linguistic criteria. Over time, this interrelatedness of the sense of community in Cantonese Central Gwongdung mirrored a substantial interconnectedness, within a complex pattern of development, to the extent that it provided a well-defined and strong material basis for theorizing about *Tong-Shaan* as a Cantonese fountainhead.

## The "idea" and "ideal" of "*Tong-Shaan*," as the traditional Cantonese fountainhead

In the nineteenth-century, there existed a bifurcated view of what the Pearl River Delta Region represented, and how it related to Cantonese experience at home and overseas. First, Central Gwongdung, and especially the Pearl River Delta Region (PRDR), existed as a "Cantonese Homeland," where Cantonese speech, Cantonese traditions, Cantonese experience, and Cantonese core values were essential metrics by which Cantonese identity was defined and experience measured. This frame of reference bound Cantonese people together and guided their movements both leaving and returning home in Central Gwongdung. Second, nineteenth-century large-scale Cantonese overseas emigration originated chiefly from within this pivotal area. This dichotomous situation, where Cantonese society encountered major geo-demographic changes, amid increasingly troubled times, stimulated a major shift in how Cantonese people in Central Gwongdung, and elsewhere, thought about home and the dilemma of leaving it. This involved a conscious change in thinking about what the Cantonese homeland represented, and how one related to it. It also involved an unconscious subjective response to changing perceptions of reality in flux, where instability and change replaced stability and permanence, as new milestones of emigrant/sojourner life on the road.

The nexus linking the contemporary Cantonese diaspora with homes scattered all across the Cantonese rural landscape, gave rise to the notion of a Cantonese Fountainhead, as a changing perspective about "home." This new idea of a Cantonese fountainhead contrasted with the earlier view regarding "home" as the Cantonese homeland. The latter centered on the material facts of a Cantonese dominated turf, located in Central Gwongdung, specifically in the Pearl River Delta Region. This was understood historically in terms of a place associated with daily life, agricultural production, and commercial activity, framed by traditional Cantonese thinking and conduct. In the newly emergent idea of a Cantonese fountainhead, there developed an alternative context for understanding what "home" represented in the Cantonese mindset. Due largely to the accelerated expansion of Cantonese overseas emigration, as framed within a transnational/diasporic context, the earlier notion of a Cantonese homeland seemed too myopic in its perspective, and too parochial in its construction. Attention had revolved around the fact that the Cantonese were from a particular location, where fixed spatial features and established social parameters mattered most in the construction of the Cantonese persona, all of which ignored the facts of a changing reality.

In the expanded context of mid-late nineteenth-century overseas emigration, the physical link between people and the place they left was all too obvious. In contrast, the newer view of a Cantonese fountainhead called attention to the organic nexus between Cantonese emigrants and their home, which focused not only on physical separation, but also emphasized and valued the many ties that bound Cantonese people together, (see chapter 5.) In this context, the notion of a Cantonese Fountainhead, underscored the need to preserve historical, social, cultural, communal, and ethno-linguistic ties between those who left and those who remained behind. This new perspective was dynamic, yet also subtle, because it was a more realistic understanding of the metaphor for "home," where the calculus of adversity and opportunity engineered a new iconic graphic representation of *Tong-Shaan*, as the Cantonese Fountainhead.

This new perspective embraced a two-way transnational organic flow of emigrants, material goods, and finances between *Tong-Shaan* and *Gum-Shaan*, and other Cantonese outposts scattered around the world. It underscored the essence of what a "fountainhead" represented, by way of a starting place from which identities, experiences, traditions, and practices originate and flow outward. It was also the place where emigrants, and their progeny located elsewhere, could look back with inspiration and appreciation, regarding their deep sense of historical legitimacy, cultural authenticity, socio-communal continuity, and ethno-speech purity.

## The Cantonese Sojourner Dilemma Syndrome (CSDS)

The intimate nexus between the Cantonese overseas emigrant and "home" provided both the structural basis and a useful framework for the notion of an historical Cantonese Fountainhead. This relationship revealed itself through a series of complex mental and emotional changes in how Cantonese emigrants thought about self, home, and sojourning. These changes were embodied in a clinical condition, which I label as the "Cantonese sojourner dilemma syndrome" or CSDS. An understanding of CSDS can help us better appreciate the meaning of the historical Cantonese Fountainhead, as both the location of Cantonese society and source of the *Yue*/Cantonese identity, as well as a metaphor for one's permanent home in Central Gwongdung.

The Cantonese sojourner, beyond mirroring the emigration-immigration experience, represented a new chapter in the Cantonese tradition of leaving home, as "migration." He embodied a new, evolving persona, which re-defined the sojourner experience, and reconfigured the traditional relationships associated with it. This arose from the dilemma of trying to reconcile elements of that experience with the myth that it gave rise to.

Traditionally, most works on Chinese emigrants/immigrants have focused on the mechanics of departure, arrival, settlement, and adjustment in the face of adversity. Little attention has been given to the sojourner's mindset and outlook, regarding his own changing self-perceptions about "self, home, and sojourning." This has been due largely to the paucity of documentary materials on this subject, which in turn results from the fact that few Cantonese overseas emigrants ever thought about, much less wrote or articulated their feelings about the sojourner dilemma.[2]

In introducing the concept of a "Cantonese Sojourner Dilemma Syndrome (CSDS), I call attention to the personal subjective dimension of sojourning abroad. Beyond the immediate tasks of living and working in a strange place, and coping with a new language and culture, the Cantonese sojourner also had to come to terms with his feelings about the experience of sojourning. Over time, Cantonese vernacular rhyme poetry became a common vehicle for expressing a wide array of personal feelings and emotions about the ordeal of overseas emigration and sojourning. In the remainder of this chapter, I utilize such poetry, translated into English, as evidence of a wide range of feelings, perceptions, and responses of Cantonese immigrant/settlers, regarding their sense of dilemma in later Nineteenth and early Twentieth-Century China and Chinese America. Much of the content of this poetry expressed itself in a personal sense of predicament, often expressed as a contradictory mixture of intense anxiety and numbing ambivalence. The unforeseen and unpredictable only complicated and intensified this sense of predicament.

### *The Cantonese Sojourner Dilemma*

Each Cantonese sojourner shared in a common purpose and promise. Again, the "purpose" was to gain material success overseas, via good luck and hard work.[3] The "promise" underscored a commitment to return home with enough money to settle down in comfort and security. The common expectation assumed that sojourning overseas would involve hardship and self-sacrifice. Thus, sojourner experience carried with it an implied contradiction, where good intentions, grand visions, and happy dreams of success were juxtaposed with a very harsh and grim reality of life overseas. Given the reality of long-term, or even permanent residence abroad, the contradiction presented a great challenge to the Cantonese sojourner. Over time the "promise" to return became harder to keep amid radically different material conditions (e.g., Chinese Exclusion). This reality also mirrored a parallel uncertainty, regarding the validity of the "purpose" motivating overseas emigration. The resulting sense of confusion and uncertainty embraced both the sojourner and his family members back home.

> My son, Take notice: …Your mother worries about you all the time…You have been away from home for years. During that time, your second elder brother died, then your father died, and then your eldest brother died too…I am old and weak now and I may die at

any moment...You should save some money and should come back at least next year. I know my days are numbered. You won't see me anymore; I may already be gone, by the time you come back. Would you feel sorry then? ...Come back, don't forget your mother, please. Your Mother [4]

My son, your business has proved profitless for a long time now... Come home as soon as you can. Don't say "no" to me any more... You are my only son. You have no brothers, and your age is now forty, but still without a male offspring. You should think carefully. If you neither make a fortune abroad nor have a son at home, your loss is double. So why not come home before it is too late? ...You have been away from home for seventeen years, you know nothing about our domestic situation.... We need you, you must come back. Your Father [5]

Take Notice, My Son: You have been away for more than a decade. Men go abroad in order to earn money to support their families, but you have never sent us money or letters since then...Are you intending to let us starve to death?... Even if you don't think of your mother and me, you should think of your wife and son... I remember what you had said when we were both in Gold Mountain. You said, "Let the old go back home and rest. Let the young seek fortune abroad."... I have been back and you have sent no money...Send some money immediately to meet the urgent need at home.... Your Father[6]

When both the "purpose" and the "promise" were undermined and divorced from a radically altered reality, then the sojourner experienced a profound emotional/psychological dilemma. This took a variety of forms, ranging from a shift in the construction of ethnic group identity, to various emotional and psychological clinical conditions.

In the 1970s many Asian American fiction writers and social science specialists intentionally deemphasized Old-World linkages, because they were anachronistic distractions. They chose instead to focus on the New-World challenge of being an "Asian American," i.e., "Chinese American." Issues of acculturation and assimilation were social processes that merited study, as a means of both explaining the dilemma of sojourning and the best means of overcoming it.[7] These alternative experiences and expectations were viewed as a useful way to undermine, and beneficially distract, from sojourner anxieties. In short, if Chinese immigrants were here to stay, then it would be better to focus on ways on how to get on with it, rather than dwell on the moot questions of the purpose and promise of sojourning.

Admittedly, this later twentieth-century rationale does little to help us understand the nineteenth-century precedent and its associated sense of predicament, where different material conditions and emigrant-immigrant mindsets prevailed. These alternatives to sojourning, (i.e., acculturation/assimilation,) did not remedy or mitigate the dilemma of Cantonese-Chinese emigrant sojourner life in America, rather they complicated and expanded it, by adding new problems requiring even more challenging responses, from already emotionally stressed and psychologically burdened sojourner-settlers. In a more personal and subjective context, anxieties stemming from the frustrations of overseas sojourner experience took many forms, including depression, intense anxiety, and a deep sense of loss, helplessness, frustration, and ambivalence.

> Born into a rotten life,
> Coming or going, all without leaving my mark.
> Even after leaving the village for a foreign country,
> running about east and west, I've gained nothing.
> Everything's turned upside down;
> it's more disconcerting being away from home.
> I have gone to the four corners of the world;
> Alas, I am neither at ease while resting nor happy while moving.[8]

It is this latter category of responses that invites my attention, because they focus on the subjective area of personal perspectives, as mirrored in thoughts, and feelings- an area of recent interest by mental health professionals, (but unfortunately, not so among historians) after seminal changes in American immigration laws impacting Chinese and other Asian groups in the late 1960s.[9] Here, I argue that the anxieties of nineteenth-century overseas Cantonese emigrants, as manifested in a set of clinical responses to sojourning overseas in America and elsewhere, took the form of a syndrome (i.e., a condition or disorder) with clinical characteristics, conditioned by traditional Cantonese beliefs, practices, and experiences.

## Components and Operation of CSDS

The key elements of CSDS (Cantonese sojourner dilemma syndrome) are: 1) motion and emotion; 2) adversity and nostalgia; 3) nostalgia and the iconographic reconstruction of home as landscape; 4) the iconographic reconstruction of landscape as a sacred place; 5) the iconized Cantonese landscape, with *Shaan* as a metaphor for a special or sacred Place; 6) *Tong Shaan* and *Gum Shaan*, as later nineteenth-century and early twentieth-century Cantonese metaphors for home in China and in America; and 7) CSDS and the dilemma of sojourning and its iconographic reconstruction.

### *Motion and Emotion*

An essential feature of the sojourner experience involved the challenge of continuous movement. From the very outset, the Cantonese sojourner existed in a state of perpetual motion. Departing home for a long difficult trans-Pacific journey merely opened a door to endless travel. Cantonese sojourners spent most of their time on the road, traveling from job to job, or searching for opportunities to start a small business. Such movement might take the form of a solitary sojourner on the road, or more typically it involved sojourners traveling together in well-organized teams, under the sponsorship and direction of their own bosses. In the early 1850s this meant traveling and working all over Northern California, and from the 1860s onwards Cantonese migrants were a common sight throughout California.[10] By the 1870s, they worked in the Pacific Northwest, the Great Basin, the Rocky Mountain region, the American Southwest, Western Texas, the northern Great Plains, and in parts of the Deep South.[11] After the mid-1880s, they were common in urban centers in the Midwest. By the

1890s, they established their own ethnic communities all along the Atlantic coast.[12] Over time, links were forged with other overseas Cantonese communities in Hawaii, Western Canada, Mexico, and the Caribbean, with constant movement among and between them. Movement also involved, when time and money allowed, return trips home, either for brief temporary visits after a few years overseas, alternately one could make a permanent return after making a sum of money, or because of old age or death. Cantonese emigrant/immigrant movement occurred every day, every week, every month, all year round.

> Drifting around, all over the place,
> Seeking food everywhere, in all four directions.
> Turning east, going west, always on an uncertain road;
> toiling, rushing about, much ado for nothing.
> Fed by wind and frost,
> I search for wealth, but all in vain.
> If fate indeed has excluded me so, what more can I say?
> After years of sojourn, I sigh in fear. [13]

The constant motion of sojourner movement involved a parallel emotional adjustment. The life of a sojourner required "traveling light," of not being weighed down with excess material and emotional baggage. Emphasis centered not only on mobility, but also maintaining an unfettered inner self. Emotions were not allowed to surface, to distract, or to compromise one's work.[14] This should not be taken to mean that the Cantonese sojourner became a robot, devoid of human feelings. On the contrary, there is much evidence to suggest that, if emotions were held in check, they were never far below the surface and were often ready to burst forth.[15] Indeed, one could argue that while the sojourner tried to keep his emotions under wrap, the constant motion of travel and movement often unavoidably triggered unintended emotional responses. The many stresses of sojourner life invariably stimulated different kinds of emotional and psychological responses. For some, it resulted in a deep anxiety over one's well-being; and for others, emotions were numbed by ambivalence, resulting in a cold stoic countenance.

> Toiling in pain, east and west, all in vain;
> hurrying about, north and south, still more rushing.
> What can a person do with a life full of mishap?
> Searching, scheming, on all four sides, not one good lead in sight.
> Eyes brimming with tears:
> O, I just can't get rid of the misery.
> My belly is full of frustration and grievance;
> When life is at low ebb, I suffer dearly.[16]

Sojourner emotions were alternately switched on and off. When switched off, the emotions became cold, ambivalent, often underscored by a self-fulfilling fatalism, as commonly identified with the notion of "eating bitterness."[17] In doing so, the sojourner could tap new reserves of strength via untapped sources of energy. There was no wasted energy in wild emotions. This helped protect the inner self and made it more resistant to the ravages of emotional conflict. Alternately, given the right timing and conditions, the emotions could be switched on. Especially good times or bad events could trigger the release of strong emotions. An especially bad event or experience, e.g., news of the death of a loved one or close friend, and repeatedly voiced complaints about hardships at home, could release a torrent of sad feelings. This predicament centered on reminders about desperate family members back home and the parallel lack of material success overseas.

> Letters from home are frequent and urgent:
> Urging me to return to Tong-Shaan (China).
> I hesitate: my purse is not full.
> I am ashamed: I have no excuse for my fault.
> But, how am I to explain it all?
> So, my homebound journey is postponed.
> I am only afraid my parents will be waiting with ever longing eyes.
> O, why don't I just pack up for home now, while there is still time?[18]

## Chapter 6

The stupefying effects of opium, alcohol, or sex could also release pent-up emotions regarding, regret, helplessness, lost opportunities, and poor choices made.

> Face haggard, turning yellow and puffy,
> waist, bent like a drawn bow.
> Lying on his side next to a small lamp,
> He holds the pipe as his family fortune goes down its hole.
> Look at him:
> Soon he will be six feet underground.
> Lazy, remiss, he won't move even if you drag him.
> He is about to meet King Yimlo at hell's tenth palace.*[19]

* King Yimlo is the ruler of the underworld and renders final judgement over the deeds of the dead. The 10th palace hands out the most severe punishments.

> Opium is the most poisonous;
> Ruining families, weakening the race.
> Once you are addicted to it, your life is gone to waste.
> Before the smoking lamp, you are constantly in a daze.
> O, strike the warning bell-
> Shape up, don't be an addict to it anymore!
> If you still cannot make this move,
> you will sink deep into a bitter sea, and suffer endless remorse![20]

> Life is a dream, an illusion:
> A twenty-year span of fun and games.
> Hugging the one in red, leaning on the one in green,
> O what joy and gaiety!
> Treasure the youthful years: once they are gone, they never return
> Before that time comes—
> What man won't hanker after pretty faces

like a butterfly lingering around lustrous flowers?
A death from passion is really nothing.[21]

The passage of time was an especially persistent and vexing source of anxiety for men who had left home in their late teens and early twenties, but who many years and even decades later were still chasing their dreams of financial independence and material well-being.

Who could have guessed the sojourn would last so long?
Had I known, I wouldn't have come at all.
Separated by many mountains and seas,
I have forsaken wife and children to seek my fortune.
Heart bleeds in pain.
A sojourner thousands of miles from home.
Time passes ever so quickly, but a reunion is so hard to come by;
I just don't know when I can start my homebound journey.[22]

Intense feelings of loneliness, heartbreak, disappointment, impatience, frustration, betrayal, pain, unfairness, and unhappiness were easily aroused, because they underscored the harsh realities of sojourner life in America. They invariably distorted perceptions and colored experiences.

Now that I have thought everything over:
I am all confused.
Needless to say I feel concern for my parents,
I am also burdened with thoughts of my wife and children.
Why so?'
'Cause I cannot make it home.
I look around- north, south, east, west- and
I don't know which direction is home.[23]

Conversely feelings of excitement, anticipation, pride, success, good luck, were infrequent and short-lived. Similarly, drug/alcohol induced euphoria were also typically transitory in nature, where the aftermath of a "reality check" was even more stark and painful. Temptations, in the form of prostitution, opium, drinking, and gambling were easily available, one only had to have some cash handy. These diversions provided emotional drifts via hard-to-resist hedonistic impulses. Again, the rapid passage of time, the loss of one's youth, and the vagaries of an uncertain future opened the door to many such temptations.

> At eighteen or twenty-two,
> Young man, don't forget:
> It's best to enjoy life when the time is right.
> Should you wait til old age comes,
> There won't be any more fun.
> Just think about this, each of you-
> All of the singing and dancing in places of merriment,
> If you pretend to be upright and won't lay your finger on this,
> You're wasting a splendid moment and you are but a fool.[24]

An exception to the rule of constant motion and its impact upon sojourner emotions existed in traditional Cantonese Opera. Despite the fact that the Cantonese community in mid-later Nineteenth-Century America had only recently established itself, and had only a token presence in small concentrations, spread over an immense area, it had managed however, to quickly resurrect a familiar façade of communal institutions and practices. In this context, Cantonese opera, quickly became a much sought after and much appreciated form of entertainment for scores of Cantonese emigrant/immigrants in Northern California, and subsequently all over the American West. Cantonese opera aroused strong emotions among Cantonese audiences both at home in *Tong-Shaan* and also overseas in *Gum-Shaan*.

> For Cantonese opera, the latter half of the nineteenth century witnessed a revolution toward a distinctive form of musical drama in its home region of the Pearl River Delta. Amazingly...[it] also marked the dawn of diaspora history...unmatched by any other

genres of traditional Chinese opera...[in] North America... like their counterparts in Guangdong [Gwongdung], the visiting troupes were equipped to travel lightly so that they could reach out to entertain their countrymen scattered in mining settlements in California.[25]

Cantonese opera had enormous appeal among popular masses, many of whom were uneducated and lead mundane lives in poor rural and urban areas. Its glittering color, rich array of stunning costumes, make-up, props and scenery, mechanical devices, aerobatics, orchestral music, singing of arias, and story-telling attracted and delighted large loyal audiences. Among Cantonese audiences everywhere, but perhaps especially so among those overseas, e.g., in Canada and America, certain aspects of Cantonese theater/opera were especially compelling and much appreciated. This included: humor and satire, the expanding vernacularization (use of Cantonese) in stage dialogues and in operatic singing, and the need for happy endings.[26]

Happy ending [in Cantonese opera], in the sense of seeing justice done, broken families or separated couples reunited, and reward for the good and punishment of the bad, was seemingly an important source of psychological reassurance, pleasure, and comfort to [Cantonese] audiences.[27]

Nineteenth-Century Cantonese opera in its expanded transnational setting both institutionally contextualized and logistically transported home-sick Cantonese emigrant sojourners back home with emotional affirmation and psychological conditioning, all tailored to fit their situation.

a theater allowed the audience to congregate, to be boisterous and even rowdy, and to have fun...[it] allowed the participants and onlookers alike to gain a measure of momentary pleasure and psychological release...[28]

Cantonese opera, with its lewd suggestiveness, coarse language, and vulgar references, [29] as well as its glittering visuals and the loud, often jarring, yet still comforting sounds of its music and song, was irresistibly alluring for the nearly-all-young-male audiences in distant overseas Wah-Q communities. Indeed, the compelling attraction of Cantonese opera flowed from its ability to excite Cantonese sensibilities, while cushioning Cantonese insecurities. It entertained in an especially compelling way because it manipulated emotions with ample doses of nostalgia, where ideas, visions, and memories of home came alive in a make-believe nineteenth-century prototype of virtual reality. Such entertainment, like prostitution, drinking, opium, and gambling, offered a momentary respite from the rigors of an unforgiving harsh reality encountered by most Cantonese sojourners in America and elsewhere overseas. Significantly, the cost to attend performances of Cantonese opera, unlike the price of admission/participation in the vice trades,[30] was cheap and it did not endanger the health and well-being of its legions of loyal fans. Local Cantonese Opera performances were much sought after, as emotionally satisfying experiences.

Intense Cantonese anxiety about self and home also expressed itself in a new sense of urgency and engagement in ethnic community daily life.[31] Significantly, Cantonese opera/theater played a critical role in the development of a new civic culture, because it enhanced local Cantonese homosocial engagement. It did so paradoxically by providing positive strokes of socialization within the context of a "bachelor society," which helped to mitigate the adverse consequences of competition and conflict, commonly identified with Cantonese web-group institutional affiliations.[32] In this regard, Cantonese opera/theater, offered itself as "a new public space" in overseas Cantonese community life. It did so physically, where the theater offered a particular location and physical space dedicated exclusively to public spectacle within the ethnic community. It also provided a nurturing emotional/psychological space, where locals could in a manner of speaking, "let themselves go" without the usual restraints of social conformity and fear of embarrassment, resulting from uncontrolled emotions.

> For an immigrant population that consisted predominantly of adult males, Cantonese opera could not be more welcome as hometown entertainment… The indulgence in nostalgia and fantasy offered unspeakable pleasure, and so did the opportunity for socializing among peers… It was the pleasure of amnesia, to forget the distance from home that entailed separation and loss, and to forget the immediate drudgery, alienation, and loneliness in the land of ghosts. A theater was eagerly sought as a refuge and a home, even for just a moment, in the life of a sojourner….[33]

Beyond the immediate distractions of local Cantonese opera and homosocial civic engagement, the stark realities of sojourning persisted. In the extreme, they could contribute to madness, self-inflicted harm, or danger, made unavoidable by either inattentiveness or carelessness. Misfortune was ever present to wreak havoc on good intentions and happy dreams. In order to avoid such dangers, defensive mechanisms were developed.

One tactic involved the adoption of an external facade of passive acceptance, marked by silence and forbearance. In this manner, there was little that anyone else might say or do to bother or hurt the Cantonese sojourner, short of physical violence. This stance mirrored the traditional belief that best way to deal with matters beyond one's ability to control, was to adopt an outward stance of seeming compliance, while simultaneously embodying cynical acceptance.[34] The former manifested a tactical move to accept and conform to conditions beyond one's ability to change or mitigate, whereby conformance and compliance were necessary and expedient. The latter mirrored a strategic move, whereby passive/aggressive engagement was effectively camouflaged by a passive, but cynical acceptance, as a means of self-preservation, until conditions changed.

> To be hard pressed by poverty is truly disgusting.
> Yet it's all due to fate.
> Since antiquity, great men have often
> had to contend with adversity;

Remember, the cycle of life is Heaven's way.
So, there is no need to complain.
All matters will turn around in the end, they always do;
One day, Heaven's eyes will no longer wink at me,*
and we'll go back to Tong-Shaan (China) with enough money.[35]

*A Cantonese expression meaning positive retribution for a good deed

The traditional tactic of seeming compliance and the strategy of cynical acceptance was a cardinal feature of the traditional Chinese socialization process, which Cantonese society fully embraced. In this process, children were taught from an early age that it was essential to maintain guarded emotions and avoid exposed sentiments, by separating passion and action. The socialization process, first within the immediate family, then in the expanded lineage, the village/hamlet or urban neighborhood community, and more generally society respectively, instilled in each individual the need for self-discipline, which required complete control at all times over one's emotions. This experience was shared by legions of Cantonese overseas emigrants.

> …once a child has reached the age of awareness he[/she] is taught that controlled behavior is more likely than emotional outbursts to bring results and rewards…pressure is brought …to make him[/her] inhibit all emotional displays and to understand that correct conduct is affectively neutral. The…critical distinction between a child and an adult is that the child acts in direct response to his emotions and an adult acts without any apparent emotion. Childlike behavior involves the…coupling of passion and action, while in adult behavior these are separated.[36] … Also, the child learns from observing the ways in which adults handle their own feelings (,) that reserve and emotional impassiveness are appropriate ways to discipline these inner urges.[37]

The ability to control one's emotions conserved one's limited energy, while enabling one to think more clearly about a dilemma and how best to carefully respond to it. This ability provided Cantonese immigrant/sojourners in America a useful coping mechanism for encountering the harsh rigors of immigration interrogation during the Chinese Exclusion Era, 1882–1943.

> There are tens of thousands of poems composed on these walls.
> They are all cries of complaint and sadness.
> The day I am rid of this prison and attain success,
> I must remember that this chapter once existed.
> In my daily needs, I must be frugal.
> Needless extravagance leads youth to ruin.
> All my compatriots should please be mindful.
> Once you have some small gains, return home early.[38]

This stance offered an effective shield against a hostile environment. Internally, however, there existed a complex blend of confidence and apprehensiveness, springing from cynical hyper-sensitive defensiveness. There evolved over time, a new functional relationship between "motion" and "emotion," whereby each helped propel and sustain the sojourner overseas. They did not materialize as static, unrelated elements, but merged as connected entities with convergent and divergent pulses, in ever-changing combinations, impacting how the sojourner saw himself, his sense of dilemma, and his changing world.

> Dispirited by life in my village home,
> I make a journey to the United States of America.
> Separated by mountains and passes,
> I feel an extreme anxiety and grief;
> Rushing about east and west does me no good.
> Turning in all directions-
> An ideal opportunity has yet to come.
> If fate is indeed Heaven's will, what more can I say?'
> Tis a disgrace to a man's pride and dignity.[39]

Life is like a vast, long dream.
Why grieve over poverty?
A contented life soothes ten thousand matters.
Value the help from other people.
In all earnest, just endure:
You can forget about cold and hunger, as you see them often.
After lasting through winter's chill and snow's embrace,
You will find joy in life when happiness comes and sorrow fades.[40]

***Adversity and Nostalgia***

Sojourner adversity stimulated, among other things, a heightened and exaggerated sense of nostalgia. It did so by stimulating visions of home, as a distraction from the rigors of daily life. In the process of dreaming about home, an imaginative reconstruction often took place, where ascribed images took the place of reality. In time, this changing perception of home affected how the Cantonese sojourner viewed and related to people and places that were important to him. The result was an ongoing mental and emotional reconstruction of "home," as a means of compensating for a life of adversity overseas.

Often I dream of the moment I return to South China.
When the dream ends, my eyes are in a daze.
In dream after dream, I'm back in Sunning*
Wife, children, the village well- all in my dream.
O, let the dreams never end.
Dream again, another wonderful dream.
But dreams of my prolonged incarceration here set my heart aflame.
Dream, dream- How I would like to dream of home again![41]
*In 1914 the *Say-Yup* district of Sunning was re-named Toi-Shaan.

Adversity came in many forms and along many fronts. It might flow from personal physical and/or mental health problems, financial hardship associated with unemployment, mounting debts from unpaid loans, a business venture gone sour, or bad luck at gambling or with women (or both).

A brave man meeting an untimely adversity,
All day long, unable to eat or sleep.
Rushing about over ten thousand miles, deep in sorrow.
Every hour, every minute, mind and body toil in pain.
Heaven's will is extreme!
This big Roc wants to spread its wings.*
Yet scores are not evened up; the mind is not at ease.
Alas, I can't rest in peace, I just can't rest in peace.[42]
*Roc" is an allusion from the classical work Zhuang zi, it refers to
a person about to seek out a great future.

Misfortune could also result from compromised relationships with family and friends, who have simply lost touch, or who have severed ties out of ignorance or some unforeseen misunderstanding. News of an unexpected crisis, illness, or death back home, made worse because of helplessness, resulting from being so far away and being unable to help resolve difficulties back home, was a common challenge facing Cantonese sojourners in America. Similarly, illness, injury, and death of a relative or friend either in the same local overseas Cantonese community, or elsewhere in some other distant location could also release raw feelings of sadness and regret.

Shocking news, truly sad, reached my ears.
We mourn you. When will they wrap your corpse for return?
You cannot close your eyes.
Whom are you depending on to voice your complaints?
If you had foresight, you should have regretted coming here.
Now you will be forever sad and forever resentful.
Thinking of the village, one can only futilely
face the terrace for Gazing Homeward. *
Before you could fulfill your ambition,
you were buried beneath clay and earth.
I know that even death could not destroy your ambition.[43]

*refers to story of two princesses who fled civil strife to distant place, married and settled down in a village, but they still missed home, so locals built a terrace facing their homeland, so that they could gaze in that direction.

There also existed a host of difficulties that flowed from dysfunctional relationships within the ethnic community, or with American society beyond it. Insecurity could arise alternately from incurring the resentment and wrath of an individual, group, or organization within a local overseas Cantonese community. It could also result from the hostility of a crazy, hot-headed American drunk, or the irrational frenzy of White American mob violence.

Since coming to the frontier land,
I have taken all kinds of abuse from the barbarians.
have come across the horizon to the flowery flag nation;*
The surroundings still fill me with thoughts of home.
All we need is profit and money.
Should our purses be stuffed with gold,
we'll pick out a date and have our homebound whip ready.[44]

*Flowery flag nation refers to the American flag, over time it became a nickname for US during the period 1890–1940

Ongoing suspicion, interrogation, and intervention by prejudicial local/state/federal authorities also made sojourner life very stressful, sparking added feelings of pain and resentment.

America has power, but not justice.
In prison, we were victimized as if we were guilty. *
Given no opportunity to explain, it was really brutal.
I bow my head in reflection but there is nothing I can do.[45]

*Prison refers to interrogation at US Immigration detention centers

At times when someone happened to anger the barbarians,
they would beat us with fists and feet.
If they felt a brutal impulse, they would aim a gun at us.[46]

Among sojourners, relative to the passage of time and the loss of one's youth, there always persisted a personal sense of helplessness and bitterness. When the months rolled into years, and the years into decades, many sojourners could not help but be saddened by the fact that the passing years robbed many of them of their robust health and energetic youth. There only existed so much time and energy in each person's life. Each sojourner at some point in time asked himself difficult questions, "Is my time well spent?" or even harder to ask, "Has it been well spent?" "Is the best already past, without having resulted in success?" "Are the best years really gone?" "Is there a second chance for me?" Everyone only has a finite amount of energy, against so many lost opportunities. In America, adversity was the sojourner's constant companion.

As a rule, a person is twenty before he starts making a living.
Family circumstances have forced me to experience wind and dust.
The heartless months and years seem bent on defeating me
It is a pity that time quickly ages one.[47]

Look at that face in the mirror:
My appearance so completely changed.
Hair white as frost, long beard hanging;
Disheartening are the bald spots sparkling like stars.
Old age has arrived.
No longer is my face young and handsome.
Without my noticing, I am already over forty.
Shame in toiling in hardship, across the vast and distant oceans.[48]

There were many ways of responding to adversity and the many unhappy feelings identified with it. Most sojourners chose to work even harder and longer, tightly focused on their goals and dreams, via endless self-sacrifices.

I have walked to the very ends of the earth.
A dusty, windy journey.
I've toiled and I am worn out, all for a miserable lot.
Nothing is ideal when I am down and out.
I think about it day and night-
Who can save a fish out of water?
From far away, I worry for my parents, my wife, and my boy;
Do they have enough firewood, rice, salt, and cooking oil? [49]

Some sought a measure of solace in different sources of inspiration and comfort, e.g., traditional Taoist/Buddhist religious rituals and practices, others in the fellowship of new ethnic Christian churches (late in the nineteenth century).[50] Many became actively involved in their local community civic culture. Hyperactive homosocial engagement via various associations and clubs took on greater importance and meaning, beyond mere affiliation. There also developed a variety of music, literary, and martial-arts clubs, for those interested, knowledgeable and proficient.[51] For many, there was the temptation of short cuts and sure bets through gambling, or joining the tongs, as a member of organized crime. Regardless of how one responded to adversity, there was always the image and memory of home that surfaced to stir up deeply moving feelings.

Though I have journeyed to the very ends of the earth,
I cannot forget my ancestral home.
The traveler, in the still of the night, thinks of his family.
Tossing and turning, thoughts whirling asleep, awake.
In dreams, my soul flies back to the village.
Fields and gardens seem so barren and abandoned.
O, why didn't I go home? Why don't I go home? [52]

These images borne out of adversity formed the basis of a very powerful nostalgia. Over time nostalgia formed a complementary relationship with adversity, where both helped to shape Cantonese sojourner outlook and experience. Overseas, amid adversity, it was increasingly hard, to remember clearly and accurately the prevailing conditions that originally prompted one to leave home and emigrate overseas. Amid the difficulties of sojourning in America, one easily and conveniently, repressed thoughts about the particulars of poverty, desperateness, unhappiness, insecurity, and instability back home. The memory of overcrowded villages, with their stench and filth, the lack of adequate food and money, the pervasive sense of hopelessness, and the chronic lack of opportunity for improvement, often faded with the passing of time.

> The journey is thousands of miles of vast distance.
> From afar, I remember my home garden.
> My dear wife must be tossing and turning in her sleep for me.
> O, how I wish my business will bring me fortune.
> To South China, I would return:
> My young son would stare at me by the door.
> Brothers would meet, like geese after a long journey.
> And, my parents would beam happy in the living room.[53]

Over time, one's memory could begin to play tricks. Soon, it was hard to distinguish between the reality of things as they were, and the reconstructed make-believe images of lonely hard-working nostalgic sojourners.

> The cool wind and bright moon make a pitiful night
> The desolate feeling is aggravated by my solitary body
> under the quilt in the wooden building.
> The traveler thinks of his native village,
> where he once kept company with a willow.
> You, my dear, had no intention of travelling because of
> your fondness for the banana plant by the window.
> Su'e* does not know the suffering among mankind.
> The whites only imprison sojourners from Dongya.**
> It is unlike living in the village, ploughing and studying.
> A leisurely life, with firewood and rice, one is content
> using a basket and gourd.[54]

*Su'e Better known as Chang'e, a goddess who lives in the moon.
** Dongya was a village in Chung-Shaan (Zhongshan) district/county.

The constant mixing of adversity and anxiety in the daily lives of masses of poor Cantonese emigrants/immigrants typically resulted in a relentless obsession with striking it rich. In this context, every thought, every action revolved around dreams of getting rich. It served as a much sought-after distraction from the rigors of endless work and personal sacrifice. This distraction, unlike drinking, opium, gambling and sex with prostitutes, cost nothing, but its allure was perhaps even more compelling and its hold even more tenacious and all-consuming.

> At the moment, I hardly have enough grub to eat.
> But I won't take it as my fate, my final destiny.
> I don't believe I will live like this till my hair turns white;
> It's only the low ebb in my life.
> When luck strikes, with the whole world behind me,
> I will be rich in a few years' turn.
> And then, I will buy property and build a Western mansion.* [55]
> *Western mansion means a modern style house, like those in America

> In the beginning I was just a poor soul.
> Suddenly, I am rich and noble.
> It's not an illusion to have a splendid mansion or a luxurious home;
> I think fate must be the cause of my past ill fortune.
> With a push from luck, gold and silver will fill my lot.
> As life changes for the better, wealth accumulates in heaps;
> Clothed in silk, with a hundred thousand dollars wrapped around my waist,* I'll return in triumph.[56]
> *The phrase of "a hundred thousand dollars wrapped around my waist" is a euphuism for having a fortune in cash to take home.

## Seeking Tong-Shaan, While Encountering Gum-Shaan

> I am red hot under the wealth star.
> In no time I have made a million.
> My savings, kept in a vault, are all yellow gold.
> O, far away, my wife and children must be
> waiting for me anxiously.
> I'll prepare the traveling clothes.
> I'll set out within a few days by boat.
> With favorable winds, I will reach Hong Kong safe and sound;
> Everyone will rush out to greet this wealthy sojourner coming home.[57]

In time, there emerged in many sojourners' mind an intoxicating nostalgia, supported by the engineering of a new reconstruction of "home." In place of the ugly and smelly, there emerged the beautiful and inviting. In the minds of countless sojourners, nostalgia helped replace bitter-sweet memories of home with beautiful fantasies. Over time, their own adversity and sense of predicament overseas contrasted sharply with an ascribed wholesome goodness and charm of one's native village. Arbitrarily and artificially, the sojourner recreated his image of home as a vision of serenity, beauty, stability, where the dignity of tradition and custom bound family and community together. Home was viewed ideally as a happy and secure place, where the only missing element was the sojourner himself.

> O, no way is such a life better than that of farming at home:
> Toiling for half a year, relaxing the rest;
> You greet your parents in the morning;
> You are with your wife at night;
> Everyone is happy, with smiles all over their faces;
> Festivals, parties, New Year's Eve celebrations-
> You and I, husband and wife,
> O, how loving would that be![58]

This recourse to reconstructing an idealistic vision of home, via a very creative and imaginative nostalgia, helped mitigate the many adversities of sojourner life overseas. It helped keep alive the sojourner myth, with its imperatives of "purpose" of leaving and the "promise" to return. It did so by providing a highly personalized, idealistic, and graphic representation that could be easily identified with. It cost nothing, but provided perhaps one of the few really harmless pleasures in sojourner daily life. It was perhaps the best tonic for what ailed the sojourner. In effect, nostalgia provided a needed diversion, a helpful respite from the rigors of a hard life overseas.

### *Nostalgia and the Iconographic Reconstruction of Home as Landscape*

Beyond the vision of a happy place and content people, the Cantonese sojourner's sense of nostalgia represented an effective tool for reconstructing not only his vision, but also his understanding of home. The reconstruction of an enduring image of home meant much more than the specifics of a particular setting or place. The reconstructed image of home took shape as a wide-angled *panoramic* view, in the form of a highly representative and symbolic graphic landscape.

In art, "landscape" is an attempt by an artist to represent his/her notion of how we might see a setting or a place (real or imagined).[59] In the context of Cantonese-Chinese sojourning, we might think of "landscape" as the idealized subjective reconstruction of a place, or more abstractly, a new conceptualization of it. In this reconstruction, "place" serves as a convenient graphic symbolic representation for a community of people. In this way, there is, perhaps unconsciously, an effort to caricature the human essence of a place or setting, via a reconstructed vision of it. This reconstructed landscape can be "… recognized not only in terms of its character, but also… contextually… [as a product] of nature…"[60] The Cantonese Sojourner in mentally reconstructing an ideal image of "home" not only re-created a graphic representation with enduring positive characteristics, but also went on to invest in that ascribed image a heightened respect and awe. In time, a nostalgic sentimentality, borne out of adversity, became itself a new source of inspiration.

> Human beings give shape and pattern to natural space and passing time...some places are thought to standout from their surroundings and become associated with special experiences and part of an ordered geography... reflect[ing] central ideas about time, space, and sacred power...[61]

"Home" then, existed not merely as a physical place from which one came from, it was also an idealized vision of family, friends, extending to embrace a whole community. Similar to a painting of a landscape, which captures an artist's view of a setting, the Cantonese sojourner captured within a single frame in his mind and in his memory, an idealized vision of what "home" meant. Among Cantonese sojourners of the late nineteenth and early twentieth century, there was a favorite poem that nostalgically identified the sojourner with home in an especially poignant and melancholy way. It may have been the most celebrated poem in the overseas Cantonese world. Although it was not composed by a nineteenth-century Cantonese sojourner, it was created by one of the greatest Tang Dynasty masters of poetry. It captures exquisitely the essence of the Cantonese sojourners' sentimental feelings about being away from home. [62]

> "Quiet Night Thoughts"
>
> Before my bed
> there is bright moonlight
> so that it seems
> like frost on the ground:
> Lifting my head
> I watch the bright moon,
> lowering my head
> I dream that I am home.[63]

The reconstruction of "home" took place on a personal level, with each sojourner embellishing his vision with the particulars of his own experience. This personal mental engineering took place within the broader context of Cantonese sojourner experience. It also took place on a public or communal level, where a commonly agreed upon consensus about these matters resulted from the common experience of sojourning overseas. In this context, it did not matter which village one came from, what the configuration of one's village was, where it happened to be located, or even what it looked like. "Home" in its essence was amorphous. It did not need to be visualized as a recreation of any one specific place, in any one form/format, at any one point in time. Over time, there evolved a commonly agreed upon image of what "home" was. It was one that any Cantonese sojourner could relate to and identify with. The commonality of Cantonese sojourner discourse, with its assortment of images, loaded references, and symbolisms, engineered the sojourner's image of "home." Cantonese sojourner poetry captured the essence of this discourse and the mental reconstruction of "home," via a nostalgically recreated landscape.[64]

The idealistic landscape obscured the realities of poverty, sickness, despair, and desperation. All of these things, the sojourner conveniently forgot, or just did not want to be reminded of. Missing home was a powerful feeling that did not need to be complicated by a reality check. Thus, landscape, as a nostalgically recreated image of "home" became over time a much-venerated icon. In time, this mentally reconstructed and emotionally charged image of "home" as an iconized landscape, was transformed from a mere place into a sacred place. In this context, emigrant emotions and experience, while embracing adversity with nostalgia, embodied underlying positive elements of resilience and optimism. This paved the way for a new, more positive subjective perception of "home" in the abstract.

> The male eagle is also easy to tame. One must be able to bend before one can stretch. China experienced calamities for a thousand years. Confucius was surrounded in Chen for seven days* Great men exhibit quality, Scholars take pride in being themselves. Gains and losses are entangled in my bosom. My restlessness is a sign of self-illumination.[65]
>
> * Confucius himself encountered dilemmas and overcame them.

## *The Iconographic reconstruction of Landscape as a Sacred Place*

The nostalgic reconstruction of "home" represented much more than the hyper-active imagination of a lonely and unhappy person. Over time, not only the color and contours of home changed in the eyes of the sojourner, but perhaps more importantly, the meaning and associations of home also underwent change. "Home" came to be viewed more than merely a serene and secure place that one missed dearly. Memories of home did more than delight and entertain- they also inspired awe and veneration. This transformed memory of home came to represent over time a newly fashioned icon worthy of veneration, because it served more than a mere reminder of home. In this altered context, "home" embraced more than one's own family, or the physical structures of a community. It expanded beyond the confines of one's own village, hamlet, neighborhood, or town to represent something more moving and more compelling in the mind of the sojourner.

As a product of the imagination, it easily escaped the limitations of time and space. Given the circumstances of sojourner experience, it is not surprising that this transformation was largely an abstraction, couched in ambiguous and amorphous terms. It was a transformation that was widely shared, easily recognized, and deeply etched on the sojourner persona, but one beyond articulation, and also one without the benefit of principle or textual explanation. I describe this phenomenon as the "iconization" of landscape as a sacred place.

## *The "Iconized" Cantonese Landscape, with Shaan as a metaphor for a Sacred Place*

The re-creation of a place as a sacred or special place has historically taken shape on two separate, but not unrelated levels of perception. One level is the intellectual, and the other is the emotional. In the former, "thought" provides "form," and in the latter "feeling" injects "meaning." It may be that "thinking" initiates the iconographic reconstruction of "home" as a place, in the shape of an iconographic landscape; but it is "feeling" that sculptures it into an icon, worthy of awe and wonder. It is also emotion that transforms landscape from an inert, static image, into a highly evocative and inspirational image of "home" as a very special or sacred place. "We [should] think of landscape, not as an object to be [merely] seen...but [as] a process by which social and subjective identities are formed."⁶⁶ Thus, the iconographically reconstructed landscape mirrors the essence of human experience, relative to the physical world, and its perceived relationship with it. Historically speaking, one could argue that there has always been the impulse for us to,

> Shape the world, even if only with our minds and not our hands. When we shape the world, we create places... "To be human, is to live in a world that is filled with significant places: To be human is to have and to know your place."... "to be without a relationship to a place is to be in spiritual exile."⁶⁷

The vision of a sacred place, is one in which one sets a particular place, setting, or landscape aside from the ordinary, thereby investing in it a special aura and/or other ascribed qualities.⁶⁸ Additionally, such a place is viewed as possessing the ability to both stimulate and attract a wide range of powerful emotional responses, e.g., dread or fascination.⁶⁹ For the Cantonese sojourner, "home," as a sacred place, stimulated feelings of harmony, reconciliation, wholesomeness, certainty, hope, and stability. This inspired vision of "home" might start with a concrete reference to particular things and places; but it ultimately became a view that lacked reference to anything concrete or specific, because it arose from a subjective view of object reality. It did, however, possess a heightened sense of specificity for those attracted to it, relative to its imagined forms, boundaries, and ascribed traits.

> The world outside my village is vast, without a boundary in sight. I' am cut off from my village by mountains and seas. Away from my village, searching for gold and silver. In melancholy, I long for the sight of the village gate tower. I think of things back in the village. Since leaving my village, I haven't returned. Messages from the village are filled with ten million complaints. Remembering my village, I wish to follow the geese home.⁷⁰

Paradoxically, visions of home also represented an expanded context for merging discrete entities across time and space. As the Cantonese sojourner came to identify "home" as a sacred place, he remembered and vicariously linked up with the living community of family and friends. Simultaneously, he also unconsciously connected with the invisible community of his ancestors.

> A Sacred place...always has a defined boundary and a centre. At its perimeter lies the threshold...Rituals accompany the crossing of the threshold, guardians protect the passageway. At the centre of the sacred place is the *axis mundi*, the world axis, the link between heaven, earth, and the underworld... allow[ing] access to imaginal depth and meaningfulness whilst holding chaos at bay. Sacred places provide an essential continuity with the past, with the Ancients of one's cultural tradition.[71]

The nostalgically driven iconographic reconstruction of landscape revolves around a number of metaphors, which are used to establish useful graphic images. Typically, natural objects served as useful metaphors, e.g., trees and mountains, in the iconographic reconstruction of landscape. They help bridge the gap between "thought" and "feeling." It has been common to use metaphors, when talking about such abstract things such as knowledge, truth, or spirituality. They are easily interchangeable, because while a particular metaphor offers a specific graphic representation, as distinguished from other representations (e.g., a tree as opposed to a mountain,) their respective functions are the same. As such, "Mountains" and "trees" are examples of this interchangeability of metaphors.

> In scaling the [mountain or tree] of knowledge without getting too far out on any [ledge or branch], in exploring the many [pathways or extensions] of thought, and in attempting to get at the [base or roots] of the matter, we pursue a [uphill battle or arduous climb]. For not only do we show

how certain [mountains or trees] have served as symbols, but we also reflect on some of the complex aspects of symbolic thought itself.[72]

Historically and culturally, the Chinese have demonstrated a special preference for using "mountain" as a metaphor, to represent a special or sacred place. In Chinese culture, *Shan* (in Cantonese *Shaan*) as mountain(s) has traditionally served as a concrete representation of a sacred place and has thus over time come become its most common metaphor. Traditionally, the classic form of a Chinese pilgrimage to a sacred place involved a journey to a temple on a mountain.[73] The actual Chinese term *Shan* (*Shaan*) represents a wide range of forms and meanings.

> A mountain (*shan*) in the Chinese context can mean [either] a single peak ([as at] Miao-feng shan), a cluster of hills ([as in] Chiu-hua Shan), or a whole mountain range ([as in] Wu-t'ai Shan), not to mention caverns in a mountain [as in] Mao Shan) or [even] an island ([as in] P'ut'o Shan).[74]

The vast majority of the Cantonese people were, by preference, and long-established tradition, long-time residents of the Central Gwongdung's alluvial plains, and lowlands. While many areas where they were concentrated were studded with hills, plateaus, mountainous spurs, and low-lying foothills, most Cantonese people lived considerable distances from soaring peaks and massive mountain ranges. In this way, there developed different Cantonese perceptions and responses to what *Shaan* meant.

In traditional Cantonese society, there were two common views of "mountains." First, there were many hills, rocky-spurs, and low-lying coastal mountain ranges, in the form of jagged, craggy projections in irregular formations of varying heights, sprinkled randomly across the landscape. This characterized the coastal *Say-Yup* or *Ng Yup* region of the southwest quadrant of the Pearl River Delta region, as well as other areas of the inner *Baak-wah* zone, most notably to the north, north-east, and east of Canton. Second, in the outer-most areas of the outer *Baak-wah* zone and the non-*Yuet* peripheral border areas along Gwongdung's borders with neighboring provinces to the far north-east, north, and northwest, there were higher more massive mountains, often characterized by towering ranges with soaring peaks. These mountains served as the source of Central Gwongdung's major river systems (i.e., the West, North, and East rivers), where towering precipices carved out deep, twisting canyons in their higher elevations.

These two contrasting physical realities, regarding how mountains presented themselves in the Cantonese environment, helped shape two contrasting views about mountains in Cantonese society. The first perception of mountain(s) arose from, and revolved around, daily life, where they existed as a barrier or problem to be overcome, relative to farming, transporting goods, or merely traveling across the landscape. There was nothing special or sacred about this perception of mountain(s). In the second view, high mountains, often towering in the distance, very far away, not only conjured up a different perception of mountain(s), but also a different kind of response to them. Many of them were imbued with a mystical quality, as their summits thrust up above the clouds and mists. The impressiveness of their size, location, and ascribed character lent a transcendental aura that inspired awe and veneration. Consistent with elsewhere in China, over time, some of these peaks in Central Gwongdung came to be regarded as sacred places, e.g., *Lo-fu Shan* to the east of Canton.[75] We should remember, that while "[n]ot all… sacred places in China were mountains, …they were [however] the prototype and most typical sort."[76]

## *Tong-Shaan* and *Gum-Shaan*, as later nineteenth and early twentieth-century Cantonese metaphors for "home" in China and America

In the Cantonese lexicon, *Shaan* functioned as a graphic representation of "home" as a solid fixed entity, representing security, stability, and roots. The idea of *Shaan* also functioned as a concrete place marker, a visual reminder that "home" was an actual place located somewhere in Central Gwongdung. The term *Shaan* also functioned as an abstract iconographic symbol for rendering the idea of "home" as a sacred place. It conjured up symbolic, subjective images of home in much the same way that traditional Chinese landscape painting might evoke special feelings in the eye of the beholder. Here "home" was sensed, by way of constructed mental images, and it was also intuitively felt by way of strong emotional feelings. While there might be a delight in suggestions of harmony, beauty, and serenity, there was also an irreconcilable distance of time and space that invited abstract fantasizing, often giving rise to introspective contemplation, with a sense of the melancholy.

These two different, but closely related perceptions of *Shaan* in the Cantonese sojourner experience mirrored an ability to service sojourner perceptions of "home" on two different levels. First, *Shaan* underscored immediate sojourner concerns about stability, security, harmony, and the well-being of one's family/friends back home. Second, *Shaan* represented enduring, time-honored traditions and conventions about self, home, and sojourning, relative to concerns about authenticity, purity, and legitimacy, as they were reproduced in Cantonese speech, represented in Cantonese identity, and recorded in Cantonese experience.[77] These perceptions and conventions square well with traditional conservative contrarian (C4) thinking and experience, (see chapter 4).

In America, among Cantonese sojourners of the mid-late nineteenth century, the particular use of *Shaan* as a metaphor for home, as a sacred place, resulted in the creation of a new set of terms, specific for the Cantonese sojourner identity and experience in North America. Two of these new uses involving the term *Shaan* were: 1) **Tong-Shaan** (Tangshan), which literally meant respectively a) [the] Tang Mountain(s), b) the Mountain(s) of [the] Tang, or c) the land of [the] Tang mountain(s); (Here, *Tong-Shaan* or "Tong Mountain" served as a convenient metaphor/euphemism for home in Central Gwongdung- where *Tong (Tang)* ideals were strongly embraced and *Tong* models were deeply revered); and 2) **Gum-Shaan** ( *Gaam-Shan*) [standard Cantonese romanization]) (*Jin-shan*) (Pinyin), which literally means a) Gold or Golden Mountain(s), or b) land of [the]Gold[en] mountain(s). In this manner, *Gum-Shaan* or "Gold Mountain" served as a convenient euphemism for "home in America."

In daily use, on a practical level, the term *Tong-Shaan* emerged as a new convenient code word or nick-name for references to what we would describe variously as; 1) back home, or 2) the old country.[78] Its literal meaning meant "homeland of the *Tong (Tang)* people" (i.e., Cantonese people). For Cantonese sojourners in North America, it became simply a convenient reference to "home," with reference to one's real or permanent home, somewhere in Central Gwongdung. Today we make a similar distinction between one's current place of residence and one's permanent residence. In this regard, *Tong-Shaan* referred to the Cantonese sojourner's "home" in the context of a permanent residence. This arose from the belief that for every Cantonese sojourner, regardless of the length of his stay overseas, his "real home" was back home in his native village or town in Central Gwongdung. References to *Tong-Shaan* unequivocally embodied this belief.

> Come to think of it,
> What can I really say?
> Thirty years of living in America-*
> Why has life been so miserable and I, so frail?
> I suppose that it's useless to expect to go home.
> My heart aches with grief;
> My soul wanders around aimlessly.
> Unable to make a living here, I'll try it in the East,
> With a sudden change of luck,
> I may make it back home to Tong [Shaan].** [79]

*translator uses the term United States, but the Chinese character is "Mei," which typically can be understood to mean "America"

** the translator uses the term "China," but the term written here is "Tong" (tang), which literally means "Tong-Shaan."

In similar fashion, *Tong-Shaan* also functioned as a subjective term, heavily laden with Cantonese symbolism (e.g., the use of metaphors, such as *Shaan* to represent stability and security) concerning home, as a sacred place. Here *Tong-Shaan* was not a particular place. Indeed, there was no such place on the map. It did not refer to, nor mean "China." Neither did it refer to Gwongdung province or any of its administrative sub-units, (e.g., *Namhoi* or *Toi-Shaan*) or geographical sub-region (e.g., The Pearl River Delta, or the Inner *Baak-wah* zone).

As a symbolic term, it possessed no explicit, concrete reference. Instead, it represented, by way of implication, the sense or essence of "home," relative to the commonly agreed upon recognition that there existed such a place, indeed a very special or sacred place, a home base for Cantonese society, and fountainhead for Cantonese culture. *Tong-Shaan*, as a symbolic term, cast a wide net, catching within its folds many elements of history, culture, ethnicity, speech, and community, as they sculptured the Cantonese sojourner persona. To adequately represent these things, *Tong-Shaan*, as a metaphor, evoked strong feelings by identifying Cantonese sojourners with their home, back in Central Gwondung.

The term *Gum-Shaan* also mirrored the dichotomous union of concrete reference and abstract symbolism, regarding Cantonese sojourner life in later nineteenth and early twentieth century America. As a practical matter, the term *Gum-Shaan* served as a code word or nickname for a variety of names associated with sojourner life in North America. Consistent with the basic term "*Shaan*," *Gum-Shaan* also had many different meanings, depending on the context in which it might be used.[80] Initially, the term *Gum-Shaan* referred to the vague, ill-defined area of the western part of North America, which in the middle of the nineteenth century specifically meant parts of northern California, and/or southern British Columbia in which Cantonese sojourners, as gold miners, had settled/worked in large numbers.[81] In time, however, *Gum-Shaan* generally came to mean any reference to any part of North America inhabited by Cantonese-Chinese sojourners. It did not, however, include Hawaii, which had its own name, *Tan-heung-shaan* (*Tanxiangshan*) (or [the] Sandalwood [Mountain(s)] Islands).[82] The use of *Shaan* in the Chinese name for Hawaii and the English title, Sea of Sterile Mountains, for a book about Chinese experience in British Columbia, Canada, effectively underscore the prominent role of *Shaan* (or mountain), relative to Cantonese sojourners in North America (and Hawaii). Because a far greater number of Cantonese sojourners migrated to America, than Canada, traditionally, *Gum-Shaan* has historically been used more commonly as a more specific reference to America, but again, it has often been applied to Canada as well, especially western Canada.

## Seeking Tong-Shaan, While Encountering Gum-Shaan

The term "*Gum-Shaan*," had its immediate origin in the California Gold Rush of 1848–49, where it mirrored a very practical application of the term "Gold Mountain," where it had a very specific, concrete point of reference. The early Cantonese sojourner literally went to *Gum-Shaan* or Gold Mountain to make his fortune, and return home. Hence, the name had a simple common-sense identification. It was very easy to use and relate to. If the term *Tong-Shaan* echoed back to symbolically laden historical precedents and cultural imperatives of classical Tang models, *Gum-Shaan* by contrast, conspicuously lacked any such implied associations. In the early mid-nineteenth century, it had originally referred primarily to northern California, where the gold fields were located. This early reference was useful because of its vague, and yet expansive application. It had originally referred to the gold country or gold fields located on the Sacramento and San Joaquin Rivers in Northern California. Subsequently, likely after 1870, *Gum-Shaan's* representation embraced successively, first- all of Northern California, then California in general, and then the Western United States, (which included the Pacific Northwest, the Rocky Mountain Region, the American Southwest respectively.) It finally embraced all of North America (both America and Canada). In the context of this study, however, and as generally understood in the fields of Chinese American Studies, and more generally Asian American Studies, *Gum-Shaan* has come to mean the "historical Chinese America" of the later nineteenth and early twentieth century or more specifically and correctly "Cantonese-Chinese America."

In later years, the term *Gum-Shaan* became more technical and narrowly focused in its application, and sophisticated in its meaning. In the aftermath of the Australian Gold rush of 1851, prefixes, "old" and "new" were added to *Gum-Shaan* to distinguish between the different places to which the term might be applied to. *Gau Gum-Shaan* (*Jiujinshan*) or "Old" Gold Mountain was used to represent respectively, a) San Francisco, b) California, c) America, or d) North America. In contrast, *Sun Gum-Shaan* (or in standard Cantonese, *San-Gaam -shan*) (in *Pinyin*, *Sinjinshan*) or "New" Gold Mountain, specifically referred to Australia.[83] Curiously, today, official agencies of the Peoples' Republic of China (PRC) (e.g., the Consulate General in San Francisco) refers to

San Francisco as *Jiujinshan* (The Peoples Republic of China uses mandarin Pinyin forms) (I use a more user-friendly Cantonese form *Gau Gum-Shaan*.)[84]

After 1900, Cantonese sojourners referred to America by way of three distinct and different terms. When referring to America in the context of "America" as a country or geopolitical entity (e.g., The United States of America, or the US), they utilized the formal term *Mei-kwok* (*Meiguo*) (literally, the Beautiful Country,) as used universally throughout the Chinese-speaking world. The term *Mei-Gwok* meant literally America or the United States of America, relative to the fact that America was a place, or the country of the American people. *Mei-Gwok* became popular in the rapidly growing (Cantonese) Chinese language press in the period 1900–1945, e.g., its growing use in the vernacular Cantonese press, <u>Young China</u>, *Sai-Gai Yat Bo* and *Chung Sai Yat Bo*.[85]

When making reference to America in an informal manner, more as an adjective than as a noun, as in "American" versus "America," Cantonese sojourners used the euphemistic term *Fa-kei* (*Fa-chi*). The term literally means "multicolored flag," referring to the American flag, with its stars and stripes.[86] Today it is a term used only among the old time Cantonese (pre-WWII) in America. Recent immigrants from Hong Kong or other Cantonese speakers do not use this term.

Over time, the term *Gum-Shaan* came to represent a stubborn conservative, even parochial habit of thought, where pre-WWII Cantonese in America referred to themselves as "*Gum-Shaan hak*" (*Gaam-Shan-haak*) (literally, [a] guest of [on] Golden Mountain(s), (i.e., an [old-timer] [Cantonese-Chinese] sojourner in America). In this context, *Gum-Shaan* took on added meaning and value, as a complement of *Tong-Shaan*. On one hand, one was a *Tong-Yan* or "Tong Person" in America, because one came from and identified with a place known as *Tong-Shaan*. In the same token, as a *Tong*-person living in America, one was also a *Gum-Shaan hak* (i.e. "guest on Golden Mountain" or a sojourner in America.) Thus, *Gum-Shaan hak* shares a similar functional role with that of *Tong-yan*, relative to identifying the Cantonese sojourner with his home in America. . In the former (*Gum-Shaan hak)* it did not link the Cantonese sojourner with his "home" back in *Tong-Shaan*; rather it linked him with his current, temporary "new home" in America, i.e., *Gum-Shaan*.

> O, [*Gum-Shaan Haak*] sojourner returning from Gold Mountain:
> If you don't have one thousand dollars,
> You must have at least eight hundred.[87]

In this way, in America, over time, the term *Tong-yan* (a "*Tong*" (*Tang*) person, i.e., Cantonese Chinese person, related less to the idea that such a person was from *Tong-Shaan*, and more with the idea that such a person now comes from or lived in *Tong-yan fow* (i.e., "Chinatown"), or on *Tong Yan-gai* ("Street(s) of the Chinese"). This meant that in America, the term *Tong* had two references, one distant- as in back home in *Tong-Shaan*, and one local, as in *Tong Yan fow* (Chinatown) or *Tong yan gai* (Street(s) of the Chinese). In a sense, the term *Gum-Shaan hak* both embodied and linked together these two representations of *Tong,* i.e., *Tong-Shaan* and *Tong-yan*.

Conceptually speaking, the terms *Tong-Shaan* and *Gum-Shaan* were not polar opposites, in their geophysical positioning, or mutually exclusive in their symbolic references to "home." They were referents placed along a continuum of experience, with associated memories. In this way over time, *Gum-Shaan* became the natural complement to *Tong-Shaan*, whereby the Cantonese sojourner mentally reconstructed two images of "home," via the term *Shaan*, as a metaphor for "home." *Tong-Shaan* meant my real or permanent home in China, and *Gum-Shaan* meant my new temporary current home in America. It was unlikely that Cantonese sojourners ever thought about these matters in this way, but evidence in sojourner letters, literature, and especially poetry clearly show that many instinctively believed in them, and intuitively felt them to be real and meaningful.

> At home [in *Tong* Mountain] I was in poverty, constantly worried about firewood and rice, I borrowed money to come to Gold [*Gum-Shaan*] Mountain.[88]

> Swallows and magpies, flying in glee: Greetings for the New Year. Daddy has gone to the Gold Mountain to earn money. He will earn gold and silver…. When he returns, we will buy a lot of land.[89]

> Father has gone to Gold Mountain. Hurry up and send money home: The whole family is depending on you; [90]

Over time, the use of the terms *Tong-Shaan* and *Gum-Shaan* became useful outward symbols for the complex internal reordering of what must have been regarded as an extraordinarily chaotic world. This development did not occur very quickly, nor very easily. Its evolution defies quantification concerning when, where, how such perceptions first came about. Consistent with a hard life overseas, it could not have been easy for Cantonese sojourners to grasp their sense of dilemma, much less critically evaluate it. It seems clear, given the rigors of daily life that even hazy impressions and superficial thinking were not easily processed. Indeed, it may be misleading to think that these reconstructed categories were ever so clearly perceived, so-well articulated, and so systematically formulated.

Despite these observations, we should remember that the relevance and value of the *Tong-Shaan* and *Gum-Shaan* labels lay in their practical daily application. Everyone knew what these labels referred to and what they represented. As convenient colloquial expressions, they were simple, easy to use, and universally recognized by all Cantonese people. As symbolic complementary references, they embodied important clues about Cantonese sensibilities about self, home, and sojourning overseas.

> My husband, pressed by poverty, took off to Gold Mountain. With a pretty sum of money, he cannot make the journey home. The road to Gold Mountain is extremely perilous and difficult; at home [in Tong-Mountain], in grief and pain, my longing eyes pierce through to the horizon, waiting for his return.[91]

**CSDS and the Dilemma of Sojourning and its Iconographic Reconstruction**

If CSDS (Cantonese sojourner dilemma syndrome) was simply a matter of calling attention to Cantonese sojourners missing their homes, then there would be no CSDS. It arises from and reflects an inherently more complex and multi-dimensional situation. As discussed earlier, it arises from the interplay between motion and emotion, and from the interaction of adversity with a nostalgically driven notion of "home," as an iconographically reconstructed landscape. This was expressed through culturally authentic symbolic metaphors, which serve as both concrete representations and abstract symbols of mentally reconstructed images of home. This activity took place on both a personal/individual level, and also on a collective/communal level of awareness. The resulting perceptions helped the Cantonese sojourner to better understand his situation. Rapidly changing material conditions after 1900 undermined an earlier simplistic, one-dimensional world view, characterized by increased uncertainty and a greater sense of helplessness. This gave rise to intense anxiety about one-self and the dilemma of choosing between two loci for "home,"*i.e.*, *Tong-Shaan* (one's permanent home back in Central Gwongdung, China) and *Gum-Shaan* (one's current, temporary home in America).

Given the perpetual movement of the Cantonese sojourner, especially in the period 1850–1930, it seems likely that any effort at an iconographic reconstruction of home was from the outset very problematic. This is not to say that the process did not get underway, nor that it did not ultimately materialize as a key feature of sojourner life. It underscores however, the fact that such thinking was neither easy nor simple. There evolved over time a problematic relationship between "motion" and "home," relative to the changing perceptions of "home." In this context, *Tong-Shaan,* as a metaphor for home, as a sacred place, initially remained constant, as an enduring focal point of respect and intense longing.

By the last decades of the nineteenth century, it had become a venerable icon, worthy of awe and loyalty. In this way, home was less "what it actually was," and more "how it was ascriptively remembered." It served as a fixed point on the Cantonese sojourner's compass. Similarly, *Gum-Shaan*, as a metaphor for "home," as a "new" special place, also became over time a widely recognized and increasingly accepted focus for the Cantonese sojourner's loyalty.

This perspective changed after 1900, previously *Gum-Shaan* had been perceived as a temporary stop, a place where a job was located, involving a temporary seasonal abode. After 1900, *Gum-Shaan* came to be increasingly regarded by most Cantonese immigrants as a kind of more-or-less fixed home for the foreseeable future with fellow Cantonese sojourners. It would not be until after the critical period 1945–1950, (after the end of WW II in 1945 and the Communist take-over of mainland China in 1949), that Cantonese immigrants living in America would begin to see themselves as bona fide immigrants, and no longer as sojourners.

They ceased to think of themselves as sojourners, because they no longer saw themselves as living only temporarily in America. Few if any thought that they would live long enough to return to China. The rupture in Sino-American relations, the aging Cantonese immigrant population, consisting mostly of men aged forty to sixty, living in a "Bachelor society," and changes in US Chinese immigration policies and laws in the succeeding years (1952–1965) initially undermined, and then later destroyed the "sojourner myth," because it nullified both its original "purpose" and "promise."

After 1945, the majority of Chinese immigrants in America were no long single young men, chasing the dream to get rich and then return home to settle down. Instead, among the few Chinese that could come to America after 1945, most were wives and children of re-unified families. After US immigration law changes first in 1952, and then even more radically in 1965, almost all Chinese immigrants coming to America were identified with re-unified families. By the mid-1960s the last generation of sojourners had either returned home to Central Gwongdung, or Hong Kong. Many had died, or were rapidly dying off, such that very few of them remained.

Over the course of a century (1850–1950,) generations of Cantonese Sojourners traveled the long journey from *Tong-Shaan* to *Gum-Shaan*, and back. Whether the journey abroad was a one-way or round-trip affair, was in part a reflection of one's fate, via a stroke of good luck, or some bad joss. It also resulted from decisions made, both wise and foolish, on the part of the sojourner himself. In sojourning, there was no predetermined schedule. The choice to return or to stay were decisions best left to each sojourner to decide. To some extent, prevailing conditions were controlling, e.g., ill health, unpaid debts, or some inextricable tangled relationship could prevent return. A lucky turn of the dice at the gambling table, an especially good year of choice jobs, or a good return on a modest investment in a cafe or laundry, could mean an unexpected early return home. Beyond the realities of finance and personal health, the Cantonese sojourner also had to face a bewildering array of thoughts and feelings about home in a constantly changing context.

Given life overseas for years, or even decades at a time, it should come as no surprise that ongoing changes have also taken place at home, in one's native village or town. Material changes have also shaped the sojourner's own personal situation, in his local sojourner community. Amid all of these changes, visions and ideas about "home" also changed, re: their imagery, meaning and value.

In time, *Tong-Shaan* came to represent a bifurcated view of home. On one hand it existed as a highly venerated icon of an ideal vision of home; and at the same time, it also existed as a concrete reference to home as a real place, with real people forming a community. Depending on the context, mood, and reason for making reference to *Tong-Shaan*, one view or the other could be summoned, used, and then discarded.

Similarly, references to *Gum-Shaan* were also dichotomous. In one context it might refer to the reality of a hard life somewhere along the Cantonese-Chinese frontier in America, e.g., working in a gambling hall in San Francisco, waiting on tables in a restaurant in Chicago, or toiling alone in a laundry in Washington D.C. Alternately, it could also represent an idealized view of a place, where great expectations drive fantastic dreams of money and success.

In both cases, *Tong-Shaan* and *Gum-Shaan* fulfilled concurrent, but contradictory, needs of the Cantonese sojourner in America. These metaphors served alternately as convenient slang terms or nicknames for very real places, relative to the realities of daily life; and they also served as icons, inspiring hopes, dreams, and great expectations about "home." This dualistic vision of home embodied alternating and competing perceptions of home, as they were manifested on both sides of the Pacific, within an evolving transnational framework.

After 1900, the *Tong-Shaan* metaphor served less as a concrete representation of "home," but instead became more and more an abstract symbol of what "home" meant to the sojourner. Its reference figured prominently in communal/public discourse in meetings, gatherings, and celebrations in scores of clan/family associations, *Wooi-koon*, secret societies and tongs. There emerged the unspoken, but widely recognized distinction between the reality of home, and its reconstructed idealized version. Old time sojourners knew that home could be perceived as any number of images. Mixed feelings now replaced earlier sure convictions.

In place of simple black-white contrasts, (of the mid-later nineteenth century) now there existed (post 1900) many shades of gray. *Tong-Shaan* might mean family, friends, but it also meant poverty and even greater hardship than life in *Gum-Shaan*. Life might be very lonely and hard in *Gum-Shaan*, but the decision to return home permanently didn't necessarily help the sojourner or his family back home. While wives, and family would be over joyed by the return of a long absent husband and father, such a homecoming also meant the end of a much relied upon source of income by way of monthly remittances. Additionally, it also meant an end of a stream of much appreciated "care" packages with lifebuoy soap, Virginia hams, Hershey bars, Almond Rocca, chewing gum, cosmetics, clothing, and other assorted treats. Some *Gum-Shaan Haak* might return home with anywhere from a few hundred to several thousand dollars. Obviously, with generous gift giving, lavish banqueting, and endless requests for financial help from scores of relatives- whatever money a sojourner brought home after retiring home to *Tong-Shaan* could be quickly exhausted, unless some of the money was set aside for investment (e.g., in a new enterprise, or building a new house or renovating an existing one) and savings for a "rainy day." Money brought home, didn't last forever.

The end of remittances meant a reduced income that a family might have at its disposal. Some of the slack in income might be picked up by the emigration and hard work of others, e.g., sons, grandsons, or other male relatives in *Gum-Shaan*. Neither newly created immigrant sons or established collateral male relatives were as able, generous, and reliable, as husbands/fathers and sons in making regular timely remittances or sending "care" packages home to *Tong-Shaan*. Many returning sojourners only brought back a modest sum of money, or hardly any at all. Some only returned with their suitcase filled with some treats, but with little or no cash to spare. Others may have met with misfortune on the return home, where they were robbed or swindled out of what cash they had. In this context, the return home was not always, and perhaps only seldom so, a financial boom to the waiting family at home.

For many sojourners, the return home meant a brief moment of joy and triumph, however, when the welcome home celebrations were over, a difficult-to-accept reality often set in. First, after a life time of hard work and self-sacrifice, now the sojourner encountered a new life of enforced "leisure" in the form of not having to get up early and toil all day, which also meant having to adjust to a new schedule, a new lifestyle. If he was somewhat wealthy, managing his wealth via investments, acquiring property (new houses), and business opportunities beckoned. Undoubtedly, for most, such was not the case. While a modest retirement meant freedom from want, of having to work so hard at manual labor, it also meant enforced leisure of free time and boredom. Locals back home had moved on with their lives, wives had grown old, children had grown—everything previously so familiar had changed, where both people and things now seemed so different and strange.

Perhaps most distressing of all was the souring of martial relationships. Young, innocent, attractive wives at the time of departure, years, or even decades ago, were now old, unattractive strangers. In one case, when a *Gum-Shaan Haak* (old timer Cantonese sojourner in America) had returned home from America, only then did he realize how Americanized he had become and how unhappy he was with his uninteresting and unattractive Cantonese country wife.

> My ugly Chinese wife (*huanglian bo*) knows nothing. We have nothing in common. What I like, she doesn't. Where she likes to go, I don't. We often fight over things like that. Imagine a man like me, working from morning till night for a living (in *Gum-Shaan*) and suffering from such a wife at home. How can I face the world? I have thought many times of divorcing her, but my son is still young. All sorts of feelings well up in my heart and I suffer so much. Please give me guidance.[92]

## Chapter 6

In *Gum-Shaan*, one might miss one's family in *Tong-Shaan*, amid a life of hard work, but there was always the "adopted family" of real or fictive male relations and close friends. When one returned to *Tong-Shaan*, there was always the recent memory of life in *Gum-Shaan*, in San Francisco, Boise, Portland, New York, Chicago, or elsewhere in America. In *Gum-Shaan*, there were fellow sojourners who were now sorely missed, especially the lost camaraderie within the "bachelor society." In *Gum-Shaan*, there might have been the image of dependent family and friends in *Tong-Shaan*, but they were only images divorced from reality. In America and elsewhere overseas, there were no outreached hands, tearful faces, and emotional tensions in the form of needy relatives, strange old unattractive women, adolescent or grown children, all of whom had become strangers.

In *Gum-Shaan* there were flushing toilets, hot and cold running water, gas-lit stoves, iceboxes, buses, cars, and subways. After 1920, there were radios, night clubs, the horse races, and movie theaters. One could always enjoy a cup of coffee, a donut, a waffle or stack of pancakes, a hamburger and French fries, a bowl of chili, a shot of whisky or a mug of beer. One could move about freely, either alone, or with a friend or two. One could always socialize over a game of *Mahjong* or *Pai-gow*, enjoying a good Cuban cigar or chain-smoke American cigarettes. There was no one to scrutinize and criticize. One only had to worry about oneself. Some sojourners in America hooked up with a White or Black woman, as a common-law wife, despite having a wife back in *Tong-Shaan*.[93]

Upon returning home to *Tong-Shaan* again, one was reunited with a wife and children and a larger circle of family and relations. In the intervening years and decades, many of the people back home in *Tong-Shaan* had changed. They had developed their own intimate circle of social relations, while others had died or moved away. Those remaining were essentially social strangers, where shared interests and familiarities were not of the present, but rather from a distant and diminished past- dimmed by memories thorough the passage of time. At home again in *Tong-Shaan*, many returned sojourners missed their peers in *Gum-Shaan*, because at home one encountered a physical setting, daily life schedule, and social scene that was less inviting, because it was estranged from the returned sojourner. His nostalgically constructed image of home in America clashed with the reality of his home, when he got there. After the initial euphoria of returning home had evaporated, the returned sojourner had become an out-of-place stranger.

I do not mean to suggest the same response for all returning sojourners. To be sure for many, they returned happily to their home villages and resumed their lives as husbands and fathers, with varying degrees of material comfort and financial success. I have heard, however, many tales of regret, lost camaraderie, lost freedom and autonomy, and material comforts among returned sojourners.[94] The sense of anxiety among sojourners occurred not only among those who returned permanently to *Tong-Shaan*, it also materialized among those who made periodic visits home. Among both types of sojourners, those who returned home permanently and those who remained in *Gum-Shaan*, there developed a numbing ambivalence associated with sojourning.

Herein lay the crux of the Cantonese sojourner dilemma, anxiety about self, home, and sojourning. *Tong-Shaan* and *Gum-Shaan,* as metaphors for "home" and "home away from home" respectively, mirrored a growing ambivalence in Cantonese sojourner life. They did so by confronting the sojourner with a series of alternatives, with little or no sense of resolution or closure, with regards to his personal life. Life routinely consisted of alternating feelings of temporary elation followed by greater frustration and deeper melancholy. This expressed itself most commonly in the contradiction of, "being here, but wishing I was there; and/or being there, but wishing I was here." When in *Gum-Shaan*, the sojourner dreamt of *Tong-Shaan*, as an idealized vision of home. In letters and photographs from home, unpleasant and uncomfortable news were conveniently minimized or glossed over by alternating feelings of helplessness. In the novel, <u>Eat a Bowl of Tea</u>, *Wah-Gay*, an elder long-time "Bachelor" sojourner, regrets his long stay in America, where he misses his wife and family. He feels ambivalent about it, because while he misses home, and wants to help out with remittances and gifts, he also feels helpless for not being there, and also for not going home for regular visits. In response to letters from home chronicling difficulties, he rationalizes "So what can I do about it? I'll just work harder and send a little more money this month, that will take care of things!" Paradoxically, he is also content with his bachelor life, where he enjoys many material comforts and modern conveniences, takes pride in his numerous homosocial relationships, amid an active homosocial life in New York City's Chinatown.[95]

Sojourner visits home relieved the tension of loneliness, but also served as a reality check, arousing feelings of, "being here (in *Tong-Shaan*), but wishing I was back there (in *Gum-Shaan*)." In similar fashion, sojourners in *Gum-Shaan*, without the opportunity to visit home, or when the memories of home visits have frayed with the passing of many years and decades, developed the all too frequent feeling of "being here (in *Gum-Shaan*), but wishing I was back there (in *Tong-Shaan*)."[96] "Should one stay in *Gum-Shaan*, or return to *Tong-Shaan?*" paralleled the equally perplexing question of whether to "stay in *Tong-Shaan* or to return back to *Gum-Shaan*? Both decisions were interrelated in a complex way, where rational thinking easily shaded into emotional feelings.

Among scores of Cantonese sojourners, this resulted in clinical signs of intense anxiety about what to do, and a numbing ambivalence regardless of what choice is made. Given the elements of constant motion, adversity, and nostalgia, then it is easy to see how such conditions could produce in the Cantonese sojourner a contradictory desire for secure roots, with a pronounced inability to be satisfied with them, even when such security was available. Elements of the unforeseen and unpredictable only complicated and intensified this predicament.

The predicament of *being here, but wishing I was there*, and the inability to find comfort and solace anywhere, was shared by many Cantonese after 1900, perhaps more so in the 1920s through the end of WW II. It not only materialized among Cantonese overseas migrant sojourners, it also surfaced among Cantonese merchants, foreign students, and peripatetic politicians. Given the unstable character of the times after 1900, with Chinese Exclusion in America (1882–1943), the American Boycott in China (1905) a stillborn Republic of China (1912–1916) followed by chaos during the Warlord years (1916–1927), with endemic Nationalist-Communist civil wars (1927–1937 and 1945–1949) and the Japanese invasion (1923–1945) the notion of "home," in its dichotomous metaphors of *Tong-Shaan* and *Gum-Shaan* became more fluid, enigmatic and increasingly meaningless in their ascribed representations and imagined usefulness. In this context, "home" remained an ideal, but one always in flux, constantly shifting focus and changing in meaning. It had become an elusive and enigmatic icon, seemingly close enough to visualize, but always just beyond one's grasp. This was especially so in regards to the metaphor of *Tong-Shaan* for "home."

*Tong-Shaan*, for many, remained a pipe dream about one's real "home." Regardless of whether one was located far away in *Gum-Shaan*, or even when one actually returned there. After 1900, but perhaps especially so after the early 1920s, *Tong-Shaan*, as the iconic Cantonese fountainhead had lost its inspiring allure. Its iconic image sent mixed messages, most of which were lost in translation, where absent Cantonese people seemed confused and lost in their thinking about "home." Returning "home" remained an ideal, and for many an impractical reality.

This perspective, was not confined to Cantonese emigrant-sojourners in America and elsewhere, but significantly also mirrored itself even among famous Cantonese peripatetic political leaders. Both *Kang Yu-wei*, the leader of the Radical Reform Movement of 1898, and Dr. *Sun Yat-sen,* the leader of the Republican Revolution in 1911, were unable and unwilling to return and remain home, even when they could. *Kang*, never returned home to his native *Namhoi* (*Nanhai*), near Canton. He died in *Qingdao* in *Shandong* in 1927. Similarly, Dr. Sun never returned to his native home in *Chung-Shaan*, near *Macao* (*Macau*). He died in *Beijing* in 1925.

Amidst chaotic conditions of the 1920s, futile wandering seemed to be the order of the day for maverick Cantonese politicians and Cantonese sojourners alike. The act of returning home to *Tong-Shaan* remained elusive, and problematic. *Kang's* words below, although quoted for use in another historical context, still resonate regarding the changing meaning of *my home, back home*, as it related to the ideal and reality of a Cantonese fountainhead in the historical context of the 1920s, a time when iconic inspirations lost their luster, and even more sadly their relevancy.

## Chapter 6

How can I live with men whose hearts are strangers to me?
I am going on a far journey to be away from them....
I set off in the morning from the Ford of Heaven;
At evening I came to the world's western end....
But when I ascended the splendor of the heavens,
I suddenly caught a glimpse of my old home...
Enough! There are no true men in the state;
no one to understand me.
Why should I cleave to the city of my birth? [97]

Many Cantonese people during the later nineteenth and early twentieth centuries encountered a perplexing and troublesome dilemma, regarding their positioning and engagement in an expanding Cantonese-speaking transnational world. This protracted sense of dilemma revolved around the notion of "home," as represented by the two iconic metaphors of *Tong-Shaan* (one's permanent home in Central Gwongdung) and *Gum-Shaan* (one's temporary, but increasingly more-or-less defacto permanent new home in Chinese America).

***Tong-Shaan*, a Cantonese metaphor for one's permanent home in Central Gwongdung**

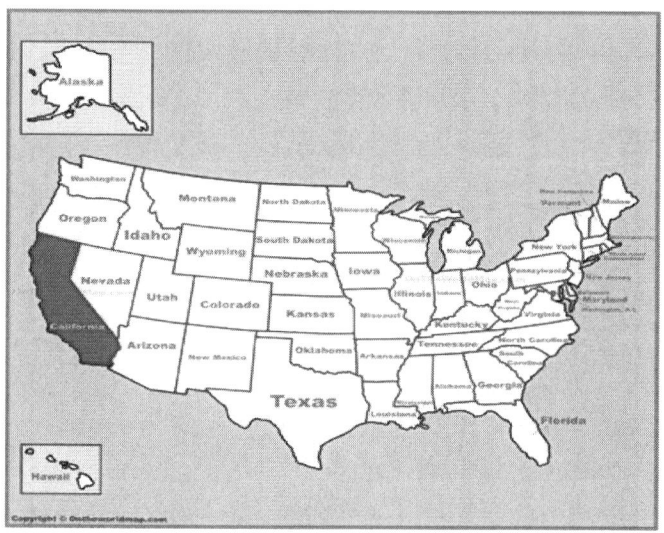

***Gum-Shaan*, a Cantonese metaphor for one's temporary home, first in northern California, and then later in all America**

The Cantonese immigrant-sojourner, i.e., *Gum-Shaan Haak* (Guest of Gold[en] Mountain[s]) represented the person most commonly identified with this dilemma. As he faced his demons, he did so with a set of pre-packaged ethno-culturally charged emotional and psychological assets and liabilities. In this context, the Cantonese Sojourner Dilemma Syndrome (CSDS) offers a useful construct for reconsidering Cantonese group identity and experience along the advancing transnational Cantonese-Chinese frontier, extending from *Tong Shaan* to *Gum-Shaan*, and back. In doing so, it also helps us to better appreciate the tangled and enigmatic relationships involving self, home, and sojourning, within a distinctly Cantonese transnational/diasporic historical and cultural context.

## Conclusion

In looking beyond objective geophysical indicators, I relocate the notion a Cantonese Fountainhead within its larger historical transnational/diasporic context, where the roots of the Cantonese community and *Yuet* culture lie deeply buried. This is evident in my identification of *Tong-Shaan*, as the graphic representation and historical embodiment of the notion of a traditional Cantonese fountainhead. Thus, *Tong-Shaan* is reflective of many converging points of focus. First, it is a graphic reminder of a particular place, inhabited by a particular people evolving through time. Second, it is a place, characterized by its own structural elements, which include geophysical, demographic, socio-cultural, and ethno-linguistic communal variables. Third, relative to mid-late nineteenth and early twentieth-century diasporic movements and transnational relationships/activities, the notion of the historical Cantonese Fountainhead takes on an expanded meaning and enhanced value for better understanding Cantonese identity and experience, in both Central Gwongdung (*Tong-Shaan)* and America *(Gum-Shaan).*

The layering of contested spaces and challenging ideas about self, society, language, and ethnicity reveals a dual track of development for both the idea and reality of an historical Cantonese Fountainhead, as it flowered in the later nineteenth and early twentieth century.

One track reflected the notion of a Cantonese Fountainhead, as viewed by non-Cantonese neighbors in Gwongdung, and other Han Chinese elsewhere in China. Here the emphasis centered on Cantonese distinctiveness, amid Cantonese concerns about Cantonese cultural authenticity, historical legitimacy, and ethno-linguistic purity. The other track, is the idea of the Cantonese fountainhead, as a conceptual construct regarding traditional *Yuet*/Cantonese identity and experience. Here the focus centered on the difficult task of forging, maintaining, and extending the constructs of that identity and experience, as they supported evolving Cantonese perceptions, identifications, and responses to the idea of "home" in its many changing forms and contexts. This task underscores this book's central theme of "what it meant to be Cantonese" in both China and America during the mid-later nineteenth and early twentieth-century.

For Cantonese people, both back home in Central Gwongdung and those elsewhere overseas- but especially for those in North America, they collectively understood that the idea of a Cantonese Fountainhead formed a key construct of traditional Cantonese identity and experience, because it embodied both a physical connection and a socio-cultural expression. Thus, *Tong-Shaan* served as a very graphic representation of the notion of a historical Cantonese Fountainhead, which served to inspire, to motivate, to comfort, and to unify and reconcile Cantonese people with their roots. Their reliance on this perception of reality provided invaluable benefits of solidarity, consensus, and continuity, which bound together those still back home in *Tong-Shaan* with those in *Gum-Shaan*, and elsewhere, via the idea of "enduring ties that bind, Cantonese style," (see chapter 5.) Actions, words, and feelings might mirror diversity and discord in many ways, on different levels and in varying degrees, however, they also simultaneously blended them into a harmonious collection of shared experiences and expectations.

In re-examining Cantonese pre-emigrant identity and experience, as it has sprung from and revolved around the idea of a Cantonese Fountainhead, two concerns have been paramount.

The first has been to properly identify, with as much specificity and accuracy as possible, the particular geophysical and demographic elements of pre-emigrant Cantonese experience, by zeroing in on a particular place and its people, as they evolved through time. This in turn involves two separate, but related tasks. The first to establish a realistic and representative socio-demographic profile of the Cantonese population in the nineteenth century, using quantitative data analysis to examine a re-constructed demographic profile within of a particular geophysical context, (see chapter 1). In this manner, evidence of prevailing material facts and conditions assist in the construction of a useful graphic representation of a heretofore vague and enigmatic notion of a Cantonese fountainhead in Central Gwongdung. The second has been an investigation of the evolving relationship between key geophysical and the geo-historical elements, which have historically crafted *Yuet*/Cantonese identity/experience in Central Gwongdung, (see chapter 2).

The second concern has been to investigate the construction of the traditional Cantonese identity, as it has factored into the unfolding of the historical narrative that gave it expression, and which also nurtured its development over time. This analysis centered on the complex and often nuanced relationship between the construction of Cantonese ethnic group identity, and the parallel ongoing development of the larger distinctive self-ascribed Cantonese cultural persona. The former relates to a series of ethnic and speech community labels, which alternately both divide and unify groups commonly identified with the broader rubric of Cantonese ethnicity (see chapter 3). The latter focuses on self-ascribed qualities of Cantonese culture, which have historically represented that culture as a distinctively conservative contrarian counter-culture (C4) (see chapter 4).

These elements have exerted tremendous influence over traditional Cantonese group identity formation, relative to those ascribed identity characteristics, which identify who the Cantonese are among themselves, and in the eyes of others. These matters have also been critically significant in orchestrating Cantonese interactions and relationships with others beyond the Cantonese community, both at home in *Tong-Shaan* and in *Gum-Shaan*.

The historical construction of the Cantonese persona took place during the later nineteenth century at the Cantonese fountainhead in Central Gwongdung, in advance of its replication in other parts of Gwongdung, the *Lingnam* region, elsewhere in China, and finally transnationally throughout the Cantonese-speaking world. This suggests a dynamic and enduring linkage between the conceptualization of *Tong-Shaan*, as the fountainhead of Cantonese society and culture, and the reality of a vital nexus between *Tong-Shaan* and *Gum-Shaan*, as co-contemporary transnational historical realities.

The real value of re-examining these matters lies not so much in their simplistic chronological/situational juxtaposition, but rather in the effort to better understand how these elements alternately work together and/or against each other, to bring about distinct and different solutions to the same set of challenges encountered by various different co-contemporary emigrant-immigrant groups.

This proposition underscores the view that efforts at successful decision-making, problem-solving, and conflict resolution tasks in early Cantonese-Chinese America flowed from both a conscious application of Old-World strategies and unconscious maintenance of Old-World values, which again is not intended to suggest a predetermined agenda or the operation of a predictive function. It is rather a situation, where pre-emigrant experiences back home provided helpful building blocks for enabling Cantonese emigrants to move forward in constructive ways, to meet the many challenges of being immigrants in distant alien, often hostile, societies. These elements were evident in how Cantonese immigrants responded to their sense of dilemma, by way of the alternatives they considered, the options they chose, the opportunities they capitalized on, and the tools they fashioned to achieve their goals.

Precedents at home, as they were later replicated in America, mirrored both long-term interests and short-term needs; collective imperatives and individual preferences; material necessities and non-material requirements, while addressing both ethnic community extra-communal threats and ethnic intra-communal tensions and conflicts. Thus, earlier experiences back home provided a formula for communal growth elsewhere, by promoting ethnic solidarity and economic prosperity, under manifestly adverse conditions.

Experiences back home regarding the development of numerous social and civic community organizations provided a basis for the comforts and constraints of family life, in the face of their conspicuous absence overseas. They also helped to preserve an essentially conservative mindset and values, while at the same time promoting a "can do" pragmatic, common-sense, goal-orientated approach to the challenges and tasks of everyday life in new distant locations. These contradictory elements were not easily summoned to service in alien geophysical and socio-cultural settings, nor were they automatic in their application. They were however, sufficiently applicable and useful to the task of replicating vital elements of traditional Cantonese society and culture in America.

I conclude my revisionist discussion about *Tong-Shaan*, as the traditional Cantonese fountainhead, with a caveat, that the iconic representation of "home" via the metaphor of "*Shaan*" appeared more enigmatic and elusive than ever in the eyes of many Cantonese after 1900, due to rapidly changing material conditions and chaotic times. In this context, the *Tong-Shaan* metaphor *for home,* and/or *back home*, still mirrored the idea of a Cantonese fountainhead- but with a significantly different meaning and sense of relevance. If *Tong-Shaan* persisted as a beacon of shared inspiration and mutual longing among Cantonese overseas sojourners and other Cantonese, it did so in new and unforeseen ways, which alternately complemented and complicated "what it meant to be Cantonese in the later nineteenth and early twentieth century."

Similarly, *Gum-Shan*, as a metaphor for home in America, also underwent change relative to its representation and application. In this context, home in *Gum-Shaan* was no longer regarded as, "my temporary home away from home, but in reality, my real home now and for the foreseeable future," due to the new reality of Chinese Exclusion in America. Cantonese immigrant-sojourners in America and elsewhere overseas, might agree that *Tong-Shaan* remained a much revered and beloved iconic representation of "home," as one's "real home," but that perspective became increasingly fossilized over time after 1900, precisely because it was iconic. In contrast *Gum-Shaan* represented the harsh reality of Cantonese immigrant-sojourner life, far beyond *Tong-Shaan*.

In a sense, the two heretofore symmetrically paired metaphors representing Cantonese notions of home were no longer on a par, relative to their ascribed meaning, representations, and reproduction. In the transnational context of the early twentieth century, they were no longer simplistic metaphors, representing different conditions and experiences, but rather they manifested new, if still enigmatic, sign posts pointing to shifting loyalties, and new priorities, amid momentous changing conditions after 1900. Consequently, the notion of a traditional Cantonese fountainhead, identified as *Tong-Shaan*, meets many standards, confirms many precedents, represents many changing connotations, and fulfills many expectations regarding the historical reality of what it meant to be Cantonese in the later nineteenth and early twentieth-centuries, in both China and America.

While the nature and meaning of the paired metaphors of *Tong-Shaan* (my home in China) and *Gum-Shaan* (my home in America) were significantly transformed after 1900, they still persisted as a unique open-ended, if largely unarticulated and subconscious, shared enigmatic representation of Cantonese life in its expanded transnational/diasporic context. Quite simply, among Cantonese people, *Tong-Shaan* and *Gum-Shaan* both represented pivotal locations where "reality" and "fantasy" met, co-existed, and over-lapped. This subjectively imagined and virtually experienced proposition formed the corner stone of "What it meant to be Cantonese" in China and America, in the later nineteenth and early twentieth-century.

**Mountainous landscape of *Tong-Shaan* (Central Gwongdung), where "reality" and "fantasy" met**

**Rolling hilly landscape of *Gum-Shaan* (Northern California), where "reality" and "fantasy" met**

Chapter 6

[1] "Political Development in Chinese America, 1850–1900," by Douglas W. Lee (PhD dissertation Modern Chinese History, University of California, Santa Barbara, 1979).

[2] Letters home also provide a rich source of evidence about how immigrant-sojourners felt about their situation, and how family members left at home viewed the difficulties of their fathers, sons and husbands emigrating overseas. Some of these have been collected and published. See, Chinese American Voices, From the Gold Rush to the Present, Compiled and edited by Judy Yung, Gordon H Chang, & Him Mark Lai, (Berkeley: University of California Press, 2006), see especially, "Kam Wah Chung Letters (1898–1903)," pp. 97–102. Letters are valuable because they provide a prose narrative of personal difficulties and experiences. However, because I want to emphasize the common denominator of a shared perspective and mutual experience, I have chosen to focus more on poetry, as a more effective and evocative expression of feelings and emotions. Poetry effectively touches upon both personal feelings and collective sensibilities in an especially forceful and meaningful way. Cantonese Poetry carved on the wooden walls of immigration detention facilities on Angel Island in San Francisco Bay are especially evocative in their ability to link personal feelings and public sentiment, regarding frustrations, anxiety, and hardship. They express these matters in an unmistakably dignified and poignant way.

[3] See, Ellen Oxfield, Blood, Sweat, and Mahjong: Family and Enterprise in an Overseas Chinese Community, (Cornell Anthology of Contemporary Issues), (Ithaca, NY: Cornell University Press, 1993).

[4] Selective excerpts from a letter from a mother in Gwongdung, to her son in John Day, Oregon February 2, 1898, see Kam Wah Chung Letters (1898–1903) from John Day, Oregon, pp. 99–100, in Chinese American Voices, From the Gold Rush to the Present, edited by Judy Young, Gordon H. Chang, and Him Mark Lai, (Berkeley: University of California Press, 2006).

[5] Ibid., see pp. 100–101. (this letter is dated July, 1899).

[6] Ibid., pp.101–102. (this letter is dated May 28, 1903).

[7] This expressed itself in a variety of ways ranging from literary creations to social science conceptualizations. See the following novels: Jade Snow Wong, Fifth Chinese Daughter, (originally published in 1945) (Seattle: University of Washington Press, 1989); Monica Sone, Nisei Daughter, (originally published in 1953) (Seattle: University of Washington, 2014); John Okada, No No Boy, (originally published in 1957) (Seattle: University of Washington, 1981); Amy Tan, The Joy Luck Club, (New York: Ballatine Books, 1989); Chang-Rae Lee, Native Speaker, (Berkeley Books, 1995); Eric Liu, The Accidental Asian, Notes of a Native Speaker, (New York City: Vintage Books of Random House1998); also see plays by Frank Chin, "The Chickencoop Chinaman," (1972) and "The Year of the Dragon," (1974) (Seattle: University of Washington Press, 1981). For social science works of the 1970s, see the following: Victor Low, The Unimpressible Race, A Century of Educational Struggle by the Chinese in San Francisco, (San Francisco: East/West Publishing Company. 1982); Sue Fawn Chung, "The Chinese American Citizens Alliance: An Effort at Assimilation, 1895–1965," in Chinese America: History and Perspectives (San Francisco: Chinese Historical Society of America, 1988), pp.30–57) (Annual Journal of the Chinese Historical Society of America); Betty Lee Sung, The Story of the Chinese in America, (Originally published as Mountain of Gold, 1967) (New York City: Collier Books, division of Macmillan Publishing, 1971). This work is very much outdated in both its contents and perspectives about Chinese Americans and assimilation, but it is the best representative general work in the period (1950–1970) when cultural assimilation was viewed as the signpost of Chinese American

success in American society. The following contemporary (post 1990s) works offer either contrasting or opposing views regarding the appropriateness/usefulness of cultural assimilation for Asian Americans. Gary Y. Okihiro, Margins and Mainstreams, Asians in American History and Culture, (Seattle: University of Washington Press, 1994); Ann Anlin Cheng, The Melancholy of Race: Psychoanalysis, Assimilation, and Hidden Grief, (New York: Oxford University Press, 2001); Shehong Chen, Being Chinese, Becoming Chinese American, (Urbana, Illinois: University of Illinois Press, 2002); Andrea Louie, Chinese-ness Across Borders, Renegotiating Chinese Identities in China and the United States,) (Durham: Duke University Press, 2004); Daryl J. Maeda, Chains of Babylon, The Rise of Asian America, (Minneapolis: University of Minnesota Press, 2009); Stephen Murphey-Shigematsu, When Half is Whole: Multi-Ethnic Asian American Identities, (Stanford, Ca: Stanford University Press, 2012); Asian American Identities and Practices: Folkloric Expressions in Everyday life, edited by Jonathan H.X. Lee and Kathleen Nadeau, (Lexington Books, 2015); Ellen D. Wu, The Color of Success, Asian Americans and the Origins of the Model Minority, (Princeton New Jersey: Princeton University Press, 2015);

[8] Marlon K. Hom, Songs of Gold Mountain, Cantonese Rhymes from San Francisco Chinatown, (Berkeley: University of California Press, 1987), Poem 19, page 95 (JSGJ II.12b). Hereafter, regarding the JSGJ abbreviation, see Translator's note about these abbreviations after the acknowledgments, as follows JSGJ I: *Jinshan ge ji* (1911); JSGJ II: *Jinshan ge erji* (1915).

[9] See following: Stanley Sue and James Morishima, Mental Health of Asian Americans, Contemporary Issues in Identifying and Treating Mental Health Problems, (Jossey-Bass Publishers, 1988); Laura Uba, Asian Americans, Personality Patterns, Identity and Mental Health; (Guilford Press, 1993); Asian American Mental Health, Assessment Theories and Methods, Edited by Karen S. Kurasaki, Sumie Okazaki & Stanley Sue, (International and Cultural Psychology Series) (Spring, 2002)

[10] See generally, Sucheng Chan, This Bitter-Sweet Soil, The Chinese in California Agriculture, 1860–1910, (Berkeley: University of California Press, 1986.)

[11] Re: Chinese in the American West, see the following: Rose Hum Lee, The Growth and Decline of Chinese Communities in the Rocky Mountain Region,(originally PhD dissertation Sociology, University of Chicago, 1947), (New York: Arno Press, 1978); The Chinese in Arizona, 1870–1950, A Context for Historic Preservation Planning, prepared by Melissa Keane, A.E. Rogerset. Al, for the Arizona State Historic Office and the City of Phoenix Planning Department (May 1992); Chris Friday, Organizing Asian American Labor, The Pacific Coast Canned Salmon Industry, 1870–1942, (Philadelphia: Temple University Press, 1994); Liping Zhu, A Chinaman's Chance, The Chinese on the Rocky Mountain Mining Frontier, (Niwot, Colorado: University of Colorado Press, 1997); Chinese on the American Frontier, Edited by Arif Dirlik, (with the assistance of Malcolm Yeung), (New York: Rowman & Littlefield Publishers, 2003) (Pacific Formations series); Liping Zhu and Rose Estep Fosha, Thenic Oasis, The Chinese in the Black Hills, (Pierre: South Dakota State Historical Society Press, 2004); Jean Pfaelzer, Driven Out, The Forgotten War Against Chinese Americans, (New York: Random House, 2007); Sue Fawn Chung, In Pursuit of Gold, Chinese American Miners and Merchants in the American West, (Urbana: University of Illinois Press, 2011); Sue Fawn Chung, Chinese in the Woods, Logging and Lumbering in the American West, (Urbana: University of Illinois Press, 2015); William Wei, Asians in Colorado, A History of Persecution and Perseverance in the Centennial State, (Seattle: University of

Washington Press, 2016). Re: Chinese settlement in Mississippi and Louisiana, see following: James W. Loewen, The Mississippi Chinese, Between Black and White, (Cambridge, Mass: Harvard University Press, 1971); also see Robert Seto Quan, Lotus Among the Magnolias, The Mississippi Chinese,(Jackson, Mississippi: University Press of Mississippi: 2007)(originally published 1982); also see, Lucy M. Cohen, Chinese in Post Civil War South, A People Without A History, (Baton Rouge: Louisiana State University Press, 1984); John Jung, Chopsticks in the Land of Cotton, Lives of Mississippi Delta Chinese Grocers, (2nd edition) (Yin-Yang Press, 2011);

[12] Re: overview of Chinese migration and settlement of Midwest and Atlantic coast region, see following: Huping Ling, Chinese St. Louis, From Enclave to Cultural Community, (Philadelphia: Temple University Press, 2004); Huping Ling, Chinese Chicago, Race, Transnational Migration, and Community Since 1870, (Stanford, California: Stanford University Press, 2012); Peter Kwong, Chinatown, New York, (New York: Monthly Review Press, 1979); Douglas W. Lee, "The Early Chinese Community in Washington D.C., 1880–1930," in The Annals of the Chinese Historical Society of the Pacific Northwest, (1983), pp. 89–92; John Kuo Wei Tchen, "New York Chinese: The Nineteenth-Century Pre-Chinatown Settlement," in Chinese America: History and Perspectives (1990) (Annual Journal of the Chinese Historical Society of America), pp. 157–192; Xinyang Wang, Surviving the City, The Chinese Immigrant Experience in New York City, 1890–1970, (New York: Rowman & Littlefield Publishers, 2001); Wing-kai To, (with Chinese Historical Society of New England) Chinese in Boston, 1870–1965 (Arcadia Publishing, 2008); Shirley J. Yee, An Immigrant Neighborhood, Interethnic and Interracial Encounters in New York Before 1930, (Philadelphia: Temple University Press, 2012);

[13] Hom, Songs of Gold Mountain, poem 25, page 101. (JSGJ II.11b)

[14] See generally the following works: Lucian Pye, The Spirit of Chinese Politics, A Psychocultural Study of the Authority Crisis in Political Development, (Cambridge, Mass: MIT University Press, 1968); Richard Solomon, Mao's Revolution and China's Political Culture, (Berkeley: University of California Press, 1969).

[15] See following: Marlon Hom, folk lit; Lai, Lim, and Yung ISLAND, Poetry and History; and Wing Chung Ng, The Rise of Cantonese Opera, (Urbana, Illinois: University of Illinois Press, 2015).

[16] Hom, Songs of Gold Mountain, poem 24, page 100. (JSGJ II.11a)

[17] "Eating bitterness" is a traditional Chinese phrase representing the idea of enduring and embracing present hardship, for the sake of future improvement. There is also the metaphor of eating a bowl of tea, where one eats (or drinks) bitter Chinese herbal medicine to recover from illness or injury. In both instances, there is the idea of enduring the unpleasant, the "bitter" in order to gain the pleasant or the "sweetness" that life has to offer. See generally, Louis Chu, Eating a Bowl of Tea, (Seattle: University of Washington Press, 1968).

[18] Hom, Songs of Gold Mountain, poem 83, page 165. (JSGJ I.12b)

[19] Ibid., poem 203, page 302, (JSGJ II.48b)

[20] Ibid., poem 196, page 295, (JSGJ I.1b)

[21] Ibid., poem 162, page 255. (JSGJ II.26b)

[22] Ibid., poem 75, page 157, (JSGJ I.12b)

[23] Ibid., poem 81, page 163, (JSGJ I.13a)

[24] Ibid., poem 163, page 256, (JSGJ II.25a)

[25] Ng, The Rise of Cantonese Opera, pp. 131, 132, 133; also see Ronald Riddle, "The Cantonese Opera: A Chapter in Chinese-American History," in The Life, Influence and Role of the Chinese in the United States, 1776–1960, Proceedings/Papers of the National Conference held at the University of San Francisco, July 10–12, 1975, sponsored by the Chinese Historical Society of America, pp. 40–47.

[26] Virgil K.Y. Ho, Understanding Canton, Re-Thinking Popular Culture in the Republican Period, (New York: Oxford University Press, 2005) (part of series on Studies of Contemporary China), see chapter 6, "Cantonese Opera as a Mirror of Society," see specifically section, "Why was Cantonese opera so Popular?" pp. 320–327; also see Marjorie K.M. Chan, "Cantonese Opera and the Growth and Spread of Vernacular Written Cantonese in the Twentieth Century," in the Proceedings of the Seventeenth North American Conference on Chinese Linguistics (NAC11-17) pp. 1-18, edited by Qain Gao (Los Angeles: Gsil Publications, University of Southern California, 2005).

[27] Ho, Understanding Canton, p.325

[28] Ng, The Rise of Cantonese Opera., pp. 173.

[29] Ibid., pp.81–82; also see Ho, Understanding Canton, pp. 301–304, 327–331.

[30] The "vice trades" refers to commercialized prostitution, opium, and gambling in Cantonese overseas communities, which were typically institutionalized commercial enterprises of secret societies, the "tongs"(autonomous renegade secret society groups) and criminal syndicates both in China, in America, and elsewhere within the transnational setting on both sides of the Pacific.

[31] Re: new "Civic Culture," see Douglas W. Lee, "Political Development in Chinese America, 1850–1900," PhD dissertation (History) University of California, Santa Barbara (1979), pp. 276–287.

[32] See following works: Stanford Lyman, "The Structure of Chinese Society in Nineteenth-Century America," PhD dissertation, University of California, Berkeley (Sociology) 1961; also by Lyman, "Conflict and Web of Group Affiliation in San Francisco's Chinatown, 1850–1910," in Asians in North America, Stanford Lyman editor (Santa Barbara: ABC Clio, 1977), pp.103–118.

[33] Ng, The Rise of Cantonese Opera., pp. 173.

[34] Lucian W. Pye, The Spirit of Chinese Politics, A Psychocultural Study of the Authority Crisis in Political Development, (Cambridge, Mass: MIT Press, 1968), p. 113.

[35] Hom, Songs of Gold Mountain, poem 32, page 108. (JSGJ I.20a)

[36] Pye, The Spirit of Chinese Politics, P.100

[37] Solomon, Mao's Revolution, p. 62.

[38] Island, Poetry and History, (First edition, 1980) p. 66, poem #31. (note, the reference to prison refers to the US Immigration detention center on Angel Island in San Francisco Bay.)

[39] Hom, Songs of Gold Mountain, poem 18, page 94. (JSGJ II.12a)

[40] Ibid., poem 30, page 106. (JSGJ I.20b)

[41] Ibid., poem 84, page 166. (JSGJ I.12a)

[42] Ibid., poem 31, page 107. (JSGJ I.20a)

[43] Island, Poetry and History, (First edition, 1980), poem #55, page 106.

[44] Hom, Songs of Gold Mountain, poem 34, page 110. (JSGJ I.12a)

[45] Island, Poetry and History, (First edition, 1980), poem #22, page 58.

[46] Ibid., from long narrative poem, lines 3–5, page 140.

[47] Island, Poetry and History of Chinese Immigrants on Angel Island, 1910–1940, edited by

Him Mark Lai, Genny Lim, & Judy Yung, (Second edition) (San Francisco: HOC DOI (History of Chinese Detained on Island- a project of the Chinese Cultural Foundation of San Francisco, 1980), P. 34, poem #3.

[48] Hom, Songs of Gold Mountain, poem 26, page 102, (JSGJ II.59b)

[49] Ibid., poem 23, page 99, (JSGJ II.12a)

[50] On the internet, search for following: Reverend William Speer, Ng Poon Chew, Presbyterian and Baptist missionary work in San Francisco Chinatown 1870–1920, also see the following works: Carol Green Wilson, Chinatown Quest, The Life Adventures of Donaldina Cameron, (Stanford: Stanford University Press, 1950) (Revised edition); Lorna Logan, Ventures in Mission, the Cameron House Story (1976); Corinne K. Hoexter, From Canton to California, The Epic of Chinese Immigration, (This book has some biographical material on Reverend Ng Poon Chew) (New York: Four Winds Press, 1976); Mildred Crowl Martin, Chinatown's Angry Angel, The Story of Donaldina Cameron, (Pacific Books, 1977); Kristin & Kathryn Wong, Fierce Compassion, The Life of Abolitionist Donaldina Cameron, (New Earth Enterprises, 2012);Julia Flynn Siler, The White Devil's Daughters, The Women Who Fought Slavery in San Francisco Chinatown, (New York: Knopf, 2019).

[51] "Civic Culture," see Douglas W. Lee, "Political Development in Chinese America, 1850–1900," pp. 276–287.

[52] Hom, Songs of Gold Mountain, poem 69, page 151. (JSGJ I.11.b)

[53] Ibid., poem 86, page 168. (JSGJ I. 12a)

[54] Island, Poetry and History, (First edition, 1980), poem #14, page 153.

[55] Hom, Songs of Gold Mountain, poem 100, page 185. (JSGJ II.44a)

[56] Ibid., poem 107, page 192. (JSGJ I.6b)

[57] Ibid., poem 105, page 190. (JSGJ I.53a)

[58] Ibid., poem in the introduction, at the top of page 45.

[59] See generally, Landscape and Power, edited by W.J.T. Mitchell, (Chicago: University of Chicago Press, 1994), pp.1–3, and 212–213.

[60] Alan H. Baker and Gideon Biger, Ideology and Landscape in Historical Perspective, Essays on the Meanings of Some Places in the Past, (London, UK: Cambridge, 1992), p. 2

[61] Pilgrims and Sacred Sites in China, edited by Susan Naquin and Chun-fang Yu, (Berkeley: University of California Press, 1992), p. 1.

[62] The famous poet is Li Po, a ninth-century poet from Sichuan. He was one of the greatest Tang dynasty poets, which lent additional special meaning for Cantonese people.

[63] Li Po and Tu Fu, Poems Selected and Translated with an Introduction and Notes, by Arthur Cooper, with Chinese calligraphy by Shui Chien-Tung, (New York: Penguin Books, 1973), p. 109.

[64] Hom, Songs of Golden Mountain, see, "Introduction to Cantonese Vernacular Rhymes from San Francisco Chinatown," pp. 3–73

[65] Island, Poetry and History, (First edition, 1980), poem #28, page 64.

[66] Mitchell, Landscape and Power, p. 1.

[67] Peter Bishop, The Myth of Shangri-La, Tibet, Travel Writing and the Western Creation of Sacred Landscape, (Berkeley: University of California, Press, 1989), p. 1.

[68] James Harpur. The Atlas Of Sacred Places, Meeting Points Of Heaven And Earth, (New York: Henry Holt Reference Book, Henry Colt Co. 1994.)

[69] Ibid., p.10.

[70] Hom, Songs of Gold Mountain, poem 85, page 167. (JSGJ I.11b)

[71] Harpur. The Atlas of Sacred Places, p.10.
[72] Douglas Davies, "The Evocative Symbolism of Trees," in The Iconography of Landscape, Essays on the Symbolic Representation, Design, and Use of Past Environments, edited by Denis Cosgrove and Stephen Daniels, (New York: Cambridge, University Press, 1988), p.32.
[73] Naquin and Yu, Pilgrims and Sacred Sites in China, p.11.
[74] Ibid., p.11.
[75] Ibid., see map of China with sacred mountain(s) located at the front of the book.
[76] Ibid., p.11.
[77] See chapter 4, "Cantonese Culture as a Conservative Contrarian Counter-Culture."
[78] *Tong-Shaan* did not have the connotation of "Motherland" or "Fatherland," because these terms imply reference to a nation or a country, which the geographical term Central Gwongdung certainly does not (i.e., it is a micro-region within a province). In this context, *Tong-Shaan*, did not have any ideological meaning or political point of reference.
[79] Hom, Songs of Gold Mountain, poem 21, page 97. (JSGJ II.44a)
[80] Harpur. The Atlas of Sacred Places, Meeting Points Of Heaven And Earth, p.10.
[81] In regards to British Columbia, see generally James Morton, In the Sea of Sterile Mountains: The Chinese in British Columbia, (Vancouver, Canada: J.J. Douglas, 1974); also see, Harry Con, Ronald J. Con, Gordon Johnson, Edgar Wickberg, et. al., From China to Canada, A History of the Chinese Communities in Canada, (Toronto: McCelland and Stewart, 1988).
[82] See generally, The Sandalwood Mountains: Readings and Stories of the Early Chinese Immigrants in Hawaii, (Honolulu, University of Hawaii Press, 1975).
[83] Sucheng Chan, Asian Americans, An Interpretative History, (Boston, Twayne Publishers (G.K. Hall, 1991), p.28.
[84] The routine transliterated term *Saam Fan-See* (*San-fan-tzu*) (San Francisco) is used by many Chinese today, in place of *Dai Fow*, ([the]Great [or Big] Seaport[town]). commonly used among the older *Longtime Californ'* or pre- WW II, the older Cantonese community. Today, when making reference to Chinese America, as an ethnic community in America, historically and culturally the term *Gum—Shaan* is still used and respected as an authentic historical term/label.re: term "Longtime Californ," see Victor Nee and Brett de Bary Nee, Longtime Californ': A Documentary Study of an American Chinatown, (New York: Pantheon Books, Random House, 1972); Re: term "Dai-Fow," see, Marjorie K. Chan and Douglas W. Lee, "Chinatown Chinese: A Linguistic and Historical Re-Evaluation," Amerasia Journal, 8:1 (1981), pp. 111–128.
[85] See generally, Karl Lo and H. Mark Lai, Chinese Newspapers Published in North America, 1854–1975, (Washington D.C.: Center for Chinese Research Materials, Association of Research Libraries, 1977).
[86] Sidney Lau, A Practical Cantonese-English Dictionary, (Hong Kong: Hong Kong Government Printer, 1977), p. 636. item #34.
[87] Hom, Song of Gold Mountain, p.41, as cited from *Taishan ge yao ji* (A collection of Taishan folk songs) ed. By Chen Yuanzhu, (Taibei, Taiwan, Folklore Books, 1969) (originally printed in 1929), song 59, p. 72.
[88] Hom, Song of Gold Mountain, p.77, poem 4;
[89] Ibid., p.41, as cited from *Taishan ge yao ji* (ed. by Chen), song 87, p. 104.
[90] Ibid., Chen, Song 127, p. 146.
[91] Hom, Song of Gold Mountain, p.44, as cited from, Anon. (Tan Bi'an), "Jinshan (*Gum-*

*Shaan*) fu xing" ("Songs of the wife of a Gold Mountain man (*Gum-Shaan Haak*), Xinning zazhi 1100 (January 1949): 68.

[92] Chung Sai Yat Po (a San Francisco Chinese language newspaper), October 23, 1950, as cited in Xiaojian Zhao, Remaking Chinese America, Immigration, Family, and Community, 1940–1965, (New Brunswick, New Jersey: Rutgers University Press, 2002), p. 141, endnote #49

[93] In Washington, DC's Chinatown, my father was deeply involved in local social/civic organizations. He owned a restaurant. On many occasions, I recall being asked to greet "Uncle" so and so, and his "wife" who I addressed as "Auntie." Most of these "aunties" were not Chinese, but instead were White or Black ladies. At the time, it all seemed so natural and "normal." I did not know that they all had Chinese wives back home in *Tong-Shaan*. The fact that my mother was Chinese and also co-owner of the largest Chinese restaurant in Washington, DC's Chinatown was extraordinarily unique. At the time, all of this was quite unknown to me. It is also well documented that Cantonese Chinese in the South, such as the Mississippi Delta also took local black ladies as common law wives, with whom they had children. In cases where Chinese wives later joined their husbands, the black ladies were sent back to their families, either with their kids- or in some cases the Chinese wife would raise the half-black half-Chinese children with her own. See, James W. Loewen, The Mississippi Chinese, pp. 135–138.

[94] I visited my father's ancestral village of Nam Tsun in 1978 in Toishan County, where I met a distant "Uncle" (actually second cousin), who had sojourned/settled in America from 1928–1948. He returned to Nam Tsun in 1948 and stayed for a year, expecting to return to New York in 1949–1950. However, because of the Communist revolution in 1949, he was unable to leave for Hong Kong. He shared with me his regret for the lost opportunity to return to *Gum-Shaan*, and was envious and resentful that my father, his cousin, had "made it so successfully" there, as a restaurant owner and community leader in Washington, DC's small Chinatown, while he was "stuck" back in the village back in Toi-Shaan.

[95] See Louis Chu, Eat A Bowl of Tea, (Seattle: University of Washington, 1979 [originally published 1961] (latest edition 2002) This dilemma is portrayed vividly in a Movie, with the same title, based on the book.

[96] The situation is analogous to the new college student, who when leaving a positive home environment, feels lonely and out of place in his/her first semester away at college. Consequently, the first semester is spent missing home, dreaming of old high school times and friends. Return home for the Christmas break yields a kind of shock, people and things weren't quite the way they were remembered, and the holidays are spent in anticipation of returning to college, with new friends and an exciting life. Return to college after the holidays often meant a new round of melancholy, "being here, but wishing I was there."

[97] David Hawks, trans. Ch'u Tz'u: The Songs of the South, (Oxford UK: Clarendon Press, 1959) also (Boston: Little Brown and Co., 1962), pp.33–34, lines 171,174,184 and 186., as cited by Kung-chuan Hsiao, A Modern China and A New World, K'ang Yu-wei, Reformer and Utopian, 1858-1927, (Seattle: University of Washington Press, 1975), p.36, footnote #87.

# CONCLUSION

At the end of this study, we return to the initial provocative, yet enigmatic, proposition of "What it meant to be Cantonese in the later nineteenth and early twentieth-century." This intriguing rhetorical question has been a problematic challenge to decipher, for two reasons. First, its simplicity belies a complex nuanced view of a historical narrative, which although possessing an abundance of material facts, has remained resistant as an evidentiary basis for fruitful investigation. This results from the lack a suitable analytical framework, in which to establish a creditable rationale for this proposition. Second, the search for meaning in this proposition has been expanded and complicated by its transnational and diasporic contextualization.

Given the proposition, that Cantonese people were historically distinct, even unique, when compared with other Han Chinese, it logically follows that we should inquire about how this came about, and why it mattered so much. In seeking to answer these threshold questions, I initially focused on identifying and assessing various constructs that contextualized the Cantonese sense of shared group identity and experience. These elements serve as a useful Segway to educating us about the meaning of being Cantonese.

The foundational super structure of Cantonese identity and experience is located in the historical intersection of geophysical and socio-demographic patterns of development over the course of two millennia. This view links a specific place, i.e., Central Gwongdung, with a particular people, i.e., the Cantonese, and their *Yuet*/Cantonese regional culture/language. While this perspective is irrefutable, both as historical fact and as a theoretical construct, we still need to understand how these factors contextualized and helped construct traditional Cantonese group identity, and experience(s).

Beyond the obvious concrete link between a place and a people, there remains the critically important, but as yet unanswered question of the evolving relationship between these physical connections, (between a place and people)

Conclusion

and how Cantonese people thought about, remembered, and subjectively viewed them in the construction of their group identity. Geophysical and sociodemographic determinants sculptured traditional Cantonese group identity and experience, by way of historic settlement and distribution patterns in Central Gwongdung. Both regionally and locally, geography and demography defined and distinguished local Cantonese group identity/experience. The historical development of Cantonese core areas and peripheries, defined macro regional identifications and synchronized them with micro local identities. They were also critical to the construction of divergent, but often overlapping, views about "us" and "them." In this way, the collective memory of the historical nexus between Central Gwongdung, Cantonese people, and their *Yuet* language/culture respectively, served as an enduring basis for the construction of Cantonese group identity and experience. This shared understanding, about the objective historical relationship, and the subjective graphic representation of "a place" and "a people," formed the first and foremost construct of Cantonese identity.

The distinctiveness of nineteenth-century Cantonese group identity was underscored by bold claims regarding the authenticity of *Yuet* language/culture, and the purity of Cantonese speech. Beyond serving as a vehicle for communication, a regional language, and its varieties of local speech, also existed as something to be respectfully treasured and enriched by continuous use. In this way, *Yuet* language technicalities and Cantonese speech conventions underscored the atypical persona of Cantonese people. This distinctiveness of language and speech collectively represented itself as South China's only true bona fide regional language/dialect. Consequently, neither the *Wu* community in *Jiangnan*, nor the *Min* community of Fujian (and in East and West Gwongdung) could rival the scale of use, and high status of *Yuet*/Cantonese in Central Gwongdung and throughout the *Lingnam* region.

In this way, Cantonese people were immensely proud, indeed often arrogant, in their high regard and deep affection for their speech/language. They often took delight in using Cantonese speech, not merely to communicate, but also as an opportunity to demonstrate technical proficiency, and as evidence of an appreciation of the aesthetic beauty and subtle art of expression.

## Conclusion

Both Cantonese people and other Han Chinese recognized the inherent difficulties and vast distance separating *Yuet*/Cantonese dialects from mainstream Han Chinese language/speech. This uneasy co-existence dates from the Ming-Qing dynasties, when the effort to identify what constituted mainstream Chinese language/speech was first identified as *Guanhua*, (*Kuan-hua*), (the *Beijing* dialect, or "speech of the officials.") In the Republican era, Chinese speech was identified as *Guoyu*, (*Kuo-yu*), ("the national language.") Finally, it became *Putonghua ("common language")* in the PRC. This historical sense of separateness and distinctiveness of Cantonese speech and *Yuet* Language, clearly identified who was Cantonese, and who was not, to the extent that it definitively exemplified what it meant to be Cantonese, in the period, 1850-1900.

Among Cantonese people, ethnic and local speech community identifications existed as important corollaries to native place identifications, whereby contradictions of ethnic/speech rivalry, competition, and conflict could be negotiated and overcome to obtain degrees of compromise and cooperation. This pattern of regional/local social engagement often brought about beneficial degrees of ethnic/speech solidarity and unity. This served as another example of a widely shared consensus of what it meant to be Cantonese in the period 1850-1920.

The enduring force of a conservative contrarian counter-culture (C4) provided a shared basis, and common frame of reference, for how Cantonese people viewed their world and their place in it. In this perspective, Cantonese cultural authenticity, historical legitimacy, and purity of speech and language, were basic constructs for preserving an uncompromised conservative mindset and an untainted contrarian outlook. This collective confidence flowed from ascribed Tang period standards and models, which shaped *Yuet*/Cantonese character, thinking, and conduct with power and precision. These determinants permeated Cantonese popular mass culture, as well as its antithetical, yet also complementary, elite high culture, such that there existed overlapping shared sensitivities, representations, and expectations, regarding what it meant to be Cantonese.

Among Cantonese people, both at home in Central Gwongdung, and elsewhere in distant overseas locations, there existed a persistent and compelling shared sense of appreciation of the "ties that bind, Cantonese style." Again, these linkages belong to one of two broad categories, relative to where and how they impacted Cantonese social engagement with other Cantonese.

The first category consisted of shared experiences in dealing with impersonal objective material conditions, (e.g., geography, climate, environment, and ecology.) Cantonese society could only try to mitigate the adverse effects of situations beyond their ability to forecast, control, or negate.

The second category of linkages that bound Cantonese people together arose from the dynamics of social engagement. This ranged from the complex and nuanced, to the simple and mundane, and from the remote to the commonplace. Some were manifest in the broad constructs of identity and experience, such as: 1) Cantonese speech, and *Yuet* language and culture, 2) regional ethnic identity and local speech community labels, 3) Marginalized homosocial relationships and the construction of Cantonese communal solidarity, 4) Enduring ties between Cantonese agnatic lineages and their associated local villages, 5) Traditional Cantonese rural marketing systems, as essential hubs for local economic activity, and 6) The primacy of native place, as a critical identification label among Cantonese people. Other considerations of enduring ties consisted of established shared proclivities, interests, and passions. This included: 7) Cantonese cuisine and the Cantonese obsession with food preparation and consumption, 8) The Cantonese mania for gambling, as a fast track for obtaining *Fa-choy,* 9) Cantonese opera: communal social engagement and the glittering centerpiece of popular culture, and 10) Cantonese popular culture, as a series of traditions, customs, and practices. These diverse aspects of traditional *Yuet*/Cantonese social engagement, clearly show that the "ties that bind, Cantonese style," constituted a rich potpourri of shared experiences and expectations, which further underscored what it meant to be Cantonese.

One of the most formidable and enduring illustrations of what it meant to be Cantonese in the period of 1850-1920, consisted of a refurbished and redirected way of thinking about Cantonese people, relative to the shifting contextualization of their group identity and experience. This involved a complex process of transition and transformation, with strong revisionist impulses, resulting in new ways understanding what it meant to be Cantonese.

## Conclusion

The lynchpin of this transformative process centered on the extended contextualization of *Yuet*/Cantonese identity and experience, within the "then" contemporary Cantonese *Wah-Q* (*Huachao*) (*Hua-ch'iao*) (Overseas Chinese) transnational-diasporic experience. Here, I identify and utilize an expanded frame of reference, linking traditional Cantonese identity with notions about self, home, and sojourning. In doing so I employ popular metaphors, to graphically represent the changing meaning and loci of "home," relative to notions of loyalty, longing, and loss. Specifically, I utilize *Tong-Shaan*, as a metaphor for one's permanent home in Central Gwongdung; and I adopt *Gum-Shaan*, as a metaphor for one's temporary home in America. I revisit the familiar refrain, about "a place and its people," but with a revisionist bias and agenda.

In expanding the context for viewing the broad sweep of Cantonese experience, and the changing nature of Cantonese group identity, there is the expectation that a multi-dimensional revisionist perspective can offer an improved, more accurate and authentic understanding of what it meant to be Cantonese. This is especially true, because I choose to let past Cantonese voices speak for themselves, via deeply personal and emotionally laden sentiments, expressed through Cantonese thinking and evocative poetry. While these voices remain nameless, they speak powerfully on behalf of the group identity and collective experience of Cantonese people in diverse and distant locations.

"*Seeking Tong-Shaan, while encountering Gum-Shaan,*" represents more than a clever and delightful play of words. Concretely, it represents conceptual bookends of "home," as a place, where I am from, (*Tong-Shaan*) and "home," as a place where I am now located or "stuck at," (*Gum-Shaan*). Both these views of home connect and contextualize different loci for the evolution of Cantonese identity and experience in the transnational context of the period 1850–1920. As subjectively ladened metaphors, they also reference difficult to grasp abstractions, concerning what identity and experience meant and why it mattered, in an era of shifting priorities and sliding loyalties, amid rapidly changing material conditions. Both underscore a revisionist view of reality, as it objectively existed, and as it was subjectively imagined and experienced.

Among the masses of Cantonese people, on a more practical level of experience, and in a more pragmatic frame of reference, the proposition of "what it meant to be Cantonese" revealed itself as an affirmative, simplistic outlook about one's self and how one approached the challenges of a difficult life. This dimension of experience revealed itself most often within a transnational/diasporic context, in China, America, and elsewhere. The above referenced factors of geography, demography, language/speech, ethnicity, history, environment/ecology, and economics might serve as critical determinants orchestrating Cantonese daily life, but for the vast majority of people, they remained variables beyond the ability of most to understand, other than by way of practical responses of mitigation and avoidance.

Typically, the vast majority of Cantonese people lacked the luxuries of free time, intellectual curiosity, rational thinking, and a desire to reflect on life's many adversities. In this sense, what it meant to be Cantonese meant something entirely different from what was presented earlier. It is not a matter in which previous comments were false or without merit. It is rather a case, where we need to recognize that there existed a "real" reality of what it meant to be Cantonese, as understood and represented by the thinking of the masses of Cantonese people themselves, especially among the rapidly growing numbers of Cantonese overseas emigrant/sojourners. Among these people, the proposition of what it meant to be Cantonese existed more as a subjective feeling, an emotional experience, a psychologically framed perspective, all of which contributed to a deeply personal frame of mind. This situation became amplified and nuanced when it presented itself in the form of a communal consensus, or as an unarticulated matter of public opinion.

Whenever Cantonese people, especially Cantonese menfolk, venturing out into a strange new expansive world, considered their own personal difficulties and challenges, they unknowingly internally processed the proposition of "what it meant to be Cantonese." In this context, the proposition represented itself as an affirmative, simplistic, and deeply personal outlook about oneself, family, and friends. This can be summed up in a number of constructs.

First, it was a given that life was very hard, economically speaking and situation-wise, where adversity dogged every step, every thought, and every action. This reflected itself both collectively and individually, whereby a sense of desperation pervaded daily life, where even adequate food was an uncertainty, and always a challenge to provide for. The struggle for life's necessities was ongoing, and time consuming.

Second, there existed a profound sense of "connection" between oneself and one's group, such as one's family, lineage, ethno-speech community, and native place. Enduring bonds bound each individual to the collective of the present, the past, and the future, which manifest itself in a tremendous sense of pride, with onerous burdens of responsibility. One's own sense of desperation was invariably compounded and intensified, because desperation was not just an individual matter, but also a collective experience. To be Cantonese was to be mindful and appreciative of these binding and unalterable linkages between oneself and the Cantonese collective.

Third, while desperation and loyalty guided one forward, there also existed an unmistakable sense of confidence, pride, and faith in one's decision to move forward to seek a remedy to one's sense of desperation at home. This did not mean that one was not apprehensive, even fearful of the unknown future, but the sense of apprehension did not undermine or void the contrasting sense of "can do" optimism. This is to say, despite one's misgivings and apprehension about the uncertainty of one's prospects for material success, one still moved forward, often with one's head held high, cautiously optimistic, and unafraid to venture forth. While the situation at home might be dire, not venturing forth to address it was not an option, collectively or individually. This calculus for action mirrored elements of courage and audacity.

Fourth, in almost every case, there existed an unmistakable air of confidence and hope, borne out of a gritty determination, yoked to a well-developed habit of self-discipline, hard work, deep commitment, and a patient deferral of immediate socio-economic gratification for long-term success. Armed with these positive assets, one could take on the challenge of adversity, by moving forward, out into the uncertain, strange, new, and uncharted world beyond home in *Tong-Shaan*.

Fifth, the payoff for the Cantonese migrant, emigrant-immigrant sojourner was a comforting assurance of what it meant to be Cantonese. In this context, pride, not shame, confidence, not apprehension, conviction, not disbelief, and a sense of hope and not despair fueled one's energy, commitment, and hopes. This deeply personal subjective sense of what it meant to be Cantonese is what made the Cantonese people (i.e., the men folk) so distinct, even unique.

This collective history of personalized Cantonese experiences, located in an expanded transnational and diasporic context, is a useful guide for deciphering the tangled relationships and overlapping meanings of what it meant to be Cantonese in the period 1850–1900, in the widely separated, yet powerfully linked worlds of *Tong-Shaan* (China) and *Gum-Shaan* (America).

## On "Being Cantonese," where the past and present meet and merge

While I offer the proposition of "What it meant to be Cantonese," as a novel conceptual tool for deciphering Cantonese identity and experience in both China and America, within the transnational/dasporic context of the later nineteenth-century (1850-1900), to advance a revisionist agenda for re-thinking elements of both Modern Chinese History and Chinese American History, I would be remiss if I did not expand on this line of thinking beyond these historical parameters.

I am mindful of the fact that the enumerated constructs of traditional Cantonese group identity and experience, while decidedly shaped by later nineteenth-century material conditions and situational developments, were not fully constrained by them, or limited to that historical context. In this light, I would suggest that the strength and relevancy of the proposition of "What it meant to be Cantonese" is that while it arose from within, and identified with the particular historical context of the later nineteenth-century, it continues to resonate, well beyond that time frame, well into the twentieth, and early twenty-first centuries, as an enduring limus test for deciphering Cantonese identity and experience. It does so because this ability to resonate mirrors a continued relevancy of its application and usefulness for assessing "What it means to be Cantonese" in contemporary, as well as historical terms.

The relevancy of which I speak starts with the nexus between such theoretical constructs as "The ties that bind, Cantonese style," and "Cantonese culture as a conservative contrarian counter-culture (C4)," as they relate to the transnational/diasporic context of Cantonese identity and experience in contemporary

America and China (the PRC). In short, the revisionist perspective regarding how we might re-think traditional Cantonese identity and experience in its later nineteenth-century context, has relevancy and expanded value, when also utilized to analyse Cantonese identity and experience in its contemporary, twenty-first century context. This is especially evident in the earlier mentioned conundrum of the "national" versus the "ethnic" in both the Chinese and American settings. I would argue that the conceptual categories adopted for assessing Cantonese identity and experience in the later nineteenth-cenury are relevant and useful for assessing such matters in the contemporary context.

In today's China, despite radically different geo-political, socio-economic, and cultural differences, there persists meaning and value to the proposition of "What it means to be Cantonese." Again, as in the past, it matters less what other Chinese and foreigners think, and more about what and how Cantonese think about themselves, both historically and culturally speaking about their place and role in the larger scheme of things. Today, ostensibly speaking, the identifying label of *Tong-Shaan* no longer resonates like it did in the past. However, if the label lacks concrete meaning and usefulness, the idea of a Cantonese "homeland" and "fountainhead" is not without value and relevancy. Cantonese people in China still regard Gwongdung, especially Central Gwongdung, as their own special place, because of its powerful historical and cultural identifications. In a manner of speaking, while the concrete term *Tong-Shaan* has largely disappeared from the Cantonese daily lexicon, the abstraction of a *Tong-Shaan* remains an important part of the contemporary Cantonese mindset, relative to where and how one relates oneself, both individually and collectively, to a particular place, as the center of gravity of one's socio-cultural identity.

Whether one refers to the persistence of a Cantonese popular culture, by way of obsession with Cantonese food preparation and consumption, the Cantonese mania for gambling, the nuanced linguistic and literary anachorisms sprinkled about in contemporary Cantonese media (i.e., newspapers, TV, social media) and entertainment (i.e., music and film), or the durability of Cantonese speech and *Yuet* language, Cantonese identity is still cherished and Cantonese experience is still relished. These matters are evident in a variety of locations and situations, from the pro-Democracy movement in Hong Kong in 2014-2020, to the dynamic economic growth in the pivotal Greater Pearl River "Bay Area" (bewteen Canton, Macau, and Hong Kong). Whether in economic/commercial, geo-political, or socio-cultural matters, Cantonese people in Central Gwongdung, and more generally elsewhere in China, remain committed to effectively personifying "What it means to be Cantonese" with great creativity, dexterity, and loyalty.

In America, despite radical changes in the place and role of Canonese people, in both American society and within a different and expanded manifestation of what constituts an ethnic Chinese community, Cantonese sensibilities and loyalties persist, albeit in altered and attenuated forms. Starting in the post WW II period (1950-1970), the *Gum-Shaan* identifying label also became increasingly anachronistic, and consequently also increasingly irrelevant. The 1949 Chinese Communist revolution, which effectively severed the *Tong-Shaan/Gum-Shaan* nexus, together with the powerful allure of American acculturation/assimilation among many of the American born progeny of remote Cantonese pioneer immigrant-sojourners resulted in a new focus of Cantonese interests and loyalties. Yet, despite the powerful attraction of aacculturation/assimilation, and the loss of a meaningful connection between the Cantonese community and *Tong-Shaan*, there persisted evidence of meaningful and fruitful ties between the "us" of Cantonese people in America, and the "them" of the Cantonese in China.

The continued, but weakened, nexus linking Cantonese people and communities in America with those in China, i.e., in Central Gwongdung, might be less apparent, less dynamic, and less important than in the past, but this is not to say that it has effectively disappeared or that it lacks relevancy and value. In the period 1965-2000 scores of new Cantonese immigrants, chiefly via Hong Kong, flooded into America. These new immigrants, numbering in the hundreds of thousands, helped engineer a new renaissance of Cantonese society and culture in Chinese America, via its contemporary (Hong Kong) Cantonese guise. This development reversed a trend that had been in effect from 1920-1970, where the American-born, acculturated and assimilated Cantonese-Chinese had become the predominant segment of Cantonese society in America, as the older pre-existing foreign born Cantonese sojourner community passed on. Despite the arrival of growing numbers of non-Cantonese Chinese immigrants from elsewhere in China, primarily from Fujian and Taiwan, as well as from Vietnam and elsewhere in Southeast Asia, the massive increase of Cantonese-Chinese after 1968 firmly and conclusively re-imposed a decidedly Cantonese stamp on much of Chinese American life and culture during the later twentieth and early twenty-first centuries.

Cantonese proclivities and sensibilities regarding Cantonese food, fashion, media, entertainment, gambling, and pop culture abound among immigrant Cantonese people and their communities. These developments helped re-enforce, modernize, and popularize the older pre-existing (1850-1900) Cantonese society and culture- which had become increasingly anachronistic by the 1960s.The renaissance of Cantonese culture in Chinese America came about because of a burst of new energy and creativity by and among the new Cantonese immigrants in America after 1965. New updated versons of traditional Cantonese food, e.g., new Hong Kong cuisine, such as a greater variety of *Dim-Sum,* new Hong Kong cinema (martial arts, animated films, historical dramas) and pop-music and entertainment, and the example of both Hong Kong and Taiwan high tech were increasingly attractive and cost effective, e.g., cell phones, appliances, TVs, computers, and a wide variety of electronics. They all bore the unmistakable imprint and influence of Cantonese tastes, interests, and needs, as both consumers and beneficaries.

These developments not only attracted the gratitude and loyalty of Cantonese immigrants and their immediate families and communities, but also helped to reshape and redirect the interests and investments (financial and time) of the American-born Chinese American community. While the America-born lacked Cantonese speech and language skills, this did not prevent the development of useful links and meaningful identifications between this group and the new nexus between Chinese in America and Cantonese society and culture, as re-defined and re-configured in China (Central Gwngdung, especially Hong Kong).

Quite simply, the proposition of "What it meant to be Cantonese" as a basic construct of Cantonese identity and experience in the later nineteenth-century, is still relevant and meaningful for understanding "what it means to be Cantonese" today. While the referents of the past i.e., *Tong-Shaan* and *Gum-Shaan*, are no longer viable and/or useful as signposts for the locus of Cantonese identity and experience, there remains a great deal of evidence supporting the reality of a revived nexus between "them and there" (Cantonese in China) and "us and here" (Cantonese in America). In this sense, there remains yet, a viable concrete and beneficial Cantonese nexus between the widely separated, yet powerfully linked historical worlds of China (*Tong-Shaan*) and America (*Gum-Shaan*). In similar fashion, the proposition "What it meant to be Cantonese" in China and America in the later nineteenth-century does indeed resonate with the parallel proposition of "What it means to be Cantonese" in China and America today in the early twenty-first century.

# BIBLIOGRAPHY

**English language sources**
*Authored books*

Anderson, Kay J., Vancouver's Chinatown, Racial Discourse in Canada, 1875–1980, (McGill-Queens's University Press: Montreal, Canada, 1991).

Armentrout Ma, Eve, Revolutionaries, Monarchists, and Chinatowns, Chinese Politics in the Americas and the 1911 Revolution, (Honolulu: University of Hawaii Press, 1990).

Baker, Alan H. and Gideon Biger, Ideology and Landscape in Historical Perspective, Eassays on the Meanings of Some Places in the Past, (London, UK: Cambridge, 1992).

Bauer, Robert S. &. Benedict, Paul, K., Modern Cantonese Phonology, (Berlin/New York: Mouton de Gruyter, 1997).

Belsky, Richard, Localities at the Center, Native Place, Space, and Power in Late Imperial Beijing, (Cambridge, Mass: Harvard University Press, 2005) (Harvard East Asian Monographs 258).

Bergere, Marie-Claire, (French edition) (Paris: Fayard, 1994); (Marie-Claire Bergere, Sun Yat-sen, Janet Lloyd, translator) (Stanford, Ca: Stanford University Press, 2000);Memoirs of a Chinese Revolutionary, (autobiography) (no place cited: Silver Street Media, 2012).

Bishop, Peter, The Myth of Shangri-La, Tibet, Travel Writing and the Western Creation of Sacred Landscape, (Berkeley: University of California, Press, 1989).

Boretz, Avron, Gods, Ghosts, and Gangsters, Ritual Violence, Martial Arts, and Masculinity on the Margins of Chinese Society, (Honolulu: University of Hawaii Press, 2011).

Brindley, Erica, Ancient China and the Yue: Perceptions and Identities on the Southern Frontier, c 400 BCE-50 CE, (Cambridge UK: Cambridge University Press, 2015).

Chan, Sucheng, <u>This Bitter Sweet Soil, The Chinese in California Agriculture, 1860–1910</u>, (Berkeley: University of California Press, 1986).

Chan, Sucheng, <u>Asian Americans, An Interpretative History</u>, (Boston, Twayne Publishers (G.K. Hall, 1991),

Chang, Jason Oliver, <u>Chino, Anti-Chinese Racism in Mexico, 1880–1940</u>, (Urbana: University of Illinois Press, 2017).

Carroll, John M, <u>Edge of Empires, Chinese Elites and British Colonials in Hong Kong</u>, (Cambridge, Mass: Harvard University Press, 2015).

Chen, Han-seng, <u>Agrarian Problems in Southmost China</u>, Shanghai, 1936 (also published as, <u>Landlord and Peasant in China</u>, New York, 1937).

Chen, Shehong, <u>Being Chinese, Becoming Chinese American</u>, (Urbana, Illinois: University of Illinois Press, 2002).

Cheng, Ann Anlin, <u>The Melancholy of Race: Psychoanalysis, Assimilation, and Hidden Grief</u>, (New York: Oxford University Press, 2001).

Chi, Ch'ao-ting, <u>Key Economic Areas in Chinese History, as Revealed in the Development of Public Works for Water Control</u> (New York: Paragon Book Corp., 1963 reprint).

Chin, Frank, (author of two plays) <u>The Chickencoop Chinaman</u>, (1972) and <u>The Year of the Dragon</u>, (1974) (Seattle: University of Washington Press, 1981).

Chow, Kai-wing, <u>The Rise of Confucian Ritualism in Late Imperial China, Ethics, Classics, and Lineage Discourse</u>, (Stanford, Ca.: Stanford University Press, 1994).

Chung, Sue Fawn, <u>In Pursuit of Gold, Chinese American Miners and Merchants in the American West</u>, (Urbana: University of Illinois Press, 2011).

Chung, Sue Fawn, <u>Chinese in the Woods, Logging and Lumbering in the American West</u>, (Urbana: University of Illinois Press, 2015).

Cohen, Lucy M, <u>Chinese in Post-Civil War South, A People Without a History,</u> (Baton Rouge: Louisiana State University Press, 1984).

Cohen, Paul A., <u>Discovering History in China, American Historical Writing on the Recent Chinese Past</u>, (New York: Columbia University Press, 1984).

Cooper, Arthur, *Li Po and Tu Fu, Poems Selected and Translated with an Introduction and Notes*, with Chinese calligraphy by Shui Chien-Tung, (New York: Penguin Books, 1973

Cowles, Roy T, *A Pocket Dictionary of Cantonese* (Hong Kong: Hong Kong University Press, 1992 paperback edition).

Cressey, G.B, *Land of 500 Million*, Geography of China, (New York: McGraw Hill, 1955).

Dong, Hong Yuan, *A History of the Chinese Language*, (New Jersey: Routledge University Press, 2014).

Eberhard, Wolfram, *The Local Cultures of South and East China*, (Leiden: E.J. Brill, 1968).

Elman, Benjamin, A., *A Cultural History of the Civil Examinations in Late Imperial China*, (Berkeley: University of California Press, 2000).

Elvin, Mark., *The Pattern of the Chinese Past, A Social and Economic Interpretation*, (Stanford, California, Stanford University Press, 1973).

Fairbank, John King, *Trade and Diplomacy on the China Coast, The Opening of the Treaty Ports, 1842–1854*, (Cambridge, Mass: Harvard University Press, 1964).

Faure, David, *The Rural Economy of Pre-Liberation China, Trade Expansion and Peasant Livelihood in Jiangsu and Guangdong, 1870–1937*, (Hong Kong: Oxford University Press, 1989).

Freedman, Maurice, *Lineage Organization in Southeastern China*, (London, UK: Athlone Press, University of London, 1958).

Freedman, Maurice, *Chinese Lineage and Society: Fukien and Kwangtung*, (New York: Humanities Press, 1966).

Friday, Chris, *Organizing Asian American Labor, The Pacific Coast Canned Salmon Industry, 1870–1942*, (Philadelphia: Temple University Press, 1994).

Fuller, Michael A., *An Introduction to Literary Chinese*, (Cambridge, Mass: Harvard East Asian Monographs # 176,) (Harvard University Asia Center, 2004).

Glick, Clarence E, *Sojourners and Settlers, Chinese Migrants in Hawaii*, (Honolulu, Hawaii: University of Hawaii Press, 1980).

Goodman, Bryna, *Native Place, City and Nation, Regional Networks and*

Identities in Shanghai, 1853–1937, (Berkeley, California: University of California Press, 1995).

Harpur, James, The Atlas of Sacred Places, Meeting Points of Heaven and Earth, (New York: Henry Holt Reference Book, Henry Colt Co. 1994).

Hashimoto, Ann Oi-kan yue, Studies in Yue Dialects 1:Phonology of Cantonese, (New York: Cambridge University Press, 1972).

Ho, Ping-ti, Studies on the Population of China, 1368–1953, (Cambridge, Mass: 1959).

Ho, Virgil K.Y., Understanding Canton, Rethinking Popular Culture in the Republican Period, (New York: Oxford University Press, 2005).

Hoexter, Corinne K., From Canton to California, The Epic of Chinese Immigration, (This book has some biographical material on Reverend Ng Poon Chew) (New York: Four Winds Press, 1976).

Hom, Marlon K, Songs of Gold Mountain, Cantonese Rhymes from San Francisco Chinatown, (Berkeley, California: University of California Press, 1987).

Honig, Emily, Creating Chinese Ethnicity: Subei People in Shanghai, 1850–1980, (New Haven: Yale University Press, 1992).

Hsiao, Kung-Chuan, Rural China, Imperial Control in the Nineteenth Century, (Seattle: University of Washington Press, 1960).

Hsiao, Kung-Chuan, A Modern China and a New World, K'ang Yu-wei, Reformer and Utopian, 1858–1927, (Seattle: University of Washington Press, 1975).

Hsu, Francis L.K., Under the Ancestors' Shadow, Kinship, Personality, and Social Mobility in China, (Stanford, Ca: Stanford University Press, 1971).

Hsu, Immanuel C.Y, The Rise of Modern China (4th edition) (New York: Oxford University Press, 1990).

Hsu, Madelyn Y, Dreaming of Gold, Dreaming of Home, Transnationalism, and Migration Between the United States and South China, 1882–1943, (Stanford, Ca: Stanford University Press, 2000).

Hu-DeHart, Evelyn, Across the Pacific, Asian Americans and Globalization, (Philadelphia: Temple University Press, 2000).

Huang, Martin, W., <u>Negotiating Masculinities in Late Imperial China</u>, (Honolulu: University of Hawaii Press, 2006).

Jones, Charles Sheridan & James Cantile, <u>Sun Yat-Sen and the Awakening of China</u>, (no place cited: Andesite Press, 2017).

Joniak-Luthi, Agnieszka, <u>The Han, China's Diverse Majority</u>, (Seattle: University of Washington Press, 2017 (Studies on Ethnic Groups in China).

Jung, John, <u>Chopsticks in the Land of Cotton, Lives of Mississippi Delta Chinese Grocers</u>, (2nd edition) (Yin-Yang Press, 2011).

Jung, Moon-Ho, <u>Coolies and Cane, Race, Labor, and Sugar in the Age of Emancipation</u>, (Baltimore: John Hopkins University Press, 2006).

Kayloe, Tjio, <u>The Unfinished Revolution: Sun Yat-sen and the Struggle for Modern China</u>, (no place cited: Marshall Cavendish International (Asia) pte ltd, 2018).

Kroll, Paul, W., <u>A Student's Dictionary of Classical and Medieval Chinese</u>, (Leiden, The Netherlands: Brill Publication, 2017) (Revised edition).

Kuhn, Philip A, <u>Chinese Among Others, Emigration in Modern Times</u>, (Boulder, Colorado: Rowman & Littlefield Publishers, Inc, 2008).

Kurpaska, Maria, <u>Chinese language(s): A Look Through the Prism of "The Great Dictionary of Modern Chinese Dialects,"</u> (Walter de Gruyter: 2010).

Kwong, Peter, <u>Chinatown, New York</u>, (New York: Monthly Review Press, 1979).

Lai, Walton Look, <u>The Chinese in the West Indies, 1806–1995, A Documentary History</u>, (Barbados: The Press of the University of the West Indies, 1998).

Lasser, Jeffrey, <u>Negotiating National Identity, Immigrants, Minorities, and Struggle for Ethnicity in Brazil</u>, (Durham, North Carolina: Duke University Press, 1999).

Lau, Sidney, <u>A Practical Cantonese-English Dictionary</u>, (Hong Kong: Hong Kong Government Printer, 1977).

Lee, Chang-Rae, <u>Native Speaker</u>, (Berkeley Books, 1995).

Lee, Douglas W., <u>Facing Cantonese Adversity, Fleeing Tong-Shaan: Cantonese Society and the Root Causes of Nineteenth-Century Overseas Emigration</u>, as volume 3 of <u>The Gum-Shaan Chronicles, The Early History of Cantonese-Chinese America, 1850-1900</u>, (Pittsburgh, Pa: Dorrance Publishing, 2023),

Lee, Douglas W., <u>Departing Tong-Shaan: The Organization and Operation of Cantonese Overseas Emigration to America (1850-1900)</u>, as volume 4, <u>The Gum-Shaan Chronicles: The Early History of Cantonese-Chinese America, 1850-1900</u>, (Pittsburgh, Pa: Dorrance Publishing, 2023).

Lee, Douglas W., <u>Establishing *Gum-Shaan* at Dai-Fow (Cantonese San Francisco) The Genesis of Chinese America (1845-1865)</u>, as volume 5 of <u>The Gum-Shaan Chronicles: The Early History of Cantonese-Chinese America, 1850-1900</u>, (Pittsburgh, Pa: Dorrance Publishing, 2023).

Lee, Rose Hum, <u>The Growth and Decline of Chinese Communities in the Rocky Mountain Region</u>, (originally PhD dissertation Sociology, University of Chicago, 1947), (New York: Arno Press, 1978).

Leong, Sow-Theng, <u>Migration and Ethnicity in Chinese History, Hakkas, Pengmin, and Their Neighbors</u>, (Stanford, California: Stanford University Press, 1997).

Lewis, Mark Edward, <u>The Early Chinese Empires, Qin and Han</u>, (first volume in series on the History of Imperial China), (Cambridge, Mass: Belknap Press of Harvard University Press, 2007).

Ling, Huping, <u>Chinese St. Louis, From Enclave to Cultural Community</u>, (Philadelphia: Temple University Press, 2004).

Ling, Huping, <u>Chinese Chicago, Race, Transnational Migration, and Community Since 1870</u>, (Stanford, California: Stanford University Press, 2012).

Liu, Eric, <u>The Accidental Asian, Notes of a Native Speaker</u>, (New York City: Vintage Books of Random House 1998).

Lo, Karl, and H. Mark Lai, <u>Chinese Newspapers Published in North America, 1854–1975</u>, (Washington DC: Center for Chinese Research Materials, Association of Research Libraries, 1977).

Loewen, James W, <u>The Mississippi Chinese, Between Black and White,</u> (Cambridge, Mass: Harvard University Press, 1971).

Logan, Lorna, <u>Ventures in Mission, The Cameron House Story</u> (1976).

Lopez, Kathleen, <u>Chinese Cubans, A Transnational History</u>, (Chapel Hill: University of North Carolina Press, 2013).

Louie, Andrea, Chinese-ness Across Borders, Renegotiating Chinese Identities in China and the United States, (Durham, North Carolina: Duke University Press, 2004).

Low, Victor, The Unimpressible Race, A Century of Educational Struggle by the Chinese in San Francisco, (San Francisco: East/West Publishing Company. 1982).

Lyman, Stanford, The Asian in the West., (Social Science & Humanities publication No. 4, Western Studies Center, Desert Research Institute,) (University of Nevada, Reno, Nevada: University of Nevada Press, 1970).

Lyman, Stanford, Chinese Americans, (New York City: Random House, 1974).

Lyman, Stanford, Chinatown and Little Tokyo: Power and Conflict and Community Among Chinese and Japanese Immigrants to America (Minority Structures and Race Ethnic Relations),New York City: Associated Faculty Press, Inc. 1986).

Mackerras, Colin, The Chinese Theatre in Modern Times, (London: Thames and Hudson, 1975).

Maeda, Daryl J., Chains of Babylon, The Rise of Asian America, (Minneapolis: University of Minnestota Press, 2009).

Mar, Lisa Rose, Brokering Belonging: Chinese in Canada's Exclusion Era, 1885–1945, (London, UK: Oxford University Press, 2010).

Martin, Mildred Crowl, Chinatown's Angry Angel, The Story of Donaldina Cameron, (Pacific Books, 1977).

Matthews, Stephen and Yip, Virginia, Cantonese: A comprehensive Grammar, London/New York: Routledge, 1994).

McKeown, Adam, Chinese Migrant Networks and Cultural Change, Peru, Chicago, Hawaii, 1900–1936, (Chicago: University of Chicago Press, 2001).

Meagher, Arnold, J., The Coolie Trade: The Traffic in Chinese Laborers in Latin America, (Xlibris Corporation, 2008).

Meskill, Johanna Menzel, A Chinese Pioneering Family, the Lins of Wufeng, Taiwan, 1729–1895, (Princeton, New Jersey: Princeton University Press, 1979).

Morris, Peter T., Cantonese Love Songs, An English Translation of Jiu Ji-yung's Cantonese songs of the early 19th Century, (Hong Kong: Hong Kong University Press, 1992).

Morton, James, In the Sea of Sterile Mountains, The Chinese in British Columbia (Vancouver B.C.: J.J. Douglas Ltd, 1974).

Munn, Christopher, Anglo-China, Chinese People and British Rule in Hong Kong, 1841–1880, (Hong Kong: University of Hong Kong, 2009).

Murphey-Shigematsu, Stephen, When Half is Whole: Multi-Ethnic Asian American Identities, (Stanford, Ca: Stanford University Press, 2012).

Nee, Victor, and Brett de Bary Nee, Longtime Californ': A Documentary Study of an American Chinatown, (New York: Pantheon Books, Random House, 1972).

Newman, Jacqueline M., Food Culture in China, (Westport, Connecticut: Greenwood Press, 2004).

Ng, Wing Chung, The Rise of Cantonese Opera, (Urbana, Illinois: University of Illinois, 2015).

Norman, Jerry, Chinese, (New York: Cambridge University Press, 1993, (Cambridge Language Surveys).

Okada, John, No No Boy, (originally published in 1957) (Seattle: University of Washington, 1981).

Okihiro, Gary Y., Margins and Mainstreams, Asians in American History and Culture, (Seattle: University of Washington Press, 1994).

Oxfield, Ellen, Blood, Sweat, and Mahjong: Family and Enterprise in an Overseas Chinese Community, (Cornell Anthology of Contemporary Issues), (Ithaca, NY: Cornell University Press, 1993).

Perkins, Dwight, H., Agricultural Development in China, 1368–1968, (Chicago: Aldine Publishing Company, 1969).

Pfaelzer, Jean, Driven Out, The Forgotten War Against Chinese Americans, (New York: Random House, 2007).

Pye, Lucian, W., The Spirit of Chinese Politics, A Psychocultural Study of the Authority Crisis in Political Development, (Cambridge, Mass: MIT Press, 1968).

Quan, Robert Seto, Lotus Among the Magnolias, The Mississippi Chinese,(Jackson, Mississippi: University Press of Mississippi: 2007) (originally published 1982).

Ramsey, Robert S., <u>The Languages of China</u>, (Princeton, New Jersey: Princeton University Press,1989).

Rhoads, Edward J.M, <u>China's Republican Revolution, The Case of Kuang-tung, 1895–1913</u>, (Cambridge, Mass: Harvard University Press, 1975).

Rowe, William T., <u>Hankow, Commerce and Society in a Chinese City, 1796–1889,</u> (Stanford, Ca: Stanford University Press, 1984).

Rowe, William T.,<u>Hankow, Conflict and Community in a Chinese City, 1796–1895</u>, (Stanford, Ca: Stanford University Press, 1989).

Schafer, Edouard, <u>The Vermilion Bird: Tang Images of the South</u> (Berkeley: University of California Press,1967).

Schafer, Edouard, H., <u>Shore of Pearls, Hainan Island in Early Times</u>, (Berkeley: University of California Press, 1970).

Schiffrin, Harold Z, <u>Sun Yat-sen and the Origins of the Chinese Revolution</u>, (Berkeley: University of California Press, 1970).

Sharman, Lyon, <u>Sun Yat-Sen, His life and Its Meaning, A Critical Biography</u>, (Stanford: Stanford University Press 1934, 1973 printing).

Siler, Julia Flynn, <u>The White Devil's Daughters, The Women Who Fought Slavery in San Francisco Chinatown</u>, (New York: Knopf, 2019).

Sinn, Elizabeth, <u>Pacific Crossing, California Gold, Chinese Migration, and the Making of Hong Kong</u>, (Hong Kong: Hong Kong University Press, 2013).

Solomon, Richard, H., <u>Mao's Revolution and the Chinese Political Culture,</u> (Berkeley: University of California press, 1971) (originally published in the Michigan Studies on China series).

Sone, Monica, <u>Nisei Daughter</u>, (originally published in 1953) (Seattle: University of Washington, 2014).

Sparks, Douglas Wesley, <u>Unity is Power: The Teochiu of Hong Kong</u>, (unknown binding) University Microfilms International (1975) ASSIN B00073D1LU.

Stockard, Janice E., <u>Daughters of theCanton Delta, Marriage Patterns and Economic Strategies in South China, 1860–1930</u>, (Stanford, Ca: Stanford University Press, 1989).

Struve, Lynn, The Southern Ming, 1644–1662, (New Haven: Yale University Press, 1984).

Sue, Stanley, and James Morishima, Mental Health of Asian Americans, Contemporary Issues in Identifying and Treating Mental Health Problems, (Jossey-Bass Publishers, 1988).

Sun, Chao Fen, Chinese, A Linguistic Introduction, (Cambridge UK: Cambridge University Press, 2006).

Sung, Betty Lee, The Story of the Chinese in America, (Originally published as Mountain of Gold, 1967) (New York City: Collier Books, division of Macmillan Publishing, 1971).

Tan, Amy, The Joy Luck Club, (New York: Ballatine Books, 1989).

Theiss, Janet, M., Disgraceful Matters, The Politics of Chastity in Eighteenth-Century China, (Berkeley: University of California, 2004).

To, Wing-kai, (with Chinese Historical Society of New England) Chinese in Boston, 1870–1965 (Arcadia Publishing, 2008).

Tregear, T.R., Geography of China, (Aldine Publishing co., 1966).

Tsin, Michael, Nation, Governance, and Modernity in China, Canton 1900–1927, (Stanford: Stanford University Press, 1999)

Uba, Laura, Asian Americans, Personality Patterns, Identity and Mental Health;(Guilford Press, 1993).

Van Der Sprenkel, Sybille, Legal Institutions in Manchu China, (London: University of London, Athlone Press, 1962).

Vitiello, Giovanni, The Libertine's Friend, Homosexuality and Masculinity in Late Imperial China, (Chicago: University of Chicago Press, 2011).

Vogel, Ezra, F, One Step Ahead in China, Guangdong Under Reform, (Cambridge, Mass: Harvard University Press, 1989).

Vogel, Ezra, Canton Under Communism, Programs and Politics in a Provincial Capital, 1949–1968, (New York, Harper Torch books, 1969; (also issued by Harvard University Press, as part of the Harvard East Asian Series #41, 1969); also reprinted by Harvard University Press 1980).

Wakeman, Frederic Jr, Strangers at the Gate, Social Disorder in South China, 1839–1861, (Berkeley: University of California Press, 1966).

Wang, Xinyang, Surviving the City, The Chinese Immigrant Experience in

*New York City, 1890–1970*, (New York: Rowman & Littlefield Publishers, 2001).

Wei, William, <u>Asians in Colorado, A History of Persecution and Perseverance in the Centennial State</u>, (Seattle: University of Washington Press, 2016).

Wilbur, C. Martin, <u>Sun Yat-sen, Frustrated Patriot</u>, (New York: Columbia University Press, 1974).

Wilson, W. Richard, <u>Learning to be Chinese, The Political Socialization of Children in Taiwan</u>, (Cambridge, Mass: MIT Press, 1970).

Wiens, Herold J, <u>China's March to the Tropics</u>, (New Jersey: Shoe String Press, 1954); also see, later edition with a different title, <u>Han Chinese Expansion in South China</u>, (New Jersey: Shoe String Press: 1967).

Wilson, Carol Green, <u>Chinatown Quest, The Life Adventures of Donaldina Cameron</u>, (Stanford: Stanford University Press, 1950).

Wolf, Margery, <u>The House of Lim, A Study of a Chinese Farm Family</u>, (New York: Appleton-Century-Crofts, 1968).

Wong, Jade Snow, <u>Fifth Chinese Daughter</u>, (originally published in 1945) (Seattle: University of Washington Press, 1989).

Wong, Kristin & Kathryn Wong, <u>Fierce Compassion, The Life of Abolitionist Donaldina Cameron</u>, (New Earth Enterprises, 2012).

Woon, Yuen-fong, <u>Social Organization in South China, 1911–1949: The Case of the Kuan Lineage in K'ai-p'ing [Hoiping] County</u>, (Ann Arbor, Michigan: University of Michigan, 1984).

Wu, Ellen D., <u>The Color of Success, Asian Americans and the Origins of the Model Minority</u>, (Princeton New Jersey: Princeton University Press, 2015).

Yang Mou-Ch'un (Martin Yang) <u>A Chinese Village: T'ai T'ou, Shantung Province</u>, (New York, 1945).

Yee, Shirley J., <u>An Immigrant Neighborhood, Interethnic and Interracial Encounters in New York Before 1930</u>, (Philadelphia: Temple University Press, 2012).

Young, Elliott, <u>Alien Nation, Chinese Migration in the Americas from the Coolie Era Through World War II</u>, (Chapel Hill: University of North Carolina, 2014).

Young, Judy, <u>Unbound Feet, A Social History of Chinese Women in San</u>

Francisco, (Berkeley: University of California Press, 1995).

Young, Judy, Unbound Voices, A Documentary History of the Chinese Women in San Francisco, (Berkeley: University of California Press, 1999).

Yun, Lisa, The Coolie Speaks, Chinese Indentured Laborers and African Slaves in Cuba, (Philadelphia: Temple University Press, 2008).

Zhang, Weiwen, and Qingnan, In Search of China's Minorities, (Beijing: New World Press, 1993).

Zhao, Xiaojian, Remaking Chinese America, Immigration, Family, and Community, 1940–1965, (New Brunswick, New Jersey: Rutgers University Press, 2002).

Zheng, Yangwen, The Social Life of Opium in China, (UK: Cambridge University Press, 2005).

Zhu, Liping, A Chinaman's Chance, The Chinese on the Rocky Mountain Mining Frontier, (Niwot, Colorado: University of Colorado Press, 1997).

Zhu, Liping, Rose Estep Fosha, and Thenic Oasis, The Chinese in the Black Hills, (Pierre: South Dakota State Historical Society Press, 2004).

**Edited books**

A History of the Chinese in California, A Syllabus, edited by Thomas Chinn, H. Mark Lai, and Philip Choy, (San Francisco: Chinese Historical Society of America, 1969).

Asian American Identities and Practices: Folkloric Expressions in Everyday life, edited by Jonathan H.X. Lee and Kathleen Nadeau, (Lexington Books, 2015).

Asian American Mental Health, Assessment Theories and Methods, Edited by Karen S. Kurasaki, Sumie Okazaki & Stanley Sue, (International and Cultural Psychology Series) (Spring, 2002).

Asian Diasporas, Cultures, Identities, Representations, edited by Robbie B.H. Goh and Shawn Wong, (Hong Kong: Hong Kong University Press, 2004).

Asian Diasporas, New Formations, New Conceptions, edited by Rhacel S. Parrenas and Lok C.D. Siu, (Stanford, Ca: Stanford University Press, 2007).

Chinese American Transnationalism, The Flow of People, Resources, and

Ideas between China and America in the Exclusion Era, edited by Sucheng Chan, (Philadelphia: Temple University Press, 2005).

Chinese American Voices, edited by Judy Young, Gordon H Chang, and Him Mark Lai, (Berkeley: University of California Press, 2006).

Chinese Historical Micro-Demography, edited by Stevan Harrell, (Berkeley: University of California Press, 1995).

Chinese on the American Frontier, Edited by Arif Dirlik, (with the assistance of Malcolm Yeung), (New York: Rowman & Littlefield Publishers, 2003) (Pacific Formations series).

Cities in Motion, Interior, Coast, and Diaspora in Transnational China, edited by Sherman Cochran, David Strand, and Wen-hsin Yeh, as General Editor, (Berkeley: University of California, 2007) (China Research Monograph, no. 62, Center for Chinese Studies, Institute for East Asian Studies, UC Berkeley).

Critical Han Studies: The History, Representation, and Identity of China's Majority (New Perspectives on Chinese Culture and Society) co-edited by Thomas Mullaney and James Leibold, (Berkeley: University of California Press, 2012).

Death Ritual in Late Imperial and Modern China, edited by James L. Watson and Evelyn S. Rawski Margery Wolf,(Berkeley: University of California Press, 1988).

Displacements and Diasporas, Asians in the Americas, edited by Wanni W. Anderson and Robert G. Lee, (New Brunswick, New Jersey: Rutgers University Press, 2005).

Down to Earth, The Territorial Bond in South China, edited by David Faure and Helen F. Siu, (Stanford, California: Stanford University Press, 1995).

Ethnic Groups and Boundaries, edited by. Frederick Barth, (Boston: Little Brown, Co., 1969).

From China to Canada, A History of the Chinese Communities in Canada, edited by Edgar Wickberg et. al, (Toronto: McClelland and Stewart publishers, 1982).

Island: Poetry and History of Chinese Immigrants on Angel Island, 1910–1940 (Naomi B. Pascal Editor's Endowment- Second Edition) edited by Him Mark Lai, Genny Lim, and Judy Yung, (Seattle, Washington: University of Washington Press, 2014).

Landscape and Power, edited by W.J.T. Mitchell, (Chicago: University of Chicago Press, 1994).

Negotiating Ethnicities in China and Taiwan, edited by Melissa J. Brown, (Berkeley: University of California Press, 1996) (Institute of East Asian Studies, China Research Monograph 46).

Pilgrims and Sacred Sites in China, edited by Susan Naquin and Chun-fang Yu, (Berkeley: University of California Press, 1992).

Popular Culture in Late Imperial China, edited by David Johnson, Andrew J. Nathan, and Evelyn S. Rawski (Berkeley, California: University of California Press, 1983).

Remapping China, Fissures in Historical Terrain, edited by Gail Hershatter, Emily Honig Jonathan N. Lipman, et. al., (Stanford, Ca: Stanford University Press, 1996).

The Cambridge History of China, vol. 1; The Ch'in (Qin) and Han Empires, 221 BC-AD 220, (edited by Dennis Twitchett and Michael Loewe, (New York: Cambridge University Press 1986).

The Chinese and Japanese, Essays in Political and Cultural Interactions, edited by Akira Iriye, (Princeton, New Jersey: Princeton University, 1980).

The Chinese City Between Two Worlds, edited by Mark Elvin and G. William Skinner, (Stanford, California: Stanford University Press, 1974).

The Chinese in Arizona, 1870–1950, A Context for Historic Preservation Planning, prepared by Melissa Keane, A.E. Rogerset. Al, for the Arizona State Historic Office and the City of Phoenix Planning Department (May 1992).

The Chinese in Latin America and the Caribbean, edited by Walton Look Lai and Tan Chee-Beng (Leiden, the Netherlands: Brill, 2010).

The Chinese in the Caribbean, edited by Andrew Wilson, (Princeton, New Jersey: Markus Wiener Publishers, 2004).

The City in Late Imperial China, ed. G. William Skinner (Stanford, Ca: Stanford University Press, 1977).

The Living Tree, The Changing Meaning of Being Chinese Today, edited by Tu Wei-ming, (Stanford, California: Stanford University Press, 1994).

The Sandalwood Mountains: Readings and Stories of the Early Chinese Immigrants in Hawaii, edited by Char, Tin-Yuke, (Honolulu, University of Hawaii Press, 1975).

Times Atlas of China, ed. J.M. Geelaw & T.C. Twichett, (N.Y. Times Books, 1974).

Violence in China, Essays in Culture and Counterculture, edited by Jonathan N. Lipman and Stevan Harrell, (Albany, New York: State University of New York Press, 1990).

## *Articles, Essays*

Aird, John S., John S. Aird, "Population Growth," pp. 247–266, in Economic Trends in CommunistChina, edited by Alexander Eckstein, Walter Galenson, and Ta-chung Liu, (Chicago: Aldine Publishing Company, 1968).

Anderson, Eugene N. Jr, "The Complex Causation of South Chinese Foodways," pp. 147–158, in The Annals of the Chinese Historical Society of the Pacific Northwest (Seattle:1984).

Bodman, Nicholas, C., "The *Nam Long* Dialect: A Northeastern Min Outlier in Zhongshan Xian and the Influence of Cantonese on its Lexicon and Phonology," in Tsing Hua Journal of Chinese Studies (New Series) (1982) 14.1 to 2:1–19,

Buell, Paul D, "The Sung Resistance Movement, 1276–1279: An Episode in Chinese Regional History," in The Annals of the Chinese Historical Society of the Pacific Northwest, vol 3: 1985–1986 (Bellingham, Washington: Western Washington University, Center for East Asian Studies).

Chan, Marjorie K.M., and Douglas W. Lee, "Chinatown Chinese: A Linguistic and Historical Re-Evaluation," pp. 111–131, in Amerasia Journal, 8:1 (1981).

Chan, Marjorie K.M., "The Chinese in North America: A Preliminary Ethnolinguistic Study," pp. 232–254, in Annals of the Chinese Historical Society of the Pacific Northwest, (Seattle, Washington, (1984).

Chan, Marjorie K.M., "Cantonese Opera and the Growth and Spread of Vernacular Written Cantonese in the Twentieth Century," in the Seventeenth

North American Conference on Chinese Linguistics (NAC 11-17), pp. 1-18, edited by Qain Gao, (Los Angeles: Gsil Publications, University of Southern California, 2005).

Chan, Ming K., "A Turning Point in the Modern Chinese Revolution: The Historical Significance of the Canton Decade, 1917–27," pp. 224–241in, Remapping China, Fissures in Historical Terrain, edited by Gail Hershatter, Emily Honig Jonathan N. Lipman, et. al., (Stanford, Ca: Stanford University Press, 1996).

Charsley, S.R., "The Formation of Ethnic Groups,"pp. 337–368, in Urban Anthropology, ed. A. Cohen, (London: Tavistock Publications, 1974).

Chung, Sue Fawn, "The Chinese American Citizens Alliance: An Effort at Assimilation, 1895–1965," pp.30–57, in Chinese America: History and Perspectives (San Francisco: Chinese Historical Society of America, 1988).) (The Annual Journal of the Chinese Historical Society of America).

Cohen, Myron L., "Being Chinese: The Peripheralization of Traditional Identity," chapter 4, pp. 88–108, in The Living Tree, The Changing Meaning of Being Chinese Today, edited by Tu Wei-ming, (Stanford, California: Stanford University Press, 1994).

Cole, James H., "Competition and Cooperation in Late Imperial China as Reflected in Native Place and Ethnicity," pp.156–163 in, Remapping China, Fissures in Historical Terrain, edited by Gail Hershatter, Emily Honig Jonathan N. Lipman, et. al., (Stanford, Ca: Stanford University Press, 1996).

Davies, Douglas,"The Evocative Symbolism of Trees," in The Iconography of Landscape, Essays on the Symbolic Representation, Design, and Use of Past Environments, edited by Denis Cosgrove and Stephen Daniels, (New York: Cambridge, University Press, 1988).

Guldin, Gregory E., "Seven Veiled Ethnicity: A Hong Kong Chinese Folk Model," in Journal of Chinese Studies, 1:1 (June 1984).

Ho, Virgil K.Y., "Gambling in Canton: Myth and Reality of a Calamity," pp. 156–218, and the "Black Hole of Impulsive and Compulsive Gambling," pp. 189–218, in Ho, Virgil, K.Y., Understanding Canton, Rethinking Popular Culture in the Republican Period (Oxford Studies on

Contemporary China series), (UK: Oxford University Press, 2005).

Honig, Emily, "Native Place and the Making of Chinese Ethnicity," pp. 143–155 in, <u>Remapping China, Fissures in Historical Terrain</u>, edited by Gail Hershatter, Emily Honig Jonathan N. Lipman, et. al., (Stanford, Ca: Stanford University Press, 1996).

Hsieh, Winston, "Peasant Insurrection and the Market Hierarchy in the Canton Delta, 1911–1912," pp. 79–101, in <u>Studies in Chinese Society</u>, edited by Arthur P. Wolf, (Stanford, California: Stanford University Press, 1978).

Hsu, Madeline Y, "Unwrapping Orientalist: Restoring Homosocial Normativity to Chinese American History," <u>Amerasia Journal</u> 29:2 (2003): 230–253.

Jue, Willard, G, "Chin Gee-Hee, Chinese Pioneer Entrepreneur in Seattle and Toishan," in <u>The Annals of the Chinese Historical Society of the Pacific Northwest</u>, (1983), pp31–38.

Kim, Jae yoon The Heaven and Earth Society and the Red Turban Rebellion, pp.1–35, in Late Qing China," in the <u>Journal of Humanities and Social Sciences</u>, 3:1 (2009).

Kwan, Man Bun, "Mapping the Hinterland: Treaty Ports and Regional Analysis in Modern China," pp. 181–193 in, <u>Remapping China, Fissures in Historical Terrain</u>, edited by Gail Hershatter, Emily Honig Jonathan N. Lipman, et. al., (Stanford, Ca: Stanford University Press, 1996).

Lee, Douglas W., "The Early Chinese Community in Washington D.C., 1880–1930," pp.86–120, in <u>The Annals of the Chinese Historical Society of the Pacific Northwest</u>,1:1 (1983).

Leong, S.T., "The Hakka Chinese: Ethnicity and Migrations in Late Imperial China," unpublished paper, Annual Meeting of the Association for Asian Studies, Washington, DC 1980

Li, Fang-kuei, "Languages and Dialects," in <u>The Chinese Yearbook</u>. (Shanghai: Commercial Press, 1937).

Lyman, Stanford, "Conflict and Web of Group Affiliation in San Francisco's Chinatown," pp. 473–499, in <u>Pacific Historical Review</u>, 43:4 (1974).

Lyman, Stanford, "Urban Change at the Sinitic Frontier: Social Organizations in the United States' Chinatowns, 1849–1898," pp.107–136, in

Modern Asian Studies, vol. 17. (1983).

MacDonald, John S., and Leatrice D. MacDonald (1964). "Chain Migration Ethnic Neighborhood Formation and Social Networks." The Milbank Memorial Fund Quarterly. 42 (1): 82–97.

Patterson, Orlando, "Context and Choice in Ethnic Allegiance: A Theoretical Framework and Caribbean Case Study," pp.305–349, in Nathan Glazer and Daniel P. Moynihan, eds., Ethnicity and Experience, (Cambridge, Mass: Harvard University Press, 1975).

Potter, Jack M., "Cantonese Shamanism," pp.321–345, in Studies in Chinese Society, edited by Arthur P. Wolf, (Stanford, California: Stanford University Press, 1978).

Reeves, Caroline, "Grave Concerns: Bodies, Burial, and Identity in Early Republican China," pp. 27–52, in Cities in Motion, Interior, Coast, and Diaspora in Transnational China, edited by Sherman Cochran, and David Strand. Wen-hsin Yet, General Editor, (Berkeley, California: Institute of East Asian Studies, University of California, Berkeley: 2007).

Rhoads, Edward J.M., "Merchant Associations in Canton, 1895–1911," in The Chinese City BetweenTwo Worlds, edited by Mark Elvin and G. William Skinner (Stanford, California: Stanford University Press, 1974)

Riddle, Ronald, "The Cantonese Opera: A Chapter in Chinese-American History," pp. 40–47, in The Life, Influence and Role of the Chinese in the United States, 1776–1960, Proceedings/Papers of the National Conference held at the University of San Francisco, July 10–12, 1975, sponsored by the Chinese Historical Society of America.

Sinn, Elizabeth, "Moving Bones: Hong Kong's Role as an "In-between Place" in the Chinese Diaspora," pp. 247–271, in Cities in Motion, Interior, Coast, and Diaspora in Transnational China, edited by Sherman Cochran, and David Strand. Wen-hsin Yet, General Editor, (Berkeley, California: Institute for East Asian Studies, University of California, Berkeley: 2007).

Skinner, William G., "Marketing and Social Structure in Rural China," in three parts. Part I, Journal of Asian Studies, 24:1, November 1964, pp. 3–43.

Skinner, William G., "Marketing and Social Structure in Rural China," part II, Journal of Asian Studies, 24:2, February, 1965, pp. 195–228.

Skinner, William G., "Marketing and Social Structure in Rural China," and Part III, Journal of Asian Studies, 24:3, May 1965, pp. 363–399.

Skinner, G. William, "Regional Systems in Late Imperial China," paper given at the Second Annual Meeting of the Social Science History Association, Ann Arbor, Michigan, 1977.

Struve, Lynn "The Southern Ming, 1644–1662," pp. 641–725, as chapter 11 in The Cambridge History of China, Vol 7 The Ming Dynasty 1368–1644, Part I (Cambridge: UK, Cambridge University Press, 1988).

Tchen, John Kuo Wei, "New York Chinese: The Nineteenth-Century Pre-Chinatown Settlement," pp. 157–192, in Chinese America: History and Perspectives (1990) (Annual Journal of the Chinese Historical Society of America).

Topley, Marjorie, "Marriage Resistance in Rural Kwangtung," pp. 247–268, in Studies in Chinese Society, edited by Arthur P. Wolf, (Stanford, California: Stanford University Press, 1978).

Wang, Ling, "Teahouse Culture," pp. 82–83, in Tea and Chinese Culture, (San Francisco: Long River Press, 2005).

Ward, Barbara E., "Regional Operas and their Audiences: Evidence from Hong Kong," in Popular Culture in Later Imperial China, pp.161–187, edited by David Johnson, Andrew J. Nathan, and Evelyn S. Rawski, (Berkeley: University of California Press, 1985.

Yip, Hon-ming, "Institutionalizing Charity, Hong Kong and Homebound Burial of Chinese Americans, 1900–1949, pp. 1–11, in Chinese America, History and Perspectives, 2018 (special dedicated volume, This Land is Our Land, Chinese Pluralities Through the Americas).

Yue-Hashimoto, Ann, "The Yue Dialect," in Languages and Dialects of China, in Journal of Chinese Linguistics Monograph Series Number 3: 1991, edited by William S.Y. Wang (Berkeley: University of California), pp.294-324.

## Bibliography

***Unpublished sources***

Chan, Marjorie K.M., "Zhong-shan Phonology: A Synchronic and Diachronic Analysis of a Yue (Cantonese) Dialect," (M.A. thesis, University of British Columbia, 1980).

Lee, Douglas W, "Political Development in Chinese America, 1850–1911," (PhD dissertation, University of California, Santa Barbara, Modern Chinese History 1979).

Lee, Douglas, W, "Fleeing Tong-Shaan, Traditional Cantonese Society and the Root Causes of Nineteenth-Century Overseas Emigration. (1988 manuscript)

Lee, Douglas, W., "Departing Tong-Shaan, Cantonese Overseas Emigration to America, 1850-1900," (1991 manuscript)

Lee, Douglas W, "The Cantonese Settlement of Chinese America, 1865-1880," (1997 manuscript)

Lee, Russell D., "The Perils of Ethnic Success: The Rise and Flight of the Chinese Traders in Jamaica," (PhD dissertation (sociology) Harvard University, 1979).

Li, En, "Betting on Empire: A Socio-Cultural History of Gambling in Late Qing China," (Washington University, St. Louis Missouri, PhD dissertation, (History) December 2015).

Lyman, Stanford, "The Structure of Chinese society in Nineteenth-Century America," (PhD dissertation, University of California, Berkeley, Sociology, 1961).

Mei, June, "Researching Chinese-American History in Taishan: A Report," pp. 57–60, in The Chinese American Experience: Papers from the Second National Conference on Chinese American Studies, edited by Genny Lim, H. Mark Lai, Daniel Chu, and Ted Wong, (San Francisco: Chinese Historical Society of America and the Chinese Cultural Foundation of San Francisco, 1984).

Roberts, J.A.G., "The Hakka-Punti War," PhD dissertation., Oxford University, Queen's College, 1968.

Te-Chao, David, "Acculturation of the Chinese in the United States, A Philadelphia Study," (PhD dissertation, University of Pennsylvania, 1948).

Worden, Robert, "A Chinese Reformer in Exile: The North American Phase of the Travels of K'ang Yu-wei, 1899–1909,"PhD dissertation (Georgetown University, 1972).

**Chinese language sources**

Ch'en, Hsu-ching, "*Kuang-tung yu Chung-kuo*," (Kuang-tung [Gwongdung] [Guangdong] and China), *Tung-fang tsa-chih*, (Eastern Magazine) 36:2: pp. 41–45 (January 1939).

Chen, Zhiping, *Kejia yuanliu xinlun* (A New Discussion of the Origins of the Hakka), (*Naning Gwangxi jiaoyu chubanshe*, 1995).

*Guang-zhao gongsuo zhengxinlu* (Account-book of the Canton(ese) [Regional] Association),"*Linian jinzhi shumu*" (record of yearly income and expenditures), 1873 and 1877, hand copied manuscript, courtesy of Du Li, Shanghai Museum; Shanghai *Siming Gongsuo si da jianzhu zhengxinlu* (Account-book for the four major construction projects of the Shanghai *Siming Congsuo*) (Shanghai, 1925).

Kuan, Wei-lan, *Chung-hua min-kuo hsing cheng ch'u hua chi t'u ti jen k'ou tsung chi piao*, (Administrative Units and local Population Statistical tables for Republican China) (Taipei, Taiwan: 1955).

Liang Ch'i-ch'ao, (Liang Qichao) (Leung Kai-chew in Cantonese) *Hsin Ta-lu yu-chi* (Journey tothe New World) as found in *Chin-tai Chung-kuo shih liao tsung-k'an* (Historical Materials in Modern Chinese History), edited by Shen Yun-lung (vol. 96–97).

Liu, Heng, *Huahuxing* (Flower Lottery) *youyanggyu shanfang shichao* in QGB, vol. 124, p. 632.

Luo, Xianglin, (Lo, Hsiang-lin,) *Kechia yanjiu daolun* (*K'o-chia Yen-chiu Tao-lun*) (An Introduction to the Study of the *Hakkas* in its Ethnic, Historical and Cultural Aspects) (Sunning (Toishan) Kwangtung, China: *Xishan shucang* 1933) (Taipei, Taiwan: *Ku-t'ing shu-wu*, 1975 reprint).

Luo, Xianglin, *Kechiashiliao huipian* (Historical Sources for the study of the Hakkas) (Hong Kong: *Zhongguo xushe*, 1965).

*Ming-Ch'ing Kwangtung she-hui ching-chi yuan-chiu* (Research on Kwangtung (Guangdong) Society and Economy in the Ming-Ch'ing (Qing) period), compiled by the Society for research on Kwangtung Society and Economy in the Ming and Ch'ing Period) (Kuangchou: Kwangtung [Guangzhou: Guangdong] People's Press, 1987).

Tan, Qixiang, editor, *Zhongguo Lishi ti tu ji,* (Historical Atlas of China), vol. #8 The Qing Dynasty, (Shanghai: Cartographic Publishing House, 1987).

*Taishan ge yao ji* (A collection of Taishan folk songs) ed. By Chen Yuanzhu, (Taibei, Taiwan, Folklore Books, 1969) (originally printed in 1929).

*Taishan shang Nan-ts'un Li-shih Tsu-pu,* (Genealogy of the Lee Clan of Nam Tsun Village of Toishan District) (Gwongdung Province), compiled by Lee Fung-nam (1964) (Unpublished manuscript)

Yen, Chung-p'ing, et. al., (compliers) *Chung-kuo chin-tai ching-chi shih t'ung-chi tzu-liao hsuan-chi* (Selected Compilation of Statistical Data of Modern Chinese Economic History), [hereafter cited as CSDMC] (Taipei, Taiwan: *Ko Hsueh* Publishing House, 1955).

Yuan, Jiahua, *Hanyu Fangyan gaiyao* (An Outline of Chinese Dialects), (Beijing: *Wenzi Gaige Chubanshe*, 1960).

Zhao, Songqiao, *Zhongguo zi ran deli,* (Physical Geography of China,) Beijing: Science Press, 1986).

*Zhongguo yuyan dituji (di 2 bn) Han yu fangyan juan* (Language Atlas of China) (2nd edition) Chinese Dialect(s) volume (Beijing: The Commercial Press, 2012), p. 125. (A joint work by the Australian Academy of the Humanities & the Chinese Academy of Social Sciences, 1987–1989).

**Internet Source Materials**

Andrus, Tony, et. al. Language Specific Peculiarities Document for Cantonese as Spoken in Guangdong and Guangxi Provinces of China, (developed by Appen Butler Hill), pp. 1-9. This text is part of IARPA (Intelligence Advanced Research Projects Activity) Babel Cantonese Language Pack IARPA-babel 101b-v0.4c, LDC2016S02 web download Philadelphia Linguistic Data Consortium, 2015 (copyright held by US government) (developed by Appen Butler Hill for IARPA Babel Program, containing 215 hours of Cantonese conversational and scripted telephone speech collected in 2011).